Y0-AGK-674

Volume 14
of fifteen volumes

YOU AND YOUR CHILD

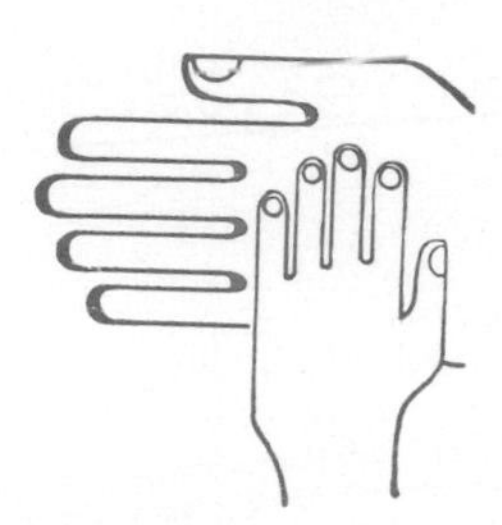

CHILDCRAFT

The How and Why Library

Managing Editor, George S. Amsbary
Art Director, Gordon J. Kwiatkowski
Volume Editor, Patricia M. Chesley
Assistant Editors, Joyce C. Berry
Jane Mayer
Volume Layout Artists, Neal Cochran
William Hammond

FIELD ENTERPRISES EDUCATIONAL CORPORATION
Merchandise Mart Plaza • Chicago 54, Illinois

1964 EDITION

CHILDCRAFT®
The How and Why® *Library*

Printed in the United States of America

FDA
LIBRARY OF CONGRESS CATALOG NO. 64-10001

Acknowledgments

The publishers of CHILDCRAFT, *The* How and Why *Library*, gratefully acknowledge the courtesy of the following publishers for permission to reprint excerpts from copyrighted materials. Full illustration acknowledgments for this volume appear on page 448.

Cassell and Company, Ltd.: *The Nursing Couple* by Dr. Merrell Middlemore, page 80 in this volume, copyright 1953 by Cassell and Company, Ltd.

E. & S. Livingstone, Ltd.: *A Way to Natural Childbirth* by Mrs. Helen Heardman, page 79 in this volume, copyright 1949 by E. & S. Livingstone, Ltd.

YOU AND YOUR CHILD

THIS VOLUME IS FOR YOU

Are you expecting a baby? Or do you already have one or two or more? Are you a grandparent or an aunt or an uncle? Or perhaps a teacher or other adult concerned with the welfare of infants and children?

Then you'll welcome *You and Your Child* for the reasons enumerated in this statement of objectives—objectives that guided the editors and contributors from beginning to end:

WHY THIS BOOK WAS WRITTEN

- To help parents, grandparents, and other relatives create a warm, comfortable climate in which family concerns and interests can be handled with grace, understanding, and humor.

- To help parents recognize that each child is different—born different, different at various ages and stages, different from his brothers and sisters, different from the child next door.

- To make parents aware of the many things a child has to learn, and understand the process by which he learns.

- To help parents and teachers identify and stimulate the gifted child, and encourage and help the slow, "average," or handicapped child.

- To help parents understand the roles of the home and the school in helping their child achieve his full potential.

- To help parents understand how their child's progress in school is tested and evaluated.

- To help parents and teachers safeguard and improve the child's physical, mental, and emotional health at home and at school.

ABOUT THE AUTHORS

Obviously, no one person is qualified to meet all these objectives. To do so, the editors called on 109 men and women representing the best thinking available today from wide areas of research, observation, and practical experience: psychologists, psychiatrists, physicians, dentists, educators, most of them actively engaged in their specialties, many of them parents themselves or actively working with children. The name of the author appears at the close of his or her article. A complete list of contributors follows this foreword.

In addition, a panel of distinguished consultants counseled with the editors from the inception of the volume and critically reviewed many of the articles. The contribution made by these consultants is immeasurable.

EASE OF USE

The 109 authors have contributed 495 articles, which are in alphabetical order from ABILITIES to ZWIEBACK, making it possible for you to find a particular subject without referring to an index. Guide words are printed in the margins at the top of each page. The guide word on the left page shows you the first entry on that page; the guide word on the right page shows you the last entry on that page.

Of course, there is no way to know for sure what word you will think of when you are, for example, concerned with a gifted child. Chances are that you will find the desired information immediately under GIFTED CHILD. But for the reader who thinks first of "exceptional child," an entry in the E's, under EXCEPTIONAL CHILD, *See* GIFTED CHILD, will speed that reader on his way. At the same time, the reader concerned with a handicapped child or a slow learner will have no difficulty in going directly to the subject.

If a child's giftedness is the only subject of interest at the moment, there is no need to read further. The discussion on giftedness is complete in itself, but at the conclusion of this entry is *See also* ACCELERATION; BOOKS FOR CHILDREN; BOOKS FOR PARENTS; CURIOSITY; INDIVIDUAL DIFFERENCES; SCIENCE; TESTS AND MEASUREMENTS. Thus, the reader is lured on and on, usually from a specific problem, which may be mental, emotional, or physical, to a view of that problem in relation to the child's life. In other words, what is life like to this child? What makes him shy, overly agressive, or jealous, or causes him to suck his thumb? Probably nothing in these articles will enable the reader to turn a shy child into a friendly, outgoing person overnight; an overly aggressive youngster into a friendly playmate; or the jealous one into a loving protector of his baby sister—and the thumb-sucker indeed may go right on sucking his thumb. But the reader will get a child's-eye view of the problem which, compounded with memories of his own childhood, will enable both child and adult to live in closer harmony.

So much for the references that follow the words *See* or *See also.* But there are additional helpful cross references to other volumes in this 15-volume set of CHILDCRAFT and to related articles in the 20-volume WORLD BOOK ENCYCLOPEDIA. The article on CONVALESCENT CHILD, for example, is referred to Volume 9, *Make and Do,* where specific directions are given for dozens of fascinating activities suitable for the child who must remain in bed. The article on SCIENCE is referred to Volume 3, *World and Space;* Volume 4, *Life Around Us;* and Volume 8, *How Things Work* as well as to WORLD BOOK's major discussion of "Science," together with its complex of related articles. And after reading Volume 14's article on TRAVELING WITH CHILDREN, let your children familiarize themselves with the lore, the scenic wonders of the states or countries you plan to visit. Let them lose themselves in WORLD BOOK's colorful maps and illustrations and amaze you with their on-the-spot travelogues.

IT'S NEW! IT'S OLD!

All the material in this book is new in the sense that it was prepared expressly for this edition and that it represents current thinking. But much of what you will find here is reassuringly old. Mother knows best, and father does, too—if they will have faith in their judgment—is the underlying logic of *You and Your Child.* No author-expert advocates "spare the rod and spoil the child," and none recommends complete permissiveness. Rather, there is a comfortable interpretation of what is meant by permissiveness very close to a point of view held in high esteem by generations of sensible parents—a philosophy compounded of love and laughter and even cleansing anger when occasion demands.

THE LANGUAGE IS CLEAR

Today's sophisticated young parents can understand just about any language the experts want to use, but the trouble is, not all the experts use the same terminology to mean the same thing. Besides, words take on new meanings rapidly in this space-age era. For these reasons, technical terms have been held to a minimum in this volume. Every effort has been made to present writing that the lay reader will find refreshingly clear and that the professional will find equally readable. Except where the reference specifically applies to girl children, "he" is used throughout the volume for the sake of convenience.

VISUAL AIDS

Photographs, drawings, and tables are used whenever possible to supplement the text. The photographs illustrate the text; the drawings do, too, including those of the "how-to-do-it" variety; tables provide information at a glance. The tables on pages 16–19, "Protect Your Infant" and "Protect Your Child," present accident prevention in a new dimension.

VOLUME 15

An extremely important adjunct to this volume is the one that follows—*Guide and Index,* which contains the "Children's Interest Guide" (pages 49–52) and the "School Study Guide," (pages 53–75). Volume 15 also tells you how you and your child can get the most out of CHILDCRAFT.

The Editors

CONSULTANTS

Special consultants for *You and Your Child* were:

JOSEPH CHRISTIAN, M.D., Chairman of the Division of Pediatrics, Presbyterian–St. Luke's Hospital, and Professor of Pediatrics, University of Illinois College of Medicine (for all medical and pediatrics articles).

WILLARD C. OLSON, Ph.D., Dean of the School of Education, University of Michigan.

CONTRIBUTORS

The person whose name appears at the end of an article in *You and Your Child* either wrote the article originally or became responsible for its accuracy as a critical reviewer. These contributors are listed here in alphabetical order. In addition, the CHILDCRAFT Consultant Committee (listed on page 4 of Volume 1) reviewed many of the articles in this volume.

Abraham, Willard, B.A., M.Ed., Ph.D.
Coordinator, Special Education, and Chairman, Department of Educational Services, Arizona State University. Author, *Common Sense About Gifted Children.*

Ahmann, J. Stanley, B.A., B.S., M.S., Ph.D.
Head, Department of Psychology; Professor of Psychology, Colorado State University. Author, *Evaluating Pupil Growth,* Second edition.

Allen, Roach Van, B.A., M.A., Ed.D.
Director of Curriculum Coordination, San Diego County, California. Author, *Independent Activities for Creative Learning.*

Artley, A. Sterl, B.A., M.Ed., Ph.D.
Professor of Education, University of Missouri. Author, *Your Child Learns To Read.*

Auerbach, Aline B., B.A.
Assistant Director for Program Development, Child Study Association of America. Author of child development publications.

† Baruch, Dorothy W., Ph.D.
Clinical Psychologist. Author, *New Ways in Sex Education.*

Bauer, William Waldo, B.S., M.D., LL.D. (hon.)
Director Emeritus, Department of Health Education, American Medical Association. Columnist, *Health for Today;* Author, *Stop Annoying Your Children.*

Bayley, Nancy, B.S., M.S., Ph.D.
Chief, Section on Early Development, Laboratory of Psychology, National Institute of Mental Health. Coauthor, *Growth Diagnosis.*

Beers, Dorothy, B.S., M.A.
Chief Consultant on Day Care, American Joint Distribution Committee. Author of child development publications.

Berlo, David K., A.B., Ph.D.
Professor and Chairman, Department of Communication, Michigan State University. Author, *Process of Communication: An Introduction to Theory and Practice.*

Bettelheim, Bruno, Ph.D.
Principal, Sonia Shankman Orthogenic School; Professor, Departments of Education, Psychology, and Psychiatry, University of Chicago. Author, *Dialogues with Mothers.*

Beyer, Evelyn M., B.A., M.A.
Director of Nursery School, Sarah Lawrence College. Author of child development publications.

Black, Irma Simonton, A.B.
Chairman, Publications Division, Bank Street College of Education. Author of child development and juvenile publications.

Bland, Jane Cooper, B.S., M.A.
Instructor, The Institute of Modern Art, New York City. Author, *The Art of the Young Child, Three to Five Years.*

Blatz, William E., B.A., M.A., M.B., Ph.D.
Professor of Psychology, University of Toronto. Author, *Understanding the Young Child.*

Blos, Joan Winsor, B.A., M.A.
Associate, Publications Division, Bank Street College of Education.

Brieland, Christine, B.A., M.A.
Parent Education Consultant, former CHILDCRAFT Advisory Service.

Brogan, Peggy
Director, American Toy Institute, New York City; Educational Consultant. Coauthor, *Helping Children Read.*

† Deceased

Burgess, Helen Steers
Parent educator and writer.

Cain, Leo F., A.B., M.A., Ph.D.
President, South Bay State College, Los Angeles.

Caldwell, Bettye McDonald, B.A., M.A., Ph.D.
Research Associate, Department of Pediatrics, Upstate Medical Center, State University of New York at Syracuse.

Castendyck, Elsa, B.A.
Writer. Coauthor, *The Handicapped Child: A Guide for Parents.*

Chesley, Patricia M.
Editor, *You and Your Child.*

Chilman, Catherine Street, M.A., Ph.D.
Assistant Professor of Family Relations, Syracuse University. Author, family relations publications.

Cole, A. Elliston, A.B., A.M., S.T.B.
Rector Emeritus, Trinity Church, Bloomington, Indiana. Author, *How To Tell Children There Is a Santa Claus.*

Coleman, Lester L., B.S., M.D.
Attending Surgeon, Manhattan Eye, Ear and Throat Hospital. Author, *Freedom from Fear.*

Conley, Veronica Lucey, A.B., M.N., M.A., Ph.D.
Executive Director of the National Association for Practical Nurse Education and Service.

Cooley, Donald G.
Medical-science writer and consultant.

Dale, Edgar, A.B., M.A., Ph.D.
Professor of Education, Ohio State University. Author, communication publications.

Day, A. Whittier, B.S.
Deputy Commissioner, Department of Corrections, St. Paul, Minnesota.

Dinkmeyer, Don, B.S., M.A., Ph.D.
Chairman, Psychology Department, National College of Education. Coauthor, *Encouraging Children to Learn: The Encouragement Process.*

DuBois, Eloise Barclay, B.S., M.A.
Director of Dramatics, Mary Institute, St. Louis, Missouri.

Duvall, Evelyn Millis, B.S., M.S., Ph.D.
Family Life Consultant. Author, *Family Development.*

Fabricant, Noah D., B.S., M.S., M.D.
Editor of *Otolaryngology* and *Eye, Ear, Nose and Throat Monthly.* Author, *13 Famous Patients.*

Finigan, Alma O., B.Ph.
Supervisor, Home and Hospital Instruction, Chicago Board of Education.

Fraiberg, Selma, B.A., M.S.W.
Supervising Child Analyst, Baltimore Psychoanalytic Institute. Author, *The Magic Years.*

Frank, Mary H., B.S., Ed.M.
Coauthor, *How To Help Your Child in School.*

Franklin, Adele, B.A., M.A., Ed.D.
Director, All-Day Neighborhood Schools of New York City Board of Education. Author, *Your Best Friends Are Your Children.*

Fromme, Allan, M.A., Ph.D.
Psychologist. Author, *The ABC of Child Care.*

Gallagher, J. Roswell, B.A., M.D.
Chief, The Adolescent Unit, Children's Hospital Medical Center, Boston. Author, *Emotional Problems of Adolescents.*

Goodlad, John I., B.A., M.A., Ph.D.
Professor of Education; Director, University Elementary School; Coordinator, Program on the Education of Teachers, University of California, Los Angeles. Coauthor, *The Nongraded Elementary School.*

Grams, Armin, B.S., M.A., Ph.D.
Faculty, The Merrill-Palmer Institute of Human Development and Family Life. Author, *Children and Their Parents.*

Grant, Eva H., B.A., M.A.
Editor-in-Chief, *The PTA Magazine,* National Congress of Parents and Teachers.

Gross, Elizabeth H., B.A., B.L.S., M.Ed.
Regional Librarian, Prince George's County Memorial Library, Bladensburg, Maryland.

Guttmacher, Alan F., A.B., M.D.
Consultant in Obstetrics and Gynecology, The Mount Sinai Hospital, New York City. Clinical Professor of Obstetrics and Gynecology, Columbia University, College of Physicians and Surgeons. Author, with others, *The Complete Book of Birth Control.*

Harris, Dale B., A.B., M.A., Ph.D.
Professor of Psychology, Pennsylvania State University. Author, *Children's Drawings as Measures of Intellectual Maturity: A Revision and Extension of the Goodenough Draw-a-Man Test.*

Hartley, Ruth E., B.A., M.A., Ph.D.
Associate Professor of Psychology, Long Island University. Author, *The Complete Book of Children's Play.*

Havighurst, Robert J., Ph.D.
Professor of Education, University of Chicago; Committee on Human Development, University of Chicago. Coauthor, *Psychology of Character Development.*

† **Hellmer, Leo A.,** B.S., M.S., Ph.D.
Professor of Psychology, University of Illinois.

Hinrichs, Marie A., B.A., M.D., Ph.D.
Consultant, Health Education, American Medical Association; Lecturer, Health Education, Roosevelt University. Author, subjects dealing with alkaloids, student health, and public health.

Hoover, Mary Bidgood, A.B., M.A.
Free-lance magazine article writer.

Hsia, David Yi-Yung, A.B., M.D.
Professor of Pediatrics, Northwestern University Medical School.

Hymes, James L., A.B., M.A., Ed.D.
Professor of Education and Chairman, Childhood Education, University of Maryland. Author, *The Child Under Six.*

Ilg, Frances L., M.D.
Director, Gesell Institute of Child Development. Coauthor, *Parents Ask.*

Jackson, Edith Banfield, M.B., M.D.
Clinical Professor Emeritus, Pediatrics and Psychiatry, Yale University; Visiting Professor, Pediatrics and Psychiatry, University of Colorado Medical Center.

Jenkins, Gladys Gardner, B.A., M.A.
Lecturer, writer, teacher in parent education and child development. Author, *Helping Children Reach Their Potential.*

Johnson, William G., A.B.
General Manager, National Safety Council.

Kehm, Freda S., B.A., M.A., Ph.D.
Director, The Association for Family Living. Lecturer, Marriage and the Family, Northwestern University.

Kempe, Ruth Irene S., A.B., M.D.
Assistant Professor of Child Psychiatry, University of Colorado Medical Center. Coauthor, *Healthy Babies, Happy Parents.*

Kesel, Robert G., M.S., D.D.S.
Professor-Head, Department of Applied Materia Medica and Therapeutics, University of Illinois, College of Dentistry.

† Deceased

Kilbride, Robert E., B.A., M.A.
Director of Public Information, Chicago Chapter, American Red Cross.

Landeck, Beatrice, B.A.
Music educator. Author, *Children and Music.*

LeShan, Eda J., B.S., M.A.
Parent educator, free-lance writer. Consulting Psychologist, Colonial Nursing School, New Rochelle, New York. Part-time Mental Health Education Consultant (formerly, Director of Education), Manhattan Society for Mental Health.

Levine, Milton I., B.S., M.D.
Associate Professor of Clinical Pediatrics, New York Hospital–Cornell University Medical Center. Coauthor, *The Wonder of Life.*

Liss, Edward, M.D.
Child Psychiatrist and Educator.

Lowenberg, Miriam E., Ph.D.
Head, Department of Foods and Nutrition, Pennsylvania State University. Author (with Benjamin Spock), *Feeding Your Baby and Child.*

Lowenfeld, Berthold, Ph.D.
Superintendent, California School for the Blind, Berkeley. Author, *Our Blind Children.*

Mace, David Robert, B.S., B.A., M.A., Ph.D.
Executive Director, American Association of Marriage Counselors. Coauthor, *Marriage: East and West.*

Margulis, Elizabeth S., A.B., B.S. in L.S.
Coordinator of the Children's World of the American Library Association's exhibit at the World's Fair (Seattle); Field Service Representative, American Medical Association.

Mayer, Jane, B.A.
Author, editor.

McCarthy, Dorothea, Ph.D.
Professor of Psychology, Fordham University.

McGuigan, R. A., B.S., M.S., M.D.
Associate in Pediatrics, Northwestern University Medical School.

Menninger, William C., M.A., M.D.
President, The Menninger Foundation. Author, *How To Help Your Children.*

Montagu, Ashley, Ph.D.
Formerly Chairman, Department of Anthropology, Rutgers University. Author, *Man in Process.*

Neisser, Edith G., B.A.
Free-lance writer, lecturer. Author, *The Eldest Child.*

Novak, Julius B., B.S., M.D.
Medical Director, The Tuberculosis Institute of Chicago and Cook County.

Novinger, Virginia B.
Author, writer.

Ojemann, Ralph H., Ph.D.
Professor, Iowa Child Welfare Research Station, State University of Iowa. Author, child development material.

Osborne, Ernest, Ph.D.
Professor of Education and Associate in the Guidance Laboratory, Teachers College, Columbia University. Author; columnist, *The Family Scrapbook.*

Pasamanick, Benjamin, A.B., M.D.
Professor of Psychiatry, Director of Research, Psychiatric Institute and Hospital, Ohio State University, Columbus, Ohio. Author, psychiatric publications.

Peck, Elizabeth, B.S., M.A.
Formerly Associate Professor of Maternity Nursing, Syracuse University.

Pierce, Mila I., M.D.
Professor of Pediatrics, University of Chicago.

Popenoe, Paul, Sc.D.
Founder and President, American Institute of Family Relations. Author, *The Child's Heredity.*

Potts, Willis J., A.B., S.B., M.D.
Consultant, Pediatric Surgery, Children's Memorial Hospital, Chicago. Author, *The Surgeon and Child.* Medical Columnist, *The Doctor and Your Child.*

Richmond, Julius B., B.S., M.S., M.D.
Professor and Chairman, Department of Pediatrics, Upstate Medical Center, State University of New York. Coauthor, *Pediatrics Diagnosis.*

Ross, Helen, A.B., B.S.
Consultant in Education, American Psychoanalytic Association, New York, New York. Columnist; coauthor, *Psychoanalytic Education in the United States.*

Sauer, Louis Wendlin, A.B., M.A., M.D., Ph.D.
Associate Professor Emeritus, Pediatrics Department, Northwestern University Medical School. Honorary Staff Attendant, Pediatrics Service, Variety Children's Hospital, Miami, Florida. Author, *From Infancy Through Childhood.*

Scholz, Roy O., M.D.
Ophthalmologist in Charge, Outpatient Department, The Johns Hopkins Hospital; Assistant Professor of Ophthalmology, The Johns Hopkins University Medical Faculty. Author, *Sight: A Handbook for Laymen.*

Senn, Milton J. E., M.A., M.D.
Director, Child Study Center, Yale University. Author, medical and child development materials.

Sherwin, May Reynolds, A.B., M.A., Ph.D.
Advisory Editor, *Parents Magazine.* Author, *Children from Seed to Saplings.*

Sherwood, Dorothy Dale, B.A., B.S.
Former teacher.

Shover, Jayne, B.A., M.A.
Associate Director, National Society for Crippled Children and Adults, Chicago.

Shriner, Mildred, M.A.
Teacher, physically handicapped children, Sunset School, San Lorenzo, California. Author, *Foundations for Walking.*

Sigel, Irving E., B.A., M.A., Ph.D.
Chairman of Research, The Merrill-Palmer Institute of Human Development and Family Life. Author, child development publications.

Sillman, John H., D.D.S., M.A.
Orthodontist, Associate Visiting Dentist, Bellevue and Beth Israel Hospitals. Consultant Orthodontist, New York Infirmary, New York City. Visiting Lecturer, University of Pennsylvania. Author, *Series on Growth and Development of Jaws: From Birth to Adulthood.*

Smart, Mollie S., A.B., M.A.
Associate Professor, Child Development and Family Relations, University of Rhode Island, College of Home Economics. Coauthor, *Living and Learning with Children.*

Smart, Russell C., A.B., M.A., Ph.D.
Chairman and Professor, Department of Child Development and Family Relations, University of Rhode Island. Coauthor, *Living and Learning with Children.*

Sondergaard, Arensa, B.S., M.A.
Elementary School Staff, Bronxville Public School, Bronxville, New York. Author, educational subjects.

Stern, Edith M., B.A.
Free-lance writer; Special Consultant, National Institute of Mental Health. Author, *Mental Illness: A Guide for the Family.*

Stoner, Marguerite, B.S., M.A.
Director, Teacher Training, John Tracy Clinic, Los Angeles.

Sunshine, Irving, B.S., M.A., Ph.D.
Toxicologist, Cuyahoga County Coronor's Laboratory; Assistant Professor of Toxicology, School of Medicine, Western Reserve University; Technical Director, Academy of Medicine, Cleveland Poison Information Center.

Tenny, John W., A.B., M.A., Ed.D.
Professor, Special Education and General Advisor, College of Education, Wayne State University. Author, exceptional children subjects.

Vasilakes, William Steve, B.S., M.A.
Teacher; author, science instructional materials.

Wineman, David, A.B., M.S.W.
Associate Professor of Social Work, Wayne State University. Author (with Fritz Redl) of *The Aggressive Child.*

Witty, Paul A., A.B., M.A., Ph.D.
Professor of Education, Director, Psycho-Educational Clinic, Northwestern University. Vice-President, American Association for Gifted Children. Associate Editor, *Highlights for Children.*

Wolf, Anna W. M., B.S.
Formerly, staff Child Study Association of America, *Woman's Home Companion.* Author, *Parents' Manual.*

Work, Henry H., A.B., M.D.
Associate Professor, Department of Psychiatry, School of Medicine, University of California, Los Angeles.

Yauch, Wilbur Alden, B.S., M.A., Ed.D.
Educational Consultant and Professor of Education, Northern Illinois University. Author, *Helping Teachers Understand Principals.*

Zeichner, Gwendolyn B., M.S.
Psychiatric Social Worker, Ittleson Center, New York.

ABILITIES

Your wonderful child, your pride and joy, seems unique to you. You are right; he is. No other person, now or ever, was or is exactly like him either physically or in abilities. But his differences from others are far greater in what he is capable of doing than they are in his physical make-up.

For this reason, then, you want to know as much as possible about the quality and character of his ability to do or perform. And you want to know how your efforts, added to those of his school, can help him develop his potential to the utmost.

Your Child's Special Abilities

It is neither possible nor necessary to list the many different abilities your child can have. Instead, it is better to take a look at those outstanding abilities that do most toward his success at home and at school; namely, general ability and a group of special abilities. General ability, usually called intelligence, is primarily verbal, mathematical, and probably spatial—the ability to think about and visualize how objects—or shapes and forms—are related.

Special talents include mechanical, musical, artistic, and clerical abilities. There is also a group of "psychomotor" abilities, such as skill in using the hands, making eyes and hands work together, muscular strength, speed of response, and steadiness. Many of these psychomotor skills are highly important in semiskilled or skilled vocations.

Tests of mental ability are given frequently in the schools, usually as paper-and-pencil tests. Only rarely are tests of mechanical comprehension, artistic ability, and musical ability given. Tests of psychomotor abilities are, as you would expect, not of the paper-and-pencil type but instead make use of apparatuses, some of which are quite elaborate. These tests, too, are seldom given to a child during his early years.

Heredity and Environment

For many years biologists, geneticists, physiologists, and psychologists have argued about whether heredity or environment makes your child the kind of person he is. Today it is generally agreed that a child's traits are the product of heredity and environment combined, and that both heredity and environment set limits on the kind and quantity of abilities he will have.

Although limits are set by heredity, the degree to which anyone develops his inborn aptitudes can be increased or decreased by a long-time exposure to an environment.

Athletic ability and musical ability, for example, are heavily influenced by heredity because bone and muscle structure play so much part in them. But environment will have to provide playing fields, athletic equipment, musical instruments, instruction, encouragement, example, or any of a dozen other things you can easily think of, before your child will make full use of that which heredity gave him. His environment, despite some hereditary factors, will also set his entire style of life, his attitudes, values, idiosyncrasies, his whole complicated pattern of behavior.

How Can You Help Your Child?

Of all the many powers that your child has, the most important is his general mental ability. Helping him to develop this ability and other highly related special abilities is a challenging task. But your way may be made easier and the results may be better for both you and him if you follow some of these suggestions:

1. Encourage your child to develop his basic skills; that is, his ability to read and his use of mathematics, for these skills make an enormous contribution to successful development. The public library, the school library, or your home library can be your allies in increasing his reading skill. Mathematics can regularly come into many games; for instance, those using play money as well as into family activities, such as computing distance traveled and automobile gasoline mileages when you are taking a trip.

2. Provide opportunities for your child to display his creativity. No doubt he has repeatedly shown flashes of creativity. Provide every opportunity for him to produce short plays, draw, paint, or model, and to compose

stories and songs. Show your interest in his creativity by keeping the things he makes. For example, pin up pictures that he may have drawn and, when possible, keep costumes or sets he may have constructed. And try very hard to judge his artistic work by a child's standards instead of by your own.

3. Encourage his avocations. It may annoy you sometimes to provide space for collections of all kinds, but these collections are part of highly important avocational pursuits. Someday, of course, he may push aside insects and even stamps and coins as "childish," but in the meantime he has been through an important learning process. This process often serves as a splendid springboard for future academic success and even vocational success. On the other hand, collections are not necessary if they do not interest him. The child who participates in athletics, crafts, and camping, to say nothing of drama and music, is also developing his abilities in an extremely desirable way. If the family can go to plays and concerts, you have another obvious way of encouraging your child to develop his artistic and musical abilities.

4. Expose your child to the world. Maybe you haven't considered the value of travel. Visiting distant cities, local parks, and historical monuments offers the finest of all chances to explore the history, geography, and culture of his country as well as the plants and animals in it. Tours of business, industrial, and government facilities, many of which may be less than an hour away from your home, can give him a glimpse of the commercial and social worlds about him in a manner superior to books or motion pictures. Let him see the world, hear the world, touch the world, and even smell the world.

5. Provide opportunities for your child to make independent decisions where he can. Or at every practical opportunity, let him contribute to a family decision in such matters as the entertainment in which the family participates, perhaps the menu for the evening meal, or the selection of his clothing. Give him a weekly allowance, too, however small; this "independent income" will allow him to make many decisions, for how he spends and saves his allowance should be mostly his own affair.

Encouragement doesn't mean grimness or do-or-die determination. True, you do want to have a plan for your child's development and your part in it, but the gentle touch will make both of you happier. Don't regiment his life in the name of encouragement. Plenty of encouragement and guidance can be given without rigid schedules, without officially organized activities, or even private lessons. After all, doesn't he have enough regimentation in his formal schoolwork? What he wants and needs from you, so that new vistas of experience can open up to him, are a few words of praise, some ways of having your time fit in with his, and small amounts of inexpensive materials and equipment. You can help him develop his God-given abilities without subjugating yourself to him, denying the rights of other family members, or overlooking his responsibilities to all other members of the household. J. STANLEY AHMANN

See also HEREDITY; INDIVIDUAL DIFFERENCES; INFERIORITY COMPLEX; RESOURCEFULNESS; TESTS AND MEASUREMENTS

ABSCESS

When pus collects as a result of infection in any part of the body, an abscess forms after a few days. An abscess may occur in the skin (a boil is a type of abscess), around a tooth, or around the appendix as a complication of appendicitis.

To prevent an abscess, avoid infection. Thus, keeping the skin clean helps to prevent skin infections and abscesses. Early diagnosis and treatment of appendicitis helps to prevent abscess formation in the abdomen. And a well-timed visit to the dentist may forestall an abscess in the gums.

Once an infection develops, the use of antibiotics, such as penicillin, may prevent the occurrence of an abscess, but such drugs should be given only at the direction of your doctor. Also, should an abscess form and drainage be desirable, let your doctor carry out the surgical procedure. JULIUS B. RICHMOND

ACCELERATION

Acceleration is often spoken of in connection with the education of gifted children. For acceleration has been recommended again and again as a way to give a gifted child academic work that is interesting and challenging enough to stimulate full use of his exceptional learning powers. An accelerated program gives a child the schoolwork required in all grades but offers it in less time than is customary. A pupil who has been accelerated may, for example, finish the eighth grade after six years of elementary schooling, but in those six years he will have completely covered all the subjects necessary for entrance into high school.

A bright student of high-school age may be accelerated, too. In some cases acceleration is done by letting him go on to college after two or three years of high school. In others he is permitted to take tests in certain college subjects and upon passing them, he is given college credit.

And in college, exceptional students sometimes are allowed to complete four years' work in three.

Parents appear to worry less about acceleration at the high-school and college levels than in the elementary school. They think of acceleration as perhaps solving one problem for their child only to create new ones. They ask: Will his social life suffer? Will he be able to get along with older children and have any friends? Will he really obtain a thorough grounding in the fundamentals if he goes so fast? Will the other children in the family come to think of themselves as dull because he is going forward so rapidly?

Each family has to solve within itself the several problems caused by family members being unlike. Essentially, differences in mental ability are similar to those in sex or in age, and ways should be found to have each individual feel appreciated for what he is rather than to be unfavorably compared for what he is not.

The fear that an accelerated child may not get a thorough grounding in fundamentals fails to consider that the very reason a child is being passed to a higher grade is because he learns so much faster than the average child. The average child usually needs more time to master the fundamentals.

The fear of a disrupted social life fails to take into account the fact that a brilliant child often has more in common with children a year or two older than he does with those of his own chronological age.

Many studies of the uses and effects of acceleration have been made and others are still being made. To date, the findings are that acceleration is largely satisfactory and that children who have been accelerated up to two full grades have had academic success and good personal adjustment. Increased use of acceleration is relatively recent, but even so, the evidence seems to justify its more frequent use as an educational method in caring for superior students. PAUL A. WITTY

See also GIFTED CHILD

ACCEPTANCE

It is the birthright of every child to be accepted by others. Acceptance by others is the basis for all that is desirable in his development. From acceptance by others, principally parents and other adults close to him, comes acceptance of self. And on acceptance of self a child's happiness and effectiveness as a person hinge. It is often difficult for parents to take the child as he comes, to understand his needs and his problems as *he* sees them. It means helping a child to develop into the sort of person *he* wants to be and can be.

Acceptance means taking the trouble to learn how to guide a child in his development so that he does not feel that he has failed to fulfill the expectations of those he loves. It means helping him follow his interests and live up to his abilities. This is a tall order, for it demands sensitivity to another person and true selflessness—the putting aside of our own desires. RUTH E. HARTLEY

See also GIFTED CHILD; HANDICAPPED CHILD; INDIVIDUAL DIFFERENCES; SELF-CONCEPT

ACCIDENT PREVENTION

Every child is going to get his share of cut lips, bruised shins, and sprained fingers. He would be abnormal if he did not. And minor injuries, although momentarily catastrophic, usually respond to simple first-aid procedures. In fact, they are in the long run quite educational, for they teach the child valuable safety concepts—that he can't swat the cat without getting scratched or defy gravity without receiving a painful jolt. In the "school of hard knocks" your child acquires both knowledge and skills that will keep him safe while he is out of your sight.

Parents' Responsibility

Serious accidents, however, are another matter. No child should ever be allowed to risk one such accident; the stakes are too high—facial disfigurement, crippling, or death. Parents must take all precautions to protect their child from senseless tragedy. Accompanying this article are two tables, *Protect Your Baby* and *Protect Your Child*, which will supply many helpful reminders of how serious accidents can be avoided.

The younger the child, the more you must protect him. A baby, of course, is completely helpless and requires total protection. You must see that he comes in touch with no hazards whatsoever, especially those that could cause severe falls, suffocation, or drowning—the "big three" baby-killers.

A baby's high chair and stroller should have straps to prevent his tumbling out. His crib should have sturdy sides. As soon as he starts crawling, you will also need portable gates for the tops and bottoms of stairways. And there's nothing better than a playpen to fence him out of mischief.

Even then, he could get into trouble if his toys aren't safe. Be sure he doesn't handle beads or rattles so small that he can jam

PROTECT YOUR BABY

	BIRTH TO 4 MONTHS (Wriggles, rolls over)	4 TO 7 MONTHS (Begins to sit and crawl)
DANGEROUS OBJECTS	Let no sharp objects come in contact with baby.	Keep buttons, pins, and beads from baby's reach. Check floors and playpen for small objects before letting him play there.
FIRE	Watch cigarette ashes around baby. Check materials used in sweaters and blankets for flammability.	Never leave a child alone in house. Don't leave cigarette where baby can brush it from tray to floor.
FIREARMS AND EXPLOSIVES	Never clean or repair a gun when baby is in the room.	Never point even a toy gun where baby can see you. He is an ardent imitator!
MOTOR VEHICLES	Never park a buggy where it might roll into traffic. In car, baby's safest spot is in his bed in rear seat.	Keep baby in bassinet or harness attached to seat. Never leave him alone in car.
PLAY AREAS	Best are padded playpen, blanket on floor, or big bed. Never leave baby alone.	Playpen. Will love yard or porch. Keep clean and free of things that might hurt him.
POISONS	Not much of a problem, but watch that no one accidentally mixes poisonous substances in baby's formula.	Baby beginning to grab. Don't leave poisons within his reach.
STAIRS, DOORS, WINDOWS	Don't put cribs or playpens by open doors or windows. Don't park buggy near open stairway.	Put gates at stairways, driveways, porches, and seldom-used storage areas. Never leave baby alone near open stairway.
TOYS	Allow only large soft toys and sturdy rattles. No sharp points or edges.	Soft rubber squeak toys, plastic toys. Beware of toys small enough to swallow. No strings of beads across crib.
WATER	During bath, check water temperature with elbow to prevent scalding; hold him securely, and don't take eyes off him for an instant.	Same bath routine. Never leave him alone near water; he can drown in a few inches.
SPECIAL HAZARDS	Keep crib sides up so he can't roll out. Don't let him lie on couch or bed alone.	No pillows on bed. No filmy plastic sheets or covering on mattress.

7 TO 12 MONTHS
(Crawls, sits, stands, walks)

DANGEROUS OBJECTS
Put knives, scissors, breakable objects high out of reach. Beware of dangling tablecloths and appliance cords. On clothing, no bells, pompons, loose buttons that he can swallow.

FIRE
Empty ashtrays before baby does. Never leave him in room with open, burning fireplace. Use fireplace screen.

FIREARMS AND EXPLOSIVES
Guns are not playthings. Keep them out of a toddler's reach. Lock them up.

MOTOR VEHICLES
Encourage him to sit quietly in car. Prohibit suckers or ice cream or candy on sticks while riding. Put safety locks on doors. At home, never leave him alone on lawns.

PLAY AREAS
Playpen still safest place.

POISONS
Put everything poisonous up high. Don't keep household chemicals under sink. Don't leave medicine bottles or tins where he can get them, not even in your purse.

STAIRS, DOORS, WINDOWS
Keep all gates and add needed new ones. Keep screens locked or nailed. Keep dark stairs lighted.

TOYS
Large blocks. Sandbox. Wide-wheeled tricycle to begin on. Never let him out alone on his tricycle.

WATER
Watch him in bath or back-yard pool. Every child should wear life jacket in boat.

SPECIAL HAZARDS
Safety caps for wall sockets. Prevent him from chewing on cords. Don't leave plastic bags lying around.

1 TO 2 YEARS
(Crawls, walks, runs, climbs)

DANGEROUS OBJECTS
Watch everything he plays with. Keep sharp tools, glass objects out of reach. Don't let him eat popcorn, peanuts, or candy with nuts.

FIRE
Keep matches, lighters out of reach. Never let baby near trash burner or leaf fire. Teach him fire is hot! It will hurt him.

FIREARMS AND EXPLOSIVES
Never play with or tease anyone with a gun. And *never* keep a loaded gun in the house.

MOTOR VEHICLES
Teach him not to stick arms out car window nor to stand on seat. Outfit him in a car safety harness. Insist he not run into the street, play in driveway, etc. Punish if he does.

PLAY AREAS
Fence section of the yard where he plays so he can't wander into traffic. Keep an eye on him.

POISONS
He will eat anything and climb great heights to get it! Lock up medicines, insecticides, household chemicals. Never get him to take pills by telling him they are candy.

STAIRS, DOORS, WINDOWS
You may need taller gates now. Watch baby carefully. Lock gates faithfully. No wax on stairs.

TOYS
Everything goes in mouth! Avoid toys with removable parts—wheels on toy cars. Don't repaint toys with poisonous lead paint.

WATER
Same as for younger child. Also fence in ponds, pools, cisterns.

SPECIAL HAZARDS
Keep all hot appliances—toasters, irons—out of reach. Guards around heaters and radiators.

PROTECT YOUR CHILD

2 TO 3 YEARS (Always investigating)	3 TO 4 YEARS (Always in motion)
DANGEROUS OBJECTS Turn in handles of pots on stove. Lock up power-operated tools. Don't allow him near operating machinery.	**DANGEROUS OBJECTS** Same as for 2-year-old.
FIRE Don't let child play with matches. Never let him poke fire. Beware of fluffy skirts around fire.	**FIRE** Same as for 2-year-old.
FIREARMS AND EXPLOSIVES Dismantle guns. Lock ammunition and guns in different places so if child finds one, he can't find the other. Don't let him touch a gun.	**FIREARMS AND EXPLOSIVES** Same as for 2-year-old.
MOTOR VEHICLES Never let him touch car controls. Help him learn to cross the street, but *never* alone. Teach him meaning of traffic lights. Don't let him play near streets.	**MOTOR VEHICLES** Can begin to learn safety rules—never to chase ball into street. Watch him closely. Insist he obey instantly. From this age on, insist he wear seat belt in car.
PLAY AREAS Keep play area in yard free of dangerous debris—broken glass, tin cans. Check play equipment for slivers, loose bolts, nails.	**PLAY AREAS** A closed gate means to stay in yard. Check his activities frequently. He is now good at climbing fences and opening locked gates.
POISONS Keep poisons locked up, including cleaners and insecticides. Never leave empty containers where he can find them.	**POISONS** Same as for 2-year-old.
STAIRS, DOORS, WINDOWS This child can open doors. Lock those that lead to danger. Burglar locks on windows. Clear stairs.	**STAIRS, DOORS, WINDOWS** Never let child lean out open windows. Caution him about running up and down stairs. Tack down carpeting. No throw rugs.
TOYS Balls, blocks, stuffed animals without bead eyes or other ornaments that he can swallow.	**TOYS** Can use simple playground equipment. Check for sharp edges. Buy swings of soft canvas, not of wood. Supervise play.
WATER Supervise bath closely. Don't leave him alone in bathroom. Begin to teach floating. Never leave him alone near body of water.	**WATER** Start teaching him to swim. Don't let him use inner tube or inflated toys alone.
SPECIAL HAZARDS Teach him to play gently with pets and to avoid strange animals.	**SPECIAL HAZARDS** Never leave trunks, large picnic coolers where child can crawl in and suffocate. Stress dangers of abandoned refrigerators.

	4 TO 6 YEARS (Getting independent)	6 AND OLDER (Goes to school)
DANGEROUS OBJECTS	Caution him about picking up sharp or rusty objects. Tell him to avoid broken glass.	Continue to lock up hazardous objects. Don't let him use dangerous tools or power mowers. Stress that safety rules apply away from home.
FIRE	Store flammables out of reach. Begin to teach safety rules about fire—that he should not go near brush fire, turn on stove, etc.	He can learn first aid for burns, what to do if his clothes catch fire, how to call fire department.
FIREARMS AND EXPLOSIVES	Teach the danger of guns—that they kill. Never let him point even a toy gun at anyone. Continue to lock up your gun and ammunition.	Same, but also teach him not to handle fireworks, bullets, or other explosives he may find, such as grenades or blasting caps.
MOTOR VEHICLES	Teach him to obey traffic signals, patrol boys, policemen. Remind him to be careful away from home.	Be sure he looks both ways before crossing a street. Teach rules for riding a bike—on right side of street, single file, with traffic signals. School safety training will help.
PLAY AREAS	Take him to park playgrounds. Teach him to use swings, slides. Supervise carefully.	Warn him about playing in dangerous construction areas, around holes, and in caves.
POISONS	Same as for 2-year-old.	After 6, a child usually loses his appetite for distasteful substances that can poison him, but take no chances.
STAIRS, DOORS, WINDOWS	Teach him never to lock door to his room or bathroom, and not to pound glass.	Tell him to go up and down stairs *one* at a time. Have him sleep with bedroom door closed to keep out smoke in case of fire.
TOYS	Keep toys in good repair or discard. He can throw, catch ball. Warn him not to dart into street after ball.	Games, puzzles, creative toys, sports equipment. Teach him to handle balls, bats safely—that skill, not roughhousing, is the object of a game.
WATER	Can swim fairly well, but never let him swim alone. Watch him closely.	Sign him up for formal Y or Red Cross swimming lessons. Stress "Always swim with a buddy."
SPECIAL HAZARDS	Let him participate in home fire drills and practice escaping out bedroom window. For second floors, get portable ladder.	Be sure he knows how to care for himself away from home—what to do if lost; never to go with strangers; how to handle emergencies.

them down his throat—or stuffed animals with tiny button eyes that he can pull off and swallow.

A very young baby who can't raise his head should never sleep on a pillow, for he could bury his head in it and suffocate. Nor should you cover a baby with heavy blankets or set his crib near heavy draperies that could blow into his face. Thin plastic, of course, is taboo in a baby's world. It should never cover a crib mattress, nor should it be left where a baby could grab it and pull it over his face.

Surprisingly, more children drown at home than in public pools. These are usually young tots left alone in bathtubs or wading pools—sometimes for only a few minutes. No baby can be trusted with more than a cupful of water, and even that is enough to cause drowning. When your child gets together with water, keep a constant watchful eye on him.

Curiosity and Caution

As soon as a child can creep, he becomes an uncontrollable menace to himself. He peeks into every corner and is especially fond of sticking his fingers and toys into electrical wall outlets. Your chances of squelching his curiosity are slight, but you can eliminate the hazard. Simply cover the sockets with child-proof caps, available at any hardware store.

To further safeguard children from shock, see that frayed cords and damaged appliances are repaired promptly, for a defect can produce a lethal jolt. Have large appliances, such as washing machine, dryer, television set, and power tools, equipped with ground wires that divert current harmlessly into the earth. Then if a short develops, there is no danger to a child who touches the faulty appliance. Another important rule: Don't allow electrical appliances near water, especially when a child is present; for example, at bathtime. He can too easily touch wet hands to the appliance or pull it into the tub, electrocuting himself and perhaps others.

Burns Are a Hazard

Burns are another hazard to small tots. Sensing little danger, they walk right up to flames, which can fly out and catch their clothing. For this reason you should never leave a child alone in a room with an open gas fire or a burning fireplace. Make him keep his distance from burning trash, bonfires, and barbecues. Also, protect him from hot substances—turn the handles of pots and pans toward the back of the stove and put the cords of appliances, such as automatic coffee makers and skillets, beyond his reach.

Protect Them from Poisons

Until your child is at least 4, he has little discriminating taste and will eat anything, including poisonous bleach, medicines, insecticides, and cosmetics. A crawler easily invades low spaces such as under-sink cupboards, so never keep household chemicals there. Older children climb incredible heights, mainly in search of sugary pills that they think are "candy." Flavored baby-type aspirin is by far the greatest menace to a child; he can down a lethal dose of 30 or 40 tablets in minutes. Best precautions are: Put locks on medicine cabinets, don't leave children alone in bedrooms where night stands hold drugs or with purses containing drugs, and never encourage a child to take medicine by telling him it is candy.

A child of 5 is less likely to pour terrible-tasting substances down his throat. But he develops new fascinations just as dangerous, among them guns, machinery, fire. He is no longer idly curious; he is intensely serious about discovering how things work. What's more, he is extremely ingenious; to keep him out of trouble, you must anticipate his ever-increasing ingenuity.

Guns and Children Don't Mix

It's not enough just to hide a gun, no matter how secret the spot. Many a child has found not only the gun, but also the right-size bullets, inserted them, and fired away, killing playmates or parents. *Empty guns and bullets should be locked up in separate places so a child can't discover both at the same time.* Needless to say, a loaded gun should never be allowed in the house. Other explosives such as "live" war souvenirs and fireworks are illegal in most states and should not be given to children to play with.

Power Machinery Is Treacherous

A child has no business around treacherous power machinery—and that goes for farm implements, power tools, and power mowers. In fact, you should not allow your child in the yard while a power mower is operating, for it often throws off missiles—stones, wire, even broken blades—that soar at speeds of 200 mph and find their mark in a child's body. You can lessen the hazard, however, by raking the lawn before mowing.

Certainly, no child should operate a power mower or other hazardous machines. He may attempt to sneak into a workshop and try his skill, just like "daddy." So it is best to equip stationary tools with key-operated switches or plugs and to lock portable tools in a cabinet.

Fire Safety

What can you do about your child's fondness for fire? Primarily, don't give him the opportunity to experiment on his own. Keep matches and cigarette lighters hidden. Equip gas stoves with safety-lock knobs. At the same time let him learn about fire under your supervision. Let him strike matches while you watch. Let him help burn trash and start the barbecue. This removes some of the mystery of fire and discourages secretive match-playing that could burn him up.

Most important, never leave a child alone in a house. In minutes he could kindle a fire or one could spring up, trapping him. Children panic easily in fire and when parents are not there to rescue them, they do foolish things like hidding under beds and in closets. When he is old enough, a child should be taught exactly how to escape fire, especially from his bedroom. If he sleeps on a second floor, you can buy him an inexpensive rope ladder to fling out the window and climb down in case of fire. You should hold home fire drills and make him practice scrambling down the ladder.

Also, insist that he sleep with his bedroom door closed because a door provides a great barrier against fire and smoke. Teach him never to throw open the door if he suspects fire. He should first place his hand against the knob and panels to determine if the door is warm. If it is, he should not open it, for flames and superheated air are on the other side. One whiff of hot air would fell him in an instant.

Swimming Safety

Probably the most important lifesaving skill your child will learn is swimming. You can take on the teaching job yourself (which is easier than you think). (Your ability is of little significance; patience is what counts.) Or you can put him in a class run by professional instructors. At the same time issue strict orders about swimming—that he should never swim alone but always with a "buddy," and never in unsupervised areas such as quarries. Be sure he knows elementary first-aid procedures, mainly lifesaving artificial respiration.

Street and Automobile Safety

From the time a child is 2, gradually teach him to fend for himself. Show him how to look both ways before crossing a street, to cross with the green light, to obey patrol boys, and to walk on the left side of the road when there is no sidewalk. Try to inculcate respect for the killing power of an auto. Point out the hazards of playing in the street and chasing balls into the road without first looking in both directions. If he rides a bicycle, teach him safe riding and rules of the road.

Of all threats to your child, by far the greatest is an automobile accident. Here again, no matter what his age, he needs absolute protection. He is helpless and dependent entirely on the good judgment of an adult driver.

Every child should have a car seat, harness, or seat belt to restrain him in an emergency stop or accident. Such a device increases his chances of survival eight times. Don't allow your child to stand on a seat, climb over seats, hang out windows, or play in the rear of an open station wagon or a truck. These antics are not only distracting to a driver, but also they could cause the child to fall out or plunge through the windshield in a quick stop. Special safety catches on doors are not necessary if the child is strapped in, but if you want to be doubly sure, install them. Don't remove handles from inside doors. In an emergency, children couldn't get out and adults couldn't get in.

In the long run your intelligent driving is what counts. Scrupulously obeying traffic signs and laws will keep you out of most scrapes, but that is not enough. It is really your attitude toward driving that determines whether or not you have an accident. Are you courteous and respectful of the rights of others? Will you sacrifice your legal right to avert an accident? Are you more cautious than the law demands? "Yes" answers mean that you probably have a fairly safe driving personality.

Good driving attitudes and habits will pay not only immediate but also long-term safety dividends. Your attitudes strongly influence how your child will one day behave behind the wheel of an auto. A child as young as 2 is very perceptive and begins to imitate his parents. If you set a good example for him, he is not likely to grow into an irresponsible hot-rodder.

In fact, your child's entire safety outlook will reflect your own. The best formula for keeping your child alive is to live safely yourself. WILLIAM G. JOHNSON

See also ARTIFICIAL RESPIRATION; EMERGENCY; FIRST AID; GUILT FEELINGS

Related article in WORLD BOOK: "Safety"

ACHIEVEMENT TESTS *See* TESTS AND MEASUREMENTS

ACNE

Most young people are inclined to worry about minor skin disorders, although few are serious. Occasional blemishes are to be expected, and young people should be encouraged to accept them as a normal, if annoying, part of growing up.

True acne, however, is a condition of the skin in which the oil (sebaceous) glands become inflamed and overactive. Pimples develop, mainly on the face, but often on the chest or back as well. In severe acne, infections and abscesses form in the oil glands. When the abscesses are large and many, the disease may leave scars. Although acne is more common in boys, it frequently is seen in girls, too. Acne can occur at any age, but it develops mainly during adolescence as an accompaniment to growth and sexual maturation when, it is believed, hormones produced by the adrenal glands increase the activity of the oil glands. It is not known why some individuals develop acne.

Complete prevention of acne does not seem possible, although cleanliness is an important requirement to keep the openings of the oil glands from becoming clogged.

If your boy or girl develops acne, a general health checkup is in order. Careful attention to the skin is important in reducing the severity of the case and consequent scarring of the skin. The skin should be cleansed gently at least three or four times a day with warm water and soap. The hair also should be kept scrupulously clean. Medication should be used only if and as directed by your doctor. A balanced diet with a lessening of sweets is often advised. The pimples must not be squeezed or pinched. JULIUS B. RICHMOND

See also HAIR CARE; NUTRITION

ACTING *See* DRAMATICS

ADENOIDS

The adenoid tissues grow at the back of the nasal passages where they cannot ordinarily be seen. This tissue is the same as that of the tonsils (lymphoid tissue). It has the function of helping to prevent or overcome infection. If the adenoid tissue becomes unusually large, it may block a child's nasal breathing and thus force him to breathe through his mouth. Also, the adenoids may block the opening of the passageway leading from the nose and throat area to each middle ear and bring about ear infections.

If a child has had frequent nose and throat infections, the adenoid tissue might itself become chronically infected and cause fever. Obstruction to nasal breathing, obstruction to the ears, or chronic infection may necessitate surgical removal of a child's adenoids. The adenoids are frequently, but not always, removed when the tonsils are removed. Your doctor's advice should be followed. X-ray treatments are no longer used to reduce the size of adenoid tissue. JULIUS B. RICHMOND

See also TONSILS; OPERATION

ADJUSTMENT

Most parents hear a good deal about "good adjustment" and "poor adjustment" these days. They are urged to concern themselves with the "adjustment" of their children. Yet how many know what the term really means?

A dictionary definition of the word tells us that it is "a change made to conform to some standard or norm." Bearing this in mind, we might ask what it means to say a person is "well adjusted" or its opposite. Well adjusted to what? Obviously a person has to be adjusted to *something;* he cannot be simply "adjusted" or "not adjusted." Hence, when we speak of the "adjustment" of a particular individual, we are implying that we have a specific situation or a certain desired pattern of conduct in mind. A person may show poor adjustment in one set of circumstances but excellent adjustment in another. Many a child who seems to show good adjustment at home is judged to have poor adjustment by his teachers in school. Or good adjustment on the playground may show up poorly in the parlor. The quality of adjustment depends on what one measures it by.

In addition, because adjustment is usually evaluated by people, whether it is "good" or "bad" depends on who is making the judgment. A teacher's standards may be quite different from those of a mental health expert. Even parents often disagree about whether or not their child is well adjusted.

Keeping these qualifications in mind, good adjustment usually means flexibility—that the individual is able to recognize the demands of reality and adapt to them. It also means that he is aware of his own abilities and limitations, accepts himself, and expects that others will accept him.

Good general adjustment does not mean slavish conformity. The self-accepting person will have his own standards and his own interests. In some situations, the best adjustment, from a mental health viewpoint, is shown by refusing to "adjust" and by leaving or changing the situation. RUTH E. HARTLEY

See also INDIVIDUAL DIFFERENCES; MENTAL HEALTH; SOCIAL PRESSURES

ADOLESCENT *See* TEEN-AGER

ADOPTION

The first step for any couple considering adoption is to be reasonably certain that they cannot have a child of their own. Adoption agencies will want fairly conclusive evidence that this is the case. Thorough medical examinations and consultations are necessary, for with the development of more knowledge about sterility and the improvement of medical techniques, many couples who thought they could not have a child have had their thinking happily reversed.

A couple considering adoption should try to be as clear as possible about their own motives and feelings. Adopting a child cannot save a shaky marriage or replace a lost child. A child must be wanted for himself, not to fulfill unrealistic expectations. It is important for prospective parents to feel comfortable about adoption, not that it is the "last resort" or that they have failed as people to have a baby of their own. Adoption is a wonderful road to successful and fulfilling parenthood if the adoptive parents are happy about it, if they are free of misgivings, and if they can accept what every parent really has to accept—that there is no way to know in advance what a child will be like.

Social Agencies Can Help

This fact—that feelings are so important—is one of the many reasons why it is always wise to consult recognized social agencies about adopting a child. Here, carefully trained and experienced social workers can provide guidance in helping a couple to explore and understand their needs and feelings, as well as the legal protection and guidance that is of such vital importance. While it is true that many states permit legal adoption of children obtained through other sources, such as a doctor or a lawyer, these are never the procedures of first choice; the adoption of a child is too important a concern for both parents and child not to warrant every possible safeguard of professional advice and supervision.

Information about recognized adoption agencies is available in each state from the State Department of Public Welfare. This agency will also be able to supply necessary information about state adoption laws and requirements. In larger cities, a Council of Social Agencies will also be able to provide information and referral. While it is true that most adoption agencies have long waiting lists for babies, older children are often available. In addition, some agencies now are placing handicapped children in adoptive homes. Foreign-born children and children of mixed racial and religious backgrounds may also be available for adoption—all these possibilities can be explored with the adoption agencies. Costs (if any) are minimal and are usually based on ability to pay. Adoption agencies are more concerned with the emotional climate of the potential adoptive home than with material considerations.

It's How You Feel That Counts

Adoptive parenthood provides all the joys and satisfactions of natural parenthood; adoptive parenthood also presents all the normal problems, challenges, stresses, and strains. Living and loving in a family—any family—offers rich rewards and fulfillments as well as difficulties. It is important for adoptive parents to keep a sense of perspective and to recognize that all children are sometimes adorable and lovable and sometimes irritating and exasperating. The fact of adoption need be of no greater or less consequence than any of a hundred other special, unique variations in families. Good feelings about this particular difference—adoption—grow out of a child's experiences. If he feels surrounded by love and approval, he will assume that whatever the circumstances of his arrival in the family, everything must have been all right. If he feels accepted for himself, if his parents are flexible and understanding of human frailty, he will feel good about all the things that are part of his life and himself.

No two children in any family are alike. And children in any family can be totally different in temperament and interests from their parents. All parents wonder sometime if they are doing a good job, because every child has difficult times and is on occasion naughty and unhappy, fearful, shy, jealous of other children, bossy, and angry. In the process of growing up, all children experiment with some lying, stealing, or fighting against adult authority—being generally objectionable. All parents get tired, lose their tempers, are impatient, and make mistakes. But none of these things have anything to do with adoption. The challenge to all parents is to weather occasional storms without feeling threatened by them. If adoptive parents have faith in their love, support, and guidance as the basic ingredients for healthy growth, if they can anticipate the unfolding of a child's unique qualities with interest, spontaneity, and joy, they need have no fear.

To Tell or Not To Tell

It is important to tell a child that he is adopted; sooner or later he suspects or finds out anyway. When he does, he can only

assume that his parents' silence has meant that there is something wrong with being adopted. Children can face any reality when it is shared with loving parents. Adoption can be a fact of life without being unduly painful or shocking and without assuming undue importance in a child's life. There are times when a child may feel sad about being adopted, but there are also times when he will feel sad about being the shortest boy in his class or about failing his math exam or about not playing baseball as well as somebody else. But feelings of difference occur in everyone's life and are not fatal. In general and in the long run, a child's feelings about adoption reflect his parents' feelings.

Many parents find that the easiest way to introduce the word "adoption" to their child is to tell him stories about himself when he was a tiny baby—a source of never-ending fascination to all children. Sometimes the opportunity may grow out of looking through a baby book or picture album, sometimes a made-up story will serve the purpose, sometimes a storybook about adoption will be helpful.

The child's own questions about adoption will change as he grows. At first he is interested only in the happy circumstances that brought him to his parents; at 7 or 8 he may begin to ask questions about why the biological parents placed him for adoption. The most important goal for parents, in answering these questions, is to keep the lines of communication open so that their child will feel free to come back again when he is confused or troubled. If the questions are hard to answer, there is no reason for trying to hide your feelings from a child. The information asked for and received is really secondary to the sharing of real feelings between parent and child. Whatever information may be given or withheld, the important thing from the child's point of view is that past history is not nearly so important as the wonderful fact of being a family here and now. Parents can indicate that there were good reasons for the adoption—that whatever these may have been, the biological parents were deeply concerned with the child's welfare, and that their giving him up was an act of responsible caring, not in any sense a rejection of the child.

Adoption Will Out

An important reason for explaining adoption lies in the fact that children are bound to hear many explanations and interpretations of adoption from others. If they feel free to come and talk to their parents, they will feel secure about their information, and distortions are much less likely to occur. When a child is very young and cannot handle the subject himself, it may be wise to tell others about the adoption, such as a nursery school teacher or the pediatrician. Certainly, close relatives and friends should be told.

Waiting to make such explanations later on, without any apparent reason, may serve to exaggerate the importance of the fact of adoption to the child.

Because feelings of difference from others are often hardest to bear during adolescence, a teen-ager may become temporarily secretive about being adopted, but the phase will pass as he feels more sure of himself with others. Since adolescence is also a time of rebellion against parental authority, there may be times when parents are made to feel that they committed a terrible crime in dooming this child to be theirs, but they should take comfort from the thought that natural parents are being made to feel just as low and wicked. Because communication is often difficult during these years, questions about adoption can sometimes be handled with more ease through outside resources: books, family physician, or religious counselor.

If at any time in the course of growing up a youngster seems unhappy and unable to deal with his problems, parents may want to gain a new perspective on the situation by consulting a specialist. The adoption agency is always a resource for consultation and referral. So are community guidance centers, school guidance departments, family doctors, or religious counselors. Problems arise in all families. They are rarely related to any one factor but have multiple causes. When parents feel stymied, they should seek help without feeling that they have failed in any way.

Many books and pamphlets dealing with adoption are available, including a memory book specially designed for the adopted baby (*All About You* by Marion A. MacLeod, C. R. Gibson Company, Norwalk, Connecticut); storybooks for the young adopted child (*The Chosen Baby* by Valentine Wasson, J. B. Lippincott, 1951, and *The Family That Grew* by Florence Rondell and Ruth Michaels, Crown, 1954); and pamphlets for teen-agers (such as *So You Are Adopted* by Eda J. LeShan and Mildred Rabinow, Guidance Center of New Rochelle, 91 Centre Avenue, New Rochelle, New York). EDA J. LESHAN

See also BABY; BIRTH CERTIFICATE; BOOKS FOR PARENTS; COMMUNITY RESOURCES

AFFECTION *See* LOVE

AGE-HEIGHT-WEIGHT TABLE *See* GROWTH

AGENCIES AND ORGANIZATIONS

Most of the time, help is only as far away as the telephone—if you know whom to call. Illness, while the most serious problem, is often the easiest to do something about. You call your family doctor or pediatrician, the nearest hospital, or the local board of health. If you are new in the community, your county medical society will provide you with sufficient information to aid you in selecting a doctor, and usually he, in turn, will be able to refer you to the source of specialized health information you may need.

Hundreds of agencies and organizations, including your state (provincial or territorial in Canada) and federal government, provide information, guidance, and sometimes assistance in specialized areas. Before writing to a state or a national agency, look in your telephone directory to see if a local chapter is listed. Or talk with your minister or your child's teacher. They are usually well acquainted with local agencies and the services they provide.

Here is a partial list of the major national associations, societies, and foundations directly or indirectly concerned with the welfare of children.

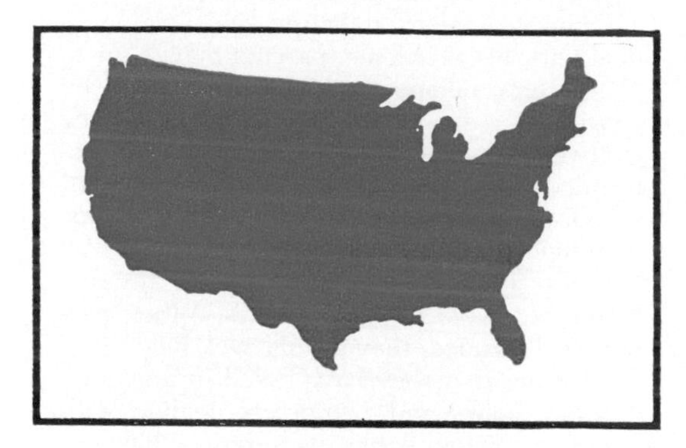

Alexander Graham Bell Association for the Deaf, Inc.
1537 35th Street NW, Washington 7, D.C.
Encourages the teaching of speech and lip reading to deaf children. Helps parents and teachers understand the special problems of the deaf. Assists schools with better educational facilities for deaf children. Encourages people to become teachers of the deaf. Free information kits and publications on speech and hearing are available to parents and teachers from the Association. A monthly magazine for parents, teachers, and educators is available from the Association.

American Academy of Pediatrics
1801 Hinman Avenue, Evanston, Illinois
Works with physicians and health organizations on child health problems. The Academy also provides information and assistance on child health problems to parents and teachers.

American Association for Gifted Children, Inc., The
15 Gramercy Park, New York 3, New York
Members are leaders in education, law, industry, the theater, art, music, and many other fields. The Association assists parents and teachers with the special problems of gifted children. Helps set up special schools for the gifted. Publications are available from the Association.

American Association of Marriage Counselors, Inc.
27 Woodcliff Drive, Madison, New Jersey
Refers married people to reliable marriage counselors and marriage counseling services. This service is available to those who write to the Association enclosing a stamped, self-addressed envelope.

American Association on Mental Deficiency
1601 West Broad Street, Columbus 16, Ohio
Is an organization of professional people who encourage research in mental deficiency. The Association assembles the latest information on prevention, care, treatment, and training of the mentally retarded.

American Association of Psychiatric Clinics for Children, The
250 West 57th Street, New York 19, New York
Is a standard-setting nationwide membership organization of psychiatric clinics for children. Local approved clinics, which may be both inpatient and outpatient, vary as to age range and services. The Association guides parents and teachers in the selection of an appropriate local clinic.

American Camping Association, Inc.
Bradford Woods, Martinsville, Indiana
Promotes the improvement and development of organized camping for children and adults. Furnishes information to parents about reputable camps for their children. Publications are available upon request.

American Cancer Society, Inc.
521 West 57th Street, New York 19, New York
Seeks to control cancer through research, education, and service. Filmstrip kits, pamphlets, and manuals are available.

American Dental Association
222 East Superior Street, Chicago 11, Illinois
Is an organization of members of the dental profession. Provides information on dental treatment, dental hygiene, and dental products. Refers those who ask to local dental care. Literature on dental health is available from the Association.

American Diabetes Association, Inc.
1 East 45th Street, New York 17, New York
Encourages education and research in diabetes. Seeks to educate the public in the early detection of diabetes. Helps the diabetic patient understand the condition better. Local affiliates sponsor meetings for diabetics and camps for diabetic children. Booklets, a bimonthly magazine, and a cookbook are all available from the Association.

American Friends Service Committee, Inc.
160 North 15th Street, Philadelphia 2, Pennsylvania
Is a world-wide Quaker organization. Programs include voluntary service projects and seminars for teen-agers and educational kits

for children 6–12, describing projects to help children in countries where American Friends Service Committee is at work. Literature is available from the Committee.

American Hearing Society
919 18th Street NW, Washington 6, D.C.
Seeks to improve and expand the services available to people with hearing and speech problems. Local organizations give scientific hearing tests, hearing-aid evaluation and orientation, speech instruction, and lip-reading instruction. Parent counseling and preschool deaf programs also are provided. Literature is available from the Society.

American Heart Association, Inc.
44 East 23rd Street, New York 10, New York
Seeks to control heart and blood vessel disorders. Counsels and rehabilitates cardiac children. Local chapters offer information and educational services to parents, teachers, physicians, and allied professional groups.

American Institute of Family Relations, The
5287 Sunset Boulevard, Los Angeles 27, California
Is a marriage counseling, education, and research organization. Offers classes to parents in preparation for childbirth. Provides premarital counseling and marriage counseling. Offers classes in developing good study habits to children. Bulletins and reading lists are available from the Institute.

American Medical Association
535 North Dearborn Street, Chicago 10, Illinois
Is an organization of members of the medical profession which seeks to advance the practice of medicine and to better the public health. Services to the public include health education materials, a question-and-answer service, monthly bulletin for teachers, conferences on health subjects, campaigns on health and safety problems, and publication of *Today's Health* Magazine.

American National Red Cross, The
Washington 6, D.C.
Is a national organization charged by the Congress of the United States of America to assist members of the armed forces and their families and to provide for disaster preparedness and relief. Other health, safety, and welfare programs are carried on by local chapters. The work is supported by adult, junior, and high school members. Publications are available from the national headquarters or your local chapter.

American Podiatry Association
3301 16th Street NW, Washington 10, D.C.
Is a national association of chiropodists. Provides literature, filmstrips, films, and slides pertaining to the growth and care of the feet to parents, teachers, and children.

American Psychiatric Association
1700 18th Street NW, Washington 9, D.C.
Does not provide psychiatric treatment or care for children and their families but helps to maintain standards in psychiatric services.

American Public Health Association, Inc.
1790 Broadway, New York 19, New York
Is a national organization of professional public health workers. Publishes special guides for teachers and health workers pertaining to handicapped children, emotionally disturbed children, and children affected by cerebral palsy, epilepsy, and heart diseases.

American Public Welfare Association
1313 East 60th Street, Chicago 37, Illinois
Is a national organization of public welfare employees, agencies, and others interested in public welfare. Provides information about public welfare programs and services for children and families. Does not provide financial assistance to families. Direct public welfare services such as financial assistance, foster care, or adoption planning are provided through state and local departments of public welfare.

American Social Health Association
1790 Broadway, New York 19, New York
Is a national health, education, and welfare organization. Works with schools and communities on training programs in family life education. Helps communities organize family life services. Works for the eradication of venereal disease and on the narcotics addiction problem.

Arthritis and Rheumatism Foundation, The
10 Columbus Circle, New York 19, New York
Seeks to control arthritis and rheumatism through education, research, and service. Refers people to local treatment clinics. Answers questions pertaining to particular types of arthritis and rheumatism. Films and publications are available from the Foundation.

Association for the Advancement of Blind Children, Inc.
520 Fifth Avenue, New York 36, New York
Is an organization of parents of blind children. Seeks to improve educational and recreational services to blind children. Provides a scholarship fund for people interested in teaching blind children. Literature is available from the Association.

Association for Childhood Education International
3615 Wisconsin Avenue NW, Washington 16, D.C.
Is an organization of parents, teachers, school administrators, teacher educators, and community workers concerned with the education of children 2 to 12. Encourages desirable conditions and programs in nursery and elementary schools. Informs parents and teachers of the needs of children and how the school program can be adjusted to fit those needs. Books and pamphlets are available from the Association.

Association for Family Living, The
32 West Randolph Street, Chicago 1, Illinois
Is an organization concerned with family welfare. Offers family life education and individual counseling on personal, premarital, marital, and parent-child problems. Monthly newsletter, pamphlets, and film guides are available from the Association.

Big Brothers of America
Suburban Station Building, Philadelphia 3, Pennsylvania
Is a national organization that helps boys between 8 and 18 who do not have fathers. Supplies men with information on how to be a substitute father to a boy. The essence of the method is "One Man—One Boy."

Boys' Clubs of America
771 First Avenue, New York 17, New York
Is a national organization concerned with helping boys from 7 to 18. Local Boys' Clubs

offer programs in physical fitness, hobbies, vocational skills, reading, music, dramatics, arts and crafts, and many other activities.

Boy Scouts of America
New Brunswick, New Jersey
Is a national organization that provides an educational-recreational program for boys 8 to 17. Offers programs in character building, citizenship training, and physical fitness. Pamphlets are available from the national headquarters.

Camp Fire Girls, Inc.
65 Worth Street, New York 13, New York
Is a national organization that provides an educational-recreational program for girls 7 through high-school age. The program combines fun and friendship with constructive, character-building activities.

Catholic Youth Organization
1122 South Wabash Avenue, Chicago 5, Illinois
Is a private organization that seeks to instill in the American Catholic youth love of God and love of country. Local parish priests direct religious, educational, recreational, and social service programs.

Child Study Association of America
9 East 89th Street, New York 28, New York
Is a child development and family life organization. Counsels parents on problems they are having with their children. Trains nurses, teachers, social workers, and psychologists in leadership. Book lists are available from the Association.

Child Welfare League of America, Inc.
44 East 23rd Street, New York 10, New York
Is a national federation of child welfare agencies. Develops standards, conducts research, provides consultation to agencies and communities, publishes professional materials, works with national and international organizations to improve policies affecting the welfare of children. Local agencies give services to parents and children, including counseling, adoption, and foster care.

Family Service Association of America
44 East 23rd Street, New York 10, New York
Is a national federation of family counseling agencies. Local agencies offer counseling to couples for various marriage problems. Provide help to neglected and dependent children and work for the prevention of juvenile delinquency. Accredited and competent social work counselors are available to help parents and teachers when serious problems of children arise in school or in the home.

4-H Clubs, See U.S. Department of Agriculture

Girl Scouts of the United States of America
National Headquarters, 830 Third Avenue, New York 22, New York
Is a national organization that provides an educational-recreational program for girls 7 through 17. Offers programs in character building, citizenship training, and community service. Pamphlets are available from the national headquarters.

Girls' Friendly Society of the U.S.A., The
815 Second Avenue, New York 17, New York
Is an organization sponsored by the Episcopal Church for girls 7 to 21. Offers programs in family life education, worship, recreation, and creative activities. The Society offers programs in more than 30 countries.

John Tracy Clinic
806 West Adams Boulevard, Los Angeles 7, California
Is an educational center for preschool deaf and hard-of-hearing children and their parents. The clinic's program consists of a consulting service that studies each child; hearing tests that determine what the child can hear; parent classes that are open to all parents of deaf and hard-of-hearing children; a demonstration nursery school that operates throughout the school year. A correspondence course is available to parents of children 5 years old and under anywhere in the world. Parent education films and records available to groups of four or more parents. There is no charge for any service to parents of deaf or hard-of-hearing children.

Leukemia Society, Inc.
405 Lexington Avenue, New York 17, New York
Seeks to control and check leukemia through research, education, and service. Local chapters offer counseling, guidance, and aid to patients and families affected by leukemia. Literature is available from the Society.

Maternity Center Association
48 East 92nd Street, New York 28, New York
Offers consultation on all questions pertaining to childbearing and maternity care. Conducts classes in preparation for childbirth and parenthood. Books, booklets, movies, filmstrips are available from the Association.

Muscular Dystrophy Associations of America, Inc.
1790 Broadway, New York 19, New York
Seeks to control and check muscular dystrophy through research, education, and service. Local clinics provide examination, physical therapy, medical advice, and assistance with personal and family problems. Literature is available from the Association.

Myasthenia Gravis Foundation, Inc., The
New York Academy of Medicine, 2 East 103rd Street, New York 29, New York
Seeks to control and check myasthenia gravis through research, education, and service. Local chapters offer patient-aid programs. Literature is available from the Foundation.

National Association for Gifted Children, The
8080 Spring Valleydrive, Cincinnati 36, Ohio
Is an organization that helps schools, parents, and communities plan educational and recreational programs for gifted children. Encourages the parents of gifted children to keep abreast of the latest information. Books and pamphlets are available from the Association.

National Association for Mental Health, Inc., The
10 Columbus Circle, New York 19, New York
Is an organization of mental health associations. Local associations give information about the treatment and education available to mentally ill children. Sponsor parent education programs. Pamphlets and films are available from the Association. The National Association for Mental Health, Inc., recently consolidated with the National Organization for Mentally Ill Children.

National Association for Retarded Children, Inc.
386 Park Avenue South, New York 16, New York
Is a national health organization dedicated to improved welfare, education, habilitation, and recreation for the mentally retarded on all age levels. Sponsors research into causes and prevention of mental retardation. Works through local and state units, which provide direct services to children and guidance to parents.

National Conference of Christians and Jews, Inc., The
43 West 57th Street, New York 19, New York
Is a national organization that educates people about racial, religious, and nationality prejudices. Works with parents on a project called "Rearing Children of Good Will," the purpose of which is to make parents aware that their attitudes about persons of differing race, religion, and national origin are transmitted to their children at an early age. Books and pamphlets are available from the Conference.

National Congress of Parents and Teachers
700 North Rush Street, Chicago 11, Illinois
Is the national organization of Parent-Teacher Associations. Local PTA's encourage cooperation between home and school. Sponsor discussion groups in such areas as family life education and health. Seek to improve children's environment in home, school, and community.

National Cystic Fibrosis Research Foundation
521 Fifth Avenue, New York 17, New York
Seeks to control and check cystic fibrosis through research, education, and service. Local chapters provide drugs and equipment, and refer patients to local clinics and centers. Literature is available from the Foundation.

National Education Association
1201 16th Street NW, Washington 6, D.C.
Is a national organization of teachers, administrators, and specialists in all types of schools, colleges, and educational agencies. Publishes periodicals and pamphlets primarily of interest to teachers; some for parents. List of publications sent free.

National Epilepsy League, Inc.
203 North Wabash Avenue, Chicago 1, Illinois
Is a national organization that collects all the available information on epilepsy. Has names of medical specialists. Locations of epilepsy clinics and psychiatric clinics. Operates a nonprofit pharmacy. Free literature is available.

National Foundation, The
800 Second Avenue, New York 17, New York
Is concerned (now that polio is under control) with medical scientific research, professional education, and medical care, primarily in the fields of birth defects, arthritis, and virus diseases.

National Foundation for Asthmatic Children at Tucson, The
P.O. Box 12337, Tucson, Arizona
Provides complete medical, educational, and recreational care for asthmatic children between 6 and 13. Accepts children from all areas of the United States. Children from low- and middle-income families are accepted with no cost to the family. Pamphlets are available from the Foundation.

National Foundation for Neuromuscular Diseases, Inc.
250 West 57th Street, New York 19, New York
Seeks to control and check diseases of the nerves and muscles through research, education, and service. Local chapters provide clinics, home physical therapy programs, and recreational programs for handicapped children and adults. Pamphlets are available from the Foundation.

National Jewish Welfare Board
145 East 32nd Street, New York 16, New York
Is the national association of Jewish community centers and Young Men's and Young Women's Hebrew Associations (YM–YWHA). Local centers conduct nursery schools and education programs for preschool children. Also conduct summer day and country camps, physical education programs, and social work programs for school-age children.

National Kidney Disease Foundation
342 Madison Avenue, New York 17, New York
Seeks to control and check kidney disease through research, education, and service. Local chapters provide drug banks and renal clinics. Literature and films are available from the Foundation.

National Multiple Sclerosis Society
257 Park Avenue South, New York 10, New York
Seeks to control and check multiple sclerosis through research, education, and service. Local chapters refer patients to proper clinics, which provide counseling to the disabled homemaker. Literature is available from the Society.

National Recreation Association
8 West Eighth Street, New York 11, New York
Is a national service organization that helps individuals and groups set up adequate recreational facilities and programs for children and adults. Booklets and pamphlets on family recreation are available from the Association.

National Safety Council
425 North Michigan Avenue, Chicago 11, Illinois
Is a national cooperative organization chartered by the Congress of the United States of America as the focal point of the safety movement in the United States. Its services include information on the prevention of accidents to children at home, at play, and at school.

National Society for Crippled Children and Adults
2023 West Ogden Avenue, Chicago 12, Illinois
Seeks to assist parents and families of crippled and physically handicapped children through education. Counsels parents and families of crippled and physically handicapped children. Offers scholarships to therapists interested in teaching handicapped children. Publications, films, and filmstrips are available from the Society.

National Society for the Prevention of Blindness
16 East 40th Street, New York 16, New York
Is a national health agency concerned with the prevention of blindness and with eye health and eye safety. Offers program consultant services. Publications and films are available from the Society.

National Tuberculosis Association
1790 Broadway, New York 19, New York

Seeks to control and check tuberculosis through research, education, and service. Local affiliates help parents and teachers develop child health programs. Booklets, films, and filmstrips are available from the local affiliates.

New York Association for Brain Injured Children
305 Broadway, New York 7, New York

Is a parent organization concerned with educational, medical, and recreational facilities for brain-injured children. The Association provides parent counseling courses, sponsors play groups, and helps to establish clinics and treatment centers. It also sponsors special teacher training courses. Literature is available from the Association.

Planned Parenthood Federation of America–World Population Emergency Campaign
501 Madison Avenue, New York 22, New York

Is an organization concerned with family planning. Local affiliates offer programs on medical birth control and provide consultation service to childless couples. Offers education programs on marriage and parenthood. Literature and films are available from the Federation and from local affiliates.

Play Schools Association, Inc., The
120 West 57th Street, New York 19, New York

Is an organization concerned with adequate recreational facilities for children. Provides workshops and discussion groups for parents, teachers, and volunteers. Pamphlets and films are available from the Association.

United Cerebral Palsy Associations, Inc.
321 West 44th Street, New York 36, New York

Seek to control and check cerebral palsy through research, education, and service. Local affiliates offer therapy, medical, educational, recreational, vocational, social work, and other services. Help patients and their families with special problems.

United Community Funds and Councils of America, Inc.
345 East 46th Street, New York 17, New York

Is the national organization of United Funds, Community Chests, and Community Welfare Councils in the United States and Canada. Local organizations help finance the work of health and welfare agencies.

United States Department of Agriculture
Federal Extension Service, Washington 25, D.C.

Sponsors 4-H Clubs for boys and girls between 10 to 19, who "learn by doing" through projects in farming, homemaking, personal improvement, community service, and citizenship. More information may be obtained from any county extension office or the extension service of any state land-grant college.

United States Department of Health, Education, and Welfare
Washington 25, D.C.

Children's Bureau

Provides grants-in-aid to all states for child health. Funds are used to help pay for prenatal clinics, public health nurses, well-child clinics, school health programs, and immunization programs. A booklet, *Infant Care,* is available from the Bureau.

Representatives take part in local and national conferences concerning educational needs of mentally retarded, emotionally disturbed, and physically handicapped children.

Provides grants-in-aid to all states for child welfare. Funds are used to help pay for the services of social workers, adoption agencies, and foster home agencies. The Bureau also provides consultation services on youth problems and assists agencies concerned with juvenile delinquency.

Office of Vocational Rehabilitation

Provides grants-in-aid to all states to help the handicapped.

The American Printing House for the Blind

Publishes braille books, including the entire WORLD BOOK ENCYCLOPEDIA, in braille, braille music, braille slates, and other educational needs for the blind or the partially seeing.

Young Men's Christian Association of the U.S.A.
291 Broadway, New York 7, New York

Is a voluntary national organization composed of locally autonomous associations that provide spiritual, social, recreational, and physical programs for members.

Young Women's Christian Association of the U.S.A.
600 Lexington Avenue, New York 22, New York

Is a national association that seeks to help young women. Local associations provide physical, educational, and creative programs. Literature is available from the Association.

The following Canadian agencies serve somewhat the same purposes as their counterparts in the United States.

Boys' Clubs of Canada
6 Weredale Park, Montreal 6, Quebec

Boy Scouts of Canada
P.O. Box 3520, Postal Station "C," Ottawa 3, Ontario

Canadian Arthritis and Rheumatism Society
La Société canadienne contre l'Arthrite et le Rhumatisme
900 Yonge Street, Toronto 5, Ontario

Canadian Association for Retarded Children, The
L'Association canadienne pour les Enfants arriérés
317 Avenue Road, Toronto 7, Ontario

Canadian Association of the Deaf, Inc.
562 Roselawn Avenue, Toronto 12,
Ontario

Canadian Camping Association
4322–4A Street S.W., Calgary, Alberta

Canadian Cancer Society, The
La Société canadienne du Cancer
790 Bay Street, Toronto, Ontario

Canadian Council of Christians and Jews, The
229 Yonge Street, Toronto, Ontario

Canadian Council on 4-H Clubs
Suite 300, 185 Somerset Street West, Ottawa 4,
Ontario

Canadian Cystic Fibrosis Foundation
263 McCaul Street, Toronto 2B,
Ontario

Canadian Dental Association, The
L'Association dentaire canadienne
234 St. George Street, Toronto 5, Ontario

Canadian Diabetic Association, The
477 Mount Pleasant Road, Toronto 7,
Ontario

Canadian Education Association, The
L'Association canadienne d'Education
151 Bloor Street West, Toronto 5, Ontario

Canadian Eye Research Foundation
2401 Bloor Street West, Etobicoke, Ontario

Canadian Federation of the Blind, Inc.
210 Northern Crown Building, Regina,
Saskatchewan

Canadian Hearing Society, The
60 Bedford Road, Toronto 5, Ontario

Canadian Heart Foundation
1130 Bay Street, Toronto 5, Ontario

Canadian Home and School and Parent-Teacher
Federation
370 Dundas Street West, Toronto 2B, Ontario

Canadian Mental Health Association, The
National Office
L'Association canadienne pour la Santé Mentale
52 St. Clair Avenue East, Toronto 3, Ontario

Canadian Mothercraft Society
616 Avenue Road, Toronto 7, Ontario

Canadian National Institute for the Blind
L'Institut national canadien pour les Aveugles
1929 Bayview Avenue, Toronto 17, Ontario

Canadian Physiotherapy Association
64 Avenue Road, Toronto 5, Ontario

Canadian Podiatry Association
3017 Bathurst Street, Toronto 19, Ontario

Canadian Public Health Association
1255 Yonge Street, Toronto 5, Ontario

Canadian Red Cross Society, The
La Société canadienne de la Croix Rouge
95 Wellesley Street East, Toronto 5, Ontario

Canadian Rehabilitation Council for the Disabled
Conseil canadien pour la Réadaptation des Handicapés
263 McCaul Street, Toronto 2B, Ontario

Canadian Tuberculosis Association
Association canadienne antituberculeuse
343 O'Connor Street, Ottawa 4, Ontario

Canadian Welfare Council, The
Conseil canadien du Bien-être
55 Parkdale Avenue, Ottawa 3, Ontario

Child Health Society of Canada, The
684 Church Street, Toronto 5, Ontario

Child and Maternal Health Division
Department of National Health and Welfare
Ministère de la Santé nationale et du
Bien-être social
Copeland Building, Ottawa, Ontario

French-Canadian Association of the Blind
Association canadienne-française des Aveugles
900 Beaubien East, Montreal, Quebec

Girl Guides of Canada—Guides du Canada
50 Merton Street, Toronto 7, Ontario

Health League of Canada, The
La Ligue de Santé du Canada
111 Avenue Road, Toronto 5, Ontario

Muscular Dystrophy Association of Canada, The
L'Association canadienne contre la Dystrophie musculaire
160 Bay Street, Toronto 1, Ontario

Victorian Order of Nurses for Canada
5 Blackburn Avenue, Ottawa 2, Ontario

(Young Men's Christian Association)
National Council of Y.M.C.A.'s of Canada
2160 Yonge Street, Toronto 7, Ontario

Young Women's Christian Association of Canada
571 Jarvis Street, Toronto 5, Ontario

Young Men's–Young Women's Hebrew Association
750 Spadina Avenue, Toronto, Ontario

AGGRESSIVENESS

We all have a built-in tendency to satisfy our needs by acting in an aggressive manner—and it's a good thing we do, too. Aggressiveness should not be confused with anger, hostility, rage, or hatred, emotions that arise when normally aggressive attempts to satisfy our needs are blocked. Your infant is aggressively demanding when he cries to be fed. Later, he will need a degree of aggressiveness to defend his rights, to earn a living, or perhaps to explore outer space—all aggressive acts in response to differing needs: self-protection, economic self-sufficiency, curiosity.

Aggressiveness, then, is natural and necessary; yet parents and teachers must nurture and support a child's aggressiveness if it is to develop properly, if it is to lead him toward sturdy independence.

Children seem to overproduce aggressive behavior at three different stages in their development, although not all children show their defiance at the same age, to the same degree, or in the same way. The 2½- to 3-year-old's defiant "no," is really short for "Look! I'm somebody, too. I can say *no,* just like you."

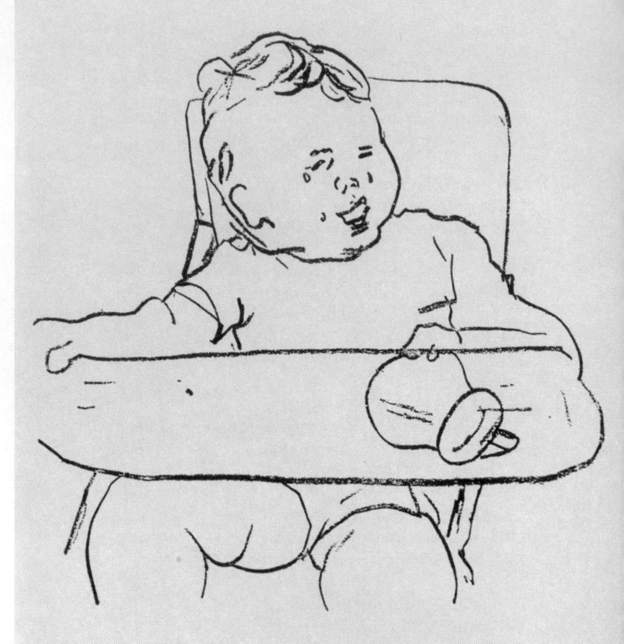

"Look, I'm somebody, too!"

True, most children can be "broken" to outward obedience and docility, but the price is too high. The child who is forced or frightened into meek obedience will only bury his resentments—perhaps to have them come out in a less acceptable form later on. Therefore, it is never wise to oppose aggressive behavior in principle or just to show who is boss. Instead, try to help your toddler find ways to keep and strengthen his healthy desire to be somebody while restraining him from acts that would be physically or emotionally harmful to himself or to other children. Tell him firmly that he may not hit, or strike, or bite, or kick. But usually, there is no good reason why he should not be permitted to pound or yell, cry or blow off steam in some other manner emotionally satisfying to him.

Around 10 or 11, children, especially boys, again may show intense signs of aggression. They become more defiant and argumentative, testing both open and less obvious ways to do—or not to do—their parents' and teachers' bidding. At times, a preadolescent will try to prove that he is beyond adult control and supervision. Such behavior shows, again especially in a boy, a desire not only to establish that he is somebody (just as he did at 3) but that he also is a special kind of somebody: resourceful, knowledgeable, mature; no pushover; competent.

A sensible adult dealing with aggressive behavior in a preadolescent relies on the same guiding philosophy he used with the 3-year-old: maximum freedom except where danger threatens the child or those about him. Obviously, there is a difference in the kind of behavior the parent has to deal with at the preadolescent stage. The child has more control and greater intellectual maturity. He can understand good reasons for his parents' yes or no, but he can also see through phony or foolish excuses more readily than at 3.

The final stage of marked aggressiveness is reached between 14 and 16 years—and boys are still more outwardly aggressive than girls. It is natural for children this age to behave in an aggressive manner, for what age range has more complex and hard-to-meet needs than the mid-adolescent? With an adult body and, in many cases by 16, a fully developed intellect, he is deprived of a role and privilege system for meeting these fully adult needs. Sexual needs are almost totally blocked, status is not clearly defined, relationships with parents and teachers often undergo severe strain.

The main risk at this time is that parents will panic and become overauthoritative, or freeze and become overyielding. Either extreme increases a young person's confusion and fearfulness and hence his aggressiveness. Now is the time for parents to do a little remembering, for most of the time it hasn't been very long ago since they, too, faced

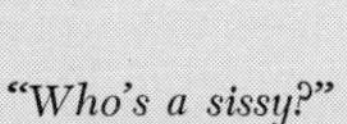

"Who's a sissy?"

"It's just an old doll!"

these same bewildering problems. When parents can communicate to their child that they understand his problems, that they will do whatever they can to help him acquire the satisfactions that can be legitimately had, there is every chance that he will come through this tricky period as a self-confident, self-reliant individual, well in control of his emotions. DAVID WINEMAN

See also ANGER; DISCIPLINE; HOSTILITY; PROBLEM CHILD

ALIBIS *See* EXCUSES

ALLERGIST *See* MEDICAL SPECIALISTS

ALLERGY

A child who has an allergy displays an unusual and abnormal reaction to various substances that he may eat, inhale, or come in contact with. Hay fever, asthma, eczema, and hives are some of the allergic conditions. Rheumatic fever and related diseases are believed to result from an allergic reaction of the tissues of the body to bacteria, particularly to the bacteria causing "strep throat."

Heredity plays a part in allergic reactions. Thus, children subject to allergic reactions often have a family history of allergies, although the family's allergies may differ.

A child's age seems to have some effect on the kind of reaction he develops. Eczema is more common in the infant; bronchial asthma and hives usually occur after the first year of life; hay fever usually develops in later childhood or adult life. Rheumatic fever usually develops after a child is 5. Each of these conditions is somewhat different in each child, and the reaction may range from brief-and-mild to long-and-severe.

Allergic reactions may also follow shots—particularly if the child has had similar injections before. Penicillin shots and tetanus antitoxin are examples of injections that may produce reactions. Fortunately, most children are now immunized to tetanus so that when they are injured, they do not need antitoxin but only a booster shot, which usually does not cause allergic reactions.

For a child with a history of allergy in the family, new foods and injections should be introduced cautiously. If allergic reactions such as eczema, asthma, or hay fever develop, the physician may test the child for sensitivity to various substances and then try gradually to reduce the sensitivity. He does so by the injection of small amounts of these substances over a long period of time.

If allergic conditions are well controlled, they have little effect on the general growth and activity of the child. JULIUS B. RICHMOND

See also HEREDITY; INTRODUCING NEW FOODS; MEDICAL SPECIALISTS; SHOTS

ALLOWANCE

A regular, predictable amount of money in the form of an allowance is one of the most worthwhile educational experiences parents can provide their children. As a child learns the possibilities and limitations of his allowance and as his needs multiply, the amount of the allowance can be increased.

What Is an Allowance?

An allowance, in the true sense of the word, is a child's share of the family income, and it should be an amount no larger than the family can afford. It should be considered the child's to do with as he pleases; it should never be withheld because of disobedience, poor grades, or unwise spending. An allowance is never a bargaining tool to guarantee a child's good behavior.

His allowance will give a child a realistic, firsthand experience in planning how his money is to be spent and how to get full value for what he spends. It will provide a natural place to learn arithmetic, an area in which he has to use logic, and it will eventually show him that sometimes a pleasure postponed is a pleasure increased. The child will make mistakes or buy unwisely at first. He may rush to spend all his money the minute he gets it, forgetting that no more will be forthcoming for several days. From such unwise haste, however, he will learn to be selective in his purchases and prudent in his spending.

When To Begin an Allowance and How Much

Sometime around his fifth birthday your child may ask you for an allowance such as his friends or his older brothers and sisters enjoy. Or he may have driven you to consideration of the necessity for an allowance by the daily demand process. You may wish to start him on a 10-cents-a-week allowance, but a nickel twice a week may prove a blessing to the child who finds a week unbearably long. The word "allowance" implies a margin of choice. A child will soon figure out that he can have two candy bars this week, or he can save his allowance for two weeks and buy a toy airplane, but he cannot have both candy and toy.

By the time a child enters school, if he has managed his own allowance for a year or so, he is ready to take on the additional responsibility of managing money he will need for school expenses—bus fare, supplies, lunches, or milk money. The family council offers a good opportunity to discuss what a child is expected to do with his newly increased allowance. Experiences of older brothers and sisters often will be valuable to him as he estimates his weekly requirements.

GUIDELINES

- Don't control your child's buying. Let him make mistakes, for in this way he will learn.
- Don't insist that a small child save something out of his allowance. "The future," "college," "a rainy day" mean nothing to a young child. A savings program will appeal to him when he has something special to save for.
- Don't associate money with discipline in any way. Don't withhold allowance money for misbehavior.
- Don't confuse a child's allowance with money he gets for chores done about the house.

Some Spend, Some Save

Each child is different. Each handles money not only according to the kind of person he is, but also according to what money has come to mean to him. Is your child one of these?

The efficiency expert. This child can handle good-sized sums of money, planning in advance for haircuts, piano lessons, his savings program, and his daily expenses, both school and social. He keeps a record of the money he gets as an allowance, money he earns, and money he spends. He totals the columns weekly and always balances his accounts. He is apt to grow stuffy about his financial genius. It would not hurt him to learn about some of the deeper values of money.

The hoarder. This child saves his money just for the sake of seeing the pile get bigger or the piggy bank get heavier. Such hoarding is not always healthy. If a child is saving for a specific purpose, his thrift is commendable. If, however, hoarding is done with a miserly attitude or because of feelings of insecurity, he needs more education about what money is really for: to exchange for something that contributes to his own or another's happiness and well-being.

The spendthrift. This youngster spends his week's allowance the minute he gets it. He may spend it all on himself or he may rashly treat his friends. He, too, needs parental guidance to curb his impetuosity. If he is "buying friendships," he may need your help in straightening out his values.

The borrower. This child spends all his money and then remembers that he has made

FOR PARENTS

- Do plan your child's allowance with his expanding needs in mind.
- Do encourage generosity.
- Do consider your child's small financial problems worthy of your attention. Help the hoarder by taking him on a gay splurge. Tell the spendthrift that he can have the special microscope if he will save for it.
- Do stress to your child that money isn't everything. There are things that money can buy, but there are many things that no amount of money will buy, and these include loyalty, friendship, respect, and love.

plans to see a movie with his friends. He manages to borrow the money from his parents. When the next allowance day comes, it is much better for him if he is shown firmly what a loan is, that when he borrows money, he has an obligation to pay it back as promptly as possible. His resultant slim allowance will make him think twice before he borrows again. He has, then, learned another important lesson about money.

See also FAMILY DISCUSSIONS; RESPONSIBILITY

AMMONIA RASH *See* DIAPER RASH

ANEMIA

The substance that is made up of iron and protein and gives the red color to red blood cells is called hemoglobin. When the hemoglobin level is lower than normal, the condition is called anemia. Although all pale children are not necessarily anemic, the child with anemia is usually pale, and he may not feel as energetic and playful as usual. If the anemia is severe and comes on suddenly, the child may be without energy, short of breath, and critically ill.

Some of the many causes of anemia and the treatment, depending upon the cause, are:

Not enough iron in the diet. In the second half of the first year of life, a baby may become anemic if he receives only milk, for milk—almost a complete food—lacks iron. Meats, egg yolk, and vegetables may be necessary and can be added to the diet if recommended by your doctor. Early anemia also responds to iron given in medicinal form.

Not enough iron absorption. In some chronic diarrheas, iron may not be absorbed by the intestines, and the diarrhea must be corrected before the anemia can be cured. Iron given in medicinal form or, in severe cases, a blood transfusion, is desirable.

Loss of blood from an injury or from an ulcer or in hemophilia or other bleeding diseases. The cure lies in an attempt to stop the bleeding and, if necessary, the giving of blood transfusions.

Destruction of red blood cells. In a number of hemolytic anemias, red blood cells are destroyed unusually rapidly within the body. Some of these conditions are common to a family and others are acquired in ways that are obscure. Some cases occur because of sensitivity to drugs or plants. The afflicted child needs a doctor's care. JULIUS B. RICHMOND

See also BLEEDING; BLOOD COUNT; CANCER; NUTRITION

ANGER

When a child's normal, active attempt to satisfy an important need is blocked, he is frustrated. And his frustration leads to that powerful emotion, anger. For example, your infant cries for help when he is hungry, when he is wet, or when he is cold. If his cry is not heeded, he becomes anxious and then angry. His cries become louder, his body movements more agitated. His crying and agitation can rise to the point of rage where he appears simply to be a "screaming mass of protoplasm." Sometimes, as when the source of discomfort is more hidden—if he has colic, for instance—he will cry and toss until he wears himself out and falls into a fitful sleep or until he gets medical help.

A toddler can become angry simply because a toy won't work for him in the way he would like. Then he may show his anger in a different way. He may attempt to destroy his toy by smashing or stamping on it. What he is really doing is trying to remove the very source of the painful stimulation and temptation that the toy exerts over him. In being destructive, a child also actually relieves the painful tension of the anger itself, for once anger begins because of a need that cannot be satisfied, it becomes a substitute for the need in its own right. And there is something "satisfying" about the expression of anger, once stirred to a certain point.

The preschooler has learned to express his feelings, and so words may replace a physical show of anger. "I hate you" or "I'm going to kill you" are statements whose angry basis are quite obvious. Even the young child in his early experimentation with language, may say to you in a moment of anger: "Me gonna t'ro you in garbage can!" While you may be shocked by such outbursts, it is important to realize that your child, in changing from physical to verbal expression of anger, has made a giant step toward becoming a socialized person. When a child says he intends to do harm or wants to do harm, he may be as much asking for help in controlling the impulse as he is threatening to release it. What he wants is some adult help so that he does not have to adopt such desperate measures.

As children grow older they improve in their abilities to do things and also in their ability to tolerate not being able to do some things. Hence they tend to become less subject to anger. But a chronically angry child may be throwing up a danger sign that asks for assessment of what is going on within him and also around him, perhaps by a child psychologist. Chronic anger and deep uncontrollable anger should not be ignored.

At the same time a child is learning to deal with his own anger, he is also learning to cope with anger in others. He finds that there is an end to a parent's patience, especially one who is overly tired or who has been provoked too far. It is far better for a cross or irritated parent to admit angry feelings, not only to get them out of his or her system, but to make a child more comfortable with his own reactions under similar circumstances. For there is nothing more damaging to a child's peace of mind than to be around a parent who is repressing or denying righteous indignation. DAVID WINEMAN

See also PUNISHMENT; TEMPER TANTRUM

ANIMAL BITES *See* BITES, ANIMAL

ANIMALS, FEAR OF

For most children, an animal is something to love. Though a dog or a cat is the usual pet, a child's affection may extend to turtles, guinea pigs, birds, insects—even toads or snakes. There is seldom any fear of animals found in children who are brought up in a family that cherishes pets. If the parents are afraid for their children or for themselves, however, or if the child has been pounced upon by a dog or severely scratched by a cat, he is likely to become fearful.

This state is unfortunate, since pets are a great source of consolation as well as of delight to children. When the grown-up world seems unfriendly, a little child often turns to a pet, which he endows with the feelings of a human being. Indeed, a live animal may become a bridge from the child to people beyond his parents. The beloved dog is a stepping stone to the warmth and confidence the child wants to find in people.

Just to hear about big, ferocious, or cunning animals as they are pictured in some fairy tales may be frightening to some children. It is easy for a child to transplant the fears he may have of some strong person he loves, such as his father, to an animal. A little boy at night says he is afraid of wolves, though no real wolves are in his experience. It is uncomfortable to be afraid of one's father, hence the transference of his feelings to an imaginary wolf or lion or whatever he regards as powerful. The child does not say or know, "I am afraid of my father," especially since he also loves his father. When he

imagines that an animal will bite him if he does something bad, he saves himself from fearing his father. A child will often conjure up such a fantasy when he has been scolded or punished, for example, for masturbation.

Parents have been known to use the threat of harm by an animal to make a child conform to their wishes. This method of discipline is a poor one, for it threatens a child's security and makes him afraid. As he gets older, he usually corrects these notions but not always completely.

In their fear of allergies, some parents avoid pets for their children altogether. This avoidance may be necessary, but pets do not have to be made despicable or threatening. Children can learn much from pets: patience, loyalty, the value of obedience. HELEN ROSS

See also FEAR; PETS; SHYNESS AND TIMIDITY

ANIMALS *See* PETS

ANIMALS, CRUELTY TO *See* CRUELTY

ANTHOLOGIES *See* BOOKS FOR CHILDREN

ANTIBIOTICS *See* DRUGS

ANXIETY

An infant gets restless when he is hungry; he cries as a signal of distress. If he has been neglected and allowed to go beyond feeding time to the point of pain, his body remembers and he becomes tense. If this happens often, he may get "anxious" about feeding even before his stomach is empty. Thus, anxiety might be called anticipated discomfort or danger.

Later, when he has had a few uncomfortable early experiences—as for example, routine shots in the doctor's office—he will show anxiety if he recognizes his mother's preparations for the checkup visit. If he falls from his high chair, he may resist being put in it.

A child tries to avoid pain. He cannot say, "I am anxious," and even when he can talk, he would not use those words. But he would react in some characteristic way, with resistance or crying or maybe downright panic.

Children differ in their tolerance of discomfort. Some seem able to weather almost any amount; others are more sensitive and respond quickly with panic or even tantrums.

One of the important lessons taught us by psychiatry, especially from studies since World Wars I and II, is this difference between human beings: how much they can bear.

This difference can be seen even in children of the same family. To all appearances their rearing has been the same. Yet it can never be identical. Both the external and the internal circumstances of their lives vary: Each has his own physiological and psychological make-up. Parents do not feel exactly the same about each child, though they try to play fair and outwardly show no difference. Parental attitudes, however, play a big part in shaping a child's disposition.

"Mother, why do you lock the doors?"

Because of these many variations, anxiety cannot be limited to general terms. It is highly specific for each child.

Anxiety cannot be entirely avoided. Even with the best intentions, parents say or do or feel something about their child that causes him to wonder and worry. A mother who was going out for the evening said to her nervous little son, "We always take good care of you. We lock all the doors when we leave." After a few minutes, the thoughtful child asked, "Mother, why do you lock the doors?" Unwittingly she had given him some of her own anxiety.

Anxiety gathers first about a child's basic needs—for food, for care, for protection against hurt. Later, when he is about 4 or 5, he becomes anxious also for assurance that he is doing the right thing. Though these anxieties begin at different phases of development, they may continue for a long time, even into adulthood. They start little, but they may grow big and even interfere with normal activity. The child who was often hungry in early life may never quite recover from the fear that there won't be enough to eat. His apprehension started with food; it may lead to anxious effort to amass enough money to cover all possible lacks. The child who suffered from humiliation because he was smaller than his big brother may in adulthood have to contend with a continuing discomfort in the presence of tall men. The little girl whose mother was always scolding about dirtiness may later develop a compulsion for cleanliness that interferes with her husband's peace at home.

Anxieties do not stand still; they are likely to spread and they may result in emotional crippling. The anxious child has little of the normal venturesomeness that brings growth and pleasure; he restricts his interests. He is unsocial because he is afraid of not pleasing people. Maybe he has tried to secure his mother's or his father's love and feels he has failed; this failure makes him anxious about the esteem of others, too. Children normally wish to please.

Children rarely know what they are anxious about. One can observe their behavior and still not be sure, though a parent who knows his child well listens with an inner ear and often catches on to the difficulty. Then reassurance is needed, not just in matter-of-fact words, such as, "You know there is no bear behind the door," but rather, "Maybe you think there is a bear behind the door because you fought with your little brother today." Then he can be reassured that his parents know the baby is annoying and they will try to keep the younger child from knocking his toys about. No one can make up a formula for every anxiety a child suffers. But one can remember that he is miserable and needs kind words to relieve his distress.

Sometimes, too, many anxieties are heaped on a child at once, and it may be hard to avoid this combination of circumstances. Mother has to go to the hospital, a new baby arrives, father is called away because of the illness of his brother, the family is about to move into a new house, and a well-meaning grandmother thinks it a good time to toilet train the 2-year-old in order to save trouble after mother gets home. Try not to pile too many new things on a young life at once. Even adults find a rapid series of untoward happenings hard to digest. Probably everyone can reach a point at which he knows he has had too much.

To avoid the uneasiness of anxiety, a child develops his own characteristic ways and these help to shape his personality. Just why he chooses one way or another is a subject of great interest to psychologists. Some children deny their fears. They feel weak; they deny the weakness in pretending always to be brave and strong. Or they make fantasies of their prowess; they are giants or wild animals who can terrify others. When they are about 5 or 6, they usually give up this make-believe and try to avoid any competition that will show them up. Sometimes they are able to hide from these feelings; that is, they suppress the thoughts of weakness throughout life. Or they blame the other person for being against them or planning harm to them. Since these devices are developed in the early years, they seem childish and unrealistic, and indeed they are to us who observe them, but they are not to a child, who seeks always to get along with comfort and ease. These characteristic methods are called defenses. It is important to help a child face events realistically so that he uses his powers of adjustment and enlarges his scope of interests. This adjustment and enlarging is called ego strength. The weak ego seeks defensive ways and further weakens itself. The strong ego tries to extend itself. HELEN ROSS

See also ADJUSTMENT; FEAR; MENTAL ILLNESS

Related article in WORLD BOOK: "Ego"

APPENDICITIS

Most commonly, appendicitis occurs in older children and young adults, but it can occur at any age.

The symptoms of acute appendicitis usually begin with vague, general abdominal pain, which localizes within four to eight hours in the right lower abdomen. There may be tenderness of the abdomen, vomiting, fever, and a feeling of constipation. Exact diagnosis may be difficult during the very early stages, and laxatives may aggravate the condition, so *no laxatives or cathartics should be given for any ailment unless specifically advised by a physician.* If treatment is not provided within 24 to 48 hours, the appendix may perforate and cause an inflammation of the abdominal cavity called peritonitis. The most effective treatment is surgical removal of the inflamed appendix. The operation usually is not associated with complications.

"Chronic" appendicitis is quite rare, and when children complain of chronic or recurrent abdominal pain, the pain is usually due to other causes. Yet because of the hazards of delaying the diagnosis of acute appendicitis, call the doctor when a child complains of abdominal pain. JULIUS B. RICHMOND

See also OPERATION; STOMACH-ACHE

APPETITE

Whether your child has a good or a poor appetite depends on his experiences with food. From babyhood he gradually forms impressions of food based on emotional reactions. If his experiences with certain foods are pleasant, he will again want to eat foods associated with those experiences.

A baby has painful sensations when he needs food. The pain is relieved by food; therefore, the infant's first reaction to food is fraught with pleasure. Gradually, he recognizes his mother as the giver of food. If mother is loving and tender when she feeds him, he begins to associate food with love. But if she later fails to feed him when he is hungry, he may have mixed feelings.

How can you promote good appetite?

First, give food only to allay hunger; do not force it; do not use food as reward or punishment.

Secondly, help your child to develop a desire for high-content vitamin, mineral, and protein foods that nourish the body. Also help him to control a craving for foods high in sugar.

Thirdly, when preparing food, consider color, odor, texture, and arrangement on the plate. Young children are sensitive to these qualities. A mother who recognizes this sensitivity will respect her child's opinion about food. MIRIAM E. LOWENBERG

See also FEEDING SCHEDULE; INTRODUCING NEW FOODS; NUTRITION

APPROVAL

Approval makes the world go round. A pat on the back, a friendly smile, a word of praise—these are the things that make us feel good inside, spur us on to do our very best, and give us a deep sense of our own worth.

Have you ever stopped to think what you'd be like if it hadn't been for the expressions of approval that people gave you as you were growing up? Bet you wouldn't be nearly so nice a person, so active or so educated as you are, without those smiles, pats, and words of approval.

Nobody can amount to much unless he has faith in himself. Approval is one important way of developing a child's belief in his own worth.

There was a time when parents were afraid to give a child too much approval or praise lest he become conceited. Some parents still feel that way.

But they needn't worry. Psychologists tell us that we should always approve the child himself, but that we should not approve of everything he does. There's an important difference. Only the wrong kind of approval spoils a child. The right kind at the right time builds up his self-confidence.

The baby says, "ma-ma" and his parents' smiles and exclamations of approval encourage him to keep on saying "ma-ma" and other words, too. Your 7-year-old daughter helps you make cookies. And if you want her to help you in the future, you had better be lavish with your approval of her fumbling efforts and not point out her faults and failures. When your child does something you don't approve of, your attitude should be, "I still like *you* but I don't like what you did." That way you teach him that he's worth something, but there are certain things he must not do.

Some parents spoil a child by thinking that everything he does is cute. They give in to him, which is a form of approval. They laugh when he does naughty things. They never teach him what is acceptable behavior and what is not.

Ideally, the approval you give a child should be suited to his personality. Watch a good teacher at work. She looks at the paper of a shy, unhappy youngster and comments, "That's good—the best you've done. Don't you think so?" To another, more self-confident child, she says, "Your answers are correct but that paper's pretty messy. Next time, try to make your work neater." And to the bright youngster whose work habits are not up to his ability, she says, "Are you pleased with this report? I'm not. You can do better than that. I'd like to see you develop this point further; explain this one and this one, too."

Sometimes, it is hard to find anything to approve in the behavior of problem youngsters. One kindergarten teacher, at her wits' end with a trouble-making child, said to him, in a flash of genius, "You're such a good rester. I'm proud of you. Now, let's see if you can sit still as nicely while I'm telling a story." The pleased smile the youngster gave her warmed her heart and told her that at last, she was getting through to him.

The trick is to make each child feel that he's all right but that he can improve himself.

We mothers would do well to use this technique more often. We're usually so busy that when a child brings us his work to admire, we do just that, without encouraging him to better efforts.

I once heard a child say to herself as she tidied up her clothes closet, "It's still pretty messy, but Mom will say 'That's fine!' "

Children need lots of approval when they are little. As they grow older, they should develop self-confidence and need less approval from others. Grownups shouldn't be dependent on the approval of others at all. But most of us are—a little. MAY R. SHERWIN

See also DISCIPLINE; LOVE

APTITUDE TESTS *See* TESTS AND MEASUREMENTS

ART EXPERIENCES

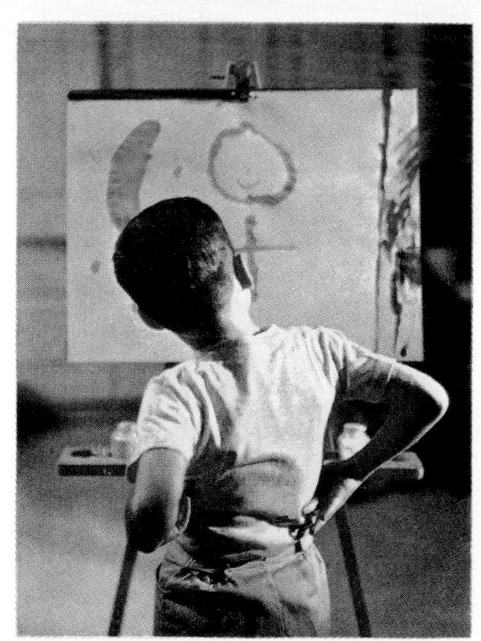

Painting and drawing are as natural for a child as speaking. When a young child paints a picture of an automobile and decorates it with beautiful colors, perhaps he is expressing his delight in the new family car more vividly than he could in words. That child is lucky, indeed, whose parents are as thrilled with each forward step in the language of art as they are with each new venture into speech.

We are learning that the more ways children have to express their feelings, the better.

Of course children often paint or model or cut and paste for sheer pleasure. Not everything they make represents deep emotion, but a picture that appears to be only streaks of color may mean a great deal to the child who painted it. Perhaps it is the way he feels about a train or his dog or his mother. A child gains a tremendous sense of satisfaction when what he has made is respected, particularly in art, where his emotions are involved. If you stand back and watch him, you may discover what he is trying to say in his picture. Then it will have more meaning for you, too.

Shall We Criticize the Work?

What shall you say to a child when he proudly shows you something he has made? A picture may look strange, or even funny, to you. If so, it is safer to say too little than too much. You might ask, "Would you like to tell me about it?" If he does not want to talk about it, he should not be pressed.

You can always find something good to mention, such as a beautiful color or an unusual form. Then a child will feel your interest and pleasure. Perhaps you can hang the picture on the wall. Giving children's pictures a place in the home is the best evidence of your approval and helps build confidence in their ways of seeing and doing. You don't have to tell them their work is "marvelous."

Painting Takes Courage

Many children will start out painting boldly and soon bring you something to admire. But how about the child who timidly dips his brush into a color and makes only a few marks with it? This first attempt appears feeble, but it may have taken all the courage he could muster.

A casual remark, such as, "What a beautiful color!" particularly if he has mixed it himself, might make him glow with pride. If he is encouraged to develop at his own pace, his effort may be a first step toward a joyful and releasing experience.

Where Do You Begin in Art?

Although everyone can imagine countless things to make, sometimes neither grownups nor children can get started. One good way is to squeeze and punch clay and see what happens to it. It is exciting to mix colors and see how they look next to each other or on paper in various shapes and forms. Trying such things often suggests ideas. There is a great deal of pleasure in putting shapes and colors together into a satisfying design. Such creativity has always been a basic concern of true artists.

Experimenting with colors and forms will also help the child who keeps repeating a skillfully drawn picture because he has been highly praised for it. He is really afraid that he will not be able to make anything else as "good." Concentrating on shapes and colors will help him to break away from repetition of what he can do and to start exploring new possibilities.

Repetition does not always indicate reluctance to go forward. When a 5-year-old, after visiting a farm, models crude little lambs over and over, he may only be reliving a new experience until he feels at home with it.

Some children experiment for a while and then turn to making recognizable objects. Other children continue to put together different colors, shapes, and lines into increasingly beautiful but abstract pictures.

Shall We Show Them How To Draw?

Some people have the false notion that only children whose work shows talent should be encouraged. The essential point is not what children make, but what is happening to them while they are making it.

Unless a child expresses dissatisfaction with what he has made, you certainly should accept it without criticism. A child dissatisfied with his clay horse may ask his father to show him how to model it. Father might say, "Let's look at a horse and see what shape he is. Is he curved or square? Is he longer than he is high? Make it the way he looks to you, because if I should show you my way, it would be my horse and not yours."

Copying Pictures

Sometimes a parent asks, "When I see my child making a shapeless blob for a boat, why shouldn't I draw one for him to copy?" If what the child has made means "boat" to him, the feeling that it is not "good enough" will be a crushing blow to his pleasure in having made it. He may come more and more to distrust himself and to lean on and copy others.

Some children have been led to believe that copying is all right. They like it. What shall we say to the child who copies a monkey from a circus poster? Even though his picture may be neat and competent, it is only an attempt to copy someone else's lines. If he paints a monkey as he knows or imagines it, his picture may be crude, but it is his own. We might say, "Even if you can't paint so well as the man who made the poster, you could make a monkey all your own, and I'd love to see it."

We should not make children feel guilty about copying. If we ourselves do not confuse copying with art, in all likelihood our children will discover it is just busy work and will lose interest. Art is not a copy of objects. It is a combination of color, lines, and shapes put together into a sensitive expression of an artist's response to his world.

How Artistic Ability Grows

When a 3-year-old makes sweeping marks across paper, he is enjoying moving the brush back and forth and watching the color come from it. At this same stage of development he squeezes his clay, pats it, and rolls it, enjoying the feel of it. It would be wrong to tell

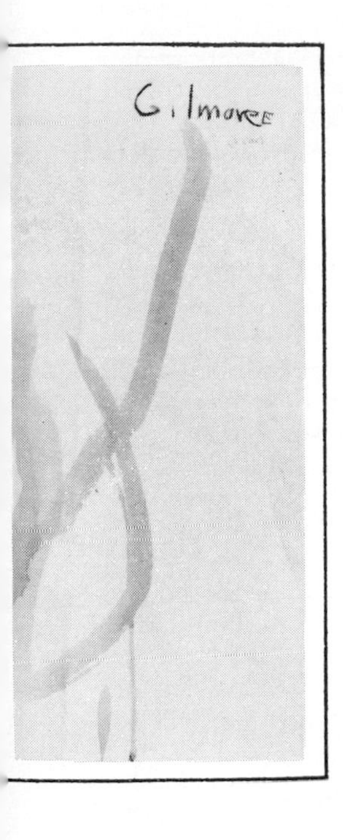

him to make something real, like an animal or a tree. You would not say to a child babbling his first beginnings of speech, "Say something sensible"!

When he is a little older, brushmarks and shapes suggest objects to him. He may say, "I am making a house." Before he finishes, it may turn into a truck or a forest, or he may dab his brush on the paper and say, "Now it's on fire! It's raining!" Yet when he began, he probably had nothing particular in mind.

Sometimes parents and teachers attempt to use children's art as a means of getting at personality problems. A mother may have read, for example, that a child's use of certain colors or color combinations indicates trouble. But in her child's case, his use of color may bear no relation to his personality.

It would be a pity to mar our enjoyment of our children's creative expression and their pleasure in the activity by a feeling that we must examine every painting for indications of behavior problems. We should no more feel free to attempt this kind of diagnosis than we would in the field of medicine.

What Are They Saying in Paint and Clay?

If a child does not bother with a body or arms or legs when he paints a picture of his mother, we should not assume that he is unaware of them. Hands and face mean mother love to him and are enough. Young children often paint or model a kind of shorthand picture, putting in only what to them are essentials. To a 6-year-old girl the essential thing might be her pretty dress and she would include enough of herself to display it.

Another child who had begun to be concerned with what was happening around him might paint himself standing in a real place. The line at the bottom of the paper means ground to him, and he would put the sky overhead where he knows it belongs. When he models himself playing ball, he may, as a matter of course, make his throwing arm longer than the other. Young children are not concerned about the actual size of things in relation to one another. Making things large in relation to their importance is not new in art. Artists in the Middle Ages, for example, pictured God enormous and the people small.

Children also like to draw things in the way that they feel explains them most clearly. For example, in his picture of a village square, one 8-year-old drew the fronts of the houses. Because they are all around the square, naturally they appear to be lying down. He has seen the square with a kind of "inner eye" and has painted it as it actually is.

Can a Child Understand Perspective?

Perspective has no meaning for young children. They will draw railroad tracks the way they are, in parallel lines. The converging lines of receding tracks drawn in perspective make a triangular shape. This may look like a railroad to us, but it is only a triangle to the average child under 7 or 8, who may ask, "What's that?"

Many older children and adults continue to see with their "inner eyes." The actual form is so vivid in their minds that they disregard surface appearances and represent things as they "know" them to be, rather than as they appear in perspective. One way of seeing is as valid as the other, and both should be accepted with equal respect.

Perspective is no longer taught in most elementary schools. Teachers are beginning to realize that art must be a personal expression. They discourage copying and never hold up children's paintings and point out where one is "better" than another. They teach a technique only when it can help a child to say more easily what he wants to say. If techniques are learned as they are needed and used, they will be remembered.

If School Stresses Technique

Sometimes we must face the problem of what to say to children who find themselves in a classroom where copying and dictated artwork are accepted practices. Naturally, children do not want to be "different." We might say, "Of course when you are in school you will want to do it their way, but at home let's use our own ideas. It's more fun."

What Equipment and Materials?

If we want our children to paint and model, we must provide materials and an inviting place to use them. Perhaps we can find a free corner, even if it has to be in the kitchen or living room. When a child wants to paint something vivid, having to wait until elaborate preparations are made may dampen his enthusiasm for the idea that stirred his imagination. If possible, keep the materials where they are readily available. You need not be disappointed if a boy or girl is soon satisfied with his painting. The intensity of children's feelings and the values they get from painting or modeling cannot be measured in time.

Equipment need not be elaborate. An easel, perhaps homemade, is desirable because it allows free arm movements and holds the child's painting up where he can see what he is doing. A piece of wallboard standing against the wall, with oilcloth or paper under it to protect the floor, makes a good substitute for an easel.

If space is available for a low cabinet or shelves, the wallboard can be attached to the top and the materials stored underneath. When children prefer to use a table or the floor, newspapers or oilcloth can be spread under their work. A smock, or one of dad's old shirts with sleeves cut short, will protect the child's clothes.

How Can You Keep Clay at Home?

Clay can be stored in a can or a crock. A tight cover, or plastic material wrapped around the clay will prevent drying. Use oilcloth or a small board under the clay when your child models. Tongue depressers, each cut to a point, and orange sticks make good modeling tools.

Clay comes powdered to be mixed with water, or ready mixed. The latter, while more expensive, is more convenient. Dried, used clay can be soaked in water to be reused and too-wet clay can be left uncovered until firm.

Plasticine, although less messy than the clay mentioned earlier, is less satisfying because it is rubbery to the touch and will not harden.

Palettes and Brushes

A muffin pan is a fine "palette" or, better still, glass furniture coasters that hold small quantities of different colors may be placed on a tray. Some mothers prefer small glass jars that can be covered so that the paint does not dry up. At least one flat bristle brush, approximately seven-eighths of an inch wide, is advisable for a child up to 6 or 7. Older children should have half-inch and quarter-inch brushes as well, and finer brushes for detail.

There should be a container for water to wash brushes, and a jar or tray to hold them. Children should wash all the paint out of their brushes and never put them bristle-end down. Young children need help in getting out and putting away materials. As they grow older, they can take responsibility for pouring their own paints and keeping their brushes and other materials in order.

Suggestions for using many everyday materials in making things can be found in Volume 9, *Make and Do,* pages 39–92.

What Kinds of Paint?

Paint comes in many forms, and, of course, no family would need all the kinds described here at once. *Poster paint,* or "show-card color," is best for children. It helps the child to express freely his feelings and ideas, because it flows readily and covers the paper easily. The colors are opaque, so a youngster can change any part of his picture by painting one color over another. Black, white, red, blue, yellow, and green are the only colors needed. Even though the initial outlay may seem large, it is economical to buy paint in pint or half-pint jars. Jars must be kept covered or the paint will dry out.

Powder paint is less expensive than poster paint and, mixed with water to the consistency of heavy cream, is almost as good but less convenient, for it spoils quickly and must be mixed often.

Oil paint is expensive. It cannot be washed off the child or his clothes with water. The brushes, if not thoroughly cleaned with turpentine, become stiff and unusable.

Water color, usually bought in a narrow box of cubes, lacks the freeing quality of poster paint. While it is no substitute for poster paint, water color at times is more convenient and its use should not be denied to children.

Finger paint helps timid children to get started and to gain courage for other types of painting. The recipe for making finger paint at home can be found in Volume 9, *Make and Do*, pages 44–45.

What About Chalks, Crayons, and Paper?

Colored chalks respond easily to the touch and cover surfaces quickly. They are best used on an upright surface so the child will not rub his arm across his picture and smear it. Since chalk dust does not clean off easily, wearing a smock is essential. The floor should be protected, too.

Crayons or *colored pencils* are less expensive than paint and not so messy, but they have less freeing power than paint. A crayon or pencil must be pressed hard to get a rich color. The child tends to grip more and more tightly and to become tense as his interest increases rather than to relax as he does in painting.

Paper sheets should be large and plentiful. For most children, unprinted newspaper or wrapping paper is thoroughly satisfactory. You can prepare old newspapers for painting by covering them with calcimine paint and spreading them flat to dry. Bogus or other rough-surfaced paper is good for chalks.

Other Materials Are Everywhere

Children should have a box to collect yarn, feathers, shells, wire, cloth, bottle caps—the list is endless. Children delight in rough and smooth surfaces. When they combine paper and burlap pieces with cellophane and bark, for example, they can enjoy both touching and looking at the designs they make. Anything that, through shape and texture, stimulates the child's urge to invent or create, is material for art.

Innumerable suggestions for helping a child enrich his art experience through the use of paints, modeling clay, chalks, and crayons, as well as bits and scraps to be found about the house, are contained in Volume 9, *Make and Do*.

The child who feels free to paint, model, or create with other materials the things he sees or feels, will be able to use his leisure time more happily and constructively now and in later life. He will have, too, a valuable channel to help drain off anger and resentment, work out doubts and fears, and express joy and satisfaction. JANE COOPER BLAND

See also APPROVAL

Related article in WORLD BOOK: "Art and the Arts"

ARTIFICIAL RESPIRATION

When a child's breathing stops for any reason, the parent's very first act should be to try to restore natural breathing as quickly as possible—to apply artificial respiration.

The various techniques of artificial respiration are all aimed toward the same end—to get an open air passageway from the lungs to the mouth and to move air in and out of the lungs by alternate expansion and contraction in the size of the chest.

The mouth-to-mouth technique, taught to all Red Cross trained people, has been the approved method of artificial respiration of the American Red Cross since 1958.

Mouth-to-mouth has several advantages over earlier methods. It provides positive pressure to inflate the victim's lungs immediately. It also enables the one giving respiration to judge more accurately the volume, pressure, and timing needed to inflate the victim's lungs.

To apply artificial respiration, you must first be sure the air passages are clear. When a child is unconscious and not breathing, the base of the tongue tends to press against and to block the upper air passageway. Foreign matter in the mouth may also form a block.

To assure free passage of air, your first step in artificial respiration is to wipe out any foreign matter that is visible in the mouth, using your fingers or a cloth wrapped around your fingers (Photo 1). Then tilt the child's head back so that the chin is pointing upward, and pull or push the jaw into a jutting-out position (Photo 2). This maneuver should move the base of the tongue away from the back of the throat.

Open your mouth wide and place it tightly over the child's mouth. If the child is small, you may be able to place your mouth over both the mouth and the nose. If this is not

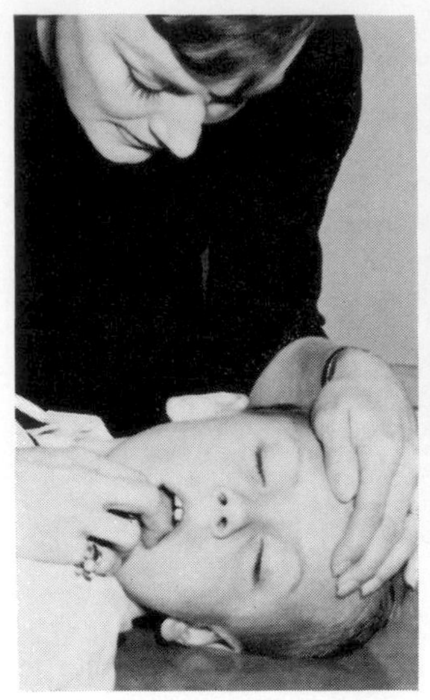
Photo 1

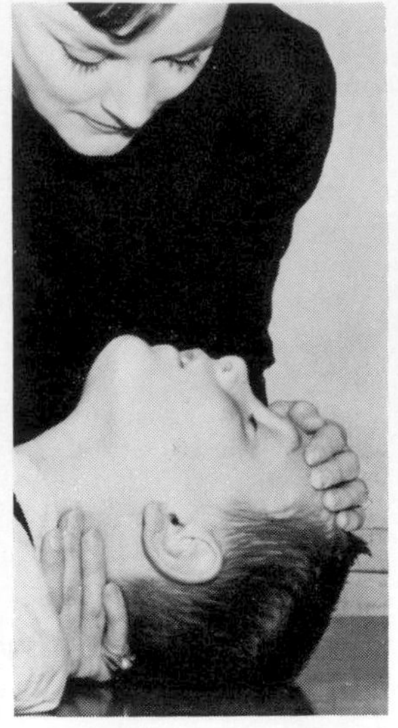
Photo 2

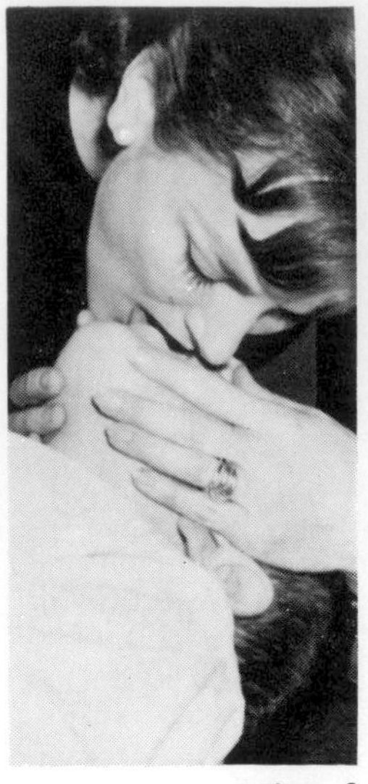
Photo 3

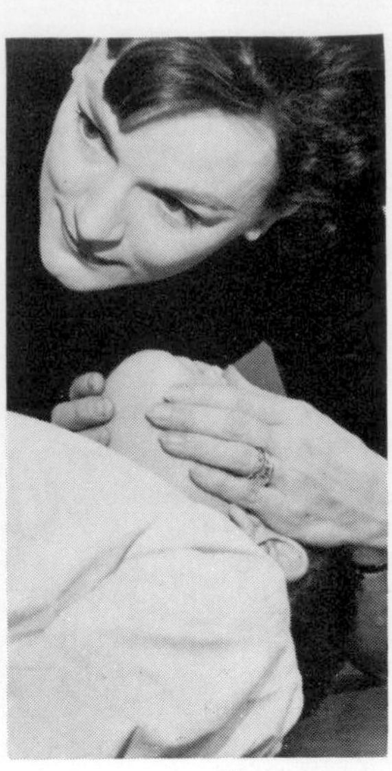
Photo 4

possible, it will be necessary either to pinch his nostrils shut or close them by pressing your cheek against them (Photo 3). Blow into his mouth (or mouth and nose).

This blowing effort will tell you immediately whether or not there is an obstruction to the passage of air. If there is, check again to be sure there is no foreign matter in the mouth, and again pull the jaw forward.

After the first attempt, remove your mouth and turn your head to the side, listening for the sound of the return rush of air as the lungs contract (Photo 4).

Now, repeat the blowing effort, alternately inflating the lungs in this manner, and listening for the return rush that indicates air exchange. When administering artificial respiration to a child, take relatively shallow breaths appropriate to the child's size, at the rate of about 20 per minute. (The older the victim, the deeper and slower the breathing. The adult average is about 12 breaths per minute.)

If, after rechecking the head and jaw position, you still have been unable to get an air exchange, quickly turn the child on his side and slap or punch him sharply, several times, between the shoulder blades. This should dislodge any foreign matter in the upper throat. Again, wipe out the mouth and repeat the preceding steps. With a very small child you can clear the air passageway by suspending him for a moment by the ankles or by holding him, head down, over one arm and giving him two or three sharp pats between the shoulder blades.

Artificial respiration should be continued until the child's normal breathing resumes or until the doctor arrives.

This mouth-to-mouth (or mouth-and-nose) technique has been thoroughly tested through research projects supported by the Department of the Army, the American National Red Cross, and others. It is the most practical method for emergency resuscitation of an individual of any age who has stopped breathing for any reason. ROBERT E. KILBRIDE

See also EMERGENCY

ASPIRIN POISONING *See* POISONING AND POISONS

ASTHMA

In an asthmatic attack the air passages to the lungs become narrowed. Air can usually be inhaled into the lungs, but there is difficulty forcing it out. The wheezing sounds are caused by this difficulty in expelling air.

Why some children develop asthma is not known, although children with asthma may have other allergic disorders, such as hay fever, and may have had eczema earlier in their lives. The offending substances are usually inhaled particles such as dust, pollens, and animal dander, but the substances can be many, including, for instance, foods.

Through skin tests a physician can often discover some of the substances to which the child reacts. To avoid these substances completely is usually difficult, so the physician sets up a resistance in the child by a careful injection of very weak amounts of the offending substances.

If asthmatic attacks are frequent and severe, comprehensive medical care is important, for such attacks may keep the child from growing normally in height or weight and may cause his chest to become "barrel" shaped because of the chronic distention of his lungs. In acute attacks some drugs are helpful, but they must be prescribed and supervised by the physician.

Asthma may have both emotional causes and emotional effects. The undesirable emotional effects can come about because the child is limited in his physical activity or is missing school or because of his reaction to invalidism. Every effort should therefore be made to minimize his handicap. The emotional factors that sometimes cause asthma are varied and numerous; among them are rivalry with sisters or brothers. In many cases of asthma it is extremely helpful to consult a child psychiatrist. JULIUS B. RICHMOND

See also ALLERGY; SHOTS

ASTIGMATISM

Contrary to popular belief astigmatism, a condition in which images are distorted or blurred, is a common disorder found in two out of three children. Both nearsighted and farsighted eyes can be astigmatic. The condition seldom represents a serious handicap.

Astigmatism is difficult, if not impossible, to diagnose without a medical eye examination, but there are some signs that indicate the possibility. Occasionally, in more severe forms, a child may hold his head at an angle to make up for a blurred image. In milder forms the constant effort on the part of the eye to overcome the irregularly blurred image may result in various symptoms, such as headache, fatigue, irritability, or general eye inefficiency. But these symptoms can also come from other forms of eye difficulty, so do not attempt to do your own diagnosing. Your ophthalmologist (medical eye doctor) will make a diagnosis and if necessary, prescribe glasses to help your child to see well and comfortably. ROY O. SCHOLZ

See also EYEGLASSES; EYE HEALTH

ATHLETE'S FOOT *See* RINGWORM

ATHLETICS

Physical activity contributes to good health; good health contributes to physical activity. Such a circle is desirable in the life of a child. And the way to make the circle most desirable is to have the physical activity fit the age, the emotional and physical maturity, and the interests of the child.

Physical education in the beginning grades has two objectives: to increase the child's coordination and skills and to allow him to enjoy a game as a member of a group. But a first-grade child will later in his life need to know about teamwork and cooperation, so his earliest physical education at school also includes gaining some sense of discipline. The child is taught through athletics why and how one gets along with others, why and how one controls tantrums, and how group spirit can take the place of the individualistic attitude. At the first-grade level this is the beginning of the sportsmanship concept.

Physical educators rarely attempt real team play for children before the children are 8 years old. In the first place, there are few team games suitable for children under 8; in the second place, very young children are still overcoming their "me first" stage. But by the time a child is 8 or 10 years old, he can begin to play team games with an appreciation of the fundamentals of team play—not, however, under highly competitive conditions, for to him the important aspect of any game is still that it is fun. Because organized sports put into practice some of the principles that the children learn in their earlier physical education, team games for fourth graders, or even better, fifth or sixth graders, can be definitely beneficial, provided—and this is important—provided such games are not overstressed. After-school games that are played at the children's own school, among their friends and classmates, with only an occasional casually interested parent as spectator and with not too much emphasis on the need to win are fine. But interschool or intercommunity games played before large groups of spectators, with cheers, bands, and adulation of stars, give the players an entirely wrong perspective.

Games involving body contact are unsuitable for children below high-school age. The elementary school child's skeleton is not mature and he is, therefore, especially susceptible to bone and joint injuries. Injuries, of course, can be incurred in any kind of game, but in body-contact games injuries are likely to be more severe. Equally detrimental in body-contact games is their greater competitive stress. Young children can gain almost nothing from games that send them into tempers or tears.

Aside from these concerns, however, competition on a reasonable level, in the right kind of game for his age, is good for a child, and sports have a specially important role in teaching him to compete. Most children in the upper grades of elementary school, when given a chance, organize and enjoy games of their own. Trouble comes when the wrong kind of organization—organization according to adult standards—is provided. Children do not need uniformed leagues, nor do they need to perform before adult audiences on a scheduled basis and with competition beyond their own neighborhood or school district. Such stressful athletics will not only cause serious emotional upsets in some children, but they may also destroy the child's love of a game before he has reached the stage where he can really benefit from it. Disappointment sometimes drives an adult to better his performance, but it seldom does so for a child, and a child in a very competitive atmosphere who fails to make the team may lose his incentive to play.

Although schools do not generally provide such highly competitive sports for young children, there is a strong tendency for baseball, football, and basketball leagues to be organized as outside programs. Few of these leagues are manned by professional physical educators, and they are rarely approved by the educators. The leagues frequently develop into the adult idea of what children need and want. But a child is not merely a small adult, and just to shorten the periods, cut down the size of the playing field, and modify the rules does not make a child's game out of an adult sport. Out of school, misdirected athletic activities can produce a child who is tense, tired, and not enjoying a game that should be fun. His schoolwork often shows the results of this stress.

In elementary schools that do provide the more intensive body-contact type of sports, such as tackle football, the parents of children participating should look at the program carefully to be sure certain qualifications are met. To begin with, the child should have an especially thorough physical examination by his own physician before participating. The examination should be repeated any time the child shows evidence of abnormal fatigue or injury. Parents should demand the presence of a physician at all games. They should insist that such athletics not be allowed to interfere with the school program—including homework. No large audience of adults should be permitted, no night games allowed, and no coaches employed who are not qualified physical educators. And before any such after-school activity is sanctioned for a few boys, parents should demand that the school provide a well-balanced physical education program for *all* children, a program that stresses good physical development and teaches skills in activities that can be continued in adult life. ROBERT A. MC GUIGAN

See also CAMP; COMPETITION; SOCIAL PRESSURES

ATTENTION SPAN

When you say about your child, "He was perfectly satisfied with his blocks for an hour," or "He'll look at a book for only a minute," you are talking about his attention span. A more formal idea of attention span includes not only the ability to keep attention focused on an object or activity but also the ability to learn while focusing. Attention, therefore, becomes an important aspect of mental development. Attention span is clearly not a simple or single ability, because it varies greatly depending on what the child is doing and his situation while he is doing it, on his interest in the project, his age, and his energy and health.

As a child grows, his attention span changes. Your child at 5 will stay with a self-chosen activity two or three times as long as he would have stayed with an activity when he was 2. But, measured in minutes per activity, his periods of concentration, even at 5, are relatively short. His attention characteristically shifts from activity to activity. Moreover, his attention span is not going to be the same as that of all other children his age.

Any given child will also vary greatly in the amount of time he will spend with different kinds of activities or he will vary in the amount of attention to the same activity at different times. You may know your child and his habits quite well and still not always be able to predict how interested he will be by some new activity or by old ones on different occasions. Nursery schools recognize that a young child must have a variety of activities and many opportunities to change from one occupation to another. This is why the good nursery school provides free play as a large part of its educational program.

Your child's attention span will depend, too, on the intrinsic interest an activity has for him or on the incentive or reward to be found in it. Although a kindergarten child usually turns from an activity after a few minutes, he may on a certain day and under certain circumstances persist for a long time, up to an hour and a half, for example, picking out a one-finger tune on the piano. Often an adult cannot understand why such an activity should be so intrinsically rewarding.

External rewards clearly influence the attention span also. In one type of study where the reward was systematically changed for several planned tasks, the average time spent by a child on the tasks was 7 minutes when no incentive at all was offered, 11 minutes when he was praised, and 17 minutes when he performed the tasks in competition with other children.

When children grow older, their ability to stay with a task can be considered a significant sign of responsibility and maturity. In school and in those home tasks involved with learning, the ability to concentrate—that is, the ability to stay with a task with prudent interruptions for rest but without wool-gathering—becomes of great importance. How to train the ability to concentrate is not fully understood. But this much about it is understood: It is probably not wise to hold a child arbitrarily to unrewarding or unpleasant tasks simply for the sake of discipline. The child may achieve some success that he can recognize, but enforcing work is much more likely to build dislike of work than to build good habits or moral character. On the other hand, praise for the child after periods of concentrated study, extra recognition for bringing activities to a successful completion, and making the success of his efforts obvious to him are useful devices, valuable in helping a child to form good study habits and to increase his attention span. DALE B. HARRIS

See also MENTAL DEVELOPMENT; REWARDS

ATTITUDES

A child's attitudes toward life and living develop out of his experiences in his home and the world adjacent to it, experiences in which he has been made to feel he either is or is not acceptable, accepted, and worth while.

If the child's attitudes are not sound and healthy, he will believe himself to be unlovable or "bad." He may express his unhealthy attitudes by striking out at others in order to punish himself or by being too withdrawn in order to spare himself the consequences of his supposed unlovableness.

Healthy attitudes are those in which the child feels that he is a worth-while person, able to play his role in his family, in his work, and among his friends and equals. With these attitudes he can accept other people and respect their rights. He will have a sense of purpose, a knowledge of what he himself believes in, and goals that are possible for him to reach. RUSSELL C. AND MOLLIE S. SMART

See also MORAL AND SPIRITUAL DEVELOPMENT; SELF-CONCEPT; SEX EDUCATION

AUTHORITY *See* OBEDIENCE

AVERAGE CHILD *See* NORMAL CHILD

AWKWARDNESS

A parent is often caught between laughter, pity, impatience, and worry as he comes in contact with the awkwardness of his child. "Isn't he funny, poor thing, how can he stumble there every time; doesn't he see the step?" If the child laughs over his awkwardness, it may be fine to laugh with him; otherwise, kind adults keep their own counsel.

When a very young child cannot at first hold a cup and drink from it, he is not labeled "awkward." His ineptitude, however, stems from the same conditions that later are called awkwardness in the preadolescent and adolescent—immaturity in development and not enough experience.

In preadolescence growth slows. At the same time strength increases and coordination improves. Energy is enormous. With his added strength and better coordination and exuberant vitality, the preadolescent child can take on many more activities. He is apt to want to swim, ride horseback, play baseball and football. His lack of experience at these sports will make him look awkward and uncoordinated until he gains more skill and ease, through trial and error and through practice, perhaps under adult guidance. Besides, his vigor, crying to be spent, makes him restless, unable to sit still, hasty, careless. As he tears about, he can seem to be extremely awkward when he is merely operating under a full head of steam.

The adolescent, although he often appears to be more awkward than he was in a previous period, has usually gained in strength and in a more coordinated use of his muscles. His trouble is that his body is now growing fast again, and he may not know what to do with so much recently acquired arm or leg or neck or elbow. The adolescent can also be made awkward by his uncertainties, not being sure what are the correct social procedures in his group, not being sure how he will get along on dates, not even being sure whether he is grownup or not grownup.

Awkward children are often pleased to have some assistance from adults. They can enjoy instruction, demonstrations, and opportunity for practice in various muscle-using skills. They can profit from encouragement and from praise for something they have accomplished. They would only be set back by frustration, damage to self-esteem, or practice that is too difficult or too repetitious.

Some children never outgrow their awkwardness, nor do some adults. IRVING E. SIGEL

See also SELF-CONSCIOUSNESS; TEEN-AGER

BABY

It isn't always love at first sight when parents gaze upon their newborn. But love has a close ally—compassion. The human heart is rare indeed that fails to respond to a new arrival—weak, helpless, utterly dependent. You want to take care of him, to shield him, to help him grow up to be all that he is capable of becoming.

During the early weeks and months, a baby's needs are largely physical and emotional. These needs should be satisfied promptly, fully, and with affection. Crying, the universal language of babies, is the only means he has to let you know that he is in distress. When he is hungry, he will cry. When he is wet or otherwise uncomfortable, he will cry. When he is bored or feels forsaken, he will cry.

There is a rhythm to his needs, a depth to their intensity, which you will soon discover by watching him closely. And gradually you will be able to satisfy these needs before his fear and anger can bring on acute tension or full-fledged anxiety. If you accept him as he is, seek to understand and fulfill his needs, and cherish him, he will reward you in countless ways.

Physical Development

The early physical development of your baby likely will receive closer attention than any other aspect of his growth. Second only to "Boy or girl?" you will hear the question, "How much does the baby weigh?" From a birth weight probably ranging somewhere between 5½ to 8½ pounds (boys are, on the average, a little heavier and longer at birth than girls), a baby's weight will increase to around 20 to 26 pounds by the end of the first year. During this time, his body proportions will change rather dramatically, with the trunk and limbs growing proportionately more than the head, which at birth represents about one-fourth of total body weight. The size at birth, however, is of little importance and does not predict adult height. The length of an infant at the end of a year, though, foretells adult height moderately well.

Your newborn after a day or two can hear. He may immediately respond with a startle or quiver to loud sounds. Even sounds of lesser intensity, such as footsteps, may cause him to become alert; if sucking, he may suddenly stop, or he may try to turn his eyes or his head to the source of the sound. Contrary to popular belief, he can see to some extent right after birth. He senses light and dark and will blink at strong lights. He will also move his eyes back and forth in an effort to follow a moving object held near his face. Focusing, though, is still difficult. He is sensitive to the feel of things: soft, warm blankets, the temperature of his bath water, a slippery rattle. And he knows the difference between tender, loving hands and those that handle him roughly or indifferently.

After six to eight weeks you may be pleasantly surprised to find your baby staring intently at your face, especially when you look straight at him. In a few more weeks, his eyes will follow you around the room, and he may burst out crying if you leave his field of vision. He will also take a sudden interest in objects, fixing his gaze on them and perhaps grabbing at them. But he probably will not be able to coordinate eye and hand movements enough to pick up objects until he is 5 or 6 months old.

Your newborn possesses a variety of responses to different tastes and smells. For example, if you offer milk to him, he will make strong sucking movements, but a bitter solution likely will cause him to make a face. Face-making, however, means nothing when it comes to discriminating against poisonous solutions. He will eat or drink anything, no matter how evil-smelling or tasting, as soon as he is old enough to find it. From the moment your child can creep or crawl, he needs to be protected from contact with any substance that can cause stomach disturbance and possible death.

Very early in his first year—usually by 2 or 3 months—your baby will acquire a sort of daily schedule that matches his general physical maturity. The pattern of this schedule seems to grow out of his natural inclinations and the needs of his mother and other members of the family. He will take in more calories at one feeding and will, therefore, be able to wait longer between feedings. At the same time, he will learn to sleep more

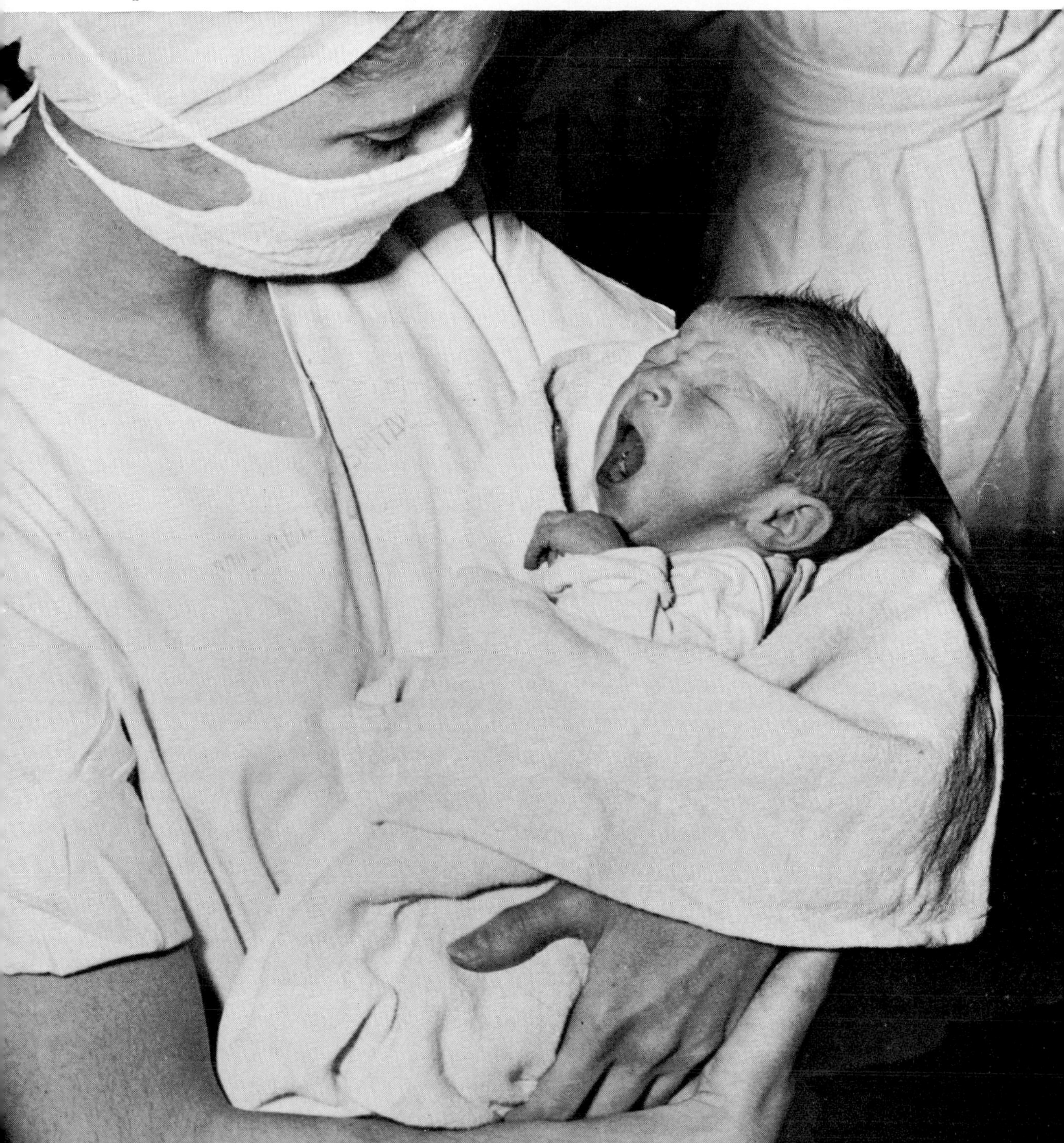

soundly—and will permit other members of the household to do the same. His sleep schedule will be closely related to his feeding routine, and undoubtedly the nature of the mother-infant relationship is affected by the smoothness of the feeding-sleep routine.

Motor and Mental Development

If you delight in watching your baby's physical development, you will rejoice in watching his motor or muscular development. Muscular activities offer the best visible reassurance that your baby's development is proceeding properly. With awe and excitement you notice when your baby pushes his head and chest up from the mattress, rolls over, reaches for a mobile dangling over his crib, grasps a rattle or takes it into his mouth. Then, of course, the days when baby first sits, stands, crawls, or walks are red-letter occasions indeed.

Why should parents get so excited over a baby who has just accomplished a turn from his back to his stomach? For more important reasons than the fact that a neighbor child of the same age did the same thing a week ago, to be sure! Such an event signals that the infant's nervous system—his control and communication center—has matured to a stage where coordination of his muscles is now possible. It means, too, that he has attained some independence of action: If he is uncomfortable in one position, he can change to another. And even more important to him, he can now maneuver himself into a position to look at the world about him, to scan his surroundings (few interesting events occur on the ceiling) and begin to interpret what is going on there. Soon, by the time he is 3 or 4 months old, he will enjoy being propped up for short periods.

Similar small miracles of growth and development happen almost daily during babyhood. And each develops out of preceding events and paves the way for succeeding events. For example, achievement of the prone, or face down, posture is essential for getting ready to sit up or to creep. A baby must have gained control of certain eye muscles and have had success in holding onto objects placed in his hand before he is able to pick up something he wants.

No one can predict precisely how your baby's motor development will take place. Although experts have worked out a development timetable for the typical baby, each child follows his own growth pattern. A perfectly normal baby often does not conform to the standard timetable. Drastic deviations from this table, however, may indicate either that he is precocious or somewhat retarded.

Generally, a baby sits up between 7 and 9 months of age. He may begin creeping when he is 6 months old, or he may wait until he is a year old to crawl. Some babies never creep at all. Somewhere between 10 and 12 months of age many babies will stand. But one with much energy and determination may get to his feet as early as 7 months, whereas an easygoing infant may wait for more than a year. All these babies may be healthy and normal; there is usually no need to worry about a baby who takes his time to develop muscular skills. Remember, though, that motor development is complex, and a child doesn't progress at the same rate in all ways. Even though a baby sits up at an early age, he may, for example, have difficulty in learning to grip small objects.

A baby's ability to control his body depends partially on heredity and to a great extent on environment. You can definitely influence your baby's motor development by providing physical and mental stimulation. For example, you can give him your finger or a small toy to grip, let him kick his legs during bathtime, pull him gently up and let him down by his arms, and let him practice sitting up when he is able.

The appearance of a baby's first tooth is a time of great excitement for his parents, but actually the event is only the reflection of a hereditary pattern. One child may without previous notice sprout a tooth in the third month, just as daddy did. Another baby may drool and fuss and not produce a tooth for a year—like mother.

Most infants, however, get their first two teeth (lower incisors) around the seventh month. A few months later, four upper front teeth appear. After a lapse of a few more months, the other two lower incisors and four molars usually come through. Although tooth cutting seldom causes much discomfort, some babies experience sore gums. These babies understandably are irritable and may cry or seek something to chew on. A rubber ring or other safe object may ease their distress somewhat.

Although crying is a baby's chief means of communication during the early weeks of his life, he also has other distress signals: Once he has you at his cribside, he can squirm, wave and kick angrily, suck on his fist, arch his back. A little later he will acquire another important communications skill—ability to smile or even to laugh out loud.

Gradually, your infant will learn to interpret the sounds he hears about him. He can distinguish between the angry and the friendly pitch of adult voices by the time he is 6 months old. At about this age, too, he has already randomly produced all the sounds he will need to speak, plus many others he will discard. His first efforts at speech are just babblings that parents often mistake for words. He may stumble on the combination "ma-ma" or "da-da" and receive such praise that he repeats these happy sounds. On the other hand, saying "ta-ta" or "ga-ga" will elicit no response, so he forgets these combinations. Sound thus becomes language, a new skill to be used in your child's attempt to master his environment.

The age at which children first speak comprehensible words varies from eight months to over two years. If your child doesn't form speech early, there is usually nothing to be alarmed about. He may still catch up with his more talkative age-mates by the time he is 3.

A child's progress in learning to speak is related to his emotions, which in turn are influenced by parental affection and attention. It helps a baby's mental progress to show him picture books, sing to him, let him hear music, point to objects and say their names—in short, to give him a wide variety of sensory experiences. The surest way to retard his mental development is to deprive him of these experiences.

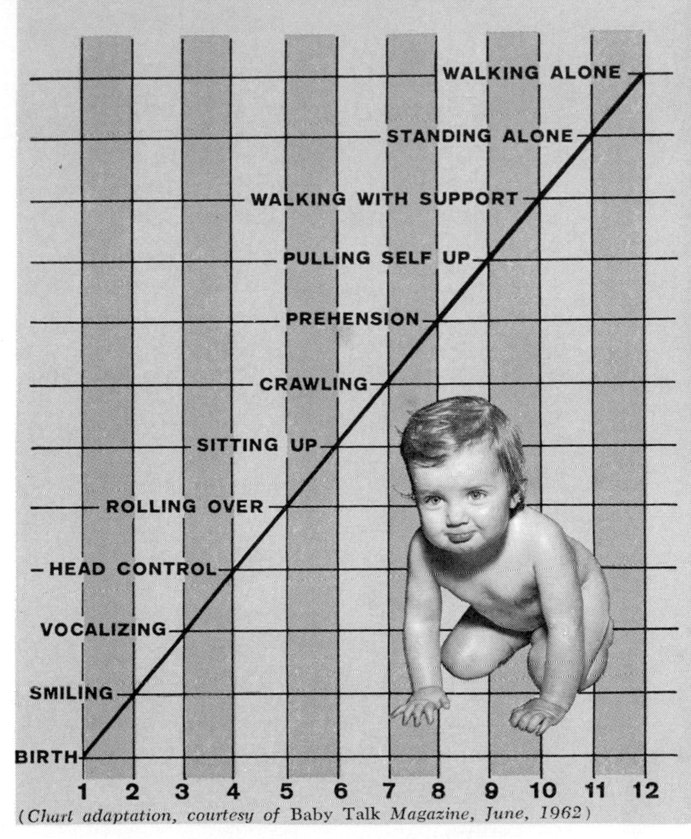

(*Chart adaptation, courtesy of* Baby Talk *Magazine, June, 1962*)

Most babies develop according to this timetable, but there are many variations.

Emotional Development

Despite a great deal of research over a long period of time, the emotional life of an infant remains a secret. He cannot tell anyone what he is thinking, and when he is old enough to talk intelligently on the subject, he will not remember what it was like to be an infant, just as you cannot.

But there is nothing subtle about a new baby's emotional reactions. He seems to be either in a state of tension and distress or the extreme opposite—calm and contentment. Between these two extremes, however, there is usually a transition phase that heralds the disappearance of one state and the imminent appearance of the other. If you study your baby carefully, you will soon learn to respond to the signals he gives before the storm so that he does not become tense and angry. Should you miss the cues he provides, it then becomes necessary to learn how to comfort him and thus restore his equilibrium. While most babies like to be cuddled when they are unhappy, some do not. They may be soothed by gentle pats on the back or by soft lullabys or soothing "conversation."

At any rate, this simple war-or-peace phase does not last for long. And one day just the sight of your face will bring forth a heart-warming smile, perhaps accompanied by a host of ecstatic body movements. These emotional reactions represent your baby's first attempts to socialize—to tell you that all is well with his emotional world and that he thinks you are pretty nice, too.

The responses an infant gets from those around him, particularly his mother, produce his first impressions of what to expect from other people. The pleasant outcome of each distressful situation not only dissolves the baby's tension, but it also leads him to believe that something will be done to help him the next time he is uncomfortable: A breast or bottle will appear to do away with hunger contractions, a cold and wet diaper will be replaced by one that is warm and dry, the monotony of a quiet and dark room will be relieved by the appearance of an animated and friendly face.

It is of course possible that the outcome of tension states can lead to just the opposite set of expectancies. The cry that communicates hunger may be ignored, or the cold sensation against a tiny body may remain, or the face that appears may bristle with displeasure. Such outcomes, especially if they occur more often than the friendly, loving kind, produce lasting ill effects in a child. He comes to believe that all social relationships must be unpleasant. To protect himself, he may withdraw, become shy, listless, or even defensively aggressive. In his early months, an infant probably won't show fear of human beings, although a gruff male voice may frighten him. Fathers and grandfathers shouldn't feel offended. They can talk more softly or pitch their voices slightly higher while they are winning the baby's friendship.

Toward the end of his first year, even the most sociable baby may go through an anxiety phase by reacting violently to strangers who come near his crib. He may cry or try to hide his head. Parents are often shocked to see that their previously friendly offspring has become so fearful and shy. But his reticence is quite usual. He is merely showing for the first time a sense of discrimination—that he, like everyone else, prefers familiar faces.

A baby's fear of strangers soon passes. In the meantime, however, it is best not to make him go to a stranger, even if it is his grandmother, for being forced only intensifies his fears. Usually, if a person appears at his cribside often, he becomes less fearful and more willing to make friends.

Protecting Your Baby's Health

Throughout this marvelous and exciting first year, a baby is wholly dependent on his parents; no other living thing is totally dependent for such a long period as the human infant. Although it is well for parents to be relaxed and comfortable in providing essential care, it is equally important for them to be alert to situations in which their baby's curiosity or lack of appropriate concern will endanger his safety.

Protecting the health of your baby also requires close cooperation between parents and family physician or pediatrician. Usually, a mother will have selected the doctor or health center even before her baby is born. If not, she should do so within the first week or two of life, and then adhere faithfully to a schedule of well-baby visits as well as seek speedy medical service in the event of accident or illness.

Records Are Important

Many mothers and fathers find an exciting scientific and literary sideline to their parental duties in maintaining developmental records. Baby books are favorite shower gifts, although a simple calendar, appointment book, scrapbook, or loose-leaf notebook may serve your purpose as a convenient place to record significant developmental items and achievements: when the first tooth appears, the first word is spoken, the first step is taken—all with appropriate photographs, of course.

But why bother with such records if the family is not historically inclined, you may ask. Often, situations arise in later years which make the keeping of at least simple developmental records extremely worth while. To have some sort of record of major illnesses, of times when accidents caused possible injuries, when shots were given, when important developmental milestones were reached—all may well be of tremendous value.

About the time you are pasting in the picture of your baby blowing out the single candle on his first birthday cake, you'll look at him in surprise. He has evolved from a totally dependent creature into an individual with a mind of his own, curiosity to spare, a word or two at his command, some degree of locomotion, and an ever-expanding comprehension. BETTYE M. CALDWELL

See also BOOKS FOR PARENTS; EMOTIONAL DEVELOPMENT; GROWTH; MENTAL DEVELOPMENT; NURSE; READINESS; SELF-CONCEPT; SOCIAL DEVELOPMENT

BABY EQUIPMENT *See* LAYETTE AND BABY EQUIPMENT

BABY-SITTER

In the language of baby care the term "baby-sitter" has become as firmly fixed as baths, booties, and bottles. Baby-sitter cooperatives have flourished in some communities; parents exchange the service on an hours-earned, hours-served basis. But in most families a competent baby-sitter is queen by the hour, sometimes by the day. She not only has stature in the household, she also has the love and respect of the entire family.

A competent sitter who loves children usually is adept at winning them over quickly, but no child, with the exception of a tiny baby, should be asked to accept sudden change in care without a show of tears. And to awaken at night or from a nap to find a stranger standing over his bed would frighten anyone. It is therefore desirable to invite the sitter to your home just to get acquainted or, if that is impossible, to come early for her first engagement. Children are quick to sense that their parents like and trust this new person. Usually they can be counted on to relax in the pleasant atmosphere created by quiet, friendly conversation, free from last-minute admonitions and instructions.

Inform your baby-sitter of any special problems or habits your child may have. Is he normally a restless sleeper? Does he cry out in his sleep? Do you wake him for a trip to the bathroom at a certain time each night?

It is helpful to a sitter to know which books or records are a small child's favorites. Often a familiar record will soothe a child who misses his mother. A sitter should know if a child clings to a particular object for comfort. If he falls asleep hugging his "banky," she won't be apt to remove it if she knows it is part of the bedtime ritual.

When a sitter is to supervise bedtime for children of varying ages, parents should establish bedtimes before they leave. Permission to watch television programs should be clearly given by parents, as should instructions about what children may have to eat or drink before going to bed.

A sitter should be told where extra supplies of food, bed linen, diapers, and clothing are kept, and where the flashlight is in the event the electricity fails. She should know whether medicine is to be given and when and how to give it. There should be ample formula made for infants, and the sitter should be told when and how to heat it and feed the baby.

When a sitter is to take over a household for several days, the parents should leave a detailed daily outline of all children's activities and privileges.

Seldom is too much information given to a baby-sitter, but often there is something that she wishes had been made more clear. What are a child's allergies? Is he required to wear a cap every time he goes outdoors because of a tendency to earaches? Is he permitted to have friends in after school or naptime? If so, how many may come and where may they play?

Parents should, of course, leave the name, address, and telephone number where they may be reached. A sitter should know the family doctor's name and telephone number and the name and number of a substitute doctor, should your own not be available.

Despite the fact that baby-sitting has become "big business" in the last decade, the parent-child-sitter relationship should remain very personal. Parents should get away from their children once in a while. And babies and small children can learn that it is fun to be independent of their parents occasionally. Thoughtful consideration on the part of the parents and a little ingenuity on the part of the substitute mother will result in a mutually satisfying experience.

See also BOOKS FOR PARENTS

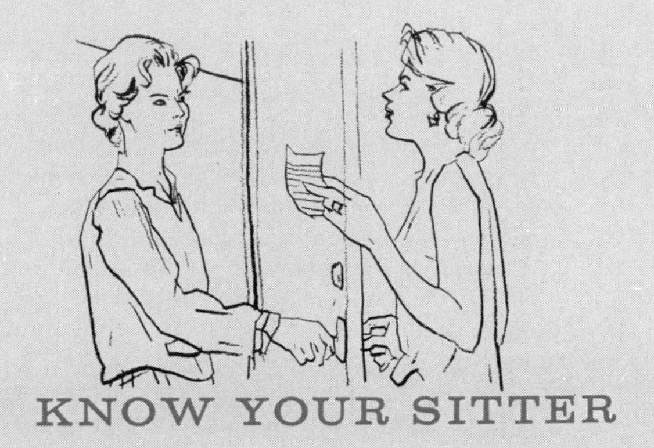

KNOW YOUR SITTER

A baby-sitter should come well recommended if you are not already acquainted. These are the things you will especially want to know about her:

- Has she had some experience with children?
- Does she really like them?
- Is her health good?
- Is she clean and neat?
- Are her morals and conduct acceptable?

Reassured on these points, it is well to remember that as she has obligations to you, so also have you obligations to her. These are some of the things that should be discussed and agreed upon:

- Her duties and privileges
- Household routines that affect her services, including how to operate equipment and appliances
- Rate of payment (and she should be paid promptly without expecting her to make change for a large bill)
- Approximate time parents will return
- Whether or not she will be escorted home, particularly if the hour is late

INSTRUCTION SHEET

(These are the major things your baby-sitter should know.)

- Telephone number where you can be reached
- Family doctor's name and telephone number (a substitute doctor's name and telephone number)
- Telephone number and name of nearest neighbor
- How to operate stove, heat regulator, or other appliances she may need
- Where extra clothing and bedding are kept
- Where candles or flashlight are kept in case lights should go off
- Telephone numbers for police and fire departments

BABY TALK *See* TALKING

BABY TEETH

Baby teeth have several other names: primary teeth, milk teeth, deciduous teeth. They develop as tooth buds in the baby's jaw about six months before he is born. Before and after his birth, calcium is gradually deposited around the buds. During the first two or two and a half years of his life this full set of 20 baby teeth will push through the gums. These teeth influence the shape of his mouth and face, and are needed for proper chewing and proper bite. A child usually begins to lose his baby teeth when he is about 6.

Your child should begin regular visits to the dentist as soon as his baby teeth have all come in. ROBERT G. KESEL

See also TEETH AND TEETHING

BACKWARD CHILD *See* SLOW LEARNER

BAD LANGUAGE *See* BAD WORDS

BAD MANNERS *See* MANNERS

BAD WORDS

"Bad" language in childhood ranges from childish toilet talk to genuine obscenity and profanity. But words as such are not "bad" to children. No young child is intentionally obscene or profane; he hardly knows what the words mean any more than the babbling infant realizes until somebody tells him that his accidental "da-da-da" could refer to his father.

Thus, obviously, it is the reaction of adults to obscene or profane language that is important. A shocked or violent reaction will undoubtedly fix a term in a child's mind as will a hearty guffaw. In either case the child is justified in feeling that he has hit upon something very special.

If your child uses an objectionable expression once, it is probably a good idea to ignore it on the even chance that he will forget it. If he continues to use the expression, a calm statement to the effect that most people do not care for those words will be more effective than drastic punishment. In the past a child who swore was made to wash his mouth with soap. The absurdity of this remedy is fairly apparent, but it does make the point that people sometimes confuse the use of dirty words with dirty-*ness.*

The only time bad words need to be taken seriously is when they are used persistently by the preadolescent or adolescent as his stab at maturity or daring. Then such words may be a symptom of a real problem; for although the 13-year-old who makes obscene remarks to girls probably knows what he is saying, it is most unlikely that he realizes that his verbal bravado is a cover for his ignorance of how to get along with girls. And it is here that the boy may require assistance, intervention, or guidance of adults.

Profanity is best dealt with on the grounds of consideration for other people. "These words have special meanings for some people and it hurts their feelings when you say them," is a statement that even a young child can understand. Parents may also offer him an alternate, acceptable expression.

Special mention must be made of children's own "toilet talk." Such words as "weewee" and "number two" are almost invariably used in periods of silliness. This is hardly surprising in a culture that bans mention of bathroom or sex terms in the average polite group. Since this talk is a mixture of attention-getting and release, it is probably best if parents assume an attitude of indifference. This is not too difficult because these words do not bother most adults in the same way as references to sex. In any case, it is helpful to remember that such silly talk is usually limited to the younger years. By the time a child is 9 or 10, he will have arrived at a point where such terms, if used, are whispered to friends and no longer disrupt dinnertime conversations. IRMA S. BLACK AND JOAN W. BLOS

BARBER *See* HAIRCUT

BASHFULNESS *See* SHYNESS AND TIMIDITY

BASSINET *See* LAYETTE AND BABY EQUIPMENT

BATHING THE BABY

Bathtime can be a most pleasant interlude —a time when you can play with your baby and when he feels lively and responsive.

Until the navel is healed, a new baby can have only a sponge bath, but after that he can be bathed in a tub every day. There is one important rule for the baby's safety. He should never, never be left on a high place from which he can tumble, nor should he ever be left alone in a tub of water. It is wise to place everything needed for the baby's bath and dressing within easy reach ahead of time so that there will be no necessity for turning your back. It is also wise to have bathtime completely free, even to the point of ignoring the telephone and doorbell.

Supplies for the bath include:
Mild unscented soap and soap dish
Soft washcloths and towels
Complete change of fresh clothing
Lotion or powder (if you use them)
Receiving blanket

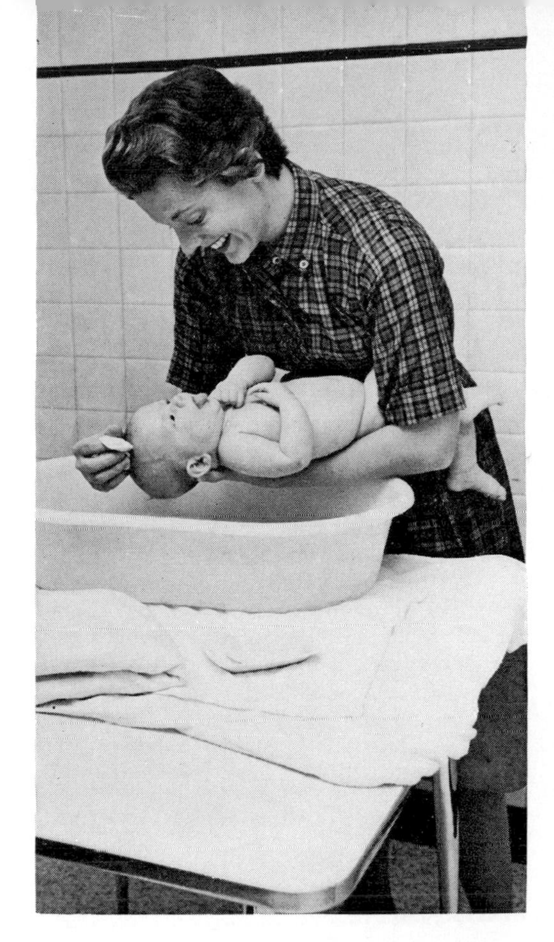

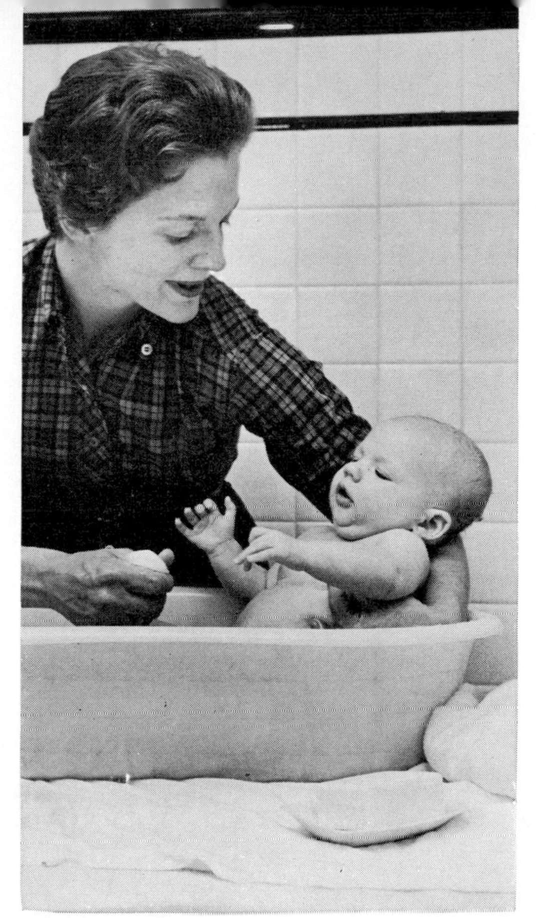

Although bathinettes can be convenient, they are not really necessary. A well-scrubbed kitchen sink plus drainboard or a small tub on a convenient table will do very well. The water should be about body temperature (100° F.), which will seem neither warm nor cold when you test it on your wrist or inner elbow.

For a sponge bath, undress your baby and wrap him in his receiving blanket. Wash him with a washcloth and bland soap (no soap is used on the face as a rule), and rinse him off with a wet washcloth. The inside of his ears, nose, and mouth are usually best left alone. Even cotton-tipped applicators can slip and injure delicate mucous membranes.

Start giving a tub bath when you feel confident about handling your baby, even though he is wet and soapy. Before washing his body in the tub, first wash his face and scalp as in a sponge bath. To wash his head with your right hand, secure his legs between your left arm and chest and support his head on your left hand (this is often called the "football hold"). Holding him in this way over the basin of water, you can rinse his scalp thoroughly. To bathe his body, let him sit in the tub, and support his head by holding your left arm behind his neck and gripping his left arm under the armpit with your left hand.

Some babies are a little afraid of the water at first or resent being wet and cold. You will minimize both problems if you keep the room warm and free of drafts, if you use only a little water in the tub, do most of the slower washing of face and scalp before the baby is completely undressed, and have all his clothes laid out so that redressing is quick and easy and relaxed. Occasionally, a baby cries a great deal at bathtime. If yours does, try to make his tub bath as quick and painless—and as much fun—as possible. If he still protests, try giving him sponge baths for a while.

RUTH S. KEMPE

See also LAYETTE AND BABY EQUIPMENT; NURSE

BED *See* CRIB; JUNIOR BED; LAYETTE AND BABY EQUIPMENT

BEDDING *See* CRIB; LAYETTE AND BABY EQUIPMENT

BEDSIDE TEACHING *See* HOME AND HOSPITAL INSTRUCTION

BEDTIME *See* SLEEP

BED-WETTING

Daytime dribbling may come about when a child is so deep in play that he fails to recognize and obey his own signals of discomfort. It isn't at all unusual, either, for a child to wet his clothing in the excitement and laughter of play, and there's not much you can do to help him except, perhaps, interrupt the merriment occasionally to head him toward the bathroom.

The child who wets his bed at night often does so in response to fear and anxiety caused by troubles of the day carried over into sleep. Punishment or efforts to force control are likely to increase his anxiety and make wetting more persistent and habitual. Drugs without other therapy have not been very successful. Most children outgrow bed-wetting as they learn bladder control or when their lives become happier and free of unnecessary stress.

If your child continues to wet during the day or to wet his bed at night after he is 5, he may be physically ill or he may be suffering from a disease of the genitourinary system. Repeated wetting both day and night, frequent urination, increased thirst, loss of weight are signs of physical illness. A physician should be consulted, not only under these circumstances, but also whenever a child complains of such urinary symptoms as pain or burning, difficulty in starting or stopping a stream, or whenever discoloration of the urine is noted.

More often, though, the problem is emotional, particularly if the child's wetting is limited to bed-wetting, or nocturnal enuresis. Parents should suspect emotional problems particularly when a healthy child who has been toilet trained for several months or years backslides.

There are many reasons for children to get upset. Usually, some difficulty in their relations with others is involved—especially with their parents, but also with teachers, brothers or sisters, or age-mates. It is useless to threaten, punish, use ridicule, or plead with a child to stop wetting. You can help him most by searching out those areas in his life that are particularly stressful to him. Is he properly placed in school? Is he trying too hard to meet competition in the classroom or on the playing field? He may feel that he is failing in his social as well as in his school relationships. Help him to meet the competition more successfully. Give him a greater feeling of self-confidence in other ways. Perhaps he needs only to know that you love him, to have you spend a little more time with him, or show more interest in his needs. When his anxiety and tensions are reduced, wetting will stop.

Although occasional bed-wetting occurs in healthy children up to age 8 or 9 years, persistent bed-wetting in the child older than 5 very often is a symptom of emotional disturbance and is accompanied by other signs. If your attempts to relieve the difficulty are not successful, seek help from your family physician, who may recommend a child psychiatrist, but remember that results are not always immediate. Sometimes a child continues to wet his bed even though he shows improvement in other ways. In fact, wetting may be the last symptom to disappear. Parents who do not understand become impatient with psychiatric help, even when they are able to see that their child has improved generally. Since they brought him to treatment chiefly for the wetting, they are disappointed and dissatisfied until a solution to the problem is finally found. MILTON J. E. SENN

See also ANXIETY; CHILD GUIDANCE CLINIC; FEAR; REGRESSION; TOILET TRAINING; URINARY DISTURBANCES

BEE STING *See* BITES, INSECT

BEHAVIOR PROBLEMS *See* PROBLEM CHILD

BELLYBAND *See* NAVEL

BIRTH

It is often reassuring for an expectant mother to know some of the facts and statistics of childbearing. Human beings are much alike physically, and a young woman can ordinarily expect what billions of other women have already experienced and will experience.

In human beings, about 280 days elapse from the beginning date of the last menstrual period to the birth of a baby. Since ovulation —the time at which an egg is ready to be fertilized—normally occurs two weeks after the first day of a menstrual period, human pregnancy actually lasts 38 weeks; that is, from conception to birth. The expected day for birth may be determined by adding seven days to the beginning of the last period and counting back three months (Nägele's rule). This is simply a quick way to calculate 280 days. Here is an example. Onset of last menstrual period, November 1. November 1 + 7 = November 8. Counting back three months = August 8.

Miscarriage, or spontaneous abortion, is the description applied if the human fetus emerges before the 28th week, when it usually weighs a little over 2 pounds. If the baby is delivered from the 28th to 36th week, he is said to have had a premature birth. The premature infant's weight usually ranges from 2 to 5½ pounds. After the 36th week the delivery is called a term birth.

As the end of a pregnancy approaches, a mother usually wants very much to know on just what day or during what week she will have her baby. Statistics say that of pregnancies carried to maturity (beyond the 36th week), 4 per cent will deliver on the calculated date, 53 per cent before the date is reached, and 43 per cent after the calculated date.

Expectant mothers quite naturally want to know the why and wherefore of labor pains. Labor consists of painful, rhythmic contractions of the muscular uterus, alternating with a painless, relaxed state of the muscle. When labor begins, the pains are infrequent—10 or 15 minutes apart, and toward the end come much more frequently—3 minutes apart. During a contraction the pressure within the uterus—a large gourd-shaped organ—is increased a great deal. This pressure gradually dilates or stretches the elastic funnel-shaped end—the cervix. The cervix connects with the vagina just as the throat connects with the mouth. When the cervix becomes sufficiently dilated to allow the infant to pass into the vagina, the force of the uterine contractions plus the voluntary, bearing-down efforts of the mother complete the birth by gradually stretching the vaginal entrance enough to allow the baby to pass through it and out into the world. After the baby is born, the doctor clamps and cuts the umbilical cord.

The length of labor—that is, from the time painful contractions begin until the placenta is finally delivered—differs greatly with various women. In first births the average length of labor is 14 hours and in subsequent births, 8 hours. Labor is divided into three stages—the first stage, from the beginning of painful contractions until the cervix becomes fully dilated; the second stage, from full cervical dilation until the infant is born; and the third stage, from the birth of the baby until the placenta is expelled.

Ordinarily, the bag of waters (sac formed from membranes that grow from the circular edge of the placenta) surrounding the baby breaks of its own accord during labor; sometimes it breaks before labor commences and occasionally it must be broken artificially by the physician. After the infant has been delivered, the placenta, or afterbirth, which weighs about a pound, separates from its attachment inside the uterus, enters the vagina, and is pushed out of the vagina. This delivery doesn't take long and is usually painless.

Nearly all babies are born headfirst, although once in a while the buttocks, or breech, of the baby presents; even more rare is the baby who lies crosswise (transverse) at the time of labor's onset. ALAN F. GUTTMACHER

See also CESAREAN SECTION; PREMATURE BABY

BIRTH CERTIFICATE

It is important, as a famous humorist once said, to know the "when, where at, and who to," besides the actual fact of a baby's birth. These vital statistics, when filed, become the legal record of your baby's birth and proof of his citizenship. They can help to establish proof of parentage, identity, the right of inheritance, and legal dependency. Accuracy is extremely important when giving the information that will be officially recorded. Check all information for spelling. If you want an "e" on Anne's name, be sure to say so, or she will be forever legally "Ann."

When you adopt a child, a new birth certificate is issued giving his new name and the names of the adoptive parents. This certificate replaces the old one.

During his life, your child may have many occasions to make use of his birth certificate. Probably the first time will be when he enters school. Later he will need proof to get his first work permit, driver's license, or perhaps a passport. And he may have to prove the date of his birth in order to cast his first vote—or one day, to marry.

See also NAMING THE BABY

BIRTHMARK

Many newborn babies and children have birthmarks. The most common kind is a reddish, flat area that has its color because of slightly enlarged or prominent blood vessels in the skin. The back of the neck and bridge of the nose are common locations for these marks. Most birthmarks are small and will not impair a child's health in any way. If the birthmark is large, parents may want to have a doctor remove it to improve the child's appearance, although removal of this type of mark is not a simple matter.

Some red birthmarks are elevated from the skin surface and are spongy in texture. These marks may grow rapidly and require careful attention. The physician may reduce their size by X-ray or radium treatments, by freezing with carbon dioxide snow, or he may occasionally remove them surgically.

Birthmarks that are black or brown in color are different from red ones. These, often called moles, occur because of abnormal amounts of pigment in the skin. Most of these may be left alone without treatment. *If any new birthmarks appear, or an old one suddenly seems to be growing, medical care should be obtained promptly.*

Mothers of children with birthmarks frequently wonder whether experiences or thoughts they may have had during pregnancy could have caused the marks. There is no evidence to support such a theory. Parents of children with extensive birthmarks may take some comfort from the fact that results of treatment to improve appearance are much better nowadays. JULIUS B. RICHMOND

See also MOLES; PRENATAL IMPRESSIONS

BITE *See* MALOCCLUSION

BITES, ANIMAL

Children are frequently scratched or nipped by their own dogs or cats. Such minor wounds seldom require more than washing with soap and plenty of warm water and rinsing with cold water. The wound may then be covered with a dressing of sterilized gauze, held in place with adhesive strips or, if it is very small, by a finger dressing. If the bite or scratch mark heals promptly, there is no other cause for concern. If it becomes inflamed, a physician should be consulted without delay.

The mouths of most animals contain a variety of germs and some viruses that may cause local infection, especially if the bare skin is broken. Where the bite goes through clothing, trouble is less likely.

Aside from ordinary infections, there are two serious diseases that may be transmitted by the bites of animals. One is rabies, or hydrophobia. This disease is most commonly transmitted by dogs, but it may also be spread by cats, squirrels, bats, or other mammals with which human beings may come in contact. After a bite from any animal suspected of rabies, certain precautions should be taken immediately in addition to first-aid treatment of the actual bite. A physician should be notified and so should the local health department. It is customary to keep the animal under observation by a veterinarian in order to find out if it has rabies.

Another vicious disease that is transmitted through bites is rat-bite fever. Any bites by rats, mice, or other rodents should immediately be reported to the physician and to the local department of health.

In case of snake bite it is important to know, if possible, whether the snake is poisonous, or venomous. A bite from a nonvenomous snake is no more significant than the bite of any other animal. But a bite from a poisonous snake calls for immediate medical attention because there are now antivenin preparations available to combat snake venom. If no medical care is available, or until the doctor comes, keep the patient quiet. If the bite is on an extremity, a tourniquet should be applied above the bite by wrapping a rubber tube or a towel rolled into a tight cord around the limb and twisting it until circulation is partly obstructed. Such a tourniquet must be released at least every quarter-hour to prevent injury to the tissues from lack of blood. If no medical aid is immediately available, a cut should be made with a sharp knife into the skin lengthwise of the limb, deep enough to bleed, but not deep enough to injure vital structures. This incision should be sucked—a procedure that involves little danger if the individual rinses his mouth occasionally.

The giving of whiskey is not advisable; whiskey merely helps spread the venom faster through the circulatory system. A cold application or ice pack gives relief and may slow the absorption of venom. W. W. BAUER

See also RABIES

Related article in WORLD BOOK: "Snakes"

BITES, INSECT

Most insect bites are more annoying than serious, but the pain of stings from bees, wasps, and hornets can be very distressing to children, and the itching of mosquito bites is annoying. Although spiders are not insects, their bites have practically the same effect. You can, however, distinguish between insect and spider bites. Insects make one puncture in the skin with a single stinger, while spiders bite with pincher-like jaws and make two holes close together.

First aid for most bites consists of the immediate application of an ice cube, or a drop of household vinegar, or a thick paste of baking soda and water. If subsequent inflammation results over the bite, medical care may be necessary; in rare instances a person may be so allergic to the venom of insects or spiders that serious or even fatal general reactions occur. Such individuals should be protected against the possibility of insect bites by clothing that covers the entire body, plus veils and gloves, and by insect repellent applied to the clothing.

Multiple bites, as from a swarm of bees or wasps, may also prove serious. A dangerous spider common in some parts of the United States is the black widow, whose bite causes symptoms resembling appendicitis or other serious abdominal diseases. W. W. BAUER

See also TICKS

BITING

Biting is the business of babies. They need to practice biting as a preliminary exercise for effective functioning of teeth and gums. And while babies are babies, we usually sanction biting. We call it "teething." Since babies are fairly indiscriminate and unselective in the objects they bite—that is, anything within mouth reach—they need help in being given legitimate biting objects. Fortunately, there are many such things available for practice biting: hard rubber rings and biting beads as well as spoons and similar objects.

When an adult ear gets bitten just because it happens to be within biting range, the baby needs to be discouraged—not by being "bitten back" but by moving the ear out of biting range with an air of "no biting ears," whether spoken or implied by firm and immediate action.

Biting back may seem to be an effective counterattack, but it is more likely to be confusing and fear-provoking to the baby. How can a child learn that he must not bite people when people bite him?

The toddler who continues to bite when teething is no longer his problem has probably learned that biting is an effective (for him) method of attack. He needs help in learning other ways of expressing his anger. "You must not bite *people!*" needs to be said and meant. Offering biting substitutes is not always effective as the child gets older.

The preschool child who continues to use biting as a way of either getting his way or expressing his anger may need more than verbal prohibitions and suggestions. Sometimes continued biting at this stage can be related to some fairly obvious disturbing factor; for example, too severe discipline or a new baby in the family or as a means of self-protection from older children. When the cause is known, a lifting of pressures or a shift in expectation or perhaps just more time with the "biter" often will bring about a change. When biting persists, it is probably a signal that this child needs more understanding.

Sometimes the family doctor or pediatrician can make suggestions that will prove helpful. The chronic biter *needs* help; he is *asking* for help. EVELYN BEYER

See also ANGER; TEETH AND TEETHING

BLADDER CONTROL *See* BED-WETTING; TOILET TRAINING

BLADDER INFECTION *See* URINARY DISTURBANCES

BLANKET SUCKING *See* SUCKING

BLEEDING

Bleeding is always an alarming experience. It is worth while for parents to realize that a little blood may look like much more than it is. In many cases the child who is bleeding will be frightened, and a calm parent will go a long way toward reassuring the child as well as insuring that the right steps will be taken to control the bleeding.

Bleeding may come from arteries, veins, or capillaries. Blood from arteries is bright red because of its high oxygen content. It comes in spurts if the bleeding vessel is of any size. Blood from veins is darker in color and flows more evenly and more slowly. Blood from capillaries is usually a minor oozing, which creates little alarm.

Profuse bleeding, or hemorrhaging, must be controlled promptly; otherwise, loss of blood may become serious. Control of hemorrhage, therefore, takes precedence over precautions against infection. With modern drugs and antibiotics an infection can be overcome later, but profuse bleeding is an immediate threat.

During World War II, first-aid instruction received by many persons included a drill in the location of so-called pressure points where hemorrhage could be controlled. These were locations where principle arteries were close enough to the surface to be readily compressed by pressure. Experience has shown, however, that persons who do not use first-aid knowledge regularly tend very soon to forget it. Fingers soon tire from maintaining pressure on an artery. Present teaching is much simpler. With a folded towel, handkerchief, or other cloth pad, clean if available, bleeding can be controlled by sustained pressure directly over the bleeding tissues. The pad or cloth can be held in place with the hand until there is opportunity to fasten it in place with a bandage. If bleeding is severe, and the blood is red and spurting, do not wait to find a bandage or pad; use your thumb.

If this direct pressure does not control the bleeding and the bleeding is in a limb, it may be necessary to use a tourniquet, although

Sometimes it is necessary to use a tourniquet.

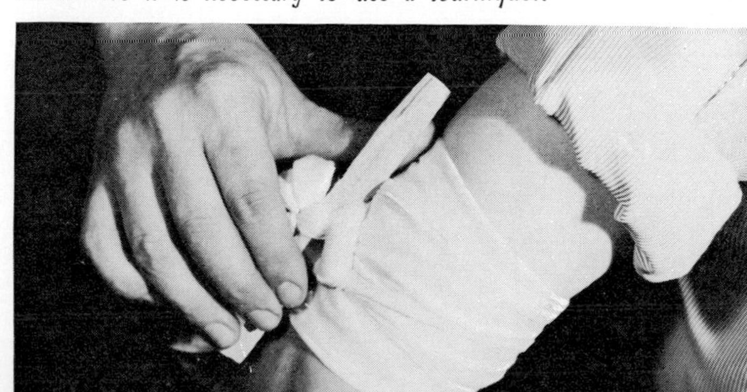

this procedure is not recommended for routine use.

A tourniquet can be made in an emergency from a twisted handkerchief or a strip of cloth tied in a knot around the limb and then tightened until the bleeding stops. It is of the greatest importance that a tourniquet, if used, be released briefly every 15 minutes, even if bleeding starts again. If this precaution is not observed, lack of blood in the tissues may cause serious injury.

The child should be kept at rest, since activity encourages bleeding. A physician should be called at once if the bleeding seems to be severe or persistent or to come from a large vessel. W. W. BAUER

See also FIRST AID

BLIND CHILD

A blind child is first of all a child. He has the same basic needs for parental affection and guidance as any other child. During infancy and the very young years, a blind child's parents do not need special apparatus, nor do they need specialized training in the care of the blind, but they do, however, need patience and understanding. And they need to know how best to guide their child in areas where he will need special help and attention and consideration because of his blindness—how to help him acquire a workable knowledge of the world around him, how to get about in it, and how to conform to generally accepted behavior patterns.

We know, from practical experience and research, that the blind child does not yearn for sight and that he takes things in stride. He acts and reacts with all his other senses, gaining most of his knowledge of the world around him through touch experiences. He hears about many things, but to acquire concrete experiences, he must apply his touch. For this reason the blind child should be encouraged to make use of his hands from early childhood on. Give him playthings that appeal to the touch. Allow him to get messy by playing with wet sand and finger paints. Let him finger-feed himself, getting used to the softness of cereal, the crispness of a cracker, the slipperiness of gelatin, and the crunchiness of celery.

Give your blind child opportunities to handle models of cars, boats, airplanes, buses, and trains. He will acquire a comforting knowledge of the conveyances that transport him from place to place. The blind child also hears, smells, and tastes. Encourage him to apply these senses. He can hear the rustle of dry leaves as he walks under a tree in the fall, he can make out in which direction a passing car goes, and he can enjoy music and the voices of his loved ones. He can smell the seashore, the gasoline as the station attendant puts it into the family car, the smoke of a burning birch log, the corn as it is popping. He can taste the good things his mother prepares for him—cookies, ice cream, hot chocolate, or cold orange juice.

Give your blind child every opportunity to share experiences with sighted persons. By this sharing he will be better prepared for a life that will inevitably include persons other than his own immediate family. The blind child need not live in isolation or confusion.

The blind child learns to walk when he is ready for it just as other children do. He may need to be shown how to move his legs. He will also want things to hold on to and free space in which to move. As the child's area of activity gradually expands from his crib to his playpen, see that he has opportunities to move about and explore. Don't be anxious about him as he attempts to get around a coffee table or ventures out into another room, but keep things in their places so that he knows where to expect them. Guide him carefully, speak softly and encouragingly to him, but do not hesitate to be firm when firmness is needed. Your reward will be to see your blind child become competent in his movements around his home and yard.

When it comes time to see to the blind child's formal education, you will find that almost every state has some kind of program for blind or partially sighted children. Nearly all states have residential schools; in many larger communities visually handicapped children attend regular classes in public schools where a resource teacher especially trained in the education of visually handicapped children is available. Both facilities provide for blind children an education equal, grade by grade, to that offered to the sighted. They also follow the same course of study. In some areas, methods specially developed for blind children must be used. (The American Printing House for the blind publishes braille books, including the entire WORLD BOOK ENCYCLOPEDIA, in braille.) This means not only braille reading and writing but also the teaching of other skills such as mobility.

Whether a child should go to a residential school or to a public school program for blind children depends upon the qualities of these facilities and upon such factors as location, home environment, and also on the child himself. BERTHOLD LOWENFELD

See also COMMUNITY RESOURCES; HANDICAPPED CHILD

BLINKING *See* TIC

BLISTER

A blister is caused by chafing or pinching the skin, or results from burns or certain skin diseases. A blister is formed by separation of the superficial layers of the skin from the underlying layers and filling of the space with clear serum. If a small blood vessel is injured, the fluid may be filled with blood. Blisters may be caused by a poorly fitted shoe or other pressure or friction. A severe pinch may cause a blood blister. Infants, not infrequently, get blisters on their lips from sucking. Ordinarily, a blister requires no special treatment except eliminating the cause and providing temporary protection.

It is usually best not to open a blister, since to do so may introduce infection. If a blister becomes infected or does not heal, medical aid should be sought.

In some circumstances where no medical service is available, it may become necessary to open a blister. In such a case, the area should be carefully washed with soap and warm water, followed by 70 per cent alcohol. With a sharp steel needle that has previously been sterilized in alcohol, make a puncture at the base of the blister, holding the needle parallel to the skin. Gentle pressure will cause the fluid to flow out. A protective dressing may then be applied. W. W. BAUER

See also BURN; POISON IVY, OAK, AND SUMAC

BLOCKS *See* TOYS AND PLAY EQUIPMENT

BLOOD COUNT

Blood contains many formed elements or special cells that have special jobs to do in the body—red cells, white cells, and platelets are important among them. Red cells get their bright coloring from hemoglobin, which contains iron. The hemoglobin absorbs oxygen and carries it to the body tissues. White cells attack germs. Platelets, which look like tiny disks, make blood coagulate, or clot. Healthy blood contains these specialized elements in normal proportions.

Almost every patient has a "blood count" from time to time, though he may not know it, since all he does is furnish a blood specimen to the doctor. A routine blood count is a literal countdown of red and white cells seen in a precisely measured drop of blood under a microscope.

A blood count can give the doctor vital information, as in determining the nature of anemias, of which there are many kinds. For instance, a deficiency of hemoglobin lessens the oxygen supply to the tissues and leads to symptoms of anemia—pallor, weakness, and easy fatigue. A rise in white cell count may indicate an infection. Some disorders may require a complete blood count of different kinds of white cells and platelets, and study of abnormally formed cells, to arrive at a diagnosis. Blood counts serve many medical purposes. A normal blood count is one sign of good health. DONALD G. COOLEY

BLOOD POISONING

When the blood stream is invaded by bacteria or other microbes, the resulting condition is called blood poisoning, but since the term does not suggest what bacteria are in the blood or how they entered the blood stream—matters of considerable medical importance—blood poisoning is a term not generally used by physicians.

Although it is possible for microbes to gain direct entry to the blood stream at the time of an injury—and this is good reason for the prompt and proper cleansing of wounds—usually there is an infection somewhere in the body from which the microbes enter the blood stream. They may enter it from an infection of the skin such as a boil or a pimple, from an infected tooth, a sore throat or tonsillitis, appendicitis, or pneumonia. In some diseases, such as meningitis, there is a short period during which the blood stream is infected. Young babies seem less able to localize infections, and invasion of the blood stream whenever there is an infection is more frequent than it is in older children or adults. Also, in rare instances, some children lack the ability to produce antibodies to protect themselves against infection and have blood stream infections repeatedly.

Fever with a skin infection, or red streaks up an arm or a leg, or tender lymph glands in the armpit or groin are signs that the infection is spreading rapidly. The child with these symptoms is in need of immediate attention by a doctor. JULIUS B. RICHMOND

BLOOD TYPE

Everyone's blood contains chemical substances known as "blood factors." We inherit them just as we do eye and hair color. Your own red blood cells contain, or lack, various factors in combinations that give you your particular blood type. Perhaps you know your blood type and your children's. It is a good thing to know.

One type of blood is just as healthy as another. But if a blood transfusion is necessary, it is important to know that the bloods of patient and donor are compatible. If they are not, antagonistic factors in certain combinations may cause the patient's blood cells to clump together or result in other serious transfusion reactions. Blood typing makes safe transfusion possible by insuring that the bloods of donor and patient will not clash dangerously.

There are four major human blood groups —A, B, AB, and O—and many subdivisions. Blood is further classified as Rh-positive and Rh-negative. Blood is typed by mixing a little of it with test serums under standardized laboratory conditions and observing effects upon blood cells. Blood samples of patient and donor may also be cross matched by similar techniques. DONALD G. COOLEY

See also FAMILY HEALTH RECORD; RH FACTOR

BLUE BABY

A baby is blue because not enough blood gets to his lungs for oxygenation.

The typical blue baby, about whom so much has been written, is one who was born with deformities inside the heart. The disease is called tetralogy of Fallot. In this condition the pulmonary artery (the vessel that carries blood to the lungs) is so small that all the blue blood returning from the body can't get through to the lungs. The blue blood escapes through a hole in the wall that separates the right and left ventricles of the heart. This blue blood that crosses over from the right ventricle into the left ventricle is pumped along with some red blood through the aorta to all parts of the body. Naturally, the smaller the pulmonary artery and the larger the escape hole between the ventricles, the bluer the child will be.

In 1945 and 1946, surgeons invented operations for shunting more blood to the lungs. These operations were successful in relieving blueness, called cyanosis, but they put an extra strain on the heart.

Since 1955, open heart surgery has been perfected, and it has been more successful for treating tetralogy of Fallot. While an artificial lung and mechanical pump carry on oxygenation and circulation outside of the body, the heart is opened and the defects inside are corrected. WILLIS J. POTTS

"BLUES" AFTER CHILDBIRTH *See* DEPRESSION

BOASTING

A little girl, all dressed up in her new red velvet party dress, looks at herself in the mirror and with spontaneous joy and shining eyes, says, "Why, I'm pretty!" Another youngster tells her teacher that she is a ballet dancer. When the teacher asks where she is studying, the child replies, "I don't need lessons—dancing came with me when I was born!" A young teen-age boy, on being told to clean up his room, turns to his mother and says, "How can you be so mean to me when I'm such a nice guy?"

Is this what we mean by "boasting"? Not at all. These are genuine and lovely feelings of well-being, expressed with the candor of childhood. They are really quite the opposite of boasting, for they express wonder and joy at being oneself.

Boasting, on the other hand, usually carries some feeling of unsureness, a sense of inadequacy. A boast that meets some inner need is frequently repeated, and with a good deal of intensity and conviction. It rarely has much basis in truth. One of the most common and normal kinds of boasting is expressed in the preschooler's challenge, "*My* daddy can beat up *your* daddy!" This boast is recognized for what it is—the natural sense of frustration with being small and helpless, the sometimes overwhelming need to feel dominant and full of power. The 13-year-old wallflower, still overwhelmed by shyness with boys, tells her parents that she danced every dance with the most popular boy in the class. A third-grade teacher is amazed to hear that a little girl's mother has two mink coats—almost as surprised as the mother would be to hear that she had even one! The stories of wealth and luxury begin to diminish when this child who has felt she was "too dumb" to understand subtraction is taught subtraction and can be given the praise and attention she craves for her real accomplishment.

Occasional boasting—making up tall tales about one's own accomplishments and successes—is a normal part of childhood. When it occurs once in a while, parents can accept it as healthy imagination, mixed with wishful thinking. The normal feelings of fear, uncertainty, and inadequacy which are a part of growing up can find a harmless outlet in boasting. It is natural to try to reassure oneself with such fantasies—up to a point. Parents can help their children enjoy the experience, even to capitalize on this kind of creativity, by encouraging them to write stories about great adventures and marvelous accomplishments. Parents can share with their children some of their own childhood fantasies and wishful dreams of greatness. But at the same time, they can also help their children to differentiate between such glorious fantasies and reality. They can point out that all children are sometimes afraid, sometimes feel they are failing, sometimes need to bolster up their courage; that it is fun to pretend and to imagine, but that it can also be satisfying to work toward mastery of real problems.

When a child is unable to control the impulse to boast continually, despite the fact that the boasting may cause discomfort and embarrassment, it may be important to look more closely at his life. Have standards and demands and expectations been set too high for him so that he feels inadequate or a failure? Are there real concerns, such as difficulty in schoolwork, problems in making friends, matters about which he may need direct help? Does he need more realistic goals and a genuine sense of his own real strengths and potentialities?

The occasional boasting of childhood can be viewed without alarm as one of the many ways in which children find expression for their normal uncertainties. It is a creative way of setting goals for oneself, of expressing worth-while ambitions and dreams for the future. But when the boast becomes more significant than the real successes of life, a child quite likely needs greater satisfactions, a greater sense of personal well-being, so that reality can be as filled with delight as any fantasy. EDA J. LE SHAN

See also INFERIORITY COMPLEX; LOVE

BOIL

When a sweat gland, an oil gland, a hair follicle, or a small wound becomes infected and develops pus, the result is a boil. If one boil develops, others often follow. Several boils very close together constitute a carbuncle. Boils and carbuncles are usually caused by pus-forming bacteria that may be on the skin normally but cause infection only occasionally. Irritation of the skin or failure to keep the skin clean may let the bacteria set up an infection, especially in the hair follicles. Every child who has frequent boils should be examined by a doctor.

When a boil is developing, the area first looks red and is tender. In a day or two considerable swelling and pain may develop. Gradually, pus forms and the center of the boil becomes yellowish. If the doctor sees the child as the boil is developing, he can prescribe medication to arrest its progress. If the boil goes on to develop pus, however, it may be necessary for the doctor to drain it surgically. JULIUS B. RICHMOND

BOOK CLUBS

There are several values in a subscription to a children's book club. Good books are selected by an advisory board from the flood of books, good and not-so-good, published each year for children: Club membership insures that a book is regularly added to the child's own library, and club membership offers a convenient way for those who do not live near a bookstore to buy books. Because books continue to arrive at intervals throughout the year, subscriptions to clubs make long-remembered gifts.

Two features of adult book clubs are often imitated by those for children: One is the requirement that a minimum number of books be bought each year; the other is the inducement to subscribe by reduction in the price of the first book or books or by gifts of various kinds. Some clubs sell books at list prices, more sell at some reduction, and only a few are truly inexpensive. These last include the popular paperback book clubs sponsored by Scholastic Book Services (Lucky, Arrow, Teen Age, Campus, Science World book clubs), but these operate only through classrooms, and individual subscriptions are not available.

Among the established book clubs are:

BEST-IN-CHILDREN'S BOOKS, Nelson Doubleday, Inc., Garden City, New York. Books for boys and girls from 3 to 10.

JUNIOR DELUXE EDITIONS CLUB (a division of Nelson Doubleday, Inc.), Garden City, New York.

PARENTS' MAGAZINE PRESS, Inc., 80 New Bridge Road, Bergenfield, New Jersey. Three age groups: Read Aloud Book Club for children up to 6; Book Club for Beginning Readers, up to 8; Calling All Girls Book Club for girls 8–12; All American Boy Book Club for boys 8–12.

THE BOOKPLAN, 921 Washington Avenue, Brooklyn 25, New York. Personalized service for children and young people from 8 months to 18 years.

THE JUNIOR LITERARY GUILD, 575 Madison Avenue, New York 22, New York. Books for children, 5–6, 7–8, 9–11, and boys or girls 12–16.

WEEKLY READER CHILDREN'S BOOK CLUB, Education Center, Columbus 16, Ohio. Three age groups, kindergarten through grade 2; grades 3 and 4; grades 5 and 6 (Young America Book Club).

YOUNG PEOPLES BOOK CLUB, 155 N. Wacker Drive, Chicago 6, Illinois. For boys and girls 8–13.

YOUNG READERS OF AMERICA, 345 Hudson Street, New York 14, New York (Book-of-the-Month Club.) "Landmark Books" (history and biography) and "All-about Books" (science).

ELIZABETH S. MARGULIS

See also BOOKS FOR CHILDREN

BOOKS FOR CHILDREN

One of parenthood's most rewarding tasks is to guide a child's first hesitating steps into the land of literature. First come nursery rhymes, probably those you treasure from your own childhood. And the next thing you know, you've kindled a spark which only books and more books can fan into a flaming urge to read, to learn, to explore.

There's no need to tell your child that you are going to build a library for him. Tell him that you are going to buy him a book. Buy it. And then on another day or another occasion, buy him another book. In the interval between the purchases, go with him to the public library or read with him a book he has brought home from school, or listen to what he and his friends are saying about a book. You will find out what books interest him, what book, among those he has seen or borrowed or has had read to him, he would like to possess. On your own, find out about other books that follow his lines of interest, but that, thus far, are books he has not heard of. Expose him to books containing additional ideas and interests, on the chance that some of these will kindle his imagination. Know how well he reads. Know which kinds of books bore him because they are too easy. Know which kinds frustrate him because they are too difficult. Buy a book for him whenever you can. As the years go by, he will have acquired a library, and you and he will have "built" it, but nothing in the process will have seemed ponderous, or overly sanctified, or anything but totally natural to him.

Why is it important to own books and have them in your home when so many books are readily available outside? The answer is many-sided. First, few children seek knowledge for its own sake without some form of stimulation and example at home. The attitudes toward learning found in the home affect a child's learning throughout his life. Children pick up these attitudes long before they go to school. So if books are an integral part of childhood, they are most likely to be an integral part of adulthood, and a book owned, carried about, taken to bed, available for many rereadings, often practically memorized, becomes part of the child himself. If a child has books of his own, in his section of the family library, he is automatically given an opportunity to imitate admired adults.

Secondly, when books belong to the family as a whole, the child is given a way of knowing he is an important part of that whole. Books owned, kept, and read at home provide sources of information for all the family. But their value goes far beyond mere information. Home reading can broaden and deepen the lives of all family members by providing vicarious experiences in a variety that no one human being could know firsthand, even in a long lifetime. And home reading can convince a child that books bring pleasure. Books that are there, available, are apt to be read.

Thirdly, when very young children live in a home in which there are books, they usually get the benefit of being read aloud to. Reading aloud to children from books and sharing pleasant experiences in reading as a family are the obvious ways to introduce even toddlers to the delights of books. But it is not enough, as some parents might hope, to impose reading on children as a sort of vitamin, good only for growing children. Youngsters should learn that the value of books is lasting; there is no better way to learn than through the example set by parents. The child who sees both mother and father reading for pleasure and information themselves, buying and borrowing books for their own and their children's use, usually copies what he sees. This child does not think of reading as something he "has to do," but as a grown-up activity that he also can enjoy. It is especially important to associate reading and an appreciation of books with men so that children do not develop the misconception that books are a feminine and therefore a "sissy" interest.

In addition to buying books for themselves and their children, parents can demonstrate that they value books by giving them as gifts on the important occasions, since gift-giving is a symbolic sharing of one's own treasure.

Choosing the Books

The very number of books available is the source of the biggest problem of those who would begin or add to a child's library. Each year about 1,600 new titles especially for children are published, some of them excellent, some poor, but most of them mediocre. Add to these the books considered "classic" and the good ones of more recent times not yet seasoned enough to deserve the classic label, and you have a sea of possibilities in which the book buyer can flounder hopelessly, unable to choose.

But these seas have been charted by specialists in children's books who work with children constantly, who keep aware of changing interests and fads among young people, and read and evaluate books as they are published. These specialists publish reliable lists of selected children's books, each title usually accompanied by a note on the distinguishing features of that book and for what interests and ages it is suitable. Among the good lists in print are *Let's Read Together*, a selection of 500 good titles for children of all ages, compiled by committees of the National Congress of Parents and Teachers and the Children's Services Division of the American Library Association and available from either of these organizations or from public libraries.

For children interested in science, *A Science Booklist for Boys and Girls,* compiled by the American Association for the Advancement of Science, is available from the Association's Washington office.

The articles on children's literature in the leading young people's encyclopedias also publish lists of good books to add to a child's library, and most bookstores and large public libraries have short lists for free distribution.

Throughout the year Sunday book review supplements of the large city newspapers publish reviews of the new children's books. Then during Children's Book Week in November and National Library Week in April, many of the leading popular magazines, as well as most newspapers in large cities, publish lists of children's books. These lists are usually confined to the most recently published books.

Librarians in public and school libraries are willing to help in the choice of books, and frequently, because they know your child and his reading preferences, are able to suggest titles that he would like to own. Many teachers have a broad knowledge of the world of children's books outside of textbooks, and they can be helpful in making suggestions.

In some communities, book fairs are held during Children's Book Week or National Library Week. Here is a good chance to see quantities of new books in great variety and to obtain guidance from librarians and teachers. And, a book fair is a festive occasion where parents and children may browse through the books together, sharing a delightful experience. Your child's spontaneous reactions to the array of books often gives strong clues to his reading tastes.

Although most bookstores carry a fairly adequate stock of children's books, space limitations make it impossible to have a complete selection. All bookstores, however, have directories of books currently in print and can order any specific title for your child.

In those communities where there are no bookstores at all, book buyers order by mail from stores in metropolitan areas. The names of such stores can be had from local librarians, teachers, or even merchants, who have directories of other retail merchants.

At the beginning you might feel bewildered in trying to choose good children's books from among thousands of titles. But you can, if guided by librarians' and teachers' suggestions and their lists and by reviews, develop discrimination and make choices almost sure to please your child.

To parents trying to build a library for their children, books may seem expensive. Yet the cost of most toys equals or even surpasses the cost of a good book. A casually purchased toy often may end broken or forgotten in a corner, while a carefully chosen book will be something a child will cherish all his life. One way to insure that additions will be made to your child's library without painful expense outlay is to set up a simple budget for the regular purchase of books. Another is to have a subscription to one of the several children's book clubs. Most clubs select and mail a book monthly.

Few budgets will allow for the purchase of all the books a child reads. Few homes could house them. But the habit of regular library use will extend a child's own book collection endlessly. The library will also give him easy access to those books that might be of only passing interest.

Schoolbooks at Home

When a child enters school, some parents may feel that he should have duplicates of his school readers or supplementary readers as his sole reading diet. They are sometimes confirmed in this mistaken belief by those who advise parents to buy or borrow books that use only the words on the child's grade reading list. As a result, parents may find themselves poring over books, trying to decide which are "too old," or "too young," or best fitted to the school program, when attention might better be devoted to deciding if these books are appealing and interesting enough to a youngster. Once a child has learned to read, it is not necessary that he know every word he encounters, for he will broaden his vocabulary by seeing new words in the context of those he already knows.

Standard of Quality

How can parents recognize good reading material for their school-age children? Here is a simple but accurate yardstick for measuring the value of a child's literature: If a children's book is interesting to an adult, it will probably be interesting to a child, too. And it is especially important that parents choose books written in a way that is stimulating to read, for the appreciation of words and language is keen in childhood, when the music and mystery of words are fresh, and the child himself possesses an inborn sense of wonder. Too many authors feel that writing for children demands little creative talent and that anything written in words of few syllables and in an uncomplicated style, no matter how insipid, trite, or condescending, is suitable for children. The language of the best writers for children is rhythmic and rich.

Parents who are concerned that their child read only "good" books are often dismayed when he begins to devour the books in a "series," which may be poorly written. Not all these books, however, lack in literary quality, and as long as a child mixes them into a rich diet of literary fare, they serve their purpose in developing discrimination, for he soon finds such literature pallid beside his more vital, robust books.

A one-sided collection of any kind does not meet the rapidly changing, multiple interests of a child. Under the pressures of the space race, great new emphasis has been placed upon the study of science and mathematics. And along with children's natural interest in science, this emphasis has created a great demand for literature in scientific fields. Such books are, of course, valuable, but a wide variety of literature is needed to stimulate the minds and imaginations of future scientists. So a desirable goal for any home library is to have a balanced collection of good books, with some emphasis on the special interests of each family member.

By the time a child begins to choose his reading from among his parents' books, his own much-read and treasured library, housed in his own bookshelves, should include some ABC and nursery rhyme books, which have introduced him to books and a delight in reading as well as given him an early appreciation of rhythm and delightful language. He should be acquainted with many fairy tales, folk tales, and tales of the great heroes, all of which introduced him to differences in countries and some of the universal likenesses in human nature. From such stories he has learned positive values and profound lessons in human behavior. True, these stories may often portray cruelty, wickedness, and sorrow, along with heroism, sacrifice, and happiness, but they serve a vital psychological function in giving children an outlet for some of their socially undesirable impulses by allowing them to identify with imaginary or mythical characters.

The well-rounded home library will have good "family" stories, "girl" stories for girls, adventure stories for both boys and girls, sports stories, historical novels, and animal stories of all kinds. It will have books on nature study and other fields of science, "how-to" and other hobby books. And it will have histories and biographies. Such books can often be a source of inspiration to a child as he reads about the lives and accomplishments of the world's great men and women.

The number of books and the different kinds represented in your child's library will depend to a great extent on him. Perhaps the greatest function of parents in guiding the purchase and selection of their children's books is to be sure that each child has the kinds of books that meet his changing needs.

Reference Books

The foundation of your home library should be carefully selected reference books chosen especially with your child in mind, but which will also meet the need for information of other family members. There should be a good dictionary (preferably one with word derivations), not compiled especially for children, to be used by all family members. A good young people's encyclopedia is a necessity in these days of increased amounts of homework, even in the early grades, and in view of the emphasis on academic excellence that is current. Having these sources of information in his own home makes it possible for a child to establish the habit of study and encourages him to assume responsibility for doing his homework.

Encyclopedias and dictionaries, although they are primarily sources of information, have always given the fortunate children who possess them endless hours of recreation, browsing at random among the pictures and articles. Although such browsing will leave a child with numerous, often unrelated, bits of information, his reading can awaken him to the enormous breadth of the field of knowledge and act as a sharp stimulus to his imagination as he experiences other worlds than this—older ones, and ones not yet seen, as well as myriad aspects of the present wonderful world.

Reference books should be chosen with care. The authenticity of the information presented, both in pictures and text, should be guaranteed: Learn how often the material is brought up to date to keep it authentic. The care with which the articles are written will be obvious in the grammar and punctuation, which is also important. This kind of information about encyclopedias is available from any librarian. If there are no local public libraries and no school librarians, the state library agency, usually an extension library in the state capitol, will provide evaluations of several encyclopedias that have been judged by these high standards. Your set of WORLD BOOK and the WORLD BOOK ENCYCLOPEDIA DICTIONARY meet these standards.

Parents want to provide the best for their children: the best parents, the best home life, the best schools, the healthiest communities. These riches of life enjoyed in childhood, they know, will enable their children to live their lives fully in a world changing so rapidly that one cannot even predict what their adult world will be like. Parents have met a part of their obligation when they recognize that one of the greatest gifts of life in any kind of world is a love of reading and a store of the world's great books to read.

And one word more: Don't be overly concerned about a few finger smudges, a crayon mark, a rumpled page or two. Few children wantonly destroy their prized possessions. But they can't very well prize a book on the top shelf of the bookcase. Much-loved books are bound to pick up a few signs of use.

The list that follows includes both old-time favorites and newer titles, many of them for reading aloud, all of them for children, with emphasis on the young child and school-age youngsters. ELIZABETH S. MARGULIS

See also BOOK CLUBS; BOOKS FOR PARENTS; MENTAL DEVELOPMENT

Related article in WORLD BOOK: "Literature for Children"

Activities and Behavior

Back-Yard Games and Activities by Sylvia Cassell. Harper and Row, 1958. Good ideas for outdoor fun.

Codes and Secret Writing by Herbert S. Zim. William Morrow, 1948. How to write in code. How to write secret messages.

Fun for One, or Two by Bernice Carlson. Abingdon Press, 1954. Inexpensive ideas for travel and home fun.

Fun with Magic by Joseph Leeming. J. B. Lippincott, 1943. An easy approach to magic.

Pencil, Pen and Brush by Harvey Weiss. William R. Scott, 1961. Drawing for beginners.

What Do You Say, Dear? by Sesyle Joslin. William R. Scott, 1958. Etiquette for very young children. Humorous situations and illustrations.

See also Volume 9, *Make and Do*

Animals and Plants

Birds in Their Homes by Addison Webb. Garden City Books, 1947. Birds and their nests.

Dinosaurs by Herbert S. Zim. William Morrow, 1954. Facts about dinosaurs.

Houses from the Sea by Alice E. Goudey. Charles Scribner's, 1959. Scientific information about shells and seashore life.

Insects: A Guide to Familiar American Insects (revised edition) by Herbert S. Zim and Clarence Cottam. Golden Press, 1961. Comprehensive nature study manual.

Let's Go Outdoors by Harriet E. Huntington. Doubleday, 1939. Nature book for the young child. Photographs.

Pagoo by Holling Clancy Holling. Houghton Mifflin, 1957. The life cycle of the hermit crab.

Pets: A Complete Handbook on the Care, Understanding, and Appreciation of All Kinds of Animal Pets by Frances N. Chrystie. Little, Brown, 1953.

Play with Plants by Millicent E. Selsam. William Morrow, 1949. Experiments with plants.

Small Pets from Woods and Fields by Margaret Waring Buck. Abingdon Press, 1960. Care and feeding of animal pets. How to raise plants.

The Golden Treasury of Natural History by Bertha Morris Parker. Golden Press, 1952. Natural history for beginners. *See also* Parker's *The Golden Treasury of Science.*

Zoo Babies by William Bridges. William Morrow, 1953. True stories about animal babies born in the New York Bronx Zoo.

See also Volume 4, *Life Around Us*

Folk and Fairy Tale Books

Fairy Tales Told in England by Virginia Haviland. Little, Brown, 1959. Familiar fairy tales. *See also* Haviland's tales told in France, Germany, Ireland, Norway, and Russia.

It's Perfectly True, and Other Stories by Hans Christian Andersen (translated from the Danish by Paul Leyssac). Harcourt, Brace & World, 1938. Excellent read-aloud tales.

Just So Stories by Rudyard Kipling. There are several editions of these nonsense stories about the wonders of nature.

Pecos Bill, the Greatest Cowboy of All Time by James C. Bowman. Albert Whitman, 1937. Tall-tale adventure stories.

Picture Books by Randolph Caldecott. Frederick Warne, n.d. Four volumes of many favorite stories.

Rootabaga Stories by Carl Sandburg. Harcourt, Brace & World, 1922. Tales full of wisdom, poetry, and nonsense.

Tales from Grimm freely translated and illustrated by Wanda Cág. Coward-McCann, 1936.

Tales from Silver Lands by Charles J. Finger. Doubleday, 1924. Legends from South America.

The Blue Fairy Book by Andrew Lang. Looking Glass Library, also Random House, 1959. Favorite fairy tales.

The Fables of Aesop: Selected, Told Anew, and Their History Traced by Joseph Jacobs. Macmillan, 1950. Some well-told and well-selected old favorites.

The Rainbow Book of American Folk Tales and Legends by Maria Leach. World Publishing Co., 1958. A collection of tall tales.

See also Volume 2, *Stories and Fables*

Machines

A Book of Moon Rockets for You by Franklyn M. Branley. Crowell-Collier, 1959. Simple explanation with accompanying drawings of rockets and the moon.

Big Book of Real Boats and Ships by George J. Zaffo. Grosset & Dunlap, 1951. An oversized picture book that is one of a series about all kinds of machines.

The First Book of Airplanes by Jeanne Bendick. Franklin Watts, 1958. Elementary aeronautics, principles of flight, engines, and different types of planes.

What Makes It Go? by Rose Wyler and Gerald Ames. McGraw-Hill, 1958. Explanation of the power that makes machines move. Experiments, glossary of scientific terms.

See also Volume 7, *How We Get Things;* Volume 8, *How Things Work*

Music and Art

Famous Paintings: An Introduction to Art for Young People (revised edition) by Alice Elizabeth Chase. Platt and Munk, 1962. Paintings, drawings, and sculpture of the past five thousand years.

Fireside Book of Folk Songs edited by Margaret B. Boni. Simon and Schuster, 1947. Familiar ballads, marches, nursery rhymes, and carols with words and music.

The Wonderful World of Music by Benjamin Britten and Imogen Holst. Garden City Books, 1958. History of music.

Treasures to See: A Museum Picture-book by Leonard Weisgard. Harcourt, Brace & World, 1956. Fine arts museums and the things seen in them.

Tune Up: The Instruments of the Orchestra and Their Players by Mrs. Harriet E. Huntington. Doubleday, 1942. Photographs of instruments and performers. Origin and construction of instruments. Seating arrangement of an orchestra.

Myths and Bible Stories

A Book About God by Florence Mary Fitch. Lothrop, Lee & Shepard, 1953. Wonders of nature aid the child in his understanding of God.

Small Rain: Verses from the Bible by Jessie Orton Jones. Viking Press, 1943. Passages from the King James version of the Old and the New Testaments.

Stories from the Bible by Walter de la Mare. Alfred A. Knopf, 1961. Stories about Old Testament heroes.

Stories of the Gods and Heroes by Sally Benson. Dial Press, 1940. Tales about the Trojan War.

The Christ Child: As Told by Matthew and Luke by Maud and Miska Petersham. Doubleday, 1931. Story of the Nativity. Catholic and Protestant editions.

The Lord Is My Shepherd: Stories from the Bible, Pictured in Bible Lands arranged and illustrated by Nancy Barnhart. Charles Scribner's, 1949. Stories from the Old and the New Testaments.

People and Places

America Begins: The Story of the Finding of the New World by Alice Dalgliesh. Charles Scribner's, 1959. Discoveries and explorations of the New World. *See also* Dalgliesh's *The Fourth of July Story.*

Dancers of the Ballet by Margaret F. Atkinson and May Hillman. Alfred A. Knopf, 1955. Sketches with photographs of prominent ballerinas and danseurs.

Leif the Lucky by Ingri M. and Edgar P. d'Aulaire. Doubleday, 1951. Discoveries and explorations of a Viking.

Little Brother of the Wilderness: The Story of Johnny Appleseed by Meridel Le Sueur. Alfred A. Knopf, 1947. The Johnny Appleseed story of frontier life and pioneers.

Story of the Presidents of the United States of America by Maud and Miska Petersham. Macmillan, 1953. Sketches of the Presidents from Washington to Eisenhower.

The Story of the Southwest by May McNeer. Harper and Row, 1948. Geography and life in the southwestern United States.

This Is New York by M. Sasek. Macmillan, 1960. A picture book about the city of New York. This author has several good books about cities throughout the world.

See also Volume 5, *Holidays and Customs;* Volume 6, *How Things Change;* Volume 10, *What People Do;* Volume 11, *Scientists and Inventors;* Volume 12, *Pioneers and Patriots;* Volume 13, *People To Know*

Picture Books

ABC by Bruno Munari. World Publishing Co., 1960. Good first ABC book.

And To Think That I Saw It on Mulberry Street by Theodor Seuss Geisel (Dr. Seuss, pseudonym). Vanguard Press, 1937. A small boy's active imagination turns a horse and wagon into a circus parade.

Andy and the Lion by James H. Daugherty. Viking Press, 1938. Modern version of Androcles and the lion.

Angus and the Ducks by Marjorie Flack. Doubleday, 1930. First book of a series about a little Scottie dog and his adventures.

Ask Mr. Bear (revised edition) by Marjorie Flack. Macmillan, 1932. Mr. Bear gives Danny a wonderful idea for his mother's birthday present.

Billy and Blaze by Clarence W. Anderson. Macmillan, 1951. Story of a boy and his pony.

Book of Nursery and Mother Goose Rhymes illustrated by Marguerite de Angeli. Doubleday, 1954. Most complete book of nursery rhymes.

Curious George by Hans A. Rey. Houghton Mifflin, 1941. One of several books about a mischievous little monkey.

The Golden Goose Book by L. Leslie Brooke. Frederick Warne, n.d. Classic nursery tales.

Goodnight Moon by Margaret Wise Brown. Harper and Row, 1947. A little rabbit says good night to all the objects in his room.

Hercules: The Story of an Old-fashioned Fire Engine by Hardie Gramatky. G. P. Putnam's Sons, 1940. An old horse-drawn fire engine becomes a hero.

Lavender's Blue: A Book of Nursery Rhymes compiled by Kathleen Lines. Franklin Watts, 1954.

Little Bear by Else H. Minarik. Harper and Row, 1957. Stories about a childlike cub.

Madeline by Ludwig Bemelmans. Simon and Schuster, 1939. Madeline's adventures in a Paris boarding school.

Make Way for Ducklings by Robert McCloskey. Viking Press, 1941. Mrs. Mallard creates an amusing traffic jam as she moves her family to the Boston Public Gardens.

Mike Mulligan and His Steam Shovel by Virginia L. Burton. Houghton Mifflin, 1939. Mike and his red steam shovel solve a serious problem.

Mother Goose illustrated by Gustav Tenggren. Little, Brown, 1940.

Mother Goose; Seventy-Seven Verses with Pictures by Tasha Tudor. Henry Z. Walck, 1944.

Over in the Meadow by John M. Langstaff. Harcourt, Brace & World, 1957. Old counting rhyme song with a copy of the tune.

Petunia by Roger Duvoisin. Alfred A. Knopf, 1950. First of several books about an appealing and silly goose.

The Biggest Bear by Lynd K. Ward. Houghton Mifflin, 1952. Johnny discovers a problem and an unexpected solution when his little cub turns into a huge and sometimes destructive bear.

The Camel Who Took a Walk by Jack Tworkov. E. P. Dutton, 1951. A camel fools the other animals who are ready to pounce on it.

The Country Bunny and the Little Gold Shoes by Dubose Heyward. Houghton Mifflin, 1939. A country bunny wants to be an Easter bunny.

The Little Engine That Could by Watty Piper. Platt and Munk, 1954. A little engine makes every effort to pull a cargo over a steep mountain.

The Little Train by Lois Lenski. Henry Walck, 1940. One of several books about Mr. Small.

The Real Mother Goose illustrated by Blanche Fisher Wright. Rand McNally, 1941. Over 300 rhymes. One of the most popular editions.

The Story About Ping by Marjorie Flack. Viking Press, 1933. A Chinese duckling comes home safely after a harrowing adventure.

The Story of Babar, the Little Elephant by Jean De Brunhoff. Random House, 1937. A little elephant is made king when he returns to the jungle from Paris.

The Story of Ferdinand by Munro Leaf. Viking Press, 1936. A gentle little bull loves flowers rather than fights.

The Tale of Peter Rabbit by Beatrix Potter. Frederick Warne, 1904. Tale of Peter's misfortune in Mr. McGregor's garden.

Poetry

A Child's Garden of Verses by Robert Louis Stevenson. There are several editions of this book of verse about a child's own world.

Laughing Time by William Jay Smith. Little, Brown, 1955. Verses about everyday incidents.

Time for Poetry (revised edition) by May H. Arbuthnot. Scott, Foresman, 1959. A selection of poems and nursery rhymes.

The Complete Nonsense Book: Containing All the Original Pictures and Verses, Together with New Material by Edward Lear. Dodd, Mead, 1942. All of Lear's famous limericks and funny verses.

The World of Christopher Robin: The Complete When We Were Very Young and Now We Are Six by A. A. Milne. E. P. Dutton, 1958. Complete books in one volume with Shepard illustrations.

See also Volume 1, *Poems and Rhymes*

Science

Experiments in Science (revised enlarged edition) by Nelson F. Beeler and Franklyn M. Branley. Crowell-Collier, 1955. Science experiments using odds and ends around the house.

Find the Constellations by H. A. Rey. Houghton Mifflin, 1954. Astronomy for beginners. Charts, tables, and views of the sky. *See also* Rey's *The Stars: A New Way To See Them.*

Fun with Science by Mae and Ira Freeman. Random House, 1956. Easy science experiments using household objects.

The Rainbow Book of Nature by Donald Culross Peattie. World Publishing Co., 1957. A nature book useful for family trips and discussions.

The Wonderful Story of How You Were Born (revised edition) by Sidonie Matsner Gruenberg.

Garden City Books, 1959. Explanations of sex and reproduction. Has a guide for parents.

What's Inside the Earth? by Herbert S. Zim. William Morrow, 1953. Material on geology. Alternating pages of more detailed information for adult readers. *See also* Zim's *What's Inside of Me?*

You Among the Stars by Herman and Nina Schneider. William R. Scott, 1951. Explanation of the system of the universe.

See also Volume 3, *World and Space*

Storybooks

Alice's Adventures in Wonderland and Through the Looking Glass by Lewis Carroll, illustrated by John Tenniel. Alice's experiences when she follows a rabbit down the rabbit hole.

All-of-a-Kind Family by Sydney Taylor. Wilcox and Follett, 1951. First book of a series about five daughters in a Jewish family.

"B" Is for Betsy by Carolyn Haywood. Harcourt, Brace & World, 1939. First book of a series about the everyday activities of a little girl and her friends. "Eddie" series for boys.

Call It Courage by Armstrong Sperry. Macmillan, 1940. A Polynesian boy conquers his fear of the sea.

Charlotte's Web by E. B. White. Harper and Row, 1952. A lonely pig is befriended by an endearing spider.

Five Boys in a Cave by Richard Church. John Day, 1951. Exploring an unknown cave brings exciting adventure to the "Tomahawk Secret Society."

Heidi by Johanna Spyri. There are several editions of this classic story of the little girl and her grandfather who live in the Swiss Alps.

Henry Huggins by Beverly Cleary. William Morrow, 1950. Day-to-day laughter in the life of a typical American boy.

Homer Price by Robert McCloskey. Viking Press, 1943. Inventive Homer gets in and out of funny and curious predicaments.

Many Moons by James Thurber. Harcourt, Brace & World, 1943. Story of a princess who wanted the moon.

Mary Poppins by Pamela L. Travers. Harcourt, Brace & World, 1934. When nursemaid Mary Poppins blows in on an east wind, incredible and amazing things begin to happen to the children. First book of a series.

Miss Pickerell Goes to Mars by Ellen MacGregor. McGraw-Hill, 1951. One of a series about the incredible and hilarious experiences of Miss Pickerell.

Misty of Chincoteague by Marguerite Henry. Rand McNally, 1947. Two children's dreams of owning a wild mare and her colt come true.

Mr. Popper's Penguins by Richard and Florence Atwater. Little, Brown, 1938. A housepainter receives a penguin who brings excitement and hilarious adventure to the family.

My Father's Dragon by Ruth Stiles Gannet. Random House, 1948. The adventures of a boy who learns to fly and goes off to rescue a baby dragon.

Rabbit Hill by Robert Lawson. Viking Press, 1944. A story of excitement among the animals who learn that people are coming to live in a house nearby.

Strawberry Girl by Lois Lenski. J. B. Lippincott, 1945. A story of family life, feuds, and fun in the Florida cracker country.

Tales from Shakespeare by Charles and Mary Lamb. Macmillan, 1950. Introduction to Shakespeare for younger children.

The Adventures of Pinocchio by Carlo Collodi (Carlo Lorenzini). There are many editions of this Italian classic about a wooden doll that becomes a real boy.

The Bears on Hemlock Mountain by Alice Dalgliesh. Charles Scribner's, 1952. Adventure tale based on an American legend.

The Black Stallion by Walter Farley. Random House, 1941. One of a series of books about a wild black horse.

The Book of King Arthur and His Noble Knights by Mary MacLeod. World Publishing Co., 1950. An introduction to King Arthur for younger children.

The Borrowers by Mary Norton. Harcourt, Brace & World, 1953. First of a series about miniature people who live in secret places and sometimes communicate with "big" people.

The Family Under the Bridge by Natalie S. Carlson. Harper and Row, 1958. An old Paris tramp helps a homeless family.

The Hundred Dresses by Eleanor Estes. Harcourt, Brace & World, 1944. A little girl pretends to own a hundred dresses.

The Incredible Journey by Sheila Burnford. Little, Brown, 1961. Adventures of two dogs and a cat who trek across the wilds of Canada to their home.

The Little House in the Big Woods by Laura I. Wilder. Harper and Row, 1953. Pioneer family life. First of a series.

The Matchlock Gun by Walter D. Edmonds. Dodd, Mead, 1941. A 10-year-old boy protects his mother in a terrifying Indian raid.

The Moffats by Eleanor Estes. Harcourt, Brace & World, 1941. First book of a series about an amusing and realistic family.

The Saturdays by Elizabeth Enright. Farrar, Straus & Cudahy, 1941. Each week the Melendy children pool their allowances so that one of them can afford something special once a month. First book of a series.

The Valentine Cat by Clyde R. Bulla. Crowell-Collier, 1959. A modern fairy tale of a little black kitten with a heart on its forehead.

The Wind in the Willows by Kenneth Grahame. There are many editions of this book about the adventures of Mole and Water Rat.

The World of Pooh: The Complete Winnie-the-Pooh and The House at Pooh Corner by A. A. Milne. E. P. Dutton, 1957. The escapades of this lovable bear complete-in-one volume with Shepard illustrations.

Trouble with Jenny's Ear by Oliver Butterworth. Little, Brown, 1960. Jenny's capacity to "hear things" creates a story of fun and suspense.

BOOKS FOR PARENTS

A great many people have had a great deal to say about child development and related subjects dealing with child guidance, family living, sex education, and health. What these people have said has found its way into books, pamphlets, and magazine articles. The books listed here are but a small sampling of the wealth of interesting, informative reading to be found in bookstores and libraries. Notice that many of these books have been written by the distinguished men and women whose names you will find on the contributors' pages in the front of this volume. Space will not permit a listing of the hundreds of splendid pamphlets available. But if you will turn to AGENCIES AND ORGANIZATIONS, you will see that literature is available from many specialized sources.

The book list that follows has been compiled by Doctor Freda S. Kehm, director of The Association for Family Living.

A Child Development Point of View by James L. Hymes, Prentice-Hall, 1955.

Adoption and After by Louise Raymond, Harper and Bros., 1955.

American Folk Songs for Children: A Book for Children, Parents, and Teachers by Ruth Seeger, Doubleday, 1948.

A Parent's Guide to Children's Reading by Nancy Larrick, Pocket Books, 1958.

Babies Are Human Beings: An Interpretation of Growth (second edition) by Charles Anderson Aldrich, M.D. and Mary M. Aldrich, Crowell-Collier, 1962.

Baby and Child Care (revised edition) by Benjamin Spock, M.D., Pocket Books, 1957.

Brothers and Sisters by Edith Neisser, Harper and Row, 1951.

Childhood and Adolescence: A Psychology of the Growing Person by L. Joseph Stone and Joseph Church, Random House, 1957.

Children of Divorce by J. Louise Despert, Dolphin, 1962.

Dialogues with Mothers by Bruno Bettelheim, Crowell-Collier, 1962.

Dr. Spock Talks with Mothers: Growth and Guidance by Benjamin M. Spock, M.D., Houghton Mifflin, 1961.

Fathers Are Parents, Too by O. Spurgeon English, M.D. and Constance J. Foster, G. P. Putnam's Sons, 1951.

50 Years of Children's Books by Dora Smith, National Council of Teachers of English, 1963.

Health and Safety for Teen-Agers (revised edition) by Gladys Gardner Jenkins; W. W. Bauer, M.D.; Helen S. Shacter, and Elenore T. Pounds, Scott, Foresman, 1962.

Helping Children Reach Their Potential by Gladys Gardner Jenkins, Scott, Foresman, 1961.

Helping Your Child Improve His Reading by Ruth Strang, E. P. Dutton, 1962.

Helping Your Gifted Child by Ruth Strang, E. P. Dutton, 1960.

How to Help Your Child in School by Mary Frank and Lawrence K. Frank, Viking Press, 1950.

How to Live Through Junior High School by Eric W. Johnson, J. B. Lippincott, 1959.

Poetry in the Elementary Classroom by Flora Arnstein, National Council of Teachers of English, 1963.

Problems of Parents by Benjamin Spock, M.D., Houghton Mifflin, 1962.

Sex Ways in Fact and Faith: Bases for Christian Family Policy by Evelyn M. Duvall and Sylvanus M. Duvall, Association Press, 1961.

Teaching Your Child Right from Wrong by Dorothy K. Whyte, Bobbs-Merrill, 1961.

The Art of Dating by Evelyn M. Duvall and J. D. Johnson, Association Press, 1958.

The Children's Bookshelf: A Parents' Guide to Good Books for Boys and Girls by the Child Study Association of America, 9 East 89th Street, New York 28, New York.

The Eldest Child by Edith G. Neisser, Harper and Row, 1957.

Love and the Facts of Life by Evelyn Millis Duvall, Association Press, 1963.

The Happy Child: A Psychoanalytic Guide to Emotional and Social Growth by Irene Josselyn, M.D., Random House, 1955.

The Happy Family by John Levy, M.D. and R. L. Munroe, Alfred A. Knopf, 1956.

The Magic Years: Understanding and Handling the Problems of Early Childhood by Selma Fraiberg, Charles Scribner's, 1959.

The Parents' Guide to Everyday Problems of Boys and Girls: Helping Your Child from 5 to 12 by Sidonie M. Gruenberg, Random House, 1958.

The Parents' Manual (second revised edition) by Anna W. M. Wolf, Frederick Ungar, 1962.

The Vanishing Adolescent by Edgar Z. Friedenberg, Dell, 1962.

The Widening World of Childhood: Paths Toward Mastery by Lois Barclay Murphy and others, Basic Books, 1962.

These Are Your Children (expanded edition) by Gladys Gardner Jenkins and others, Scott, Foresman, 1953.

Toys, Toddlers and Tantrums: The Babysitter's Book by Emily R. Dow, William Morrow, 1962.

What To Tell Your Child About Birth, Death, Illness, Divorce and Other Family Crises by Helene S. Arnstein, Bobbs-Merrill, 1962.

BOREDOM

There's probably nothing wrong with a bored child who is otherwise healthy that a change won't mend—new scenery, a new game, new playmates, or a new challenge. A child isn't likely to say, as would an adult, "I'm bored silly." But he may ask what seems to you an endless number of silly questions, without bothering to wait for the answers. If the questions are asked in an increasingly whiny voice and accompanied by restless behavior, listen closely, for the child may really be saying, "I feel unimportant around here. Tell me I'm somebody special to you."

Often a bored child takes his boredom or feelings of unimportance out on other children. He is tired of playing; the game is no longer fun, so he hits the dog, knocks over his playmate's building blocks, tears books or your newest magazine.

To rule out the possibility of oncoming illness, check a child's temperature if his boredom continues or his bad humor seems unusual. Often a nap in a darkened room, with a favorite stuffed animal for company, will bring him back to his normal interested and interesting self.

Perhaps you have put away a Christmas toy or a birthday gift when he received too many. Now may be a good time to introduce it or to plan a surprise for daddy when he comes home or to get acquainted with the new neighbors down the street.

Gifted children often become bored. If your child is a preschooler, perhaps a nursery school or play group would help to keep him busy and challenged. If he is of school age, you may want to talk with his teacher. Some children need extra stimulating projects or chores to keep them from becoming bored.

See also GIFTED CHILD; NURSERY SCHOOL; PLAY GROUPS; RESOURCEFULNESS

BORROWING

"Neither a borrower nor a lender be," is stating the case against borrowing and lending a little strongly, but there is merit to the maxim. Borrowing can become a habit. If a child's tendency to borrow is not curbed very early, it can continue until friendships are broken and the child's integrity questioned.

To borrow something with the promise to return it within a certain time is a solemn trust. It is also assumed that the borrowed item will be returned in the same condition it was in when borrowed. To be late returning something, or to return it damaged, is almost unforgivable.

In a community where there are many children, toys sometimes have a way of straying. A child may come home with another child's tricycle. "I just borrowed it," he may tell his mother. A wise mother will question this statement, and accompany her child, with the tricycle in tow, to the other child's home. If this kind of "borrowing" is condoned, the child will find it easier and easier to continue to take things under the guise of borrowing.

A child may well be told by his parents, "Do not borrow anything from anyone unless it is absolutely necessary. And then, return it as soon as possible—in good repair."

See also HONESTY; RESPONSIBILITY

BOSSINESS

Bossiness in children can mean many different things. When, for instance, a 5-year-old tells all the other children in kindergarten that they don't know how to ride a bicycle and they had better watch him if they want to learn, he may really be saying, "Gee, kids, I just learned how myself, and I'll get scared if I don't act like a big shot."

A 10-year-old who keeps telling his classmates what to do, who cannot bear it if they don't accept his leadership, and who looks with dismay on his failure to make friends because of his exuberance and need to control, may be a child with unusual gifts of leadership, one of those especially bright and gifted youngsters who seem to be "bossy" only because they are ready for a more demanding and challenging environment. Perhaps he should be placed with an older group of children. On the other hand, an 8-year-old who will play only with younger children whom he can order around at will may be bossy because he is the youngest child in a large family and is always being told what to do at home.

Frequently, bossiness in children comes about from lack of experience in working and playing with others. Sometimes the most sensitive, creative, and exuberant youngsters simply don't know how to express themselves, how to play without taking over. Parents can help by explaining how other children feel, by offering concrete suggestions for ways in which the child can express his ideas and still give others a chance to express theirs. Bossy children often cannot understand the reactions of their playmates. "All I wanted to do was to show them how to build a tree house, but they wouldn't listen to me," says one bright 10-year-old boy, puzzled by unfriendly responses. "I only wanted to start a cooking club, but the girls got mad when I said I would be the chairman of the first meeting," reports a confused 12-year-old culinary enthusiast. "I'm the best hitter, so why shouldn't I be the captain of the team?" asks a budding baseball player.

These children have leadership qualities, but they need their parents' help in understanding the feelings of others, in learning how to lead and how to, at the same time, be part of a democratic group. Eventually they may see that real leaders want to encourage others to make a contribution, that a real leader does not make all the decisions for the group.

Bossiness that stems from inner feelings of uncertainty and powerlessness calls for a different kind of help. If a child has just moved into a new neighborhood and entered a new school, and is nervous and uneasy about how to make new friends, his tension and anxiety may take the form of bossiness. Here again, someone who understands his real fears can help him to find more acceptable ways of making friends.

Leadership, a quality to be encouraged in those who have it, is an important asset in a democratic society. As children gain in self-confidence, become more skilled in group living, and find outlets for their talents, they will discover the important distinction between bossing and leading. EDA J. LE SHAN

See also ANXIETY; COMPETITION; LOVE

BOTTLE FEEDING

For the first month or so of a baby's life, he awakens chiefly in order to eat. Food is of vital importance to him because of his tremendously rapid growth. The doctor is interested in the feeding of your baby and may spend a lot of time discussing the subject because he knows the importance of good nourishment. He also knows that a good adjustment for both mother and baby to his feeding will go far in making the rest of their mutual adjustment satisfactory.

Feedings involve much more than getting the right number of calories into the baby. Feeding represents a major part of a young baby's experience with the outside world and especially with his mother. The relief of unpleasant hunger pangs is something he soon associates with his mother, with her warmth and her pleasant voice. Feeding is also associated with being securely but tenderly held. Feeding, thus, quickly becomes associated with being loved. In addition, feeding is an experience in which gradually the baby learns how to adjust to someone else. The inevitable delay of a few minutes between the first hunger pangs and his mother's being able to feed him are something he learns to tolerate without feeling insecure about eventually getting his supper. This ability to adjust to delay while still trusting his mother to meet his needs is a very important part of personality development. Feedings are important not only to the baby but also to the mother, for a lot of her satisfaction in her new baby quite naturally comes from her pride in her ability to care for him well.

For the first few months, a baby's total diet can be made up of milk or a milk substitute, with vitamins and some sugar added. The sugar is advisable because it is not good for a small baby to get all his calories from protein. Most common formulas consist of some form of cow's milk, with water and sugar added to make the cow's milk similar to breast milk and easy to digest. Different forms of milk vary chiefly in the ways of processing and the amount of butterfat or cream they contain.

How Does Milk Vary?

Whole milk contains all the cream and is a fairly satisfactory milk to use in formulas. Homogenized whole milk has had the fat droplets broken up and is therefore sometimes more digestible. One-half skimmed milk is made by removing half the cream from regular whole milk. It cannot be made from homogenized milk. Some doctors prefer it, especially for small babies, because it may be more easily digested. All these milks are safe if pasteurized, fresh when purchased, and kept clean and well refrigerated. Since many serious illnesses can be transmitted by raw milk, only pasteurized milk should be used.

Certified milks, premium milks, condensed milk, and skim milk are either expensive or not suitable for the average formula.

Evaporated milk is probably the most popular base for formulas today. It is whole milk from which one half the water has been removed. It is pasteurized and sterile, inexpensive, easy to store and to prepare, and easy for the baby to digest.

There are many special milk formulas on the market today in liquid, canned form. Most of these are quite expensive and, although they are usually digestible and convenient to use, they are not necessary for the average baby.

Some formulas are made with milk substitutes for the rare baby who is allergic to cow's milk. Goat's milk, available in cans, and several different soybean preparations can be used under special circumstances.

Choice and Preparation

The choice of a formula should always be left up to your doctor. He will be the one to decide if, instead of the usual formula that

the bra, do not flatten the breasts; rather, support them by raising them upward and inward.

Cotton flannel or moisture-resistant material is sold with some bras as protection against the flow of colostrum or milk during the nursing period. Avoid this material, for it is rough and prevents free circulation of air. It is better simply to place a soft, porous, clean tissue over the nipples to keep them clean and absorb secretions.

The nipples are sensitive and should be treated gently. Wash them during your bath or shower and dry them carefully. Most physicians discourage the use of soaps, oils, or alcohol, for nipples are provided with an abundant supply of glands whose secretions have germ-killing properties. Moreover, mother's milk contains an excellent antiseptic that provides a remarkable degree of protection.

If Your Doctor Advises Massage

Doctors differ about the advisability of massaging the breasts and intentionally expelling colostrum. Some physicians and mothers feel these activities improve the milk flow in the first week after birth and give the mother experience in handling the breast. Should your doctor advise massaging, Mrs. Helen Heardman in her book, *A Way To Natural Childbirth,* suggests a simple procedure:

- Wash your hands thoroughly.
- Sit in a comfortable straight chair.
- Lubricate your hands with a bland hand cream.
- Place one hand on top of the other above the breast.
- Draw hands apart with firm, even pressure.
- Turn hands downward, one on each side of the breast, and press firmly and evenly.
- Cup your breast as your hands swing downward toward the areola and nipple, drawing the breast forward and upward.
- Allow the breast to fall gently as fingers and thumb glide off without touching the areola and nipple.
- Start with 2 or 3 times once a day and gradually increase to 10 or 12 times.

Expelling colostrum, should your doctor advise it, is also simple. Using your right hand on your left breast and vice versa, place your fingers below the areola and your thumb above the areola. Apply gentle, rhythmic pressure, alternately compressing and releasing the collecting reservoirs of colostrum located behind the areola. Removal of the colostrum helps to clear the ducts and keep the passage open for milk. The high degree of thickness of colostrum is thought to be one of the main reasons for congestion and failure of milk to flow during the week after birth.

Factors Essential to Success

What are the factors of successful breast feeding? First, a hungry baby; second, lactation (the yielding of milk); and third, easy expulsion of milk. None of these present much of a problem.

For the first few weeks a baby may be so hungry he will nurse 6 to 10 times a day. Each day the feeding times will be different, but soon you will be able to guide him into a routine schedule. Remember also that he will cry for other needs besides food, so if you think it too soon to nurse him, try changing his position, burping him, or rocking him.

Expulsion of milk is also easy—yet misunderstood. Many think milk comes because the baby sucks, but this is not true. Through activity the breast empties itself into the baby's mouth. As the nipple is stimulated by the baby or by the mother's handling, the smooth muscles of the breast automatically contract and expel the milk.

This reaction is called the "letdown reflex," and like other reflexes is controlled psychologically. That is why emotions can determine the ease or difficulty with which the baby gets milk. Embarrassment, discomfort, or too short or infrequent nursing periods can disturb the working of the reflex. Therefore, it is important during nursing to have privacy, quiet, assurance of relaxation, and freedom from discomfort. Music and a rocking chair help nursing as does a cup of tea or other warm drink at the end of a tiring day.

How To Nurse Your Baby

When baby comes, you may be too excited to know when or how to nurse him. If you, like many mothers today, are awake when the baby is born, you may want to nurse him immediately. He will probably be a bit upset by the birth process, and you can give him comfort and bring joy to yourself and your husband by nursing your baby in the delivery or recovery room. The first time and until the milk comes (on about the third day), nursing for three to five minutes is recommended on one or both breasts, depending on the baby's needs. Nursing for this short period will satisfy his sucking urge, remove colostrum, and prevent sore nipples.

If your hospital has a rooming-in unit, you may want to try this kind of maternity care. For one thing, having your baby beside you enables a feeding schedule agreeable to both you and your baby and not one fitted to a routine schedule. During the first days you may need a "pain pill" to help you forget the stitches and make feeding the baby more enjoyable, so don't hesitate to ask your doctor for one. It's extremely important also to have clean hands, clean perineal pad, and a clean, dry baby.

For the early feedings you will lie in bed, your head and back supported by pillows (perhaps with the bed slightly elevated), with the baby cradled in your arms. Later you may be more comfortable sitting up in bed or in a rocking chair, with your back and arms supported by pillows as you cuddle your baby. Supporting your breast with your hand may provide added comfort. Remember to take a couple of deep breaths, relax, and rock to your heart's content. Before the baby begins to nurse, it will be easier for both of you if you expel a little colostrum or milk (of course, with clean hands) to make the nipple erect and the areola soft. You need not cleanse the nipple before or after feeding.

The baby should be swaddled loosely in a blanket, with his arms and hands free. Don't let him become too warm or he will fall asleep. He is like the rest of us who enjoy our meals more at an outdoor picnic than in a stuffy, hot restaurant.

To direct the baby to the nipple, touch his cheek nearest your breast and he will turn and root. Let him take his time grasping the nipple. Do not force him; he may need a few moments of tasting and practicing. As he latches on, you may feel a momentary sensation of biting on the nipple. Some mothers also feel "afterpains" during nursing, caused by contraction of the uterine walls.

As the baby nurses, his lips will be far up on your breast, with his gums pressing the areola rather than the nipple. You may need to pull his lips out to the position for playing the flute. This enables him to compress the sinuses and squeeze the milk as he sucks it into his mouth. So he can breathe easily, use your finger to make a small dimple in your breast near his nose. To remove the nipple, place your finger between his lips and gums, thus breaking the vacuum.

After a while your nipples will become accustomed to nursing, the baby will eat more, and your milk supply will increase. Frequent stimulation and emptying of the breasts augments the manufacture of milk. Then you will want to increase the nursing sessions from 5 minutes to 10 or 20 on one or both breasts. If the baby starts on the left breast and finishes on the right, start him on the right next time. A safety pin on your bra will remind you where to begin.

During the first weeks avoid a formula, for the baby may become so fond of the easy nipple that he will refuse your milk. But after you and the baby are used to each other, a "relief" bottle is a must. A pacifier can also help satisfy the sucking instinct, so strong in the early months. If given only when the baby needs to suck and removed when he loses interest, you need not pay any attention to comments that in-laws or neighbors might make.

Surprisingly, tiny babies have personalities of their own which they display at feeding times. Dr. Merell Middlemore describes these in *The Nursing Couple*. It will be fun to see which type your baby is.

> First, there is the "barracuda," who, when put to a breast, nurses vigorously and promptly for 10 to 20 minutes.
>
> Second, is the "excited ineffective," who grasps and loses the nipple and starts screaming. He needs to be comforted and calmed, then put back to breast.
>
> Third is the "procrastinator," who puts off until the third or fourth day what he could do on the first day. Do not push or prod this one. He waits for the milk to come in, then does well once he starts.
>
> Fourth is the "gourmet," or "mouther," who tastes and smacks his lips. After a few minutes of this, he settles down and nurses very well.
>
> Fifth is the "rester," who nurses, then pauses to rest. If unhurried, he does well, although nursing takes longer.

These descriptions emphasize that each baby is an individual and nurses differently. Parents should accept their baby as he is. To do so may not be easy, but time, patience, and mutual understanding help make parenthood rewarding.

Nursing and Your Figure

You may be under the misconception that breast feeding will cause you to lose your girlish figure and force you to alter your diet. The truth is, breast feeding helps you regain your usual size sooner. And your menu during nursing is not much different from your diet during pregnancy. A well-rounded diet, high in protein and with extra vitamins and iron, makes perfect milk for your baby. You should drink milk, of course, and if you dislike it, simply disguise it in soups and puddings. For extra nourishment add dry skimmed milk powder to milk, casseroles, or meat loaf. Your doctor may also suggest the use of vitamin B complex, such as brewer's yeast or wheat germ, or that you eat three small meals daily, with snacks in between. Nursing makes you thirsty and you will require a large quantity of liquid—usually about three quarts a day. Otherwise, breast feeding need not interfere with normal routine—smoking, a cocktail, exercise.

For the first few days after leaving the hospital, your milk supply may be low because of excitement and readjustment. This can be a discouraging time. It is a time when every bit of moral support helps—an understanding husband, a mother or friend to help with housework, a visit from a public health nurse who can answer some of your perplexing questions about breast feeding. But probably the biggest morale booster is a phone call or visit from someone who has been a successful breast feeder.

Right Attitudes Are Important

Unfortunately, many mothers who wish to nurse their babies are held back by the attitudes of friends and the belief that breast feeding is old-fashioned. These factors shouldn't deter you if you're properly informed. Bone up on the subject before the baby is born. Ask questions of your doctor and nurse. Enter group discussions on the subject. Together with your husband enroll in a class to prepare for childbirth and parenthood. ELIZABETH PECK

See also BURPING; COMPLEMENTARY FEEDING; WEANING

BREATH-HOLDING

Few things are more frightening to a parent than a child holding his breath. To the worried parent, a 15-second episode will seem more like 15 minutes. The child, ever alert to new means by which he can control his parents, is more than likely to know how anxious his breath-holding makes them.

One single effective rule can be given on what to do when a child holds his breath: Do nothing at all. The worst that can happen is that the child can pass out briefly—at this time the reflex mechanisms of breathing will take over and do an adequate job until he comes to again. If the breath-holding episodes continue, it is probably a good idea to bring them to the doctor's attention. He may be able to help you discover why the youngster finds it necessary to try to control his parents by such a drastic technique as breath-holding. BETTYE M. CALDWELL

See also TEMPER TANTRUM

BRIBES *See* REWARDS

BROKEN BONE

Fractures are classified as simple and compound. The simple fracture is one that does not perforate the skin; in the compound fracture a sharp end of the bone may protrude. A compound fracture is, of course, much more serious, since it may become infected. Fractures extending into joints are more serious than those involving only bones.

Because of the immature development of children's bones, they suffer a common type of fracture called a "greenstick" fracture because the bone breaks only partially, like a green stick of wood. Another fracture common in children is the so-called epiphysial fracture, which consists of a separation at the growing ends of the long bones in the limbs.

A broken bone, of course, requires immediate attention, but in the meantime parents may need to take steps to prevent further injury or to deal with shock. If there is suspicion of a broken bone, do not try moving it about to confirm your fears; to do so may injure nerves, blood vessels, and muscles, or the skin may be perforated.

If at all possible, a child with a suspected fracture should be made as comfortable as possible where he is and should not be moved until he has been seen by a doctor. This precaution is doubly important if there is suspicion of neck or head injury. Contrary to popular belief, a person with severe pain is not more comfortable in his own bed than he is anywhere else. Unwise efforts at moving the patient may convert a simple fracture into a compound one or, in cases of fractures involving the neck, may seriously damage the nerve tracts in the spinal cord. W. W. BAUER

See also FIRST AID

BROKEN HOME

A home can be broken by dissension while all the family members continue to live under the same roof, but we usually reserve the term for circumstances that have removed one or both of the parents and may even have made it necessary to separate brothers and sisters. Extreme cases are not common. The household that must operate with only one parent is, however, a frequent phenomenon in today's world, a fact that brings no comfort to the particular family involved. To the father or mother deprived by death of a partner, the patterns of the present and the plans for the future are jolted and distorted and perhaps for the moment in utter chaos; in the case of separation, desertion, or divorce, there is likely to be, in addition, the pain of recasting the past, of being forced to recognize that what had seemed like a happy home had in it the seeds of dissolution.

Practical Problems and Their Solutions

The practical problems that beset each family, the details of financial arrangements —of whether a mother should get a job outside her home, or whether a father should try to find a housekeeper to care for his children—these and countless other problems are so personal that it is hard to find any generalities to cover the circumstances of a particular household. In general, however, it is well to keep in mind these things:

Disrupt as little as possible the patterns that are familiar to the children. If a mother must for personal or financial reasons get a job, she should try to get one that will permit her to be with her children at some of the accustomed times. If a move must be made, it would probably be better to move to a familiar and well-liked place than to a totally strange environment. (Brothers and sisters, it should be noted, are part of the environment; separating them from one another at such a time is a further disruption to be undertaken only in instances of extreme difficulty and with extreme caution.) Each case is, of course, special. If a child has been eagerly anticipating going away to school, for instance, a family break-up might be the perfect moment to initiate the program. If, on the other hand, he is likely to feel that he is being sent away to get rid of him, this would be the worst possible time to corroborate such fears.

One further "rule": WAIT. Whatever decisions have to be made will be better made a little later. In the inevitable shock of death —even one long expected, or of divorce— even long desired, there is often a sort of terror of inaction, and so action is undertaken in the wrong way, toward the wrong end. Even if a parent is herself convinced of the action she must take ultimately, whether it be moving back home with her parents, cutting expenses by selling possessions, getting married, getting a job, whatever it is, she will do better not to hurry into it and not to hurry her children into it.

For almost anyone in the throes of coping with a serious break in her life and her home, talking with an objective outsider will be beneficial. Friends and loving relatives can be comforting and often helpful, but they cannot ever be as objective as an outsider. A minister, a psychiatrist, a social worker in a family agency, a family or personal counselor, may be of inestimable value in times of crisis. HELEN STEERS BURGESS

See also DEATH; DIVORCE AND SEPARATION; FAMILY SERVICE AGENCY; GRANDPARENTS AND OTHER RELATIVES

BRONCHITIS

An inflammation of the lining of the tubes leading to and within the lungs is called bronchitis. It may be caused by bacteria or viruses or by chemical substances that get into the lungs by accident or through various forms of air pollution. Most commonly, however, bronchitis is caused by a cold or a lingering virus infection. Especially in infants, bronchitis following a cold may hang on for six or eight weeks after the patient seems to have recovered from the cold.

Although bronchitis varies in severity, most cases are fortunately mild and of short duration. The most bothersome symptom is coughing. A child may develop pus in the bronchi and cough up considerable amounts. This may not be noticeable in an infant or a very young child, for youngsters usually swallow the material that they cough up. In severe cases, the cough may weaken the child a lot and may even start him vomiting. The cough may be more severe during the night and very disturbing to the parents.

If bronchitis persists for more than a few days, the doctor should be consulted. Increasing the humidity of the room by use of a humidifier may be helpful, especially for infants. In severe cases, X-ray examination of the chest and bronchoscopy (that is, looking into the air passages with a special instrument) may help the doctor to find the cause and treat the patient. Medicine to reduce the cough should be given only upon specific advice of the doctor, since the cough usually serves a useful function in ridding the bronchi of irritating material. Medicines to increase the effectiveness of the cough or to make the sputum more liquid are of questionable value. JULIUS B. RICHMOND

See also COUGH; STEAMING; VIRUS

BROTHERS AND SISTERS

Lucky is the child who has brothers and sisters with whom to share toys and treats, share father's time and mother's attention. There's even much to be said for feelings that are less than friendly between brothers and sisters, for while a child is learning to control his anger and resentment, he is also learning respect for another's rights and how to defend his own. And this kind of learning will smooth many a rough spot in the years to come when you aren't around to keep the peace.

Children growing up together in a family are drawn close by common background and traditions, by companionship and shared fun, and, even more strongly, by the way they come to feel part of one another and to imitate one another's feelings and behavior.

Yet at the same time, inner pulls and outside pressures create rivalry and resentment. A child would like to have his parents entirely to himself. Giving comes hard to the young. Conflicting feelings of liking and disliking someone, of wanting to be independent and wanting to be cared for, are present in everyone—beneath the surface if not consciously, contributing to the mixed feelings that brothers and sisters have about one another. The intense competitiveness of our world presses upon even small children.

A child's early relationships with brothers and sisters serve as a way for him to find out what is acceptable or unacceptable or what works—be it acceptable or not—in getting along with others. As children grow in love and in friction, they lay foundations for respecting one another's rights and for defending their own. A child who has shared toys or candy bars, father's time or mother's attention, and who has found sharing both satisfying and not unbearably painful, will find that sharing in larger ways will come more readily as he grows up. Those first experiences in expressing and controlling the love, anger, and fear that a child feels for his brothers and sisters influence his later attitudes and help to shape his personality.

Accepting the Unfamiliar

Certain situations tend to heighten tensions among the junior members of the household. The arrival of a new baby is likely to bring forth feelings and behavior that are both disagreeable and agreeable in the youngsters already on the scene. No matter how carefully parents try to give the impression that the new baby is not taking first place, it often seems to the older child that another baby is so much excess baggage. "If I'm all right, why do they need another one?" is a possible unspoken query in the mind of the 2- or 4- or 6-year-old.

Some youngsters find the baby quite acceptable while he stays in his crib. But when he begins to crawl around and to interfere with their play and their possessions, they find his presence upsetting. Such resentment of the baby is no reflection on parents. Jealousy can usually be kept within bounds, but rarely can it be avoided completely, nor is such avoidance necessary. One of the fundamental facts of living is that no one can have sole claim on the attention of another. That fact is perhaps learned most economically when a child shares his parents with brothers and sisters.

Mothers and fathers can make sharing bearable for the older child by accepting calmly his statement that the baby is a nuisance. Feelings that are aired tend to be less explosive. If the displaced child is given an extra measure of affection and time to be alone with mother or father, he will know he is still loved. If parents provide tangible evidence that being an older child provides its own pleasures, and if they avoid frequent exhortations to be "mother's big girl," they set the stage for friendliness to the new baby.

Smoothing Out Difficulties

Disputes among youngsters often arise from an overdose of one another's society. If some privacy is possible, the company of one's brothers and sisters becomes more welcome. Disputes also arise many times from sheer lack of space. When toys, dolls, and games are thrown higgledy-piggledy about the house, they may become constant sources of contention. Everyone needs to feel that a few things belong to him and are safe from raids by brothers and sisters. Sharing also comes more readily to those who are sure that what they share will be returned. Mothers and fathers find that a small amount of thought and energy devoted to providing each child with a shelf or corner of his own usually reduces disagreements. Plainly labeled clothing removes arguments over "He swiped my sweater," or "She's wearing my socks again."

If one child in the family has developed a talent for sliding out of responsibilities around the house, and another feels he is continually saddled with the most burdensome tasks, tempers are likely to be short. Allowing the children a voice in the rotation of household jobs often diminishes squabbling.

Temporary breakdowns in amiability may come about because of events totally unrelated to the home. The child who feels he is bullied or left out by playmates often takes out his outraged feelings in bullying a brother or sister. One who is pushed at school to do as well as some other member of the family did previously, or one who feels he is treated unfairly by a teacher, may lash out at home at anyone who gives him half a reason for doing so.

What Is "Being Fair"?

Parents, being human, can hardly avoid finding one certain age or sex or temperament especially appealing. Probably as long as no one offspring is a full-time favorite for life, no one need worry about a bit of favoritism shown here or there. A greater danger today may lie in that sterile kind of fairness that leans over backward to avoid playing favorites. "I can't do it for you because it wouldn't be fair to the others," is not always a sensible line of reasoning if what is asked is some special comforting or assistance. When a youngster is ill or troubled, when he has suffered a disappointment or a loss, he may benefit from extra encouragement, affection, and attention. If the spirit in the family is, "Mother or father will stand by you, too, when you are in need," the other children are far less likely to feel they are being discriminated against when one of them is temporarily given a larger share of support. "Tempering the wind to the shorn lamb" is not playing favorites.

Special Considerations

In a family consisting of one girl with several brothers, one boy with a bevy of sisters, or one child far younger than the others, it may be necessary to give consideration to the tastes and the requirements of this "minority" in planning schedules, recreation, and perhaps sometimes in the use of family funds.

The lone girl can profit from the company of other girls in Camp Fire circles, Girl Scout troops, or similar organizations as a welcome relief from proving she is "as good as a boy." She may need occasions when she can have her friends in the house without being teased by her brothers. She and her mother can enjoy feminine pursuits as she gets old enough for sewing and for making the home cozier and more attractive. She need not be the only one to whom housework is allotted, nor need she wait on her brothers hand and foot.

The son who is surrounded with sisters can be supplied with opportunities to associate with males. Excursions with his father will be appreciated. It is a temptation to make him the protector of his sisters, but he need not play that role to the exclusion of activities more congenial to his age and sex.

Being the eldest, middle, or youngest has potential disadvantages and also advantages, but what the family makes of the position carries more weight than the position itself. No one is fated to be gay or serious, successful or inept, just because of his place in the order of birth. A wide variety of traits is characteristic of each position. Children tend to live up to what is expected of them and to conform to the mental picture they have of themselves. If an individual's shortcomings are attributed to his relative age, being eldest, middle, or youngest, and the constant refrain is, "What can you expect of a middle child?" or, "Of course he's spoiled; he's the baby," the unfortunate aspects of the position will be highlighted. If the part the youngster is expected to play challenges his powers, adds to his self-confidence and self-respect, and makes life more interesting for him, where he ranks in age can be one of his strengths. "He's our eldest and he shows us the way," is a far better attitude—spoken or unspoken—than, "Poor boy! We had to learn by practicing being parents on him."

Preventing Discord

Disagreements cannot be eliminated when four or six or eight persons live together, but parents can often take a few simple steps, besides those already mentioned, to create a climate in which friendliness among children can take root—even though it may blossom slowly. In a family that allows for and respects individual differences, the unique personality of each member can be taken into account. Mothers and fathers can stress and give scope to the special bonus each child adds to family life. If parents see the variety in the personalities of their youngsters as an enrichment to family living, their sons and daughters will tend to have a higher regard for one another, too.

When differences are cherished and nourished, no one child is held up to the others as an example of all virture. Comparisons that undercut good feelings rarely enter into conversation—or thinking.

Children in the family tend to get along together better if parents avoid using competition as a means of handling the day's routines. To offer a reward for the best report card or the best behavior devastates morale and engenders bitterness far more than it promotes efficiency.

Older children can take responsibility for looking after the younger ones, but they do so more effectively and cheerfully if left plenty of time to pursue their own interests with children their age.

Good feeling between the children in the family is furthered, too, if each child is encouraged to make friends for himself outside his home. It may be necessary to do some planning so that each one has a turn to invite playmates to the house. A Saturday at a schoolmate's home refreshes not only the child who goes visiting, but also those who remain at home.

The more arguments and quarrels you can forestall, the fewer you will have to settle. You can often make it easier for the children to play pleasantly if you try to find activities that seem satisfying to a twosome or threesome among them. Then, when tensions seem to be rising, you can suggest those pastimes or jobs that a particular team or perhaps the whole lot finds most enjoyable. You can often deflect coming trouble if you are aware of the low points of the day or the week, or sensitive to the danger signal of overexcited voices or uncontrollable dashing about. Some mothers arrange their work so that they will not be busiest in the late afternoon if that is the hour when brotherly love is at the lowest ebb. Being available to read a story or propose a quiet game may avert some stormy scenes. A family chore, such as making breakfast on Sunday morning while their parents sleep late, can give children something to do together. Pleased with being on their own, they may work with more cooperation and cheerfulness than they customarily show.

Given a setting and a way to enjoy themselves together, friendliness between the children tends to snowball and they learn how to live together with fewer clashes. Many mothers find it worth the extra effort to introduce surprises into daily life. An impromptu picnic, a spontaneous family stunt night or dress-up party, or a new guessing game varies the humdrum. Whatever it may be that substitutes good fellowship for teasing, and laughter for faultfinding, can give a lift to members of a family group who are on the way to becoming grumpy with one another.

How much bickering is to be overlooked and at what point should parents take stock of their children's relationships to see if anything is basically wrong? If a chip-on-the-shoulder attitude is the dominant one, and name-calling and fighting are the *only* ways of communicating the children seem to use, you may well wonder if pressures can be eased. If you can help each child find enough satisfactions in life so that he can *afford* to let others have some of the good things, too, quarrels may become less frequent. A child who likes himself finds it easier to like his sisters and brothers. The youngster who knows there is at least one thing he does well, can more easily admit someone else's competence. It is not so hard to grant someone else a place in the sun if one is sure of one's own place.

In a family where antagonism is not deep, the usual bickering decreases when pleasant events are taking place. The children can make common cause—either against an outsider or at times against their parents. It is gratifying if they generally come to the aid of the one of their number who is beset with troubles. It is a good sign, too, if from time to time they seem able to share one another's joys and sorrows. If they can do some of these things, at least a part of the time, parents can set their own minds at rest. Within the alternating currents of warmth and estrangement between the children, the youngsters are probably learning more than they could put into words about working and playing, giving affection and receiving it, forgiving and forgetting, and weathering the small crises of their daily lives. EDITH G. NEISSER

See also BOOKS FOR PARENTS; FAVORITISM; JEALOUSY AND RIVALRY; NEW BABY

BRUISE

A bruise, or contusion, is the result of a bump that does not break the surface of the skin but is sufficiently hard to cause small blood vessels to break and allow blood to ooze into the tissues. Bruises may be red to start with, turning black, blue, lavender, or yellow as changes occur in the blood while it is being absorbed. An ordinary bruise requires no treatment, but the small patient may be reassured and comforted by cold applications. If a child seems to bruise too easily, or if bruiselike spots appear in the absence of any observable cause, some interference with normal clotting of the blood may be responsible, and medical investigation is in order. W. W. BAUER

BRUSHING TEETH *See* DENTAL CARE

BULLYING *See* AGGRESSIVENESS; REJECTION; TEASING

BUMPERS *See* CRIB; LAYETTE AND BABY EQUIPMENT

BURN

A burn is the reaction of living tissues to excessive heat in any form. Burns are the same whether caused by flame, dry heat, electric sparks, hot liquids, sunlight, or overexposure to X rays. A first-degree burn is one that reddens the skin but does not produce blisters. A second-degree burn is one in which blisters are present in addition to the first-degree redness. The third-degree burn is one that involves deeper destruction of skin tissues.

Small first-degree burns are usually of little consequence. The best home remedy for them is to put the burned area immediately under running cold water or to apply an ice pack. If pain continues, a small child may be comforted by the application of petroleum jelly and a light cloth covering.

Second-degree burns of small extent may have the same first-aid treatment.

Third-degree burns and burns of first and second degree which cover a large area are more serious and should have immediate medical attention. While waiting for the doctor or when no medical attention is available, it is best to avoid application of any of the remedies recommended from time to time for burns; namely, oily mixtures, tea poultices, or other home remedies. The general condition of the patient is of greater consequence with severe burns than the burn itself because poisonous products of tissue destruction are absorbed and make the patient ill. In the absence of medical care, the affected area or the patient's entire body can be immersed in lukewarm water, which helps to alleviate pain. If there are symptoms of shock, such as clammy skin, weak pulse, or faintness, strong coffee or tea may be given if the individual is conscious and is not burned about the mouth.

A child with severe burns should not be moved unnecessarily until the doctor has been consulted.

W. W. BAUER

See also ACCIDENT PREVENTION; FIRST AID

BURPING

Burping (or bubbling) the baby is a very important part of feeding him, whether he is breast-fed or given a bottle. It is particularly important in the first few weeks when a baby doesn't burp easily by himself. While nursing, a baby swallows a certain amount of air along with the milk. If the air is not

brought up, it may go from the stomach into his intestinal tract and cause him quite a bit of discomfort. Or it may come up suddenly when the baby is put back to bed and bring up some of his dinner along with it.

Insufficient burping is one of the common causes of spitting up and of colic or "indigestion." Your baby should be burped at least once during a feeding and at the end. The easiest way to do it is to rest him gently against your shoulder or gently sit him up in your lap, supporting his head and back meanwhile. (It is a good idea to have a diaper or cloth on your shoulder, because lots of babies bring up a few drops of milk along with the air bubble.) Sometimes slowly rubbing your hand up and down his back helps bring up an air bubble.

Some babies burp very easily and often; others find it much harder, especially at first. It is worth while to be patient at first, even if it does take 5 to 10 minutes to bring up a bubble.

Sometimes you may be tempted not to disturb your baby by lifting him to be burped if he is peacefully sleeping at the end of a feeding. But if he is put down without burping, the chances are that he may become restless again and cry in a short time because of the discomfort caused by a large air bubble. Actually, burping rarely disturbs a contented baby very much, and most babies sleep right through the process when they are satisfied with their feeding. Sometimes a baby does arouse with burping and may even seem hungry. If so, you can offer him more food, which he will take only if he really wants it.

RUTH S. KEMPE

CAMP

Every summer millions of boys and girls in the United States spend a part of their holiday in camp. It is highly probable, therefore, that as your children approach camp age you will consider whether or not you want them to have this experience, what types of camps are available to them, and what kind you should choose.

What benefits do parents see in children's summer camps, and why are they so popular? First, of course, there is escape from the restrictions of city living. With grass to run on, rocks to clamber over, and woods to explore, a child has the chance to stretch not only his muscles but also his social and emotional horizons. Camp offers him, too, his first great chance to be on his own. Removed from his home, separated from his parents, without policemen on street corners, teachers at desks, and fenced-in playgrounds, he has to develop new self-sufficiency. This liberation is what he needs, for a child can-

not develop best when he is watched and protected all the time. Many children also need something else that camp can give them and that they do not get at home—close daily living with numerous other children of about the same age. Because the children are together in their cabins, at their meals, and in their activities throughout each 24 hours, more give and take, sportsmanship, and group participation is asked of them than in even the best of schools.

Children also need relationships with adults other than their parents such as they used to have when grandparents and uncles and aunts were a part of daily living. The everyday contact with counselors at camp is a modern, desirable way for a child to have additional adults in his life. And, too, the well-run summer camp can offer many activities not to be found in most families—nature study, dramatics, crafts, horseback riding, and numerous other out-of-door and group experiences.

But these reasons for the popularity of camps are mostly adult reasons. As far as children themselves are concerned, the explanation of the popularity is simple: It's fun. If youngsters throughout this last half century hadn't found lasting satisfaction in camp living, it isn't likely that camping would be the tremendous enterprise it now is.

Variety of Camps

When you start looking into camps, you will find differences in their organization, emphasis, and programs.

The traditional camp, the one that is probably most common, is highly organized and carefully planned. There is heavy emphasis on athletics, though usually there will be a sprinkling of crafts, music, dramatics, and nature study. Campers move regularly from one activity to another summoned by whistles or bells. The traditional camp may appeal strongly to you if you value order and regularity and if you like to have your children's activities closely directed.

At the other end of the scale is the camp in which few regular activities are scheduled. Each youngster does what he wants to do—goes on a hike to a beaver dam, joins in a baseball game, rides a horse, rows a boat, or participates in any available activity that may appeal to him. Though the director and the counselors have a part in decisions, the campers themselves have the most voice. For some parents, and for some children as well, this informality and flexibility is uncomfortable and they do not like it. You may be this sort of person. On the other hand, you may be one of those who find the permissive camp far more acceptable and challenging than one with a highly organized program.

A relatively small number of camps offer only what some of them have called "camptivities." Nature study, hiking, canoeing, camp cooking, and swimming are stressed. Often, there are no regular bunks or cabins; groups live in tents, covered wagons, tepees, or woodsman's huts, which the children themselves may help build. There is no central dining room, and each group is responsible for the preparation of its own meals, getting the food to be cooked from a camp storeroom. People who favor this kind of camping are convinced that it provides a far more realistic and meaningful experience than a program of baseball, volleyball, formalized shopwork, and other city-derived and school playground activities. Opponents believe that such "camptivities" are not much use to the child in coping with his out-of-camp life.

Some camps center on a specific skill, such as music, sailing, horsemanship, or language. Games and athletics may have a minor part in the program, but the specialized activity is major. For the most part, such specialized camps are planned for older children who have particular interests and want to concentrate on them. Here again individual tastes are important. You may not feel that the specialized camp is desirable, especially for younger children, or you may feel strongly that the chance to concentrate on one skill is a great opportunity for your child.

Interfaith and interracial camps make special efforts to include representative groups in both the counselor and the camper bodies.

Work camps provide opportunities for older children to help with local crops or to help develop recreational facilities in deprived communities. There are not many of these camps, but they are gaining quite a lot of favorable attention.

Some trip camps feature hiking or canoe trips. And there are some mobile camps that travel across country to national parks or undeveloped areas by station wagon or pickup trucks, camping as they move.

Recently, churches, YMCA's, and other community organizations have been sponsoring camps for the entire family. In such camps, in addition to the activities for particular age groups, there are frequent family recreation periods and chances for the family, as a unit, to have fun on cookouts and on trips to nearby points of interest.

Coeducational camps are growing in number, too. Though by far the larger number of camps enroll only boys or only girls, more people are accepting the idea that it is sensible to have the two sexes in the same camp, since in later life they will be together in the family and in the community.

Some public schools in various parts of the country have their own camps as a part of their educational program. These camps serve a dual purpose because they are used during the school year as well as in the summer months. Often, an entire class group will spend a week or 10 days away from the classroom in out-of-door activities.

Organization camps such as those sponsored by churches, YMCA's and YWCA's, Boy Scouts and Girl Scouts, settlement houses, and 4-H Clubs make it possible for families of even limited means to provide fine camp experiences for their boys and girls. Facilities, programs, and staffs of many of these camps are as good as those in the more expensive private camps.

Camp Philosophies

Some directors of private camps run tightly scheduled camps that stress awards and competition. They feel that only through incentives will they keep the children busy and interested. "Unless," one camp director has said, "you insist that they participate in the program and unless you back this up with some system of awards for doing specific things, youngsters will lie around in their bunks and read comics."

In such private camps one is likely to find a very complicated and thoroughgoing system of awards and competition. A child who accumulates enough points is awarded some symbol, such as a felt arrow to be sewn on his camp shirt or a colored kerchief to be worn around his neck. The competitive system is applied not only in games, but also in such camp tasks as cleanup, putting on the best campfire entertainment, or being the most neatly dressed. For some children, however, the pressure of such strenuous participation is so great that they become tense and tired much of the time.

Other camp directors run less highly organized camps. In such camps the directors stress that the available activities should first of all be interesting. There is less stress on awards or competition. The chief aim is to help develop initiative, responsibility, and a give-and-take attitude.

Those in charge of the noncompetitive camp allow the child more time for relaxation and for self-chosen activity that can be enjoyed for its own sake. Some children thrive in one atmosphere and not in the other. Your knowledge of your child can help you to decide whether he should be in one type of camp or the other.

The Camp Staff

Important as the type of program is in choosing a camp, program takes a distinctly secondary place to that of camp staff, for it is obvious that the effectiveness of the activities depends on who will be directing them.

Ordinarily, the director and his counselors will be people who have had training and experience with children. Thus, they are mostly teachers, recreation leaders, and athletic directors. But even more important than the camp leaders' experience is their attitude. Do they understand and enjoy children? Though this question is not easily answered, you can get some notion of how much understanding and enjoyment there is by talking to some major staff member.

There are certain other more concrete signs of the quality of the camp staff for which you can also look. Most camp people agree that there should be at least one mature counselor for every eight children. Usually the counselor should not be younger than

19 or 20 years old and should have had previous experience with groups of children. It is helpful to check on the ratio of junior or assistant counselors, too. If the junior staff is disproportionately large, its members will have to take on responsibilities beyond their years and abilities.

You can learn a lot in a discussion with the director about how he selects and trains the counselors. If he concerns himself with attitudes of the counselors toward children, with their past experience with children, and with their ideas about what they would do in meeting common camp problems; if there are pre-camp and in-camp training sessions in which the staff members work together to develop deeper understanding of children's nature and needs, you can assume that the emphasis is being put where it belongs.

Perhaps one of the soundest ways for you to judge not only the camp staff but also the program is to talk with parents whose children have gone to the camp you are considering. While not a sure-fire method, such confabs may give you as clear a picture as it is possible to get without going to the camp yourself.

Preparing for the Camping Experience

Even when your child seems eager to go to camp, he will get more out of his camping summer if he is allowed a part in all that leads up to it. He should certainly have some voice in selecting the camp. Let him know about the different kinds there are and listen to him, in part at least, about the kind he prefers. Let him meet the director, if possible, and also let him say whether he wants to be at a camp with his friends.

Camp representatives often have movies to show. Give your child an opportunity to see these, to ask questions, and to get some feeling for what he himself will experience when he gets to camp. If he can talk to older children who have already been to camps or if he can read stories about camp, so much the better.

If he has never been away from home, good preparation for camp can be derived from spending a night or two with relatives or sleeping in a tent in a friend's back yard.

In most states camps are required by law to meet sound standards of health and safety. You can easily find out how any given camp will feed your child and what kind of housing will be provided.

Parents' Relation to the Camp

While your child is at camp, you can have a valuable continuing relationship with him and his experiences through visits—short ones are welcomed by most camps—through reports sent out by the camp, through follow-up discussions with the director and, as an alert parent, through a sensitivity to your child and his reactions.

With a few exceptions, summer camps give children an excellent combination of education and fun. Summer camps now deserve their popularity. ERNEST OSBORNE

See also LETTER WRITING

Related article in WORLD BOOK: "Camping"

CAMP COUNSELORS *See* CAMP

CANCER

Any new, abnormal growth of body tissue is a neoplasm, or tumor. Tumors may be either benign (doing no harm) or malignant (cancerous). Happily, benign tumors are more common in children, but no age group is immune to cancer. The appearance of any unexplained swelling or lump in or under the skin, symptoms of illness such as unexplained vomiting, or bruising, or pain require the skilled opinion of a doctor to determine whether a benign or a malignant tumor is the cause of the symptom. Occasionally, an observant parent can detect a tumor in a child, but far more frequently, a careful physician will find it during examination of his patient. Early diagnosis of a tumor improves the chances for successful treatment.

Acute leukemia is one of the more common malignancies of childhood. Although this disease may occur at any age, it appears most often in children between the ages of 2 and 6. The characteristic feature of leukemia is an overproduction of abnormal white blood cells that are unable to carry on the function of blood cells. Early signs of the disease are fever, anemia, and a tendency to bruise easily. As the disease progresses, symptoms of illness develop which vary according to the extent of infiltration of the leukemic cells into other tissues of the body. The course of the disease is short and rapidly fatal unless it is controlled by effective drug therapy. Within the past decade intensive medical research in the field of cancer has resulted in the discovery of drugs that are effective in controlling the growth of leukemic cells and in retarding the disease temporarily.

It is now known that other childhood cancers as well as leukemia respond well to specific drug therapy, but these drugs must be used as supplementary aids to surgery or irradiation for the best results. MILA I. PIERCE

See also CLINICS; PHYSICAL CHECKUP

CANDY *See* DENTAL CARE; NUTRITION

CARBOHYDRATES *See* NUTRITION

CARBON MONOXIDE POISONING *See* POISONING AND POISONS

CARBUNCLE *See* BOIL

CARDIOLOGIST *See* MEDICAL SPECIALISTS

CARELESSNESS

A very young child cannot really be expected to foresee that a toy left out overnight may be lost or spoiled, that he will have less fun trying to work or play in a room not picked up, that a glass left at the table's edge may tip over and break. But by the time a child reaches school age, he should begin to be mindful of such matters. If he is not, his parents might ask themselves some questions: Does he, perhaps, have so many games that one more or less doesn't matter? (Store the excess items, agree upon where the remaining few will be kept.) Does mother regularly and speedily attend to the picking up herself? (Resist, even though it's true, the idea that picking up is often done faster and better without the help of children. They don't learn anything that way. Regular pickup times can be useful; so can the specific assignment of responsibility.) Are play and mealtimes being organized and arranged in such a way as to help your child avoid damage or breakage? (If not, give him a place to use the best equipment you can provide, and then do not hesitate to make the limits clear. Older children may have to use part of their earnings to purchase replacements of items they have damaged or destroyed through carelessness, give up time with their friends to straighten the mess they've made, be deprived of the right to use something they have abused.)

Sometimes parents describe as careless the child who is always falling, tripping, or bumping into things. "He just doesn't watch where he's going," they say. Usually the problem isn't so simple. The child may not be so well coordinated as others; he may be so intent on where he is going or on keeping up with the other children that he doesn't think how to get there; sometimes he's been so overprotected as a toddler and very young child that he hasn't had a chance to learn to see danger for himself. Here, as with the kind of carelessness that has to do with taking care of things, it's a good idea to try to discover the underlying cause for the problem and then to set up situations in which the necessary learning—or relearning—can take place.

IRMA S. BLACK AND JOAN W. BLOS

See also AWKWARDNESS; CHORES; RESPONSIBILITY; RULES AND REGULATIONS

CARRIAGE *See* LAYETTE AND BABY EQUIPMENT

CAR SICKNESS *See* MOTION SICKNESS

CATHARTICS *See* LAXATIVES

CAVITIES *See* DENTAL CAVITIES

CEREBRAL PALSY

Cerebral palsy is a general term. It is used to define a condition resulting from abnormal brain development or brain damage that may occur before, during, or after birth. In all cases there is impaired motor function and abnormal muscle action. If the child is a "spastic," his muscles will be tense and contracted or he may suffer from random involuntary movement.

Cerebral-palsied children have the same needs and problems as normal children. Like all children, they want and need to learn to do for themselves and to become increasingly independent of their families.

The fact that they are handicapped, depending upon the degree, presents additional problems in learning to talk or to use their hands or in being able to sit, creep, stand, or walk. Problems in hearing or in seeing may be present, and even a child's ability to learn may be affected.

Cerebral palsy is the result of an accident that probably could not have been prevented. It is not contagious. With patient understanding care and training a child may be helped to improve his condition. With adequate educational and medical treatment, many of these children may complete their schooling, including college.

If a child lacks balance and ability to move about, exercises or physical therapy may be recommended. A physical therapist, working under a doctor's direction, will show parents what exercises their child needs. These exercises will be an aid in learning more normal motor development.

If a child cannot use his hands, he may have difficulty in reaching, grasping, placing, and releasing his toys. He may be unable to feed or dress himself or hold a pencil for writing. An occupational therapist, working under the doctor's supervision, may be called upon to help.

Speech, in all children, is developed in stages, from the first babbled "ba-ba" to putting sounds together in words and sentences. A cerebral-palsied child whose speech is affected will probably need the help of a trained speech therapist who will suggest to parents ways in which they can provide their child with experiences that will stimulate speech and language development.

Many large cities, and an increasing number of smaller communities throughout the United States and Canada, now provide some educational facilities for the cerebral-palsied child. For the child who is severely handicapped, some states provide residential schools where he may live for a period of time. Intensive therapy and special education are given.

When a child is severely handicapped, and no provisions are made in the local community or in the state, a home-bound program may be the solution. A qualified teacher comes several times a week to teach the child in his home.

To discover medical and educational facilities for a cerebral-palsied child, parents may call upon their doctor, the local health department, the state department of health, or the local, county, or state department of education. MILDRED SHRINER

See also COMMUNITY RESOURCES; HANDICAPPED CHILD; HOME AND HOSPITAL INSTRUCTION; MENTAL DEFICIENCY

CESAREAN SECTION

Sometimes a mother's birth passages are not wide enough to permit the birth of the baby. In such a case, a cesarean operation is performed. An incision is made in the mother's abdomen, then an opening made through the wall of the uterus, and the baby is brought out of that opening instead of being born through the vagina. But the vast majority of mothers have normal, uncomplicated pregnancies and give birth to their babies without difficulty. MILTON I. LEVINE

See also BIRTH

CHAFING

Irritation, redness, and roughness are signs of chafed skin. Chafing may occur from clothing that rubs against the body—at the belt line, for example, or by irritation resulting from contact between two skin surfaces, as in the armpit or groin. The condition may be made worse if sand or other irritating substances or perspiration are in contact with the affected areas. Chafing tends to be worse in hot weather because of perspiration. Fat children may have more chafing because of irritation between skin folds. If a child is very fat, he may have to lose weight before the chafing will disappear.

Careful cleansing of the skin and application of soothing medicines prescribed by the doctor are helpful in clearing the condition. The child should be helped to avoid irritating the roughened skin further—especially by scratching. JULIUS B. RICHMOND

CHAPPING

Exposure to cold, wet, windy weather is likely to cause a child's skin (particularly his cheeks, lips, and hands) to crack and roughen, or chap. Staying in when the weather is bad, of course, will prevent chapping. But it isn't always possible to avoid exposure, especially for the school-age child. Mittens and mufflers will help, as will an effort not to lick the lips. But mittens get wet and mufflers slip down. The child whose skin chaps easily will welcome applications of protective creams and oils. If his skin has already chapped, it is sometimes necessary to apply medicines prescribed by a doctor until the condition clears. JULIUS B. RICHMOND

CHARACTER *See* MORAL AND SPIRITUAL DEVELOPMENT

CHEATING

Expect your child to do some cheating, but if it is excessive and constant, it must be recognized as a problem. How important a child's cheating is depends upon many factors, such as amount of self-confidence, emotional adjustment, what is to be gained, and the opportunity to cheat.

All children will cheat to one extent or another under conditions of easy opportunity and strong motivation. A child who may not cheat on a school test may cheat in a contest to win a prize. Or a child may cheat on a test with one teacher and not with another. Children cheat more in grading their own papers when they find large mistakes than when the mistakes are small. Even among college students only a relatively small per cent hold to rigid standards of honesty on tests, preparing reports, and writing papers.

Learning to refrain from cheating is a gradual process, and a child must be helped by parents and teachers to know what honesty is in many different situations. For example, the child who shows his answers on a test to a less well-prepared friend should be helped to see that it is disservice rather than helpfulness which he is displaying; that he is helping his friend to be dishonest. The standards of young children depend almost entirely upon an uncritical application of rules given to them by adults. There is no attempt to modify them to fit new and unique situations. As children grow, they gradually acquire standards that allow them to modify the "rules of the game" to fit the needs of the people involved and the demands of new situations. Thus, the goal in training is to help a child learn to use his problem-solving and creative ability to determine what is the honest thing for him to do in a particular situation. For we know that in the more complex situations, even adults will show honest disagreement about what is the more honest course of action. Problems of honesty can be so complex that it is impossible to view them in "all-or-none" terms. Individual interpretations and judgment are necessary.

The importance of a good example from parents cannot be overemphasized. What might appear to adults as petty cheating on their parts can loom large in the eyes of a child. The casual comment about "beating the parking meter" or deliberately keeping excess change through the error of a store clerk may deeply impress a child; winning unfair advantage over friends in business can influence a child much more in his attitudes about cheating than will a great deal of time spent in voicing platitudes.

While it is sometimes necessary to punish a child for cheating, generally, reward is more effective as a training technique. A child should be rewarded with acceptance and commendation when, in spite of easy opportunity to do so, he refrains from cheating. This course will reinforce honest behavior in future situations. There are times, however, when punishment is required following a dishonest act. While punishment, like reward, can be an aid in helping a child to discontinue a specific form of undesirable behavior, punishment, unlike reward, does not help a child to generalize to new and varied situations. LEO A. HELLMER

See also HONESTY; MORAL AND SPIRITUAL DEVELOPMENT; REWARDS

CHECKUP *See* PHYSICAL CHECKUP

CHEMICAL BURNS *See* POISONING AND POISONS

CHICKEN POX

Chicken pox (*varicella*) is a virus-caused disease that is extremely common and contagious. Although chicken pox is a disease in itself, it often follows immediately upon some other one of the infectious diseases. Most children are not very sick with chicken pox.

The symptoms of chicken pox are mild fever, upset stomach, headache, and loss of appetite. A blister-like rash appears suddenly on the body, face, or scalp—sometimes in the mouth. The blisters itch intensely. They later develop crusts, or scabs.

Often a child has such a light case of chicken pox that there is no need to keep him in bed. (This decision, of course, is at the discretion of the doctor, who should be called as soon as chicken pox is suspected.) Everything possible should be done to help the child keep his hands off his rash, for scabs that are pulled off leave scars, and scratching and the infection that comes along with scratching may also scar the child's skin. MARIE A. HINRICHS

See also COMMON COMMUNICABLE DISEASES; SICK CHILD; VIRUS

CHIGGER BITES *See* BITES, INSECT

CHILDBIRTH *See* BIRTH

CHILD GUIDANCE CLINIC

Child guidance clinics are centers for the diagnosis and treatment of children who need professional help in overcoming emotional, social, or behavior problems. Staff psychiatrists, psychologists, and caseworkers work together to help children who are referred to them.

The psychiatrist assigned to a case seeks to learn all he can about the child and his worries or problems. A psychologist is often asked to test the child to determine his strong and his weak points. A social worker will visit the child's school and his home to gather still other clues to the trouble the child is having. All this information is useful to the psychiatrist as he tries to help the child understand and outgrow his problems.

Some child guidance clinics are connected with schools, others with hospitals, and some with social welfare agencies. Traveling guidance clinics function in many areas where no such clinic is permanently located.

See also COMMUNITY RESOURCES

CHILD HEALTH CONFERENCE

A child health conference, also referred to as a well-baby clinic, offers health supervision for well babies and preschool children who would not otherwise receive continuous health supervision. Child health conferences may be sponsored by public health departments, service clubs, and hospitals. The professional staff includes physicians, public health nurses, nutritionists, and others. The principal services are health appraisal, including history taking and physical examination; immunization; screening for the early detection of handicapping conditions; parent counseling on all aspects of a child's health, including disease and accident prevention; dental health; behavior problems; nutrition; and normal growth and development.

For information about the child health conference nearest you, consult your city or county health department or the Visiting Nurse Association.

See also COMMUNITY RESOURCES

CHILDHOOD DISEASES *See* COMMON COMMUNICABLE DISEASES

CHILDREN'S BOOK CLUBS *See* BOOK CLUBS

CHILDREN'S ENCYCLOPEDIAS *See* BOOKS FOR CHILDREN

CHILDREN'S MAGAZINES *See* MAGAZINES

CHOKING

Children may choke from accidentally breathing or coughing substances such as food or foreign objects into the windpipe. Encourage your child to chew his food thoroughly and not to try to talk while eating. Peanuts, and even talcum powder, when accidentally drawn into the lungs, cause a dangerous form of respiratory trouble called inhalant pneumonia.

Your small child's toys should be shatterproof. Dolls and stuffed animals should have eyes embroidered or appliquéd rather than made of buttons, beads, or glass. Babies and toddlers should be safeguarded with special care against the danger of swallowing small objects around the house—marbles, rings, safety pins, cuff buttons, favors in packaged confections, and the like. If a child finds a small object, teach him to give it to you or to other adults. Thank him and substitute a more desirable prize.

If your child has actually begun to choke, turn him upside down and strike him sharply a few times between the shoulder blades. If this effort does not work, give it up; calm the child as much as you can and start for the nearest hospital, if possible leaving someone else to phone the doctor to meet you there. It is seldom advisable to reach into a child's throat with your finger unless you can see the offending object clearly and grasp it easily.

W. W. BAUER

See also ACCIDENT PREVENTION; EMERGENCY

CHOREA *See* SAINT VITUS'S DANCE

CHORES

There are certain chores that must be done regularly to keep a home running smoothly. Routine dusting and cleaning, shopping for groceries and household supplies, planning and preparing meals, setting the table, washing and drying dishes, making beds, and doing the laundry are all necessary everyday chores.

Major responsibility for these chores falls to the mother of the family. But every family member, in some way, can relieve her of some of these tasks. A 3-year-old can smooth a bed, empty wastebaskets, put soiled clothes

into the hamper, pick up newspapers and magazines, and put away his toys. Little ones can bring in the morning paper, put out milk bottles, plump up couch cushions, and empty ash trays. Very young children like the feeling of helping adults, so wise parents will build from that premise, letting little ones help whenever possible.

At times the chores given the young child may seem to parents to be more play than work. But the little girl who rolls out cooky dough and sprinkles the cookies with cinnamon and sugar and watches mother pop them into the oven is learning a skill she will need in later years. The little fellow who holds the board while dad saws away at the other end learns cooperation and a carpentry skill at the same time. As children grow, they can take on more chores, more responsibilities, and become more important to the smooth functioning of the home. Using this system of increasing the complexity of the chores assigned to a child, it is not unlikely that a boy of 14 can have charge of yard work, keep the basement and garage clean and in order, keep walks shoveled of snow, and carry out the trash regularly. A girl of this age can help with the family washing and ironing and can plan and prepare a meal when necessary. Little girls, from babyhood, can be taught to take pride in their homes, and when they see what satisfaction their mothers gain from a well-run home, they will like to share in keeping it that way. A mother's illness will not unduly upset a family if a daughter can step in to prepare meals, wash and iron clothes, and keep the home an orderly, pleasant place.

In the family where cooperation is the keynote, there is virtually no dividing line between women's work and men's work. Boys and their fathers do dishes, teen-age daughters run lawn mowers, boys wash windows, and girls wash dogs. The whole family cleans house on Saturday, making short work of this weekly chore. When members of a family work together to clean the basement or the garage, they will enjoy an activity that, for one person, would be a dreary chore.

The ideal situation is achieved when each child does his assigned chores willingly. But, or course, the ideal must be reached through much planning and working. "How do I get my children to follow through on chores?" is a question often asked by parents. Some parents install a chart on the kitchen wall where chores are outlined, with spaces for an "X" or a star when the chore is completed. Other families withhold privileges until the chores are done. Some parents curb the viewing of television until assigned tasks are finished. A trip to the zoo or a family picnic may be postponed until all work is done. Each family must find the system that works best in that family.

Children occasionally say, "But, mother, I'm too busy to work at home." Or, "I have too much homework." Or, "I have a project for Camp Fire." These are probably valid statements, but if parents are firmly convinced that children should have some set responsibilities around the home, they will help their children find the necessary time to carry them out. When the work habit is started in the very young child, when the habit of sharing responsibilities is begun early, children will usually take for granted that work at home is just part of family life.

It takes imagination to give children tasks that stimulate them rather than endless bedmaking and dishwashing. In general, they like chores that show results. If something dull and grimy can be made bright and shiny, the task seems worth while. All chores, to be meaningful learning experiences for a child, do not necessarily have to be dismal and disagreeable. Children can learn just as much, if not a great deal more, doing chores they like to do and enjoy as they can from doing something unpleasant.

Some families tie in chores with allowances, but most families feel that chores are done by family members simply because they are living together, under one roof, and they agree that certain things must be done to make that living pleasant and happy. Praise for regular fulfillment of chores is a sure way to build up a child's self-esteem—especially when criticism is kept at a minimum and the child is shown the approval of other family members. VIRGINIA B. NOVINGER

See also ALLOWANCE; RESPONSIBILITY; WORKING MOTHER

CHRISTMAS *See* SANTA CLAUS

CIGARETTE *See* SMOKING

CLASSICS *See* BOOKS FOR CHILDREN

CLAY, MODELING *See* ART EXPERIENCES

CLEFT PALATE

An opening in the roof of the mouth which keeps the nose and mouth from being adequately separated is described as cleft palate. The opening can be very small or so large that the mouth and nose are practically one cavity. Sometimes the tendency toward cleft palate is hereditary, but often something has interfered with normal development of the mouth before the baby was born.

An infant with cleft palate requires good professional care. At first, he may have difficulty in nursing and may need special feeding. Also, children with cleft palate tend to have middle-ear infections and should be watched carefully for this complication. Closing of the palate by surgery often may be delayed until the second or third year. In some instances a dental appliance may be advisable instead of surgery, or both procedures may be used. The aim is to give the child a good appearance, ability to eat normally, good speech patterns, and normal physical, emotional, and social growth. Although treatment may take a long time, results nowadays are often gratifying. In many states, special provision for the care of children with cleft palate has been made by teams of experts working in cleft palate centers. JULIUS B. RICHMOND

See also DEFORMITY; HARELIP; OPERATION; SPEECH DIFFICULTIES

CLIMBING

Instinctively, a child loves to climb. Rather than thwart his wishes, encourage him. Climbing gives a child confidence and skills that will help make him safer in future physical activities.

Provide sturdy, splinter-free boxes for the toddler to crawl around on while you watch. Or let him go up a few stair steps while you back him up. But at first, try to prevent solo ventures when you aren't around. Certainly, prohibit his climbing on high objects from which he could take a bad fall.

Older children can give vent to their climbing desires on monkey bars and in trees. Usually they scamper around these with great agility. Most of the danger comes when the equipment is faulty and breaks, or when tree branches are too small to support weights or too slippery to grasp. Purchase only good equipment and keep it in good repair. Teach children to choose trees with rough bark, easy to grip, and to test a limb before applying full weight on it.

One good general rule is: Never urge a child to climb higher than he wants to; he usually knows his limitations better than you do. WILLIAM G. JOHNSON

See also ACCIDENT PREVENTION; TOYS AND PLAY EQUIPMENT

CLINICS

Some clinics are staffed by physicians who specialize in a certain illness and practice as a team to diagnose an illness and to treat patients afflicted with it. A cancer clinic is an example.

Other clinics offer help in the form of advice or treatment, as in a domestic-relations or psychiatric clinic. Some clinics, frequently called medical arts clinics, are staffed by a number of doctors including, perhaps, an obstetrician, a pediatrician, an internist, a surgeon, an ophthalmologist (medical eye doctor), and an ear, nose, and throat specialist. Here families can find the care they need "all under one roof."

The outpatient department of a hospital, where patients who do not require hospitalization are treated, is often called a clinic.

Certain clinics are operated solely for those persons who are unable to pay for medical care, with doctors donating their services. Sometimes there is a small fee for medicine, but the charge is usually based on a patient's ability to pay.

There are many special clinics to help persons with health or personal problems. A pediatrics clinic is a medical service especially designed for children. There are also child health conferences (popularly known as well-baby clinics), eye clinics, dental clinics, reading clinics, and child guidance clinics. One of the newest on the scene is a "walk-in" psychiatric clinic, where troubled persons can talk with experienced counselors.

Families needing help may be referred to a specific clinic by a doctor, a hospital, or a local public health or public welfare department. Local grade and high school guidance and counseling personnel often help troubled school-age children and will, if additional help is needed, refer the child and his family to the proper clinic.

See also CHILD GUIDANCE CLINIC; CHILD HEALTH CONFERENCE; COMMUNITY RESOURCES

CLIQUES *See* CLUBS AND CLIQUES

CLOTHING *See* LAYETTE AND BABY EQUIPMENT

CLUBFOOT

When a baby is born with an abnormal, underdeveloped foot that is turned inward or outward, the foot appears to be stubby, or clubbed; hence the term "clubfoot." The condition may occur in one or both feet and varies in severity from a very mild deformity requiring little treatment to a severe case requiring extensive care. An orthopedic surgeon, or bone specialist, usually directs the care of a child with a clubfoot. Treatment ranges from the use of special shoes and splints to plaster casts and possibly surgery. Best results are obtained when care is started early, preferably in early infancy. If treatment is delayed, the results may not be so satisfactory. JULIUS B. RICHMOND

See also CRIPPLED CHILD; HANDICAPPED CHILD; OPERATION

CLUBS AND CLIQUES

Clubs and cliques spring up spontaneously among children during the grade school years. These associations may dissolve as quickly as they form, although some groups of neighborhood friends maintain a close bond for years.

The distinguishing features of a club are that it has elected officers, meetings, rules—of a sort—and a clear-cut, though shifting, membership. He who was excluded yesterday may be the chief promoter tomorrow. Clubs of greater stability among the middle and upper grade school children are often centered around the pursuit of a hobby.

A clique is merely a collection of youngsters who prefer playing with one another. A ringleader may unofficially hold sway. Who is "out" and who is "in" is not well defined, and tenure is even more impermanent than in a club. Cliques often become clubs. Clubs may drift into being cliques.

In spite of adult misgivings about unsupervised coalitions, they serve a useful purpose. Being included satisfies that deep-rooted human desire to belong as well as the childish enthusiasm for secrets shared with a chosen few.

Informal, loosely knit groups offer children an escape from the world of adults. Between the ages of six and ten a boy or a girl is apt to become discouraged about ever growing up. It takes so long. Parents and teachers seem to value only such tiresome goals as clean hands, neat spelling papers, and soft voices. Contemporaries who have similar ideas of what is interesting and important are a distinct relief.

In these groups of like-minded companions, a child gets the recognition and sense of achievement so vital to the growth of a healthy personality. Through the compromises, the arguments, and the hatching of grandiose schemes a youngster grows in independence and in ability to get along with others. He gains an understanding of which plans can actually be carried out and which are in the realm of make-believe.

Time spent in groups of their own choosing is usually profitable as well as happy for boys or girls. Yet occasionally you may feel that some direction is called for to cut down bickering and wounded feelings among the girls or the fights and the rowdiness among the boys. A suggestion from a friendly adult about putting on a play or a circus and inviting families and neighbors may be welcomed. An offer of assistance in making presents or decorations for an approaching holiday, or scrapbooks for hospitalized children may put a stop to brewing mischief. A group may take kindly to the idea of building up some sort of collection. Learning a skill or a sport from some adult in the neighborhood may appeal to the youngsters.

The restlessness of the members of a club or clique may be a sign that they are ripe for a more formal organization, such as Cub Scouts, Brownies, Gra-Y, Camp Fire Girls, or one of the other adult-sponsored leisure-time activities.

Not all children are equally enthusiastic about being in clubs. We can respect the tastes of those who are contentedly pursuing interests on their own, even as we recognize that belonging to a group can contribute to the enjoyment of living and to the growth and development of children who relish such participation. EDITH G. NEISSER

See also APPROVAL; DRAMATICS; FRIENDS; GANGS; YOUTH ORGANIZATIONS

CLUMSINESS *See* AWKWARDNESS

COLDS

Sneezing, a stopped-up or runny nose, sore throat, and a cough usually add up to "the common cold," a malady with which parents are all too familiar. Certain types of viruses, traveling from person to person through tiny droplets in the air, cause colds. Chilling and fatigue often are blamed when a cold develops, but exposure to an infected person suffering from a cold is the more likely culprit. Since a cold does not confer immunity, people can have repeated infections.

Infants usually suffer only mild colds—a runny nose, a slight cough, but from toddlerhood on, children average about four colds a year. Symptoms vary, but usually the cold sufferer will have some fever, and his appetite and his energy may decline.

In itself, a cold is not especially harmful, but the complications that may occur can be serious. Medical care is therefore important because of the need to detect and treat complications early. While an infant's cold may be mild, it can be very uncomfortable because eating is difficult for him when he cannot breathe through his nose. A baby also has a greater tendency to develop complications, such as middle-ear infections, sinusitis, bronchitis, and pneumonia. For these reasons, it is most important that people with colds, including members of the immediate family, stay away from a baby. Masks worn over the mouth and nose of the cold sufferer who must care for the baby are not very effective, but they are a precautionary measure, along with frequent hand-washing.

The complications of a cold may be caused by bacteria rather than a virus; therefore, antibiotics may be effective in treating the complications, even though antibiotics are not considered helpful in treating the uncomplicated cold. In general, however, these drugs should be reserved for use in serious illnesses such as pneumonia, meningitis, and other forms of severe infection.

The child with a cold should drink plenty of fluids and should get extra rest. It also may be helpful to increase the humidity of his room with a steamer, especially if he is an infant or a small child. His nose secretions should also gently be wiped away to prevent his tender skin from chafing and becoming irritated. Occasionally, nose drops or nasal sprays may prove helpful in clearing nasal congestion, but these preparations should be used only on the advice of a physician, and neither drops nor sprays should ever be used in an oily suspension. Small amounts of aspirin may provide comfort, too, but should be given only if the child is drinking lots of fluids.

A child may gradually be permitted increased activity as his energy increases. If no complications develop, a child who has had a cold is usually not considered infectious after three or four days. JULIUS B. RICHMOND

See also BRONCHITIS; COMMON COMMUNICABLE DISEASES; NOSE DROPS; SICK CHILD; SINUSITIS; VIRUS

COLD SORE *See* FEVER BLISTER

COLIC

Colic is a most uncomfortable condition that occurs in some babies during the first three months of life. The baby cries very hard and seems to be in great pain, as if he has a severe stomach-ache. His abdomen is often hard and tense and he may pass some flatus, or gas. Episodes of colic happen more often in the evening and with a few babies may occur almost every night.

Colic almost always disappears by the time a baby is 3 months old, which makes some people believe colic is due to an immaturity of the intestinal tract. As far as is known, colic usually is not due to allergy and may occur even though there are no other difficulties in feeding or digestion. It seems to happen regardless of whether a baby is breast or formula fed and regardless of the kind of formula he gets. There is some indication that anxiety or tension in the family may at times increase frequency of colic. Whatever the causes are, colic does not interfere with the baby's over-all health or development and can be considered an unfortunate but not a serious condition. This fact is important to recognize, because to worry about colic will only make it harder to cope with.

There are some things you can do that may help prevent or lessen a baby's colic. It is certainly worth while to check the feeding situation. If your baby is formula fed, his doctor should review the formula and your method of making it. Rubber nipples should be checked to make sure holes are the proper size. The baby should not be fed too rapidly or for too long, and he should be given several chances to bring up air bubbles. If the colic occurs regularly at a certain time, some quiet rocking or holding may be soothing. Sometimes a baby is more comfortable lying on his tummy, either over a partly filled hot water bottle or on his mother's lap.

Your doctor may have suggestions of his own to help with this problem. RUTH S. KEMPE

See also BABY; BURPING

COLOR BLINDNESS

When a child is color blind, he sees certain colors as gray. Although some of these children see all colors as gray, red and green are the colors that usually appear as gray to the color-blind child.

If you notice that your child has difficulty identifying colors, if he wears mismatched socks or cannot take the correct crayon from a box when asked to select one by color, it will be wise for you to have his vision checked. Some schools check children for color vision in the very early grades, a practice that should be supported and encouraged. Early detection of color blindness will prove helpful in guiding these children.

While there is yet no cure for color blindness, research studies continue. Sometimes vitamins are added to the diet or injections of vitamins are given, but such therapy should be attempted only under the direction of a qualified physician.

See also EYE HEALTH

COLOSTRUM *See* BREAST CARE AND BREAST FEEDING

COMFORTING

Comforting an anxious child is as natural as feeding a hungry one. Usually a parent or some other grown-up person and often an older child respond quickly to a hurt or frightened child. A child's cry strikes a responsive chord in almost everyone. Sometimes, unfortunately, we are not always aware of a child's need to be comforted and he has to suffer quietly and bury his anxiety. But it will appear later. It is possible to suppress hurt for a long time but not forever. One day an emotional outburst will come, maybe after the cause has been forgotten. Comforting and talking things over are emotional first aid. They will heal or help to heal many hurts and prevent trouble later on.

A child needs comfort when he hurts himself and when he is afraid and when he loses something dear to him, be it no more than a battered toy. Comforting should have its constructive side. A hurt will get well, a broken toy often can be repaired or replaced. But don't get impatient when your comforting is not immediately effective. Any grief requires some time for recovery. HELEN ROSS

See also ANXIETY; LOVE

COMICS

Comic books are here to stay. Wise parents realize that this is true and are not disturbed; they try only to cope with the situation in a sensible way. Once parents understand what it is their children like about comics and how and why children turn to comics, they will know what groups of parents, groups of teachers, or separate members of a family need to do. Comic-book reading will assume no more important role than it merits.

You need to see the child, not the comic book. Each child brings something different to his reading and takes away a different message. The important thing is not just, "Is he a comic-book reader?" but "What else does he do?" "How large does comic-book reading bulk in what he reads, the way he spends his free time—his whole daily program?" With the answers to these questions, parents can get a perspective.

Comics Are Available and Cheap

Comics are sold in almost any store today, and their price, varying from 10 to 25 cents, makes them available to the piggy-bank crowd. The trading of comics has become a going business among the youngsters who read them quickly and pass them along.

A comic-book story moves fast; it compresses a great deal of plot and action into one strip or section. With the aid of a few well-drawn lines, the child gets sufficient clues about what is happening so that reading of the text becomes relatively unimportant. He looks and understands. The world of books is not closed to him, even though his reading ability is poor. There is great satisfaction in this discovery to the child who has been made to feel incompetent in the school's approach to reading.

Comic books are many and varied in content. Children have a chance to explore, to test, and to taste many kinds of stories. Here they can find a favorite character and a favorite world of make-believe. They want to throw themselves into a world of fun, fact, suspense, and wonder. Comic books offer this opportunity.

Grownups collect china, glass, bottles, stamps, and similar objects to display before their friends. Just so, the young reader of comics often finds his prestige heightened in proportion to his hoard of comic books. His stack of books may reach from the floor to the window sill, thereby making him champion comic-book collector in his neighborhood. He can also use comic books as a means of barter. "I'll give you three Superman comics for that jackknife," is a phrase we may hear, with variations, many times.

What Effect Do Comics Have?

The comic often does for the child what the newspaper at breakfast does for some grownups. It postpones the moment of responding to a daily schedule or routine. To the child, reading a comic book can postpone that errand to the grocery store, going to school, or getting ready for bed.

For children who have many reading experiences, who enjoy reading either for pleasure or for school assignments, an occasional reading session with the less objectionable comics can be a lot of fun. The more different types of reading parents make available to their child, the broader will be his taste. He will soon learn the difference between good and not-so-good reading. In comics he finds humor, adventure, truth, exaggeration—even distortion—presented in brief and varied ways. By reading comics, children feel a kind of release from restrictions placed upon them. For example, many children would like to do some of the things Dennis the Menace does so hilariously, but they wouldn't dare. Reading about Dennis can act as a sort of safety valve.

Some comics are frightening, but so are some of the stories considered "good literature." If a child is frightened by something he reads, it would be well for his parents or teacher to find out where his fear lies. The child may have a fear about himself or about his relationships with others.

We cannot say, flatly, that comics affect a child's behavior. Many environmental forces, not just one, cause a child to behave in a certain way. When we find out *why* a child chooses one particular comic over another, then we will have a clue to why he behaves as he does. Some children break laws or engage in destructive gang play or other forms of delinquent behavior. Here, again, while the *ideas* for some of the things these children do may have been pictured in a comic book, they might just as well have come from something the child observed in his home, on the television screen, or in some book other than a comic.

Forbidden books usually manage to arouse twice the interest they would command if they were normally available. When comics are taken away from a child, when a child is forbidden to read them, the comic-book lure becomes so strong that he is going to get them at any cost. Many a parent can remember stolen minutes reading comic books under the bedcovers by flashlight. Children are going to acquire and read comics, one way or another, so forbidding them is an empty gesture. Less effort spent worrying about comics and more effort spent in supplying desirable but equally satisfying activities will prove more rewarding.

Effect of Comics on Language and Reading

Distortions of language, exaggerated remarks, colorful words, and oddities of speech are all caught and retained by a child's sensitive ear at one time or another. Home backgrounds and school experiences can give a child an interesting vocabulary of his own. Precision of speech, beauty of expression, and soundness of thought begin in a child's first experiences with language in his own family. Long before he reads, your child will show, in his speech, the patterns of language used by those closest to him. If he has heard a meager number of words, the comics may give him a wider selection from which to choose. If he has a considerable background of language, he will not be permanently affected by inaccuracies or distortions met and laughed at, or even especially relished, in the comics.

If parents, teachers, and librarians have shared stories, poems, pictures, and books with a child, comic books will not hold a place of overwhelming importance to him. Interest in comics will be temporary and the fun to be had from other reading experiences will more and more crowd out undue interest in comic books.

The more varied a child's experience with books, the sooner he will develop a taste for wholesome and satisfying literature wherever he finds it. Beauty, truth, humor, honest characterization, and all the values he has prized in family and school living will be sought in books. The adventures to be found and shared in the selection and reading of many different kinds of books can never be supplanted by comic books alone. A child who has read the thrilling original of a fairy tale or an adventure story will be disappointed in the watered-down versions available in comic-book form. ARENSA SONDERGAARD

See also BOOKS FOR CHILDREN; FEAR; MAGAZINES

COMMON COLD *See* COLDS

COMMON COMMUNICABLE DISEASES

Most of the common communicable diseases of childhood begin in much the same way, as you can see by the accompanying table.

A child may wake up in the morning with a miserable case of sniffles, or he may come dragging home from school, aching and irritable. At this stage, there's a big question about what the symptoms mean. Maybe it's only a cold. But if you are the child's mother, there is no question about what you do.

Put the child to bed in a room by himself; keep everybody else out.

Take his temperature; look for a rash on arms, face, neck, or chest.

Call your doctor.

Don't think you are being overcautious when you follow this procedure. The patient may indeed have only a cold. But even so, bed is the proper place for him.

If the illness does turn out to be a catching disease, the earlier and more complete the isolation, the better for other members of the family, especially for babies and elderly relatives. The sooner medical advice is sought, the better the chance to determine the nature of the illness and to lighten and shorten the course of the disease.

Rashes can appear and go away before an inexperienced person notices them. In some communicable diseases prompt treatment may mean the difference between early recovery and a long, severe illness. Early consultation with the doctor can be helpful to other members of the family, too. He will advise on what precautions are necessary to protect them and will notify the local health department, as required by law.

Health department regulations vary from community to community. But when communicable diseases such as diphtheria, poliomyelitis, or typhoid fever are reported to a local health department, a representative of the department usually calls to discuss precautionary measures, including disinfection after the patient has recovered.

COMMON COMMUNICABLE DISEASES

DISEASE	INCUBATION PERIOD	COMMON SYMPTOMS
CHICKEN POX (Varicella)	14-21 days	Mild fever, upset stomach, headache. Blister-like rash that appears suddenly. Blisters become crusted in 1 to 3 days.
DIPHTHERIA	1-4 days (or longer)	Severe sore throat. Fever. Yellowish-gray patches on tonsils, throat, or palate. Breathing may become tight and difficult.
GERMAN MEASLES (Rubella)	10-21 days (average, 18 days)	Begins like head cold. Headache. Rash on face and head, spreading to neck and trunk. Slight fever during rash. Rash lasts 2 to 3 days. Glands at back of head and neck and behind ears enlarged.
MEASLES (Rubeola)	Fever, 10 days. Rash, 13-15 days	Resembles cold. Fever, nasal discharge, watery eyes, cough. White spots in mouth. Pinpoint rash begins behind ears, on forehead and face on third or fourth day.
MUMPS (Infectious Parotitis)	12-26 days (average, 18 days)	May experience sudden onset of chills and fever. Headache. Swelling and pain in one or more salivary glands.
POLIOMYELITIS (Infantile Paralysis)	9-13 days—or less	Begins suddenly. Chills, fever, sort throat, dull pain on bending neck, headache, vomiting, weakness or paralysis of one or more muscle groups. Stiff back.
SCARLET FEVER (and Strep Sore Throat)	2-9 days	Begins very suddenly. Headache, chills, fever, sore throat. Vomiting frequently occurs without warning. Neck glands enlarged and tender. Tongue red and rough. Rash appears in 24 hours. Skin peels.
SMALLPOX (Variola)	7-16 days (usually 12 days)	Begins suddenly with chills, fever, vomiting, or convulsions. Severe headache and backache. Red spots that change to blisters filled with pus. Scabs in 10 to 12 days.
WHOOPING COUGH (Pertussis)	5-21 days (average, 10 days)	Increased nose and throat secretions. Spells of coughing. Cough worse at night. Slight fever. Whooping develops in 2 weeks. Coughing spasm may end in vomiting.

USUAL HOME CARE	ISOLATION PERIOD Child who has it	Child who has been exposed	PREVENTIVE MEASURES
Isolation. Prevent scratching. Trim fingernails. Apply soothing lotion.	Isolate 6 days after rash first appears.	None	None. One attack usually confers immunity.
Isolation. Hospitalize if possible. Bed rest and nursing care. High-calorie soft or liquid diet. Disinfect soiled articles and discharges.	Isolate until 3 consecutive bacteria-free cultures 24 hours apart.	Quarantine 7 days and until 2 bacteria-free cultures.	Shots of diphtheria antitoxin (usually begun as part of 4-in-1 shots in infancy). One attack usually confers immunity.
Isolation. Keep patient warm.	Isolate from first symptom to 4 or 5 days after rash.	None	None. One attack usually confers immunity.
Isolation. Keep warm and quiet. Darken room if light bothers eyes. Light diet.	Isolate from first symptom to 4 or 5 days after rash (8 days).	Quarantine 7 to 14 days under some conditions, but quarantine of no value during epidemic.	Protective vaccine is now perfected, and available. Gamma globulin in special cases for temporary immunity.
Isolation.	Isolate until swelling subsides, 7 to 10 days.	None	One attack involving both sides usually confers immunity.
Isolation. Patient usually hospitalized. Hot packs or iron lung, etc., depending on doctor's orders.	Isolate last part of incubation period and first week of acute illness.	None	Polio shots (usually begun as part of 4-in-1 shots in infancy). Oral polio vaccine. Postpone nose-throat surgery in epidemics. Avoid unnecessary travel or visits during epidemics.
Isolation. Complete bed rest. Close medical supervision.	Isolate until recovered.	None	None
Isolation. Keep warm. Sterilize personal articles.	Isolate suspects and cases until no scabs.	Revaccinate. Observe for 3 weeks.	Vaccination in infancy. Periodic revaccination.
Isolation. Small, frequent meals. Disinfect freshly soiled articles and discharges from nose and throat.	Isolate (not necessarily indoors) for 4 weeks from onset or 3 weeks from whooping stage.	If not immunized, quarantine for 14 days after indoor exposure.	Shots (usually begun as part of 4-in-1 shots in infancy). Early immunization important.

UNTIL HELP ARRIVES

While you are awaiting specific instructions, here are some general suggestions:

- Keep an apron, gown, or smock hanging inside the sickroom door to wear whenever you attend the patient.
- When care is completed, collect waste material in paper bags, gather up soiled linen and dishes, and place all this material outside the door on newspapers.
- As you empty water and wastes, grasp doorknob, faucet handles, and the like with torn pieces of newspaper, kept just outside the sickroom door for that purpose. Burn this paper, along with paper bags. Wash the patient's linen and dishes separately from the family's washing.
- When you are finished with these chores, scrub your hands with soap and hot water. Remove apron and hang it back in the sickroom, wrong side out, in such a way that you can put it on again without touching the right side.

The table accompanying this article provides information about nine of the more common childhood communicable diseases. The listing is alphabetical, with medical terms in parentheses. Incubation period means the length of time between exposure to a disease and the appearance of the first signs or symptoms—the time usually required by the germs, once they are in the body of a susceptible person, to grow and reproduce themselves in sufficient quantity to cause illness.

"Common symptoms" are the symptoms usually present—signs that will alert parents to the need for expert medical advice. Only a doctor can make a diagnosis and prescribe treatment.

Isolation is recommended for each disease. This precaution points up that people, not things, are responsible for the spread of communicable diseases. It is usually the saliva that carries infection. One well-known exception to this observation is malaria, which is spread by mosquitoes.

With two possible exceptions, prevention by immunization is the best cure. The two exceptions are German measles for girls and mumps for boys. Both these diseases are likely to be less serious and have fewer aftereffects if they occur before adolescence. Medical science may soon perfect a German measles vaccine. MARIE A. HINRICHS

See also GAMMA GLOBULIN; FAMILY HEALTH RECORD; IMMUNIZATION; NURSE; SICK CHILD

COMMUNICATION *See* CRYING; TALKING

COMMUNITY RESOURCES

Community resources available to you and to your child depend a great deal on where you live. A large city usually has many specialized services. A smaller community may have only the schools, a few professional persons, and the county department of health and welfare. Services have been extended through traveling clinics and by branch offices of urban agencies.

Schools. Your public school is the basic community resource for children over 6. Special help, particularly with problems that interfere with learning, is given by the classroom teacher or by other personnel—the psychologist, counselor, speech therapist, nurse, or school social worker (sometimes called the visiting teacher). The school social worker is most likely to be concerned with problems that involve both the family and the school. Some larger school systems have a psychiatric consultant. Schools are an excellent source of referral to agencies offering specialized services.

Professional persons. Your physician, lawyer, and clergyman are among those who not only provide counsel themselves but who also may have knowledge of other community resources.

Health and welfare departments. Functions of local, county, or regional health and welfare services differ from state to state. These organizations provide information and direct services as authorized by law. The public health nurse is helpful to families because she is responsible for community health education and consultation on maternal and child health. While welfare departments were initially established to provide financial assistance and to place children in foster care and adoption, many now offer preventive casework for children living in their own homes.

Day care centers. Centers under private or public sponsorship provide child care at a reasonable cost for mothers who need to work. The demand for day care far exceeds the supply.

Child guidance and mental health clinics. Child guidance clinics deal with emotional and behavior problems. If both children and adults are served, the term "mental health clinic" often is used. Some parents mistakenly feel that such clinics are only for the mentally ill. Clinics provide individual diagnosis and are able to be most effective in the early stages of a difficulty when improvement can result from short-term treatment. Such resources seek to forestall the development of serious emotional disturbances and to prevent delinquent behavior. Fees for these services are based on the family's income.

Mental health associations. Most mental health associations are engaged in education rather than direct treatment. They distribute books and pamphlets, sponsor workshops and study courses, and show films. They stimulate the development of clinics and hospitals for the mentally ill and the mentally retarded.

Family service agencies. Marriage and family counseling are a major concern for private family agencies. They strengthen family life through consideration of emotional problems and of such needs as budgeting and vocational planning. Skilled caseworkers help people individually. More recently they have been seeing entire families for group counseling. Families are served by many other social agencies, including those specializing in child placement, vocational rehabilitation, leisure-time activities, legal aid, child protection, and infant health and welfare. Agencies are usually affiliated with a welfare council or council of social agencies providing general information to citizens and referring them to appropriate resources.

National voluntary health agencies. Associations devoted to the study and treatment of specific diseases and conditions have local chapters that provide information and certain direct services. Among others are organizations for the blind, the deaf, and the crippled as well as for those afflicted with brain damage, cystic fibrosis, epilepsy, heart disease, mental retardation, muscular dystrophy, tuberculosis, and poliomyelitis.

Parents' associations. The National Congress of Parents and Teachers has a broad interest in education and operates the largest parent education program of any voluntary agency. The formation of parents' groups has also been important in the development of services for handicapped children and the implementation of legislation on their behalf. Parents often learn helpful techniques of child care from group members and also gain reassurance from sharing their experiences. Groups of parents of gifted children are among the newer organizations now being established.

Cooperative planning. Since specialized staffs are limited and the cost of providing services is high, smaller communities find it advantageous to work together to develop regional units to secure the specialized services they require. In some cases the county provides the best unit. In others, larger areas are needed. Service available within 50 miles—about an hour's drive—represents the ideal for every family.

Adequate community resources for children and their parents must include direct services to provide many kinds of special help, easily accessible sources of information to offer the knowledge to prevent problems, and group activities that will help develop both competence and confidence. A self-study of community organizations is often the first step in determining the gaps that need to be filled. CHRISTINE BRIELAND

See also AGENCIES AND ORGANIZATIONS; CLINICS; NURSE

COMPETITION

Every moment of the waking day, someone is urging a child on to do something as well as or better than another child. Competition is one of the most frequently used incentives to better behavior and greater achievement in homes, in schools, in camps—wherever adults have the management of children. Yet there is probably no child-handling device that has greater possibilities for inflicting damage than the urging of children to indulge in unhealthy competition with each other.

Consider for a moment the meaning of competition. In the strictest sense, competition means striving for a position or a prize, usually in accordance with fixed rules. But carried to an extreme, competition means measuring oneself constantly against the achievements of others and seeing each comer as a potential rival. Can a life ruled by the spirit of that kind of competition be sound and healthy? Yet when we urge competitiveness on a child, we may set him on the path toward just such a life.

One often hears that children must be taught to compete because they live in a competitive society. What is basically wrong with such a statement?

First, children don't have to be taught to compete. Many children compete quite spontaneously within a family setting either for approval or simply for attention. They compete with brothers or sisters or even a parent. If they are successful in their competition with the family, they are very likely to continue such behavior in school and on the playground.

Secondly, the statement's implication that a competitive attitude is the best motivation for success is not necessarily true. When a person sets out primarily to do better than others, he always risks failure. The threat of failure induces anxiety, and anxiety keeps a person from doing his best. Free of anxiety, an individual can put all his effort and ability into the task at hand.

Finally, such a statement indicates that there is too much emphasis on the "competitive society," emphasis that may cause us to overlook the amount of cooperative activity needed to keep society going. Indeed, in our close-bound system, children motivated by competitiveness are not likely to do so well in the long run as those able workers who are moved by a spirit of cooperation.

Situations in which awards are offered are by nature competitive. Only one or a few can win. But to succeed, a child doesn't have to regard others as rivals. He can enter such situations simply determined to do his best, to compete within the rules according to the strict definition of competition, all without concern for doing better than someone else. If his best is not good enough to bring the desired award, it is healthier for him to plan how to gain it in another way than to feel defeated and envious.

Two attitudes toward competition are unhealthy: to fear it and to overemphasize it. A child's fear of competition is usually based on feelings of unworthiness because his parents criticize him or seem to prefer another child. Parents who are never satisfied with their own child, who constantly hold another up as a shining example, are likely to induce a sense of hopelessness which can lead a child to avoid competition. Similarly, the experience of having always been bested in competition, which sometimes happens to a younger child in a family, is likely to cause him to turn away from competition.

Here are some signs of an unhealthy spirit of competition: (1) when a child cannot cooperate with others without being the "boss"; (2) when every kind of situation is entered competitively, whether that spirit is appropriate or not; (3) when winning over others leads to gloating and boasting; (4) when losing leads to vindictiveness and claims of having been "cheated"; (5) when only the fact of winning is important to a child. These unhealthy attitudes may develop when love, attention, and respect are not freely given in the home but have to be fought for constantly. The child who is at least sometimes successful may become a compulsive competitor—a pathetic figure who can never have friends but only rivals, and who can never rest because the threat of defeat is always with him. RUTH E. HARTLEY

See also APPROVAL; ATHLETICS; JEALOUSY AND RIVALRY; SPORTSMANSHIP

COMPETITIVE SPORTS *See* ATHLETICS

COMPLEMENTARY FEEDING

A complementary feeding is formula offered to a baby either in addition to, or in place of, a single breast feeding.

There may be times when the breast milk supply does not satisfy the breast-fed baby. If this happens during the first two or three weeks while the breast milk supply is still being established, it is wise to be cautious about using too many complementary feedings, for the best stimulus to breast milk increase is nursing. Satisfying the baby too often with formula during this period may actually reduce his mother's milk supply. Since the baby who is greatly unsatisfied with the amount of breast milk available may make his mother more tired and anxious, an occasional bottle would be wise in order to give the mother some rest. Sometimes a bottle of sweetened water will suffice, but during especially hungry or fussy periods formula may be required.

The need for complementary feedings may also arise when a breast-feeding mother has to be separated from her baby for one or more feedings. Such separation is not wise during the first month but, once the breast feeding is well established, an occasional substitute bottle causes no difficulty. Some mothers even go to work part time during the second or third month and find that they are able to nurse their babies satisfactorily with the addition of one bottle feeding a day. Before resorting to complementary feedings for any reason, it is well to consult the baby's doctor.

Complementary feedings are made up just like regular formula and must be sterilized in the same way. Every mother who nurses should have equipment and some bottles on hand and should know how to make a formula when necessary. If complementary feedings are rarely needed, one convenient way to be prepared for them is to make up one or two extra bottles of water whenever sterile water bottles are prepared. Then a small can of evaporated milk can be newly opened and a single bottle of formula made up without further sterilizing. Unless the doctor has suggested something different, proportions could be: water, 4 ounces; evaporated milk, 2½ ounces; sugar or corn sirup, ½ tablespoon. But if complementary feedings are used fairly often, it is probably best to make up the smaller amounts of regular formula. RUTH S. KEMPE

See also BOTTLE FEEDING; FORMULA MAKING

COMPULSIONS *See* ANXIETY; RITUALS

CONCEPTION *See* REPRODUCTION

CONCUSSION *See* HEAD INJURY

CONFERENCE *See* TEACHER CONFERENCE

CONFIDENCES

"Promise you won't tell, Mommie, promise." When a youngster says that to you earnestly, with serious trust in his eyes, you know you're not supposed to tell anyone. And you don't mean to, either. "Of course, I won't, dear," you promise lightly.

But if you're a person who talks too much, as most of us do, and who has lots of things on her mind, then you may forget and spill a confidence to a group of adults sometime, especially if the story seems good for a laugh.

You may not even realize you have betrayed a confidence until your child comes in a few days later with an accusing look.

"Bill's mother told him what I told you the other night about Nancy. You promised you wouldn't tell anyone."

Crestfallen you may be, and you apologize up and down, but the damage has been done. You have betrayed a child's confidence, and that's serious.

There are times when a child doesn't ask you to promise not to tell, and you're not sure whether what he told you was a real confidence. If there's the slightest doubt in your mind, don't repeat it. Even trivial things that seem humorous to grownups may embarrass a child and make him feel uncomfortable. Adolescents are especially sensitive. It is then that parents must watch their step.

Should you share a confidence with your husband? That depends on how carefully he will guard the information. Often in telling him, the confidence part is lost sight of. Then when you scold him for repeating the story to others, he may answer truthfully, "I didn't know it was a secret."

These confidences a child trusts adults with, though they may appear unimportant bits of information, are in reality one of the vital bonds that hold a child to us and make him feel that we care. MAY R. SHERWIN

See also INDEPENDENCE; PRIVACY

CONFLICT *See* INDEPENDENCE; QUARRELING

CONFORMITY *See* SOCIAL PRESSURES

CONJUNCTIVITIS

Conjunctivitis is an inflammation of the membrane covering the front part of the eye and the lining of the eyelid, caused either by a bacterial or a viral infection or by chemical irritants, such as smoke or soap.

Your suspicion may be aroused when your child complains of "something in my eye." This feeling is often a first symptom, followed by discharge or swelling accompanied by itching, burning, and discomfort from light. Symptoms, usually more intense in the evening after the eyes have been used, will vary with the amount of inflammation. In the morning, a child's eyelids frequently will be glued together from the discharge that has dried during the night.

If the inflammation does not clear in a very short time, your doctor should be consulted, for he knows how to diagnose and treat this disorder. Usually, conjunctivitis is not contagious, but if this particular case is, your doctor will give you necessary instructions to keep it from spreading to other members of the family. ROY O. SCHOLZ

See also ALLERGY; EYE HEALTH; VIRUS

CONSCIENCE *See* GUILT FEELINGS; IMAGINARY COMPANION; MORAL AND SPIRITUAL DEVELOPMENT; RITUALS; SELF-CONCEPT; TATTLING

CONSISTENCY *See* DISCIPLINE; PERMISSIVENESS; PROMISES; RULES AND REGULATIONS

CONSTIPATION

Mothers of young babies often worry unnecessarily about constipation, thinking it has something to do with the frequency of bowel movements. Also, they and others are overconcerned about "regularity" and have a tendency to blame many different physical troubles on constipation. Constipation means that the stools are small, hard, and dry, and that they are difficult for the child to expel. Babies, like adults, vary a great deal in the frequency of their bowel movements. While most small babies have one to three movements a day, some have four or five regularly every day, and an occasional breast-fed baby has one movement every two or three days. What is important, then, is that the baby seems comfortable and well and that the stools are soft and easy to expel.

Most babies will have an occasional mild episode of constipation for a day or so, with some discomfort. Usually, no special treatment is necessary for this condition except to offer the baby an extra amount of water.

If your baby is chronically constipated, it is always best to regulate his diet. Extra water is the first step. If the baby is entirely formula fed, the substitution of one tablespoon of dark corn sirup for one of the tablespoons of regular sugar in the formula may help. Do not increase the total amount of sugar given.

If your baby is breast fed, the doctor may feel that some supplementary food in his diet is needed. Cereal, if it is the only solid food, may be mildly constipating. If the baby is taking several solids, giving him more fruit (except for banana) is usually sufficient. Occasionally, one-half ounce of prune juice mixed with an ounce of sterile water can be given. *Never give your baby laxatives, suppositories, or enemas without consulting your doctor.*

Quite frequently, older children will have mild chronic constipation. Occasionally, this condition represents some resistance to toilet training, but most often it starts with the development phase around the age of 2 when the child is learning to exercise his own will and to say "no." He even says "no" to his own body needs and ignores them while he continues to play rather stubbornly. It is important never to make a battle out of this kind of constipation, because a child who feels he must defend his right to exercise his own control can become very stubborn indeed at this period. Fixing everyone's attention on his bowel habits as a battleground may help to set up a lifelong pattern of resistance expressed in body habits. Your child should have a balanced diet, active exercise, and a good fluid intake. A regular time for a bowel movement, such as the period after a meal, may help, but only if this time is calm and not rushed or filled with tension-producing activity and excitement. RUTH S. KEMPE

See also ENEMA; LAXATIVES; SUPPOSITORIES; TOILET TRAINING; WATER FOR BABY

CONTAGIOUS DISEASES *See* COMMON COMMUNICABLE DISEASES

CONTRARINESS

All parents look forward eagerly to signs of growth in their children; the first time a baby rolls over by himself, his proud mother is likely to call her husband at work to announce this exciting event. The first step, the first word, the first signs that one's brilliant progeny recognizes different members of the family—all these are cause for pride and joy. But, when another sign of growth appears—that first loud and clear, "No!"—parents are likely to be somewhat less enthusiastic. Somewhere around the age of two, the honeymoon between parent and child seems to end abruptly; Junior has discovered his own power; he suddenly stumbles on that magic word that can make him master of all he surveys.

How this early period of contrariness is handled can assume considerable importance. If parents become alarmed and feel the need to assert their authority "before things really get out of hand," they may be setting up a struggle for power, which is really not necessary or helpful. If parents can genuinely enjoy that first exultant "No!" as a healthy sign of growth and independence, they will recognize that the time has come for encouraging some initiative and freedom of choice. Contrariness in the young child has a tendency to increase if the reins are held too tight. Some opportunity for independent expression, such as selecting which overalls to wear to the playground or choosing between two kinds of cereal, make children feel that the parent is responsive to their growth, and they have less need to fight on really important issues where parents must remain firm.

Contrariness can increase from too much freedom as well as too little. Choices and opportunities that are too difficult and for which a child is really unprepared may confuse and upset him. It is very hard to find that fine line of distinction between too much and too little freedom, but the line can be found by watching a child to see what he is ready for, what he can begin to make decisions about, and where he still needs parental controls.

As children grow older, this kind of adaptation to their increasing experience, judgment, and maturity is continually needed. Some rebelliousness, some contrariness, has to be, but when this behavior is frequent enough to cause almost continual friction, parents should ask themselves whether or not they are encouraging their child to use his increasing powers to gain mastery over himself and his environment—the parents' goal as much as it is the child's.

Much contrariness can be handled with humor and a light touch. Rather than setting up enemy camps, some compromises, some bargains, some new avenues for self-expression can be offered. Sometimes contrariness occurs when a child is tired. Fatigue often can be avoided; when it can't be, the issue at hand may be postponed until the child is in a more refreshed and reasonable state of mind.

Contrariness can also be eased by experiences away from home, either in a nursery school or a play group, or in visits to other children or grandparents. Such experiences bring into the child's life the more neutral and less emotionally charged authority of other adults and give him a sense of independence, of having a life of his own.

Where there is a will, there will inevitably be a "nay!" Parents save much eventual trouble when they recognize that will is a sign of individuality, of a growing ability to make judgments, an indication that a child is moving toward responsible maturity. EDA J. LE SHAN

See also INDEPENDENCE; OBEDIENCE; STUBBORNNESS

CONVALESCENT CHILD

One of the best ways to take care of your convalescent child is to take care of yourself. "Who *me?*" you ask incredulously. Yes, you. Get as much rest as you can, take a walk when you can, eat regular meals, and don't be afraid to ask other members of the family to help you when *they* can. In this way, you will be happier and more relaxed when you are with your child, and he will be happier and more relaxed, too. And a child at ease, with an optimistic outlook, will get well faster. Your child and you will also benefit if you deliberately avoid useless rushing, if you cut down on housework, keep the family meals simple, and limit the number of visitors. Older brothers and sisters may enjoy their special responsibilities after their school day is done; the invalid may enjoy their company, too, just as he may enjoy changing to the company of his other parent or someone like a grandmother or an aunt.

If the patient's bed can be placed where you can easily see him or easily hear him, and where he can see and hear what others in the house are doing, he again will be more relaxed, this time because he does not feel exiled or isolated. To make him feel part of both indoor and outdoor life, place his bed near a window, avoiding drafts, of course. A bird feeder outside his window gives him something specific and lively to watch; so does a goldfish bowl near his bed. A growing plant or a sprouting seed will provide a reason to look forward to tomorrow.

Routine is an ally to both parent and child. Make the routine as much as possible like the one the child has when he is well, considering always his convalescent restrictions. If he has watched certain TV programs when well, and if there is no eye problem or inaccessibility to the set, let him see the same programs. If he has had stories at bedtime, bacon on Sundays, and orange juice after naps, the treats can be given at their usual times. Don't try new foods unless the doctor has prescribed them and don't try, at this time, to get the child to break a habit you have previously ignored. The more your child can feel that life is as it was before, the less apt he is to sink into the withdrawal of illness or to begin to think of himself as a person entitled to privileges because he has been sick. He will follow his schedule more willingly if he has some voice in setting it up. If he is able to read or tell time, he will probably enjoy a chart indicating when medicine is to be given, when rest period occurs, when visitors can be expected; he may even like to be the one who reminds you what comes next on his schedule.

Entertainment is an important part of the convalescent's recovery program. This does not mean that he needs a three-ring circus, nor that an adult must be constantly entertaining him. It does mean that he needs playthings that will keep him quiet, content, and occupied. Just as when he is well, the sick child should have only a few playthings at a time and should be allowed a change before he gets truly bored. He should have games and toys and books and crafts suited to his age level and abilities, so that he is neither frustrated by their difficulty nor made indifferent by their simplicity. If he is bedridden, he should have some favorites within easy reach or, if room-bound, be able to search out for himself a change in occupation. He will also need suggestions on what to read, look at, do, and make.

New toys are not necessary. If he already has blunt scissors, crayons, paper, water colors or finger paints; if he already has clay to model or beads to string; if you have old magazines and catalogues for cutting out or used gift wrappings and greeting cards with which he can make cards of his own, or cardboard and paper to use for scrapbooks, he will be able to play for hours. Sometimes he will like it if you make the basic materials for him: paste from flour and water or modeling dough (which you can color with a little food coloring if you want) from the old recipe of four parts flour and four parts salt to one part water. He may like, too, to get on with a collection he has already started, sorting specimen stones into boxes or mounting his coins or stamps. And he will probably enjoy arranging snapshots for you or tidying your thread box.

New toys can, however, be made part of the day's entertainment. Space your surprises and do not give many at one time. A new

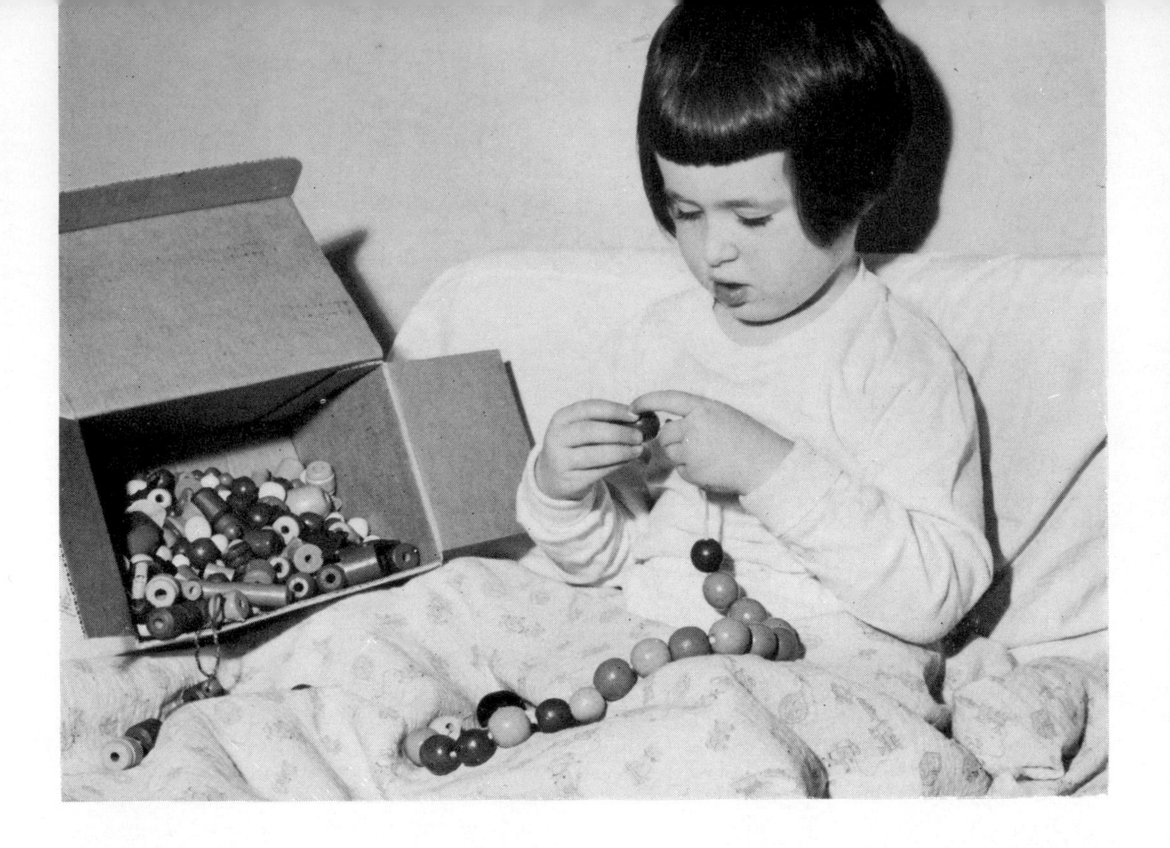

record with either music or storytelling may hold his attention for quite awhile; so may miniature cars or planes, or models of either, which he can build.

If your child goes to school, he will not want to fall behind in his schoolwork. Ask his teacher for work he can do at home, and set aside certain periods of the day when he is to study and you can be available for advice. Perhaps your school even has a home teacher system and will want to send a teacher to your house. Perhaps there is supplementary reading to be done and you can get the books from his school library.

A long convalescence can be tedious and unproductive for all concerned. But it can also, if managed with thought, be a time when a child profitably pursues old interests and happily takes up new ones.

You will find some excellent suggestions for your convalescent child's amusement and learning in Volume 9, *Make and Do,* pages 295–314.

See also HOME AND HOSPITAL INSTRUCTION; NURSE

CONVULSIONS

To parents and teachers, few signs of illness in children are more distressing than convulsions. The child may lose consciousness, his eyes roll, his muscles jerk or twitch, his teeth clench. Sometimes he urinates or his bowels move. Convulsions are a symptom, not a disease, and their causes are many and varied.

Perhaps the most common cause in infants and young children is high fever—brought on by upper respiratory infection, whooping cough, pneumonia, or scarlet fever. Convulsions may also occur in connection with such diseases as those causing unusually low blood sugar or unusually low levels of calcium in the blood. In diseases like tetanus (lockjaw) or infections of the brain, convulsions are often frequent and severe. Convulsions may also develop after birth injuries or after brain injuries resulting from accidents. Epilepsy, too, is a possibility, in which case the term "seizures" is used rather than convulsions.

Since high fever brings on convulsions in some children, it is sensible to keep and use a good thermometer so that you can call a doctor when the reading approaches 104° F. He will give you directions for further treatment. If you are unable to reach the doctor immediately, keep the child resting quietly in bed, with adequate but not excessive cover.

Whatever the cause of convulsions and however great your concern, try to remain calm and reassuring when you are in the child's presence. JULIUS B. RICHMOND

See also COMMON COMMUNICABLE DISEASES; EPILEPSY; TETANUS

COOPERATION *See* CHORES; HELPFULNESS

COORDINATION *See* GROWTH

COPYING *See* ART EXPERIENCES; CREATING; IMITATION

COSMETICS

When your little girl begs to use your perfumes or lipstick, she is obeying a typically feminine instinct. Until she is about 11 years old, she will probably not be interested in cosmetics except when she plays grownup or has a part in a school play. But when she is between 11 and 12, she very likely will tease to wear lipstick on special social occasions. Groups of mothers getting together can often agree that the use of lipstick should be postponed. Your child will not mind doing without it if her friends have to do without lipstick, too. By the time she is 13, she will run into rather well-established customs on the use of lipstick and she will probably follow the crowd, wearing lipstick for parties or even for everyday, as others in her school do.

Your daughter probably wants beauty advice from you whether she asks for it or not. Your stress on clean, well-brushed, gleaming hair and on a clean, flawless skin can give her a feminine aim and lessen some of her imitative desire to cover up natural beauty.

Little girls cherish such beauty aids as bubble bath, bath oil and powder, colorless nail polish, and a light cologne. Most mothers agree that the use of these cosmetics tends to encourage cleanliness and neatness. In fact, a pretty manicure kit has been known to discourage little girls from biting their nails. Mild shampoos that do not sting the eyes can be an incentive toward keeping hair shining clean.

Boys, of course, scoff at cosmetics, but many a small lad has enjoyed "shaving" with his father's shaving lather and dabbing on cologne when he's finished. Boys say they do not like bubble baths, but secretly they think they're kind of fun. A detergent now made for children will bubble delightfully in the bathtub and clean a small boy thoroughly at the same time.

If your teen-ager has a pimple at a time when appearance is especially important, a dab of one of the mild, medicated cover-up creams on the blemish will be a boon.

COUGH

The important thing to remember about a cough is that it is a symptom and not a disease. A cough means that something is irritating the respiratory passages, something the body would like to get rid of.

The causes of cough are many and varied. In young children, foreign bodies such as small coins, whistles, or tiny toys may occasionally be inhaled, or breathed, into the air passages and produce a cough. Food materials may also inadvertently be inhaled—vegetable particles are particularly irritating. Chemical substances, such as oils occasionally used in nose drops, may get into the air passages and cause severe cough. But by far the most common sources of coughs are infections of the respiratory tract—from mild infections like the common cold to pneumonia caused by various viruses or bacteria.

A doctor should be consulted to determine the cause of a cough. He may suggest tests and possibly X-ray examination of the chest.

The treatment of a cough depends largely on the cause. Foreign substances in the air passages should, of course, be removed. If infection is present, the doctor may prescribe antibiotics. A child confined to bed may be helped to cough up infectious materials if his position is frequently changed and the humidity of his room is increased. A baby does not have a forceful cough and therefore occasionally needs to have secretions removed by a doctor using an instrument for that purpose. Drugs to liquefy coughs are of questionable value and should be used only if a physician prescribes them for a special reason. The same is true of drugs to suppress a cough.

Occasionally, a child may cough repeatedly just to gain attention. His parents need to try to learn the basis for his emotional difficulty and to supply the attention or signs of affection he needs. JULIUS B. RICHMOND

See also COLDS; COMMON COMMUNICABLE DISEASES; CROUP; SORE THROAT; TUBERCULOSIS; VIRUS

COUNTING

Young children recognize and accept counting as part of their cultural heritage long before they are actually able to count accurately. To chant "1–2–6–7–10" is a perfectly acceptable first step for a young preschooler who is just beginning to discover counting in his world. And in today's world, when staggering numbers relating to current events fill living rooms via television, he is just as likely to say, "1–2–6–7–a million."

It is easy to tell when a young child makes accurate association between a spoken number and the actual number represented. "I am 4 years old," he will say, touching each of four fingers.

This touching of objects in relation to learning to count is very important. Early man actually dropped one pebble or something similar to represent each of the fish or other objects he was talking about. This was his way for counting before we had a number system. And this is what a child is doing when he touches each of four fingers to show the number 4. For this reason it is important not to try to talk a child out of using his fingers for counting and figuring. He will drop the habit when he no longer needs to touch concrete objects for accuracy. And until he shows that he no longer has this need, it only confuses him to have someone disparage his system of finger counting. You can find counting rhymes in Volume 1, *Poems and Rhymes*, pages 16–17.

While whole systems of arithmetic can be based on counting, it is important to know that some children never count by one's in their figuring. They immediately see and understand the group involved in a number like 3. For these children it is important not to require them to count by one's, for to do so will slow them down in later computations. PEGGY BROGAN

Related article in WORLD BOOK: "Arithmetic"

COURAGE

Courage has been praised through the ages. The Roman word for man, *vir*, is at the root of our word "virtue." So parents want their children to be courageous, not to be overcome with fear in danger and calamity.

The adult view of courage, however, is far from the child's. He is not born brave. Courage has to be learned as any other virtue. The teaching of courage demands a most realistic attitude on the parents' part. They cannot expect great courage in a small child too weak to defend himself. When he is older, parents can help their child measure his strength against odds. The young child who is really afraid often boasts of his bravery and strength. He thus denies his weakness even to himself. This boasting is not deceitfulness; it is a way of quieting his fears. Parents have to help their child be realistic about danger.

Physical courage is easier to explain to children than moral courage, which comes only with the growth of a sense of right and wrong. To own up to an error or a misdeed requires courage at any age, and in this the small child needs the example and strength of his parents. Moral standards are learned from parents, not so much by teaching as by example. A child's first models of behavior are his parents; later on, teachers become models, too.

As a child grows older, his moral strength increases, and soon he is able to make his own decisions about right and wrong. HELEN ROSS

See also READINESS; SHYNESS AND TIMIDITY

COURTESY *See* MANNERS

CRADLE CAP

Cradle cap develops on a baby's scalp occasionally if precautions are not taken to prevent it. Whitish scales on the scalp which flake off are the first signs. If allowed to continue, the scales become a heavier crust, yellowish and greasy. When the condition has progressed to this stage, the scalp may look a little red and irritated and a rash may also develop on the baby's face and chest.

The best way to prevent cradle cap is to shampoo the baby's scalp (including the soft spots) thoroughly every day at the beginning of his bath, using soap and water and a washcloth. No ointments are advisable. If a crust has already developed, mineral oil can be rubbed into the scalp in the evening. In the morning the oil should be thoroughly washed out in a vigorous shampoo. If this does not bring improvement in a few days, consult the baby's doctor about further treatment.

Although it may sometimes be hard to distinguish from early eczema, cradle cap is not a true allergy. RUTH S. KEMPE

CRAMPS *See* MENSTRUATION

CRANKINESS

Some babies and young children seem awfully hard to please. Often a mother gets the feeling that nothing she does is right. Her baby continues to be cranky and irritable all the time. Ways of showing irritability will vary with a child's age, but the most common signs of irritability are frequent crying, difficulty in falling asleep, frequent waking, an unwillingness to smile, frantic thrashing movements of arms and legs, or unusual body stiffness.

A mother's first reaction to such behavior from her baby is usually the fear that he is sick. This is a wise reaction because the early stages of many childhood illnesses are marked by increased irritability. If, however, a careful medical check shows no physical reasons for the baby to be irritable, his mother is likely to wonder if she herself is in some way inadequate, if she is doing everything wrong. The chances are that she is not, but a healthy self-appraisal of her mothering might give her some clues. The easiest way to make the appraisal is to try to discover in what type of situation cranky behavior occurs most often.

Is there a rhythm to the child's crankiness? Babies seem more likely to be irritable during certain times of the day—the afternoon or early evening hours are favored. Fatigue, then, may be one reason for irritability.

Is fussiness in any way associated with feeding? Many mothers, when a baby is fussy, are quick to change the infant's formula, making the change perhaps without medical consultation and paying little attention to the baby's growth rate and weight gain. Yet a change in feeding, made without any solid reason, may only increase irritability, introducing something new to which an already troubled baby must adjust.

What is taking place in the home at the time the baby starts acting fussy? Are there several persons and a fair amount of noise in the room? Or, conversely, is everything unusually quiet? Babies, like adults, react to changes in what is going on around them, and a baby accustomed to a fairly high noise level may object to extreme quiet. Some fussy babies seem to respond very well to a little extra warmth and to moderate restriction of arms and legs. The ancient custom of swaddling is therefore used effectively sometimes in a revised form: A receiving blanket folded diagonally is wrapped securely around the baby from the shoulders down.

Occasionally, a mother and her baby have drastically different temperaments or activity patterns. A mother who herself is active and moves vigorously may automatically assume that a fussy baby will like being rocked or bounced. Yet such behavior may simply increase the irritability of a baby whose contentment depends on quiet and the least possible outside stimulation. A bit of experimentation may show up his preferences.

A mother who "tries everything" to help eliminate crankiness in her baby may worry lest she spoil him. Maybe she should just close the door and let him cry? If the baby is very young, "spoiling" is not likely. His irritability is probably because of some difficulty in making the transition from living warm and secure within the mother's body to a strange new world. When this is the case, a mother may be able to do little more than make her baby as comfortable as possible. Normal growth processes usually help wipe out the problem by the time he is about 3 months old. If, however, this type of irritability continues, then other causes in the infant's physical or social situation are at work. Perhaps your doctor can help you search out these causes and find remedies to restore your baby's serenity. BETTYE M. CALDWELL

See also CRYING; REST

CRAWLING *See* CREEPING

CRAYONS *See* ART EXPERIENCES

CREATING

Human beings do not simply accept the world into which they are born. They are constantly at work—trying to create a better world than the one produced by preceding generations.

This creating begins early in the lives of children. The preschooler explores the kitchen pots and pans to see what they have to offer. He discovers they have sound—wonderful sound that changes the whole world in which he is living. Soon he is using this sound for his own purposes—creating patterns that, from his point of view, make the world a more significant place.

A pair of older children may put their special mark on the world by rearranging the living room chairs—this time creating a deep cave, another, a cove for crocodiles and other furious monsters.

A little girl may use clay to make a horse—not a clay copy of a horse someone else made previously but a truly creative expression of her own love for horses, her times of actually and imaginatively riding through time and space, and her hopes of someday owning a horse.

Many materials are now available to help you help your child create. Clay and claylike preparations, paint (tempera and finger paint) in convenient jars, blocks in imagination-inviting sizes and shapes, drums and other musical instruments may all be purchased at local toy, art, or music stores. And don't forget the ordinary household items that children readily put to their own creative purposes.

It will help everyone concerned if a special time and place are set aside for some types of creating. When a child is working with paint, clay, and other potentially messy substances, let him have his own small square of linoleum or oilcloth to put down on the floor while he is working. And let him wash it himself when he is through. An upside-down kitchen chair with a piece of cardboard against the four legs makes a pretty good easel. And after dinner, while mother and dad can enjoy their coffee and be the audience, the child can have a fine time and place for dancing out patterns for *The Sorcerer's Apprentice* or other favorite recordings.

Creating is a uniquely human way of thinking and doing. It is a way for a child to put his own mark on the world—actually a way to build and enhance the world he lives in. PEGGY BROGAN

See also ART EXPERIENCES; DRAMATICS; MUSIC; WRITING

CREEPING

There is a great deal of variation in the age at which babies begin to creep and also in the way they do it. A few babies crawl as early as 6 or 7 months. Others don't creep until they are about a year old. A few babies never crawl at all; they just stand up and walk. A heavy baby who is also of a placid disposition is apt to be more content to sit in the midst of his toys than the more active, curious kind of child.

Individual ways of creeping can be quite a lot of fun to watch. Some babies simply lie on their stomachs and wriggle and manage to get all around the room. Some just sit, but by pumping themselves with one leg to one side or the other they get where they want to go. The straightforward crawler gets up on his hands and knees and makes a beeline for his objective. Many a child creeps backward, and the "monkey walker" crawls on his hands and feet, with his knees straight and his bottom uppermost. The "crabwalk" takes the baby sideways, but he gets there just the same.

These are only some of the variations in creeping, but they all prove that baby is eager to get about, no matter how. He is perfectly willing to experiment until he finds the way to move that works best for him, regardless of how difficult or awkward it may look to adults. Often, he may rock back and forth on his hands and knees for a long time before he decides which way to move.

The creeper will do better if he is not hampered by awkward clothing. Sturdy overalls, which allow free movement and protect the knees, are fine for both boys and girls.

When a baby starts to creep, he gains access to many new places and things. Creeping, then, is the signal for giving thought to his safety as well as the safety of precious knicknacks. Open stairways, electrical outlets, sharp-pointed objects are examples of the hazards to be guarded against. Put away precious things and allow him complete freedom in safe rooms, such as his bedroom. The playpen will keep him safely confined when you can't watch him closely. RUTH S. KEMPE

See also ACCIDENT PREVENTION

CRETINISM *See* MENTAL DEFICIENCY

CRIB

Four questions should be uppermost in your mind when you shop for a crib: Is it sturdy? Is it safe? Is it comfortable? Is it convenient?

A well-built crib will serve three or four children in a family—and a cousin or two as well. Bars should be spaced so that there is not the slightest danger of a child's head becoming lodged between them. It is not enough that the finish be durable and washable; it should be guaranteed harmless by the manufacturer, for a baby considers the smooth top rail of his crib the finest kind of "teething ring."

Choose a crib that is large enough. Fresh from a fluffy bassinet or basket, a baby may look lost in his new crib, but before you know it he will be rolling about, pulling himself up, and crowing with delight as he learns to make the rounds. After all this exercise, it is pleasant to have plenty of room to fall flat on a fat tummy, arms and legs sprawled in all directions.

To ease the strain on adults who will care for the child, his crib should be equipped with sides that move up and down. When he's old enough to get in and out by himself, the sides can remain in the lowered position. The mattress base should be adjustable to several levels—highest for easy care of a very young baby, lower as the baby becomes more active.

Select a firm mattress for the crib—one that fits snugly so that baby hands, arms, and legs won't get caught between it and the crib. Foam rubber and hair mattresses are slightly more expensive than cotton felt. But they wear longer and retain their original firmness better, thus affecting favorably both your pocketbook and the child's comfort and posture.

Crib bumpers are advisable when the baby begins to move about. In fact, they may be used from the beginning to protect the baby from drafts.

See also JUNIOR BED; LAYETTE AND BABY EQUIPMENT

CRIB ROCKING *See* ROCKING SELF

CRIPPLED CHILD

Crippled children, like all other children, need to know they are loved and accepted. When we accept a child's handicap, we see him for what he has and not for what he lacks. The handicap may be due to a birth defect or to an injury, or it may be the result of accident or illness. Crippling may be so mild that it passes unnoticed, or so severe as to result in permanent and total helplessness. In between these two extremes are the moderate cases to which we devote most of our effort in care, treatment, and education.

Because children react emotionally in different ways to their crippling handicaps, an individual plan must be made for each child. The central figures in this plan, when the child lives at home, are his parents. It is through the affection and security given him by his parents that the crippled child will learn his most difficult but most important lesson—how to accept and live with his handicap.

Of the trained workers whose task it is to set up and carry out the plan of care, you can look first to your doctor. He will tell you what you need to know about your child's handicap, what you can expect in the way of progress and improvement, what you should do now, and what you can leave for the future. And, always, you need the doctor for regular checkups to keep you on the right path and to give you new goals as old ones are attained.

But the doctor does not work alone. He is a member of a team. Depending on a child's disability, he works with the nurse, the physical therapist, the occupational therapist, the speech specialist, the social worker, the teacher, the psychologist, and the parents. Each makes a special contribution.

There are many public and private agencies to which parents may look for assistance. In each state there is a state-wide crippled children's service to help those in need to secure diagnosis, hospitalization, and convalescent care as well as other services. The types of cases eligible for this help vary from one state to another.

Almost every state has made provisions for the crippled child who is ready for school. When he can attend regular classes and schools, he should do so. Some children need no extra attention. Others need an adjustment in their school tasks, a rest period, help in going up and down stairs, or they may require specialized equipment or transportation. When several children in a given area need extra help and attention, special schools may be set up, with buses to take the children to and from school. For those who cannot attend because they are confined to their homes, hospitals, or convalescent institutions, visiting teachers may be assigned. Other arrangements may be made also, such as the school-to-home or the school-to-hospital telephone that enables a child to share in classwork and recitations, even though confined to bed. Television stations in some communities also provide educational programs helpful to the child who cannot attend his regular classes.

For children whose disability is severe, who need intensive training, or who for a variety of reasons cannot be cared for at home, there are residential centers.

The remarkable advances made in research on crippling conditions is truly heartening. The advent of vaccine for poliomyelitis has brought giant strides in the control of residual crippling from this disease. Drugs now control other diseases that formerly caused years of hospitalization and often permanent crippling. Great strides have been made in fitting, and teaching the use of, artificial limbs. Experience has shown new ways of bracing, of bringing useless muscles back to work, and of teaching crippled children to walk, to use their hands, and to talk. New techniques in special education are opening a whole new world to these children.

One of the most important things parents can do for a handicapped child is to help him to help himself. Help him to realize that he is not alone in being handicapped, that there are other children and adults who are struggling with problems such as his. Help your crippled child to talk about his handicap but not to the point of capitalizing on it to gain concessions or as a means of seeking sympathy from family or outsiders. Let your child know that you expect him to maintain reasonable standards of behavior; do not let him "get away" with behavior you would not tolerate in a child who is not handicapped. Teach your child that you see him as a lovable person, a person with promise in certain areas, although limited in others. Give this child the best possible health care. Be sure that his diet is adequate, that he gets rest and relaxation, that he exercises to the limit of his capabilities, and that he has opportunities for contacts with friends and companions that bring the social life so important for development to maturity. JAYNE SHOVER

See also COMMUNITY RESOURCES; HANDICAPPED CHILD; HOME AND HOSPITAL INSTRUCTION

CROSS-EYE (STRABISMUS)

If the eyes of your newborn child are out of line for a few months, don't worry about it. If, however, by the time he is 6 months old his eyes are still not straight—if they turn in, float up or down, or swing out—he should be examined by an ophthalmologist (a medical eye doctor). If treatment for crossed eyes is started early, chances of correcting the disorder are excellent.

If crossed eyes are not corrected, the sight of the child may not develop as well as it could, or the crossing may become worse. Children with badly crossed eyes can be made very unhappy by the ridicule of their schoolmates. When you take your child to a medical eye doctor, the examination probably will be made with the aid of drops to insure an accurate diagnosis. Thus, the specialist is able, even in the case of an infant, to determine the kind and degree of the vision problem. He may recommend glasses or exercise or an eye patch. Should these measures fail to straighten the eyes, an operation may be needed. ROY O. SCHOLZ

See also EYE HEALTH; FARSIGHTEDNESS

CROSSING STREETS

Crossing streets safely is something a child begins to learn in babyhood. Unknown to you, he watches and unconsciously remembers your every move—for example, when you jaywalk or when you look both ways before you push his stroller across the street. Later, when he stands on his own two feet, he will follow your example—so be sure that example is a safe one.

For children of 5 and under, you should establish definite rules for crossing streets. Most important, the child must always ask your permission to cross and be strictly punished if he fails to do so. You must have absolute obedience on this point, for the danger of his running wildly into the street and being struck by an auto is too great.

Before stepping off the curb, always take the youngster's hand and hold it all the way across the street. Explain that you cross at corners only, never in the middle of the block, and always with the green light or walk sign. "Sound off" your every act as you go. Say, "We always stop at the corner. We look both ways. We go when the light flashes green. We watch for cars that may be turning the corner. Now it is safe to go." After several sessions, let your child tell *you* when it is safe to cross.

Then the day comes when he must go off on his own—a day of apprehension for any parent. But an average child of 6 or 7 years should be able to cross streets alone. Walking with him all the way to school every morning, for example, can embarrass an older child after a while.

During the first lone crossings, watch your child to be sure he does everything correctly. Insist that he never step off the curb until the light changes, that he look both ways, and that he cross quickly rather than dawdle in the center. Also, instruct him to obey police officers and patrol boys. Then relax. There's no need to worry about him if you have taught him well. WILLIAM G. JOHNSON

See also ACCIDENT PREVENTION

CROUP

Although croup is often thought of as a disease, it is actually a symptom of throat infection. Croup appears in the form of noisy breathing or a barking cough or both together, caused by swelling and irritation of the opening from the throat into the windpipe, or trachea, in an area called the larynx, or voice box.

Croup may be chronic and may start from birth if there is some abnormality in the formation of the larynx or its surrounding tissues. Sometimes the condition improves as the baby grows larger, but it may be necessary to increase the size of the airway in the larynx gradually by insertion of instruments.

Most cases of croup happen suddenly, usually because of some acute infection or irritation from a foreign substance. In some instances, a child has great difficulty in breathing—and may require the lifesaving measure of surgery to make an opening below the larynx into the windpipe. Because of this possibility, *croup should always be reported to the doctor immediately.* JULIUS B. RICHMOND

See also COUGH; DIPHTHERIA; LARYNGITIS; STEAMING

CRUELTY

A child's fear or anxiety shows itself in various ways, one of which may be cruelty—behavior that finds pleasure in causing pain. His victim may be a child smaller or younger than himself or an animal or an insect. The pain inflicted may be physical, as in kicking, hitting, or biting. Or it may be psychological, as in teasing, insulting, or withholding satisfaction. But the basic cause of cruel behavior lies in the child's emotional life. He feels insecure, worried, or afraid, and the more he has to prove that he is powerful, the greater will be his effort to show powerlessness in some other person or thing. The more "unpleasure" he can produce in another, the more pleasure he feels in himself.

Very young children may behave with seeming cruelty, but care should be taken to distinguish between actual cruelty and immature conscience. A 3- or 4-year-old has not had time to develop a clear sense of right and wrong, of good and bad. The mother of a 4-year-old daughter was horrified to find that the child had strung her kitten up in such a manner that the kitten was about to die. Actually, the little girl loved animals; she simply did not know about strangulation and death. In an older child, however, cruel behavior should not be ignored. Older children, especially boys around 9 or 10, sometimes feel that they have to prove their competence and power. They may have occasional temporary lapses into the desire to inflict pain as proof of superiority. At such times, it is necessary for parents to point out that cruelty comes from not being sure of oneself, and that the more an individual resorts to cruelty to prove his superiority, the more he shows that he is really unsure of himself or afraid.

The dismembering of animals or insects (pulling wings off flies, for example) can serve a child's need to prove his superiority, but this form of cruelty can also be misplaced curiosity about how things "work," especially about how his own body works.

It is usually not difficult to help normal children to establish friendly relationships with other children and kind and protective feelings toward animals and all helpless things. Example is the best teacher. A child must be shown how to be gentle, how to pick up or hold a small creature, how to assume responsibility for animals or insects in his care. It is never wise to meet, or to threaten to meet, cruelty with cruelty. "I'm going to show you how it feels to be bitten," serves no good purpose. Rather, it is far better to find out why a child resorts to cruel behavior. If the reason eludes his parents, they may want to seek the help of a child guidance clinic or a psychologist. Persistent cruelty is never as important as the meaning of such behavior in a child's personality. DAVID WINEMAN

See also AGGRESSIVENESS; DISCIPLINE; PETS

CRUSHES

During the period of preadolescence, boys and girls—but more often girls—develop strong attachments to other children of their own sex as well as to favorite adults. The attitude toward the best friend, whose status superficially may appear greater than that of the parent, provides the child with an opportunity for emancipation from parents.

Often these crushes are short-lived. Your child may develop many "best friends" over a relatively short period of time. Quarrels or separation by distance, for example, are among the factors that help break up these relationships.

Attachment to another child of the same sex is generally viewed as a normal developmental phase. It is another necessary way for the child to gain independence from his parents. There is some evidence that girls retain these crushes over a longer period than boys do. Usually, crushes on like-sex or older people shift to members of the opposite sex.

Parents may resent these intense situations, but it is important to realize that most often they are to be expected. In fact, too much attention and interference on your part may prevent the normal transition to usual boy-girl social contacts.

Thus, dependency on emotional satisfactions with members of one's own sex or older adults is a transitional phase to a more mature love relationship. IRVING E. SIGEL

See also FRIENDS; IMITATION

CRYING

With a cry a newborn baby makes his declaration of independence—proclaims that he has ended his physiologically dependent life. And with a cry he will continue to make many important announcements, for crying is the first vocal communication of which he is capable, a built-in response that will, all through his life, let others know what is going on inside him. Crying is the earliest expression of discomfort: Whenever hunger, stomachache, cold, or too much warmth reach a critical tension point, an infant will cry to announce his need. Unfortunately, it is difficult to know which need he is announcing.

Newborn babies show impressive individual differences in the amount of crying they do. But how much a baby cries during his first few weeks of life is not a measure of how much he will cry later on. Infants often have periods of extreme irritability up to about three months; then the amount of crying usually drops sharply.

A baby's reasons for crying change as he ages. The new infant cries because of painful sensations that accompany a physical need. Fairly soon, however, he also cries as though expecting something unpleasant to happen to him. For example, the sight of an unfamiliar person is not likely to make a 3-month-old infant cry. But an infant of 6 or 7 months, one who has learned to discriminate between his mother and everyone else, may wail without interruption at the sight of an unfamiliar face. Thus the cry lets parents know which objects and events their infant is afraid of or which ones make him feel that something unpleasant is about to happen.

There is a tendency to think of crying as "negative behavior," as something to be eliminated as completely as possible. Cutting down on crying is, of course, one of the social goals. On the other hand, crying is important in helping an infant get along in the world, for by means of his cry he develops a little control over what happens to him. That is, he cries, and (hopefully) somebody responds. Some parents worry that, in responding to a baby's cry, they will encourage undesirable behavior. Accordingly, they advocate picking up or changing or feeding the baby when he is not crying and ignoring him when he is. This procedure may be logical from an adult point of view, but it undoubtedly complicates an infant's early attempts to signal his feelings. Furthermore, if a baby is never fed and changed or in some way made more comfortable when he cries, it becomes more difficult for him to learn that what he *does* makes a difference in what *happens* to him.

Many months must pass before the emotional communication delivered via the baby's cry becomes very subtle. The frightened 2-year-old may muffle his sobs, but the message gets across. And the angry 4-year-old, under the press of social rules asserting that big children do not cry, may fight to hold back his tears. Thus new forms of communication appear and refine the message; but throughout life, crying serves the important function of transmitting information about an individual's emotional state. BETTYE M. CALDWELL

See also BABY; COLIC; COMFORTING; EMOTIONAL DEVELOPMENT; TEAR DUCTS

CUB SCOUTS *See* YOUTH ORGANIZATIONS

CUDDLING

A baby held close to his mother's body while being fed receives more than one type of gratification: His hunger contractions stop and he also gets a pleasurable sensation from the feel and warmth of her body.

Over the years, people have assumed that mother love develops largely because the mother is the person most likely to offer nourishment to the baby. But the by-products of the feeding situation—cuddling and close body contact—may be at least as important in the development of affection as the food she offers. Experiments have shown that baby monkeys "love" a substitute mother who provides warm body contact, regardless of whether the cuddly substitute gives any nourishment. Furthermore, if a noncuddly object provides milk, the baby monkeys will usually drink as quickly as possible and then hurry to their soft and cuddly mothers.

Human babies also like close physical contact with other human beings. Countless cartoons depict a baby being held and walked at 2:00 A.M., much to the discomfort of a tired father, while a bottle of milk sits rejected on a nearby table. Baby does not live by milk alone!

But the pleasurable sensations associated with cuddling are not limited to contact with other people: Cuddly animals, blankets, and towels seem to provide some of the same type of gratification. Often a child clings to a beloved blanket long after he gives up the bottle, the pacifier, or even the thumb.

It is important to recognize that most children like to cuddle as well as to be cuddled. A 4-year-old girl may carry her doll cradled snugly in her arms and cover the doll with its own blanket. Traditionally in our culture such cradling and cuddling are considered feminine activities. Young boys, therefore, may learn to resist receiving or offering a hug, yet these same boys may continue to need their stuffed toys or blankets at bedtime.

Children differ greatly in their need for the pleasures that physical contact brings. Enjoyment of some degree of close body contact with loved persons persists in one form or another throughout life. The baby who stops crying when he is snuggled into his mother's arms is not too different from the young adult who seeks to hold close and caress his or her loved one. BETTYE M. CALDWELL

CURIOSITY

The insatiable curiosity of a child can sometimes be terribly irritating to a parent or other adult who fails to see the end such curiosity serves. Child and adult go for a walk together. The child runs here and there to look at something or stops dead to pick up and examine something else. The adult has a destination in mind or an errand to do; he feels he is being held up by unnecessary and undesirable dawdling. He forgets that a young child's strong curiosity is the child's best means toward learning and mental growth. Or if he remembers, he feels that some more appropriate and convenient moment for learning could be found. He tries to hurry the child and provokes only resistance in the small human whose investigations are as important to him as the adult's interests are to the adult.

Questions can also irritate parents, particularly when a child is around the age of 4 or 5 and can ask as many as 300 a day. But not all questions are asked to gain information.

Some apparent curiosity may be shown just to make social contact with another child or adult or to hold attention.

Fortunately, just about the time parents feel that the questions are getting beyond them in both quantity and difficulty, the child goes to school. One of the many roles of the school is to satisfy curiosity and to stimulate more curiosity. A parent can learn a good deal about this dual art by watching how a good school performs. The teacher listens carefully and answers partially, then sends the questioner on to seek information for himself through additional reading, observation, or experimentation. The materials toward which the child is directed are on his intellectual level, complicated enough to preserve his interest, simple enough to encourage it. He is taken on trips to see those things he is curious about and those he will become curious about when he has visited them. He is encouraged to tell stories at school about outside experiences and to bring to school objects that have awakened or satisfied his curiosity.

The good school also knows—and here again the parent can find a lead to follow—that some curiosity can involve physical danger. The child is encouraged to try new activities, but his age and degree of reasonableness are taken into consideration and he is not left too much on his own.

Sexual curiosity, even in the very young, is now accepted by most parents as normal and to be expected. But so much emphasis has been placed on the answering of questions by adults that some parents are a bit disturbed when, after they have discussed the matter as best they can with a child, he still wants to discuss it with his friends. This wish of the child is also normal and to be expected. In resatisfying his curiosity through conversation with friends, he also satisfies himself that adults have been honest with him, that he is on a basis of equality with others his age, and that he is developing toward the kind of adulthood he should properly have.

Curiosity is an important aspect of learning. In general, any child handles the concrete aspects of his experience much better than he does the more remote, abstract, and ideational aspects. These abstractions will come in time. His early curiosity assures that he gains the materials with which to carry on mature thinking. The child who has learned that his parents will be considerate of and helpful to his curiosity has a good start toward intellectual development. DALE B. HARRIS

See also MENTAL DEVELOPMENT; SCIENCE

CURRICULUM

In return for supplying the local school system with good teachers and buildings and equipment, parents have a right to expect an educational program that will result in maximum development of their children. This educational program is called the curriculum.

With an understanding of children and of the local community and knowledge of the fundamentals of good citizenship, teachers, under the skillful leadership of the principal, proceed to construct a curriculum for the entire school. This curriculum is a carefully organized series of planned activities. It begins with the kindergarten or first grade and continues to the last grade in the school. These activities are centered around five fundamentals:

- Knowledge of things and people
- Ability to solve daily problems
- Development of the spark of creativeness
- Ability to get along with others
- Physical and emotional well-being

Each step in the curriculum is identified by a descriptive theme, or center of interest. Of course, the details of the curriculum vary from community to community and from school to school.

Home and family living is usually the first theme. At the earliest stage of a child's development, he is naturally concerned with experiences near home. These need to be enlarged and made more understandable to him. He studies his own home, the work of father and mother, the different kinds of homes in the community, and the activities that go on in a home.

The neighborhood is the second theme. Homes are enriched by many goods and services coming from the outside, such as milk, groceries, and mail. These are studied in order to gain an understanding of the interdependent nature of modern living. The home is still the center of interest, but attention is shifted to the surrounding activities that enrich it.

The community as a unit is the third theme. The child is encouraged to understand how people live together in groups beyond the family, and how different groups live together. If the community is small enough, it is studied as a whole; if large, communities within the city are first studied as examples of the whole.

As the scope of learning widens, the children are taken to the *extended community,* to learn of factors outside their local communities which influence their lives. The goods and services that flow in from outside are studied. A teacher may take her pupils to a local supermarket where they can examine merchandise on the shelves, identifying each item and finding out where it came from. Visits to neighboring manufacturing communities provide children with information about how and why things are made, and where they go upon completion.

The nation in the world is next, with emphasis on the fact that every nation depends upon its neighbor nations for many of its needs and some of its cherished customs.

The community of nations is the final theme. Older children are encouraged to understand the essential relationships among nations, with their diverse customs and their difficulties in learning to get along together.

Throughout each of these themes, the central concern is that the children understand the interdependence of man and the means of achieving harmony and cooperation. To assure understanding and to learn in practice how this understanding may be achieved, individual classrooms are often operated as laboratories of life, exemplifying what is being taught. Instead of merely handing out assignments and hearing lessons learned, the skillful teacher tries to involve the children in planning and carrying out the program.

Children participate in the curriculum as much as their maturity and abilities allow. The entire curriculum is built with the intention of creating in children an understanding and respect for their backgrounds and customs. Teachers respect their children's interests; at the same time, teachers recognize their responsibility for developing within children a keen desire to learn what the faculty has planned for them.

In individual classrooms, children often are given the opportunity to choose a phase of the particular center of interest being studied. When studying the community, one child may want to study government, another transportation. In Volume 15 of CHILDCRAFT some of the most frequently taught curriculum units are presented, along with reference to the places in CHILDCRAFT where the subject matter can be found. See the "School Study Guide" section and the portions of the general index printed in blue.

A curriculum is a carefully thought-out, patiently planned guide, by intellectually responsible people, whose aim and desire is to send children out into the world to take their rightful places as contributing members of society. WILBUR A. YAUCH

See also HOME-SCHOOL RELATIONS; LIBRARIES

CUTS AND SCRATCHES

Because most cuts and scratches will heal by themselves, parents tend to neglect them. But minor injuries may, on rare occasions, become serious. Every object inflicting an injury carries germs capable of infecting the human body; even a minor cut or any break in the skin may turn serious. The wise course, therefore, is not to neglect any cut or scratch that your child may have.

To lessen the chances of infection, wash your hands thoroughly before treating any wound. Discourage your child from placing his mouth over a cut or scratch. The mouth harbors germs that can infect a wound.

If the cut is not deep, there will be a little oozing of blood, which does no harm. Simply washing with soap and warm water and subsequent protection with a finger dressing or small gauze square is all that is necessary. Popular reliance on antiseptics is traditional, but, in general, antiseptics are not necessary and are best reserved for medical use. If in spite of this advice antiseptics are desired, the best ones are the new iodine preparations, which are relatively painless—2 per cent water solution of mercurochrome, 70 per cent alcohol (which stings), or one of the new antiseptic creams or spray disinfectants. Some of these contain mild pain relievers. The choice of these substances for your medicine cabinet should be discussed with your physician, and they should be provided in advance and replenished often enough to keep fresh whether or not they are used.

A deep cut or scratch may bleed somewhat profusely. Such bleeding is not too alarming; for a short time it is good because it helps to cleanse the cut. Unless very large vessels are involved, bleeding is usually easily controlled by direct application of a sterilized dressing over the bleeding point.

If small wounds do not heal promptly or if inflamed areas appear around them, they should have prompt medical attention. Inflammation means infection.

When such wounds do not bleed readily or when they may have been contaminated with soil from pastures, barnyards, lawns, gardens, or other areas fertilized with animal manure, they should always have medical attention because of the danger of tetanus. Tetanus immunization has long been part of the health treatment for every infant, but it is now recommended that adults as well should be immunized. W. W. BAUER

See also BLEEDING; FIRST AID; MEDICINE CABINET; TETANUS

CYSTITIS *See* URINARY DISTURBANCES

DANCING

For the very young child, dancing should be a free and natural form of expression. Children love to dance, and they do not even need music to perform rhythmically. Dancing is a wonderful way to let off steam indoors on a rainy day. Even father, mother, sisters, and brothers can join in a lively dance to records or they can sing their own tunes.

Many a mother, watching her little girl dance gracefully, is impelled to enroll her in dancing school. While the social experience of a dance class is fine, you may find that a child's natural growth and ease of expression can be blocked by forcing her to take formal lessons in dancing. A child's natural sense of rhythm may be "trained" out of her by giving her set forms to do too early in life. Too often the emphasis is on performance and not on the joy and emotional release that result from the right kind of experiences in dancing. Ask yourself why you are eager to give your young child formal training. Even if you believe you have a potential star, it is still questionable if early formal training is desirable. Classes that emphasize natural body movement and music interpretation are usually more suitable for the young child.

Another kind of dancing which seems to begin earlier and earlier in the life of the school-age child is social, or ballroom, dancing. Dancing classes for very young boys and girls exist in some communities. There they are taught the social graces almost before they have lost their baby teeth. Some children enjoy this early social exposure, but many are bored by it. Social pressures in some communities demand that boys and girls attend dance classes, but there is doubt that children younger than their mid-teens need this type of experience.

See also SOCIAL PRESSURES

Related article in WORLD BOOK: "Dancing"

DANDRUFF

Simple dandruff, with or without mild itching, is not regarded as a scalp disease but more as a threat to good grooming. As adolescence approaches, or sooner, the normal scalp will show a mild degree of scaling. Oily secretions of the scalp and external dirt particles make the scales more obvious.

Proper and regular hair and scalp care are usually adequate to control simple dandruff. A shampoo once a week is usually sufficient, but parents can best determine their child's shampooing needs as well as what cleansing agent will be best for him. Encourage him to brush his hair and scalp or to massage the scalp gently with his fingertips. Approximately 10 minutes a day of either is adequate. Excessive manipulation of the scalp through either brushing or massage is not advisable. Though authorities disagree on whether dandruff is infectious, each member of the family should have his own brush and comb.

There is no sharp dividing line between normal and abnormal dandruff, but excessive, uncontrollable dandruff and itching, accompanied by inflammation of the scalp, strongly suggest that a scalp disease is present. If you suspect that your child has a scalp disease, you should, of course, consult your doctor. VERONICA L. CONLEY

See also HAIR CARE

DARK, FEAR OF THE

Darkness does not have to mean danger. To be sure, a child cannot see what is there, but he does not need to be frightened. With your hand as he goes into a dark room and with your confidence that he will encounter nothing bad, your child probably will go freely into the dark and soon learn how much he can see without a light. Total and complete darkness does not often happen, and most children find it exciting to discover how much they actually see in the "dark."

Fear of darkness is not a thing in itself; it is akin to other fears that something terrifying can happen, especially when a child has been naughty.

Even a little child appreciates a flashlight, which will give him some control over darkness. A small night light is helpful if he must go to the bathroom. There is no virtue in maintaining complete darkness just to make a child stoical.

Fear of darkness is one ruse used by some children to keep their parents with them at night. Every child likes the bedtime intimacy with father or mother, a story or a prayer—

which should not be denied—but the timing should be consistent so that a child knows what to expect. Parents who can be cajoled into prolonging bedtime create trouble for themselves. Fathers and mothers who vie with each other in granting these bedtime favors are not playing fair. HELEN ROSS

See also FEAR

DATING

The growing-up process goes faster and faster as time goes by. In many places, 10- and 11-year-olds are invited to boy-girl parties and date dances. It seems even to be an accepted pattern in some places that preteen-agers should date.

But are children of these ages really emotionally ready for dating? These years are the years when your child comes up against all the painful problems of physical growing up and when he struggles with the disturbing problems of emotional growing up. Surely a child doesn't need to add to his burdens and conflicts the pressure to start dating.

Actually, for children of these early ages, dating is a kind of make-believe—a "let's-pretend-we're-grownups" activity. Such children are simply not emotionally ready to get the real values of dating. They are imitating the patterns of young people in their late teens, but they attach childish meanings to these patterns.

What does a date mean to so young a child? For some children it is simply a prize, a trophy, a symbol that they have reached a certain status; for these, dates are collected in quantity and have no real qualitative meaning. For other youngsters, the early age date is a burdensome test. The girl (already anxious as the result of the physical and emotional changes of puberty) has to test her femininity before she is fully feminine—indeed, the girl of 12 who is not sought after when others her age are dating may well feel that her worst fears have been confirmed and that no boy will *ever* want to date her. And the boy of 12 (forced to date at the same time he is going through the puberty stage of "hating" all girls) may well begin to feel that there is something wrong with his masculinity—just another torment to add to the rest of the torments of puberty.

Generally, a child is not emotionally ready to get real value, to say nothing of real pleasure, out of dating until the middle teens. By this time the difficult part of puberty is past; many of the inner conflicts, anxieties, and puzzlements have been resolved; the child has lived with his changing self a little longer and is more used to himself, and more sure of himself. Now he can look upon dating with pleasure, and his anxieties can be healthier.

Parents can help. They can discourage dating in the preteens and early teens simply by refusing to support the date dances and the boy-girl parties that seem to be the style in some communities. In fact, in those communities where parents have banded together to withdraw support from such activities, the children do not object. There was little impetus from the children themselves to date at an early age. They seemed not at all unhappy about waiting until they were older. One wonders, indeed, if they were not also relieved! SELMA FRAIBERG

See also PREADOLESCENT CHILD; PUBERTY; TEEN-AGER; SOCIAL PRESSURES

DAWDLING

Dawdling is more annoying than serious, but, like the common cold, it can lead to complications.

It helps to remember that efficiency is not the highest good in life. Some time-wasting, some daydreaming are actually necessary for growing boys and girls—or anybody else, for that matter. The trick is to separate important obligations from the ones that can easily be put off. Family tension will be a lot less if the difference is clearly understood.

Getting up promptly on school mornings, dressing in the allotted time, appearing at the table at mealtime, arriving at school and club meetings on time—these are kinds of things that affect others. We live in an ordered world, and even a small child has to learn to adapt his behavior to the needs and patterns of other people.

You are not inconsistent, however, if you balance a moderate amount of pressure to get up and dress promptly on school days with a moderate amount of leeway on Saturdays. No harm will come of poking along at a task such as weeding. There's buried treasure in the sweet-smelling earth, and time stands still on a golden day.

Some children are slower by nature than others, although every child seems to go through at least one stage when he is prone to dawdle. He may be bored. Perhaps certain things that were fun and grownup when he first learned to do them, now seem hard or just dull routine. He may need help in organizing his time so that the boring things can be done quickly. Show him how to lay out tomorrow's clothes and where to assemble what he plans to take to school the next day.

It's a wise parent, too, who takes time to put a few sparks into a bored child's life. An alarm clock of his own can be fun to set for getting up in the morning and to reset for making the dressing finish line. Small, gay surprises are often effective lures to the breakfast table, where an upside-down plate conceals "Your fortune for the day," or "You and your Best Friend are invited for snacks immediately after school."

If these tactics are not effective, it may be that a good letting alone is in order. Let him be late for school a time or two. Let him miss the special bus headed for a special event. His chagrin may be harder on you than it is on him, but it is easier on both of you than nagging, which only results in anger or in a kind of absent-minded withdrawal.

As children assume more responsibility for what they do, feel, and think, they need increasing opportunities to act on their own—to do things in their own way and in their own time and to experience the consequence of misjudging time. Each child will do many things differently from the way his parents do. (Often, when he does things as his parent does them, that parent is annoyed.) The point is, children are far more likely to assume responsibility for important obligations if they are allowed freedom to waste time in their own sweet way when there's no good reason why they shouldn't.

See also BOREDOM; CHORES; CURIOSITY; DAYDREAMING; LAZINESS; NAGGING

DAY CAMP

The day camp might be called the little brother of organized camping. It can provide almost all the experiences of organized camping save that of sleeping away from home. For younger children and for those older children whose families find the full-time camp not feasible, the day camp can be a lifesaver.

Two factors, at least, differentiate the day camp from the resident camp. Daily transportation is necessary. And in most instances use is made of public facilities, such as parks, swimming pools, and other outdoor spots. The conscientious parent, in choosing a day camp for the child, will want to be sure that daily travel does not exceed an hour each way and that health and safety precautions are followed. Similarly, a look at the facilities used to see if they are suitable is in order. Crowded playgrounds, pools, and parks are clearly less desirable than less used ones or open fields and woods.

Most important, of course, are the counselors. College students or older men and women are generally to be preferred. Though it is not easy to be certain of the quality of the staff, it will help to meet the director and, particularly, to learn what you can from parents whose children have been in the camp previously.

Second only to the staff in importance is the nature of the activities carried on. Certainly, swimming, group games, and athletic activities have their place. But these should not constitute the whole program. Most children need opportunities for individual activities, for less highly organized play. Crafts of various kinds, painting, and informal, imaginative play are essential to a well-rounded program. And these should provide creative experiences in which children can work out their own ideas rather than follow printed directions or those of the counselor.

Day camping, whether it is sponsored by church, the "Y," other community organizations, or as a private venture, has an important role in the summer life of children. If used intelligently, the day camp can add richly to the growth and development of your child.

ERNEST OSBORNE

See also VACATION, SCHOOL

DAYDREAMING

Daydreaming as an occasional way of coping with the difficulties of life, dealing with frustrations, disappointments, and hopes, may be expected as a child approaches the beginning of his school years. But it is the adolescent who is the daydreaming champion. His motionless idleness does not mean that his mind is as slack as his body. He is doing something, going somewhere inside that skull of his, and it is a good idea to let him alone to do or to go. For a normal amount of daydreaming is not harmful; it can definitely be constructive. It lets off steam; it broadens a child's world and permits him to set his own high goals.

But too much of anything is not healthful. If a child daydreams at the expense of playing with friends or getting his schoolwork done, or if he's not quite sure which are his daydreams and which his realities, he's probably exceeding a healthy limit of fantasy.

Teachers are usually aware of the over-dreamy child in their classrooms, and they know that such a youngster is retreating from his problems rather than meeting them constructively. Parents and teacher working together can try to find out what the pressures are on this child, why he has to have relief, and how relief can be given to him. Frequently, when school and home give a child their patience and support, and reduce their pressures on him, his daydreaming can be brought back to a more reasonable level.

Don't forget, however, that many of the best things in the world have materialized out of someone's daydreams. IRVING E. SIGEL

See also DAWDLING; FARSIGHTEDNESS; LAZINESS; PATIENCE; TEEN-AGER

DAY NURSERY *See* COMMUNITY RESOURCES; NURSERY SCHOOL

DEAF CHILD

Since the child who is deaf looks and acts like any other child, his handicap sometimes can remain undetected for too long. But he needs special help, and the sooner he gets it, the better off he will be. These signs warn parents that their child may be deaf:

WARNING SIGNS

To 6 months—is not startled by noises; is not responsive to pleasant or cross voices.

To 18 months—does not understand words; babbles with few sounds; his own voice becomes less musical.

From 18 months onward—does not progress from saying a few words to speaking in sentences.

General characteristics—depends on sight more than on hearing; becomes more and more silent.

If there is any doubt about your child's ability to hear, take him to an otologist (M.D. specializing in hearing) for examination. If he feels that it is necessary, the doctor can also refer you to an audiological (hearing) center for further testing and guidance.

Parents who continue to search for something that will give their deaf child hearing are obeying the most natural impulse in the world. Unfortunately, at the present time, nothing of such a nature exists.

The treatment of deafness lies in education. It is never too early to find out what schools for the deaf are available in your community. School entry is usually at 2 or 3 years of age. Certain schools have parent education programs to help you guide the deaf child before he enters school. If there is no program of this type locally, an excellent parent education program is available by correspondence.

It is important to remember that a deaf child is first of all a child. He has the same needs as his brothers and sisters have: to be loved, to explore and learn, to grow and *be* in a world of people and events. He should be treated on an equal footing by all members of his family. Although he cannot understand words yet, he can understand situations of eating, sleeping, dressing, toileting, and thus assume responsibilities as do other children his age.

The deaf child can learn to talk. The first step along this long road is for his parents to talk to him. Talk whenever he looks at your face. Talk about whatever he is seeing, thinking, or feeling at a particular moment. This is the beginning of language—understanding words as spoken by other people. In the deaf child's case, language learning will come through sight or lipreading, his main avenues of learning.

Later on, he will use the words whose meaning he understands to express his own ideas. The single words that he first uses will gradually become complete sentences. This is the other side of language—expressing.

As soon as he uses words to express, he needs help in using his voice, in articulating sounds, and in combining all into the rhythmic flow that is speech. Normal speech depends essentially on normal hearing, and the aim here is to develop as much intelligibility as is possible.

It is through the medium of language that the deaf child will gain knowledge, communicate with other people, and even think. Special teachers will play a major role in building language and speech throughout the school years, yet the child's parents will always be the key people who provide the opportunity for him to use, as well as to enrich, his language learning. With special schooling and guidance, the child handicapped by deafness can grow into a mature, self-supporting individual. MARGUERITE STONER

See also COMMUNITY RESOURCES; HANDICAPPED CHILD; HARD OF HEARING

DEATH

Today's young children have very little contact with death. Neither brothers and sisters nor parents are likely to die before a child has become an adult, because the death rate of children has dropped and most adults live on into their 60's and 70's.

Nevertheless, accident, illness, and old age exact their toll. Some member of the family *may* die, and it is sensible to be prepared to help children face death if it should occur. Most parents, though, are inclined to avoid thinking about such an unpleasant possibility and are not prepared to help their child at the time of bereavement.

While there are no simple formulas, it is possible to offer guidelines to help youngsters face the death of someone they love.

The parent needs, first, some notion about the concepts children may have concerning death. A study made in Budapest by Maria

Nagy indicates some of the common reactions of children of various ages:

"The young child from 3 to 5 denies death as a natural and final process. To him, death is like sleep; you are dead and then you are alive again. Or, as on a journey, you are gone and then you come back again. Consequently, children of this age may seem to be rather callous when they are told of the death of a member of the family. They express an immediate sorrow, but soon forget all about it, or at least give the impression of so doing.

"Between 5 and 9, roughly, youngsters appear to be able to accept the idea that a particular person has died, but don't accept it as something that happens to everyone—and particularly not to themselves.

"Only as they reach 9 or 10 years of age do they begin to recognize death as inevitable for all persons and as something that can come to them."

One should realize, of course, that not all children will follow the pattern Maria Nagy discovered in her study of Hungarian children. As a matter of fact, isn't it true that there are adults who, on the emotional level at least, cannot admit to themselves that death is really inevitable?

Some Side-Stepping Answers

In a way quite similar to that of using the stork story to explain birth to children, adults have tried to soften the reality of death. For instance, a 5-year-old child may be told, when his beloved grandfather dies, that the old man had gotten very tired and had quietly gone to sleep. But the child observes that this sleep has taken his grandfather away for good and that everyone is sad. What will be the child's reaction about sleep? It can happen, and often has happened, that a child becomes afraid of bed, afraid of falling asleep, for he feels that he, too, might go off into his grandfather's kind of sleep and never return.

Similarly, a youngster told that his grandmother has gone away to another city may suffer grievously from a sense of desertion. He may at least suffer some hurt over his grandmother's failure to invite him along or even to say good-by.

Even the religious explanation that seems desirable to the adults in many families is not always helpful to a child. Few children find comfort in such explanations as, "God took him," "Jesus wanted him," or "He has gone to be an angel in heaven." Inherent in such explanations is the risk of building in the child feelings of resentment, fear, and even hatred toward the God who may strike down without warning someone for whom a child cares deeply.

These explanations fail a child because they are basically evasive. The natural desire to spare a child the pain of facing realistically the death of someone dear to him usually only makes the feelings of fear or resentment stronger and last longer. Difficult though it may be for you, a direct and honest answer is usually best.

In explaining the cause of death to a child, you usually have to deal with either accident, illness, or old age. Rather than to give philosophic or religious interpretations, immediate causes may be discussed. Thus, in talking about a fatal accident, you can place emphasis on good judgment, carefulness, and thoughtfulness. In talking about old age as a cause of death, you might point out that eventually everyone's body grows old and tired and can no longer go on.

Of course, the words you use are important. Just because someone has died of an illness or an accident does not mean that there is considerable chance that the child, too, may meet a similar fate. It is very important that a child not misunderstand or misinterpret any explanation given to him.

Naturally, children will be more deeply affected by certain deaths than by others. If a playmate has died, youngsters need more reassurance, since they may well see themselves threatened. Or if the father of one of their friends dies, they are likely to feel that their own father may die. Children's anxiety can be soothed if their parents stress the fact that very few young parents die and add to this the assurance that if anything should happen, arrangements have been made for the children to be well taken care of.

Guilt Feelings

Children often come to feel that in some way or other they were responsible for the death of a member of the family. A child whose dying grandparent may live with the family will probably have been "shushed" a good deal during the illness. Understandably, he has not always been completely quiet. This, in itself, for a sensitive child may bring feelings of guilt that can be most disturbing upon the death of the grandparent. Or should a brother or sister die, some of the natural feelings of hostility that are to be found among brothers and sisters may haunt the living child. It is as though something he did or thought contributed to the death. If parents bear this possibility in mind, they can help their child to deal with his guilt feelings.

There are differences of opinion and practice about children's participation in family gatherings of mourning relatives and funeral ceremonies. One common practice is to send the children away to friends to spare them what it is feared will be the upsetting effects of grief and mourning. In some instances, this course may be wise. Generally, however, such a procedure makes a child feel alone and shut out, adding confusion about death and a deepening of disturbing feelings of mystery. To be with the family but protected against some of the more extreme demonstrations of grief that may occur is more reassuring than to be spared the experience.

If, then, you find yourself facing the necessity of helping your child understand death in a firsthand situation, honesty is the best policy. And, if there is added to this, recognition that the child in a bereaved family is in special need of love and affection, he will be helped to come through the experience in a positive way. The value of the feeling of belonging, in sorrow as well as in joy, cannot be overestimated. ERNEST OSBORNE

See also BOOKS FOR PARENTS; BROKEN HOME; OVERPROTECTION

DEFORMITY

Any correctable deformity a child has should be taken care of as early in his life as possible. Cleft palate and clubfoot are examples of malformations that can be corrected if they are treated early.

If your child has a physical abnormality that medical science cannot overcome, if he is too short or too tall, if he has a disfiguring birthmark or a missing finger, remember that he has the same basic needs as all other children: to be loved and treated with respect and to be encouraged to do his best. It is a mistake to keep him away from other children, to shield him from possible jeers and teasing. He needs to learn to mingle at an early age. Actually, children accept one who is different far more readily than do adults, often tailoring their games to fit the capabilities of their handicapped playmate.

Of one thing you may be certain: The deformed child will have the same attitude as his parents have toward his deformity. If they are ashamed, he will be; if they accept him as he is and are proud of what he *can* do, his strengths will grow stronger.

If parents of a deformed child need help beyond that afforded by their doctor, he will refer them to the proper agency.

See also COMMUNITY RESOURCES; HANDICAPPED CHILD

DEMAND SCHEDULE *See* FEEDING SCHEDULE

DENTAL BRACES

A dental brace is an appliance used to correct malocclusion, or poor bite. A child who has crooked teeth or a facial deformity caused by teeth that have not come in properly may have several worries. He may be uncomfortable because of some difficulty in speaking or in biting or chewing his food. He may be self-conscious because he feels he looks different from other children. He may have protruding front teeth that do not allow his mouth to close, or his teeth may be crowded into a small jaw. Some children have too much space between their teeth, resulting in large gaps that may impair speech.

Occasionally, a child will need corrective treatment because he sucked his thumb or fingers excessively when his second teeth were coming in. Some children lose their baby teeth too early because of decay. Then when the second teeth come in, they may shift out of position, causing a poor bite, or malocclusion.

If your child has these or any other forms of malocclusion, a visit to an orthodontist (a dentist who specializes in the treatment and correction of irregularities of the teeth) is definitely in order. Your own dentist can recommend this type of specialist to you. Many parents worry that their child will have to undergo severe pain if orthodontic treatment is performed or that continued use of the appliances will cause the child's teeth to decay. There is no cause for such concern.

The orthodontist will make study models and take X rays of your child's teeth before he arrives at a diagnosis. He will be very careful to see that the braces he prescribes fit properly. He will make regular and thorough examinations, adjusting the braces as needed, and he will also give instructions on keeping the teeth and appliances clean. While the child is wearing braces, sticky candy and chewing gum are strictly taboo.

Occasionally, a child may experience some discomfort during treatment, but at no time should there be pain. Your orthodontist will welcome your call should there be any questions. The doctor's instructions must be followed to insure best results. JOHN H. SILLMAN

See also DENTAL CARE; MALOCCLUSION

DENTAL CARE

Theoretically, everyone wants his child to have strong, healthy teeth; wants him to be spared cavities in childhood and adolescence; wants him to be spared extraction and gum diseases in later life. Theoretically, yes, but not always practically. Good dental health requires eating the right kinds of food, regular home care, and periodic visits to the dentist, but not everyone has the day-by-day firmness and fortitude to carry out the program. Yet dental science has now progressed to the point where if such a program were widely carried out, barring accidents, most people could keep a full set of sound second teeth for life.

Foods Build Healthy Teeth

Foods that are right for general health—milk, fruits and vegetables, meat, poultry, fish, eggs, and butter—are also right for healthy teeth and gums. Fibrous vegetables and fruits that require chewing have the value of acting as tooth-cleansing agents. Vitamin D and sunshine are strong allies.

Faulty Diet Can Harm Teeth

Sugars and starches actually feed tooth decay. Sugars are more harmful than starches because they more readily produce acids while they are in contact with the surfaces of the teeth. Sticky sweets, because they remain longer on the teeth, naturally do more damage.

Most people eat far more sugar than is necessary for good nutrition. But sugar tastes good and is inexpensive, so it is likely that many people will go right on eating it. If, however, you want to make a sincere effort to reduce dental decay in your child, you will have to restrict his sugar intake.

Frequent in-between-meal eating of sweets probably does the most harm to teeth. Substitute fruit, nuts, popcorn, cheese, and other sugarless snacks. Take for your slogan: "Cultivate a fruit tooth in place of a sweet tooth to save teeth." Make an effort to satisfy your child's appetite for sugar by supplying him with sweetened items at only one mealtime per day. If he brushes his teeth carefully immediately after that meal, his dental decay bacteria will starve, little acid will form, and his dental health will improve.

Tooth Brushing

A child should be taught to brush his own teeth soon after all his 20 primary teeth have appeared. A 3-year-old who assumes this responsibility achieves a sense of importance, thinks of himself as doing all the wonderful things that mommy and daddy do, as being grown up.

His own toothbrushes in the colors he likes, an attractive tumbler for rinsing his mouth, his own tooth paste or powder, and a sturdy stool to stand on so that he can reach the washbasin give a child a feeling of achievement and pride of ownership and belonging. Although brushing his teeth will be awkward at first, he will soon learn the proper technique from watching you and by help from you and his dentist. Do not oversupervise and do not expect a thorough job at the beginning. Encourage his efforts and let him know you are proud of him.

He will welcome and enjoy these experiences if you give him the right start. One child who had just that day gone with his mother to buy a brand-new red toothbrush and a tube of tooth paste, went up to her at a birthday party, tugged at her dress impatiently and said, "Mommy, can we go home now so I can brush my teeth?"

If the routine of proper and regular brushing is established early, it is likely to become a habit that will remain throughout life. This habit will provide protection during childhood when teeth are highly susceptible to decay. Adults, too, should continue good tooth brushing to insure the health of gum tissue and to avoid tartar and pyorrhea (a gum disease).

The best time for washing dishes is soon after they are used, before food particles cling to them. Whenever possible, teeth should be brushed right after eating for the same reason. The paste or powder used is not as important as how the brushing is done. Dentifrices serve primarily to assist the brush in cleaning and to make the performance more pleasant. The brush should not just hit the high spots but should be used carefully so that food particles are removed from between the teeth and from other sheltered areas where bits can collect and remain undisturbed. The soft modern diet does not provide the chewing and cleansing action that teeth require. Toothbrushing must, therefore, make up for this lack.

Visits to the Dentist

Regular and frequent visits to the dentist should begin early. Until new ways that do not require special rules of good diet and hygiene are discovered, tooth decay will develop in most children. The dentist can detect early signs of it and can correct the trouble that, if neglected, would lead to pain and the need for extensive and expensive treatment in the adolescent and young adult.

Your child's first visit to the dentist should be made at the age of 3, soon after he has all his primary teeth. This first visit should be a normal step in his growing up. He should not be afraid of it. Most children get their fear of the dentist from their parents or friends.

It is often helpful to take your child with you—as a special treat—on one of your routine visits to your dentist. Arrange for this visit beforehand with your dentist so that your child will be allowed to come into the treatment room, sit in the dental chair, perhaps make the chair go up and down. He can be permitted to examine some of the instruments and get acquainted with both the dentist and the surroundings so that his first real visit won't be strange and alarming. Frequent visits to the family dentist offer the surest way for your child to keep his teeth for a lifetime. ROBERT G. KESEL

See also FLUORIDE; NUTRITION

DENTAL CAVITIES

Cavities develop in teeth through a disease process known as dental caries, or tooth decay. Tooth decay begins in sheltered places where bacteria and food particles can collect and remain undisturbed. These places include pits and grooves on the chewing surfaces of the teeth, areas between the teeth, and along the gum margin on the cheek sides.

Cavities develop because of bacteria. Bacteria act upon food particles, producing substances, mainly acids, that can dissolve the very hard tooth enamel and soften and eat away the underlying dentine. The acids result from the action of bacteria on carbohydrates, principally sugars, in the diet. The amount of acid produced and the softness or toughness of your child's tooth structure largely determine whether a cavity will begin and what its rate of progress will be.

To help your child have fewer cavities, it is important that you restrict sugars in his diet and that you superintend careful tooth brushing soon after his meals. ROBERT G. KESEL

See also DENTAL CARE; FLUORIDE

DENTIST *See* DENTAL CARE

DEPRESSION

"Blues" beginning a day or two after delivery and lasting several days are common enough to be considered almost normal. There may be an organic chemical basis, but it is far more likely that the "blues" are probably due to a combination of emotional factors. The new mother has been keyed up to a high pitch by the expectation of her delivery. Now that this acme of life's experiences has been passed successfully, there is a letdown feeling. Added to this is natural concern about her adequacy for motherhood. She questions whether she will be a good parent and whether she can properly divide her love between her husband, who had all her devotion, and the baby. Then, too, there is the inevitable adjustment of in-laws and her own family to the newest member.

These "blues" ordinarily require no specific therapy. A few tears, a kindly husband, and a frank discussion between the patient and a knowledgeable and sympathetic physician are all helpful. Mild sedatives are useful, too.

Occasionally, such "blues," instead of disappearing or progressively improving in a few days, worsen and the new mother becomes agitated and depressed. Under such conditions, psychiatric consultation becomes an urgent necessity. ALAN F. GUTTMACHER

See also NEW BABY

DERMATOLOGIST *See* MEDICAL SPECIALISTS

DEVELOPMENT *See* EMOTIONAL DEVELOPMENT; MENTAL DEVELOPMENT; MORAL AND SPIRITUAL DEVELOPMENT; SOCIAL DEVELOPMENT; VOCABULARY DEVELOPMENT

DIABETES

Failure of the body to utilize sugar normally produces the disease called diabetes. Although diabetes is more common in adults, it occurs at all ages. The child with diabetes usually eats a great deal more than normally, drinks large quantities of water, and urinates frequently or in large amounts. His condition is diagnosed by analyzing urine and blood for sugar. If the diagnosis is not made promptly and treatment begun, he loses weight rapidly, gradually becomes weaker, and may become drowsy or lose consciousness; that is, go into diabetic coma.

The child with diabetes is cared for mainly through the use of insulin, a hormone produced by the pancreas, which increases the efficiency of his body's use of sugar. The discovery of insulin has been one of the great advances in medicine, for insulin enables diabetic patients to lead relatively normal lives. The insulin is usually given by injection because the oral substitutes for insulin have not proved entirely adequate for most children as yet. Insulin preparations have been developed which act for long periods so that the child may need only one or two injections a day. Care must be taken to regulate the amounts of insulin taken, for too much may lower the blood sugar to a point where the child may feel unusually hungry or nauseated, or he may faint and lose consciousness—sometimes with a convulsion. In recent years, children with diabetes have been permitted to eat a rather general diet, although some physicians prefer that their patients' food be carefully weighed and regulated.

Since the care of the child with diabetes will be lifelong, special attention should be given to his emotional development. He should be encouraged to participate in the usual childhood activities and to have the usual schooling. Famous tennis players like Hamilton Richardson and Bill Talbert were diabetics. Many diabetic children grow to adult life able to assume the same responsibilities as healthy persons. JULIUS B. RICHMOND

See also ENDOCRINE GLANDS; HANDICAPPED CHILD; HEREDITY; SPECIAL DIETS

Diapers come in small and large sizes, either square or oblong. The most adaptable size is 21″ × 40″. One kind of diaper is shaped somewhat like training pants. Another kind has a series of snap fasteners on either side, making safety pins unnecessary.

Diapers are most commonly made of a cotton knit fabric or one of three woven fabrics—bird's-eye, gauze, or cotton flannel. Bird's-eye, stiff when new, softens with laundering. It is strong and will absorb as much moisture as the gauze and knitted fabrics but is not so absorbent as cotton flannel.

Fine-mesh cotton gauze diapers are lightweight and they dry quickly. They tend to wrinkle and get out of shape, but a little extra care in folding overcomes this problem. Flannel diapers are superior to the other fabrics for absorbency. The soft nap of the flannel diaper is pleasant to the touch, but as the nap wears off the diapers become smooth and less absorbent.

Some mothers prefer knit diapers because they stretch as the baby moves. But knit diapers have several disadvantages; they take longer to dry, are not so absorbent, and they also tend to get out of shape with continued use and laundering.

Gauze diapers are the most costly of the woven diapers. Specialty diapers with snap fasteners and those with colorful printed patterns are higher priced yet.

Two dozen diapers are usually sufficient if you wash and dry them every day. Four dozen relieve the pressure of "every day *must* be washday," and give you a few extra for emergencies.

A diaper-washing service, at least for a baby's first few months, is of great help to a new mother. The service not only assures the mother that the diapers are thoroughly clean and sterile, but it saves her the daily washing and drying task. In fact, a gentle hint to doting relatives may even bring a gift of a few months' diaper service—an ideal present to mother and baby.

Washing the Diapers

Each time the baby's diaper is changed, put the wet diaper into a covered pail partially filled with water. If the diaper is soiled, scrape the contents into the toilet bowl, flush, and rinse the diaper in the bowl first. A mild soap or detergent may be added to the water in the diaper pail, but be sure the soap is thoroughly dissolved. If it is not dissolved, soap particles will stick to the diapers and be difficult to remove.

It is always wise to rinse the soaking solution out of the diapers in clear water before laundering them. Many automatic washing machines have a prewash cycle that may be used for this purpose, but a quick rinse in the laundry tub will do just as well. Stubborn stains may require a little rubbing, which may be done as you prerinse.

Use plenty of hot water and a mild soap or detergent in your washing machine for washing baby's diapers.

The most important step in the diaper laundering task is probably thorough rinsing. Three or four rinsings are necessary if the washing is done in a washtub or wringer-type machine. The normal wash-rinse cycle of an automatic washing machine will, in most cases, provide an adequate cleansing process. But, if you feel that additional rinsing is necessary, run the diapers through a second rinse cycle.

Diapers dried outdoors have the advantage of the sun's bacteria-destroying rays. Many modern clothes dryers are equipped

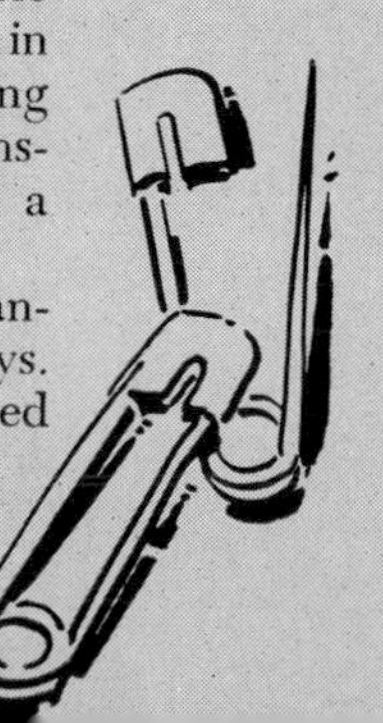

with ultraviolet light, which discourages the growth of bacteria as clothes are drying.

If your baby has developed a diaper rash that is persistent, or if his skin is especially sensitive, consult your doctor. He may suggest that you boil the diapers or use a special antiseptic in the final rinse water.

Diapering the Baby

When the image of a diapered baby comes to mind, we usually think of him in old-fashioned "three-cornered pants." This fold is no longer popular because the diaper is bulky at the front pinning point and tends to spread the baby's legs too far apart. And baby's comfort, of course, is of first importance when diapering him.

A square diaper can be folded in thirds, then folded over at one end. This will yield a diaper three thicknesses at one end, six thicknesses at the other. Inasmuch as boy babies wet the fronts of their diapers and girl babies wet the backs, place the thickest fold where needed.

Oblong diapers may be folded in several ways, depending on the size of the baby. They can be folded in half and then in half again for a tiny baby, the sizes of the folds to be adjusted as the baby grows. For a baby who seems to wet a great deal, it may be wise to use two diapers, particularly at night.

Slip the folded diaper under the baby's hips. Working first on one side and then the other, lap the back fold over the front fold. Hold two fingers under the folds, next to the baby's skin, before you stick the pin into the diaper. The baby's undershirt may or may not be secured to the diaper. If pinned, it will probably be wet the next time the diaper must be changed. If not pinned, it will creep up. You will have to decide which course is best.

See also DIAPER RASH; LAYETTE AND BABY EQUIPMENT; WATERPROOF PANTS

DIAPER RASH

Diaper rash is so frequent in its mild form that almost every baby has it once or twice. The skin in the diaper area becomes red and chafed looking, and sometimes a few pimples are present. The rash may spread and there may be a good deal of discomfort to the baby. Little boys who have the sores of severe diaper rash on the penis may have pain when urinating.

The treatment of diaper rash starts always with the same measures that will ordinarily prevent it: Change wet or soiled diapers more frequently. Do not use waterproof pants over the diapers often, especially on very young babies or on those with very sensitive skin. It is also important when washing diapers to rinse them well.

When the skin is chafed, let the baby lie two or three times a day without diapers. The air will do much to dry and heal the skin. Apply a protective ointment or one of the new special diaper rash preparations when the skin is clean and dry.

Severe diaper rash is usually the result of an interaction between the bacteria on the skin and the urine on the wet diaper. This interaction produces ammonia, which irritates the skin and causes a rash. For severe diaper rash, rinse the diapers in an ammonium chloride solution after they have been completely washed and rinsed. After rinsing in the ammonium chloride, wring out and dry in the usual way. Occasionally, diaper rash occurs because the baby is allergic to the soap or detergent used in washing the diapers, but the danger is lessened if the diapers are thoroughly rinsed.

If the diaper rash becomes infected, it is best to consult the baby's doctor. Impetigo is a fairly common complication of severe diaper rash. RUTH S. KEMPE

See also RASH

DIARRHEA

Frequent loose, watery stools signal diarrhea. Diarrhea is often caused by problems in feeding, occasionally by a food allergy. Sometimes diarrhea is a symptom of infection in the bowel or in some other part of the body. Diarrhea can be very mild and cause little discomfort. At other times and especially in very small infants, it can become a serious disease.

Sometimes a child has one or two loose stools when new solid foods are being introduced, particularly when chopped or bite-size foods replace strained ones. Cutting down on the amounts of new foods and going very slowly in introducing them will usually make adjustment to them easier. Sometimes the baby's formula is being made in incorrect proportions (too much sugar or too little water) or without adequate sterilization. It is always wise to check your formula preparation and the amounts you are feeding with the baby's doctor.

Mild diarrhea may be an accompaniment of another general infection, such as a cold or an ear infection. In addition to whatever treatment your doctor suggests for the primary infection, extra fluids (water, diluted formula, apple juice, or very weak tea) will help replace the fluid loss caused by diarrhea and fever. A very bland diet consisting of such foods as applesauce, cereal, and gelatin is usually taken best.

Sometimes diarrhea is caused by a specific bowel infection that your doctor can diagnose by a bacteriological examination (a stool culture). Certain infections can become severe, and it is therefore important to use careful techniques of cleanliness in coping with them to prevent spread from one member of the family to another. Hands should be washed thoroughly after handling the baby or his diapers, and the diapers should be placed in a covered container and washed separately. Germs are killed by boiling the diapers or ironing them.

Because diarrhea can become particularly serious in a small baby, it should always be reported to the doctor. Signs of more serious illness include frequent, watery stools, mucus or blood in the stools, listlessness, failure to eat, vomiting, fever. Any of these symptoms should be reported to your doctor so that he may watch your baby more closely and possibly prescribe special medical treatment for his diarrhea.

In older children, diarrhea is usually milder, but it occurs in the same situations —as a specific bowel infection, part of a general illness, or because of eating the wrong food. Occasionally, diarrhea is a symptom of tension or anxiety, occurring at times of stress or excitement, such as school examinations or a very special party. If these situations bring on diarrhea frequently, it is worth while to consider ways to relieve your child of his stress or to help him avoid too much excitement. RUTH S. KEMPE

See also ANEMIA; FOOD POISONING; STERILIZING

DIETS *See* SPECIAL DIETS

DIPHTHERIA

Thanks to modern drugs and sanitation, diphtheria is rarely seen these days. It needn't occur at all, for inoculation with diphtheria toxoid begun in infancy is almost completely effective in preventing infection.

Diphtheria begins with sore throat, fever (which may or may not be high), headache, and possibly backache, drowsiness, and vomiting. Yellowish-gray patches appear on the tonsils and may spread to the rest of the throat. Breathing may become tight and difficult.

Because of its very serious nature, the child with diphtheria requires prompt medical attention, skilled nursing care, and close observation. MARIE A. HINRICHS

See also COMMON COMMUNICABLE DISEASES; IMMUNIZATION; SICK CHILD

DISCIPLINE

One of the most important jobs of parenthood is to teach children good discipline. A child must learn the right and the decent ways to behave so that he becomes a constructive and contributing member of his society. He must learn to act well, first in the society of his family, then in the society of his equals, and eventually in the wider society of his community and his nation and the world. Probably no other single task of parents is of greater significance, both for the child's happiness and for the well-being of everyone else.

This basic job is complicated by two widespread misunderstandings. Many people, for example, think that discipline and punishment are one and the same. Punishment, however, is only one of many techniques for teaching children discipline. It is not the only tool available. An overreliance on punishment can build the very opposite of what a parent wants.

Another common misconception is that discipline is resented by children and makes them unhappy. Adults who believe in this error not only hesitate ever to use punishment, but they also use all the other methods of teaching discipline much too little. They falsely believe they are being good to children. The fact is that undisciplined children almost always are unhappy children. They frequently feel lost and bewildered, even frightened, because they never know what the limits are. They often feel unloved because no one seems to care enough about them to teach them what is right and what is wrong, what is allowed and what is not.

Teaching good discipline is a difficult job even without these common misconceptions. It is, however, a job that parents can do. Fortunately, it includes many basic elements that are easy for most of us.

Love Is the Basis of Good Discipline

The very foundation of good discipline is a child's sense of being well and thoroughly loved. To love and to show their love is not a hard job for most parents, yet it is a crucial part of teaching discipline. It is very difficult for a child to learn good ways of behaving unless he feels a solid, supporting sense of welcome from infancy on.

Being loved makes two contributions to good discipline. First of all, the sense of being well loved through the years spurs the child's total growth. For example, love is the basic psychological support that enables a child to use his brain power as he matures, to think things out, to remember the lessons of the past, to apply what he knows to new situations. The child who feels unloved and unsure of his own worth is pulled back continually to babyhood. He is apt to be impulsive and egocentric. It is harder for him to think clearly and to remember, and much harder for him to act like a good citizen, despite his advancing years.

Secondly, the well-loved child, from the very early months of life on, begins to feel with and to side with, to think like and to act like, the people who give him love. This process is called "identification." It is similar to, but is a much stronger and more continuous process than, what is commonly called "imitation." The loved child unconsciously puts himself inside the skin and bones of the people who care for him and begins to think and feel as they do; he takes on their attitudes and values.

Parents Should Be Well Disciplined

The process of identification suggests another and often-overlooked element in teaching good discipline: Parents themselves should be well disciplined. Even when we are not saying a word to our children, we are teaching them discipline through our actions. Children have their eyes constantly on us. They learn from what they see going on all around them, every second and every minute of their waking hours. The process of identification begins very early. The lessons sink in slowly but steadily. What is being learned does not always show in the early years, but the lessons are inside the child and they will show as time goes along.

This way of teaching good discipline—by acting wisely and well—fortunately is like showing our love for a child: It is not too hard for most of us to do. None of us is perfect; our children will not be perfect either. But most of us live reasonably decent lives. When we recognize that even very young children are becoming aware of what we do, and learning from it, we often try even harder to be good citizens and to be well disciplined ourselves.

The discipline of parents affects the teaching of discipline to children in still another way. Throughout infancy and toddlerhood children are too immature to be taught specifically many of the appropriate and approved ways of acting. They do not yet have the brain power to understand. They have not yet developed the emotional capacity to control their actions even if they did understand. They are not yet sufficiently mature to be their own policemen. Adults must be a child's policeman and his conscience, his fence and his off-limits sign, until the youngster can take on these jobs for himself.

Creating a Good Environment

During these early years, especially year one and year two, wise parents teach discipline by creating an environment in which the child can only act well, in which it is almost impossible for him to be bad. If things are not to be touched, they are put out of reach. If certain areas are out of bounds, either a fence is built or the parent stays right on hand to be the fence himself. The child is free to use almost everything he sees because the parent has fixed the child's little world to make it safe. Adult energies do not go into endless "no's" and "mustn'ts" and "don'ts." These words attempt to build the policeman inside the child, a step he is not yet ready for.

This third role also is not hard to play, but it is time-consuming and energy-demanding. When children are 1 year old, 2, and even 3, parents have to be on hand constantly, always alert and ever ready to step in with a constructive idea. Too many adults are unwilling to give this much time to a child. They try too early to teach the child discipline when what is needed is to demand more discipline of themselves.

Of course, no one can create an environment that makes all "bad" behavior impossible. Despite many precautions, infants and toddlers inevitably get into some things that should not be touched. They inevitably damage some property or hurt other children. The most fully disciplined parent can never ward off all "bad" behavior. Being on hand and alert, however, the well-disciplined parent can quickly redirect children so that their most constant practice will be in acting well.

Specific Teaching of Good Behavior

There is no one age when suddenly the adult begins to play a more active role of instruction, when he begins to teach the child to carry within himself the controls and the judgment that will enable him to act well on his own. The timing of specific teaching is the one really hard job in teaching discipline. Timing is a matter of judgment. It varies from child to child, home to home, situation to situation. There will be instances when a parent feels that his child can understand and control his behavior before he reaches 3 years of age. In general, however, specific teaching increases after 3 years of age. Around this time youngsters become more verbal, their attention span lengthens, and they begin to act with more thought beforehand. Instruction then in right and wrong ways to act, and why, becomes more important. It is more possible to reason effectively with a child, pointing out what the rules are, why they exist, why they are important, what would happen if they did not exist. It is more possible for him to control his behavior by calling to mind what he knows. This is the time to build on the base that has been laid during the earlier years.

The process of reasoning with a child, explaining and interpreting, ought to be the mainstay of a parent's approach to discipline from this point on. It is the best method for helping a child build generalizations that will enable him to act in good ways in new situations as they arise, and in situations where he is on his own with no adult policeman present. It also best respects the child's growing independence and runs the least risk of making a child disobedient, not because he disagrees with a rule, but simply to assert his independence.

Reasoning, however, is a slow method. You cannot expect a child to learn a lesson for all time because you have gone over it with him once. Learning discipline, learning anything, is complicated. The same situations may well arise again and again; this does not necessarily mean that the teaching was wrong but simply that more talking and more explaining and interpreting are needed. It takes time and patience to build an independent youngster who carries inside himself a good set of standards and who is not dependent on someone else to make him good.

Reasoning Is Serious Business

Talking with a child should not be confused with weakness or vacillation. Parents who teach through talking have to believe in what they are saying. Their way of talking must convey to the child a sense that the lesson is important and that they have convictions about it. Nor can this teaching process ever be "just talking," while the child goes on acting as before, after listening with half an ear. When a parent says "Stop" and tells why, the action must stop, at least for that incident. When a parent says "Don't" and tells why, that must be the end at least for that incident. The parent talks, explains, teaches, *and* follows through so that a child is as seriously impressed as possible from that one lesson.

Rewards and punishment are other teaching approaches that begin to be of some use during this same period. Sometimes, but not always, they are useful for adding strength to the verbal instruction that a parent has given. Sometimes a parent feels that one or the other might even teach the lesson better than the slower process of reasoning.

Experience Teaches

During these years from 3 or so on, our words or the rewards and punishment we use are not the only instructions in discipline the children are receiving. Children increasingly learn good ways of acting from their own experiences. As they begin to use materials, as they start to play with other children, they can't be expected to begin with perfect behavior. They are beginners, after all. They must experiment. They must make mistakes. But children learn from all their errors. Sometimes the learning comes explicitly from an age-mate: "You shouldn't do that. It isn't nice." Often children learn from their own quiet observation of how things have worked out. Occasionally, it is helpful to say something that reinforces what the child is learning through his experiences. As often, it is better to keep quiet and simply let the lesson sink in on its own.

Every age, of course, presents its own unique issues in discipline. Progress toward good behavior is not a steady, smooth, even path. It has its ups and downs. If a parent becomes discouraged at any one point in development, it often helps to look back to a child's infancy to realize how much he has already learned. It helps to realize the many different ways in which the child is being exposed to lessons in discipline. And it helps to remember that learning discipline is a lifelong task, the continuing and probably never-ending business of learning the good and the right and the desirable ways of responding to people and to life. JAMES L. HYMES, JR.

See also LOVE; OBEDIENCE; PERMISSIVENESS; PUNISHMENT; REWARDS; RULES AND REGULATIONS

DISCUSSION *See* FAMILY DISCUSSIONS

DISEASE *See* COMMON COMMUNICABLE DISEASES (or see specific disease)

DISHONESTY *See* HONESTY

DISOBEDIENCE *See* OBEDIENCE

DIVORCE AND SEPARATION

Divorce, regardless of the circumstances leading up to it, is almost always an unhappy experience for one or more of the members of the family who are directly involved. It is particularly difficult for children. But when you have decided there is no other solution, you have to tackle the problems divorce brings. You can get through the difficult moments. So can your child. As you gain in courage, so will he.

Nothing short of the truth is good enough when explaining to a child why his parents no longer live together in the same house. Children, being imaginative little creatures, will make up their own reasons if they are not told by one or both parents the truth about the situation. Children 3 years old or younger will need merely to be told, "Daddy has moved away to another house. He will not live with us any more."

Older children can be told, "Daddy and I made each other unhappy. We could not be friends any more." Or, "Daddy and I did not enjoy being close to each other any more. We are going to live in different houses to see if we will be happier that way." Assure your child that you will keep him informed each step of the way to final separation and divorce. He needs to feel secure, and he needs to be able to count on his parents to share the truth with him.

If possible, try to help your child feel that the other parent is a good person, even though not good for you. But don't say he has been good if he has not. It is better for a child to hear a harsh truth from the parent who loves and cares for him than to have it slip out of the mouth of a stranger. If you believe your former spouse has deserted his family, never to return, hold out no false hopes. Waiting for something that will never happen is worse for a child than any blunt explanation could be.

Don't Hide Your Feelings

If you have feelings of sadness over your separation, don't try to hide these feelings from your child. Let him know that you feel unhappy at times, but never use a child's shoulder to weep on. Don't pretend to love your estranged mate if you do not. A sweet, martyr-like attitude is usually false. A child will feel more secure if he has the sound, solid truth of your feelings right out in the open than if he senses something shaky and insincere in what you say.

It is perfectly normal for a child to become angry at his parents every so often whether or not they are separated or divorced. And it is only natural that he should feel added resentment from time to time at this upheaval in his world. In different children this resentment seeks different outlets. One child will go on a hunger strike, sitting and staring at his food. Another child will tell lies or bite his fingernails. Another child will have a cough for which a doctor can find no physical basis but which can be traced to an expression of anger. Some children, feeling that their "badness" led to their parents' divorce, continue the bad behavior indefinitely, or until they can be made to understand that naughtiness and angry feelings are a natural, normal part of life.

A wise mother, knowing that children will "act out" their feelings, will not scold her small daughter for spanking her doll, because she knows it is important for her child to keep sharing her feelings with her. If the child becomes angry, and if she can shout out the things that are bothering her, a much more healthy atmosphere will exist.

Visits Are Reassuring

Unless there are unusual circumstances, a child needs to see and visit with the parent who has left the home. These visits tend to assure the child that he has not been deserted. Ordinarily, a child needs two parents, but he should have only one home. Equal division of time is confusing to the child, who should be able to say, "This is where I live. There is where I visit." For a child under 4 or 5, the visits to his estranged parent are ordinarily best confined to daytime. As he grows older, he may spend the night if he asks to. If the experience proves comfortable and happy, and does not increase the strain between the parents, the child may be allowed to visit again.

When the child is around 7 or 8, he may want to spend several days or weeks with his other parent. At the age of 9 or 10 the child may even elect to spend more time with his other parent than he does with the one with whom he has been living. There are no hard and fast rules as to how much time should be spent with which parent at what age. Most important is that the child and parents feel easy and comfortable.

In most cases it is best to have arrangements about visits definite and to have them put in legal terms. One child's father will come at ten o'clock on Saturday morning to pick up the youngster, promising to have him back home again by six that evening. Another father and mother arrange for visits in the child's home at certain and regular hours. Some children can go away for the weekend with their other parent. As a child grows, the legal arrangements concerning visits, and possibly also custody, may well be reviewed and revised to fit changed circumstances, interests, and needs.

What About Remarriage?

A parent's remarriage brings sudden changes to a child's life—another set of parents and perhaps two new sets of grandparents as well as aunts and uncles. When a parent plans to remarry, the fact should be shared with the children involved. They should be told that the parent is thinking of marrying again, when this event is likely to occur, and what will happen to the child afterward. Security is the basis of a child's life, and at no time is it more important for him to feel secure, wanted and needed, than when his parents divorce and remarry.

In visiting the parent who has remarried, a child still needs time to be alone with his parent. A half-hour walk, a little time to talk or read together, are desirable and necessary. Resentments against the parent's new mate are logical and normal, but these resentments can be gotten through with patient handling.

New Addition Brings Problems

When a new baby arrives on the scene, jealousies are bound to enter after the first excitement subsides. Half sisters and half brothers are no more immune to rivalry than are full sisters and brothers. Letting the bad feelings toward the new brother come out into the open in words rather than in deeds is still a good procedure. "That brat! I won't walk in the park when you take him. I'm going back to my daddy!" a child may storm. But the storm will blow over if he is not made to feel "bad" for saying these things. Peace will be restored if he can harmlessly air his grudges without punishment. It is best to permit the child his griping as a safety valve and to help him as he grows to have his own interests, his own friends, and a life of his own.

Parents who have separated should not compete with each other for their child's love and attention. A father should not load his visiting child with presents and candy before he takes him home to his mother. Divorced parents should not use a child as a weapon to carry on their own battling.

In the final analysis the things that will be most important to the child of divorced parents are honest sharing, true understanding, and a straightforward, but warm, down-to-earth caring for the child. This attitude is worth more than lollipops and ice-cream cones, electric trains and walking dolls. Give your child the feeling that he is accepted. Give him a secure sense that you love him and that with you he can be himself, and you build the deeper, more enduring relationship for the long pull. DOROTHY W. BARUCH

See also BOOKS FOR PARENTS; FAMILY SERVICE AGENCY; FEAR; STEPPARENTS; WORKING MOTHER

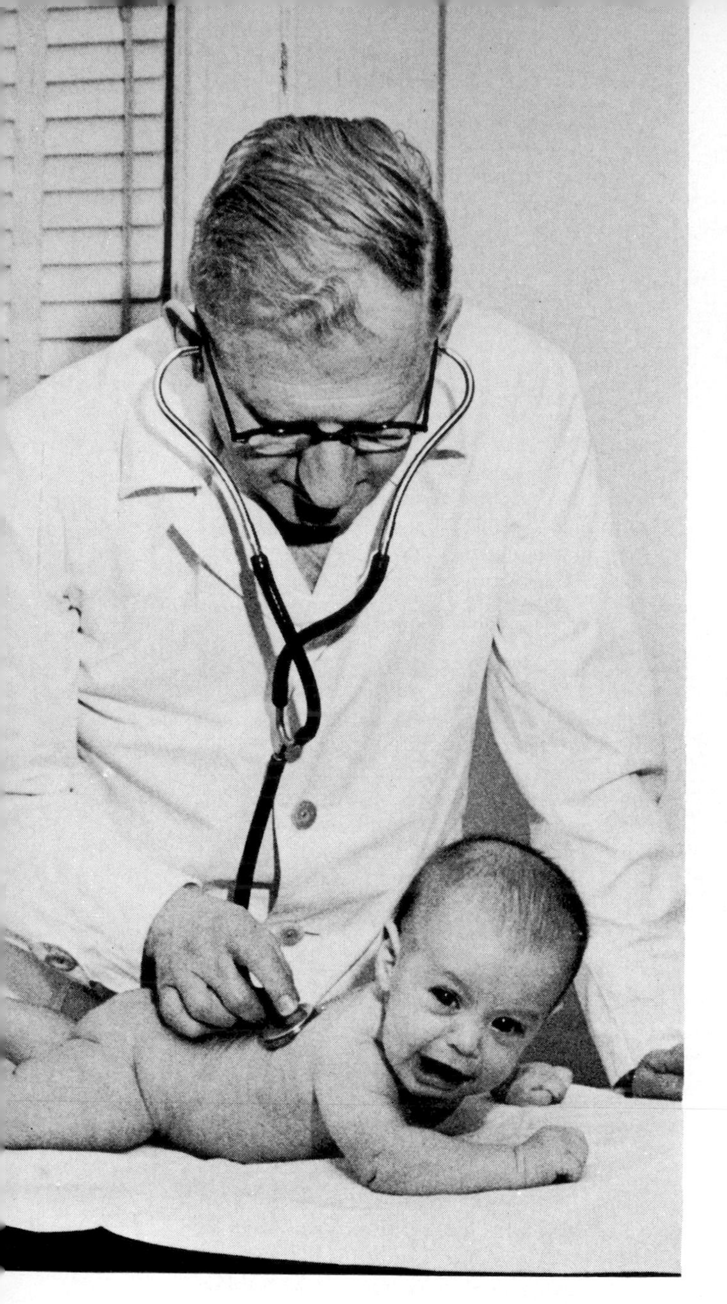

DOCTOR

Before their baby is born, most parents decide who his doctor will be. Often, he's their trusted family physician—a general practitioner. Or the mother's obstetrician may have recommended a pediatrician—an M.D. who has spent many years learning about the growth and development of children and their diseases. The important thing is that your baby have a doctor from the beginning, preferably the same doctor, to help keep him well and to care for him when he is sick.

Should the family move to another community, perhaps the former doctor will recommend a new one, or you may ask the county medical society or the local health department, even a local hospital, for the names of doctors especially good with children. These same sources can give information about well-baby clinics (also known as child health conferences) to parents who do not wish to have a private doctor, about hospital outpatient departments or clinics, and public health nurses in the new community.

Once you have placed your child in the care of a doctor, have faith in him, stay with him, and follow his suggestions carefully. If you don't understand his explanations (sometimes doctors unconsciously slip into medical jargon), ask him to use words that are clear to you. Some mothers keep a notebook handy in which they jot down questions that occur to them between regular visits. At the doctor's office they write down instructions having to do with formula changes, new foods to be added to the diet, and medications. In this book, or into a permanent health record, should also go any information concerning shots, allergies, and illnesses, which will be valuable to a child as part of his continuing medical history.

On your first visit with the baby's doctor, you and he will probably decide on a schedule of regular visits—once a month, quite likely, during the first year; at least every three months during the second year. Thereafter, checkups twice a year are sufficient for most children.

During these visits, the doctor will check your child's height and weight, advise when new foods should be introduced, when toilet training should be started, and give shots and booster shots to protect him from the common communicable diseases. The doctor will also have an opportunity to observe your child's general development and to determine whether his mental, emotional, and social growth is following a pattern that is normal for him.

During these visits, too, a youngster becomes acquainted with examination chairs, tables, and instruments. He gets used to the sights and sounds and medicinal smells that characterize a doctor's office. If children develop friendly feelings toward the doctor when they are well, they are far more likely to cooperate when they are sick. Children often are irritable during an illness, especially if the illness is acute. If the first meeting with a doctor takes place when a child is uncomfortable and distressed, you can hardly expect cooperation.

At certain ages, particularly between 1 and 3, a child may resist examination by a doctor. Don't worry. His behavior is normal, and there is no need to let temporary resistance interfere with regular visits to the doctor, nor should you change to another doctor. If your own attitude toward these regular visits remains calm and casual, chances are good that your child will soon come to feel the same way.

Under no circumstances should the doctor be used as a threat to be called if a child fails to obey. The doctor cannot be assigned the role of bogieman one day and be accepted as friend the next. Nor should a doctor be used to reinforce parental commands to stay out of mud puddles or to wear ear muffs. A physician can be more effective if the child sees him as a special kind of friend and adviser. He can play his part in guiding your child's development best if he has his complete confidence, if he is regarded as an ally rather than as another enforcer of everyday rules.

Honesty about what the doctor does is also important to the development of friendly relationships. Unfortunately, the traditional way to set a child's fears at rest has been to assure him that "nothing is going to happen" or that "the doctor won't hurt you." Sometimes, such promises cannot be kept, and a child may come to feel that his parents and the doctor are unreliable. "Nobody likes to get shots, but you know the doctor will hurt you as little as possible. Now let's get it over with so you can play with the little cars on that table." Far better is a frank but sympathetic attitude. A few tears, a shriek or two, a show of fear or anger, are no reflection on a small person's upbringing, and they relieve his feelings immensely. Older children can readily understand that it is much better to suffer a slight hurt for a minute or two than to take chances on being sick and miss out on a lot of fun.

When more serious and painful procedures are necessary, the doctor, knowing your child's personality as he does, will help you to determine how to go about explaining what is to come. As a general rule, it is not wise to tell a small child far in advance of the event, but he should know what will take place before he goes to the doctor's office. Simple, brief explanations are usually best. "That boil hasn't gone away by itself. The doctor will open it so it can clear up," or, "The doctor will take stitches in that cut so it will heal faster."

Some doctors or parents may offer rewards to children for submitting to examinations or treatment. Gifts are not necessary if the doctor has had an opportunity to establish good rapport with his small patient. Rewards in the form of candy or toys have the disadvantage of giving a child the notion that he should receive a present for doing what must be done. "When we finish at the dentist's, let's call daddy at his office," or, "How would you like to stop at the library to see if the book you wanted is there?" give a child something to look forward to. A pleasant experience ahead has none of the unfortunate features of the usual reward or bribe.

From time to time a family doctor may wish consultation with other doctors. Ophthalmologic consultation is sometimes necessary to check vision properly. Surgical consultation may be needed at various times. If psychological problems develop, consultation with a child psychiatrist, child psychologist, or social worker, often working together in a child guidance clinic, may be desirable. And a continuing relationship with a dentist, starting around 3 years of age, is also desirable, particularly since at this age painful procedures are usually not necessary and the child comes to know the dentist as a friend before any complicated treatment is required. At times you may have some question about the desirability of a consultation, as with an orthopedic surgeon about the feet or with a skin specialist about a birthmark. If so, don't hesitate to discuss the matter with your child's doctor. Most physicians welcome the opportunity to have another doctor's opinion if there is some good reason for it.

As soon as your child is old enough to answer questions himself, stay in the background during office visits. A youngster's answers to questions and his description of how he feels often provide valuable clues to the state of his well-being. When the time is right for him to answer questions, both your child and his doctor will appreciate your tact in suggesting that you wait outside the consulting room while they talk.

As a child grows older, his checkups should continue, even though he seems to be quite healthy, for it is to his advantage to realize early that the doctor is his friend, with a genuine interest in his well-being. Thus is the foundation laid for sound medical care and a continuing relationship with his doctor into adulthood. JULIUS B. RICHMOND

See also CLINICS; COMMUNITY RESOURCES; DENTAL CARE; FAMILY HEALTH RECORD; MEDICAL SPECIALISTS; PHYSICAL CHECKUP

DOG BITES *See* BITES, ANIMAL

DOLLS *See* TOYS AND PLAY EQUIPMENT

DRAMATIC PLAY *See* DRAMATICS; DRESS-UP PLAY

DRAMATICS

Few things are more fun than taking part in a play, as writer, actor, scenery painter, costume maker, or audience. Almost any child is a naturally dramatic creature who would like the chance to participate in each or all of these ways. And you can give him the opportunity to be each and all—the opportunity to have fun with dramatics while gaining in other ways as well.

The educational value of dramatics is great. Dramatized folk tales, legends, fairy stories, children's classics, Bible stories, biographies of great men and women, all can add to the child's information about the language, satire, humor, or thought in his cultural heritage. Mother Goose rhymes or works of famous poets, spoken dramatically can increase awareness of the rhythm and lyricism of language. Historical material comes to life for children when they dramatize it. The landing of the Pilgrims, The Boston Tea Party, the Declaration of Independence mean more, stay longer in the memory, when they have been dramatized. Benjamin Franklin and Jane Addams are more truly examples of individual endeavor to a child who has played that he is one of these historic figures. King Arthur and Robin Hood are romantic people to "be." Study of an early history and culture, such as that of ancient Egypt, is no longer just research to the child who has worn a pharaoh's crown.

Little plays that a child acts out after seeing television programs, motion pictures, and theater become part of his personality—this is one of the reasons he needs your guidance in avoiding overly sophisticated and sensational dramas, and equal guidance toward constructive ones.

Imaginative, faraway places appeal to children. Plays based on *Aladdin, Peter Pan,* and *Alice's Adventures in Wonderland* can carry a child off to these places. On the other hand, simple plays about nature in which the child uses the sounds of thunder and wind, and

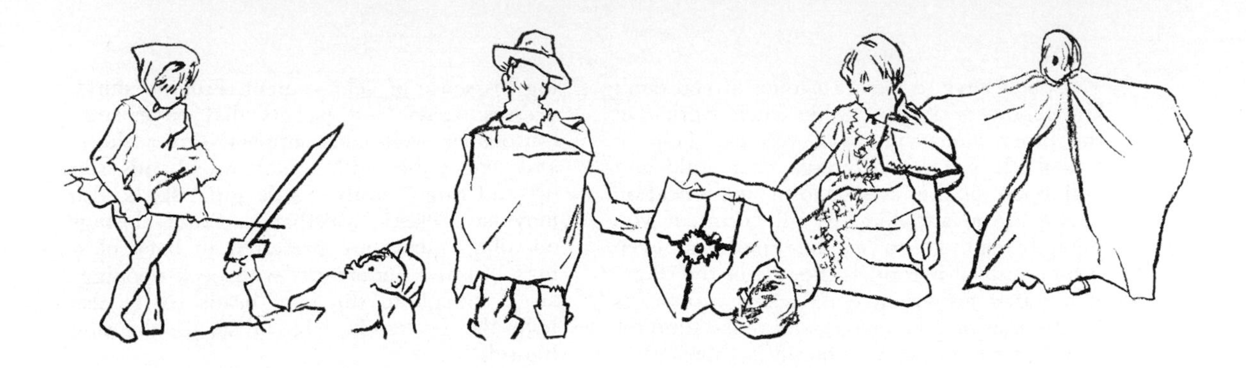

plays in which he dramatizes the ways of animals bridge for him the realistic world and the one he imagines.

Dramatics As an Emotional Outlet

Emotional release is often a valuable part of dramatics. If a child is afraid of the dentist, a simple acting out of the visit can frequently lessen the fear. Playing Pinocchio as he struggles to learn to be good appeals to both boys and girls who all have those struggles, too. Creating dramas from such stories as *The Emperor's New Clothes, The Shoemaker and the Elves,* and *The Sleeping Beauty* offer constructive outlets for imagination and feeling.

Cooperation in a simple form can be learned by the very young child through dramatic play. When he grows older and works with others to collect props or set scenes or paint faces, he also *feels* cooperation in the emotions that flow freely in group work.

All children tend to be imaginative and creative to some extent. Some are resourceful in thinking up ideas or are clever in inventing characters or in making something out of nothing for costumes and scenery, while still others can put ideas into words. Often children who don't do well with words are clever in pantomime. The creativity of one child is usually stimulating to the creativity of others.

The Shy and the Bold Benefit

Withdrawn or negative children often respond to a chance to participate in dramatics, whether as actors or stagehands or on a planning committee. They feel part of the group and try to live up to the responsibility given them. If their special abilities are noticed or needed, they have an increased sense of usefulness. Similarly, an earnest, shy child plays a role in a play, and his shyness disappears or diminishes because he can be less self-conscious while speaking the words of some interesting character.

The aggressive child learns to make a contribution without monopolizing attention. He can be helpful by acting as assistant director, as a prompter, as a scenery director, or as a make-up director.

How the Parent Can Help

How do you, the parent, fit into all of this? Principally you fit by being the background, providing the stimulus, and taking the role of appreciator. Your very young child will have his plays at home. You read stories or plays to him, turn on TV, play a rhythm record on the phonograph. You lend him his dad's old hat and a worn-out shirt. You talk to him a bit about what he hears and sees: "How does the littlest bear sound when he finds his broken chair?" "Show daddy how Christopher Robin talked to Winnie-the-Pooh." "Do you want to play cowboy?"

When he is older, most of his dramatizations will take place at school or with his friends. As he plays with his friends at home, particularly at times when they seem not to know what to do and are restless and quarrelsome, you can provide some suggestions to start off dramatics; read them *Three Billy Goats Gruff* or *The Bremen Town Musicians.* You can ask, "Can you roar like a troll?" or, "Who wants to be the dog in this story?" After you have inspired the dramatization, you can sit on a playroom chair and watch the performance. On another occasion you can provide hand puppets and let the children turn these into the characters they need. You can have a collection of old clothes and props that the children are always free to use. During summer vacation or on birthdays and holidays, you can suggest some kind of circus or stunt or patriotic story that might appeal dramatically to sisters and brothers or to friends. You may, accidentally almost, establish through this an unexpected neighborhood or family rapport.

If you are interested in your child's school plays and have accustomed him to the idea that you listen to him, he will talk to you about a play from its inception. Later you may hear, "I get to be an angel. Can you make wings?" or, "The teacher wants the mothers to come to school to make costumes."

You don't have to make costumes if you don't know how or if you dislike such work. On the other hand, any way you can help in school plays does encourage your child and will open up an avenue of communication between you and him. By all means, if you possibly can, go to see him perform, even if he is only a daffodil at the rear of the stage. If a rather grown-up child wants you to listen to lines or give cues, try to make time for it. Often the father in a family is more interested in plays than the mother. He may have, for years, been making paper hats or sketchy costumes at home for his children and may be delighted when he is asked to make props or scenery for school dramatics.

Don't Expect Perfection

It is best not to expect or demand any kind of finished dramatic performance of children. They don't need perfection to be satisfied, and you may only discourage them if you find perfection necessary. They don't need to be shown off, either. Their primary need is that you recognize the value of dramatics to them and that you encourage them toward active participation in some or several dramatic fields. ELOISE B. DUBOIS

See also CREATING; DRESS-UP PLAY; SELF-CONSCIOUSNESS

DRAWING *See* ART EXPERIENCES

DREAMS, BAD *See* NIGHTMARES

DRESSING SELF

When your child begins to show an interest in his clothing, usually before his second birthday, he will very likely find it much more fun to take his clothes *off* than to put them *on*. But there will be times when your son will insist, "Me can do," and his choice of costume will provide many hilarious moments for his family. He will wear a cowboy hat with swim fins and consider himself well-dressed. He will put his pants on inside out, his shorts on upside down, and his coat on backwards. Your little girl may offend your sense of color harmony by insisting on orange socks and a pink dress. And she sees no reason why her new party dress shouldn't be worn to the supermarket. It is natural for you to encourage socially accepted attire, and to hurry to help when your child takes an intolerably long time to get dressed. The best course however, is to allow a child time enough to dress if that is what he wants to do and to permit some choice of clothing suitable to the occasion.

There are subtle ways to help your child get dressed, while at the same time preserving his sense of achievement. Provide shirts, dresses, coats, and jackets that have large buttons or well-made zippers. Boxer shorts and long pants with elastic waistbands slip up and down easily. Little girls' skirts also may have elastic waistbands. Front closings on all garments are preferred to back closings. Knitted undershirts with neck openings large enough to slip over heads easily also help the 2-year-old who insists on dressing himself.

To make self-dressing an easier task, place a little boy's shirt on the bed with the back uppermost, and spread his pants on a chair or on the bed, ready for him to slip into them. A little girl's dress can be placed back uppermost to help her put it on easily. Loosen the laces in shoes, and be sure socks are right side out. Two-piece snow suits are easier to manage than one-piece, long-zippered ones.

A toddler may revert many times in the next three or four years to his babyish ways, which will include wanting his mother to dress him. A new baby in the family is almost certain to bring on a temporary state of helplessness. But if you make dressing as easy as possible, help the toddler with the hard jobs—small buttons, back closings, and shoe tying—and let him do what he can for

himself, he will become much more independent than if he is helped consistently. His progress will suffer setbacks, but there will be definite progress, which should be noted and praised.

See also RESOURCEFULNESS

DRESS-UP PLAY

How often have you heard your little girl say, "Let's play dress up!" A wise mother will provide a box in which to put old dresses, suits, hats, shoes, purses, shawls, scarves, and bits of lace with which little girls can become brides or dowager queens at a moment's notice. Boys, too, like to dress up, but usually at the suggestion of girls who want to include them in a play or a pageant that requires a male character or two.

Children can learn much more than that which they are formally taught in school or at home. The creative play of dressing up gives a child an opportunity to take on another identity, either that of a grownup he knows or some character from a book or play. You can find dress-up suggestions in Volume 9, *Make and Do,* pages 182–189, 192.

Children's dress-up sessions provide wonderful themes for home movies. Some children even write plays and act them out as father takes movies that will be cherished and laughed over by family members for years.

DRINKING FROM CUP *See* WEANING

DROOLING

Drooling means that so much saliva is being produced by the salivary glands that the baby doesn't swallow it fast enough and it spills over and dribbles down his chin. Babies usually start having more saliva when they are about 3 or 4 months old and they may start drooling then. Again, the amount of saliva produced varies a great deal from child to child, and large differences are entirely normal.

Saliva is an important fluid in digestion; mixed with the food in the mouth it begins the process of digestion of starchy foods and helps to make other foods moist.

Drooling is apt to be increased with teething, but it often is present long before teething starts. An increase in drooling frequently happens three to four days before a tooth is about to erupt and sometimes is one of the first signs of a new tooth. Drooling, mild fussiness, and an increased tendency to chew on anything available probably mean that your baby's gums will show the redness and swelling heralding his first tooth.

Most babies stop the excessive production of saliva that makes them drool when they are somewhere between 12 and 18 months old. Before that, drooling may seem a nuisance, but it is quite harmless and has no untoward significance. If your baby's shirt keeps getting wet, a cloth bib may help to protect his clothing. RUTH S. KEMPE

See also GAGGING; SPITTING UP; TEETH AND TEETHING; VOMITING

DROPPING *See* THROWING AND DROPPING

DRUGS

Various preparations used in an effort to provide comfort and to prevent and cure disease are classified as drugs. Some of these, such as aspirin, are single chemical compounds, while others, such as some prescriptions ordered by a doctor, are mixtures of chemical substances. Still other drugs, such as insulin and ACTH, are extracts from the tissues of animals, and their chemical composition may not be known precisely.

The so-called wonder, or miracle, drugs—the antibiotics—are extracts made from the growth of a particular mold. The sulfonamides, or sulfa drugs, are among the most important synthetic drugs used in the treatment of pneumonia and other diseases. Vaccines are made from the growth of bacteria or viruses.

Many specific drugs can now be bought over the counter, but there are dangers in giving them to children. Proper diagnosis is necessary for proper treatment. It is possible for overdosage to cause harm. Even vitamins should not be given without checking the kind and amount with the doctor.

Reports of the dramatic results achieved with the antibiotics sometimes tempt parents to demand their use for a cold or other slight indisposition. These drugs not only have no effect on a cold, but it is also possible for a child to develop allergic reactions (hypersensitivity) from repeated use of penicillin or the sulfa drugs so that they cannot be given when needed for more serious infections such as pneumonia. *Parents should keep for future reference a written record of their children's reactions to drugs.*

It is a good idea to discard unused medicines after recovery from an illness since many deteriorate with time; they also are a hazard to the child bent on exploring the family medicine cabinet. JULIUS B. RICHMOND

See also FAMILY HEALTH RECORD; MEDICINE CABINET; MEDICINE GIVING; PRESCRIPTIONS

Related article in WORLD BOOK: "Drug"

EARACHE

An earache is one of the most unpleasant experiences a child can have. By far the most frequent cause of an earache is the common cold. The trouble begins when infection from the nose travels to the middle ear cavity through a short tube, known as the Eustachian tube.

Doctors today can prescribe certain antibiotics and sulfa drugs that will effectively treat earache produced by infection. Occasionally, however, these valuable drugs are not used soon enough, or else they meet up with germs that resist them. Then it is sometimes necessary for a doctor to make a small opening in the eardrum to allow the infection to drain out. Proper drainage and adequate care of an ear infection will usually prevent serious complications from developing.

Some earaches develop from other causes. Hot, humid weather in the summer can cause a painful infection in the outer ear canal—the part of the ear you can see when you look directly into the ear.

A child can also start an infection of the ear canal by carelessly scratching and poking the ear with his fingernails, with bobby pins, matches, or other unclean objects. In these cases he might break the skin surface and cause a boil or an abscess to form.

Infection of the ear canal is often very painful, perhaps out of all proportion to the actual size of the abscess or boil that has formed. But when proper treatment is begun early enough, there is a good chance for stopping the infection before it becomes severe.

Sometimes earaches occur even when the ear itself is healthy. If your child complains of an earache, he should have his teeth, nose, throat, and voice box (larynx) examined as possible sources of his pain. A pain in the ear may be associated with an unerupted wisdom tooth, infection of the sinuses, or a bad case of tonsillitis.

Earache is seldom caused by wax in the ear. Some children produce a large amount of the stuff, just as others perspire freely. Wax in the ear should not be regarded as an accumulation of dirt; it is actually a natural body secretion.

If while swimming or bathing a plug of ear wax is moistened, a child's hearing may be affected, causing temporary deafness. Prompt removal of the wax by a physician will cure this type of defect. NOAH D. FABRICANT

See also ABSCESS; COLDS

EAR, FOREIGN OBJECTS IN

Doctors have a bit of advice: "Never put anything smaller than an elbow into your ear." This is a sound suggestion, for objects inserted into the ear can cause trouble.

Children are prone to put such things as peas, beans, or corn kernels into their ears. These vegetables swell, causing intense pain. Beads, buttons, and stones also find their way into the ears of small children. Although such objects do not swell, they may irritate the ear and cause acute discomfort. Sometimes an insect will lodge itself in a child's ear.

Fortunately, most foreign objects rarely cause trouble by themselves unless the eardrum is injured. If your child has something in his ear, don't try to remove it yourself. Often just the attempt to remove a foreign object results in injury. Your doctor has the proper knowledge and skill to remove a foreign object safely from the ear. He should be consulted promptly. NOAH D. FABRICANT

See also EARACHE

Related article in WORLD BOOK: "Ear"

EAR INFECTION *See* EARACHE

EATING *See* APPETITE; EATING PROBLEMS; INTRODUCING NEW FOODS; NUTRITION

EATING BETWEEN MEALS

There's nothing wrong with letting your child have food regularly between the customary widely spaced three meals a day. He may need more than three meals a day to keep him from showing irritability, fatigue, or other side-effects of hunger.

Feeding a child between meals simply means that you have found it advantageous to redistribute the day's total food. Giving smaller and more frequent meals has been shown in nursery schools to result in happier and healthier children.

Most children should be given between-meal feedings routinely. It's also important to see that each in-between meal contains a high-protein food, just as breakfast, lunch, and dinner should. Milk, cheese, meat, or peanut butter sandwiches, because of their high-protein content, will help satisfy the appetite for an adequate period of time. On the other hand, foods such as cookies, cake, candy, and sweet drinks pile up calories without having a long-term effect on curbing hunger.

The habit of eating sweet foods between meals as snacks or simply to relieve boredom may become an undesirable one. Candy and other sweets are not good between-meal foods and can contribute to overweight and tooth decay. MIRIAM E. LOWENBERG

See also NUTRITION

EATING PROBLEMS

Eating problems generally arise because of conflict between individuals. When children have an eating problem, the conflict is between the child who is being presented the food to eat and the adult, usually the mother, who is presenting it.

This conflict comes about naturally because the adult, usually the mother, knows what foods a child needs and attempts to impose her will on him. But she may have only limited knowledge of how her child feels about the food she is asking him to eat. She forgets that his feelings must always be taken into account.

Preventing Eating Problems

These are some of the steps that parents have found successful in avoiding eating problems:

- The mother or perhaps both parents decide what their goals are. Do they want their child to eat an adequate diet at all costs? Or do they wisely hope that he will learn to like most of the foods that together make up an adequate diet for a growing child?
- They then decide that they will *consistently* work toward the accomplishment of their goals. Consistency and persistence are indeed necessary here.
- The parents also decide that they will try to understand how their child feels about the goals they have set. If a quart of milk per day seems to be too much, they will revise their goals. Or perhaps they will separate the immediate from the long-term goals. Suppose at a given stage a child can drink only one-fourth of a glass of milk comfortably. The mother who understands would give him that much, but she would also have more milk available, perhaps in a small pitcher nearby, so that when he is ready, he can ask for more. With this technique many children who would refuse one large glass of milk will voluntarily drink their daily quota. Children usually set higher goals for themselves and fulfill them willingly when they have a voice in the matter.
- The child is not commanded to eat. Personalities are left out, and there is no "Eat this because I say so." The parent simply presents the food a child needs. This approach automatically avoids an interpersonal conflict.
- No issue is made if someday the child rebels violently. Temporary avoidance of an issue over a specific meal or food is far better than matching wits or physical strength.
- A young child must save face. He should be allowed, for instance, to say that he will not eat a certain food. This refusal can be passed over at the time. Later, the calm adult can allow him to eat the food without vindictive comment. Children who have refused food can be given to understand that when they want the food at another time, they can have it, and that they will not be reminded that they had previously refused it.
- Food is served attractively and in small portions. New foods are always introduced in small quantities, with popular foods forming the rest of the meal.
- Eating utensils are adapted to the age of the child. Plates and cups are in attractive colors. Bowls are of a depth a child finds suitable. Handles of spoons are easy to grasp and hold.
- Self-feeding is permitted and encouraged even though some spilling may result.
- The child's eating habits are not discussed in his presence.
- The parents remember certain facts about nutrition: Not every nutrient has to be given at every meal; it is the over-all pattern that counts. The child knows how much food he can eat at a given time. Some foods will frequently be accepted better if combined, as milk or eggs used in a custard. Different children have different-sized appetites. Many children eat as much food as adults and others eat far less. Also, an individual child's appetite may change from time to time. He usually wants less to eat when he is teething or when he is tired or ill. It is also characteristic of the 2- to 3-year-old occasionally to lose interest in food. Forcing food when the appetite is flagging can often mean the beginning of an eating problem.

- Parents should act as though eating successes were expected, but there is no need for effusive compliments. Children are quick to observe sincerity in adults.
- Family mealtime is a time to enjoy one another's company and to talk about many things other than food, none of which should embarrass a child.
- A child likes to eat unobtrusively without being pointed out as "good" or "bad" for what he has eaten. Food is nourishment for the body and not a sign of being good or bad. The moralistic attitude toward eating confuses a child, and there is really no basis for saying, "Be a good boy and eat your vegetables."

All the rules that apply to avoiding eating problems also apply to trying to cure them. In addition, it is wise to remember that:

- Every child is different, and no general "golden" remedy can be suggested to cause him to eat an adequate diet happily. He should be understood as a person. If parents proceed on the basis that "behavior is caused" and "the child has his reasons," progress in understanding him can usually be made.
- The parent who relaxes about family meals and expects to enjoy them can concentrate on understanding her child and not on his eating problems. Problems do not often occur under these circumstances.
- No matter how little he is eating, a child must be reached at the level where he is. If, for instance, he has been refusing almost all foods and wants an entire lunch of only mashed potatoes, he may certainly be allowed to eat only mashed potatoes. At later meals, other foods can be casually offered. MIRIAM E. LOWENBERG

See also APPETITE; FEEDING SCHEDULES; INTRODUCING NEW FOODS; NUTRITION

ECZEMA

When a child eats something or when his skin comes in contact with something to which he is sensitive, he may get a skin disorder called eczema. Eczema is therefore thought to be an allergic reaction, and children thus afflicted usually have a history of some allergic ailment in the family, although the ailment need not have been eczema. A child's eczema often begins in early infancy and usually starts on his cheeks. It may continue until there are raw, weeping lesions over much of his body. The condition is not contagious.

Eczema is difficult to manage, so it is best not to let it get started. New foods should be introduced singly and gradually. Then, if a rash develops, it is easy to identify the offending food and stop giving it. More complicated detective work may be necessary to find and eliminate offending materials such as wool, silk, rabbit hair, or soap.

The rash usually itches intensely; babies rub the lesions and thus aggravate the condition. If the rash is extensive, wet dressings are usually applied and changed frequently. Since this treatment may be difficult in the home, hospital care is sometimes advised. Medicines may be given to provide relief from itching and consequent rest for the child. Drugs are sometimes quite helpful, but they must be used cautiously and only under the direction of a physician.

Eczema requires early and careful treatment, for a severe and extensive case can slow down a child's growth and can even have considerable undesirable psychological effect on him. When eczema is allowed to become chronic, it tends to localize in the elbows and backs of the knees; the skin becomes dry, thick, scaly, and sometimes cracked. A child who has eczema in any form should be under the care of a physician, who may advise consultation with a skin specialist or an allergist. JULIUS B. RICHMOND

See also ALLERGY; SHOTS

EDUCATIONAL TOYS *See* TOYS AND PLAY EQUIPMENT

EDUCATION, PARENT *See* BOOKS FOR PARENTS; PARENT EDUCATION

ELECTRIC SHOCK

Electric shock is much easier to prevent than to treat. When a child is the victim of electric shock, it is usually because an adult has forgotten how curious and investigative a child can be, or because the adult has not realized how little a child knows of danger or caution. To a child, an electric outlet is a fascinating hole in the wall, just right for poking with a stray bobby pin. To a child, an appliance cord is for pulling—he doesn't know that it may be faulty. To a child, it is quite possible that he can find Lassie by poking into the rear of the TV set. In the mind of a child who sees a radio in the bathroom, there is no conceivable relationship between water and electricity and death.

Make your home safe, keep your eye on your child, and let him understand that in dealing with certain dangers your "No" means "Positively not!" Even the crawler learns to stay away from plugs if you repeatedly pick him up, say a firm "No," remove him to another spot, and hand him a distracting toy.

But if, in spite of all reasonable precautions, your child becomes the victim of electric shock, remember that while seconds count, it won't help to be careless of your own safety. If you find him in contact with an electric wire and unable to let go, keep calm. Pull the main switch if it is near, or jerk the plug from the socket. But do not touch either the hot wire or the victim with your bare hands while electricity is still flowing. If you can't turn it off, throw a piece of cloth or newspaper around the wire or use a stick, and pull with that. If you have to pull the child away from the wire, again use folds of cloth or newspaper, heavy gloves or tested rubber ones, or poles, boards, or branches—anything—just so it is a nonconductor and dry, and just so you are standing on a dry surface.

Electric shock stops the victim's respiration and sometimes his heart. Artificial respiration should be begun immediately while the doctor is being called. If an electric spark has caused a burn, treat it later as you would any other burn. W. W. BAUER

See also ARTIFICIAL RESPIRATION; BURN; EMERGENCY

ELEMENTARY SCHOOL *See* SCHOOL-AGE CHILD

ELIMINATION *See* BED-WETTING; CONSTIPATION; DIARRHEA; TOILET TRAINING; URINARY DISTURBANCES

EMERGENCY

In any emergency the most important advice is also the most difficult to follow—*keep calm; don't panic!*

It helps greatly to think over the kinds of parent-child emergencies you may be called upon to meet before they happen. Having faced them mentally and planned a course of action, you are less likely to panic and are more apt to do the right things.

The most common single home emergency involving children, according to records of the American Red Cross, is internal poisoning resulting from an overdose of flavored aspirin or other common medication. Next come falls, and then injuries caused by articles falling or tipping onto the child. The obvious solution to all these common accidental emergencies is prevention. Keep medicines locked in the medicine chest, out of reach of children. Safety-inspect your home, put up stairway guards and use them, and don't stack or pile heavy things haphazardly.

Emergencies caused by illness—as opposed to accident—involving children are likely to be high fever, convulsions, or appendicitis. For any of these, immediate treatment by a doctor is needed. While waiting for the doctor to arrive, keep the child quiet, in bed, warm but not overheated. Do not give him a hot-water bottle or a laxative or an enema or any medication except on competent medical advice.

When an emergency does occur, remember that help is at hand—in the contents of your first-aid kit, in your medicine cabinet, and via the telephone.

If another adult or an older child can help, one person should care for the patient while the other telephones for the doctor. If you are alone, quiet the patient as quickly as possible, administer urgently needed first aid, then telephone immediately. The doctor will want to know the nature of the injury or illness as completely as possible; the child's temperature, if you have been able to take it; and what you have already done. Be prepared to answer his questions quickly and accurately. Calling an ambulance or making hospital arrangements will usually be handled by the doctor. For night emergencies or when your own doctor is not available, call the police department, the fire department, or simply dial "0" and tell the operator the nature of your emergency. ROBERT E. KILBRIDE

See also ARTIFICIAL RESPIRATION; DOCTOR; FIRST AID

EMETICS

An emetic is a medicine or other substance that causes vomiting. Vomiting, however, is *most undesirable* if: (*a*) the patient is asleep or has convulsions; (*b*) a corrosive substance is involved (lye, ammonia, bleach, toilet-bowl cleaner); (*c*) a petroleum product is involved (kerosene, turpentine, lighter fluid, liquid furniture polish, waxes).

Vomiting is the preferred treatment in most cases of poisoning due to eating substances other than food. It is an excellent first-aid measure and is more effective than pumping the stomach.

You can get various emetic agents. The best is sirup (*not fluid extract*) of ipecac. If you don't have this preparation, you can use dry mustard or strong salt solutions. Actually, if none of these are available, you can make the child vomit by finger-tickling the back of the throat. If you try this procedure, protect your finger by placing some blunt object between the patient's jaws. Any time vomiting is induced, be sure to keep the patient's head lower than his hips so that all the vomitus will flow out of the mouth and not back into his throat. Catch and save the vomited matter for the doctor to analyze.

Vomiting is more effective if the patient is first made to drink some liquid. But remember, *be sure* of the kind of poison before inducing vomiting. IRVING SUNSHINE

See also POISONING AND POISONS

EMOTIONAL DEVELOPMENT

It is no news to mothers that even the littlest children are capable of getting all worked up about things, into a thoroughly aroused emotional state. During early infancy a baby most frequently expresses this inner excitement and tension by crying. Then as the months and years pass, he learns other ways to express his feelings. He learns certain kinds of emotional control. Both emotional expression and emotional control are learned through living closely with other people.

A newborn child's emotional life is very simple. When awake, he is either quiet or excited. When excited, he shows either a kind of delight or distress. At first, his distress signals are all pretty much alike, but as he gains greater control of his body, he learns that the more specifically he expresses his needs, the quicker help arrives.

Then an infant grows to be a toddler, and the ways in which he can express emotion change accordingly. He learns how to stamp his foot, bang his head, hold his breath, bite, and show other physical signs of rage and frustration, sometimes to the dismay and embarrassment of his parents. Eventually, the toddler is taught that physical aggression is not acceptable, but at just about this same time, he learns to speak and fortunately can air his feelings that way. The ability to speak well enough to let others know how he feels is a great boon to the 3- and 4-year-old.

A parent can learn much about emotions by watching his preschool child. At this age, reactions come immediately; they are direct, and the causes of them are fairly obvious. Angry, tearful outbursts result when a child cannot get something he wants—affection or attention or another child's toy. Fear arises when he is in any uncomfortable situation that he doesn't know how to get out of; love and affection well up in response to rather unexpected good fortune, such as a new toy or a hug. The child this age knows no other more appropriate ways to behave; he knows little of judgment and reason, so his feelings are likely to dictate his behavior.

Gradually, as a result of experience with adults and more especially with other youngsters, a child begins to suppress direct emotional expression. He learns that "big boys and girls" do not cry over every little thing or get scared easily. He learns to conceal anger—not to "take it out" on the source of the problem. He learns not to smash things because they do not work just right and not to hurt people whenever they get in his way. To some extent, of course, this kind of growing up has to happen if children are to live comfortably in society, but it must be remembered that the gradual disappearance of tantrums and "I hate you's" does not mean the end of strong feelings and emotional difficulties in the life of a child. He does become more experienced as he gets older, but he also becomes more aware. And with awareness there are happenings going on all around him that frighten or anger him, happenings he did not notice when he was younger.

A child needs to be reassured that even though civility demands self-control, emotions are legitimate and should be expressed. One important step in guiding a child is to teach him when and how to express his feelings, good or bad, and to assure him that these same feelings build up, from time to time, in everyone. ARMIN GRAMS

See also INDIVIDUAL DIFFERENCES; MENTAL HEALTH; SOCIAL DEVELOPMENT

ENCEPHALITIS *See* SLEEPING SICKNESS

ENCYCLOPEDIA *See* BOOKS FOR CHILDREN

ENDOCRINE GLANDS

Although small in size, the endocrine glands are very important because they produce vital chemical substances called hormones. Hormones regulate various functions of the body. Endocrine glands are also called the ductless glands because their hormones enter the blood stream directly instead of reaching it through ducts, as secretions from other glands do.

The "master" endocrine gland is the pituitary. It is located at the base of the brain, to which it connects by a short stalk. This gland, approximately the size of the end of your thumb, produces many hormones. One of these regulates a child's growth; other glands regulate the activity of other endocrine glands—thyroid, adrenal, pancreatic, and sexual glands.

The thyroid gland, situated in the midline of the neck, produces thyroid hormone, which regulates the general level of chemical activity, or metabolism, of the body. The adrenal glands, situated just above each kidney, produce hormones that regulate growth, sexual development, sugar metabolism, and the use of salt by the body. Part of the pancreatic gland produces insulin, which regulates the use of sugar within the body. The sexual glands produce hormones that, particularly in adolescent years, affect growth and the development of masculine or feminine characteristics. JULIUS B. RICHMOND

See also GROWTH

Related article in WORLD BOOK: "Gland"

ENEMA

An enema is a means of introducing a rather large amount of fluid into the intestine through the rectum, having it remain there for a short time, and then having it expelled. Enemas are given in the hospital when it is necessary to make the bowel as empty as possible, particularly before surgery. Occasionally, enemas are given in order to introduce medicine, but only in unusual situations.

Home enemas are rarely used, since they often increase the difficulties by producing a considerable loss of fluids. During illness the few situations in which they might be used are chiefly those in which something mildly poisonous has been eaten and its rapid elimination is important. In any case, the use of an enema during any kind of illness would depend entirely on the doctor's advice.

Enemas as a treatment for constipation are almost never used today except in the rare case of an impaction (a severe piling up of feces in the bowel). They should not be used as treatment for ordinary and chronic constipation, since they almost always help convert a mild constipation into a severe problem. Enemas produce bowel movement by severe irritation and stretching of the bowel lining. Irritation may last for several hours but is usually followed by a period during which the bowel has a tendency to react less than usual. Thus, regular use of enemas will tend to destroy the healthy muscle tone of the bowel and make constipation a much more severe problem.

There is another reason why enemas are not a good idea on a regular basis. They are not only uncomfortable physically, but they also often are quite disturbing psychologically to a young child. They may be frightening, but after regular and prolonged use they can even become pleasurable and serve to concentrate attention on the bowel in an unhealthy and undesirable way. Since constipation is best treated by dietary means, increased exercise, and attention to the child's bowel habits, the complications resulting from the regular home use of enemas are totally unnecessary. RUTH S. KEMPE

See also CONSTIPATION; TOILET TRAINING

ENURESIS *See* BED-WETTING

ENVIRONMENT *See* GROWTH; HEREDITY; MENTAL HEALTH

EPILEPSY

Most children who have epilepsy are in every other way perfectly normal. Epilepsy is not inherited, as such, although there may be a family tendency toward the disease, just as there may be toward diabetes or disabilities of the heart. There is no such thing as an epileptic type of personality.

An infant whose temperature rises to around 105° F. may go into a fit of unconsciousness, with violent spasms or movements of the body. This is known as a convulsion. If the child is younger than 3 or 4, and if the convulsions occur only with a fever, and not too often, it can be expected that they will stop. If the convulsions or seizures occur without fever and continue after the child is older, the doctor will think of epilepsy.

Medical science has recently discovered greatly improved treatment for epilepsy. It is important that any child suffering from convulsions have immediate medical attention. Parents should be completely frank in describing the child's convulsion, in reporting head injuries or illnesses involving high fevers, and in recalling any history of convulsions in the family. The doctor, who seldom is able to observe the seizure, will need this information and the results of diagnostic tests to make a proper diagnosis. He probably will request an electroencephalograph study, which is a painless tracing of brain waves or impulses of the nervous system. Treatment is usually more successful if the convulsion is associated with a family tendency rather than from brain injury. Modern drugs can eliminate or reduce seizures in about 85 per cent of the patients, but some time may be required to determine the proper combinations and dosage of drugs. Success of the treatment for epilepsy will depend largely upon how carefully and continually the doctor's instructions for controlling the disease are followed.

The two most common types of epileptic seizures are known as *grand mal* and *petit mal.* When the patient suffers a grand mal seizure, he loses consciousness, falls, and his muscles may stiffen or become rigid. He will then begin to twitch and jerk, first rapidly, then more slowly but more violently. Saliva may flow more freely during convulsions and not be swallowed, and bowel and bladder control sometimes is lost. The convulsions usually last only a few minutes, although the patient may frequently remain drowsy and perhaps will sleep for a time. There is not much to do for a child suffering an epileptic seizure—place a coat or folded blanket under his head and remove objects from the path of moving arms and legs. A folded handkerchief may be placed between the teeth to keep him from biting his tongue or cheek.

In a minor, or petit mal, seizure consciousness is lost for a few seconds, but balance is maintained and the patient does not fall. Afterward, he may appear dazed momentarily; then he resumes conversation or normal activity. The frequency of petit mal seizures, perhaps dozens in a single day, will interfere more with learning than will the infrequent grand mal seizures.

Epileptic children need the same affectionate guidance, patient understanding, and satisfactions from life that all children need.

Epilepsy itself is usually not a serious handicap, but the attitudes of the child's playmates and of adults may create difficulties. The parents of an epileptic child are wise to let friends and neighbors know of their child's condition, and to give them accurate information about epilepsy.

The epileptic child can usually go to school. Cooperation between the principal, the teacher, the school nurse, and the parents is extremely important. A note from the child's doctor will also be helpful to school personnel if the child should have a seizure at school and need help.

Some school systems provide special services of one sort or another for pupils with epilepsy, but usually, with the improved control of seizures now possible, these children attend regular classes. Unfortunately, there are still communities where school officials appear to be uncooperative and where medical services are not readily available for children whose seizures are rather severe. A local doctor or medical society can usually assist parents who seek help for their child. In extreme cases, however, parents may have to consider state-supported institutions, which will provide protection and lifetime care if it is necessary. JOHN W. TENNY

See also COMMUNITY RESOURCES; HANDICAPPED CHILD

ETIQUETTE *See* MANNERS

EVAPORATED MILK *See* BOTTLE FEEDING

EXAMINATIONS *See* SCHOOL TESTS AND EXAMINATIONS

EXCEPTIONAL CHILD *See* GIFTED CHILD; HANDICAPPED CHILD; SLOW LEARNER

EXCUSES

Everyone, at some time or other, tries to avoid the consequences of his own hasty or ill-advised actions. Understanding this, and accepting—with straight face and good conscience—a child's occasional alibi is perfectly all right. It is nevertheless important to help a child realize that an *excuse* is at best a defensive explanation, while a *reason* describes an unavoidable circumstance. It is important to help a child to acknowledge responsibility and be able to take the consequences of his actions.

When a child consistently breaks his word, comes home late, avoids his chores, and always has a ready explanation, someone had better examine the whole family atmosphere. Perhaps there is something to which the child is reacting. Perhaps the youngster feels the pressure of too many demands. If this is the case, fewer demands may be the answer. While lessening the demands, parents can see to it that the child is living up to his reduced responsibilities. Perhaps reprimand or punishment is unnecessarily harsh so that a child frantically uses any excuse out of fear. In this case, the important thing is to treat the lateness or the undone work as unfortunate but not fatal. Taking the attitude that accidents sometimes happen, that all people are occasionally late through honest forgetting, or that they may slip up on homework when the weather tempts them to postpone it too long will make it easier for a child to feel that his parents are fair and reasonable people to whom he can admit a mistake. This does not eliminate firmness. A child who is consistently late coming home from visits to friends may indeed need to be kept at home for a day so that his memory will work better the next time. But even punishments can be handled in a spirit of learning rather than vindictiveness.

Parents can also help their children by being straightforward about their own shortcomings. Many a child learns to be glib and inventive right in his own home. Father insists someone else left the basement light on —mother, that someone else left the milk out of the refrigerator.

It is especially important to maintain an approach of strictest honesty when writing excuses to a child's teacher. Many a parent who gets angry or anxious about his child's free-wheeling alibis will gloss over facts so that the child will not get into trouble with his teacher. Here, as in so many other things, parental example speaks louder than parental words. IRMA S. BLACK AND JOAN W. BLOS

See also RESPONSIBILITY

EXTROVERT-INTROVERT

Extrovert and introvert are terms used to describe two opposite extremes of personality. Every human being must have these two basic attitudes available—and flexibly—if he is to do well in life. He possesses the two in varying degrees at all times, though the amount of each will vary with his situation in life and with the different periods of his life.

The newborn infant, for example, has little interest in the external world; he is mostly concerned with his inner life, though it is still mostly vegetative. At this stage he is mostly an introvert. But from the moment of birth until grade-school age, a child turns more and more toward the outer world, and in this sense becomes more and more of an extrovert. From 4 to 10, given half a chance, he is typically full of curiosity about the world and what is in it, reaching out eagerly to one and all. Being an extrovert comes naturally to him at this time of life. But with the onset of puberty, many children become moody, more withdrawn into themselves—they become more introverted. Then in adolescence the pattern changes again. The normal adolescent swings back and forth from great extroversion to great introversion. And the fully mature person, though actively interested in making his place in the external world, may do so in widely different ways. Even within a single occupational group there is room for both—those who are mainly extroverted and others who are just as strongly introverted. The aggressive salesman who goes out after people and the quiet bookkeeper at his desk—each has his important place in life. But as they grow old, they will both withdraw some interest from the external world and again become more interested in their inner selves; life seems to end, normally, on a more introverted level, just as it began with a self-centered attitude. These, of course, are very broad generalizations. Independent of age, and depending on mood and situation, every person becomes more of one and less of the other.

Extroversion thus refers to an individual's tendency to turn outward rather than inward in coping with his needs and the demands the world makes of him. Extroversion implies a preoccupation with action, things, people, and all that pertains to the external environment rather than to inner emotions, feelings, and fantasies. Since both extroversion and introversion are needed for normal living, too much of one or the other can be undesirable. Yet most people expect their children always to be friendly, outgoing, cheerful. This tendency of parents to wish their children to be more extroverted than introverted can create an imbalance in the child's emotional make-up. An extroverted reaching out to the world, while desirable up to a point, can become undesirable if it leads to a drying up of the inner fantasy world, to an inability to live with oneself without constant external stimulation. Also, the typical extrovert tends to react to the external world only in direct ways. It is not a sign of mental health if a person is always outgoing, always cheerful, never fazed by any difficulties in living. Likely as not, he is overcompensating for depressive feelings that are closed in and denied, and that might have to break out forcefully sometime. As always, mental health resides in a middle area between the extremes.

Introversion is the tendency to seek satisfaction of one's needs by turning inward rather than looking for satisfactions in the outer world. It is that inwardness which alone allows an individual to interpret events in a deeply personal way—an inwardness he needs to preserve his inner psychic continuity. Things go wrong only if the introvert becomes so preoccupied with his own feelings, fantasies, and thought processes that he is no longer in full contact with outside reality. The always quiet, always obedient, always well-behaved child may well be too strongly introverted. This is undesirable if it is his preeminent attitude at the expense of all or most extroverted attitudes. Extreme introversion is as much a sign of emotional disturbance as extreme extroversion. BRUNO BETTELHEIM

See also INDIVIDUAL DIFFERENCES; MENTAL HEALTH; SHYNESS AND TIMIDITY

EYE, FOREIGN OBJECTS IN

By far the most common accident to a child's eye is that of a small foreign body sticking to the surface. This can happen to children at play or simply while walking in the wind. Because the condition is so painful, your child will tell you immediately if he has something in his eye. Your baby cannot tell you, but he may cry and rub his eyes. Most often such foreign substances will be washed out in a few moments by the child's own tears, which will be stimulated to flow more rapidly by the irritant. If the foreign object does not wash out, it is very important to seek professional care. Many amateur attempts to remove seemingly trivial foreign bodies have resulted in appreciable loss of sight, usually from infection. You should not attempt to remove the foreign body with the corner of a handkerchief or allow anyone else to do so. See a doctor.

If an eye is injured by an object such as a dart, an arrow, or a knife, it is vital that no one touch the eye except a trained person, nor should anything be put into the eye. Many an eye has been lost from attempts of untrained persons to open the lid of a severely injured eye. The eye should be covered and the patient taken gently to a doctor or a clinic where he can be given professional medical care.

Most of these tragic accidents are preventable. Dangerous objects such as fireworks, slingshots, BB guns, and sharp scissors should be kept out of the hands of children too young to understand danger. ROY O. SCHOLZ

EYEGLASSES

One out of four 6-year-olds who have eye examinations will be found to need glasses.

They are, therefore, worn by so many children that they are accepted casually in most cases. Some children are even very proud to wear them.

The need for glasses may be determined by an ophthalmologist (medical eye doctor) who will use drops in order to do the most accurate examination possible. Even an infant's needs (and some babies do need glasses) can be determined by examining his eyes after he has been anesthetized.

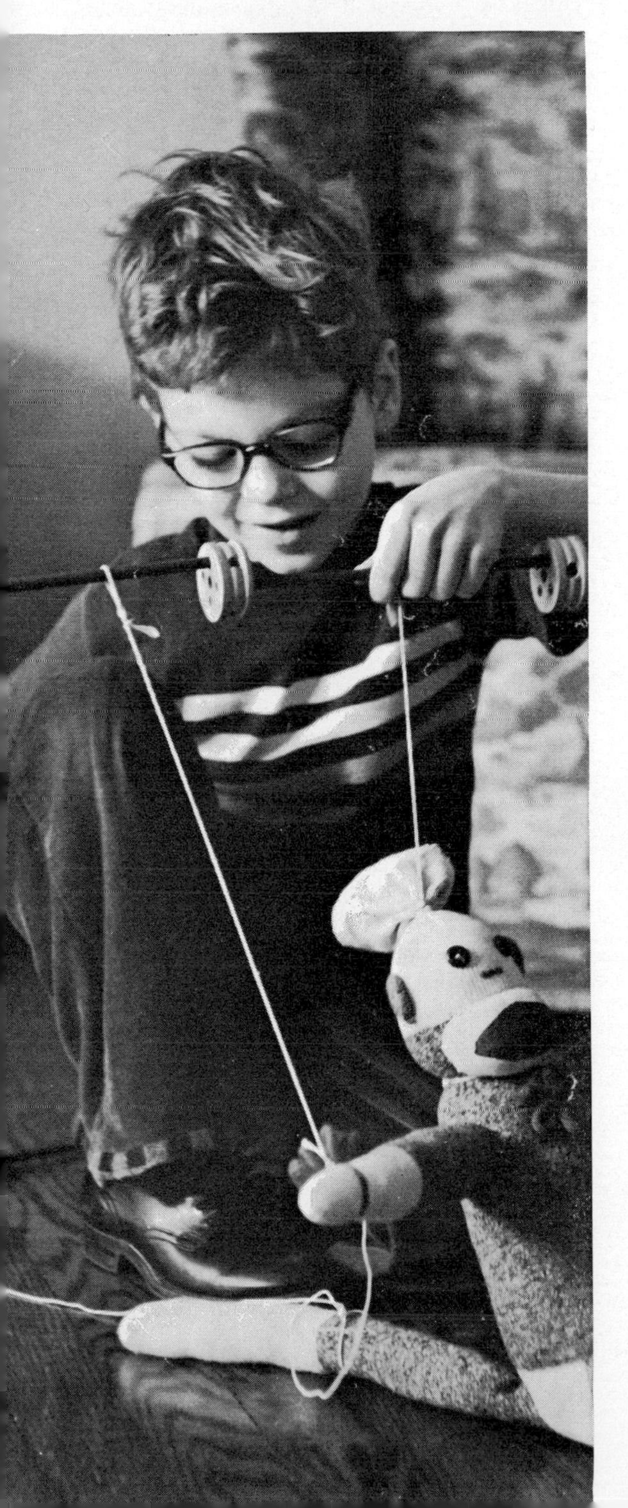

Remember that glasses make a child comfortable and enable him to see well, but they do not change the condition for which the glasses were prescribed. Nor will wearing glasses increase his need for them.

While a child should be encouraged to keep his glasses reasonably clean, it is not necessary to make a fetish of polishing off each fleck of dust. He should, however, be instructed not to put his glasses face down on any surface, for spectacle glass scratches easily and replacement is expensive.

Children who wear glasses need them through no fault of their own. Their glasses will be broken on occasion, particularly at play. Do not punish a child for breaking his glasses; adults break their glasses, too, in the normal course of living. So, grin, bear it, and replace them as soon as possible.

The child who needs glasses plays more happily and more safely if he wears his glasses. Doctors rarely find glass in the eyes of children who break them at play. For this reason, children are not usually given lenses of safety glass, although your own doctor is the best judge of whether or not your child should wear safety glasses.

Your eye physician will prescribe glasses only if they are required and will be delighted to remove them if your child outgrows the need for them. Be sure he returns for a re-examination when the doctor has asked him to, for a change in power of the glasses may be in order; the wrong strength may be worse than no glasses. ROY O. SCHOLZ

EYE HEALTH

A good general rule for the care of normal eyes is to leave them alone except for periodic medical examinations. When eyes seem abnormal in any respect, diagnosis and treatment should be made by an ophthalmologist (medical eye doctor). Self-diagnosis and self-treatment of eye disorders can be disastrous.

Contrary to popular opinion, there are no known exercises that will alter nearsightedness, farsightedness, or defective color vision. The use of lotions is unnecessary, for tears normally cleanse the eyes.

Furthermore, because of the varied diet available in the United States, vitamins or special foods are rarely of specific value in the treatment of eye disorders or in the development of normal eyes.

When your newborn baby cries, there are no tears and there won't be until he is from a few weeks to several months old. The eyes of infants produce only enough tears to keep them moist. When tears do flow, they drain through two small openings in the lid margins into a tiny sac and thence enter the nose, causing it to "run." Occasionally, this tear system will become blocked and tears will constantly run over the edges of the lids, or there may be a swelling of the tear sac at the inner corner of the eye near the nose. This disorder calls for medical treatment.

In the first few weeks of life a baby's eyes frequently look crossed at times and straight at other times. There is no need to be alarmed over this lack of eye coordination. But if at the age of 6 months a baby's eyes are constantly out of line, they should be examined by a physician. Treatment started early can often do away with the need for surgery.

All children should be examined by an eye physician before they enter the first grade. One out of four children will need help with a visual problem.

In most states children are given visual screening tests as they enter school. Through the use of these tests, a tremendous number of poorly functioning eyes have been found and given correction. Such tests, however, because they are usually given by teachers or parents, who necessarily lack the skill or knowledge of a medical eye examiner, cannot be substituted for a medical eye examination. Have an eye physician examine your child as he enters first grade and again every two years thereafter to be sure that he does not have an eye difficulty that the school eye test could not find.

In addition to the need for a routine eye test, there are other reasons for taking your child to an eye physician. Be alert to these danger signals:

DANGER SIGNALS

- Frequently stumbles or bumps into furniture
- Squints, frowns, blinks excessively while reading
- Holds reading very close
- Becomes overtired when he uses his eyes
- Continually moves closer to television in order to see (He should be able to enjoy television from a distance of eight or more feet.)

If you observe any of these or other distress signs, including sore or unusually red eyes or eyelids, consult your doctor.

Cataracts occur only on rare occasions in children. A cataract appears as a white spot in the pupil. If you see such a spot, take your child to a physician.

Needless to say, a child must see well in order to be able to learn well. But if his eyes have tested normal and his IQ is normal and he still is having difficulty in reading, there is perhaps an emotional problem. Some children who see the words clearly find it almost impossible, because of emotional difficulties, to understand their meanings.

Good lighting and correct posture make for more efficient use of the eyes and often will prevent eye discomfort. Do not restrict reading to save your child's eyesight. Restriction can actually prevent full development of his visual ability, which like muscular ability improves with practice and use.

Distinct contrasts in lighting may contribute to fatigue, as when a child watches television in a darkened room or studies at a desk where a single lamp leaves the rest of the room in darkness. Some other light should be on in the room.

Of the approximately 95,000 serious eye accidents that happen to children each year, about a thousand are severe enough to cause complete loss of sight in one or both eyes. Most of these accidents could have been prevented. Sharp-pointed scissors should not be given to children, nor should arrows or BB guns be put in the hands of children too immature to understand the dangers involved in their use.

If, in spite of your precautions, your child's eye is injured, it should not be touched by anyone except a trained person, nor should liquid be put into the eye. Gently cover the injured eye and take the patient to a doctor or to the clinic, where the injury will be given professional care. ROY O. SCHOLZ

See also ASTIGMATISM; CROSS-EYE; EYEGLASSES; EYELID, DISEASES OF; FARSIGHTEDNESS; NEARSIGHTEDNESS

Related article in WORLD BOOK: "Eye"

EYELID, DISEASES OF

The eyelids protect and clean the eyes. The eyelashes screen dust and dirt from the eyes.

Disorders of the eyelids are usually shown by redness or swelling. There may be tumors or notches in the lids. A red lid margin may be caused by a need for glasses or by an affliction similar to that seen when a person has dandruff. The glands of the lid or the eyelash follicles may become infected and cause what is called a sty. Any of these signs should be checked by a doctor who can determine the cause and give treatment. ROY O. SCHOLZ

See also CONJUNCTIVITIS; EYE HEALTH

FACTS OF LIFE *See* SEX EDUCATION

FADS *See* SLOPPINESS

FAILURE *See* SCHOOL FAILURE

FAILURE, FEAR OF

Parents' ambitions for their children to do well in school, in sports, in social contacts are normal in our culture. The baby's first steps bring beaming approval; his first sentences are a delight. There is every reason for a child to know from infancy how he can bring pleasure to his parents. But there comes a time, usually around 2 years, when he wants to please himself, too, ushering in a negative period sometimes hard to bear. Never does he lose sight, however, of his parents' expectations, and like most other children he strives to fulfill those expectations.

Parents should not expect too much too soon. A child is easily led on to trying new activities, such as climbing or swimming, when he is not forced beyond his readiness. Not every child, even in the same family, is ready at a given age. Forcing or pushing can put a child in reverse, and then some parents get discouraged and think more pressure rather than less is needed.

One way out for the child is to refuse to try, not because of fear of the activity itself but because of his dread of failing. To him, failing means displeasing his parents or his teacher. This mechanism is easily explained: A little girl failed in her first spelling lesson and went home crying, "My teacher doesn't love me anymore. I can't spell." A mother, looking disappointed when her 10-year-old son brought home a grade of 95, said, "Why can't you make a hundred?" Another lad was found crying late at night because with the bases loaded, he had struck out in a league game that afternoon—and his father had shouted in derision. All these children know better than their parents that "perfection" is an impossible goal. Improvement, yes, but not perfection.

Such parents can learn from the wise teacher who said to the youngsters in his arithmetic class. "It is all right to make a mistake; it is not all right if you do not learn how to correct it."

Little children think of failure as the inability to live up to their parents' ambitions; later, the child feels failure if he cannot keep up with his age group or with his expectations of himself.

The first time a child feels he has failed offers the occasion to help him. While he must have the experience of winning once in a while, he has to learn that not everyone can win the race; not everyone can win the prize in a competition. When he knows this truth, he is free to do his best even though he may not win. Many children lose because their eagerness to win gets in the way. HELEN ROSS

See also FEAR; READINESS

FAIRY TALES

Fairy tales are stories that have some element of the supernatural, such as fairies or "little people" or witches or animals and objects that talk and act like human beings. Myths, fables, and legends are also usually included in the broad term "fairy tale." Children themselves sometimes use the term to mean any kind of fiction.

Many fairy stories are part of the body of folklore handed down from one generation to another in song and story since before the days of printing. In addition, nearly all the great writers for children, including the modern ones, have written this appealing kind of literature. Hence, until a wave of "fact" books and realistic stories swept into the world of children's literature in the 1930's, fairy tales made up the major part of reading for most children.

Fairy stories have themes that occur over and over, no matter in which country the story originates. The beautiful peasant girl who, through her goodness and sweetness, and with a little help from a fairy godmother, marries the prince and the seemingly dull younger brother who outwits everyone and marries the princess are present in every country's folklore. The settings and details of the story reflect the customs of the country, and reading these stories helps children to understand that countries may be different but that people have many similarities the world over.

Moral lessons are plainly taught in fables in which animals retain their animal traits but talk and act like human beings. Valuable lessons are learned from nearly every kind of fairy story that within a highly imaginative setting makes observations on human behavior. Myths and legends that explain various occurrences in nature as primitive people reasoned them out are especially stimulating to the budding scientist.

Beautifully illustrated editions of fairy stories from many countries are available in libraries and bookstores. And some of the traditional editions of German, English, and French fairy tales known and loved by many adults in their own childhoods are still in print. A choice selection of these all-time favorites appears in Volume 2, *Fairy Tales*, pages 85–122. ELIZABETH S. MARGULIS

See also BOOKS FOR CHILDREN; COMICS; IMAGINATION; READINESS FOR READING

FAMILY DISCUSSIONS

Family meetings are held by a great number of parents and children and are not awesome affairs. Some families reserve a regular time to hold their get-togethers. Others have theirs at regular times but adjourn quickly if there isn't much to talk about. Some only call a meeting if a special something has come up of concern to everybody. Some families enjoy a good deal of formality, so they elect officers and have a set agenda at their councils. More informal families can discuss even the most serious items while the members—at least the younger ones—are sprawled comfortably on the floor. What most groups discover, regardless of the council's form, is that talking things over makes for more cooperation and unity. And that means a happier family.

Lots of children seem to enjoy a family get-together whose specific purpose is discussion. They feel important and equal and, as a result, quite communicative. The parents, when such discussions take place, get a chance not only to air their own points of view, but also to find out their children's—what they are thinking about, why they considered some parental decision unfair, in what ways they would like to help the whole family.

The family parley has two aims: (*a*) to come to decisions to *do* something—parents remain the final authority, but some decisions can be compromises, often acceptable to all, and (*b*) to acquaint the family members with the family's general principles, goals, problems, minor and major crises, and with all matters concerning the group or an individual in the group who needs the group's advice.

It goes without saying that everyone in the family, old enough to talk, can be invited to a conference. However, everyone does not have to take part in every conference. Some talks between parents aren't truly family conferences, for decisions arising out of such talks will simply be communicated to the children. Some discussions about money or mortgages might be over the heads of the younger children and only frighten them, whereas the same discussion could bring revelation and a warm sense of responsibility to an older child. Young members can be included in more and more discussions as they mature, as they learn reticence in public about intimate family affairs and are judged able to take on the responsibilities that go with privileges.

Everything and anything can be talked about in a family discussion, even gossip, but several important subjects keep coming up again and again—household finances, allowances, discipline, privileges, chores, recreation, entertainment, and vacations. Lucky parents with lucky children talk these things over freely, come to know each other better, to respect each other more, and to have more fun together. WILLIAM E. BLATZ

FAMILY HEALTH RECORD

When the doctor asks the young expectant mother whether she has ever had German measles, she is often unable to answer. Or when a child has a suspicious-looking sore throat, and the doctor asks whether he has received his diphtheria immunization, many a parent has a vague recollection that he got some kind of shots but cannot remember what they were.

Answers to such questions can be very important. For example, German measles in the first three months of a pregnancy can injure the unborn baby. And prompt treatment is important in other contagious diseases.

Later in life, an accurate knowledge of childhood diseases and their complications may help the doctor to assess the chronic condition of a patient more effectively than if he did not have this history. The medical "history" of a patient is so important that doctors often spend hours asking questions with which impatient patients can see no connection with their immediate pain or discomfort. When surgery has been performed, a knowledge of exactly what was done may become very important in later years.

For these reasons, physicians now advocate the keeping of a family health record in which the medical history and experiences of each member of the family can be entered while memory is still fresh and the doctor is still available for information.

In such a record would appear facts about any complications during birth, both as to mother and baby; immunizations; childhood

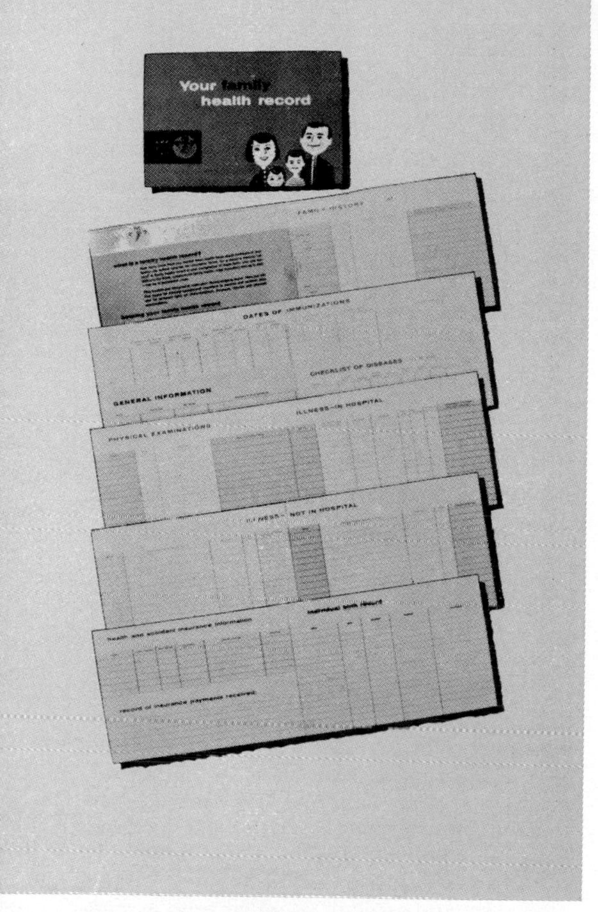

Your Family Health Record *published by the American Medical Association.*

diseases; injuries and their treatment; operations; allergies; drug sensitivities; and other pertinent information, all accurately dated. The American Medical Association has developed such a record; others have been published commercially and may be purchased in bookstores. W. W. BAUER

FAMILY LIVING

When someone says, "family," you usually think of father, mother, and children living together. "Family" also means parents and children plus grandparents, aunts, uncles, and cousins. In general, though, the people who live together in one home as the members of a group are a family in the sense that they matter the most to one another and form a solid unit.

Since marriages are built on love first rather than on considerations of wealth, social position, and parental wishes, a husband and wife expect tremendous emotional satisfaction from their life together. In countries where marriages are arranged by the elders, expectations are more modest and great love is a happy extra. In the United States, couples need the closeness of companionship and depth of love that they desire because they so often live in an impersonal world where their own small family is the one warm, acceptant, nurturing haven.

Parents live very closely with their children, giving and receiving intense love. How different from the casual feelings on a South Sea isle where every child calls all women mama, auntie, or grandma, and calls every contemporary brother or sister. Here in the United States there is only one mother, and she spends many hours alone with her babies and preschool children. She sometimes doesn't even have grandma to advise her and to hold the baby for a while, nor would she often heed grandma's advice. Very much on her own, the young woman feels the weight of responsibility and turns to her husband to share it.

Sharing is a key word in family living. Men and women are no longer very fussy about which job is male and which is female. In the seeking for closeness of the early years of marriage, the young couple do many homemaking jobs together. Later, they divide the work along more traditional lines, but each can pinch-hit for the other. Many women earn money outside the home, and the modern husband has adjusted considerably by sharing the housework.

Many failures in family life come because the impossible is expected. On the other hand, deep love, beautiful relationships, and great happiness do exist in many families where there is a realization that nothing can be perfect and where people do the best they can. Good relationships evolve because men, women, and children do the best they can. Great demands for unselfishness and self-control are placed on parents, since childhood and youth are held to be so important. Achieving justice and harmony in meeting the needs of both children and adults in the family is a constant challenge to parents, but even the challenge is fascinating and rewarding. RUSSELL C. AND MOLLIE S. SMART

See also BOOKS FOR PARENTS; FAMILY DISCUSSIONS; FATHER; GRANDPARENTS AND OTHER RELATIVES; LOVE; MOTHER; WORKING MOTHER

FAMILY SERVICE AGENCY

A local family service agency, staffed by caseworkers college trained for their jobs, helps the people of a community in numerous ways. Marital unhappiness, trouble with in-laws, unmanageable children, problems connected with illness, chronic budget worries, and teen-age problems are a sampling of the difficulties brought to family service agencies. The agency provides family counseling, working toward the improvement of family living and the prevention of family breakdown.

The family service agency is instituted and supported by citizens of a community who realize the need for this special kind of service. Voluntary contributions and support through community chest campaigns provide operating funds. Persons seeking help are charged a fee based on their ability to pay. But if a family is unable to pay any fee, the same service is given free of charge.

Family service agencies work closely with health, education, religious, and welfare services in the community they serve. Consultation and cooperation, all on a basis of strict confidence, are part of such an agency's effort to preserve family life and to raise family standards.

See also COMMUNITY RESOURCES

FANTASY *See* BOASTING; IMAGINARY COMPANION

FARSIGHTEDNESS (HYPEROPIA)

Eyes grow to various sizes, just as people grow to different heights, and a farsighted, or hyperopic, eye is merely one that has a shorter diameter from front to back than a normal eye. A slightly farsighted child will have little or no difficulty seeing. If an appreciable amount of farsightedness is present, the patient may have lowered visual acuity, and he will have to expend much greater effort to see. Farsightedness, if uncorrected, is one of the major causes of crossed eyes.

A farsighted eye will generally see well when tested at the beginning of a close task. After prolonged use of such an eye, either at schoolwork or at play, the image may become blurred and indistinct and the child experiences eye discomfort and headaches. The farsighted child may be inattentive and short-tempered after using his eyes for television, movies, or for close tasks. It is work for these children to see, and they, therefore, unconsciously will not use their eyes but would rather daydream. Farsightedness is the basic problem with some poor readers.

School vision tests often discover the farsighted, but school tests are no substitute for a regular examination by an ophthalmologist (medical eye doctor).

Once farsightedness is discovered and glasses are fitted and worn, the farsighted child will usually see well enough to improve in his schoolwork.

ROY O. SCHOLZ

See also EYE HEALTH

FATHER

There's nothing easy about being a good father—the hours are long, and many of those hours are spent far from home. But the pay is good. In fact, being a father is a richly rewarding experience compounded of the admiration of sons and the adoration of daughters, to say nothing of the shared love between the father and the mother of those sons and daughters.

In the nature of family life in our society, mother usually carries the major responsibility for the care and guidance of children, especially of the youngest. The father is out of the home working at his job all day, but mother is right on hand when the significant developments, especially of early childhood, take place. Yet father makes three broad kinds of contributions crucial to the good development of his children.

Fathers make the first of these contributions through spending as much time as possible directly with their children. Such direct participation is especially important today. The same forces that tend to pull fathers out of the home pull all men out of their children's lives. There is danger that youngsters will have almost all their important dealings with women until they reach the secondary school. This overly effeminate world is not good for boys. Boys need as many experiences with men as we can possibly provide. They need men, especially a father whom they adore, to set a pattern for them. Boys grow into manhood, in part through their physiological maturing but in large part also through seeing how men act and talk and work and plan, how they react to each other and how they react with women. The companionship of men, of a good father in particular, is an essential ingredient in a boy's growth to manhood.

Girls, too, need the companionship of their fathers. An overly effeminate world is not good for them either. Fathers, in fact, play a dual role in their daughters' development. By the contrast of their speed, strength, size, voice, muscles, fathers help their girls to know what they are not. Simultaneously,

they help their girls to know what men are like and how men respond.

Scheduling Time for Children

A father's time with his children may have to be limited to evenings, weekends, holidays. But many wise fathers try to schedule all the time they can in their busy lives for their children. They recognize that their children need experiences with them, both as a second person in the family and as a second sex, at all ages from infancy on. They take as much part as they can in the early experiences of family life: changing diapers, giving baths, feeding, pushing the baby carriage, playing with the baby. As children grow older, fathers consciously plan time for car rides with the youngsters, for walks, for games, for a story hour. As a minimum, they are glad to have the children around for conversation. In this way they know what is happening in their children's lives inside and outside school, and the children can hear their fathers chat about the important events in the wide world outside the family. Many wise fathers make the special effort to take children to their place of work to see what father does and where he does it.

Most fathers enjoy the hours they spend with their children. Fathers have a unique advantage over mothers in this regard. They usually are "something special" in a child's life, not tarnished by everyday contact. They often see children at their brightest and best and are in a prize position to enjoy their youngsters' language, their questions, their spontaneous and fresh responses.

A Member of the "Board"

This note of enjoyment is very important. Fathers do not have to be angels—ever-loving, ever-happy with their children—any more than mothers must be. Both fathers and mothers have a right to occasional moments of irritation. It is important, however, that both boys and girls see the man in their family as more than someone who is grumpy, irritable, harsh, stern, and punishing. This narrow picture of father, and of the sex he represents, sometimes develops when father's only dealings with his children are as the "court of last resort"—the final judge and punisher. This picture sometimes develops when a father spends time with his youngsters simply out of a sense of duty. He arrives home exhausted but plays a game he detests because he feels he should. Or he takes a child on a trip to the zoo when he wants nothing more than to rest his tired feet. The art of good family living lies in someone's knowing: Who is the fresher member of the team? Solutions cannot be found mechanically—now it is mother's turn, now it is father's turn—any more than good family living results when children hardly know they have a father, or a father hardly knows he has a child.

Fathers who make the time to be with their children learn that youngsters are trouble as well as fun. Boys and girls never stay "good" all the time. This important learning lays the foundation for the second contribution fathers make to their children's development. A father who keeps abreast of his child's development from the very start is an important and able member of the family's "Board of Directors."

Family life is managed much more wisely and children receive more sensitive guidance if mother and father together talk over a child's behavior and together make plans for the future. A "children's hour," usually after the youngsters are in bed, when the day's events can pass in review and be discussed, is one of the most significant times in good family life. Willing and thoughtful participation in such analyses is the second of father's major contributions to his children.

Father usually has the advantage of not having been physically or emotionally involved in the incidents as they occurred. In addition, mother and father are two different personalities. They are of two different sexes. Their daily work usually involves them in two different locations. New ideas and new approaches will emerge out of these differences which will be sounder than if the decisions were made by one alone. A mother may tend to become overprotective; father often can contribute a plug for a child's growing independence. A mother may tend to be overly patient; father may see more clearly that the child is ready for his next step. A mother may tend to magnify the importance of little events; father, hearing the story secondhand, may be able to add a needed grain of salt.

Wise fathers, of course, bring more than their common sense to such discussions. In addition to knowing their own children well, they keep in touch with the best thinking about children in general. There is some danger that mothers will be the half of the parent team which reads about children, attends meetings about children, and attempts to know good professional thinking about children. Some fathers are well informed about finance or business or politics or sports but ignorant about child development. The pooling of ignorance and knowledge seldom leads to a wise plan, but the pooling of information from two different backgrounds can lead to better living for children.

Father Works in the Family, Too

By being an informed member of the family's "Board of Directors," the father lightens the task of the mother. She does not have to make all the decisions alone, unaided and unsupported. She gets real psychological support from knowing that father cares and takes the time to listen. This is typical of the third contribution fathers make to their children—a background contribution, yet a very basic one. By becoming participating members of the total family, fathers help their wives to be better mothers.

A father, for example, can do a great deal to lighten the physical load of heavy, hard work that every young mother carries. Fathers sometimes take on household jobs they might not normally do: shopping, washing dishes, vacuuming. This is a service to mother directly, but it has important repercussions on the living of the child. A physically tired woman easily becomes grouchy, irritable, and resentful of all that children do.

Fathers can help by at least appreciating that a home with young children in it seldom has the spick-and-span look of a childless home. Fathers give valued support to their wives, and through them to their children, when they realize that a child, with all his possessions and mess, adds a new kind of beauty to a living room that once was spotless, with every magazine and book neatly in order.

Fathers can also take the lead in breaking the monotony of mother's job. Men's work has its deadly routines, but out in the community father is more apt to meet people, to lead a more varied life, and to get social and intellectual stimulation. Mother runs the risk of feeling trapped. Once a child is born, her world can seem to close in and to be bounded for months on end by the four walls of her home. A father, aware of this danger, finds ways to widen his wife's sphere so that she has moments of being a woman, a hostess, a citizen, an adult friend, a companion, a learner—and not simply a mother alone.

Those who perforce must raise a family alone—widows or widowers, for example—know best how much children miss, directly and indirectly, when only one parent is available. Yet many two-parent families do not take the fullest advantage of their opportunity. A father exists, but he plays a very small part in his children's lives. This is too bad. Whenever two sets of hands and feet are available, more of children's needs can be met. Whenever children know intimately two sets of voices, two differing degrees of strength, two differing paces, and two differing tones, their lives are richer. Life, in fact, goes more smoothly for all—for the child, for the mother, and for the father, too, for father gains a precious sense of being the father of a child, with all its joys and with its inevitable tribulations, too. JAMES L. HYMES, JR.

See also LOVE

FATHERLESS CHILD *See* DIVORCE AND SEPARATION

FAVORITISM

It is not easy for parents to admit that they have favorites among their children. They naturally like to believe they give love equally, for they are aware that playing favorites can be damaging. A less preferred child can grow up believing he never can please these two people on whom he is emotionally dependent. This belief may congeal into a chronic discouragement and sense of failure that may pursue him through life.

On the other hand, the child who is complacently aware that his parents think whatever he does is simply wonderful is in danger of assuming that he can win love and everything else in life effortlessly and without ever facing his own shortcomings.

These consequences are altogether possible though by no means certain. The less appreciated youngster may eventually develop an I'll-show-them-I'm-better-than-they-think attitude and drive ahead to a certain kind of success. The favored one, instead of growing up spoiled, often gains assurance, a constructive optimism; he sees the world as his oyster. When it comes to predictions about human beings, the best motto is, "You never can tell."

Nevertheless, favoritism exacts a price and *is* a destructive element in family life. Parents are right to be on their guard against it. When parents recognize their own varied feelings about their children, they are taking a step in the right direction. It is human and almost inevitable to find a good-tempered, responsive child enjoyable, congenial, and easy to reach. It is also human to be irritated by a child who creates constant difficulties. Friction between the personality of such a child and yours is inevitable, for he is forever defeating your efforts.

After parents have faced up to their own feelings, there are several things to do.

The first is to be scrupulously fair. Your "difficult" child isn't always at fault; the "good" one may provoke the misconduct in order to shine by comparison. Children need to know that their parents are aware of such possibilities and are sensitive to their side of any given case.

If you have to punish a child, make it quick and soon over with. Each day, even each hour, should start with a clean slate. No child should be continually in the doghouse. Nothing fails like failure. Remember also that a troublemaking child is quite aware of the look of anticipatory disapproval on your face (which you can't see) and the tension in your voice.

These things are basic, but it will help if you can go even further and be extra generous where you are perhaps least inclined to be. This doesn't mean just gifts and privileges, though it may. It means more time expended on your less enjoyed child, more imaginative sharing of his interests, and an ever-listening ear to the clues he gives you to what may be troubling him. It may even mean that you occasionally comply with unreasonable demands—not grudgingly, but with gaiety and humor. If he lies on the floor and demands that you put his shoes on when he can "perfectly well do it himself," yield to such whims now and then. Laugh and do it with a pat and a smile.

Sometimes parents actually prefer the more difficult of their children. It may be the "good" child whom they find less interesting or "cold" or somehow alien. Parents should remember that this child needs them, too. Don't decide he is this or that type and nothing you can do can change things. Childrens' potentialities for growth are frequently astonishing. ANNA W. M. WOLF

See also DISCIPLINE; HUMOR; LISTENING TO CHILDREN; SELF-CONCEPT; REJECTION

FEAR

The words "fear" and "anxiety" are often used interchangeably, but there is a psychological distinction that is helpful in trying to understand and describe a child's distress. *Fear* usually has an object; that is, a child is afraid of lightning. *Anxiety* is scattered and vague; it is a carry-over from an uncomfortable or fearful experience. The memory of a hurt of any kind is likely to persist, and the child develops a dread that the hurt might happen again. This is anxiety.

Everyone has to learn what to be afraid of. An infant approaches a hot stove with no fear until he has burned himself or has had his hand spanked by his mother, who is correctly teaching him to be afraid of harmful things. The toddler pulls out electric light plugs, even putting them in his mouth unless he has been scolded or warned. It is the job of parents to protect their children as far as possible from these external dangers.

Since a baby has had no time to learn from experience, his parents have to act on their own experience and knowledge of what is dangerous. The old adage that man learns only from experience is true enough, but this does not mean we should expose a child to harm during the process.

The toddler is an explorer; he wants to touch and taste everything. This behavior is normal; indeed, such curiosity is the mainspring of learning. Since he does not know what is dangerous, it is often better to remove harmful objects from his grasp or to take him out of harm's way. But it is not always possible nor even helpful to a child to bring him up in constant isolation. Sometimes a scolding or a spanked hand are necessary to save a child from peril and to teach him what is dangerous. The mother's frown or look of distress may be enough. Until a child can understand words, a warning is not effective; though even before he learns to talk, the normally bright child understands what his parents mean, and he learns very early that he must not do certain things. It is not uncommon for a little child to spank his own hand when he knows he has transgressed.

Parents cannot always be at hand, and a small child is bound to suffer some hurts that may produce fear. Sometimes he learns the hard way; he really gets hurt by an automobile or by a strange animal or by another child, or he gets lost in a crowd and cannot find his mother. No parent is wise enough to protect a child from all fearful circumstances, nor would it be to the child's advantage to try to anticipate all the dangers in the world. Constant talk about danger makes a child nervous and timid.

Parents' own fears are easily communicated to their child. A baby senses the uneasiness of his mother; he feels the tenseness in her body, in her tone of voice, in her restlessness, and his own nervous system responds. "Johnny is afraid of electric storms," says one mother, "but so am I. My mother used to be afraid, too." This is not heredity, as some people think; it is passed-on experience.

Fortunately, the human being from the moment of birth tries to save himself from discomfort. A baby cries when startled by bright lights or loud noises; his nervous system is protecting itself. A baby cries, too, when he is hungry, not because he understands hunger, but because his empty stomach is uncomfortable. He soon learns that his cry brings food and that with food the discomfort disappears.

Dependence on his mother for food and comfort makes her presence all-important to an infant. This helplessness, though not known to him as fear, dominates his early development. Fear of the loss of his mother seems to be primary, since the mother's presence means both food and love—his means of survival.

When his mother goes away from home, the infant who is comfortable, warm, and well fed will notice the absence little, but as soon as he is old enough to observe who brings him what he wants, he clings to that one person. This clinging may come as early as 6 months. At 1 year, the mother's leaving may be a painful experience. It is a kindness to accustom a little child ahead of time to the person who will care for him while his mother is gone.

Children who have really lost a mother or who have suffered neglect in their earliest years may carry this fear of the loss of love throughout their lives. Fear of loneliness and of death, a lonely event, are probably bound up in the fear of losing the mother. Children who have been consistently loved and protected during their early years have a better start in meeting life's later privations.

Fears can spread. One dog may have been dangerous, but the child in his logic includes all dogs. One windstorm may have blown the roof from a house in the neighborhood. The little child naturally expects another storm to be destructive. In time, and with the help of his parents, he normally corrects these impressions. Unfortunately, some adults never discard their childish logic and continue to be afraid throughout life of situations that once made them fearful. A 3-year-old boy was stung by a bee. The next day when his mother saw another bee near the child's head, she screamed in fright, but the child said trustingly, "Oh, the bad one was yesterday's bee." He had made his own correction.

Fear can be restricting. The badly frightened child is unwilling to risk trying something he feels may hurt him. Sometimes this self-protection is extreme; he closes himself in from any new experience, and a chain of fears shackles him. Fortunately, however, the physiological urge for activity in normal growth usually overcomes timidity.

To the fear of the loss of love and the fear of getting hurt, another should be added: the fear of doing wrong. But this fear is almost the same as the fear of the loss of love, because a child seeks to please his parents by doing what is right. In his mind, wrongdoing threatens the good feelings between him and his parents.

Though these fears arise in the early years of life, they may persist in a variety of troublesome forms. A child may be afraid to leave home for school; he screams at the mention of the doctor's office or maybe he develops a chronic shyness. In their bewilderment about what to do, parents often resort to shaming their child, appealing to his wish to grow up, or they try trickery to get him to the doctor or the dentist. These are poor methods. Shaming usually makes a child more miserable and less able to act spontaneously, for it makes him feel inadequate. Trickery may start a lasting distrust of the father or the mother which will color a child's life. Many adults have never recovered from the loss of confidence in the grown-up people of their childhood. A common example is the man who feels that someone is always trying to take advantage of him. From his childhood experience, he formed a lasting concept that makes it impossible for him to get along with his boss.

Occasionally, parents transfer their concern from a member of their early family to one of their own children. A mother who had a ne'er-do-well brother was constantly fearful that her young son would grow up to be like him. This kind of fear can have a crippling effect on any child.

Patience and watchfulness to see why a child is afraid, then careful dosing of new experience will help. But first, parents should examine their own fears in an attempt to understand their children's worries better. Understanding thus gained may help parents to control their fears in the presence of their children. The same is true of the anxious parent who seems to conjure up worries about health and physical safety as well as about the child's success in school and among his friends. It is hard to grow up to be spontaneous and carefree in such an atmosphere.

An ounce of prevention of a child's fears goes a long way in reducing the need for a pound of cure at a later age. HELEN ROSS

See also ANIMALS, FEAR OF; ANXIETY; DARK, FEAR OF THE; DOCTOR; FAILURE, FEAR OF; HOSPITALIZATION; LEAVING HOME, FEAR OF; NIGHTMARES; STRANGERS, FEAR OF; THUNDER AND LIGHTNING, FEAR OF; TOILET, FEAR OF

FEEBLE-MINDEDNESS *See* MENTAL ILLNESS

FEEDING *See* BOTTLE FEEDING; BREAST CARE AND BREAST FEEDING

FEEDING SCHEDULE

How often and how regularly you feed your baby will depend on the kind of feeding schedule you and he work out together. Sometimes a doctor gives very definite advice on this matter, especially in the case of a small or a premature baby who needs a carefully regulated diet. With a bigger baby, the doctor may encourage you to choose your own kind of schedule.

A strict schedule advocates feeding the baby a certain number of ounces every three to four hours, whether he seems hungry or not. Advocates of this kind of schedule feel that "training" the baby is all-important, and that training is possible from the beginning.

Self-demand feeding means that the baby is fed whenever he seems hungry. This approach sounds ideal, but some mothers have trouble knowing when a baby is hungry and they worry that every single cry signifies hunger. This situation sometimes is confusing and, for a mother who worries a lot, is apt to mean a slavish overconcern about meeting her child's needs. Enthusiastic advocates of self-demand feeding feel that a baby should never experience delay between his hunger and its satisfaction.

These are both rather extreme positions. As is often the case, a more flexible and middle-of-the-road approach is satisfactory to most mothers and babies. There is a need for some kind of schedule, or pattern, to the day for both mother and baby. A mother must be able to plan her work a little bit in order to care for her house and family as well as for the baby.

Some idea of the usual feeding patterns of babies may help a mother decide how to judge her own baby's needs. Most babies in their first two or three weeks will be hungry every three hours. Gradually, the hunger intervals lengthen to about every four hours. Most babies want to eat oftener during one part of the day (late afternoon or evening, usually) and will compensate by sleeping longer intervals at night. RUTH S. KEMPE

FEET *See* FLAT FEET; PIGEON TOE

FEVER *See* TEMPERATURE

FEVER BLISTER

Some people call them cold sores, some call them fever blisters, and doctors call them *herpes simplex.* By whatever name, these virus-caused blisters occurring on mucous membranes or skin are a source of distress to the child who has them—usually on the lips or about the mouth but sometimes inside the mouth. They also may occur—especially in girls—on the mucous membrane of the genital region and the surrounding skin. There is a tendency for the blisters to recur, particularly when the child is subjected to physical or emotional stress.

Fever blisters do not make a child feel ill except in rare instances when the lesions may be extensive or when they occur in internal organs. Then he may have a fever and be quite ill. Fever blisters also tend to occur along with certain illnesses associated with fever, such as pneumonia or meningitis.

The lesions are infectious during the blister state, so the infected child should have his own towel and otherwise try to avoid spreading the serum that comes from the blisters. Usually, the blisters dry in three or four days and develop a crust. The crust drops off in another three to five days. For fever blisters your doctor may prescribe the application of camphorated oil or a salve to make the child more comfortable. JULIUS B. RICHMOND

See also VIRUS

FIDGETING

Fidgeting is what we all do when we are too nervous, too upset, to sit still. We move our fingers, shuffle our feet, get up and walk around, or we talk too much. This behavior, especially in children, is very annoying to other people. "Stop fidgeting," says a mother to her 9-year-old daughter, but the child keeps right on. Disobedient? No, she can't stop. The nervousness inside her has to come out in action.

Usually, fidgeting is just temporary—something important is about to happen—a birthday party or daddy's return from a trip. Give the child something to do and he'll quiet down. Suggest he run around the block, anything to use up the energy pent up inside him. If this suggestion isn't feasible, give the youngster a paper and pencil and let him write or draw.

When the cause of fidgeting is not obvious (perhaps a reprimand by his teacher or a scrap with a friend has upset him), try to get him to talk about what's bothering him. Children, like adults, feel better when they have a chance to share their worries with a sympathetic listener.

But when a child fidgets all the time, that's more difficult to deal with. Then you need professional help—a doctor, psychologist, or psychiatrist—to find out what's bothering the youngster. MAY R. SHERWIN

See also CHILD GUIDANCE CLINIC

FINES *See* PUNISHMENT

FINGER PAINT *See* ART EXPERIENCES

FINGER-SUCKING *See* SUCKING; THUMB-SUCKING

FIRST AID

(NOTE: First aid for various types of emergency situations is described under the specific situation—BURN; BLEEDING; POISONING AND POISONS; SHOCK.)

First aid is defined by the American Red Cross as "immediate and temporary care given the victim of an accident or sudden illness until the services of a physician can be obtained."

In giving first aid, you do not diagnose or attempt to treat a serious injury or illness—you do what ought to be done to meet the emergency, and you get a doctor as quickly as possible.

The benefits of first aid to a stricken child (or adult) begin with the steadying effect of knowing that he is being cared for, that someone is doing something to relieve his distress.

Competent first-aid training is valuable to parents and well worth the small investment in time. Your local Red Cross office, police or fire department, or Office of Civil Defense can tell you what first-aid training courses are available in your community.

Most home accidents result in minor injuries, and the needed first aid is obvious. In

FLAT FEET

When a baby first begins to stand up and walk, his mother is very apt to look at him and exclaim, "Oh, my goodness, he's got flat feet!" Nine times out of 10 she will be wrong, for her baby's feet only look flat. A baby's foot is quite plump, and the plumpness disguises the foot arch to some extent. More important, until a child has been walking for some time (usually months), the muscles and ligaments of the arch are not strong. The arch of the foot consists of several bones, all fitting next to one another in a curve supported by the muscles and ligaments that attach to the bones. When these muscles are weak, the arch will be relaxed and flattened. Gradually, as a baby learns to walk and as he uses his feet, the muscles become stronger and hold the bones of the foot in a firmer arch. If, after walking has gone well for months, the feet still look flat, they should be checked by the baby's doctor to see if wedges need to be applied to the inner heel of the shoe. Sometimes people say that children who are learning to walk should have shoes with very firm shanks and arch supports to protect the weak ankle muscles and prevent flat feet. Actually, this is not so; the best shoes are soft and flexible, ones that allow the muscles of the foot and ankle freedom to move and become stronger through exercise. Rigid shoes are more likely to interfere with normal foot development than to foster it.

RUTH S. KEMPE

See also WALKING

FLU *See* INFLUENZA

FLUORIDE

In a number of areas throughout the world, including places in the United States, drinking water filters down through natural rock formations containing fluorides. Lifelong residents in these areas have about half as many decayed teeth as the people who were born and reared in fluoride-deficient areas. Fluoride provides this protection mainly because it combines with the tooth substance as it forms to produce a tooth enamel that is better able to withstand the acids that cause decay.

Because of what fluorides can do for teeth, many communities now add salts of

the case of serious injury, there is a definite order of action:

- *a*) **Give necessary first aid.**
- *b*) **Have the victim lie down.**
- *c*) **Check for injuries and do what is immediately needed.**
- *d*) **Call the doctor.**
- *e*) **Keep the victim quiet and continue first-aid treatment until the doctor arrives.**

You must act quickly in cases where each second of delay is important: severe bleeding, stoppage of breathing, and poisoning. If possible, have someone else call the doctor while you are taking action that may save the child's life.

First-aid kits are available in a wide variety of sizes, types, and prices. American Red Cross has designated three basic kits—16-unit, 24-unit, and 32-unit—which are packaged by a number of surgical supply manufacturers according to Red Cross specifications. The first-aid kits available in most drugstores and department stores are not standardized in any way, and you should examine the contents and type of packaging before purchase.

To do its job properly in the home, in the family car, or on a hike through the woods, the first-aid kit should contain sufficient materials for its probable use; it should be arranged so the item you want can be quickly removed without scrambling the entire kit. The kit should also have individual items separately wrapped so that unused materials do not become soiled or contaminated.

A family with small children should have, either in kit form or easily available in the home to meet most emergencies:

An assortment of adhesive compresses—the type with a sterile gauze pad centered in an adhesive strip
Several 3″ × 3″ gauze pads
Roll of sterile gauze bandage
Tube of burn ointment
Roll or package of folded sterile gauze totaling one-half square yard or more
Several triangular bandages
Tourniquet
Scissors
Tweezers

ROBERT E. KILBRIDE

See also ACCIDENT PREVENTION; EMERGENCY; NURSE

fluorine to their water supply. A concentration of fluoride of about one part per million parts of water provides fullest benefit for the teeth and is absolutely safe. It is also inexpensive—the community cost of adding fluoride averages about 10 cents per person per year.

If you live where the water supply lacks the protection of fluoride, your child should have fluoride applied to his teeth by a dentist or dental hygienist soon after the teeth erupt. Your dentist will specify at what stages of tooth development your child should have this protection. ROBERT G. KESEL

See also DENTAL CAVITIES

FOOD POISONING

When food is improperly handled or stored, it can become contaminated by bacteria or their products. This food when eaten can then cause food poisoning.

There are several types of food poisoning and the reactions are somewhat different in each. In one type of food poisoning, the attack comes on about two hours after the contaminated food is eaten. Children—and adults, too—develop severe diarrhea and abdominal cramps, become weak and pale, and may collapse. Sometimes large numbers of people at affairs such as picnics develop symptoms of food poisoning at the same time. Such foods as potato salad, custards, and cream puffs, and ground meats and cold cuts become contaminated readily, and they should either be kept refrigerated until served or they should be avoided in hot weather. Cooking destroys the substance that causes the poisoning; well-cooked food that has not been left standing is therefore usually safe.

A child with symptoms of food poisoning should lie down until you can get medical care for him. Hospitalization and fluids given intravenously may sometimes be necessary. There usually are no lasting aftereffects following recovery from an attack of food poisoning.

In another form of food poisoning, the bacteria themselves are transmitted through the food. Food handlers may carry the bacteria in their intestines without being sick and transmit through contamination of their hands. Typhoid fever and other diarrhea disorders can be transmitted by carriers, or by food, water, or milk that has come in contact with sewage. The time of onset of symptoms in this type of food poisoning is longer—usually two to seven days. The afflicted child frequently develops diarrhea and fever, and the severity of the disease will depend upon the severity of the symptoms.

A rare form of food poisoning is called botulism. It develops in canned or preserved foods, producing a poison that has severe effects on the central nervous system. Botulism must be treated by a physician. Food that has been properly canned or preserved does not contain this poison.

Some wild mushrooms and berries are themselves poisonous, and children should be taught to recognize them and to avoid eating them. JULIUS B. RICHMOND

See also POISONING AND POISONS

FOOD REQUIREMENTS *See* NUTRITION; VITAMINS

FOREIGN LANGUAGE *See* TALKING

FOREIGN OBJECTS *See* EAR, FOREIGN OBJECTS IN; EYE, FOREIGN OBJECTS IN; NOSE, OBJECTS IN; SWALLOWING THINGS

FORMULA MAKING

Making a formula is a simple procedure once you obtain the formula recipe from your doctor and learn how to manipulate the equipment so as to keep it sterile.

It is helpful if you can see pictures or actual demonstrations of the two methods of formula preparation—perhaps in a class for new or expectant mothers. Or you can obtain excellent, well-illustrated pamphlets

from many dairies or dry milk companies.

You should keep the formula preparation equipment in a special place so that you omit nothing in the sterilizing process. Minimum formula equipment includes:

10 to 12 eight-ounce bottles with their nipples and caps
Sterilizer or large covered kettle with a rack in the bottom
Measuring spoon
Large and small measuring cups
Long-handled stirring spoon
Metal funnel
Tongs
Can opener
Nipple jar for storage

There are two methods of formula preparation: terminal heating and standard clean.

In the standard clean method, you sterilize the equipment and formula separately, then pour the formula into sterilized bottles. Boil the clean bottles, caps, and measuring supplies in a sterilizer or kettle for at least 10 minutes. Nipples need to be boiled five minutes, either together with the other equipment or in a saucepan. After this, you must handle all equipment with sterile tongs and not touch it with your hands. Into the sterile quart-measuring container pour the right number of ounces of water, which has been boiled for 10 minutes. To the water add sterile milk and the sugar, again using sterile equipment. (If evaporated milk is used, wash the cover of the can thoroughly in hot water.) Pour the mixed formula into the bottles, put the nipples and caps in place (using tongs to do so), and tighten by hand. Then store the bottles in the refrigerator until needed.

In the terminal heating method, you mix the formula first, then pour it into clean bottles, and boil the bottles—formula and all—for 25 minutes. During boiling, nipples are in place but with the caps screwed on very loosely so that pressure does not build up too much. After cooking, you can tighten the bottle caps a little more and refrigerate the bottles until needed.

You may find the terminal heating method simpler and safer to use than the standard clean method because the equipment needs only to be clean and not sterile when ingredients are measured, mixed, and poured into bottles.

Formulas made by either of these methods can be stored in a refrigerator up to two days, as long as the bottles are not opened in the meantime. When you wish to use a bottle, open the cap, put the nipple in place, and warm the bottle in hot water until the milk drops feel the same temperature as the skin of your wrist.

After a feeding, it is not wise to keep the formula for more than half an hour or so before throwing it away. It should not be put back in the refrigerator and saved for another feeding. Leftover unopened bottles of formula can be used in cooking such things as biscuits, puddings, and other dishes where the small amount of sugar does not spoil the flavor. RUTH S. KEMPE

See also BOTTLE FEEDING; NURSE

FOSTER CARE *See* FAMILY SERVICE AGENCY

FRACTURE *See* BROKEN BONE

FRESH AIR

Parents often feel that fresh air is in some way essential to good health and that everyone must sleep with an open window and be outdoors at least part of every day. Although fresh air is much more pleasant than the stale air of a warm room, it is actually no more healthful. The oxygen content of air remains quite constant. Probably the most important benefits from time spent out of doors, benefits not to be minimized, are the relaxation and enjoyment, the invigorating effect, and the increased zest of a change in scenery. But remember when you feel obligated to bundle your child up and take him out in the coldest and most unpleasant weather that fresh air is not really necessary for physical health.

Most babies should be kept indoors most of the time for the first month or so, unless doing so is a real inconvenience to the mother. After this initial period, an outing or an outdoor nap every day is probably good for a baby as long as extremes of weather are avoided. Very cold, windy, damp, or hot weather is apt to cause only discomfort. Mild days, cloudy or sunny, all make an agreeable background for a stimulating ride in carriage or stroller or for a peaceful nap in the carriage.

The same principle of moderation applies to the question of fresh air in your baby's room. Opening the windows at least part of the day to freshen the air is certainly important to comfort, for no one enjoys being in a stale, overheated atmosphere. But in a very cold climate and in very cold or damp weather, it is not a good idea to leave a baby's window open all night. The temperature of his room should not be much colder at night than in the daytime, since babies do not always stay warmly covered. Probably 60° F. to 65° F. is a good nighttime temperature in his room. RUTH S. KEMPE

FRIENDS

From about the age of 2 through adolescence a child needs friends near his own age to help him in his development, both as a group member and as an individual. The need for friends is so fundamental that when a child lacks real companions he often creates imaginary ones.

Although the friendships of 2- to 4-year-olds are likely to be brief, each friendship is intense while it lasts. While no single specific relationship is likely to be significant, the experience of having friends during the preschool years is of critical importance to a child as preparation for the school years to follow. A child who has the opportunity to have friends of his own age during his early years comes to middle childhood with two major advantages: He *expects* to be accepted as a friend by others and he has learned some of the techniques needed for getting along with his age-mates.

A young child may have difficulties in making friends because he has not had enough companions of his own age, or because he is afraid and unable to protect himself in the snatch-and-grab society of the preschooler. The latter attitude may often be traced to the presence of an overprotective adult who hovers too closely in the background, watching every move the child makes. Adults who fuss overmuch about a child's small hurts do great harm to the child's social relationships. The friendships of very young children are compounded of bites and scratches and blows as well as of hugs and amiable play, and a child who is afraid of the first is not likely to experience much of the second.

There are special conditions that may interfere with a child's ability to make friends: Premature development may get in the way. A vocabulary too advanced for the other children to understand, or highly specialized interests that are more mature than those of the child's little friends may create difficulties. If, however, these differences are accompanied by a self-confident, outgoing manner and a warm interest in others, they can be turned to advantage. A child bright enough to acquire a well-developed vocabulary can, with a little friendly encouragement, learn to speak to his age-mates on a simpler level. And specialized interests can be the basis of leadership potential if handled wisely.

The breaking of friendship ties in childhood can be even more upsetting than in adulthood. A move to a new school, a new neighborhood, or a new camp often ushers in a period of social hardship. Existing cliques rarely welcome a newcomer. A boy often has to prove himself by displaying skills that are valued by the other boys. A girl may have an easier time if her parents can give a series of small parties for her new schoolmates or her neighbors. After that, of course, the child's own social skills must carry the day.

A child's friends help him to grow up. By sharing secrets and talking about common problems, he learns that his problems are not unique. This knowledge contributes to his internal comfort. Help from his friends encourages him to be less dependent on his parents—an extremely important step in growing up.

Loyalty to friends is often a bone of contention between parents and children. During and after the middle school years the values, opinions, and mannerisms of the gang seem

to be more important to the child than those of his parents. It is a wise parent or teacher who, realizing that this is a child's way of fitting into his social world, does not make an issue of these differences. If a child seems to be overdoing conformity, adult opposition will only increase it. An understanding attitude, clearly conveyed, will help a child regain and maintain an even keel.

No adult, no matter how understanding, can take the place of own-age friends in a child's life. His friends are a part of himself. Criticism of them is often interpreted as rejection of himself. If the chosen companions seem objectionable, the most effective course is to find out what their attractions are and to provide acceptable substitutes. Sometimes undesirable companions do not actually represent a child's own preference, but he accepts them because he cannot attract the friends he really wants. In such cases, parents can be extremely helpful: Making an occasion to invite the preferred children to the home and seeing that they have a good time is often enough to start mutually satisfying relationships.

If a child is having trouble making friends, discreet observation of his behavior in a play group may give clues to the reasons. To know why he is having trouble may not be enough, however. An attitude that is too aggressive or one that is too fearful may indicate need for help from an expert. The sooner such help is given, the better for the child's social development. Parents cannot do everything. It is sufficient if they are sensitive enough to make it possible for a child to get needed help. RUTH E. HARTLEY

See also ACCEPTANCE; CLUBS AND CLIQUES; COMMUNITY RESOURCES; CRUSHES; IMAGINARY COMPANION; PLAY GROUPS; SOCIAL DEVELOPMENT

FROSTBITE

It is the blood supply that keeps the tissues of our body warm. If certain body areas are not well supplied with blood or if they are especially exposed to extreme cold the way our ears, nose, fingers and toes are, they may be damaged. This damage is called frostbite. The immediate effects are that the frostbitten area becomes whitish and numb. The long-term effects can vary. The tissue of a frostbitten finger may be completely lost, or every time it is exposed to cold, you may experience a mild but painful burning sensation months after the original injury.

Prevention of frostbite is important because of the destructive nature of tissue freezing. Since dampness increases the hazard, children should be taught to come indoors to change wet or damp clothing, particularly shoes and socks. And youngsters should have adequate protection in cold weather—especially for ears, hands, and feet. A child subjected to prolonged exposure to extreme cold, as when ice skating or skiing, should also wear a protective face mask.

If a child does suffer frostbite, the area should not be touched (contrary to much folklore about rubbing the area with snow). It should be permitted to warm gradually. Consult a doctor as soon as possible. In severe cases, blistering may occur. Blisters from frostbite are usually treated in much the same way as blisters from a burn would be. JULIUS B. RICHMOND

See also BLISTER

FRUSTRATION *See* AGGRESSIVENESS; ANGER; ANXIETY

GAGGING

Gagging is a reflex action at the back of the throat which sometimes produces vomiting. Gagging also occurs if a child is nauseated and ready to vomit. The gag reflex is sometimes highly sensitive in young babies and may cause some "spitting up." Occasionally, a bit of dust or lint in the mouth or a nipple pushed too far into his mouth makes a baby gag. Sometimes babies gag during feedings simply to show that they have had enough.

Babies very often gag a good deal when first offered solid foods such as cereal. This is quite natural since the solid food is strange in consistency and at first difficult to swallow. Making the solid more fluid and offering very small amounts usually is helpful.

Gagging is really an important protection against aspiration—the entry of solids into the voice box and breathing passages where they could cause choking and suffocation. When a baby gags, it is a sign that he is not able to cope with whatever is in his mouth and may need your help. RUTH S. KEMPE

See also EATING PROBLEMS; INTRODUCING NEW FOODS; SPITTING UP; VOMITING

GALACTOSEMIA *See* MENTAL DEFICIENCY

GAMES *See* ATHLETICS

GAMMA GLOBULIN

Globulins are part of the human blood plasma. There are three globulins—alpha, beta, and gamma. Each one has antibodies to help the body throw off infections. Gamma, which has the most antibodies, is the most effective.

A person who has had a particular disease has developed more than the usual number of antibodies against that disease. So a serum made from the blood of the recovered patient can be used in another human being to prevent some diseases and to make other diseases less severe.

Because gamma globulin (GG) is present in human blood plasma, it does not give children the allergic reactions that occasionally follow the use of antitoxins that are derived from animals.

Gamma globulin gives temporary immunity to those people who have been exposed to infectious hepatitis, measles, and German measles. Where children have already contracted measles or paralytic polio, an injection of gamma globulin can diminish the severity of the disease. A special kind of gamma globulin is effective also in the rare cases where there are complications from smallpox vaccinations. LOUIS W. SAUER

See also COMMON COMMUNICABLE DISEASES

GANGS

A gang is a group of teen-age or preteen boys who spend much of their time together, are unswervingly loyal to one another, and take orders from one of their number who, though not formally elected to the position, is acknowledged as leader. Emblems, uniforms, and hangouts are important accessories to gang life. And usually, there is a mutually agreed-upon purpose, not always in defiance of law and order.

One gang may do nothing more than stand on a street corner, preferably an intersection where "something might turn up." Another may exist chiefly to fight any rival groups whose members might trespass.

Membership lines are clearly and tightly drawn. Being admitted is far simpler than getting out. Whoever is not in the gang is regarded as, at best, a threat, but more probably as a dangerous enemy. Here is where a gang differs from a clique, a crowd, or a club. Such groups may scorn "outsiders," but do not feel called upon to fight them. Defending, by any means however violent, any member who has suffered so much as a slight slur, is also one of the distinguishing marks of gang behavior.

The pattern of exclusive allegiance to those on the inside, and even more, of suspicion and mistrust of those on the outside, tends to make a gang attractive to the angry, bitterly disappointed young person who has never known the protection of a kindly, strong, older individual. If a boy has been labeled "bad" or "troublemaker" at home and in the community, if he has gained no acceptance or sense of achievement at school, if he feels that everyone is against him, the gang may appear to be his only refuge.

Girls are less likely than boys to form gangs. In some neighborhoods they, as well as younger boys, may become hangers-on of the boys' organizations.

A youngster who has a firm, loving adult to whom he can turn and who finds approval, satisfaction, and fun part of the time within his family, is not likely to be lured into lawlessness. If, in addition, he has friends his own age and the conviction that he does at least one thing well, he has sound protection against involvement in gangs with delinquent tendencies. EDITH G. NEISSER

See also APPROVAL; CLUBS AND CLIQUES; FRIENDS; INDEPENDENCE; YOUTH ORGANIZATIONS

GENEROSITY

"I don't understand," said a child's mother. "Why don't you like Mrs. Morgan? She's such a generous person." "No, she isn't," the child said. "She laughed when I hurt my knee."

The dictionary rules in favor of this child's concept. Being generous is not a matter of mere openhandedness but rather "having qualities attributed to people of noble birth—noble-minded; gracious; not mean; magnanimous." Although common usage tends to have generosity mean lavish gift giving, generosity is not simply a social technique, and it is more than taking turns to get some good out of sharing. Generosity is a quality of the spirit which embraces sympathy, tolerance, forgiveness, kindness.

From the mother's earliest "gift" of food to her complex feelings of love, the child is—at first—the recipient. The way he feels about receiving, the comfort he associates with tenderness, his first inklings of the possibility of giving—all are the root emotions from which his own capacity for generous feelings and generous behavior spring.

It is surprising how early the first compassionate impulses appear. "Me b'ing a b'anket," the toddler may say when his mother lies down with a headache. And of course it makes no difference to either of them if the covering he chooses is doll-size. "Don't cry, baby," croons a 2-year-old as she peers into the carriage of an unhappy infant. "Don't cry, baby. I pat you." Clearly both of these very young children are extending to others the solicitous attentions that have brought them solace in time of need and, perhaps even more important, are learning to give of themselves in order to help others.

Acts of sympathy and kindness are as truly generous as the sharing of material possessions. If it is delightful to see a child spontaneously give away something that he likes because he likes his friend, it is quite as touching to see him comfort a friend who has fallen or to hear him tell his little sister, "You didn't mean to break my truck, so it's all right." And what impulse could be more truly compassionate and generous than that which prompted a little girl to guide the fingers of a blind classmate over her block building so that he could feel the shape the other children were discussing? Children capable of expressing such warm feelings to others, of accepting their friends' occasional mistakes with equanimity and forgiveness, are, like those who are easy about sharing possessions, usually those whose parents have given freely of their own love, sympathy, and understanding.

Parents who are concerned because their children seem lacking in generous impulses may be defining generosity too narrowly or expecting the attribute to appear in full-blown, grown-up form. The youngster who extends half a cooky or serves others only after helping himself is moving in the right direction. So is the child who declines to let another use his crayons but eagerly hands out the pictures he has drawn.

Sometimes adults unwittingly thwart a generous impulse by being too quick to protect a child from giving his things away. ("Oh, no, dear. That's all right. You keep it.") Or they reject an offering because it has no intrinsic value. In both cases the child is deprived of the very real joy of giving as well as an opportunity to learn that generous behavior is desirable behavior. Even if mother does not want a raisin, a bobby pin picked up from the floor, or a broken crayon, she would do well to accept it graciously, put it in her purse or pocket, and say, "Thank you. I'll keep it here until I need it." Such small deceits are in a good cause, and there will be time later on for children to learn to be more discriminating in their choice of gifts.

Parents who feel that their youngsters need extra opportunity for practicing generous behavior might do well to consider some ideas that have worked for others. Providing children with a pet (or even a plant) that needs regular and devoted attention is one possibility; enrolling a child's help in preparations for birthdays and other festive occasions is another way of letting him experience the fun of doing things for others.

Sometimes a parent can take the lead in small ways, important none the less. Instead, for example, of urging a child to "say thank you for the nice party," he may be encouraged to invite the birthday child to his home sometime. Instead of telling a child how lucky he is that he got so many presents, he may be told that the baseball mitt might be a good thing for group play in the park someday, or that with his new leathercraft set he can make presents for his friends.

One 8-year-old who had agreed to contribute his Halloween trick-or-treat money to a worthy charity came home with a full container. As he sat down to cookies and milk, he said happily, "I've never felt so useful in my whole life."

And that experience, of course, is the point of it all. IRMA S. BLACK AND JOAN W. BLOS

See also SHARING

GENITALS, HANDLING *See* HANDLING GENITALS

GERMAN MEASLES

German measles (rubella) is a highly contagious, but usually mild, disease that is caused by a virus. It occurs most often in the spring among both children and adults. The first symptoms appear one to three weeks after exposure. German measles can be dangerous to an unborn child. If an expectant mother contracts the disease during the early months of her pregnancy, the child can be born with abnormalities. Usually these abnormalities occur in the eye or in the ear. A pregnant woman, therefore, should try to avoid exposure to German measles. But if she is exposed, she should see her doctor as soon as possible.

German measles is also called three-day measles because of its usual duration. Its symptoms are often those of a cold, plus low fever, headache, and a swelling and hardening of the glands in the neck and behind the ears. Some cases are so mild that there is no rash. When a rash does appear, it begins on the face and spreads to the rest of the body, and lasts two to three days.

Bed rest and isolation are usually all the care required for a child with German measles. He should be seen by a doctor, though, as the symptoms could possibly be those of a more serious disease. Any secondary complications, such as chest or ear infection, should of course, be reported to the child's doctor immediately. MARIE A. HINRICHS

See also COMMON COMMUNICABLE DISEASES; SICK CHILD; VIRUS

GERMS

"Germs" is a word rather loosely used these days to talk about any infectious agent that can cause illness. When people speak of germs, they usually mean bacteria or viruses—microscopic living organisms that multiply in the body and may cause illness. Germs, of course, are too small to be seen except under some kind of microscope, but under conditions right for them they can multiply very fast. Some germs, such as those that are ordinarily present in dust or on the skin and in the digestive tract of every healthy person, do not ordinarily cause health problems. Most older children and adults have over the course of the years built up a good deal of resistance, or immunity, to a small exposure to germs. Small infants usually have immunity, probably received from the mother, to a few of the infectious diseases. This immunity to such diseases as measles, German measles, and poliomyelitis lasts only a few months and does not include such common illnesses as colds, chicken pox, and streptococcal infections.

Because babies, especially small or premature ones, are particularly susceptible to infections and may have more difficulty in coping with illness, it is well to protect them as much as possible from exposure to germs by keeping the baby and everything about him clean. Cleanliness cuts down on the number of germs likely to be present. Most important, don't allow anyone near the baby who is suffering from a cold or any other illness or infection. This automatically means that you do not expose a small baby to large crowds of people or to close contact with strangers, since it is impossible to know about the infections they might have. The baby's formula is sterilized so that the few germs present in milk won't multiply and cause a gastrointestinal infection.

This doesn't mean, of course, that a baby can or should live in a sterile environment. That would be impossible and unnecessary. The ordinary rules of cleanliness—for example, hand washing after doing anything "dirty" and before handling food—will usually be sufficient. As your baby gets older, he will be exposed more and more, and will ordinarily have resistance to withstand exposure to germs. Any baby who is crawling about on the floor is going to get a lot of dirt into his mouth, but by now his body can cope with germs, especially the comparatively harmless kind of germs usually found in the dust of the average household. RUTH S. KEMPE

See also STERILIZING; VIRUS

GETTING ALONG WITH OTHERS *See* AGGRESSIVENESS; BROTHERS AND SISTERS; CLUBS AND CLIQUES; FRIENDS; GRANDPARENTS AND OTHER RELATIVES; MORAL AND SPIRITUAL DEVELOPMENT; POPULARITY

GIFTED CHILD

A genius and a gifted child are not the same. A genius is a very rare person, indeed. There are, however, many gifted children. It is quite possible that you have one. If there is such a child in your family, you will want to know how to identify him, how to educate him, and how you, the school, and the community can cooperate best to foster his full development and happiness.

The term "gifted" is usually applied to those children whose rating on intelligence tests is very high. But the meaning of the term has been extended until now when one speaks of the gifted, he may include children whose performance is remarkable in any worth-while field of endeavor.

Even when the intelligence test alone is used as the measure of giftedness, there is disagreement about how high a child has to score to be classified as gifted. For example, special schools or special classes for the gifted sometimes require candidates to have an IQ (intelligence quotient) of 120; others may demand an IQ of 140 as the minimum rating. The most commonly used intelligence test standard for the gifted is a minimum IQ of 130.

Characteristics of High-Ability Pupils

People used to think of the small, bespectacled recluse as the typical gifted child. But ideas on this subject have changed. For most often the pupil who is distinctly above average in his mental gifts is also somewhat above average in his physical and social development. Although exceptions are numerous, he will, on the average, stand, walk, and talk earlier than other youngsters. He may be able to manipulate things sooner or to build successfully with blocks. The gifted child is on the whole rather well adjusted. He tends, moreover, to be modest and cooperative, although there are, of course, many exceptions.

The young intellectually gifted child will display some of the following characteristics:

- Early and accurate use of a larger vocabulary than that of the average child and unusual proficiency in language expression
- Early interest in calendars and in telling time
- Keen observation and unusual retention of facts
- Tendency to question and to seek answers
- Attraction to picture books at a very early age
- Pronounced ability to give and sustain attention
- Early discovery of cause and effect relationships
- Originality in speaking.
- Early interest and proficiency in reading, and a strong liking for books, including encyclopedias, dictionaries, and atlases.

The intellectually gifted child's aptitude for language is such that he learns to read at an early age—often before he enters school. His rate of learning is so rapid that he can usually master the skills of his grade in half the allotted time and is able by fourth or fifth grade to do the work of the seventh or eighth grade pupil.

The Gifted Child at School

It becomes clear, then, that the school program for a gifted pupil should be geared to his rapid learning rate. Schools should recognize his ability and work out a stimulating and challenging curriculum that will be varied enough to interest him and foster his greatest possible development. This is the ideal, of course. And it is an ideal that is coming closer to realization.

Already in some special classes and special schools, gifted children are being offered enriched and stimulating experiences. For example, there may be opportunities for the elementary school pupil to learn another language, to discover new and varied ways of solving mathematical problems, to make special reports, to develop his individual interests and talents, to read widely, and to explore the field of science. A unique feature of this program is in the cooperation of parents it elicits. They assist in the school library in cataloguing and arranging books, plan and participate in student excursions, and help to devise interesting activities offering unusual opportunities to the pupils.

In some elementary schools partial segregation of the gifted has been tried successfully. With this system, pupils of high IQ spend a portion of each day in the regular classroom and the remainder of the school day in workshops where they engage in individual research, the pursuit of special interests, or appropriate group activity.

At the high school level, many schools are making outstanding efforts to challenge the gifted pupil who has unusual scientific ability. At this level, also, honor classes offer increased motivation and greater stimulation to talented students.

More Schooling in Less Time

Our schools have long practiced grade-skipping to a limited extent. Educators have frequently questioned the value of this practice. Parents have sometimes worried over the possible ill effects upon their child's social adjustment when he is placed with older classmates. They also fear that their child may be placed at a disadvantage physically, especially in physical education activities and sports.

There are, however, certain known advantages in speeding up learning. The bright pupil can progress through school at a rapid rate and reach the threshold of a productive life at an early age. Moreover, the higher level work in an advanced grade may give the superior pupil a greater interest in learning and make him put forth more effort.

It seems, then, that parents, too, can concede that a moderate amount of acceleration is justifiable in many cases. Acceleration should, however, be recommended and attempted only after each child has been studied carefully and expertly as to his mental, physical, and emotional readiness. Part of the study should also include consideration of the type of class he will enter.

Identifying Creativity in Children

Although a high intelligence test rating is one characteristic of the intellectually gifted child, there are some children who are gifted in art, music, writing, creative dancing, or creative dramatics. Their giftedness can be recognized chiefly by their performance. There are other children with outstanding ability and promise in mathematics, mechanics, or social leadership of whom the same thing can be said. Intelligence tests will not be adequate for their identification.

This is why it is desirable to consider any child as "gifted" whose performance in a valuable line of human activity is consistently or repeatedly remarkable. Both home and school should offer opportunities for the release and expression of such ability.

Although intelligence tests are the most effective means of finding the child with a high degree of abstract intelligence or unusual ability in science, such tests are not infallible. For one thing, they do not always provide an accurate measure of the ability of children from impoverished or underprivileged homes, nor do they make adequate allowance for differences in cultural background. Furthermore, they cannot locate all types of gifted children. Several other techniques are, therefore, being used to identify pupils with gifts in music, writing, or other arts. For example, films were used in one such effort to identify pupils who were highly gifted in writing. The films had neither narration nor dialogue. The sound track presented a musical score with special effects that accompanied the appearance of birds and animals. A guide suggested how teachers might encourage each child to express his unique feelings about a particular film.

Some compositions had such originality and beauty of expression that skeptical persons might doubt that children wrote them without help. Yet many of the most outstanding of these products were written by pupils whose IQ's were lower than 130—that standard so often used in defining the gifted. This evidence indicates that a high IQ does not necessarily mean creativity. It suggests that a child gifted in some areas may be identified only by his performance.

Parents' Role

The well-informed parent has a strategic opportunity to discover a child's gifts—and to discover them early. Parents' estimates of their children's abilities will sometimes be inaccurate, of course. Yet it is important that parents try to make judgments. They will be helped in making judgments by learning about the characteristics of gifted children and about the patterns of typical or "average" children as well. Then they will be better able to make comparisons and reach decisions about the extent and nature of a child's gifts.

Knowledge of how gifted children develop will help parents to deal successfully with perplexing problems as they arise. For example, although the gifted child tends to be superior to the average in social development, he is by no means as advanced socially as he is mentally. A gifted child of 6 whose mental age is that of a typical 9- or 10-year-old child may be somewhat superior in physical development and similarly somewhat ahead in social development; yet there will still be a marked gap between his mental and his social, emotional, and physical development. He may be able to tell what the words *loyalty* and *cooperation* mean, but he may not know how to be either loyal or cooperative. He needs patient understanding and guidance to translate language into deeds. Like all other children, the gifted child needs security, affection, encouragement, recognition, and praise from sympathetic parents. Parental insight may nourish a child's gifts and help him to develop harmoniously. On the contrary, some children's gifts are undeveloped because at home strong emotions or insecurity have blocked expression and growth.

The parents of a gifted child should not exploit their child's gifts but simply accept and encourage them. Reading aloud to a child before he learns to read by himself is a good beginning. Of course, some gifted children will learn to read independently before they start to school and should be encouraged to read when they are able to do so readily. But parents should continue to read aloud to some extent even after their child has learned to read. As the child grows older, and his parents observe his expanding interests, they can help him to satisfy them. At 8 or 9 the gifted child will be reading many books and will usually make wide use of encyclopedias and dictionaries. He may like reading about special subjects, such as astronomy, history, or photography, or he may enthusiastically collect and arrange specimens. Books and magazines on his special interests and hobbies should be made available to him at home, and he should be encouraged to use the school and public libraries. Parents should discuss with their child his favorite books and his discoveries in them. Some of his discoveries will be about himself and about other people. He will find pleasure sharing discoveries with his parents and with his teacher.

A heartening reawakening of interest in the gifted child, in identifying him and planning suitable programs for him, has already brought great rewards. Yet it is clear both that only a beginning has been made in this direction and that the pursuit of excellence should be extended and encouraged. Our greatest, but perhaps most neglected, resource lies in our gifted and talented children. For the world needs its best minds to search for truths that still await discovery, its creative artists to contribute to understanding and joy, its most brilliant minds to give new insights and affirmations.

The present-day struggle to determine the goals and ideals by which the peoples of the world will live requires the full use and wide application of the creative spirit and the services of those people most talented in human relations. PAUL A. WITTY

See also ACCELERATION; BOOKS FOR CHILDREN; BOOKS FOR PARENTS; CURIOSITY; INDIVIDUAL DIFFERENCES; SCIENCE; TESTS AND MEASUREMENTS

GIRLS' CAMPS *See* CAMP

GLANDS *See* ENDOCRINE GLANDS; SWOLLEN GLANDS

GLANDULAR FEVER

While glandular fever, or infectious mononucleosis, does not often affect infants and young children, parents stand a good chance of experiencing it with the family before their children finish school. The disease commonly strikes in late childhood, adolescence, or young adulthood, and it tends to occur in epidemics.

This infectious disease is highly variable. A typical case often begins with chills and fever, headache, dizziness, and sore throat and swollen glands in the neck, or swelling of lymph glands in other parts of the body; hence, the name glandular fever. Sometimes the symptoms are so mild that they are overlooked; thus, diagnosis of this disease may be uncertain until the doctor confirms his suspicions by means of laboratory tests.

In some cases a widespread reddish rash may also develop. Sometimes the liver may be affected and jaundice may result. Another complication may involve the central nervous system, possibly resulting in convulsions. A doctor's care is essential so that he can watch for complications.

Antibiotics do not seem to be effective against glandular fever but are constantly being tried in an effort to find one that will be. Patients who have glandular fever should be kept in bed and isolated in order to prevent the spread of the disease.

The disease may last from two to four weeks, but in some instances the patient may not regain his usual energy for several months. It is, therefore, important for parents to help a young person understand the nature of his illness, to assure him that it won't last forever, and that he will regain both his strength and his place in his school and social life. JULIUS B. RICHMOND

See also HOME AND HOSPITAL INSTRUCTION; SICK CHILD

GLASSES *See* EYEGLASSES

GRADE CARDS *See* SCHOOL REPORT

GRADE SCHOOL *See* SCHOOL-AGE CHILD

GRANDPARENTS AND OTHER RELATIVES

The value of a grandparent as a sitter or as a helper in a family emergency is well known. Grandmothers and grandfathers, aunts and uncles, too, make equally important, though less apparent and immediate, contributions to a child's emotional development and to his understanding of people and of the world around him.

Grandparents are not what they used to be. Due to the early marriages of their offspring, many men and women attain grandparenthood in their early 40's. Medical science has made it possible, and custom has made it probable, that an individual in his 40's, 50's, and even well into his 60's will be vigorous and energetic. Grandparents are not sitting, as the nursery rhyme would have us believe, with hands folded in their laps. They are likely to have occupations and interests of their own, and more power to them!

Today's child knows his grandmothers and grandfathers as more active and livelier personalities than did children in the past. He is also apt to know them for a longer time, since the span of life has been extended. More grandparents are around, too.

Substitute Parents

Some grandparents are called upon to be substitute parents. For a boy or girl who has lost a mother or a father through death or divorce, a grandparent of the same sex may almost take the place of the missing member of the family circle. Then the grandmother or grandfather becomes the trusted guide, confidant, and model. As the one who sets standards and defines "good" and "bad," the figure of the grandparent becomes woven into the child's budding conscience.

Children benefit from having adults other than their parents with whom they can share their joys and sorrows. Self-confidence and friendliness blossom as a small child feels comfortably at home at grandma's or another relative's house. Grandparents' ways are usually similar to parental ways. To a toddler, that helps to make them acceptable. Yet, every household has it unique features and traditions. In the slight variations between the routines and demands of his own home and his grandparents' (or perhaps a great-aunt's), even that arch conservative, the 2-year-old, discovers that what is new may still be agreeable.

Grandmother's House—a New World

A few years later when he enjoys novelty more wholeheartedly, the very fact that grandpa's house is different from home becomes one of its greatest charms. Here is a chance "to get away from it all," which is as necessary at 5 as at 50. Life at grandfather's is often less competitive. There is less hurrying and less pressure. Grandma and grandpa usually have more time to listen and to answer questions than has a mother who is trying to be attentive to several children at the same time. Because they are not full-time parents, grandparents usually display a high —albeit a short-lived—degree of enthusiasm for youthful conversation, which is a balm to the hearts of the young. A release from the friction of brothers and sisters is welcome, too.

In some quarters the extra attentions grandparents or aunts and uncles give are regarded as "spoiling." Encouragement and affection of the right kind can hardly be overdone and "spoil" no one. The kind of behavior we call "spoiled" usually results from inconsistency in an adult's treatment of a child or from the thwarting of a child's efforts to be independent. Besides, spoiling does not come about through brief intervals with grandparents.

The Magic Door to the Past

Grandparents open the door to the past. Hearing what it was like in "the olden days" can be fascinating (and the "olden days" begin, for a child, in those dark ages before jets, space capsules, superhighways, supermarkets, and Superman). "Tell me about mommy when she was a little girl," or "Was my daddy ever bad?" are frequent inquiries. The answers usually suggest that parents, too, were once small and erring. That they grew up gives a small person reassurance that he, too, will be grown-up someday.

Grandparents supply a feeling of having roots. "Here is a picture of your father when he was as old as you. My, you look a lot like him," or "You are the fourth Elizabeth in our family. Isn't that nice?" Casual remarks such as these are a tonic to a growing personality trying to make sure that he truly belongs.

Some difficulties may show up along with the joys and rewards in even the happiest relationships between older and younger generations. Those frequently repeated phrases, "The nicest thing about grandchildren is that they go home," and "Being a grandparent is wonderful—all the fun and none of the responsibilities," suggest that a moderate amount of the company of their grandchildren pleases most grandparents. Delightful as are the sound of small voices and the patter of little feet, most older persons find them wearing after a time.

Grandparents who are asked to take a number of children every weekend or who are expected to drop their own plans and be at the beck and call of pleasure-bound sons and daughters often feel imposed upon. Having raised their own families, many grandparents believe their responsibilities to their grandchildren should be elective unless their presence is acutely needed. One father explains the attitude he and his wife have taken toward asking for the services of grandparents: "We try not to kill the goose that lays the golden eggs."

How shall the middle generation, which often feels caught between its own parents and its children, manage so that the benefits inherent in the warm relationship of grandparents and grandchildren may be realized?

You are not likely to ask too many favors of your parents or parents-in-law if you keep in mind that grandchildren are an auxiliary interest and really should not be the chief concern of grandparents, unless a grandmother is substituting for a working, an absent, or an ill mother. You can be glad if older people have a full life of their own.

One's Company—Three's a Crowd

If grandparents have one child at a time for a visit or to take on an excursion, everyone concerned is usually happier. One child is four times easier to care for than two or three. Two cousins may be a happier combination than two brothers or two sisters.

Grandchildren and their grandparents often get along best when the middle generation is not present. There is less temptation for a child to play one off against the other when he is with representatives of only one generation.

If your mother or mother-in-law is permitting the children to do something which you honestly believe is harmful, or if your father or father-in-law is frightening a sensitive boy or girl with threats or tall tales, you may tactfully but firmly suggest a different course of action. To explain why you believe that this one thing is not good for the child is different from complaining about every detail of behavior everytime grandparents visit you or a youngster stays with them.

If grandparents object that, "She doesn't seem to know what to do with herself here," or, "He's into everything," a concrete suggestion of something your youngster enjoys which might be substituted for activities that lead to trouble may be appreciated. Keep a few toys at grandmother's or send along a favorite game, storybook, doll, or car to avoid continual begging for something on the part of the children or the buying of perishable, worthless, or unsuitable playthings by distraught relatives.

It may, as some young mothers claim, take a week to get the baby back to his usual routine after a visit from grandpa. In the long run, grandparents mean so much to a child that even a slightly fussy disposition for a few days is not too great a price to pay for getting acquainted.

If you ask some member of the family to stay with your children when you go out, the same courteous, clear-cut arrangements you would make with a paid helper are called for. Keep to the hour of your announced return, leave a note telling where supplies are, and, above all, write down in plain sight the number where you can be reached. The convenience of aunts, great-aunts, or grandparents should be considered and respected. Some quite obliging relatives will say to you, "Leave the baby with us whenever you please, but don't ask us to sit up at your place waiting for you to come home." Others are willing to "sit" where the children live—and where there are several childern this arrangement is almost a necessity, but only until a certain hour or on certain evenings. To respect these limitations will prevent abused feelings. Grandparents who were quite willing to put two children to bed a few years ago may, when they themselves are a bit older, find four or five too much for them.

No matter how well any plan worked last year, it may need to be altered this year. Needs and tastes change as youngsters grow up and grandparents grow older. The Saturday afternoon cocoa party at grandpa's, which was the high point of the week for a 5- or 6-year-old, is suddenly renounced. It may, most appropriately, need to be replaced by going to grandpa's for early supper when Saturday afternoon becomes the chosen meeting time for a 7- or 8-year-old's "club" Or perhaps it is grandpa who has joined a club!

Some families set aside a particular time for get-togethers. This may be advisable if grandparents with few interests of their own tend to expect too much of the younger generation's time. Here is a custom which needs to be frequently and frankly reviewed lest it grow stale and outlive its usefulness.

Three Generations Under One Roof

Tensions are especially apt to develop if three generations must share a home. There may be days when even the mildest suggestion from a usually reserved older person is interpreted by a daughter or daughter-in-law as "interference." At times, a houseful of children may appear as a nest of hoodlums or a madhouse to a weary or discouraged middle-aged or elderly person.

When three generations live under one roof, everyone's well-being may be served if some thought is given to dividing responsibilities and allotting privileges. Boys and girls can learn to be quiet while grandma takes a nap or grandpa writes a letter, but perhaps grandma can be encouraged to rest before the older ones come home from school and while the younger ones are napping. If grandfather usually returns home in the late afternoon, his grandson who practices the trumpet or the drums may need to do so before five o'clock, even at the sacrifice of half an hour of football.

If grandma's room is declared "off limits" except by special invitation—and being invited is something of a treat—she may more readily have the privacy she likes.

Working out when each family member shall have first claim on radio or TV, telephone or living room makes it easier to see that everyone's rights are respected.

If space is a problem, life may go more smoothly if everyone has some leisure-time activities that occasionally take him out of the house. Elderly grandparents may find a happy social life in a golden-age circle. Middle-aged ones will be welcomed in church or community activities as volunteer workers. And supervised, organized groups for the children of school age tend to keep a 7-year-old or a 10-year-old from feeling, perhaps rightly, that "there's not one thing you can do in this house without being clobbered." Even 3- and 4-year-olds are often cheerier for having a few hours in a nursery school or play group where the tastes, the endurance, and the attention span of his own age group are catered to.

Grandparents will usually be more content and less inclined to feel either superfluous or offended if they are given a definite part in the work of the household. If their advice is occasionally sought, it does wonders for their spirits. A grandmother who is a competent cook or a deft needlewoman may be pleased at having a good-sized family to feed or clothe once more. A grandfather who is a passable handyman or an astute shopper may find satisfaction in taking over minor repairs or some of the family buying.

Grandparents are an asset in the lives of children and of young parents, too, not merely as a convenience but also for what they can contribute in affectionate interest and the way they can widen horizons. Indeed, they are so important that if you are not fortunate enough to have any around, by all means go out and find one or two whom you can borrow. EDITH G. NEISSER

See also FAMILY DISCUSSIONS

GRANULATED EYELIDS *See* CONJUNCTIVITIS

GROUP PLAY *See* PLAY GROUPS

GROWING PAINS

The term "growing pains" has no medical meaning; physicians do not believe that pain occurs in the feet or legs of children because of growth. Whenever a child complains of pain in his feet and legs, therefore, his parents should try to find the cause. If a child persistently complains of such pains, it's time to take him to the doctor. He, in turn, may wish to have an orthopedic specialist examine the child.

Poor alignment of the bones, ligaments, and muscles of the feet and legs, and hence uneven weight bearing, is the most common cause of foot and leg pains in young children. Flat feet or poor alignment of the knees, either bowed or knock-knees, may also cause pains. The child who limps because of pain and complains that one or both hips hurt should be taken to a doctor for examination.

Occasionally, a child may have fleeting pain and swelling—sometimes with redness —in one or more joints. This condition might be an early symptom of rheumatic fever, a disease that often involves the heart. Pain in the joints may also indicate rheumatism or arthritis. If a child has such symptoms, a doctor should be called immediately.

Also, when a child exercises a great deal, as during summer vacations, he may become fatigued and complain of pain in his feet or legs. Sometimes he may not have pain while active during the day but will cry out with pain in the evening or during the night when the fatigued muscles may have cramps. And parents should also keep in mind sprains and bruises and bumps as a possible cause for acute pains. JULIUS B. RICHMOND

See also BOWLEGS; FLAT FEET; KNOCK-KNEE; MEDICAL SPECIALISTS; RHEUMATIC FEVER

GROWTH

Growth is one of the most obvious things that happens in the child. Our first reaction on seeing a youngster after an absence of a few weeks or months or years is likely to be, "How you have grown." Of course we often measure our own children's progress from year to year by making a series of pencil marks on the doorframe to show where the top of their heads reached at each successive measuring. Also, the pediatrician weighs and measures your child when you take him in for his regular health checks. These are the measures you can see. They are important as a part of the total evaluation of a child's progress, health, and well-being.

But there is much more to growth than the simple condition of becoming larger. As the child grows in size, his body proportions change, his features change, and often also his coloring. Teeth erupt, fall out, and are replaced by permanent ones—the list could be extended into a fairly long series. Just how do these changes take place?

The process of growth in the child may be thought of as a series of interactions between the growing organism and its environment. In this process the child *grows;* that is, he becomes larger. He *develops;* that is, he becomes increasingly complex in his body structure and its functions. He *matures;* that is, he approaches ever more closely to his mature size, organic structure, and body build.

These three aspects of growth are more or less continuously acting on and facilitating each other. As the child grows in size, the structure and functions of his body are becoming more complex, and at the same time they are continuously approaching their mature state.

The Growth Process

The ways in which these growth changes occur are inherited. The realization of this inherited potential is in many ways controlled by factors in the environment, some of which favor, and some of which interfere with, the growth process. It is not always possible to separate the hereditary factors from the environmental factors in a given instance. But if we have an understanding of the basic hereditary factors in growth, we can see better how the environmental factors may modify them.

The growth of an individual starts with the fertilized egg, and in the nine months before birth the most rapid growth and development take place. From the single original cell there is a rapid multiplication of cells. Soon several different types of cells develop and from these the characteristic human form emerges. There is the nervous system, which develops most rapidly. There are the beginnings of the bony skeleton; the muscles; the organs such as the heart, lungs, and digestive system; and the system of blood vessels which together with the heart form the circulatory system. The complex of glands which produce a variety of hormones are a part of this developmental process, and many of these hormones have profound effects on the child's growth, development, and maturation.

The heart in the fetus starts to beat about three weeks after conception; the earliest body movements may occur at about eight weeks. By 25 weeks the body structures are well defined and most of the reflexes necessary for postnatal life are present.

Birth occurs normally when the fetus is 40 weeks of age, but an infant may live if born as young as 26 weeks or as old as 50 weeks. Thus, infants, even at birth, are at different stages of maturity. But typically, the newborn is a skinny little thing with a large head and short arms and legs. He has very little muscle or fat, and his head is larger in circumference than his chest. He is about 20 inches long and weighs about 7½ pounds.

But this condition doesn't last. In a few short months the baby has become plump

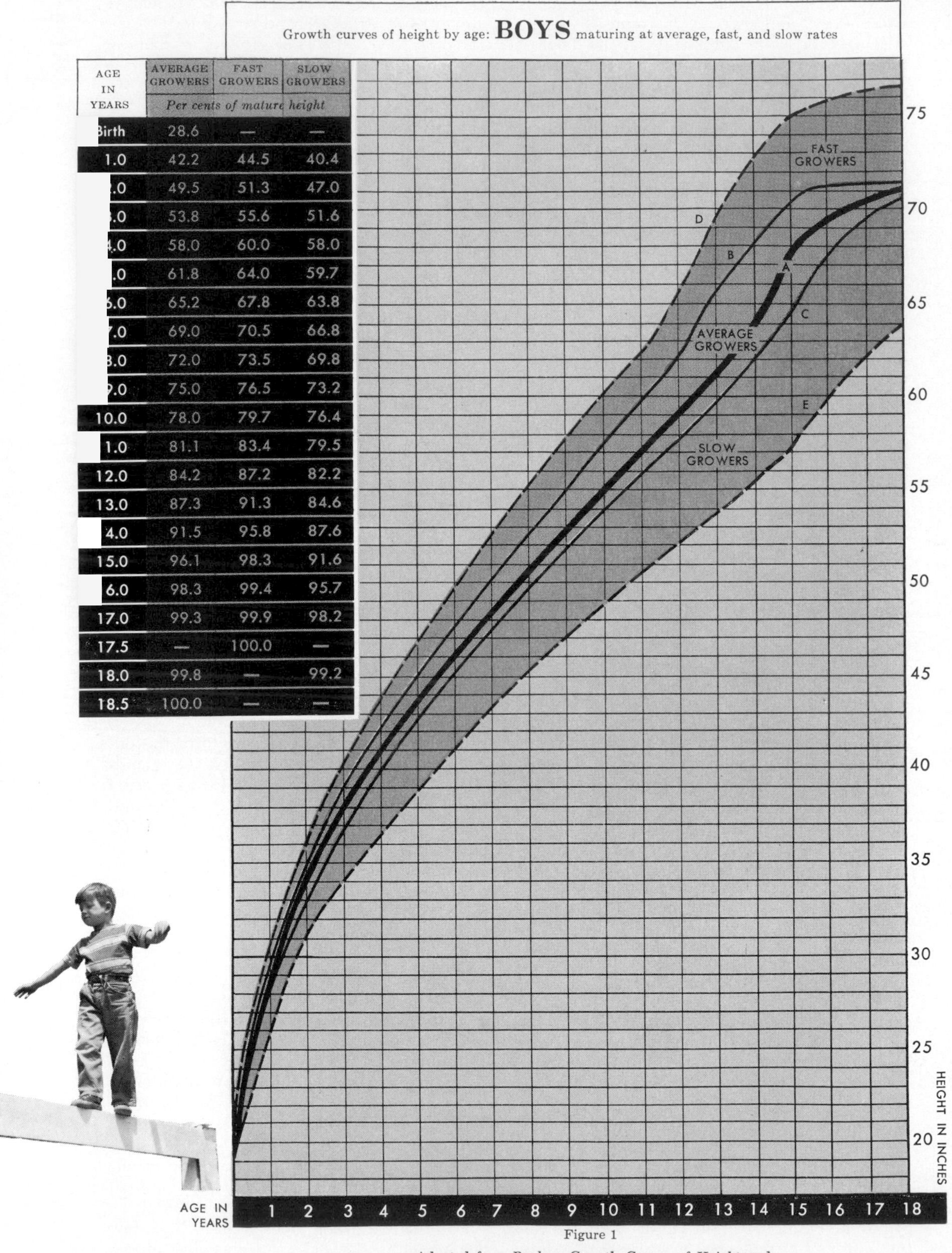

Growth curves of height by age: **BOYS** maturing at average, fast, and slow rates

AGE IN YEARS	AVERAGE GROWERS	FAST GROWERS	SLOW GROWERS
	Per cents of mature height		
Birth	28.6	—	—
1.0	42.2	44.5	40.4
.0	49.5	51.3	47.0
3.0	53.8	55.6	51.6
4.0	58.0	60.0	58.0
.0	61.8	64.0	59.7
6.0	65.2	67.8	63.8
7.0	69.0	70.5	66.8
8.0	72.0	73.5	69.8
9.0	75.0	76.5	73.2
10.0	78.0	79.7	76.4
1.0	81.1	83.4	79.5
12.0	84.2	87.2	82.2
13.0	87.3	91.3	84.6
4.0	91.5	95.8	87.6
15.0	96.1	98.3	91.6
6.0	98.3	99.4	95.7
17.0	99.3	99.9	98.2
17.5	—	100.0	—
18.0	99.8	—	99.2
18.5	100.0	—	—

Figure 1

Adapted from Bayley: Growth Curves of Height and Weight By Age for Boys and Girls, Scaled According to Physical Maturity, *Journal of Pediatrics*, 48:187, 1956, published by The C. V. Mosby Company, St. Louis.

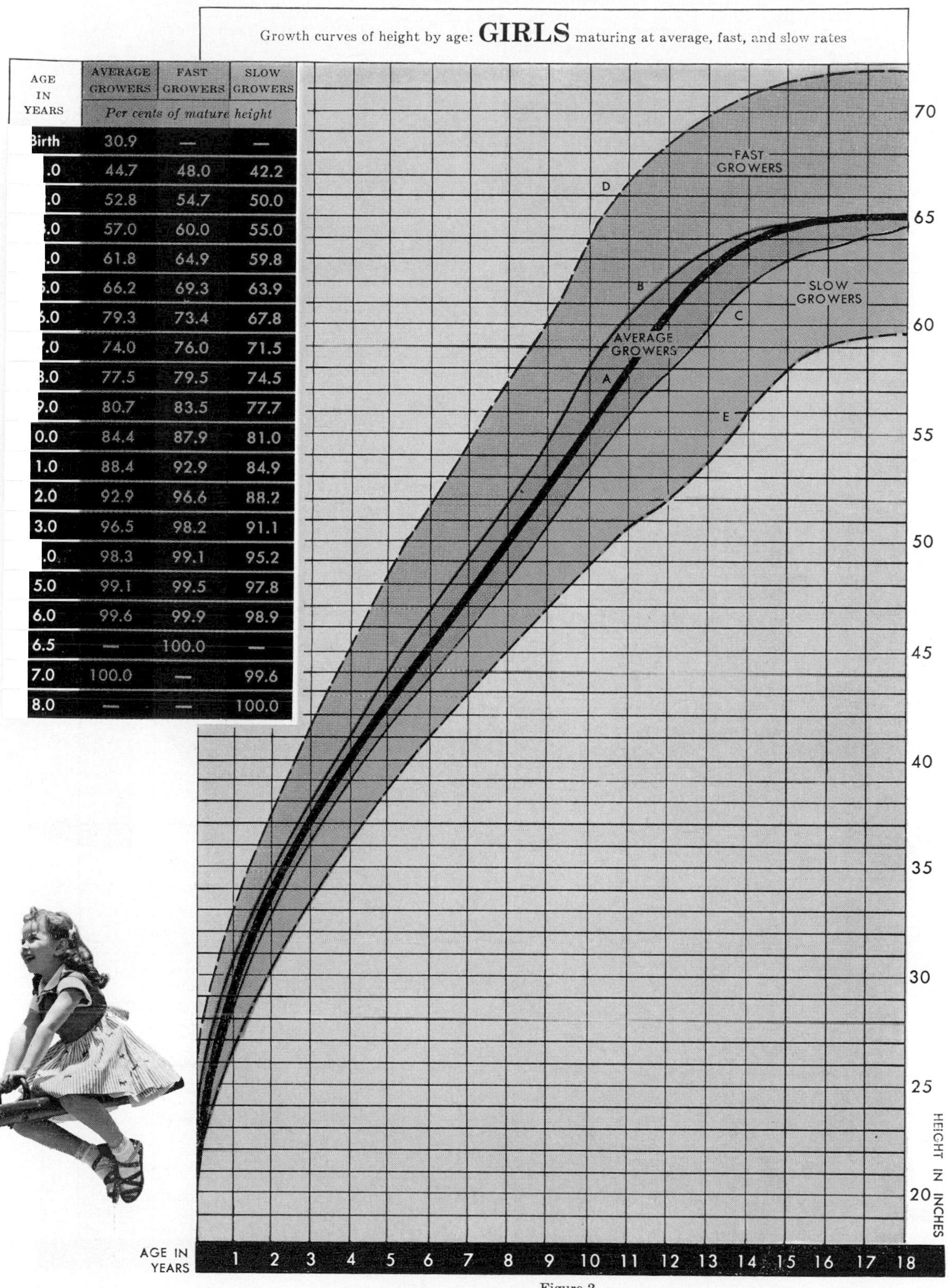

AGE IN YEARS	AVERAGE GROWERS	FAST GROWERS	SLOW GROWERS
	Per cents of mature height		
Birth	30.9	—	—
.0	44.7	48.0	42.2
.0	52.8	54.7	50.0
3.0	57.0	60.0	55.0
.0	61.8	64.9	59.8
5.0	66.2	69.3	63.9
6.0	79.3	73.4	67.8
.0	74.0	76.0	71.5
3.0	77.5	79.5	74.5
9.0	80.7	83.5	77.7
0.0	84.4	87.9	81.0
1.0	88.4	92.9	84.9
2.0	92.9	96.6	88.2
3.0	96.5	98.2	91.1
.0	98.3	99.1	95.2
5.0	99.1	99.5	97.8
6.0	99.6	99.9	98.9
6.5	—	100.0	—
7.0	100.0	—	99.6
8.0	—	—	100.0

Figure 2

Adapted from Bayley: Growth Curves of Height and Weight By Age for Boys and Girls, Scaled According to Physical Maturity, *Journal of Pediatrics*, 48:187, 1956, published by The C. V. Mosby Company, St. Louis.

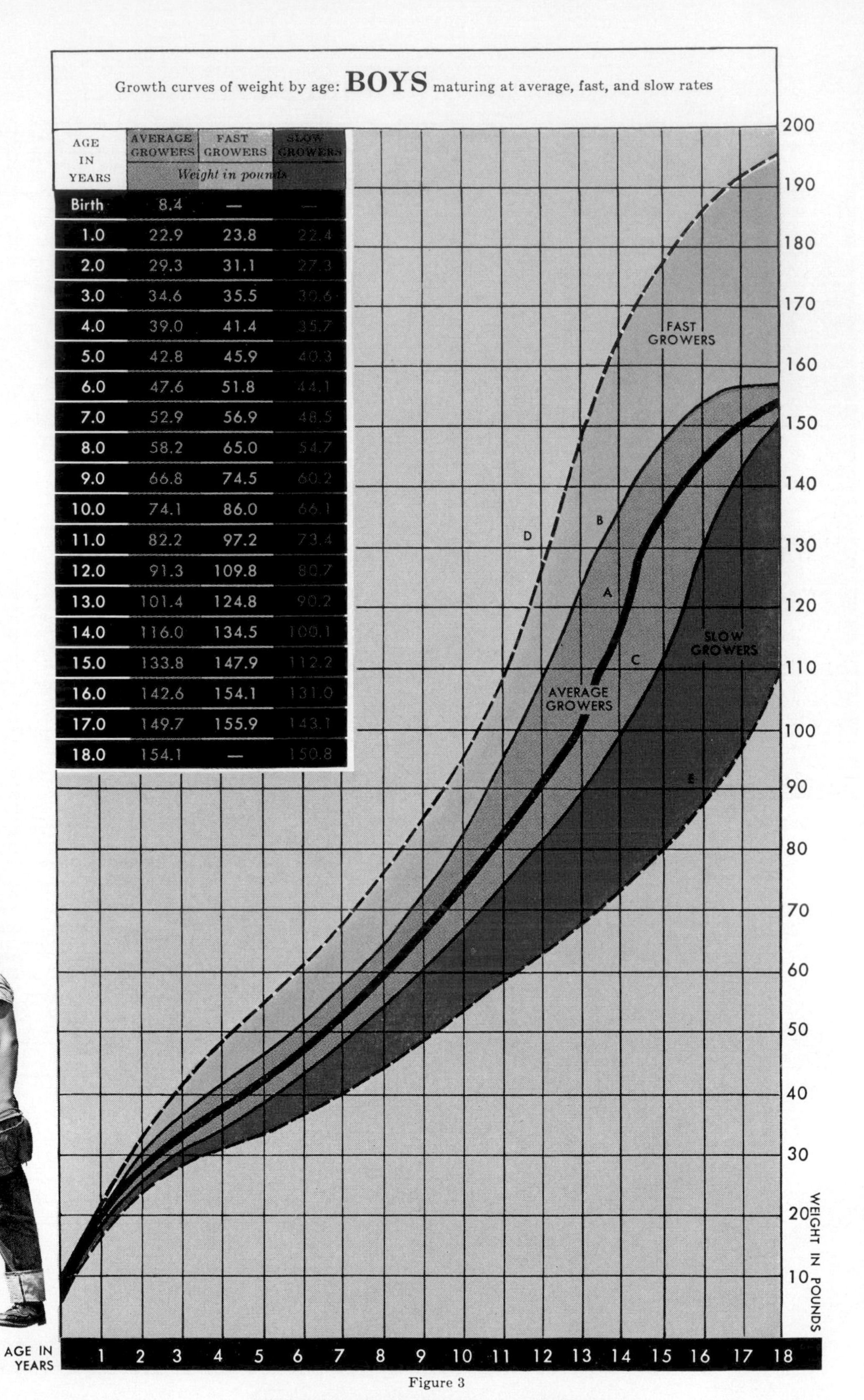

Growth curves of weight by age: **BOYS** maturing at average, fast, and slow rates

AGE IN YEARS	AVERAGE GROWERS	FAST GROWERS	SLOW GROWERS
	Weight in pounds		
Birth	8.4	—	—
1.0	22.9	23.8	22.4
2.0	29.3	31.1	27.3
3.0	34.6	35.5	30.6
4.0	39.0	41.4	35.7
5.0	42.8	45.9	40.3
6.0	47.6	51.8	44.1
7.0	52.9	56.9	48.5
8.0	58.2	65.0	54.7
9.0	66.8	74.5	60.2
10.0	74.1	86.0	66.1
11.0	82.2	97.2	73.4
12.0	91.3	109.8	80.7
13.0	101.4	124.8	90.2
14.0	116.0	134.5	100.1
15.0	133.8	147.9	112.2
16.0	142.6	154.1	131.0
17.0	149.7	155.9	143.1
18.0	154.1	—	150.8

Figure 3

Adapted from Bayley: Growth Curves of Height and Weight By Age for Boys and Girls, Scaled According to Physical Maturity, *Journal of Pediatrics*, 48:187, 1956, published by The C. V. Mosby Company, St. Louis.

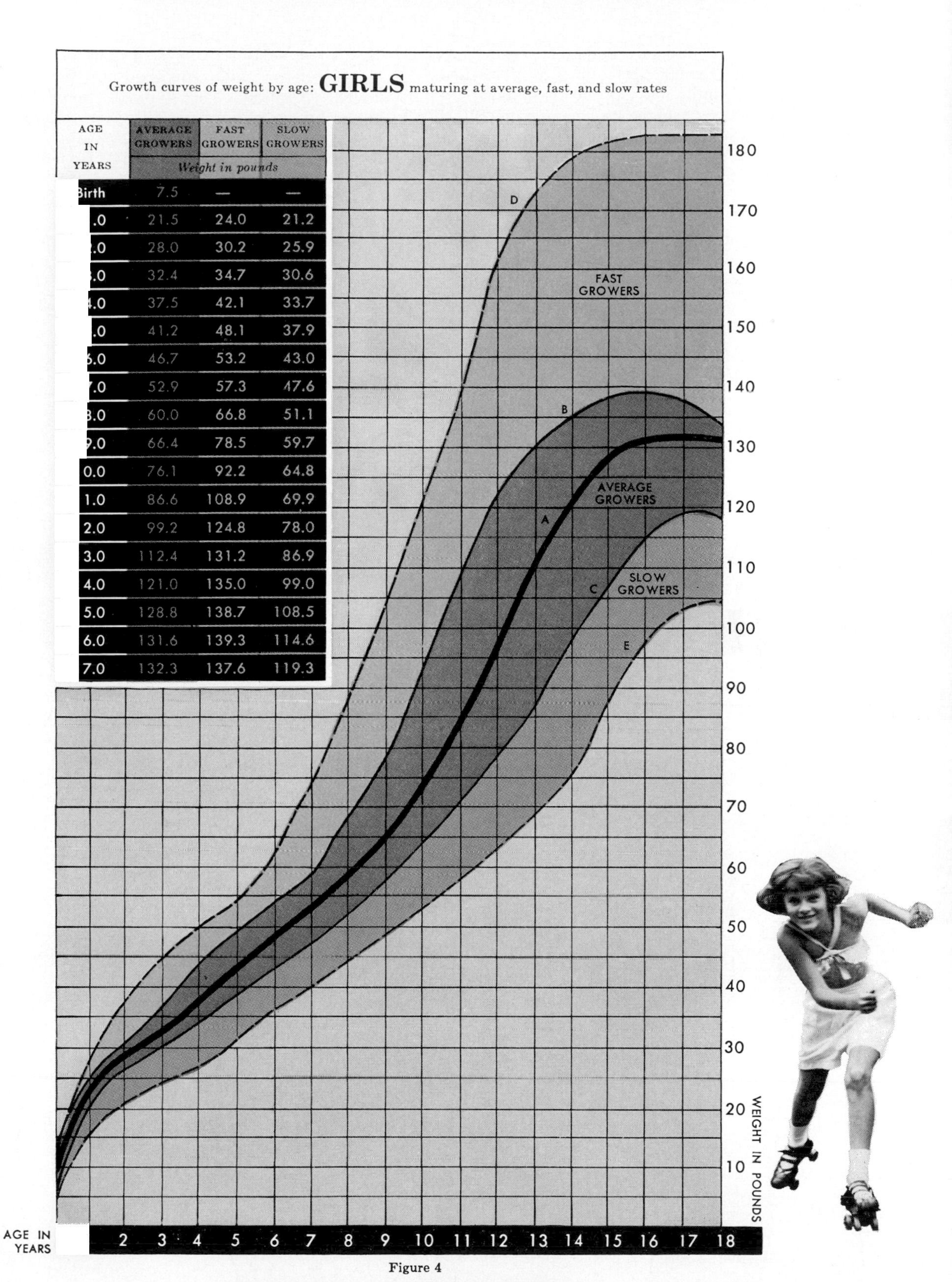

Growth curves of weight by age: **GIRLS** maturing at average, fast, and slow rates

AGE IN YEARS	AVERAGE GROWERS	FAST GROWERS	SLOW GROWERS
	Weight in pounds		
Birth	7.5	—	—
.0	21.5	24.0	21.2
2.0	28.0	30.2	25.9
3.0	32.4	34.7	30.6
4.0	37.5	42.1	33.7
.0	41.2	48.1	37.9
6.0	46.7	53.2	43.0
7.0	52.9	57.3	47.6
8.0	60.0	66.8	51.1
9.0	66.4	78.5	59.7
0.0	76.1	92.2	64.8
1.0	86.6	108.9	69.9
2.0	99.2	124.8	78.0
3.0	112.4	131.2	86.9
4.0	121.0	135.0	99.0
5.0	128.8	138.7	108.5
6.0	131.6	139.3	114.6
7.0	132.3	137.6	119.3

Figure 4

Adapted from Bayley: Growth Curves of Height and Weight By Age for Boys and Girls, Scaled According to Physical Maturity, *Journal of Pediatrics*, 48:187, 1956, published by The C. V. Mosby Company, St. Louis.

and active and his body has made rapid gains in growing up to the size of his head. By 6 months of age he has more than doubled his weight to an average of 16½ pounds and increased his length on the average to 26 inches. This general trend continues through the first year, with most of the growth occurring in the body and with a generally increasing chubbiness. These numbers represent only the typical, or average. They are not to be used for comparison.

Growth is most often measured and described in terms of heights and weights for age. These measures represent only the over-all size of the child, and they are the most easily measured. The typical growth in height for age of boys and girls is represented in the center curve *A* of Figures 1 and 2 on the preceding pages. The growth curves for weight are shown in Figures 3 and 4, where, again, the typical growth rates are shown by the heavy center lines *A*.

A glance at these curves shows immediately that there are periods of rapid and slow growth. After the fast growth of the first year, the changes are more and more grad-

Growth changes in body proportions (but not in height) shown by tracings from photographs of one boy and one girl at 1½, 4, 8, 14, and 18 years.

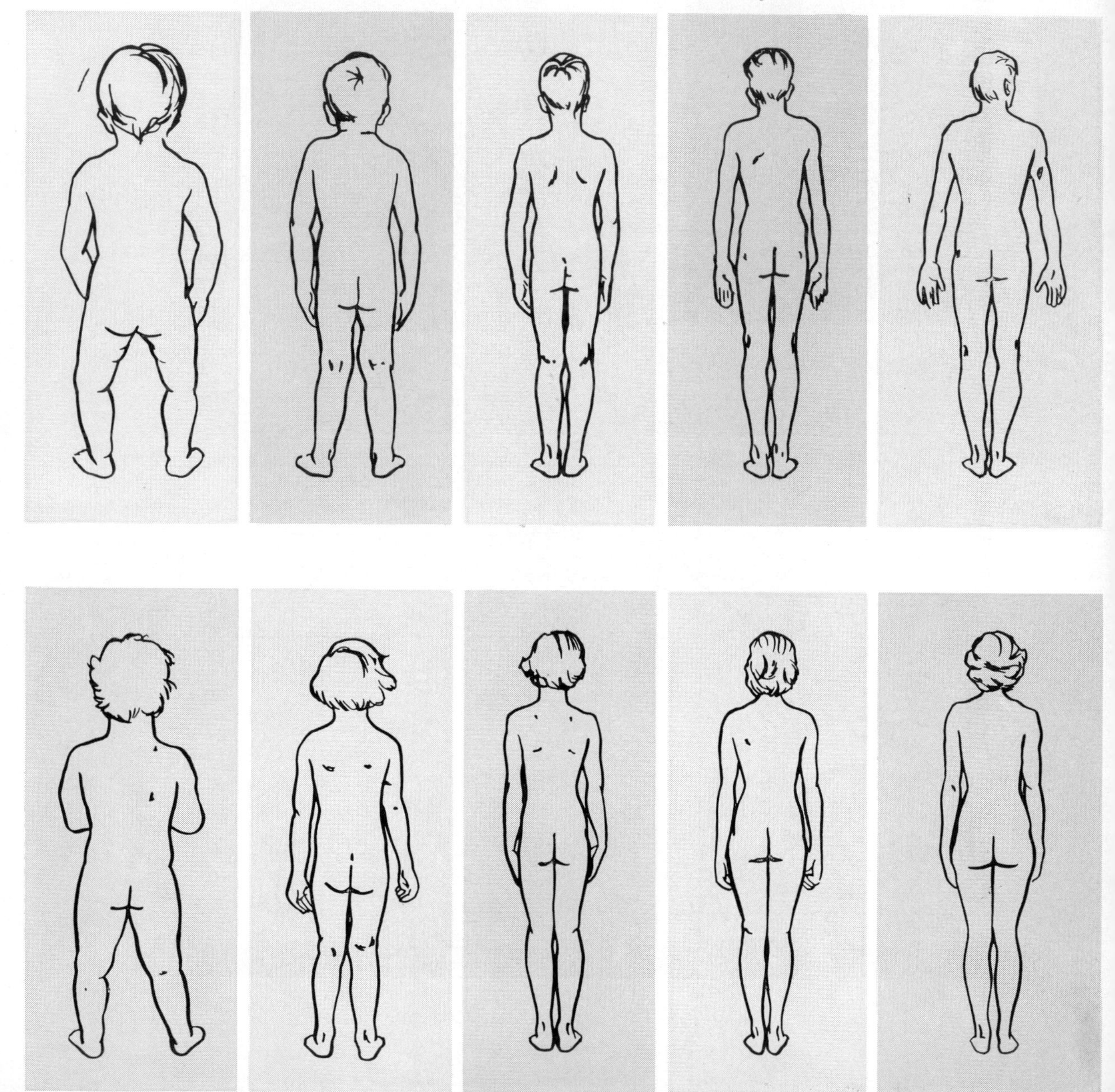

ual, becoming fairly steady between about 6 and 10 years. Then after briefly seeming to mark time, there is a spurt of rapid growth before the final slowing down and stopping. These changes in rates of growth are seen most clearly in the curves of height.

Remember that all these figures are based on averages and that there are many individual exceptions to them.

Changing Body Proportions

Because different parts of the body grow at different rates, the child's proportions are constantly changing as he grows. From the big-headed, skinny newborn he changes to the chubby, roly-poly 1-year-old. Then he loses his baby fat, his legs grow faster than the rest of him, and he emerges a lanky 9- to 11-year-old.

Adolescence brings about a rapid change in many dimensions. The entire bony structure grows larger; We become aware of this from the rapidly growing hands and feet. It may also be seen in the broadening of the boys' shoulders and of the girls' hips. There is an increase in muscles, especially in the boys, and fat, especially in the girls. The girls' breasts and the boys' genitals develop, the face enlarges, and the voice changes (these last two more in the boys), pubic and axillary hair grows. Many of these changes take place very rapidly. Often in the span of a year or two the child becomes physically an adult.

The general changes in body proportions are shown on the facing page. We see here the changes in one boy and one girl between 15 months and 18 years. Do not use these figures as a basis of comparison, but as a general rule at birth the head makes up about one-fourth of the body length, while in the adult it is only about one-eighth of the total. Length of the legs comprises about one-third at birth and one-half in the adult, of the total body length. To put it another way, the head doubles its size, the trunk triples its length, the arms increase about four times, and the legs about five times between birth and the completion of growth. Shoulders almost triple their width, hip widths are tripled, chest circumference is increased two and one-half times, and head circumference one and one-half times. These figures are, of course, very general and are not exactly the same for both sexes.

Growth Difference Between Boys and Girls

In the infant and the young child sex differences in growth and body proportion are so slight as to be of no practical significance. Although girls on the average are a little more mature than boys of the same age, boys on the average are a little larger in size. Boys and girls cut their teeth at about the same ages.

One of the few measures that may be easily used in these early ages to assess physical maturity is the series of X-ray standards for bone development. One of the most useful of these standards, by Greulich and Pyle (1959), is composed of X-ray pictures of the left hand and wrist. There are two sets of standards, one for boys and one for girls. Each picture in a series shows the bones with the characteristic stage of maturity of a boy (or girl) of a given age. There is a standard picture for each three months during the first year and a half, and there is one for each year or half year until the bones are mature. For the first eight or nine years the bony contours consistently appear to be only a little more mature for the girls. At about this time, however, the girls start maturing very rapidly. By 13 years of age there is a two and one-half year difference in degree of skeletal maturity. The girls attain adult status (the bones in the hand have fully mature contours) at an average age of 16 years, 3 months. The boys do not reach maturity until the average age of 18 years, 9 months.

Starting at around 10 years, several aspects of physical maturing are easily observed. In each of these aspects, about the same amount of difference between boys and girls in rates of maturing shows up. As we have already noted, the girls' rate of skeletal maturing speeds up at about 10 years. So does her rate of growth in size. At the same time there is a rapid change toward the mature body form. Characteristic fat deposits form, giving her soft, feminine contours. In the typical boy, starting about two years later, muscles grow on the fast-growing, bony framework, and in another year or two he achieves the broad-shouldered, narrow-hipped, muscular appearance that foreshadows the adult male build.

Individual Differences in Growth

Healthy children show wide variations from the average in all aspects of growth. Very few children are right at the average in all respects. Some are naturally tall, some short, some heavy-set, some slender; some are long-legged, some long-bodied. Some go through the processes of growth and maturing much faster; others much slower than the average. There are individual differences in the degree to which a girl's build becomes feminine or a boy's build becomes masculine, and a few retain rather childlike builds.

When you evaluate your child's build or growth, it is important to keep in mind the extent to which these differences are normal and healthy. A child may appear to be very short because he is maturing more slowly than usual, or very tall because his rate of growth is very fast. These normal variations in growth rates are shown for height in Figures 1 and 2, and for weight in Figures 3 and 4. If a boy or girl has a bone age that is one or two years advanced over the average, the height curves will look more like those just above and to the left of the center, line *B*, while if the bone age is a year or two slow, the height curves will be more like those just below and to the right of the center, curve *C*. And the weight curves of these same children will tend to follow the corresponding curves in Figures 3 and 4.

Notice that these differences occur mostly in early adolescence. That is when the starting time of rapid growth and maturing varies greatly from child to child. Girls at 10 or 11 years, or some boys at 12 or 13, may suddenly start growing fast and become much taller than their age-mates. These children are usually early maturers; they will attain their adult size and build early. But when they become adults, they will not necessarily be outstandingly tall. The relation of their heights to others of their sex will be more like it was in early childhood. It is just as possible that a girl who still remains a little girl at 13 or 14, or a boy who has not started maturing and growing fast at 15 or 16, will soon start growing and will overtake his age-mates only a year or two later. Adult heights may be estimated from the percentage tables in Figures 1 and 2.

Some children, however, are inherently large and tall. They usually are tall from early infancy and also somewhat advanced in bone age. These children usually remain relatively tall. Others are inherently short and consistently grow slowly and remain short. To a considerable extent these are inherited differences, and we find that children are much like theirs parents or other family members in their sizes and their rates of growth. The top *D* and bottom *E*, broken-line curves of height and weight in Figures 1, 2, 3, and 4, indicate approximately the normal variations. That is, about 98 per cent of children are at least as large as the lower line and no larger than the upper line for sex, age, and stage of maturation.

Sometimes growth does not follow the expected course. There appear to be three periods of growth: (1) the first three or four years of life, (2) midchildhood years, and (3) adolescent years. For each of these three periods there is a shift in the relative importance of the hormones that are influential in controlling growth: (1) The thyroid predominates during infancy, (2) the pituitary growth hormone in midchildhood years, and (3) the sex hormones in adolescent years. When a child's growth does change its course to faster or slower than the expected pattern, it is likely to be at the juncture between two periods. The timing of the new phase may be a little early or late, and the growth potential may be stronger or weaker than in the earlier phase.

At the onset of the adolescent phase of growth, many boys and girls become fat in varying degrees. This is usually a temporary condition, and as soon as fast maturing and growth in height are well started, the extra fat disappears. For some, however, it can be a time for watching the diet to make sure that the weight does not get out of control.

Environmental Influences on Growth

In general, growth is encouraged and aided by a good well-balanced diet, by adequate exercise, and by adequate rest and sleep. Children's needs for food, rest, and exercise vary. It is not good to force the same amount of food and the same hours of sleep, for example, on every child. Some need more and others, less. The child's needs can be judged by keeping a check on his health and watching his growth in relation to his own growth history.

Poor nutrition or a persistent infection, for example, can slow down growth and also leave the child in need of more rest. Periods of prolonged anxiety and emotional disturbance may have the same effects. In an acute illness a child's entire energies go into combatting the disease, and growth ceases for the period of emergency. But once health is restored, normal growth is resumed if the other requirements for healthy growth are also met. As a rule, the greatest effects on growth appear to be the long-persisting conditions. For example, children tend to be larger and grow to be taller adults in areas like some in California and Texas, where the climate is mild, allowing children to play outdoors without heavy clothing the year around, and enabling them to eat of ever-present supplies of fresh fruits and vegetables. Also, children in families who are better educated and who have larger incomes and more adequate houses tend to grow larger—probably because their parents know better how to feed and care for them and can also afford the better food and care. It is also true that children tend to be taller than their own parents, perhaps because our knowledge about ways to promote health increases with each generation.

But, fortunately, there are genetic limits to peoples' size. Improved environments help each child to achieve only his own potential. They do not create a race of giants.

When a Child's Growth Differs from the Pattern

With a knowledge of the normal variations in growth, development, and maturing, both children and their parents can know better what to expect. The 9-year-old girl who suddenly grows four inches in a year can be reassured that she will not be a giant. The 15-year-old boy who finds himself left behind when his best friend has suddenly become four inches taller than he may gain some consolation in knowing that he is not going to stay short but will soon start catching up to his friends.

When a child's growth is widely different from the pattern, of course it is wise to take him to a physician for an expert evaluation. For some of the big differences in growth pattern, effective methods of treatment now exist. For others, medical knowledge is still too incomplete.

If, according to the best evaluation, it is clear that a child will be unusually tall or short, then he should be helped to make the best of it. The short boy (or girl) can be helped to learn how to select clothes that will make him seem taller. He can be guided into sports activities that emphasize skills he can master and that do not demand size and the strength that goes with large size. The tall girl can be reminded that the best dress models are often tall; she can be encouraged to stand erect and be given dancing lessons to develop good coordination and poise.

Equally as important as these aspects of appearance, parents should help the child to realize that every person deviates in one way or another from the average or ideal, and that the best way to cope with such deviation is to accept it and turn one's efforts to developing one's good qualities. Then the defects will either not be noticed by others or will soon be forgotten or considered unimportant. Those who counsel a child should consider what his best potentialities are and help him to direct his efforts toward improving and capitalizing on them. NANCY BAYLEY

See also HEREDITY; INDIVIDUAL DIFFERENCES; NUTRITION; SEX DIFFERENCES

GUIDANCE *See* CHILD GUIDANCE CLINIC

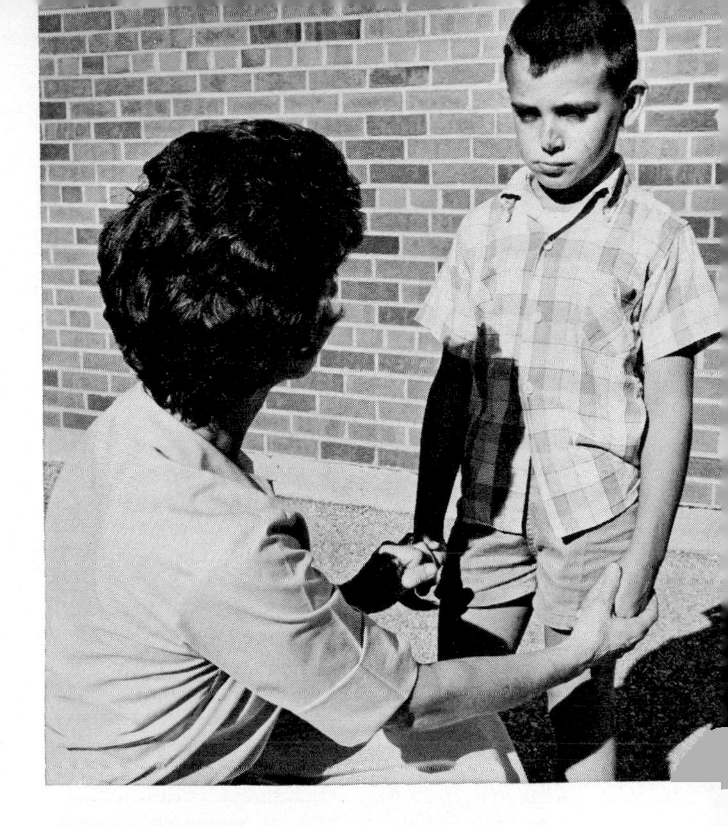

GUILT FEELINGS

One day a parent may scold his child for some misdemeanor and end his tirade with: "Aren't you sorry for what you did?" The next day the same parent may even avoid scolding because he is afraid that he is giving his child a guilt complex. Such a parent is neither irrational nor inconsistent; he is just behaving like a normal parent.

A person without any guilt feelings would be a monster; one with intensely strong guilt feelings cannot live successfully. Neither too small a sense of guilt, nor too much of it, nor guilt about the wrong issues is healthy. Thus, as parents, we should help our children to feel guilty where the issues are truly important, but we should also help them not to feel guilty about trifles. And, even where it is important, parents should help their children not to feel too severely guilty.

Guilt is an act of self-condemnation. It is the voice of conscience, or of the so-called superego. It is neither the result of punishment nor is it caused by the fear of punishment. It is rather the result of taking into oneself the standards of parents or of other people who are important to the child. The child who is afraid of punishment develops a conscience reaction against his misdeed because he fears he will lose his parents' love. Parents often overlook this fact because what they remember is that after they were punished by their parents, they mended their ways; so, too, after they have punished their child, they see an improvement. What created the positive effect was that the punishment convinced the child that his misbehavior was serious enough for his parents to stop loving him. What is effective is not the severity of the punishment but the proof that misbehavior leads to loss of love.

This, of course, presupposes that the child is loved and feels loved. It is such a pleasant and gratifying feeling that a child will go to great lengths to preserve it. He learns to avoid doing wrong because he does not want to lose the love of his parents. Parental love gives the child the feeling, "I am a good child; I am lovable," but it also gives him the feeling, "If I do certain things, then I stop being lovable." Later on in life, he will stop loving himself if he commits a bad deed just as he once lost his parents' love by doing wrong. This, then, is the origin of guilt feelings and how they deter us later on from doing wrong.

A healthy conscience, or a healthy superego, will have both parental love and morality in it as well as the threat of losing important good feelings if we violate our conscience. Whether or not the threat of withdrawal of love will be effective in creating just the right amount of guilt, and with it the right kind of conscience, depends on the amount of love and respect the child has experienced from his parents. Threats, when not balanced by respect and tender care, will produce excessive guilt and may cause a variety of disturbances, the most marked of which may be a deadening of spontaneity and initiative. The child who is too afraid he may disobey the rules of behavior will find it difficult to play and to enjoy life.

The important thing about guilt feelings is not only to have the right amount, but also that guilt should arise over important issues and not over trivial matters. To make a child feel guilty for taking candy out of the candy jar will not help him very much to be morally upright in later life. Emphasizing a few important issues and seeing to it that the child feels guilty about them will make these issues stand out as things to be avoided. Learning must proceed step by step from the most important to the less important. The same goes for how things are learned. At the beginning a child will feel guilty only for moments, later for hours, and only then will he try to avoid misbehaving altogether. Important learning takes time. That is why we should not expect too much guilt (or the avoidance of bad behavior) all at once or about too many issues.

All too often children are made to feel guilty about things that are not really immoral but are simply inconvenient to the parent or potentially harmful to the child. Danger is certainly to be avoided. But a child should not be made to feel guilty for being foolhardy, for guilt may then block off a much more sensible and simple avoidance reaction. For example, there is no reason why a child should feel guilty about touching a hot stove, but he should certainly avoid doing so because it may be painful or dangerous. Therefore to tell a child he is bad for touching a hot stove or for running into the street after a ball is totally misleading. To tell him that he is careless and invites pain is right. Some adults have guilt feelings that are much too strong because as children they were made to feel guilty about things that were really not wrong but simply to be avoided out of common sense. Some children feel more guilty about using a swear word than about stealing, simply because stealing was not part of their experience while bad language was, and they were made to feel terribly guilty about using it.

There are some particular issues where a word of warning seems in point. For example, children should not be made to feel guilty about using their initiative, nor about what they feel or wish—only about the way they act. They should not be made to feel guilty because they do not yet live up to their parents' ideals. Children will mold their personalities either in the image of their parents if they love them or in the opposite image if they hate them. But even if they love their parents, they may not follow the parental image all at once nor in the sequence the parent would prefer.

Nothing human beings do is ever *all* wrong. It is a sign of excessive guilt feelings if a child thinks what he did was *all* wrong—that there weren't some intelligent or acceptable motives present also. Therefore he should be given a chance to explain his reasoning. The parent should not reject all the child's reasoning, nor all his actions, but instead should help him to see where his reasoning is wrong, always stressing that some of it is right. In this way his guilt feelings will not extend from the specific thing he did wrong to an all-pervasive, overpowering feeling that keeps him from living successfully. He can then dare to meet the world courageously, even if it means that sometimes things will not turn out altogether right.

BRUNO BETTELHEIM

See also INFERIORITY COMPLEX; LOVE; MENTAL HEALTH

HAIR CARE

The color of your child's hair, its texture, its scarcity or abundance are physical characteristics for which his ancestors are responsible. But its luster, its vitality, and its attractiveness depend mostly on the child's own general health and on the kind of hair and scalp care he receives.

Although hair withstands everyday wear and tear remarkably well, it does require a certain amount of protection and care. It needs daily brushing to give it gloss (at least 100 strokes), to remove loose scales, and to stimulate the scalp.

Regular brushing of your child's hair should begin as soon as there is hair to brush. The bristles of the brush should be soft enough not to cause discomfort or damage to his tender scalp. You can get best results by separating the hair into convenient sections and brushing up and away from the scalp, one section at a time, moving your wrist with each stroke so that the brush goes through a rolling motion.

The comb you use should have blunt teeth because rough edges damage scalp and hair shaft. Section tangled hair, and start combing about two inches from the free end of the hair. When the comb passes freely to the ends, place it a little higher in the section and comb through to the end again. Repeat the procedure until the comb passes freely from the scalp to the ends of the hair. Combs and brushes are as individual as toothbrushes, and each child should have his own. Wash them frequently in warm soapy water to keep them clean and fresh.

Hair and scalp are probably more subject to dirt than any other part of the body. The scalp retains the dust and soot from the atmosphere as well as the excretions of the oil and sweat glands. But if the hair is well brushed and combed each day, a shampoo once a week or every 10 days should be enough for most children. Hair cleanliness is particularly important for the youngster with complexion problems, such as acne.

Use only gentle shampoos. Until puberty, a child's hair hasn't much oil, and a strong shampoo may irritate the scalp and make the hair unmanageable. And if, as almost always happens, some lather runs into a child's eyes, a strong shampoo will burn or sting. Most shampoos designed especially for children are mild.

Brisk towel drying may break and split a child's hair, so blot the hair dry. If it is the kind of hair that snarls and tangles to an unusual degree after shampooing, a crème rinse may help.

If you use hair spray for arranging and setting, be careful that it is sprayed at a distance of approximately 12 inches from your child's head and that eyes are shielded.

Encourage your child to take responsibility for caring for his own hair at the first sign of willingness on his part. Girls, especially, benefit from deftness in caring for and arranging their own hair. And don't forget the compliments: "I like the way your hair shines after a shampoo," or, "You're nice-looking when your hair is clean and brushed" will work wonders. VERONICA L. CONLEY

HAIRCUT

One day, somewhere between his first and second birthdays, daddy is going to look at his son and say, "Mom, that boy needs a haircut." Mother's reaction may be, "Oh, *no*, he's just a baby!" But there's no denying that he will have to have his first haircut sometime, and it might be good to think about it and plan for it now.

If your child is an outgoing little fellow, not timid with strangers, you may very likely take him for his first haircut without incident. But if he is shy, especially with strangers, better lay a little groundwork to get him ready for the big day. Perhaps he can watch his dad having his hair cut, or a neighbor's child to whom haircuts are old hat.

You might get him used to the sound of the clicking scissors by trimming his hair at home a few times before his first professional haircut. Show him pictures of a child in a barber chair. Put a big apron over his shoulders and give him a "pretend" haircut in front of a mirror. Sometimes children are frightened by the moving reflections in the big mirror at a barbershop—their own and the barber's and those of customers in adjacent chairs.

If, despite your careful preparation, he cries and is fearful, don't insist on the haircut that first visit. Give him a little time. The barber in his white coat, the shiny equipment, and people talking loudly are pretty confusing to a child. Most barbers want a child to get used to haircuts at an early age and will cooperate with the parents. A "ride" to get him used to the up-and-down chair might help.

Many mothers manage to keep a little girl's hair trimmed neatly at home. But if her hair is thick or unruly, the same type of preparation might be in order if she is to be taken to a barber or beauty shop. Play "beauty shop" with her or take her with you when you have your hair cut.

For those who want to practice the fine art of haircutting at home, there are many good kits available. Some parents seem to be born barbers; others acquire skill only through trial and error. But the savings, particularly in large families, often makes both the original investment in equipment and the effort well worth while.

See also HAIR CARE; SHYNESS AND TIMIDITY

HALF BROTHERS AND SISTERS *See* DIVORCE AND SEPARATION

HANDEDNESS *See* LEFT-HANDEDNESS

HANDICAPPED CHILD

A handicap is not necessarily an unbearable calamity. A handicapped person can often lead a useful and satisfying life. Limits are set by the handicap, of course, but within those limits the person with impaired sight or hearing, epilepsy, cerebral palsy, or mental retardation may be able to live happily as a member of a family and a community.

Parents' Attitude Important

Children take their viewpoints from adults. Because this is so, it is important for parents to speak of a handicap in a matter-of-fact way, with the child as well as with others. A handicapped child needs love and warmth and affection and encouragement; he needs reassurance in those moments when he is discouraged; he needs support in the things he tries to do. It is the parents' attitude toward their child and his disability that is important. Being oversympathetic, overindulgent, overly kind and solicitous serve only to point up his handicap. All the child really wants is to be considered as "just another person," able to do pretty much as other children do.

Stress What He *Can* Do

It is important to concentrate on what a handicapped child can do rather than on what he cannot do. Between seizures an epileptic child can do pretty much what other children do. The child with defective vision can still enjoy what can be heard, felt, touched, or tasted. The deaf child can see the wonders of the world about him. The mentally retarded child who has love and understanding can be helped to satisfy what may be few wants and simple needs.

Sometimes disabilities loom so large that they seem to be all there is to see about a child, but it should never be forgotten that behind and beyond and above any handicap is an individual, a temperament, a personality. The child is a person, and some of his senses and abilities are undamaged by a particular handicap. Overemphasize the handicap and its limitations, and a youngster is doubly handicapped from the start.

They Need to Achieve

Boys and girls who are handicapped need to feel a sense of achievement, as do all other boys and girls. Obviously, a crippled boy cannot compete in organized strenuous games, but he may make a fine cheer leader. A cerebral-palsied girl cannot, for her own safety, be allowed to dry dishes and glasses, but she can feel great satisfaction in drying and putting away the silverware. A parent's goal for a handicapped child should be to offer him challenges that he can accept and fulfill, while at the same time not overtaxing his capacities. As he gains dexterity, he may be given more difficult tasks.

Like all other children, handicapped ones ought to have every possible chance to become self-reliant. They should dress themselves as much as they are able; should go out alone, unless the hazards of doing so place them in danger greater than that encountered by other children of the same age; should be allowed choices of what to wear, for example, or what to have for breakfast.

Going Places and Making Friends

The handicapped child needs every chance to broaden his experience. Excursions, reading, story hours at the library, or games with other children are all possible experiences for the handicapped child. He should have fun; he should be included in group activities. Some parents feel that their handicapped child should associate with normal children only. They feel that other handicapped children might depress their child. Actually, it is good for a handicapped child to have some friends as handicapped as he is, for among them he is not pushed to undue competition.

When children come to visit a handicapped child for the first time, they are likely to display curiosity about the child's hearing aid or thick-lensed glasses or leg braces. Let the guests examine these pieces of equipment. When children understand why it is necessary for a handicapped child to wear these things, they will not be embarrassed and will feel free to talk frankly and casually with the child and his parents.

Interests and Attitudes

A handicapped child who has a particular skill or interest will meet with other children on a common ground. Mentally handicapped children usually like music and can share in group singing. Lame children, unable to participate in more active games, often become excellent chess or checkers players. A hard-of-hearing child can participate in the arts and crafts. Creative dramatics brings out the very best in children, handicapped youngsters included. Friendships flourish when handicapped youngsters and other children play together and work toward a common goal.

In promoting the interests of their child, parents must take a wise and open-minded attitude. They may feel that their handicapped child has been slighted if he is not invited to join other active children. If parents can realize that all children—the brightest, the most intelligent, the best-liked ones—receive slights at one time or another, they will not harbor resentment. At the same time, parents of handicapped children must be careful not to force their children into friendships with children who do not have limitations. As in setting goals or tasks of any kind, there is a fine line between expecting too much and expecting too little of the handicapped child.

It does not help a handicapped child to have his parents pity him. He is not helped when parents pamper him or shower him with everything he wants or let him always have his way. When a handicapped child is so handled, he becomes more dependent, more helpless, and, as he grows older, more demanding. He becomes known as a spoiled child, with an unappealing personality. At the other end of the scale are the parents of handicapped children who are overcritical, who set their standards of behavior unmindful of their children's capabilities. These children carry double burdens of their handicaps, plus the knowledge that nothing they do pleases their parents.

Finding Medical Care

Parents of a handicapped child often go from city to city, or even from country to country, trying to find a magic cure for their child. Such aimless searching is useless and is emotionally upsetting to the child as well as his parents. Many of these parents fall into the hands of quacks who promise sure-cure remedies. Often a family's entire savings are used with no improvement, much less cure. The wisest course is to find a reputable and competent doctor or clinic and follow through conscientiously on the recommended course of care and treatment.

Parents of handicapped children may feel that they need help in meeting the problem of "doing what is best for the child." All parents harbor hopes and dreams for their children's happiness and success. Their hopes and ambitions are limited by what the children are able to do—for all children have some limits beyond which they cannot go. But sometimes the degree of the limitation may be so great that parents feel their problem is overwhelming. Recognized counselors and mental health and service agencies will help these parents.

Nearly always, parents feel that they are somehow to blame for their child's handicap. But very few handicaps are anyone's fault. For many handicaps, like certain forms of mental deficiency and seizures, the cause is unknown. With others, even where a cause is recognized, the condition may still have been unavoidable.

Others Have Similar Problems

It is comforting to parents to know that there are many more couples just like themselves. Membership in a group of parents whose children are similarly handicapped holds particular solace and inspiration for parents of handicapped children. These groups of dedicated parents organize their own special schools and often staff them. They crusade for improved legislation for handicapped children and for better conditions in state institutions. They stimulate the establishment of clinics or research projects.

While interest in these special projects is a necessary and vital part of providing care for a handicapped child, parents must not so lose themselves in the child or to a project that they retreat from the world about them. A complete change of scene, an evening devoted to sheer fun, are necessary to parents' welfare.

Shall He Live at Home or Not?

The needs of others in the home of the handicapped child have to be considered if family life is to be harmonious. A family may ask itself:

Will family members have too many sacrifices to make if the handicapped child lives at home?

Will the financial strain be too great if the child needs constant or special attention?

Will a brilliant older brother or sister have to forego a college education if a mentally handicapped child goes to an expensive private school?

Will the handicapped child be able to help with his share of family chores? Or will other children have to do his work for him?

Will the wishes and the needs of the handicapped child always come before those of other children in the family? Will other children become "substitute" parents for parents who work or pursue other interests?

How happily and heartwarmingly will normal children include a handicapped child in their home entertaining? Whether a handicapped child should live away from home depends entirely on the answer to the question, "What is best for the child and the family?"

The ideal for handicapped children is a balanced life between two worlds. One is the world geared to his special needs, where he is provided with a combination of stimulation and relaxation right and fitting for his handicap. The other is the world where people are not handicapped. If a handicapped child can feel he belongs, and has his own little niche that no one else could fill in his home and community, he will be aided in his development.

EDITH M. STERN AND ELSA CASTENDYCK

See also COMMUNITY RESOURCES; HANDICAPPED CHILD IN SCHOOL; HOME AND HOSPITAL INSTRUCTION

HANDICAPPED CHILD IN SCHOOL

School is a social experience essential for the development of every child. It is heartening to know that, through the efforts of community groups and through legislation, handicapped children can share the fulfillment of the tradition of school for all.

Handicapped children include those who are blind or partially seeing, deaf or hard-of-hearing, crippled, cerebral palsied, speech handicapped, mentally retarded, or those who have serious behavioral problems. "School," to these children, may mean many things. It may mean the local public school, a private or parochial day school, a private boarding school, or a state residential school. In some instances it may mean school at home with a visiting teacher or it may mean that the parent himself assumes the role of teacher.

Begin with the Local School

Because it is usually better for a handicapped child to live with his family and go to a local day school, your own community school should be considered first as you seek educational opportunities for your child. Only after all local resources have been exhausted is it well to look beyond the community. Communities that have no organized program for handicapped children may have a clinic or a recreation center that will help. Often civic clubs provide funds for new and improved services for the handicapped.

Many times it takes a group of interested parents to alert a local school system to the needs of the handicapped child. With an active interest on the part of these parents and other civic-minded individuals, the school in the community, no matter what its size or location, should be able to help handicapped children in many ways.

Some Schools Have Special Services

Some school systems set aside special classrooms for the handicapped, while others have special school buildings for these children. Many school systems employ specialists who go from school to school to help both

children and teachers. These specialists include speech correctionists, hearing specialists, physical therapists, and others. Other services for the handicapped include the provision of home teachers for children who cannot attend school, special clinics, and medical services. Information about these services may be secured through local community organizations, both men's and women's service clubs, or local or state health departments.

A recent book, *Directory for Exceptional Children,* published by Porter Sargent, Boston, Massachusetts, gives detailed descriptions of schools for handicapped children.

The Residential School

Almost every state supports residential schools for handicapped children who, for various reasons, cannot be kept at home. The blind, the deaf, and the mentally retarded, particularly, may find the special services they need at state-supported schools. Some of these schools permit children to go home for vacations; others send some of their older boys and girls to a local high school, believing that the handicapped child's adjustment to other people is most important, especially as he approaches adulthood. The length of time a child stays in a special school depends upon the nature and extent of his handicap and the ability of the local community to provide the services he needs.

There are many private boarding schools around the country for handicapped children. Many are fine; others range from mediocre to poor. All states require some form of licensing for these schools. A check through your physician, your school, or a reliable community agency should be made before you decide to place a child in one of these private schools. Again, the decision to send him away to school should be based on the kind and extent of the child's handicap and the general situation in the family.

Schools and Parents—Partners

Close teamwork between school and parents is necessary to the education of the handicapped child. A child's medical advisers, too, should be consulted. Working together, parents and teachers can often succeed in obtaining better services for handicapped children and in awakening the community to needs that should be met.

Schools can help parents of handicapped children through parent-training classes. Here parents meet with other parents who have similar problems.

A child who is secure at home, and whose parents take an understanding interest in the development and improvement of the educational opportunities for him, is indeed fortunate. He is on the road to becoming a happy, adjusted person. LEO F. CAIN

See also COMMUNITY RESOURCES

HANDLING GENITALS

If one observes children from earliest infancy, he will note the development of the arms and hands as exploratory organs. Hands explore mouths, noses, ears, and sooner or later hands reach toward and discover the genitals.

This tendency in infancy is not masturbation, for it is not performed for any pleasurable sensation but merely as an examination of the child's own body.

Usually in infants and very young children this casual exploration is part of the learning process and of no other significance. But if a child reaches frequently for the genital area, examine the area to be certain there is no irritation of the skin or that the diaper and clothing are not too tight.

Parents should guard against pulling a child's hands away every time he touches his genitals, lest they make him feel there is something wrong or "not nice" about the genital area. MILTON I. LEVINE

See also ATTITUDES; MASTURBATION

HANDWRITING

At an early age children recognize handwriting as something very important in their world. It is not at all strange for a 4-year-old laboriously to scribble out a "story" and then expect his mother or father to be able to read it. Once he is attending school (and sometimes before), he will begin to ask how to write specific letters and words. And so a child gradually becomes a person who can write.

It is important to remember that in handwriting a person's hand and eyes have to work together. For some children this coordination is easier than it is for others. If a child is left-eyed (if he sights through the left eye and in other ways selects his left eye as his dominant eye) and right-handed, for example, he may well have difficulty teaching his hand and eyes to work together. This does not mean that he is a "slow" learner and it does not mean that he is not trying when his writing seems to lack form.

If your child seems to have difficulty with handwriting, above all be patient with him. Remember that he has to *want* to write to bring his eyes and hand actually into the required coordination, and he will soon learn not to want to write if practice sessions are

Aa Bb Cc Dd Ee Ff Gg Hh Ii Jj Kk

Manuscript writing is customary in the lower grades.

Aa Bb Cc Dd Ee Ff Gg Hh Ii Jj Kk

Later, a child learns to connect his printed letters to form cursive writing.

spent with impatient adults. Let some of his writing practice come from nonwriting activities which require hand-eye coordination and which he enjoys. Painting, for example, requires hand and eyes to work together and can be a fine activity for the youngster who is having difficulty writing.

If your child prefers to use his left hand, be sure to help him slant his paper in a way comfortable for left-handed writing instead of in the familiar right-handed slant.

Generally speaking, it seems better to help a child print (called manuscript writing by teachers) before he writes. And it is better for him to print lower-case letters rather than capitals. His next step will be connecting the printed letters, and gradually he will develop his own connected handwriting (called cursive writing by teachers). It is a good idea to check with your child's school to see the procedure followed in printing and writing before helping with printing or writing, for it will only confuse him to have you teach one kind of handwriting while his school teaches another. PEGGY BROGAN

See also LEFT-HANDEDNESS

Related article in WORLD BOOK: "Handwriting"

HARD OF HEARING

There are two groups of children with defective hearing—the deaf and the hard of hearing.

The deaf child is one who cannot hear enough sounds to be able to understand connected speech, even if he wears a hearing aid. The child who is deaf from birth does not learn to talk without special education. He does not learn the meaning of words as other children learn because he has never heard people talk. But nearly all deaf children have some slight ability to hear, called "residual hearing." If a sound is loud enough and of a certain quality or tone, they are able to hear it. Sometimes parents refuse to face the possibility that their child is deaf because he can hear an airplane in flight or he can hear a truck roll by. The child hears these sounds because he has residual hearing for the quality of sound made by the airplane or the truck. But he cannot hear the quality of sound or tone used in speech.

The hard-of-hearing child has a hearing loss. This loss will usually affect his speech, because it is natural to talk the way we hear speech spoken. A child who is hard of hearing will have a speech defect until he has had special speech lessons. He will say words in the same way that he hears them spoken, but usually he will not hear all the sounds in every word.

If there is any doubt about your child's ability to hear, take him to an otologist (M.D. specializing in hearing) for examination. If he feels that it is necessary, the doctor can also refer you to an audiological (hearing) center for further testing and guidance.

Since many hearing difficulties are caused by disease, any condition that tends to produce deafness should be investigated and remedied as soon as possible. Various tests can be made to determine the state of a child's hearing. These tests include the use of the voice, a watch, tuning forks, and the audiometer—an electronic device that accurately measures a child's response to the intensity of various sounds. An audiometric examination enables a doctor to determine whether a patient is deaf, how much hearing has been lost, the character of the hearing loss, and whether a hearing aid will be helpful in correcting the inability to hear satisfactorily. Audiometric graphs or records also provide a means of measuring hearing loss for

a particular patient over a long period of time. A record of a hearing loss can be kept and compared with new records, permitting the doctor to tell whether the child's hearing is improving, becoming worse, or remaining unaffected.

Hearing aids are devices that help the hard of hearing to hear. A modern hearing aid, of which there are many with minor variations, consists essentially of a small battery, an amplifier (also called a transmitter), and an ear receiver. The amplifier picks up sound, makes it louder, and transmits it to the ear receiver by means of a wire. The ear receiver is small and made to fit the individual ear. The amplifier is frequently worn on the lapel or some other place where it can freely receive sound.

There are two types of hearing aids—the air conduction aid and the bone conduction aid. An air conduction aid amplifies sound, transmitting it directly to the ear itself. Bone conduction aids transmit sound waves to the bony part of the head, usually in the mastoid region behind the ear. The air conduction aid is by far the more popular. But some children are unable to tolerate the molded ear insert required by the air conduction aid; therefore the bone conduction aid is usually best for them.

A hearing aid brings to hard-of-hearing children many sounds that at first seem new and strange. It is most important to realize that a hearing aid will not restore hearing to normal, but it will amplify sound so that it can be heard. Voices may sound different to a hard-of-hearing child using a hearing aid because the voices appear to lack some of the qualities and timbre he may remember before his hearing was affected. A partially deafened child can frequently hear some tones better than others, and his hearing aid can be adjusted to amplify tones he has difficulty hearing so that they sound normal to his ear.

If you are in doubt about your child's ability to hear, an ear specialist will tell you whether a hearing aid will help. The specialist can tell whether a child will be most benefited by using a hearing aid at all times, or whether wearing it when it will help him most—listening to instructions at game periods, for example—will be best.

Every hard-of-hearing child should have the benefit of a complete hearing study. The type and degree of his hearing loss must be studied, using every available and acceptable hearing test. NOAH D. FABRICANT

See also DEAF CHILD; HANDICAPPED CHILD; MEDICAL SPECIALISTS

HARELIP

A deformity of the upper lip with which the baby is born often is called harelip, although cleft lip is the preferred term. There may be a family history of harelip.

The cleft on the lip may extend to the nose on one or both sides. The defect has a tendency to occur along with cleft palate or other defects of the body; therefore the baby with cleft lip should be examined thoroughly. If there are no other abnormalities, harelip can be treated by plastic surgery, usually in the first few weeks of the baby's life. If the cleft occurs on both sides, the correction is more difficult, but the results are generally good. If the child also has a cleft palate or other defects, care of all the problems must be planned together. JULIUS B. RICHMOND

See also CLEFT PALATE; OPERATION

HAY FEVER

The child who has an allergic reaction to pollens from plants, usually ragweed in the United States, suffers severe attacks of sneezing, severe itching and redness of the eyes, and watery discharge from the nose. The condition is called hay fever, and it usually does not occur until the school years and adolescence. Other allergic disorders, such as eczema, asthma, or hives, are quite common in children who develop hay fever, and there are generally some allergic disorders in the family background.

Severity of the attacks varies with the amount of pollen in the air. Programs of ragweed control are worth while, therefore, to try to lower the pollen count in the air. If the child is sensitive only to ragweed pollen, vacationing during the height of the season in areas where the weed does not grow may

Ragweed, foe of the hay fever sufferer.

be desirable if the family can so arrange. Certain air conditioners and mask devices that remove most of the pollen from the atmosphere may provide some relief. It may also be helpful to have the child tested by an allergist who may advise lowering the child's sensitivity gradually by giving him weak injections of the pollen. This hyposensitizing may be desirable if there are other pollens from trees and grasses to which the child is also sensitive. Various drugs such as the antihistamines provide some relief from hay fever. The drugs may produce side-effects, so they should be given only on the advice of a physician.

JULIUS B. RICHMOND

See also ALLERGY

HEADACHE

Children have fewer headaches than adults, but a child whose parents have frequent headaches tends to have more than the child whose parents rarely have headaches. Many times, the precise cause of the headache cannot be determined; perhaps it is associated with tension. Such a headache is often relieved by aspirin.

Some headaches seem to be associated with eyestrain, although there is some difference of opinion among doctors as to how frequently eyestrain is responsible. If headaches are frequent, it is well to check the child's vision. Headaches may also be caused by infection of the sinuses. Sinuses should also be examined when the cause for headache cannot be found.

A few children have migraine headaches, which are often severe and are accompanied by vomiting. Usually there is a history of migraine headaches in the family. The victim of migraine may feel relieved by lying down in a quiet room. Specific medicine for this type of headache can be prescribed by the doctor. Since emotional upsets tend to bring on migraine headaches, the child's emotional life should be examined in an effort to relieve his problems.

Headaches are also frequent in acute infections with fever but subside as the infection is relieved. Rarely, a headache may be an early symptom of brain tumor, but such a possibility usually should not be worried about.

JULIUS B. RICHMOND

See also COMMON COMMUNICABLE DISEASES; EYE HEALTH; MENTAL HEALTH; SINUSITIS

HEAD-BANGING AND ROLLING

The child who bangs or rolls his head usually does so in fairly slow and rhythmic movements, but he may deliberately hit his head so hard that he produces bumps and bruises. Or he may roll his head sufficiently to wear off part of his hair. Sometimes it is obvious that he bangs or rolls in frustration; at other times he may do the same things when he is apparently at peace with himself and the world. Parents are usually afraid that there is something wrong with their child. They worry also that he might fracture his skull or in other ways seriously and permanently injure himself.

Regardless of how parents interpret the behavior or worry over it, the baby has his reasons for doing what he does, and his behavior serves some meaningful function for him. For example, rolling or banging may provide release from tension. Such behavior may also mean that the child's environment is so lacking in external stimulation that he has to turn his attention inward on his own body. With increasing age, an infant needs and can tolerate more and a greater variety of stimulation. In fact, he will seek out such stimulation of all his sense organs. He may struggle to maintain a body posture that keeps him in good visual contact, or cry if taken from a room filled with people who are talking and laughing. He will also increase the stimulation he receives by exploring his own body. The 4-month-old baby may play happily with his feet, just as an older infant will hold and manipulate a toy. Or he may stuff his fist into his mouth and chew on it just as he will chew on a rattle or a plastic doll.

The interpretation that head-banging or rolling may represent a baby's attempt to increase stimulation is supported by the fact that babies reared in institutions, where adequate attention cannot be given each child, show much more of this behavior than children in a home atmosphere where they are talked to and played with and given toys to occupy them. Often all that is necessary to stop the head-banging of the less privileged children is to provide more stimulating surroundings.

Head-banging, like many other forms of undesirable behavior, can become a technique by which a child controls adults. That is, he may learn that his parents will yield on almost any point rather than endure the torture of hearing him bang his head. If the baby continues to bang his head even after parents make certain that he has plenty of interesting objects to look at, to chew on, or to feel, that he has people around to hold him, cuddle him, and talk to him, and that he is allowed to get rid of emotional tensions through crying or by making noise or in-

dicating that he may be hungry or anxious, then it would probably be wise to seek professional help in understanding the child's problem. BETTYE M. CALDWELL

See also CRIB; EMOTIONAL DEVELOPMENT

HEAD INJURY

It is not uncommon for a baby to receive a few bumps on his head. Usually his injuries are not so serious that they cannot be "kissed away." The bumps that older children sustain may or may not be more serious. Such injuries may come from falls, collisions, automobile accidents, or athletic injuries.

The head injury may be superficial, merely cutting the scalp. Such a cut usually bleeds profusely and creates more alarm than is warranted. The immediate procedure is to wash the cut and cover it with a sterilized or clean dressing held in place by a firm bandage to control bleeding. Medical help should then be sought.

More severe injuries may fracture the skull or cause bleeding or other damage within the cavity of the skull.

A skull fracture may occur at the point where the blow is sustained or at a point at the opposite side of the skull, just as a melon dropped on the ground may crack open on the opposite side from where it hit. Skull fractures are diagnosed by X ray and may require surgery to control bleeding or to release pressure on the brain.

A severe blow may cause excessive bleeding within the skull if it bursts a blood vessel of sufficient size. In other circumstances it might cause concussion, a state of microscopic bleeding within the brain tissue. These are serious emergencies requiring medical and often surgical care.

If your child has received a severe bump on the head, he should be kept quiet for a while even if he seems to recover quickly. He should be kept in bed and watched closely for signs of dizziness, stupor, incoordination, and changes or inequality in the size of the pupils. If any of these signs occur or if there is vomiting, a physician should be called promptly. W. W. BAUER

See also ACCIDENT PREVENTION; FIRST AID

HEALTH *See* DOCTOR; PHYSICAL CHECKUP

HEALTH, MENTAL *See* MENTAL HEALTH

HEALTH RECORD *See* FAMILY HEALTH RECORD

HEARING *See* DEAF CHILD; HARD OF HEARING

HEARING AID *See* HARD OF HEARING

HEART MURMUR

A normal heart makes typical lub-dub, lub-dub sounds every time it beats. The lub sound is made by closure of two valves inside the heart (the mitral valve in the left ventricle and the tricuspid valve in the right ventricle). The dub sound is made by closure of the valves in the aorta and the pulmonary artery.

A heart murmur is a purring, rumbling, or scratchy noise that replaces the normal lub-dub and is caused by blood flowing over or through some rough place.

Murmurs can be called either systolic or diastolic. A systolic murmur is one that is heard during the time of contraction of the heart. A diastolic murmur is heard during the time the heart is resting.

The murmur, heard by the doctor with a stethoscope, is the noise made by blood going through deformed valves, through channels narrowed by disease, or through holes in the heart (defects in the walls between the auricles and ventricles).

A very important group of murmurs heard in children are so-called functional murmurs. Nobody knows what causes these murmurs, but we do know that they are harmless. It is very important for the doctor to recognize such a murmur and not confuse it with a murmur caused by disease. Otherwise the patient may get treated for some heart ailment he doesn't have. WILLIS J. POTTS

HEAT EXHAUSTION

Heat exhaustion is a state of shock. It results mostly from loss of water and salt through excessive perspiration. Heat exhaustion is not the same as sunstroke or *heatstroke* since it can happen to persons in no way exposed to the sun. The treatment for *heatstroke* is radically different from that for heat exhaustion, so it is extremely important to be able to recognize the difference between the two conditions.

Heat exhaustion occurs mainly in persons who work where it is excessively hot. In children, heat exhaustion should be easy to prevent by observing a few simple precautions.

A child shouldn't wear any more clothes than necessary for warmth or decency. Such clothing as is worn should be light in weight, light in color, and loose. Care should be taken to see that the child gets enough salt. The amount of salt ordinarily used in food is usually sufficient, but in times of extreme and prolonged heat it may be necessary for the child to take salt tablets, too. Activity should be reduced when it is extremely hot. Occasional tepid baths are helpful.

Paleness, weakness, or unconsciousness are signs of heat exhaustion. The skin is moist and clammy; the pulse is weak and often irregular. In an emergency give a tepid bath, allow rest and quiet, and administer salt and fluids. Further treatment should await your doctor's advice. W. W. BAUER

HEATSTROKE

Heatstroke, or sunstroke, is not due to the sun, but to heat. It consists of a disturbance of the nervous center in the lower brain which controls body temperature. The result is an uncontrolled rise of temperature. The human body cannot sustain a high temperature for any length of time and live. It is important, therefore, to recognize this condition and distinguish it from heat exhaustion. The child with heatstroke is red-faced and flushed, probably unconscious, and very rigid. Heatstroke is the only condition in which rising fever is accompanied by a *dry, hot* skin. Emergency treatment calls for immersion in cold water until the body temperature goes down to endurable levels, but not below 102° F., since the patient's temperature may fall too low if the cold-water treatment is continued too long.

The child with sunstroke or heatstroke should be kept in bed at rest for full recovery. Give him plenty of fluids; salt may be administered in the form of salt tablets or a teaspoonful of salt in a pint of water. Sponging with cool water is a useful help while the temperature is high. The extremely high degrees of fever which may accompany heatstroke or sunstroke may do injury to the brain, leaving an aftermath of tingling sensations or, occasionally, paralysis.

Persons who do not perspire should take special precautions to avoid exposure to excessively high temperatures. W. W. BAUER

See also HEAT EXHAUSTION

HEIGHT *See* GROWTH

HELPFULNESS

During the first year or so of life, babies have no sense whatsoever of being helpful. They need all the help they can get, and cannot give any themselves.

Quite soon, however, even toddlers take some preliminary steps toward contributing to family life. The toddler wants to feed himself, to climb up to the toilet seat himself, to wash his own face. Actually, his efforts are self-centered rather than geared toward helping others. His main concern is to reject help and to do a job himself.

But these budding ventures are the raw material out of which true helpfulness later develops. When children are 3, 4, and 5, they still want to prove how big they are. During this period, however, they have occasional moments when their motivation is truly to help others. They may want to open a door or carry a bundle (usually the largest one!), to set the table, or help prepare the food for supper. It is worth while to be patient and pleased whenever children volunteer. The beginnings of helpfulness can be squelched by stopping children from doing the jobs they want to do—adults can always do them faster and better!—or by asking youngsters to do more than they are ready to do.

Wise adults often work along with young children, lightening the task of cleaning up the play room, for example. They often cheerfully put the finishing touches on a job when a child's interest has flagged or when his strength has ebbed. This cooperative approach nourishes the child's desire to be helpful and, at the same time, teaches him about helpfulness. The child who has experienced help when he needs it is best prepared to give help when others need it. If their early efforts have been welcomed and appreciated, children are usually ready by 5 or 6 or 7 to carry some simple but regular role in the family's functioning: to empty the wastebaskets, to put the silverware away, to make their own beds, to feed their pets, or to get the newspaper from the mailbox. At no age do children carry all their responsibilities ever-faithfully with never a slip-up. As they approach preadolescence, it is not uncommon for them even to gripe a bit about "all the work" they have to do.

But despite their occasional lapses and their noise, being helpful and contributing to the family is pleasing to children. Elementary school youngsters especially grow best when they feel needed. A wise tolerance for children's "beginner's faults" keeps alive this sense of being needed. With this understanding support and good examples around him, a child grows who is helpful within his family and who slowly is laying a base that will enable him later gladly to be helpful in his community. JAMES L. HYMES, JR.

See also CHORES

HEMOGLOBIN *See* ANEMIA; BLOOD COUNT

HEREDITY

What your child will be is determined a great deal at the moment of conception, when the sperm from the father meets the egg from the mother. At that instant in time, if we could translate the chemical code inside the tiny fertilized egg, we could tell whether

the child is to be a boy or a girl, blue- or brown-eyed, color-blind or with normal vision.

Chromosomes Store Information

How can the infinitesimally small egg, roughly 1/175 of an inch in diameter and weighing 1/20-millionth of an ounce, contain all this information? The storehouse of information is in the nucleus of each body cell where we find the *chromosomes*. Under a microscope, chromosomes take up a laboratory dye more strongly than other parts of the cell and appear as dark strings in the nucleus. Only recently have the chromosomes been counted correctly; there are 46 in each cell of the human body, and these are unique for every individual.

How does the fertilized egg with its original 46 chromosomes manage to distribute the same chromosomes to all the cells of the growing baby? The chromosomes are made up of a complicated chemical, deoxyribonucleic acid (called DNA for short), which has the ability to duplicate itself. The chromosomes make copies of themselves from the material in the cell; as cell division takes place, each daughter cell gets an identical set of 46 chromosomes. The one exception to the rule of 46 chromosomes to a cell is that egg and sperm cells each have 23 and in fusing give the fertilized egg the correct number.

On the chromosomes are located the *genes* that control various specific traits, such as blood group, the ability to clot blood, sensitivity to certain tastes, etc. The situation is even more complicated because many genes may work together to produce the one trait that we observe, or one gene may affect the individual in several observable ways.

Each cell has 46 chromosomes made up of 2 sets of 23 each. One set of 23 chromosomes comes from the individual's father, and one set from his mother.

Dominant and Recessive

There will be two genes, one on each identical chromosome, for every trait. If one of these is *dominant*, it will rule over the other one. The gene for brown eyes is dominant over blue eyes and the gene for blood group A is dominant over blood group O. If an individual gets genes for brown eyes and O group from one parent and genes for blue eyes and A group from the other, he will have brown eyes and be classified as blood group A. The gene for group O is still there, however, called *recessive* because the trait it governs does not show up in the person with only one such gene. It takes a double dose of genes to make a recessive trait show up; both chromosomes must carry the gene for blood type O to have it appear in an individual. The individual with one gene for blood group A and one for O may transmit either gene to the next generation, because only one set of chromosomes goes into the sperm or egg cells.

Each child has only half of his mother's genes and half of his father's and is a unique combination of them. There are thousands of total genetic combinations possible for every child.

The last pair of chromosomes, unlike the other 22 pairs, may not be identical. Every egg bears a large chromosome known as the X chromosome and every sperm either an X or a smaller Y chromosome. When these meet in the fertilized egg, an XX baby will be a girl, an XY, a boy. Other genes occur on the X and Y chromosomes, and the traits they govern are called "sex-linked." A famous example of a sex-linked trait is the disease hemophilia, characterized by excessive bleeding, which Queen Victoria passed on to her one son, three grandsons, and six great-grandsons. She herself did not have the disease; because she was XX, the gene on her "good" X chromosome overcame the recessive hemophilia gene on the other X chromosome. Males have only one X chromosome. Those of Queen Victoria's descendants who received her defective X chromosome had the disease, and those who happened to receive the good X chromosome did not.

Hemophilia is just one example of a "bad" gene. Many disease conditions are hereditary and were once considered hopeless. Scientists are now studying these diseases, trying to discover where the body's chemistry has gone wrong. If the mistake can be corrected—by a drug or a change in diet—the person with an inborn defect of metabolism can lead a normal life. Diabetes mellitus, a condition in which carbohydrates are not utilized normally, is a hereditary disease that is controlled by giving a hormone that the body is not making in sufficient quantity, insulin. Agammaglobulinemia is a hereditary condition in which the blood does not contain gamma globulin, leaving the patient unable to fight off severe infections; in this case gamma globulin can be injected.

Phenylketonuria, or PKU, caused by a recessive gene, is a disease in which the newborn child cannot utilize part of the milk protein properly. This abnormality eventually causes mental retardation if the disease goes unchecked. Quite recently, a simple diaper test has been devised that shows the doctor

whether the disease is present. If it is, a special diet is immediately prescribed, and on it the child can attain normal development.

The study of phenylketonuria leads us to another important area of genetic research —the detection of carriers.

We have mentioned that recessive traits must be caused by two identical genes in order to appear. What of the individual who has only one of these recessive genes—does he differ from the normal? Apparently yes. In the case of the phenylketonuria gene, a blood test indicates that individuals with one gene for the disease can be identified, even though they are not sick in any way. Scientists are working out tests to detect these carriers of bad genes, for when a known carrier marries another carrier, the chances are one out of four that any child of theirs will have the disease in question. Marriage between cousins is more likely to produce an affected child because if one partner carries a recessive gene, a member of his family is more likely than usual to carry it, too. There are good recessive genes, of course, that may endow the child of a cousin marriage with better than ordinary attributes.

Exciting discoveries are being made all the time in these fields, detecting carriers and treating genetic disease once it has occurred.

Occasionally, changes will take place in the body's genes spontaneously, and this event is called *mutation*. A mutant gene will be transmitted to future generations in the regular way; all the bad genes mentioned above arose from mutations at some past time. There is evidence that radiation from X rays, ultraviolet light, and fallout may cause fresh mutations, though the number is very small. Certain new mutations are not compatible with life and cause early miscarriage in humans. These miscarriages are, of course, a great blessing, for the child could not have been normal.

In addition to mutations, there are chromosomal abnormalities consisting of too many or too few chromosomes. Mongolism is currently thought to be associated with an extra chromosome.

Heredity vs. Environment

How much influence can parents have on their children's development if a child's heredity is determined before birth? The genes are there in the child and cannot be altered, but environment plays an essential part in how these genes do their work. There is no simple relationship between genes and the effects we observe; a long series of complicated steps takes place before we see the final results of gene action, and environment influences each step. The chromosomes are directly involved in making special proteins, called enzymes, that are necessary to carry out the hundreds of chemical reactions that go on in the body. The gene effects we observe are the result of these many events.

Nutrition is one example of an important environmental factor. The increasing height of our population is not due to genetic change as much as to improved nutrition. The appearance of diabetes mellitus is definitely related not only to a hereditary factor but to diet as well. A great variety of situations from diet to emotional climate determines how genes exert their action. The question of heredity versus environment is a fascinating one, but it is clear that environment is vastly important in the development of the child. A fine genetic constitution may not be able to overcome an unfavorable environment, and conversely, a child with average genetic make-up may flourish in a congenial environment.

Each child is an individual genetically and should be helped to make the most of his genetic endowment. DAVID YI-YUNG HSIA

See also GROWTH; NORMAL CHILD; PRENATAL IMPRESSIONS

HERNIA

When body tissue pushes through an abnormal opening in any part of the body, it is referred to as a hernia. The most common type is called *inguinal* hernia, which occurs in the groin region. In boys, a loop of intestine slides through an abnormal opening around the cord that attaches to the testicle; if the hernia is large, the swelling can be seen and felt in the scrotum, often on both sides. Girls can also have inguinal hernia on one or both sides of the groin. Inguinal hernia is corrected by a surgical operation that can be done even before a baby is a year old or later, as the surgeon desires. Trusses or injections should not be used in attempting to correct an inguinal hernia in a child for they often make matters worse.

When a child has a hernia for which no operation is planned, he should be watched carefully. If at any time the contents of the sac containing the hernia cannot be pushed gently back into the abdomen and if the child is having pain, his doctor should be called immediately. The doctor probably will suggest hospitalization and possibly surgery.

The second most common type of hernia occurs at the navel and, if very small, may disappear gradually in time. If not, this type of hernia should be corrected by a surgical

operation. Tape or other pressure on the abdomen is not advisable.

Other types of hernia are quite uncommon in children, but outpouching of body tissue anywhere should be called to the doctor's attention promptly for proper diagnosis and treatment. JULIUS B. RICHMOND

See also NAVEL; OPERATION

HICCUPS

It's normal for babies to hiccup frequently —sometimes several times daily. During a hiccup, the breathing cycle stops and the child experiences a short, jerky contraction of the diaphragm—the muscular tissue dividing the chest from the abdomen. Apparently the condition occurs because of stimulation of the diaphragm, although many people have thought, without proof, that hiccups come from overfeeding, and others blame irritating foods in the stomach.

Hiccups cannot usually be controlled voluntarily, although "holding the breath" sometimes seems to stop the contractions. Usually, however, hiccuping stops of itself after a few minutes. Older children may be helped by a drink of water. In rare instances, hiccups continue for a longer time. When this happens, call the doctor. Continued hiccuping can exhaust a child. JULIUS B. RICHMOND

HIGH CHAIR *See* LAYETTE AND BABY EQUIPMENT

HITTING

Hitting is usually an effective method used by a preschooler to express annoyance, irritation, or anger even though it may not necessarily result in successful resolution of the problem according to adult standards. It is a primitive way of saying, "I want" or "I don't want" or "I don't like" or "Get out." It is a vigorous assertion of need or desire.

Hitting is even somewhat sanctioned in our culture. Prize fights and boxing are officially accepted as adult diversions. And even nursery school teachers have been known to sponsor carefully refereed boxing matches for children who seem to need to hit. Hitting in moderate degrees seems to be more acceptable than biting or kicking.

Most parents and teachers are not overly concerned with a moderate amount of hitting behavior. They are more likely to be concerned with the child who hits too much or the child who doesn't hit enough or the child who seems to be the victim of hitting, unable to defend himself or to "hit back."

Parents and teachers sometimes need help to clarify their own feelings about hitting as well as its meaning to the "hitter" and the "hittee." We need to know whether we should try to abolish hitting as a method of communicating (and if so, how?) or whether we should condone it and even encourage it ("If he hits you, you hit him back!") or whether we should teach a moderate use of hitting ("Use your hands; no hitting with sticks or shovels").

What about the child who hits? If a child finds that hitting "works," that is, if he gets what he wants as a result of hitting or if he finds that hitting is not only effective but also approved by his important adults, he is likely to continue. If, however, hitting results in getting hit and hurt, he may be susceptible to the suggestion that he try another method of persuasion.

"People don't like it when you hit them. Sometimes it makes them feel like hitting you. Maybe you could *tell* them what you want instead of hitting."

The chronically passive object of being hit may need some help in daring to be more assertive. "I know you don't like to hit, but sometimes you may need to hit John so he will know how it feels. John will also know that you don't like it when he hits you." This need not be construed as general approval or permission to become a "hitter." Rather, it is supportive to the less aggressive child who finds hitting somewhat lacking in satisfaction as a way of communicating his wants and needs. No recommendation is implied that the nonassertive child become a bully, but only that you will support him in asserting his need, and that sometimes hitting is not only justifiable but necessary for those who haven't learned to discuss their differences.

Emphasis needs to be first on recognition that most young children will tend to hit before they discuss; second, they will continue to hit if they find that it works or if they themselves are habitually hit; and third, that they are likely to respond to substituting discussion for hitting as they are helped to understand that this is something that can be learned.

Sometimes young children need to be protected from their own vigorous hitting impulses—without being blamed: "I know how you feel, but I can't let you hit the baby," or "I know that sometimes you feel angry and feel like hitting, but after awhile you will learn that you can *tell* people instead of hitting them, and I'm going to try to help you." This kind of comment will help your child to learn that hitting is something he will not be blamed for but something that he will eventually outgrow. EVELYN BEYER

See also AGGRESSIVENESS

HIVES

The child with hives has a rash. His skin is swollen and his face, if the hives are there, will look "puffy." The lesions are white or reddish, raised, and take either a circular or an irregular shape. They itch intensely.

Hives is an allergic disorder that comes on after eating some food or inhaling some pollen or other substance to which there is sensitivity, or after the injection of some immunizing material. Hives is also a reaction to certain infections, such as streptococcal sore throat. The child who develops hives as a result of sore throat should be carefully observed for the possibility of rheumatic fever. Certain medicines may also produce hives in allergic children. Penicillin is particularly likely to do so—a good reason to limit its use to times when it is absolutely necessary.

Hives may last for a few hours or for days. The doctor will usually prescribe soothing lotions or even soothing baths in an effort to control the intense itching and thus reduce the child's need to scratch. He may also prescribe various antiallergic drugs. In extremely severe cases, he may administer injections that are effective in controlling the condition temporarily.

Although hives seem to be a disorder of the skin, the condition is much more extensive, often involving internal organs as well. For this reason, it is important to consult the doctor immediately when a child suffers an outbreak of hives. Swelling may occur where it will interfere with breathing—a situation which requires emergency medical care.

It is logical, of course, after an acute attack of hives is over, to try to determine what has caused the outbreak. Efforts may then be made to avoid that substance or to reduce the child's sensitivity to it by injections of dilute amounts of the material over a long period of time. JULIUS B. RICHMOND

See also ALLERGY; ITCHING; SORE THROAT

HOARDING *See* ALLOWANCE

HOME AND HOSPITAL INSTRUCTION

What can you do to help your school-age child who is hospitalized or housebound for a considerable length of time because of a severe disability or illness? Time passes slowly for the child with a fracture, rheumatic fever, or some other handicapping condition. His lack of companionship, his fretting over inability to attend school, and his fear of possible grade failure tend to make him irritable —and often retard recovery.

Throughout the United States school boards are supporting special programs for youngsters who are ill in a hospital or at home. A qualified teacher may visit the child and conduct a teaching program as much like his regular school program as his physical condition will permit. If you are the parent of a hospitalized or housebound child, ask his physician if he would agree to some form of instruction if it is available. If he does approve, call the principal or administrator of your child's school to find out how to go about getting the service.

Usually the school agency asks that your physician fill out a special form. In addition to the vital statistics, the agency will want to know the nature of your child's illness, how long he is expected to be in need of special teaching, and any other information deemed necessary. In some communities, teachers are sent to hospitals to teach isolated cases. In big city hospitals that have large pediatric departments, it is more likely that teachers will be on the staff. Here school-age patients are automatically referred to the teacher after medical approval.

If you are fortunate enough to get a home teacher, there are several things you can do to create a pleasant teaching atmosphere. See that the teacher has a table on which to work. If your child is bedridden, arrange a bed tray or board for him to use as a desk. Good lighting is extremely important. Lessons should be kept as free from interruptions as possible. Small children must not be permitted to play in the room while lessons are in progress. Television and radio should be silenced unless they are being used in connection with a lesson. It is important that your little student cooperate and complete his lesson assignments. Follow the teacher's suggestions; she usually has good reasons for offering them.

Home learning or hospital learning may prove to be a satisfying experience for your child. Often it is the special teacher who recognizes the problems that hamper a student educationally and who is able to remedy them. But no matter how much you enjoy the home teacher, be sure to send your child back to regular school as soon as the doctor says you may. ALMA O. FINIGAN

See also LIBRARIES

HOME ENVIRONMENT *See* DISCIPLINE; FAMILY DISCUSSIONS

HOME LIBRARY *See* BOOKS FOR CHILDREN

HOMEMADE PLAY EQUIPMENT *See* TOYS AND PLAY EQUIPMENT

HOME NURSING *See* NURSE; SICK CHILD

HOME-SCHOOL RELATIONS

In the not too distant past, when a child reached school age he was "sent to school" as if school were some far-off, distant institution. The child went, the parent stayed home. The school worked alone, carrying all the responsibility for the child during the school hours. Parents became involved only if and when a youngster got into trouble. At that time a note might be sent home or the parent called in for a conference. The only other relationship between home and school occurred at report card time. Sending a child to school was similar to sending a car to the garage for repairs: The "experts" took over, and returned the finished product to its original owner once the needed work was done.

Today, almost all schools feel a need for a much closer relationship between home and school. Many schools say to parents in effect, "You cannot simply send a child to school. Parents must come along with him, sometimes literally but always at least in spirit."

There are many reasons why it is important for home and school to be close-working partners in the education of every child. The most important is that, despite the large size of classes, good teachers always try to individualize their work with students as much as possible. To do this, they need information that only parents have in full detail. A teacher needs to know each child's interests and enthusiasms, his fears and uncertainties, his past and his present home living.

Knowing the Children

Many schools establish procedures that enable teachers to become familiar with the backgrounds of all their children as early in the year as possible. Some teachers visit the children's homes; others schedule conferences with parents at school early in the year to talk about the children; other schools rely on questionnaires that give parents an opportunity to furnish background information about their children.

Learning to know children as individuals is not a job that a teacher can do once and for all at the beginning of the year. Often the goal of the initial meetings is simply to lay a groundwork so that parents and teachers find it easy to continue to talk together as the school year progresses.

A child's life does not stay fixed and stationary. New events occur which have their repercussions on how a child learns and behaves at school. Disturbing events such as illness or difficulties with playmates or family reverses, and happy events such as success in community clubs or the birth of a brother or a sister or the visits of relatives, all contribute to the ups and downs of a child's life in school. The teacher who does not know about these significant occurrences at home cannot understand the child at school, nor can she be as sensitive in planning her school assignments as she might otherwise be.

It is important, too, for the teacher to know the child's reaction to his school life as seen by the parents at home. Youngsters often express their feelings about school, their confusions or disappointments or irritations, their joys and thrills, in the bosom of the home. They may not feel as free to express their honest reactions in the less personal setting of the school. If parents and the teacher have become friends who find it easy to share information, the teacher can get a firsthand report.

In some communities this flow of up-to-date information can go on through telephone conversations between parents and the teacher throughout the school year. In some situations it must be saved for official conference times or passed on when parents and the teacher meet at the PTA meeting or other school gatherings.

Knowing the School

A teacher must know facts about each child, and it is equally important for parents to know about the school. Close home-school relationships demand a two-way flow of information: from the home to the school about the child *and* from the school to the home. The child is the parents' child, after all. Parents have a right to know the kind of experiences their youngster is having during his school hours, for their general information. They also need to know what is going on so they can play their part in supplementing the school's efforts. No school can do the whole job of education alone; the home is also a "school."

The younger the child, the more important it is for teachers to inform parents about the school's program. Young children are very bad reporters. When they come home from school, they are apt either to say nothing

about the school's academic program or to give an account of some specific highlight that was important to them but not necessarily representative of their total day's experience. Young children are also less apt to bring books home or to have comprehensive homework assignments that can indicate the program of the school to parents. But a child's life in school is too important to parents for all the information to come through children or through incidental sources.

Because parents have such a great stake in a good education for their child, it is very easy for them to worry needlessly about what is and what isn't happening at school. And it is easy for them to read critical articles in newspapers or in magazines about schools and education in general, which may or may not be typical of the school and classroom where their youngster does his daily work.

The monthly meetings of the Parent-Teacher Association are one means by which parents can learn about their child's school. In addition to learning from the specific topic under discussion, there usually is an opportunity for parents to visit their child's classroom, meet and talk briefly with the teacher, and see the products of the children's efforts as well as the books and other materials that the children are using.

As an added source of information, some schools enable the parents of a particular grade to meet as a group with the teacher of the grade. Such room meetings give the teacher an opportunity to tell specifically about his goals, his program, and the instructional materials the children will use throughout the year.

A few schools make it possible for parents to sit in the classroom to observe the children and the teacher in action during a regular school day. Such observation presents a problem as youngsters get older, but young children are usually pleased when their parents visit. Because the children are so pleased, they often become a bit excited, sometimes acting more boldly than usual and sometimes becoming more dependent when their parents are present. One visit by a parent seldom reveals a completely typical day; observation, nevertheless, is an excellent way for a parent to learn what a group's program is actually like. Following an observation, it is important for the parent and the teacher to spend some time talking together, either in person or at least over the phone, so that a parent's questions may be answered and any misconceptions clarified. Such conversations usually cannot be held in the classroom while the teacher is busy with children, but they are an important follow-up both for the teacher and for the parent.

Parents are frequently invited to come to school, not to sit on the sidelines, but to participate in the classroom program. Some mothers and fathers have specific skills such as piano playing or specific information that can enrich the daily program. Others come to help with a particular aspect of the program such as a trip. Occasionally, parents participate simply as general assistants to the teacher, a real service in today's crowded classrooms. Parents who have the opportunity to work side by side with teachers are fortunate; they get to know the school's program very well.

Some teachers find it convenient to send home a newsletter about the activities of the group, covering the highlights of the last month or so. Parents usually find this a satisfactory means of keeping in touch with the major projects, the main emphases and accomplishments of the class.

More than knowing in general about school life, parents' greatest interest usually is in knowing their particular child's place in his group. Historically the report card has been the avenue through which this information has been passed on. Through the years there have been changes in the frequency of sending report cards and in their form. No report card, however, can give as complete and clear information about a child's life in school as a face-to-face conference between the teacher and the parent. More and more elementary schools are supplementing whatever form of report card they use with conferences. These person-to-person chats occur sometimes after the report cards have been sent home and sometimes before the written report is sent home.

Some Problems

Despite the great advantages in close home-school relationships, there are some common difficulties that all adults involved need to recognize. Few schools, for example, provide enough free time for teachers to talk with parents. It is not uncommon for home visits and conferences to be scheduled after the regular school day is over. This time pressure, especially severe if classes are large, sometimes makes it impossible for home and school to get together as much as either might prefer.

The relative newness of the idea of close home-school relationships is another major problem. Adults, whether they be parents or teachers, seldom grew up themselves in schools where it was the "thing to do" for

YOU AND THE PTA

home and school to work closely together. This lack of firsthand experience can make it hard for today's parents and teachers to find a comfortable way of working together. As a hangover from the past, parents are apt to suspect that any approach from the teacher will be based on criticism of the child and of the way the parents have raised him. In reverse, teachers are apt to suspect that parents will automatically take the role of critic, attacking the teacher and his program at school. Once the ice is broken, both the parent and the teacher usually discover each other to be quite human and likable and that it is possible to build effective and pleasant working relationships.

Some basic understandings on the part of both home and school are necessary for effective home-school relationships. The first relates to time. It takes more time on everyone's part if parents and teachers are to work together for a child's well-being rather than to work separately and in compartments. Parents must be prepared to save time for meetings, conferences, observation, and participation. Schools must increasingly provide time for teachers to work with their adult counterparts.

A second understanding that must be mutually held is that neither homes nor schools can change overnight. Both parents and teachers are human. Both, to some extent, have their set ways. Although both want a child's well-being, there are limits to what both the home and the school can do. Sometimes these limits arise from the understandable difficulties that all adults have in changing their ways. Sometimes these limits are a part of the total situation: the needs of the other children for whom a teacher is responsible; the needs of other members of the family for whom a parent is responsible.

Perfection Not Always Possible

At times, too, the problems a child faces are not within anyone's power to solve. A home or a school may make some adjustments that lessen the difficulty, but a perfect solution simply may not be available. Often home and school must temper their hopes for a child by the realization that children are tough and able to withstand some difficulties and that life cannot and need not be perfect every minute of the time. There is the danger that teachers will expect perfection from the home and that parents will look for perfection in the school. Such unrealistic expectations can lead only to disappointment and to the weakening of relationships rather than to their increasing closeness.

It takes time, patience, and understanding for close home-school relationships to grow. When they do, everyone gains. Teachers do their work better and work with more satisfaction in an atmosphere of confidence and support. Not infrequently, close personal friendships develop out of close home-school relationships. Parents, in turn, feel more at peace about their children if they know that the school is open to them, sympathetic to what they have to offer and responsive to their reactions. The greatest winners, of course, are the children. Individual children gain because the close working harmony of the important adults in their lives can mean more consistency and better planning. But all the children of a community gain because no school system is ever better than the parents of that community want it to be. Only when parents are fully aware of the educational program can they aspire to the best for their children and work effectively to make that best a reality. JAMES L. HYMES, JR.

See also PARENT-TEACHER ASSOCIATION; SCHOOL REPORT; SCHOOL TEACHER; TEACHER CONFERENCE

HONESTY

Your child was not born with a sense of honesty. Nor is there a particular age at which he will reach the "age of reason"—before which he is unable to respond to character training and after which he is completely responsive to such training. He develops honesty gradually from early childhood throughout adulthood and develops it only as a result of careful home effort, guidance, and example.

But the fact that very young children have limited ability to respond to precepts of honesty is not a reason for you to wait to start some training. Early training is good, but it must be tailored to fit the child. A small child can't be expected to generalize very much from one experience to a new one. Early training must thus be a patient, careful teaching of the honesty factor in each new situation. It is only later, after the youngster has been helped to see the honesty element in a large variety of situations, that he can begin himself to generalize to the new. The more help he has, the sooner he will adopt his own set of values and work out behavior that fits them.

A child's concept of honesty depends not only upon what his parents say to him, but also upon what he notices in their attitudes and behavior. Usually, what he sees for himself is more important than what he is told. A child whose parents tell him that he must

always be honest about money will pay little attention if he is aware that they indulge in little dishonesties themselves. No good training program for honesty, or any other character trait, ever evolved out of "do as I say and not as I do."

Psychological studies have shown that honesty depends on many factors, such as age, intelligence, and emotional adjustment. A child who is limited in intelligence or one who is emotionally disturbed cannot be expected to show normal progress in character development.

Psychological studies also indicate that all children display dishonesty to some extent, in one form or another, and that a child who may be honest under one set of circumstances may be dishonest in another. For example, a child may be entirely honest in one relationship because he admires and respects and trusts the person with whom he is dealing. In another situation the same child may be dishonest out of fear or anger or knowledge of previous injustices.

As a training aid, reward is generally more effective than punishment, but more important are timing and consistency. For example, it is important to praise your 5-year-old immediately after he has told the truth about the broken glass and to follow through with a like pattern to the next similar case. You will only confuse him if you reward him for the truth in one situation and punish him for it in the next.

LEO A. HELLMER

See also IMITATION; MORAL AND SPIRITUAL DEVELOPMENT; REWARDS

HOOKY, PLAYING *See* TRUANCY

HORMONES *See* ENDOCRINE GLANDS

HOSPITALIZATION

At some time it may be necessary for your child to be hospitalized. Parents who have gone through this experience know too well the emotional upheaval involved. Understandably, they are worried and anxious, and their anxiety communicates itself to their small child.

Perhaps the hardest part for parents and child is the moment of first leave-taking at the hospital. A very young child may feel that his mother is abandoning him in a strange and terrifying world. For this reason, a mother should stay with her child if at all possible. If not, it will help you both to have a member of the hospital staff present just before your first leave-taking. A child needs a person who has time to hold him when you leave and to comfort him in his immediate grief. Don't attempt to slip away without warning the child that you are leaving, and don't linger on and on after you have told him you must go.

Some children adjust rather quickly to hospital confinement, but there are those who are consumed by the thought of their mothers. To such a child, it helps to have a hospital member say, "Your mother brought you here because you are sick. When you are well, she will come to take you home. Your mother loves you. She wants you to get well fast so you can go home." Even a toddler will understand this kind of talk and, if repeated between his mother's visits, his hospital stay will be more bearable.

The preschooler is a lively child with a lively imagination. When he is to go to the hospital, he should be prepared in a matter-of-fact way. Tell him what to expect in hospital procedure, step by step, from the time he enters the hospital foyer until he is ready to go home. If you don't know the procedure, take time to find out. It is reassuring to a child to know that his parents know a great deal about the place where they are to leave him, because always there lurks in his mind the paralyzing fear that you might not be able to find him again and that he will be lost.

Let him help pack the things he will take with him, including a favorite something to cuddle. Promise to bring surprises when you visit him—not for being good, just for being. And even if he isn't old enough to read, colorful cards from family and friends will brighten his days.

If it has not been possible for a mother to see her small child during the hospital stay, she must, upon his return home, again envelop him with her love to rebuild a secure relationship. If the toddler has not seen his mother, he may come home angry with her for deserting him. He will not forgive her completely until she can prove to him again her steadfastness and love.

If the preschool child has had a difficult hospital experience, he may regress in his behavior, act babyish, or have a temporary setback in toilet training. Soon, nightmares may appear. He may not let his mother out of his sight.

Thoughtful preparation of a child for hospitalization, followed by a hospital experience that takes his feelings into consideration, will do a great deal to lessen unpleasantness before and after.

See also CONVALESCENT CHILD; HOME AND HOSPITAL INSTRUCTION

Related article in WORLD BOOK: "Hospital"

HOSTILITY

Unlike anger or resentment, hostility is not a state purely of feeling; hostility involves a way of thinking, thinking that someone is antagonistic to one's wishes, needs, rights, and privileges, or unfriendly to one's self as a person. Hostility also involves a determination to pay back in kind what one thinks he is getting from the object of his hostility. True hostility probably does not really begin until a child is of school age, for younger children are more apt to experience anger or rage, unelaborated by thoughts of getting even or inflicting damage through spite.

Yet, from school age on, children, as an inevitable part of their growing up, enter and pass through phases of hostility toward their parents, teachers, or brothers and sisters, or playmates. A child occupies status inferior to that of an adult; this status is enough to produce hostility toward adults. The need to share love with a brother or a sister or with one or the other parent creates the basis for rivalry or enmity which forms a fertile ground for hostility.

Although hostility is natural, a hostile child requires your help in order that he may safely steer through this period without freezing a hostile attitude into his philosophy of life. Since hostility is built upon some view a child has of another or others, it is terribly important for you to try to discover with him what it is that is making him feel and act hostile. His reasons for the hostility should be brought out into the open so that they may be looked at realistically. If, for instance, a child is hostile because he feels that his sister is getting a "better deal" from his parents, the facts that he is using to support his hostility have to be examined carefully with him. Perhaps he is interpreting them wrongly. Or perhaps the mere fact that the other child is younger and a girl has caused one or both parents to interfere in the boy's rough play with her too sharply and without enough explanation at the time of interference.

By carefully exploring their relationships with their children, parents may help to replace fantasies of neglect or favoritism with reality, or they may discover that they have unwittingly been a little careless and need to modify something in their handling techniques.

DAVID WINEMAN

See also AGGRESSIVENESS; ANGER; CHILD GUIDANCE CLINIC

HOUSEHOLD CHORES *See* CHORES

HUMIDIFYING ROOM *See* STEAMING

HUMOR

A sense of humor is beyond any question a saving grace in family life, because many things that children do, at every stage of growing, can turn your hair gray if you lose your capacity to smile a bit and laugh occasionally. One-year-olds dump all their toys out of crib or playpen. Two-year-olds make messes with their food. Threes leave piles of toys scattered everywhere. Fours punch holes in screens and make unlovely crayon designs on the walls. Five-year-olds can talk and talk and talk and then begin to shout. The list could go on and on. Healthy behavior is not always aesthetic behavior, nor is it always easy to live with. Children's normal energy, their curiosity about their world, their eagerness for independence, their highly social nature, create countless incidents that call for a light touch and an easy capacity to roll with the punches. A sense of humor lets you take a "major crisis" with just a grain of salt. It helps make you glad you have children and glad those children are normal, healthy, and active. It helps your children to be glad they are alive. It saves no end of wear and tear.

A sense of humor also works wonders for parents in creating happy relationships with their children. Very often the flat command and the heavy hand can breed resistance. Serious insistence can lead to equally serious rebellion, while the same situation handled with a gay touch or a little joke can induce good-willed cooperation. Not that one has to laugh continuously or hesitate to face serious issues as they arise. Some questions, obviously, are no laughing matter. But putting away toys, getting ready for a bath, coming in from play, and no end of other simple routines of everyday living often go more smoothly when the adult introduces some pleasing element that makes the chore look attractive and bearable.

Children gain from a parent's sense of humor in still another way. To a large extent humor is a learned characteristic. Youngsters who seldom see smiles or hear laughter or experience the fun of happy family give-and-take have trouble incorporating into their own personalities the ability to smile as they go along life's way. Children who are continually surrounded by appropriate good humor can hardly escape becoming pleasant people of good will.

JAMES L. HYMES, JR.

See also DISCIPLINE

HURTING OTHERS *See* CRUELTY

HYPEROPIA *See* FARSIGHTEDNESS

IDEALS *See* MORAL AND SPIRITUAL DEVELOPMENT

ILLNESS *See* MENTAL ILLNESS; SICK CHILD

IMAGINARY COMPANION

Imaginary companions, those characters human or animal which young children invent, often make their presence felt in the homes of 2- to 5-year-olds. Parents may find it tiresome to be told that a nonexistent little man with a preposterous name is sitting on the living room couch or that a lion—albeit a very tame one—is nestled among the rubbers in the hall closet, but these creatures may be assisting your child in some important kinds of growing.

Sometimes an imaginary companion is merely an idealized playmate who is always agreeable, utterly loyal, and ready for any adventure. His "company" tides a small person over bad or boring moments and soothes many hurts. Because of his "company," a 3- or 4-year-old may be able to play contentedly by himself—and it is no small achievement to learn to amuse oneself. But children need real friends, too. You can take the trouble to provide live playmates even though your son or daughter occasionally does like to retreat to the fictitious ones; after all, fictitious companions never ask to have a turn with the toy train nor do they snatch a doll away.

The creatures that a youngster invents may have the abilities and the good qualities he would like to have. These figments of fancy serve as an ideal to be lived up to for some children. In quite the opposite way, a boy or a girl may supply himself with a veritable little demon of an imaginary friend whom he blames for whatever mischief takes place. The existence of this convenient scapegoat does not mean that your offspring is becoming adept at sliding out of the responsibility for his own acts, but rather that he is developing a conscience. He can recognize the difference between acceptable and unacceptable behavior. He does not yet have the moral strength to do the right thing consistently, but he separates himself from his own lapses by claiming that an imaginary twin or a bad rabbit is the naughty one. He relieves his properly guilty conscience by being properly severe with his erring companion. When conscience works more effectively and forestalls infractions of the rules of the household most of the time, the imaginary culprit usually vanishes from the child's life.

Another useful role the fictitious friend plays is that of the docile, timid spirit whom the small child will try to protect and reassure. You may overhear comforting words to convince the beast or the boy or whatever it may be, that the barking dog, the growling thunder, or the dark bedroom are really nothing to be scared of. What better way to keep up one's wavering courage than to feel called upon to allay the fears of a creature even more helpless than oneself? A different type of unreal playmate is the one who is so strong and clever that he becomes the protector. In either case, if the youngster is able to draw strength from these fantasies temporarily, so much the better.

Since imaginary companions are children's own property, you may take your cue from your child in such matters as addressing the nonexistent one or attempting to decide how the mythical animal will act. It is hardly fair—indeed it would be downright confusing to a child—to suggest that you have the power to do away with the imaginary friend or to turn him against his inventor. Other children in the family may joke and tease about the 2- or 3-year-old's fancied friends, but the adults can afford to go along with these pretendings. You can ask the inventor of a Mr. Bluber or a Mrs. Campermouse to please tell him or her to get out of grandpa's favorite chair or to wait outside while the family eats.

As long as a child can easily go back and forth between his world of pretending and the real world, there is no cause for concern over these nonexistent creatures. They may multiply in number and change name and form suddenly. If they are accepted casually by adults, they will usually wither away when they are no longer needed for company, to reinforce conscience, or as protection against danger. EDITH G. NEISSER

See also IMAGINATION

IMAGINARY FEARS *See* ANXIETY; FEAR

IMAGINATION

The years from 3 to 6 are the peak years for imagination. Children younger than 3 are primarily concerned with manipulating materials. Their time is spent getting the feel of clay, paint, and sand and exploring the possibilities of blocks and pots and pans. These very young children play imaginatively at times, but more often their actions are determined by the nature of the materials at hand than by their own brainstorms. After their 6th birthday, children continue imaginative activities, but two forces intervene to lessen the dominance of make-believe and "let's pretend." Children over 6 spend much of their time in school. Their work is reality-centered, and they are busily learning the right and the wrong way of performing. Imaginative, free activities have to be compressed increasingly into their after-school hours. Developmentally, too, these older children are becoming more self-critical, more concerned with how their behavior stacks up against what the outside world expects. They are becoming more interested in and capable of following rules and regulations in games.

In between these two periods is the 3-to-6 age span, when children have the time and the freedom to live their own lives in their own way. And for the first time they are able to take the initiative in thinking out for themselves how materials can be used and how people can act. They have not yet reached the stage of caring whether their ideas are "good" or "bad," "true" or "make-believe," measured by reality. The distinctive new note in development is that the child has thought up an idea. It is his idea. It originates within him rather than within the material. The result is that 3-to-6-year-old children constantly use themselves, other people in their world, and all the materials around them, freely and creatively, in whatever way strikes their fancy.

A tricycle does not have to be a tricycle. It can instantaneously become a horse or a motorcycle or an airplane or a boat, and can change from one to another in a jiffy. The child does not have to stay as he is. He can become a father, a digger, a soldier, a cowboy, a baby, a prisoner, or a sick person. Children frequently mix up their roles. A 4-year-old, without being in the least bothered, can put on a soldier's hat and say to another 4-year-old: "Let's have a bull fight."

Children very often say out loud what they are imagining: "I am the doctor and you are the sick person, and I come and make you well." But even when youngsters are alone or not talking, the chances are overwhelming that within their minds they are creating their own make-believe world. At an easel a child paints a picture that may look like nothing at all to the adult watching. It is sure to have great significance to the child—and a changing significance. He may be painting a "tree" one moment and then, as fancy suits him, change that tree into a very satisfactory (to him) "house" or "car" or "dog."

Imaginative activity has many values for children. It is a great emotional equalizer for one thing. Depending on his own need, a child is able to turn on bigness: "I must be the boss and you must do what I say"; or to turn on dependency: "I must be your baby and you must feed me and put me to bed." Through imagination the child makes up for whatever gaps he experiences in the real everyday world in which he lives.

Imagination makes important intellectual contributions, too. Through taking roles and through imposing his ideas on the materials around him, a child gains clarity and slowly develops an understanding of what things are and how they operate. He sorts out all the impressions that have come in to him and "tries them on for size" through dramatic play. This creative, purely personal organization within his own mind is, in fact, a whole series of mental practice sessions in attention span, in problem-solving, in thinking and organization, and in language. We can call all this imaginative activity of young children

A child is able to turn on bigness.

—play. But the word is misleading because youngsters are very serious, very earnest, and often quite solemn about their imaginative activities.

Imagination leads to valuable social learnings, too. Children daydream imaginatively and sometimes work alone imaginatively. But most of their best imaginative activities are with other youngsters their own age. One child's creative ideas stimulate the other child's response. Imaginative activities become one of the best ways in which children learn to get along together.

We sometimes make the mistake of thinking that the imagination of young children is spurred by fairy tales, by unrealistic and fantastic shows or movies, or by fanciful books and illustrations. These may have entertainment value, but adult imagination makes no special contribution to children's imagination. Children's imagination is mostly rooted in reality. Children play out what they have experienced. They change and distort and re-create what they know best. The basic way to stimulate imagination is to give young children firsthand experiences. House play—taking the roles of mother, father, baby—is the most frequent imaginative activity because it stems from the most familiar experience, but imagination need not stay centered around any one idea. The more children know, the more they can imagine. Trips to the firehouse, the police station, the airport, the harbor, to construction sites where houses are being built and earthmovers are at work, bring a flow of impressions. Sights and sounds such as these are the stuff with which boys and girls think and out of which they imagine.

Play materials that children are free to use in their own way are equally important boosters of imagination. Sand, paints, clay, boards, boxes, barrels—anything that has no "official" way in which it must be used—are helpful. Children make especially good use of dress-up clothes: adult hats, gloves, shoes, pocketbooks, and so on. When children have had some specific firsthand experience, such as a visit to a firehouse, it helps to have available the kinds of props and supplies that lend themselves to "firehouse play": ladders, for example, or tricycles or wagons that can become fire engines; a bell; a hose; or hats that can become firemen's hats.

The third and last major stimulus to imagination is adult attitudes. We must be glad to see children play imaginatively. We must accept what they do as *their* play. We must be patient, not expecting young children's play to be realistic by adult standards or to be governed by any set of rules other than those the child makes up from moment to moment. Children sense whether they are getting support from the adults around them. Too many children are constantly interrupted because adults feel that children are "just" playing. Too many sense that their parents are in a hurry to move them on into the next stage in development when they will learn academic skills. We must value this brief, creative time in life. The young child's highly individualistic make-believe activity is the base on which later adult creative innovations are rooted—in the arts and in the business world, in the professions, in politics, or on any kind of job. JAMES L. HYMES, JR.

See also CREATING; DRESS-UP PLAY; HONESTY

IMITATION

That bright-eyed infant looking up at you from his crib will doubtless, in due time, learn to walk, talk, laugh, sing, play tennis, ride a horse, earn his living, have a spouse, and become a dues-paying member of some organization. If it were possible for him to grow up with no one around to imitate, he would never learn to do or be the majority of these things.

Because you, his parents, are with him the most and because he loves you the most, you are the ones he will imitate most often, will strive to be most like, or even will pattern after without conscious trying. The small boy who is accustomed to hearing his father

It's natural for a child to imitate adult behavior.

speak fondly of his school days quite likely will look forward to and enjoy his own. The little girl whose mother demonstrates how wonderful it is to be a girl probably will remain forever proud of her own feminine role.

Psychologists think of imitation in two forms: (1) imitation on cue, such as standing up in a classroom because a teacher has struck a note on the piano, and (2) imitating without cue by simply modeling behavior on what is seen in or heard from an elder. One youngster, a late talker, had as his first spoken words, "Don't do that"—obviously not a phrase he had thought up for himself. Parents sometimes use the on-cue response as a teaching tool, ringing a dinner bell to announce meals or putting lights out as the signal for the final good night. But more commonly parents think of imitation as the copying of a model and they make use of this tendency of the child in training him.

A child also imitates the nonhuman. He tries to trill like a bird, chug like an engine, to be as round as a balloon, or as high in the sky as a box kite. Whatever his mode of imitation, it furthers his learning about the ways of life and the world. Imitative play activities—the toddler following his mother about the house, repeating her motions as she attends to her household chores; the older children playing house or store, being mother or father or storekeeper—help children learn attitudes appropriate to their sex and to learn roles and attitudes appropriate to certain occupations. Through playing such parts, a child increases his ability to understand the viewpoints of other people and becomes "socialized"—able to take the other person's viewpoint in feeling and attitude as well as in behavior.

Because of his relative immaturity and helplessness, a young child attaches a great deal of importance to the power and status that age and skillful performance can bring. He observes and wishes for the privileges given to older brothers and sisters and to grownups. His desire for independence and freedom is undoubtedly a strong incentive for him to imitate grown-up models. This form of imitation is an important feature of personality development. The process by which a child models himself after a loved adult in outward behavior is called identification—the process that leads him to adopt the attitudes and values of his model.

Identification with another also appears to lead a child to a deeper understanding of the feelings of other people, and thus becomes an important source of that socially and morally valuable quality, sympathy.

Although young children commonly model themselves upon their parents, they may, as they get older and as they become interested in more people, pick teachers or other admired adults to copy. Substitution of such adults for the parent is perfectly natural and is important in the child's emotional development. The discovery by a child that his parents are less than perfect is a big step toward his emotional independence and mature discrimination of important values. Parents do not always see the change this way—they sometimes resist being discarded as models and resent seeing another set up in their place.

Many parents also are distressed when their child admires and copies an older youth or young adult—one whom the parents do not admire. For the most part, such imitation does not last long. Usually, the examples of behavior and attitudes that parents themselves have expressed prove to be more enduring and command their child's loyalties in the long run. Parents, wittingly or not, are constantly teaching their children to be like them. DALE B. HARRIS

See also ATTITUDES

IMMUNIZATION

Take a look at the immunization schedule shown in the accompanying chart. Today it is routine procedure to follow this schedule closely. The purpose of such immunization is to protect the health of infants and children. You will notice that the series of shots gets started when a child is extremely young, generally when he is only a month and a half or 2 months old. You will notice, also, that the shots are combined ones, immunizing against diphtheria, whooping cough, polio, and tetanus. The combined shot is sometimes called triple (3-in-1) or quadruple (4-in-1) vaccine. When a combined dose of only three is given—to prevent whooping cough, diphtheria, and tetanus—the poliovaccine is then administered separately. As the table indicates, booster doses of all these shots are also necessary to maintain immunity. Shots to prevent scarlet fever are no longer needed because this disease responds to penicillin.

The substances used in the preventive shots are called antigens. They are prepared from the germs, viruses or their toxins (poisons), that cause the diseases. Antigens are given by inoculation.

Combined Doses

You may wonder why doctors prefer to give combined doses rather than to inoculate a child against the diseases one by one. The

IMMUNIZATION SCHEDULE
FOR BABIES AND CHILDREN*

AGE	DISEASE	WHEN GIVEN		
	PRIMARY IMMUNIZATION SERIES:	day	month	year
	against these diseases:			
First dosage at 1½ to 2 months	Diphtheria, Whooping Cough, Tetanus, and Polio			
Second dosage at 3 months	Diphtheria, Whooping Cough, Tetanus, and Polio			
Third dosage at 4 months	Diphtheria, Whooping Cough, Tetanus, and Polio			
First dosage at 6 months	Smallpox (vaccination)			
	ROUTINE BOOSTER DOSES:			
	against these diseases:			
1 year old	Diphtheria, Whooping Cough, Tetanus, and Polio			
2 years old	Polio			
4 years old	Diphtheria, Whooping Cough, Tetanus, and Polio			
6 years old	Smallpox (vaccination)			
8 years old	Diphtheria, Tetanus, and Polio			
10 years old	Polio			
12 years old	Diphtheria, Tetanus, and Polio			
14 years old	Polio			
16 years old	Diphtheria, Tetanus, and Polio			
	EMERGENCY BOOSTER DOSE: (IN CASE OF EXTRAORDINARY EXPOSURE)			
Only when your doctor advises	against these diseases: Diphtheria, Whooping Cough, and Tetanus			
	SPECIAL OTHER IMMUNIZATION (FOR SOME SPECIFIC REASON)			
Only when your doctor advises	against these diseases: Cholera, German Measles, Infectious Hepatitis, Measles, Mumps, Plague, Rabies, Tuberculosis, Typhoid Fever, Typhus, Yellow Fever			

*Based on *Report of the Committee on Control of Infectious Diseases* (1961), American Academy of Pediatrics, Evanston, Illinois combined dose makes it possible to set up immunity earlier, and the earlier the immunity, the safer for the child. Combined doses are also great timesavers for the parent and the doctor, and they cost the parent less than the many single doses would. For the child himself there are fewer needle pricks and hence less pain and anxiety. You need not worry that the combined dose is harder on a child medically than single ones would be—reactions are rarely more severe from the multiple shots, and the benefits make up for whatever more pronounced reaction might occur. Once in a while a doctor has reason to give each kind of antigen separately to a particular child. If your doctor prefers this method for your child, he will probably be glad to tell you why.

Early Immunization

You may also wonder why the shots will be given to your child so early. Why take a healthy, thriving baby and "fill him up with all that stuff," you may ask. Why, indeed? Chiefly, because you want your child immune as soon as possible. There is no inherited immunity from an immune mother for whooping cough, polio, tetanus, and diphtheria (as there is with measles) to protect a child during his first months. Immunity to these diseases is not achieved until more than a month after the final dose of the antigens, and the doses have to be given about a month apart—thus, even with an early start, the child will be several months old before he becomes immune. He will also need a periodic booster dose to remain immune. But perhaps the most important reason for early immunization is to prevent whooping cough, which still causes more deaths during the first year of life than do measles, polio, scarlet fever, and smallpox combined.

A child's first smallpox vaccination is also given early in life, a month or two after the last dose of the primary series of triple or quadruple antigen. This is done because the reaction is usually much milder than if he should be vaccinated later on. Sometimes, however, vaccination is delayed until very hot weather ends, lest profuse perspiration and accumulated dust on the blister cause a secondary infection resulting in delayed healing and a larger scar.

What About Reactions?

Whenever a reaction—swelling, reddening, or fever—occurs after a dose of triple or quadruple antigens, it is a good idea to consult your doctor, even though as a general rule everything is back to normal within three or four days, at the very most. Don't forget to remind the doctor of a previous reaction at the time of the next dose; perhaps he might prefer to give a somewhat smaller dose that time, even though to do so will require more trips to his office.

The immunization program for premature infants is handled in a slightly different way. Doctors often prefer to wait until the premature baby is older and stronger and better equipped to generate antibodies. Or he may prefer to start fairly early and give small fractional doses. Or he may prefer sometimes to give just small doses of the whooping cough vaccine while the infant is young, and then later on follow up with a complete set of the combined triple or quadruple antigens.

Booster Shots

A periodic booster dose is routine procedure (see Table). Also, an emergency booster shot might be advised when, for example, an immunized child is known to have been exposed to a disease. When a previously immunized child is bitten by an animal, steps on a nail, or has a burn contaminated by soil, most doctors quickly give him an extra dose of tetanus toxoid.

New ways of immunization are constantly appearing. For example, live polio virus (attenuated) is under investigation, both for safety and protective power. Should it be found safe, shots for polio would no longer be needed. Then the poliovaccine would be given by mouth.

Special Shots

Special immunization is needed if you and your child are going to travel to places where he might be exposed to diseases other than those for which he has had shots or where food or water may be contaminated. His immunizations against diphtheria, whooping cough, tetanus, poliomyelitis, and smallpox should also be brought up to date. A smallpox certificate, signed by the physician and countersigned by the local or state department of health, is required before entry into many foreign countries and at the point of re-entry into the U.S.A. Your destination determines which precautions should be necessary. If you talk with your doctor well ahead of the time of your departure, he will be able to provide the kinds of immunization required.

LOUIS W. SAUER

See also COMMON COMMUNICABLE DISEASES; SHOTS

IMPEDIMENT, SPEECH *See* SPEECH DIFFICULTIES

IMPETIGO

Penicillin or other antibiotics are usually effective in controlling impetigo, an infection in which small blister-like sores, or lesions, develop on the surface of the skin. The lesions contain a clear fluid at first, which quickly changes to pus. Later, the lesions usually open and a thick, yellowish crust develops over them, which drops off in from four to six days. These lesions can occur anywhere on the body, singly or in large numbers. The condition is highly contagious.

Impetigo is usually caused by staphylococcic infection. Occasionally, however, other bacteria are responsible. When babies get impetigo, they should be watched carefully, for there is a tendency for the bacteria to invade the blood ("blood poisoning"). For this reason, consult your doctor early if impetigo is suspected. Gentle cleansing of the skin is an important part of treatment. JULIUS B. RICHMOND

INCUBATION PERIOD *See* COMMON COMMUNICABLE DISEASES

INCUBATOR

Very small premature babies, especially those under four pounds, have a good deal of difficulty at first in making the change from the mother's womb to the outside world. The body systems that keep the baby in good health are not so well developed as in the full-term baby. A premature baby has little or no fat under his skin to insulate his body. One of his big problems is to maintain an even body temperature and not to lose body heat when he is exposed to room temperature.

Homemade incubators have been constructed by using a well-padded basket lined with hot-water bottles to help keep the premature baby warm. The modern hospital incubator looks rather like a glass box on legs. The box is completely closed so that the baby is in an atmosphere that can be carefully regulated in every way—not only the temperature but also the humidity and the oxygen content in the air. Glass walls allow the nurse to watch the baby carefully, without disturbing him except for feedings and diaper changes. RUTH S. KEMPE

See also PREMATURE BABY

INDEPENDENCE

One child's mother frets because he will not leave her side; another worries because her child takes chances. Still another mother whose child will gladly go alone to the corner store but still asks to be put to bed at night, is confused about the meaning of independence for young children.

Suppose a small boy is hesitant about trying the big slide at the playground. But his mother is insistent and coaxes him up the ladder. When he reaches the top, he freezes and screams in fright. His embarrassed and frustrated mother commands him to "stop acting like a baby," to be "a brave boy." But he cannot. For some reason he is fearful where other youngsters are adventurous. And when his mother implies that she is disgusted with him, she adds to his terror because he feels he has lost her love. Of course, going down a slide is not the problem—it is this youngster's feelings that matter. Perhaps he would benefit from more generous praise for the things he can and does do alone; perhaps his parents expect too much of him. Perhaps they unconsciously want to keep him dependent, although they talk about wanting him to grow up. Perhaps they treat him as if he were still a baby—are too quick to step in and take over, find it hard to accept their child's strivings for self-sufficiency.

And what about the fearless 4-year-old who is always taking chances? Where is he? Starting to cross a street, perhaps, as his frightened mother catches him, roughly brings him back to the curb, and spanks him for his disobedience. A more useful tactic might be for the mother to point out the dangers in the situation, check on the child's understanding of traffic signals, and offer to let him be the one to tell her when it is safe for them to cross.

Independence is not an all-at-once, all-or-nothing affair. It is an attitude, a state of being, which emerges when an individual develops sufficient judgment and self-confidence to go ahead on his own in some activity. It does not develop at the same time in all areas of activity. That is why the child who is sure of himself at the grocery store might still not be ready to go up to bed alone. Another child of the same age might reach for mother's hand at the supermarket but not mind the dark. Evidently these situations have different meanings for the two children. And it is these meanings, these private sets of ideas that refer to the past but still affect present behavior, that decide the way an individual will act. Independence, like other personality traits, is the result of both growth and experience. It can be encouraged; it can be restrained. But it can neither be produced upon demand nor reversed by decree. IRMA S. BLACK AND JOAN W. BLOS

See also READINESS; RESPONSIBILITY

INDIGESTION *See* COLIC; CONSTIPATION; DIARRHEA; STOMACH-ACHE; VOMITING

INDIVIDUAL DIFFERENCES

Before your newborn baby leaves the hospital someone will probably take a printed impression of his foot or thumb. This print will be different from that of any other infant previously recorded anywhere at any time; the print will also be different from that of any child who is going to be born anywhere in the future. The difference will exist even if he is one of identical twins, a pea who looks precisely like the other pea in his pod.

Your baby also has, at birth, his own particular blood type, his own particular arrangement of blood vessels, his individual anatomical structure of nerves and muscles and body chemicals and body fluids. There will be other people who duplicate him in any one of these physical characteristics, but there will be no one who has the exact combination he has, *no one!* This miracle of similarity and differentiation is part of the miracle of man the survivor, man the adaptable, man the maker and doer and changer.

At the hospital your reaction to your baby's foot or thumb print is predictable. You expect him to be unique in this respect and you glory in his uniqueness, telling yourself happily: He's mine, he's different, he's *himself*.

But then time will pass and instead of glorying you may begin to worry just because your child *is* unique. For after all, we do live in a world where standards are set up, where people are judged by standards, and are often penalized for not meeting them: Thus you'll see your neighbor's baby take his first steps at 10 months, and you'll wonder why yours doesn't do the same. You'll remember that your cousin's child was toilet trained somewhere around his second birthday and wonder why your own is oblivious to wet diapers when he is nearly 3. You'll watch some youngster in your child's nursery school draw recognizable birds and dogs, and you'll look askance at the meaningless crayon scribbles your child makes.

Or your experience could be quite the opposite and you find your child advanced in several areas. Perhaps he will be taller than the neighbor's child of the same age, or he may climb better, or seem to sing with more accurate pitch. Or, as is very likely, you will see him go fast in one direction and slowly in another; you may see, for instance, when he's 4, that he can read a number of words but cannot go to sleep without a pacifier.

If his differences from other children begin to bother you, you'll do very well by him, by yourself, and by your relationship to each other to remember his hospital footprint, and from it conclude again that he was not born to be like anyone else in temperament, in physical characteristics and development, or in mental capacity and rate of development. For although outside forces seem designed to shape a child into a mold, his drives from within seem designed to shape him into a unique individual.

It is easy to say that we are aware of individual differences among children. Indeed the idea is almost a commonplace: "It takes all kinds," we say when we see someone behave in a way we think is different. And with increasing frequency teachers, child guidance experts, and counselors are pointing out that no two individuals are built alike, no two individuals grow alike, no two individuals think alike, and no two individuals develop at the same rate.

The increasing attention paid to the *fact* of individual differences is all to the good. Articles in this volume of CHILDCRAFT make a point, at almost every turn, of reminding you of individual differences. But there is this danger: Sometimes when an obvious fact is stressed, people accept the fact but forget its importance. Thus, all of us by now may have come to accept the fact of individual differences while at the same time we forget its implications and applications in the lives we and our children lead from day to day and from year to year.

Physical Differences

The forces assuring that each individual will be different from all other individuals begin their work early, long before a child is born. Some traits are inherited. The coming together of mother and father from widely separated ancestral paths assures a child who is a little like his mother and a little like his father, but mostly different from both.

Although many families produce look-alikes with great similarity in physical build, it is not at all unusual to find families where one child is built squarely, sturdily, close to the ground, and another child has delicate bones and a long, thin frame. It is not out of the question for a mother of three to have a redhead, a blond, and a brunet, nor for one of her children to need glasses before he enters school and another to have excellent vision straight through college. Isn't it more than natural, then, that in different families children should differ markedly from one another in their body proportions and size, in their coloring, their rate of growth, their stamina, their susceptibility to disease? Isn't it less than astonishing that there will be little or great acuity of hearing, high or low morning body temperature, corresponding high or low morning energy or that one person will need 20 times as much salt on his food as another in order to achieve the same taste? It is easy enough to observe that some children take their first steps at 9 months; some are only beginning to toddle at 18 months; a boy who was one of the shortest in his class suddenly shoots up and passes some others when he is 15; a girl who seemed too tall for her age stops growing before some of her classmates do. And yet, for all their differences, what each one of these children needs is to be given the best possible over-all physical care and then to be allowed to grow up, without undue comment, at the rate and to the maturity that nature intended for him.

Emotional Differences

The same need applies to his emotional differences. Some 3-year-olds easily leave their parents to spend happy hours in a new setting. For other 3-year-olds, even the thought of being out of mother's sight is a terrifying experience. Some 4-year-olds scream in frustration when their first attempt to couple a train fails. Other 4-year-olds calmly try again. Some very young children are painfully aware of adult reactions, others seem far more able to live in their own world, largely unaffected by adult crises and emotions. If each of these children can be looked at individually, have his differences in temperament and sensitivity recognized, his path smoothed where possible, and then be let alone to develop in his own way, his chances of proper development are good indeed.

Mental Differences

The mental processes of children, their mental capacities and limitations, and their rates of mental development, differ as greatly as any other aspect of their capabilities. Some children talk better at 2 than others do at 3. Some will do "rithmetics" before they go to nursery school, others will not care in the least that two and two are four until the fact is forced upon them. In a first grade, size differences are often so great that the largest children would be physically unnoticed in a class of third graders and the smallest ones would fit physically with nursery school children, but the mental differences are equally great. In an ordinary first grade, some 6-year-olds respond intellectually like 4-year-olds, others, like 8- and 9-year-olds. And this intellectual spread among children of the same age tends to grow even greater as these children advance through the grades. This does not mean, however, that any given child will be either advanced or retarded or on a level in all his schoolwork. To say that a child is in third grade usually means that he is doing third-grade work in some subjects, second- and fourth-grade work in others. Also, a child who starts out slowly may be one who later catches up with others, or the one who starts out with a great burst of ability may level off and become more like the usual child.

There are, then, two major facts of individuality and individual differences for you to keep in mind. First, each child varies—often markedly—from all other children in all phases of development—physical, emotional, social, intellectual. Secondly, each of the many traits characterizing the individual child develops at a different rate. The great danger for parents, seeking to guide their children, is that they will want to follow too closely the expectations they build up from the behavior and accomplishments of other children. What you, as a parent, can do is to provide opportunities geared to the realities of your particular child's abilities and potentialities. Every child should experience enough success to be able to take failure in his stride. The child expected to walk, talk, toilet train, and read before he is ready to do these things may experience so much failure that he comes to see himself as unworthy. His talents wither because his only chance for self-preservation is not to try.

The knowledge of individual differences is propelling many schools and teachers away from a common set of expectation for all children of the same age or grade, is encouraging them to provide learning materials suited to the individual's abilities and interests, to abandon graded classrooms in favor of ones where a child can progress at his own speed. Parents can not only encourage the schools in these recognitions, they can also learn from what the schools have learned. By being aware of the uniqueness of each child, understanding who and what he is and what his requirements are, they can help him to happiness and success in a world that needs his special talents and skills and personality.

The lesson of the infant foot or thumb print need not be lost. It can remain in your mind forever as a symbol of the uniqueness of the individual who is your child. It can give you the inspiration to be unafraid of differences, to encourage his individuality at every point, and to let him become an adult worthy of being born with a print unlike any other in past, present, or future. JOHN I. GOODLAD

See also ABILITIES; BABY; EMOTIONAL DEVELOPMENT; GIFTED CHILD; GROWTH; HEREDITY; MENTAL DEVELOPMENT; MORAL AND SPIRITUAL DEVELOPMENT; NORMAL CHILD

INDIVIDUALITY *See* INDIVIDUAL DIFFERENCES

INFANT *See* BABY

INFANTILE PARALYSIS *See* POLIO

INFECTIOUS MONONUCLEOSIS *See* GLANDULAR FEVER

INFERIORITY COMPLEX

We all feel inferior in some respects, and to varying degrees. Such inferiority can be borne calmly if it is balanced by opposite feelings. These need not be feelings of superiority, but they should at least be feelings of adequacy. As long as a child can feel, for example, "I am inferior in spelling, but I am adequate on the playground and in reading," or "I am temporarily inferior in spelling, but I shall soon become adequate," there is no harm in his feeling inferior at spelling. If, on the other hand, feelings of inferiority extend over much or all of the total personality and to many life activities, then that person is suffering from an inferiority complex.

Without a certain sense of inferiority human beings would lose one of the strongest motives to improve themselves and to achieve in this world. Only when that feeling reaches such a degree that someone despairs of his ability to achieve at all in important ways does it become a serious disturbance.

There are many reasons why a child may feel inferior. After all, children are inferior to adults, little children are inferior to older children. Girls may feel inferior to boys because girls cannot do, or are not encouraged to do, some of the things that boys normally do. Or boys may feel inferior if their sisters, for example, are preferred by the parents. The difference between more or less normal feelings of inferiority and an inferiority complex can be recognized from a child's behavior. A child is normal if after he succeeds in an area in which he felt inferior, he drops his feelings of inferiority about that area. A boy may feel inferior because others his age have learned to swim and he has not. But, once he has mastered the sport and feels the equal of his friends, if not their better, then in this respect, at least, he is in good shape emotionally.

On the other hand, a child who never shows any signs of feeling inferior may feel intensely inferior. Some children who suffer severe feelings of inferiority try to deny or to camouflage them with boasts of superiority. A child who must always be best, who must always win in games, may be suffering from an inferiority complex he is trying to hide. Of course, some boasting is entirely normal, particularly for younger children. Again, it is when such behavior is extremely intense and of an unvarying nature that an imbalance is suggested.

All children need encouragement, but a child who feels inferior needs it particularly. The best medicine for a feeling of inferiority is not to tell a child that he is doing fine when he really isn't or to encourage him to think he is able to do what he fears he cannot do. In such a case nothing is less sensible than to call a feat "easy" to encourage the child to try. If an adult pictures as easy what to a child is a difficult achievement, and the child, despite his best efforts, cannot succeed, the child's self-esteem is further damaged. He then believes that he cannot even achieve what his parents think is easy. If, on the other hand, a parent tells the child that to overcome certain difficulties is very hard, and the child then with effort learns to master them, that will make him feel good about himself. And even if he fails, he will not feel inferior because he was told beforehand that the task was difficult.

Better than such a direct way of trying to make the child feel better about himself where he feels inferior is a somewhat more subtle approach. Children can be made to feel good about themselves and about the abilities they have that do not yet trouble them. If, for example, your daughter feels inferior to boys, it is not a good idea to tell her that she can do all that boys do, because in truth she cannot—witness only the physiological difference between the sexes. But a girl can be made to feel good about herself if the fact that only she will be able to bear children is stressed. Her pride in this—her positive ability—will eventually counteract whatever feelings of inferiority she may have about not being a boy.

Most important of all, a child should not be made to feel ashamed of himself, as opposed to feeling ashamed about some particular thing he has done. Closely as guilt and shame are related, it is important for a parent to understand the difference in their impact on a young child. He feels ashamed when he is made fun of, when he is ridiculed. He may feel ashamed if he doesn't know something, if he does something awkward and is laughed at. As adults we would hardly feel guilty just because we lacked knowledge or because something slipped out of our hands.

The difference between shame and guilt is important. We feel guilty about something we did that we shouldn't have done, but we feel ashamed about ourselves as total persons. Guilt may lead to avoidance of the act one feels guilty about; shame may lead to an inferiority complex and withdrawal. A guilty person will try to correct his behavior or apologize for it, as a child will say, "I'm sorry—I won't do it again." But a child who is ashamed will cover his face with his hands; he doesn't want people to see him and he is afraid to look the world in the face. An adult who wants to prevent the development of an inferiority complex in a child tries not to make the child feel ashamed of himself in any way. BRUNO BETTELHEIM

See also GUILT FEELINGS; MENTAL HEALTH

INFLUENZA

People of all ages seem to be susceptible to influenza, although newborn babies may be temporarily immune if their mothers have immunity. Epidemics of influenza may be found in almost every part of the world. Influenza is an acute disease caused by a virus present in secretions and other discharges from the nose and mouth of an infected person. It is thought to be transmitted through coughing, sneezing, and breathing.

The first symptoms usually include aching muscles, especially of the back; lack of energy; and fever that may become quite high—as much as 105° F. or 106° F. The child may also cough and complain of sore throat. Symptoms last several days and gradually subside if no complications develop. The sick child may, however, lack his usual energy for some time after he appears to have recovered.

The most serious thing about influenza is its possible complications. Some of these complications may not be caused by influenza virus but rather by bacteria that invade during the course of the illness. Middle-ear infections, pneumonia, kidney reactions, and inflammation of the brain are but a few of the complications. A child with influenza should be under the care of his doctor who will watch for complications and also prescribe drugs that will make the child feel more comfortable.

Effective vaccines for preventing influenza have been developed. Unfortunately, their effects last only a short time, possibly only six months to a year, so they are not recommended unless it seems that an epidemic may be developing. Also, since in rare cases there may be reactions to it, the vaccine is not generally recommended for children. But children with chronic diseases, such as tuberculosis, diabetes, and muscular dystrophy, probably should receive the vaccine if an epidemic seems likely. JULIUS B. RICHMOND

See also SICK CHILD; VIRUS

INJURIES *See* ACCIDENT PREVENTION; BLEEDING; BROKEN BONE; BURN; CUTS AND SCRATCHES; FIRST AID

INOCULATIONS *See* SHOTS

INSECT BITES *See* BITES, INSECT

INSECURITY *See* ANXIETY

INSOMNIA *See* WAKEFULNESS

INTELLIGENCE TESTS *See* TESTS AND MEASUREMENTS

INTEREST TESTS *See* TESTS AND MEASUREMENTS

INTERRUPTING

Adults usually are quite annoyed when they are interrupted in midsentence, and justifiably so. If the one doing the interrupting is a child, the adult can take the opportunity to correct him, explaining that to break in while another person is speaking is to show very bad manners. Often a child's interruption is an attention-getting device. Or if he has observed adults talking for a long time, the child may feel it is his turn to speak. Here the adult, unless sensing that the child has some "emergency" problem, can ask the child to wait until the grownups have finished what they were saying. The old adage, "Children should be seen and not heard," is out-of-date in today's world, but to expect courteous behavior from a child is definitely not out-of-date.

If children are expected not to interrupt adults, adults must not interrupt children when they are speaking. Many times a child's account of some fascinating school event is thoughtlessly interrupted by an adult who wants to know if the child has washed his hands or hung up his clothes. Adults don't think of this as an interruption, but to the child it is just that.

One small boy inadvertently taught his family quite a lesson. Every time he was interrupted in the middle of a story, he began all over again. Soon his family took care to listen to his rather long, involved tales rather than endure repeat performances.

The art of conversation in a family is not learned accidentally. To practice the courtesy of letting someone speak without interruption is part of this art. Conversations in the family should be cultivated and encouraged, and rules for courteous listening should be strictly observed.

See also LISTENING TO CHILDREN; MANNERS

INTESTINAL DISTURBANCE *See* COLIC; DIARRHEA; STOMACH-ACHE

INTRODUCING NEW FOODS

For a child, eating a new food is like taking a step in the dark. An adult has a vast fund of memories with which to compare a new food; a child has none. Suppose you are trying cooked kohlrabi for the first time. You may observe that it has a mild cabbage-like odor, a fresh white color with a tinge of green, and a texture somewhat like a cooked cabbage heart. These impressions cast some light on your step in the dark. But a child has had no time to store up experiences with foods and therefore has no chance to make comparisons.

When he does taste a new food, he remembers the experience. If it is pleasant, he may willingly try another new food. If it is unpleasant, he probably will avoid the next strange food. It is important to make your child's experiences in trying new foods pleasant ones. Here are a few suggestions:

Expect that he will eat little or none of the food at the first encounter. He may merely feel it and look at it. As other members of the family eat the food, you can ask him calmly if he would like to try it. Let him set his own goal of perhaps a bite or two. After the food is on his plate, even the unfamiliar odor may make him afraid to try it. If so, simply say nothing and either leave the food on his plate or remove it. Allow him the chance to back away without incurring your disapproval. If he feels you understand that he is getting up courage to try and that it may take several tries, his ability to take the step will be strengthened.

Don't make your child depend entirely on a new food to satisfy his hunger. For the remainder of the meal serve familiar foods he can eat easily. For example, a nursery school introducing cooked cabbage would probably include with it such familiar favorites as mashed potatoes and meat loaf. You can do the same thing at home.

Because a child usually does not learn to like a new food at the first try, introduce it again a week or so later. If others in the family relish it, your child often will, too. Repeating the opportunity to try again is very important.

Remember that no one can know exactly how one food tastes to another individual. So if your child exhibits a real dislike for the new food, simply admit it is not to his taste and don't force him to eat it. You can substitute other foods to make up an adequate diet. Although it is difficult to substitute for milk, even that can be done by encouraging your child to eat more meat and a variety of cheeses. As he grows older, you can guide him to handle his food dislikes in a socially acceptable manner. MIRIAM E. LOWENBERG

See also ALLERGY; GAGGING; NUTRITION

INTROVERT *See* EXTROVERT-INTROVERT

IQ *See* TESTS AND MEASUREMENTS

IRON *See* ANEMIA

ISOLATION *See* COMMON COMMUNICABLE DISEASES

ITCHING

Many allergic disorders such as hives and eczema are associated with severe itching, a sensation in the skin or the mucous membranes which the sufferer feels will be relieved by scratching. Many insect bites also cause severe itching. In some chronic disorders such as jaundice or unusual enlargement of lymph glands, itching tends to occur. And in some instances, the reasons for the itching and scratching seem psychological, indicating that careful study of the child's emotional life is desirable.

When itching occurs, it is necessary to find the cause and clear it up, for constant scratching causes the skin to become raw and thick. While the cause is being sought, the doctor can prescribe soothing baths and lotions in addition to other medicines that may reduce itching. JULIUS B. RICHMOND

See also ALLERGY; BITES, INSECT; COMMON COMMUNICABLE DISEASES; PINWORM; RASH

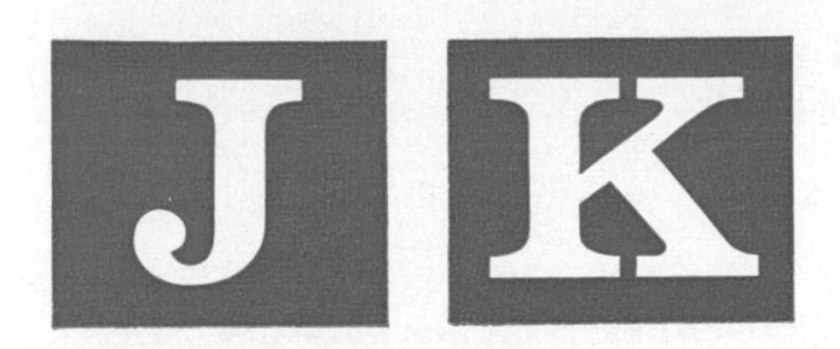

JEALOUSY AND RIVALRY

There used to be a time when we thought of human nature in the most benign and even sentimental fashion. Today we no longer shrink with dismay from the ugly side of personality. We recognize such states as jealousy, anger, hatred, and rivalry as indelible parts of our very being. We all suffer from these emotions and, in the interests of our own well-being, we must learn to handle them so that they do not exercise an unhappy force upon us.

Jealousy generally makes its first appearance in connection with the birth of a baby brother or sister. No matter what a child is told about the joys of having a brother or a sister, he nonetheless feels an acute rivalry with the newcomer. He feels "dethroned" from the central and exclusive position he formerly enjoyed in the affection of his parents. Even though they try to reassure him of their continuing love, he sees that it is now no longer his monopoly but obviously shared with the baby. Because of the child's dependence on this love, he sees the baby as a rival who threatens his status. The child becomes mistrustful and suspicious. In short, he is jealous.

Jealousy can and does assume many forms. Each of these has a double purpose: to express hostility and to attract greater amounts of parental attention, though not necessarily love. The most direct expression of jealousy is the actual attempt to do the baby harm. A second, somewhat diluted expression is to be found in the quarrelsomeness of a jealous child. He will tease his younger brother or take things from him and then try to outwit him in placing the blame. A third form assumed by jealousy is general negativism, more commonly known as plain, ordinary naughtiness. This behavior need not even be directed at one's rival to have the effect of distracting parental attention away from one's rival. Fourthly, a child reveals his jealousy by trying to be a baby again himself. We call this regression, or the opposite of growth, and its obvious purpose is to meet one's rival on his own ground. The baby is grossly dependent, and so big brother is going to try to be that way, too. Fifthly, a child's rivalry may make him feel inferior so that he withdraws from any form of competitive social life. A sixth expression of jealousy and rivalry is the opposite of withdrawal; a child may become strongly competitive and devote himself to being the best in anything he undertakes. Finally, a child's anger may easily upset his digestion or disturb other bodily functions. Once he is treated as though he were ill, he soon learns the value of illness as a seductive weapon with which to win love.

The importance of all these typical ways of expressing jealousy is that they remain virtually unchanged within us and may reappear whenever we feel the threat of rivalry again. In the classroom, the athletic field, the business office, and repeatedly in the home we remain capable of many of these expressions. They are all accompanied with feelings of self-righteousness. We feel wronged no matter how angry and hostile we may be. Along with this, we feel threatened. Our position, we feel, is always at stake so that our behavior is really designed to bolster up our deeper insecurity. Often our emotional reaction is so obviously in excess of what the situation warrants that we seek justification by referring not to the facts but to the "principle" involved.

It is clear then that jealousy and rivalry can easily get out of hand. Playing to win can get to be more important than playing to enjoy oneself. Working for success can get to be more important than working for the daily gratification of doing what one likes. Anybody and everybody can be treated like potential rivals, and when this happens, the quality of one's friendships is changed for the worse.

On the other hand, the feelings of jealousy and rivalry children suffer will, in many ways, help to equip them for a more realistic social adjustment. For example, an only child nearly always has a more difficult time weaning himself from the need for parental protection. He frequently continues to expect and demand more from people in later life than they are willing to give. Brothers and sisters who have lived through years of rivalry frequently know more about what is involved in getting along with others. They are more often better prepared for marriage. They don't flinch as easily and feel unloved at the first quarrel because they have quarreled and made up enough to know that quarrels need not be permanently damaging. In short, jealousy and rivalry can have good or bad effects upon children.

All children experience feelings of jealousy and rivalry rather intensely upon the arrival of a new baby in the family. The youngest child will in turn share his older brother's jealousy before long. An only child is exempted only relatively. Sooner or later, he becomes jealous even of his own mother or father.

In view of the universality of these feelings in our society, there is little reason for parents to become alarmed on finding jealousy and rivalry and hate in their children. These feelings will continue to exist no matter how much we talk about them. Punishment will add guilt to feelings that are disturbing enough already. Nor is it good to push these feelings underground. The best antidote for jealousy is to offer more love rather than impatience and resentment. Additionally, any good times parents help their children to have together will balance their children's emotional ledger. ALLAN FROMME

See also BROTHERS AND SISTERS; COMPETITION; HOSTILITY; NEW BABY; REGRESSION

JOBS

Jobs, as opposed to chores that are done because a child is a member of a family unit, may be assigned to a child and he may be paid for doing them. Such jobs might include clearing the yard of weeds, cleaning the stair carpeting, or making simple repairs on a younger child's bicycle. Children of 9 or 10 are capable of doing small jobs of a similar nature for a neighbor or a relative, thus earning some spending money. A child may take on the job of walking a neighbor's dog regularly, accepting pay by the week for his services. Some boys have paper routes for which they are paid at the end of the week. Girls can help during the day to amuse a neighbor's child and may accept small payment for such services.

Some adults have a tendency to overpay a child for performing some small task. "Isn't he cute?" the adult thinks, and gives a child a dollar for a 25-cent job. It might be in order to check with a child's parents before the job to agree upon the amount to be paid. Then a neighbor will not pay more for having his lawn rid of dandelions than the child's father has paid.

Compliment a child if he has done a good job. If his work needs improvement, tell him so honestly and kindly. The child will learn that he has to perform satisfactorily if he is to be paid for his work.

See also ALLOWANCE; CHORES; RESPONSIBILITY

JOINT PAINS *See* GROWING PAINS; RHEUMATIC FEVER

JOUNCING *See* HEAD BANGING AND ROLLING

JUNIOR BED

Some children willingly sleep in their cribs, with the sides lowered, until they are 4 or 5 years old. Others, especially those with older brothers and sisters, decide that a crib is "for babies," and want a big bed. A junior bed is often an answer in this situation. Also called "youth bed," this between-age bed is about as long as a twin bed, yet narrower and lower. Junior beds have half or full sides, which can be removed as soon as a child can sleep without danger of falling out of bed.

Springs and mattresses should provide a firm foundation and should not sag. Waterproof sheeting may be used if your child is likely to wet his bed occasionally.

JUNIOR FOODS *See* INTRODUCING NEW FOODS

KICKING

When a baby kicks, we are pleased, and we reward him with cooing approval. He is practicing leg movements, demonstrating that his muscles are developing, and getting ready for the next stage in using his legs. At first these seem to be random movements, but as they become better coordinated, as the muscles "learn," kicking may become a conscious accompaniment to strong feelings of either joy or rage. A very angry infant may thrash his legs in vigorous kicking movements or he may do the same thing to accompany his feelings of delight.

It is possible that a toddler's first official kick may be an experimental movement resulting in an action that brings satisfaction and pleasure. He kicks a ball or another toy, and it moves or makes a noise. He kicks a person, with no intention of hurting, and he hears a howl of pain if the kick connects with an adult. The kick that began as an easy, natural swing of leg muscles becomes invested with power to hurt and annoy as well as to express hostility.

The preschooler who deliberately kicks needs help to know that kicking people is not acceptable in our society. "I know you feel angry with Jimmy, but I can't let you kick him. Kicking hurts. You may kick a ball or kick the leaves or kick an old box—but *not people.*"

By 4 or 5, most children have learned that kicking is not an acceptable way of behaving, and they will be willing to settle for other less primitive ways of communicating their strong feelings. EVELYN M. BEYER

See also ANGER; DISCIPLINE; PERMISSIVENESS; TEMPER TANTRUM

KINDERGARTEN

A child's success in kindergarten is a two-way proposition. There are certain things he ought to know *before* he enters kindergarten, and there are many things he will gain *from* the kindergarten experience.

Mothers often ask, "What can I do to get my child ready for kindergarten?" You can:

- Teach your child to be independent.
- Teach him to get along for a few hours without you.
- Teach him to take off his outer garments and hang them up.
- Help him learn to listen to and follow directions.
- Train him to be able to go to the toilet by himself.

Parents further ask, "What will my child get out of kindergarten?" Most children:

- Learn to share and to take turns.
- Learn to accept the suggestions of others.
- Learn to talk before a group, which helps them to overcome shyness.
- Learn to experiment with different ways of getting along with others.
- Begin to learn to develop personality and talents.
- Learn about their community: the functions of a fire station, a police station, the waterworks, or sewage disposal facilities, often by taking field trips to these and other local sites.
- Learn rhythm and dancing.
- Learn to express their ideas in different ways—not only in speech, but also by using clay, paint, building blocks, paper, or other tools.

Children need the opportunity that kindergarten affords to run, jump, climb, push, and pull. That is the way their large muscles are strengthened. At the same time, they need to be carefully supervised so they do not become overtired. Kindergarten at times seems all play. But usually real learning does go on. The kindergarten teacher is especially trained to guide young children and to help them acquire knowledge and skills that will help them as they go into first grade.

See also PLAY GROUPS; READINESS FOR SCHOOL

KNOCK-KNEE

The term knock-knee describes a condition in which the knees come close together in more or less the opposite position to that of bowlegs. Usually, a knock-kneed child also looks pigeon-toed. Knock-knees usually result from the position in which the legs are held and are more common in little girls, particularly if they are plump. As a child gets older, a knock-kneed condition improves. Sometimes knock-knees go along with flat feet and sometimes, although rarely, with some general difficulty such as rickets.

Even when the knock-kneed appearance is quite marked in early years, no special treatment except muscle exercises or shoe wedging is recommended. It is only in later years and for extreme cases that specific treatment such as surgery is needed. RUTH S. KEMPE

See also RICKETS

LABOR *See* BIRTH

LANGUAGE *See* BABY; READINESS; TALKING; VOCABULARY DEVELOPMENT

LARYNGITIS

When inflammation attacks the voice box, or larynx, the organ that connects the windpipe, or trachea, with the throat and contains the vocal cords—the condition that results is called laryngitis. With this condition, the cry of a baby may have a hoarse quality, and a child's voice a definite hoarseness.

There are many causes of hoarseness: Overuse of the voice by too much talking or shouting may be a cause. This type of laryngitis responds quickly to rest. A more common cause at all ages is acute infection of the respiratory tract involving the larynx. Usually, these infections are caused by viruses. Watch babies and young children carefully during such attacks, for if the larynx swells, there may be occlusion, or closing, of the breathing passages—a matter that requires emergency treatment.

Treatment depends upon the cause. It may be necessary to consult an ear, nose, and throat specialist. JULIUS B. RICHMOND

See also CROUP; STEAMING; VIRUS

LAXATIVES

Laxatives should be given to a baby only on the special advice of a doctor. Ordinarily, the concern about "keeping regular," having a bowel movement every day, is exaggerated. A mother should not worry if her baby skips a day. Some children have bowel movements only every second or third day, but the stool remains quite soft and normal. In young children the very hard, dry stools of constipation will usually become softer with a rather minor change in diet, such as a different form of sugar in the formula or an increase in the fruits taken.

Most laxatives are highly irritating and if used repeatedly, will make the problem worse by interfering with the normal muscle tone of the bowel. For this reason, a laxative should be used rarely unless there is some special bowel problem. In that situation, your doctor will usually recommend a specific mild laxative. RUTH S. KEMPE

See also CONSTIPATION

LAYETTE AND BABY EQUIPMENT

A basic layette is much the same for any baby, although climate in certain areas may necessitate small differences.

Baby's Wardrobe

Three to four dozen diapers (If you use diaper service, have a dozen of your own on hand for emergencies.)
Four to six shirts (long or short sleeves, depending on climate)
Four to six nightgowns or wrappers
Four to six diaper sets (knitted creepers, sunsuits) when baby gets a little more social
One dress and slip for dressy occasions
One bunting or coat and hood
Two or three pairs of booties or socks
Two pairs of waterproof pants
One or two sweaters
One or two sleeping bags or crib garments
Safety pins

For Baby's Bed

Bassinet, basket, or crib
Firm mattress
Mattress cover of heavy plastic or waterproof sheeting (flannelized provides nonslip surface)
Four to six crib pads
Three to four cribs sheets (or pillow slips if you use a basket or bassinet)
Two lightweight crib blankets
One winter-weight blanket
One set crib bumpers

For Baby's Room

Chest of drawers
Comfortable chair for mother
Playpen and pad
Diaper pail
Scales
Rectal thermometer

For Baby's Bath

Folding, portable bathinette or small tub and table
Three or four washcloths
Three or four bath towels
Tray with sterile cotton swabs and cotton balls, mild soap, baby oil, lotion, and baby powder

Four to six receiving blankets
Brush and comb

For Preparing Baby's Formula

10 to 12 eight-ounce bottles for bottle-fed baby; two or three if a breast-fed baby has supplemental feedings
Two or three four-ounce bottles for orange juice and water
Nipples and caps for all bottles, with a few extra for emergencies
Sterilizer (nice but not necessary)
Bottle warmer
Bottle and nipple brush
Graduate for measuring and mixing formula
Measuring and mixing spoons
Funnel

When Baby Goes Out

Baby carriage
Carriage robe or blanket
Strap or harness when he decides carriages are for standing
Auto bed or car seat (or both) for traveling
A roomy diaper bag that is divided into compartments

A baby's trip home from the hospital will be achieved most satisfactorily if he is dressed in a minimum of clothing: shirt, diaper, diaper cover, gown, sweater, receiving blanket, and shawl or bunting.

See also CRIB; PLAYPEN

LAZINESS

It's sometimes hard to know what laziness is. Identical behavior can seem extremely lazy to one parent, only mildly so to another, or scarcely so at all to a third. Also, a parent might be bothered by laziness in one area and not mind it elsewhere. Take, for instance, a child mildly industrious both at home and at school. To a parent who values schoolwork above home chores, this child will seem diligent at home and lazy at school, but to a parent who values home help more than schoolwork, the child will seem adequately industrious at school and lazy at home. Parents also often disagree with their children about what constitutes laziness: A boy labors earnestly to earn money cutting the neighbor's grass and is considered lazy because he cuts no grass for his father; a "lazy" girl spends hours helping with costumes for her school play and sews on not one button for her mother.

No absolute judgment exists on who is right and who is wrong about laziness. But where the child's view differs from the parents' and where there is no strong reason, such as economic necessity, for the parents' views to prevail, the child should be allowed to choose where he will put forth great endeavor and where he will put forth much less.

Both laziness and what looks like laziness can come about for many, many reasons. Among them are:

- **Protest**
  Against the thing to be done
  Against the person asking that it be done
- **Physical condition**
  On-coming illness
  Failure to recover altogether from previous illness
  Fatigue as a result of a complicated or hectic life
  Rapid growth
- **Weather conditions**
  Changing of season
  Temperature: too hot, too cold
  High humidity
  Too much or too little sunshine
- **Absorption**
  In books or inventions or in creating a whole scheme of life
  In happiness over a good relationship with another person
  In unhappiness over a bad one
- **Guilt**
  For some wrongdoing, imagined or real
- **Fear**
  Of failure (refuses to work to avoid admitting that he tried and failed)
  Of reprisal from parent, teacher, or schoolmate

And sometimes a child is lazy because no one has ever insisted that he work. A father who has undergone great hardships in his youth wants to spare his child such effort. He does spare him, then becomes bewildered and annoyed when his overprotected child has no drive. Equally common is a mother who becomes a drudge for her little princess daughter. This parent, too, when her child grows up, wonders where she ever got such a lazy youngster.

See also CHORES; DAYDREAMING; FEAR

LEAD POISONING *See* POISONING AND POISONS

LEARNING *See* READINESS; TESTS AND MEASUREMENTS

LEAVING HOME, FEAR OF

The first time a child leaves home, he usually does so with his mother, and since his world is no bigger than that occupied by the two of them, he weathers the change fairly well unless something unusual happens. He minds much more if his mother leaves him behind; sometimes he is so hurt by this separation that he is inconsolable and reacts badly to any hint of her leaving him again.

The time comes, however, when almost every child must leave home without his mother. Maybe he has to stay in the hospital, or he goes to his grandmother's because his mother is in the hospital, or his parents go on a needed vacation and he stays with a relative or a friend. Since this experience can come early in life, it is well to arrange for the new circumstances to reflect home as much as possible. Let him take his toy animals or dolls or his beloved blanket or, when he is a bit older, a photograph of his mother. Much of the strangeness of the new place can thus be reduced. An occasional night at his grandparents' helps to build confidence for longer separations, even though the first try may prove too difficult and he has to be brought home. For this social blunder he should not be scolded.

Going to kindergarten or school marks another venture into a larger world, and while a beginner may have his mother with him for a while, eventually he must go it alone. Parents who had similar difficulties in childhood probably suffer as much as their children. A timid, sensitive child feels his mother's discomfort and he may capitalize on it. Most children look forward to the day when they can go to school; it is the beginning of the freedom from family that everyone must achieve in maturity. But when the long-awaited day dawns, they know only how it feels at the time to be separated from home and mother.

For whatever reason a child has to leave home, he should have some preparation. Starting to school or going to the hospital or visiting a relative should be talked over and thus rid of strangeness. An eager little girl on the eve of her first day at school said to her mother, "I hope I'll be able to do it." Talking things over is a good remedy for any kind of fear as long as the parent has the assurance that all will be well and communicates this feeling to the child. This is particularly true of the first visit to the hospital, which harbors dreadful unknowns for a child: Who will be there? What will they do? Will his mother come, too? Will it hurt? Most children's hospitals today wisely take these common fears into account.

Returning home should be a pleasurable event. Children are conservative and want everything about home to remain as it was. An anxious child observes even the slightest change as if it might be a potential danger. Adults rarely lose this wish to have things at home remain just the same. Coming back from a visit or from the hospital should be a gay affair, with perhaps a small gift. As for the daily return from school, the welcoming voice of mother makes a child feel comfortable and safe. He may wish to go out at once to play with his friends, to be sure, but most children like to touch base first for a hug and a cooky.

Even as a child gets up into the grades, he still likes to find his mother in the house. The working mother may have to make some special arrangements for her children after school. The empty house, the locked door, have often led to the beginnings of delinquent behavior. The responsibility of the parent to the child is a necessary example. It stimulates the child's sense of obligation to his home and extends itself to the time when he has a family of his own. HELEN ROSS

See also ANXIETY; FEAR; HOSPITALIZATION; READINESS FOR SCHOOL; SEPARATION FROM MOTHER

LEFT-HANDEDNESS

If you enjoy discussions that involve differing points of view, try talking over left-handedness with your family and friends. The chances are that you will hear the old-fashioned theory that everyone can and should be right-handed, the not-so-long-ago theory that interfering with handedness to any degree will cause permanent emotional upset, and the present one that many a child whose hand preference is not too great can be led gently and safely toward use of his right hand.

Heredity as a factor in left-handedness is still a controversial point, but a tendency to left-handedness does run in families and is also associated with other inherited traits such as fingerprints. Left-handedness has usually been found to be more frequent among boys than among girls, probably because of hereditary difference or the fact that mothers make more effort to teach girls the use of the right hand or because of both of these influences.

Recent increase in the frequency of left-handedness seems to be a result of parents' fear that interference with a tendency to use the left hand might lead to nervous instability or stuttering—a fear that now receives little support from careful studies. If a child is nagged, bullied, or frightened by excessive efforts to make him change over, he may well begin to stutter or otherwise show his distress and uncertainty. In other words, dealing with handedness is another case of, "It's not what you do but how you do it."

Handedness is only a part of "sidedness," and there are many complicated combinations in the use of the hand, foot, eye, and ear. Some children whose combinations are mixed up and in conflict may need retraining by a special teacher.

Babies seem during their first few months to use either hand equally; then a preference for one hand appears gradually. At this early age, preference is not well established and usually can be redirected by the parents. If, for instance, an infant tends to use his left hand, it is easy to make a point of putting everything in his right hand and thus encourage its use.

Informed opinion now leans toward leaving the child alone if he has a very strong tendency to use his left hand or after he has become 4 to 5 years old, but to shift him over from left to right hand if the shift can be done without too much difficulty during his first few years. Since he will grow up in a right-handed civilization, live in a right-handed world, there is a real advantage to him in being, in this respect, like most of his fellows.

PAUL POPENOE

LETTER WRITING

Children usually look forward to receiving letters, but all too often they will write them only because some grownup insists.

The best way to encourage a child to maintain good feelings about letter writing is to give him the help he needs, for his ideas are bound to be beyond his writing skills. Adjust your help to his age and wishes. If he is a beginning writer, take his letter down from his dictation. Let him see that you value the worth-while ideas he is creating, and don't insist that he copy the letter himself unless he especially wants to.

If he wants to write his own letter, asking you only for words he can't spell, write down the words rather than spell them aloud. In this way, he can copy correctly and can feel more independent.

Be sure that your child understands the *why* of a thank-you note, that thanking is not just hollow politeness, but that appreciation of a gift makes the sender feel good. Interest him in what he will write. Don't say just, "You have to thank grandma," but, "Tell grandma where we went the day you wore the shirt she sent you." If the child's father is away and you'd like them to keep in touch, ask, "What did you do that dad might like to hear about?" Or "Maybe he'd like to hear about our picnic plans." Almost any child will write with more originality and feeling with this kind of impetus.

If, when your child is away at camp, you can write him on subjects that involve him, the answers are apt to be more frequent, more revealing, and more personal. And if you are fortunate enough to have him establish a good back-and-forth correspondence with you from camp, he will probably continue the habit should he later go to boarding school. Don't, however, use his letters as an opportunity to teach him spelling and punctuation, for if you do, you may cut off his spontaneity and his wish to keep in touch with you.

PEGGY BROGAN

See also MANNERS

LEUKEMIA *See* CANCER

LEUKORRHEA *See* VAGINAL DISCHARGE

LIBRARIES

Your child can learn about the public library, its uses, and the pleasures and services it provides before he is able to read. He will doubtless have some books of his own at home, but he probably cannot have nearly as many as he is capable of enjoying.

If your community has a library with a children's room, let him find out how much is there for his enjoyment. He will find a room designed for his use, with tables, chairs,

and shelves of comfortable heights, and a carefully selected collection of books. As he gets older he will also find other interesting and useful materials such as maps and pamphlets and magazines. A children's librarian will help him find what he wants, whether it be a good adventure story, the latest information on rockets, or how the Mayas of Mexico built their ancient monuments. Most public libraries also have special programs such as story hours, film showings, and summer reading clubs. These programs are planned to bring child and book together, and to help establish the life-long habit of reading and of using an institution that freely serves people of all ages.

The school library is designed to provide enrichment for all aspects of the school curriculum. Usually in convenient and attractive quarters, the school library has, besides its books, related materials that frequently include films, filmstrips, and records. Children who have difficulty in reading and who are reluctant to discover the satisfactions to be had from books may, through the joint guidance of both teacher and school librarian, be led eventually to accept reading as an integral and important part of their lives. More and more schools are planning elementary school libraries, realizing the value of this close accessibility to a variety of books in relation to the ever-broadening curriculum designed to meet the growing challenge of the space era.

The ill or handicapped child, whether at home or in the hospital, needs books to brighten his day and to keep alert his curiosity about the world outside the walls of his room. Inquire of your library what it has to help him. Some large public library systems provide service to children in general hospitals and to those hospitals serving the long-term patient. Various reading aids, such as ceiling projectors, are available to enable severely handicapped children while away the tedious hours with good reading material. Many hospitals have their own libraries. Volunteers are often recruited to help wheel carts of books and magazines to hospital wards for those who are confined to their beds. Ambulatory patients may visit a small but usually attractive room where a larger and more varied collection of reading materials is kept. ELIZABETH H. GROSS

See also BOOKS FOR CHILDREN

Related article in WORLD BOOK: "Library"

LIBRARY, HOME *See* BOOKS FOR CHILDREN

LIGHTNING *See* THUNDER AND LIGHTNING, FEAR OF

LIP BLISTER *See* BLISTER; FEVER BLISTER

LISPING *See* SPEECH DIFFICULTIES

LISTENING TO CHILDREN

Listening to children is not only fun but also very rewarding. When your youngster tries to tell you something important—important to him, that is—you should listen with your whole attention—be "all ears," as it were.

At other times, you can listen with one ear while going about your household tasks. But one ear or all ears, you should listen sympathetically and not scold or discourage or laugh whenever your child tries to share his happiness or his sorrows with you.

Sometimes it is well to listen to youngsters when they aren't really talking to you. You can be busy—or just appear to be—in the kitchen, at the ironing board, or at the wheel of the car. Often, children will forget that you are there and talk freely among themselves. Call it eavesdropping, if you will, but listening when they don't realize that you are, is one important way to find out what makes children tick.

You can also "listen" to children with your eyes as well as your ears. Sometimes the droop of a shoulder, the sparkle of the eyes will tell you more than what a youngster says. He may insist emphatically, even angrily, "I'm not tired." But he's been sprawled out on the living room floor for an hour—too tired to move, your eyes tell you. MAY R. SHERWIN

LISTLESSNESS

If a child who is usually full of zest and vitality suddenly becomes listless, he may need watching for a day or two to see if he has the beginning of a cold or some other illness. Or perhaps his listlessness is a sign of simple fatigue—the result of too much excitement, an overscheduled vacation, a little too much intensity about some competitive sport. A sudden onset of listlessness usually suggests some physical change, either within the child or in his environment.

Chronic listlessness may have other possible meanings—some perfectly good and healthy, others worth watching. One child may come home from school on most days in a state of depletion; all he wants to do is lie on his bed, eat an apple, and perhaps listen to the radio. After an hour or so, he seems refreshed and is off to play. His teacher says he works and plays with great intensity and success all during school hours; obviously his temporary listlessness is simply a healthy way in which he recharges his battery. Another child, on the other hand, is often listless and seems to be off in a world of his own, in school as well as at home. He rarely seems really involved or enthusiastic about things that are going on around him. Is he bored? Is there too little that can stimulate and challenge him? Or has he, perhaps, been under too much pressure—is this his way of escaping from problems he feels he cannot solve? Listlessness can sometimes result from feeling overwhelmed by the demands and pressures of life.

Listlessness often comes with periods of great physical change and growth; it is almost as if nature requires this period of apparent inactivity when dramatic bodily changes are taking place. Think, for instance, of the lanky, slow-moving adolescent, who can lie in a hammock for hours on end, daydreaming, hardly moving a muscle except to lift a cola bottle. His "goofing off," frustrating as it may seem to the parent who wants the lawn mowed, apparently does represent a real need, especially during puberty.

It is important to distinguish between listlessness that reflects boredom or an escape from reality, and the kind of quiet daydreaming—of seeming to do nothing—that is really important to growth. Creativity is dependent on a rich inner life; time for reflection, time for imaginative thinking, time for dreaming, time for discovering one's own soul are most important. Sometimes when it seems as though nothing is happening, the most is happening. Sometimes being alone and quietly doing nothing means that one is replenishing one's own inner life. Sometimes inactivity may represent an important plateau before a new spurt in intellectual development takes place.

Occasional periods of being alone, to think one's own thoughts, to throw off for a while the pressures and burdens of life, are helpful and refreshing; they revitalize one. A general and continuing pattern of listlessness, where there seem to be few moments of joy, of exuberance, of involvement with others, may mean that growth has been blocked in some way. This listlessness calls for some careful thinking about what it may spring from and what can be done to encourage a renewed zest for living. EDA J. LE SHAN

See also BOREDOM; DAYDREAMING; PUBERTY; RESOURCEFULNESS

LOAFING *See* DAWDLING; LAZINESS

LOCKJAW *See* TETANUS

LONELINESS

When a child says he is lonely, it is usual to assume that he wants the company of other children. But he may be expressing only boredom, which is easily banished by a change of activity.

What loneliness really means depends on how and when it is expressed. The loneliness of an "only" child or of a child who has been isolated from other children for a long time may be a healthy sign, for it is normal for children to want the company of other youngsters near their own ages. But if a child is lonely while living in a neighborhood teeming with young people, he may need your help in making friends.

Still another meaning attaches to feelings of loneliness when a child and his parents do not have a close and satisfying relationship. Then he may simply need more mothering or he may need closer contact with a loving and understanding father.

Children differ greatly in their susceptibility to loneliness. A child who has been surrounded constantly by other people since birth is less likely to feel lonely than one who is accustomed to being alone. Complaints of loneliness coming the moment a child is separated from his playmates may, however, indicate a lack of inner resources and interests. A compulsive need to be with others may also be a symptom of anxieties he would rather not face.

Sometimes loneliness cannot be avoided. Then it is comforting to parents to remember that it can have a positive value. Creativity often develops out of loneliness. Out of solitude, a child can follow the paths of wonder, from the ways of a cocoon to the why's of a cloud.

RUTH E. HARTLEY

See also ANXIETY; CREATING; ONLY CHILD

LOST CHILD

When a child is about 3 years old, he should be taught his full name and that of his parents, just in case he becomes separated from you while shopping or he wanders from his own yard. As soon as he is capable of learning, he should be taught to spell these names and to recite his home address and telephone number.

Teach your child to recognize a policeman, and teach him that the officer is his friend. On one of your family excursion days take your youngster to your local police station so that he can become acquainted with the officers there.

Should your child be missing, notify your nearest police station. If family members join the search, be sure someone the child knows stays at your home in case the child returns on his own. To return to an empty house could be a frightening experience, particularly if the missing child had not considered himself lost in the first place. "I knew where I was all the time," he may say.

Try not to cause undue fear in your child's mind, but stress the importance of not talking to strangers. Tell him *never* to get into a car with someone he does not know; *never* to accept candy, food, or toys from strangers; *never* to go off with a person he does not know. Schools stress these important points, but you, as a parent, will want to begin the training early, well before your child goes to school.

If you should find a child who is obviously lost, notify the police and keep him with you right at the place where you found him, if possible. His parents may be close by, and to take the child away might further delay their reunion.

LOVE

"To live is to love, and to love is to live," said Havelock Ellis. The greatest gift you can make to your child, therefore, is to enable him, in his relationship with you, his parent, to learn how to receive and to give affection —freely, trustingly, confidently.

Children have literally died because they were deprived of love. They have withered away, like cut flowers. This has happened, of course, only in extreme circumstances. It couldn't happen in a normal home—even in a pretty bad home. We can manage to keep going with very little love in our lives. But that is not life in the fullest sense. It is mere existence.

Out of the womb—warm and protective, but dark and lonely—the child comes at birth. At first he is hardly aware of his surroundings. His hearing is confused, his vision unfocused. He has to evaluate his new surroundings in terms of touch—the warm, soft breast from which he sucks milk, the caressing hands that try to make him comfortable, the mother's body against which he nestles. It takes some time before he can recognize that this breast, this hand, these arms that hold him close, belong to another person like himself, with whom he has to establish a relationship.

But when awareness comes, the child already knows that his mother has the power to accept or to reject him, to give or to deny love. When she caresses him and approves of him, he senses that he is accepted and secure. When she finds him displeasing or has to deny him what he wants, the frown on her face, the hardening of her voice, the slight tensing of her muscles tell him that an invisible barrier has been raised between him and her.

Because his need for love is second only to his need to survive, the child responds continuously to his mother's emotional attitude toward him. He tries to please her because when she is pleased, the sun shines in his world. As long as he is able to do what she wants him to do, he will endeavor to satisfy her requirements. This is how a good mother teaches her child to behave, and it is the basis of all sound discipline. She withdraws the signs of her love a little when his actions are displeasing. But when he does what she asks of him, she rewards him with overflowing affection.

As a child grows older, he learns to respond to the other people in his life—to father, to brothers and sisters, to playmates. Gradually he becomes aware that he is not just the center of an adoring circle of older people who have nothing to do in life but to meet his needs and minister to his happiness. They also need love, and suffer if they don't get it. Therefore he learns that affection is a two-way process. There are times when his mother hasn't much love to offer him because she is in need of it herself. He discovers at those times that by loving words and loving deeds he can bring back the luster to her eyes and the smile to her face.

Thus the child learns one of life's most valuable lessons—that it is just as satisfying to offer love, and to win a grateful response, as it is to receive love free and unmerited. In the adult world few of us can expect to be continuously loved unless we ourselves make the effort to be loving and to be lovable. It is only those who give love freely who receive it abundantly.

A child can go even further. He can learn, as he grows older, to give love without expecting it to be returned. In his dealings with animals, with younger brothers and sisters, and with difficult playmates, he can understand that they are sometimes unable to respond to his warm and generous impulses. Thus he learns compassion and what we call altruism, or devotion to others. Although this is a mature form of love, it is not out of the reach of a happy, affectionate child.

As parents think of the child's point of view, they can easily see how much he depends on them in this area of the emotions. Unless they love him warmly from the beginning, it is hard for him to accept himself as a worth-while, lovable person. Unless he can learn in his relationship with them to express freely the love that is in his own heart, he may have difficulty when he is older in using positive emotion in relating to other people and may become withdrawn and "distant."

Can you, as a parent, control your power to act lovingly toward your child? Yes, you can. For some, of course, it is easier than for others. It must begin with wholehearted acceptance of the child that is yours and your sympathetic understanding of his limitations. He may not be everything you wanted or hoped for. He may not even have been planned to arrive at this time. But every child has lovable qualities, and there is something seriously wrong indeed with a parent who doesn't feel a child's helplessness and dependence tugging at his heartstrings.

Love, remember, is not just an emotional state. It is an attitude toward its object that brings about the release of outgoing emotion. By a conscious effort you can adopt attitudes and perform actions that will soften your heart toward your child, and then the tides of warm feeling will flow. Thus you will not only be creating the atmosphere in which your child can grow naturally into a happy human being, but you will also be furthering your own growth and happiness. DAVID R. MACE

LYE POISONING *See* POISONING AND POISONS

LYING *See* UNTRUTHFULNESS

LYMPH GLANDS *See* SWOLLEN GLANDS

MAGAZINES

An easy and pleasant way to please a child with a gift is to send him a subscription to one of the magazines published especially for children. The gift will arrive at regular intervals throughout the year, the child will look forward to it and will remember the sender often. He will have something lasting to put on his own bookshelf in his own room, something he can read intensively or thumb through casually, as he wishes.

Children's magazines provide new, attractive, and up-to-date reading. Many children whose attention is not yet held by a long book find pleasure in selecting and reading the short stories and short articles a magazine brings them. Even a child who reads nothing but comic books can be weaned to something better and more solid by magazines—for some of the best magazines for children have the same appeal that comic books have.

Magazines for children tempt the child with profusely illustrated stories and articles about children and their dozens of interests. Suggested activities, appropriate for children in the age group for which the magazine is intended, are always featured. So, too, are things-to-do, such as puzzles, crafts, recipes, and science experiments—features that are so popular that they make the next issue eagerly awaited by the young subscriber.

Because children's magazines are so much like the adult magazines in the kinds of articles and features they carry, a child who has formed the habit of reading periodicals in childhood may be expected to read among the many magazines published for teen-agers and adults when he reaches these ages.

Many magazines published for children are in such special fields as religion, hobbies, music, art, science, nature study, and sports. Children or parents who want information about these special magazines can find it at public or school libraries. A list of the most popular *general* magazines for children is given here. Subscriptions cost between two and six dollars a year.

The American Girl. Ages 10–16. Monthly. Published by Girl Scouts of the U.S.A., 830 Third Avenue, New York 22, New York.

Girls' interests, including scouting.

Boys' Life. Ages 8–18. Monthly. (Special rates to Boy Scouts through local councils.) Published by the Boy Scouts of America, New Brunswick, New Jersey.

Wide variety of articles; many comics; interesting to boys in broad age group.

Calling All Girls (formerly *Polly Pigtails*). Ages 7–12. 10 issues. Published by Better Reading Foundation, Inc., 52 Vanderbilt Avenue, New York 17, New York. Subscriptions should be sent to Calling All Girls Subscription Office, Bergenfield, New Jersey.

Stories, articles, and activities of interest to the preteen-age girl.

Child Life. Ages 3–12. 10 issues a year. Published by Child Life, Inc., 3516 N. College Avenue, Indianapolis 5, Indiana.

Stories and a variety of features.

Children's Digest. Ages 7–12. 10 issues. Published by Better Reading Foundation, Inc., 52 Vanderbilt Avenue, New York 17, New York.

Stories, including digests of children's books, and activities.

Children's Playmate. Ages 6–9. 10 issues. Published by Children's Playmate Magazine, Inc., 6529 Union Avenue, Cleveland 5, Ohio.

Many craft ideas suited to season.

Highlights for Children (combined with *Children's Activities*). Ages 3–12. 10 issues. Published by Highlights for Children, Inc., P.O. Box 269, Columbus 16, Ohio.

Things to do, articles, and stories.

Humpty Dumpty's. Ages 3–7. 10 issues. Published by Better Reading Foundation, Inc., 52 Vanderbilt Avenue, New York 17, New York. Subscriptions should be sent to Humpty Dumpty Subscription Office, Bergenfield, New Jersey.

Stories and activities of interest to the preschool child and the beginning reader.

Jack and Jill. Ages 4–10. Published by The Curtis Publishing Company, Independence Square, Philadelphia 5, Pennsylvania.

Variety of stories, features, things to do.

Pack-O-Fun. Ages 3–12. Published by Clapper Publishing Company, Inc., P.O. Box 568, Park Ridge, Illinois.

Answers need for craft suggestions.

ELIZABETH S. MARGULIS

MAKE-BELIEVE *See* IMAGINATION

MALNUTRITION *See* NUTRITION

MALOCCLUSION

Occlusion, or bite, is a term dentists use in referring to the way teeth are arranged in the mouth and the contact they make when the jaws are brought together. A child's occlusion may be normal or abnormal. When it is abnormal, it is called malocclusion, or poor bite.

A child with a poor bite cannot chew his food properly, his appearance may be altered, and his general well-being affected.

Malocclusion may be inherited, it may be acquired, or a combination of these factors may be responsible. The condition may be found in both deciduous (first) and permanent (second) teeth.

Your child's dentist will readily recognize signs of malocclusion during the course of periodic dental care. And he will advise you if the opinion of an orthodontist is needed. Not all malocclusions are preventable, but most can be improved. JOHN H. SILLMAN

See also DENTAL BRACES

MANNERS

Good manners are not a set of tricks to be pulled out of a hat when needed. Nor do good manners result from orders given in a disagreeable way by other persons. If you want a well-mannered child, let him see politeness and good manners in his home. When a child hears phrases such as "Please" and "Thank you" regularly and pleasantly used at home, he will soon learn that such courteous phrases act as lubricants for the machinery of living.

A child will also be helped by a little advance coaching on the proper way to act. Your child's first dinner party with adults will be more pleasant for everyone present if he is briefed at home *before* the party. Or if he is to stay overnight at a friend's house for the first time, explain to him that other families have rules and traditions that may be different from your own and that he should take his cue from his young host. If your child is to travel by plane, train, or boat, help him to understand before he starts out some of the situations he will encounter while eating on board or using washroom facilities or getting ready for bed. *Advance* training in social behavior is a kindness both to the child himself and to the people he will encounter.

Manners are not merely polite phrases and ways of handling forks. Training in manners should also include training in coming promptly to meals, respecting the rights of others, sharing, taking turns, and winning a game gracefully.

Well-mannered children are usually those who know both what is expected of them and that they are trusted to do it. A child needs reminders, of course: "Remember to take your cap off when Mrs. Jones stops to speak to us." Or, "Remember, Susie will be your guest and you can help her have fun." But it is never wise to embarrass a child by discussing his good or bad manners before other people.

A great many parents are overanxious to have their children behave correctly. Their children then suffer from parental pressure. All children have occasional spells of bad manners, but if sullenness and bad manners are the child's usual pattern, his parents should stop to ask themselves if they are expecting too much. Sometimes relaxing demands will appreciably improve manners.

It is always better to suggest than to demand or command. A friendly "Wouldn't you like to thank Auntie?" is much more effective than an order: "Thank your aunt or you can't have the candy she brought." The "thank you" Auntie receives when the child is forced to make it is quite meaningless—and sometimes grudging.

Kindergartners learn much about mannerly behavior in school. But a child should not be sent to kindergarten to learn manners. Although he will be helped by mingling and associating with other children, his basics in manners should be learned at home.

Many parents are often proud to hear that their children have far more beautiful manners when visiting other people than at home. "I guess some of the training shows up when he's away from home," a father may say. This is as it should be. Homes are places to relax, to a point, but if the fundamentals of gracious manners are instilled in children at home, they can usually be counted on to behave admirably away from home.

Manners, whether good or bad, are automatic ways of communicating with one another. In some homes children are ill at ease, not knowing how to greet people who call or how to treat a guest. In other homes, especially those where children are included in at least part of the social life, children welcome callers with a friendly smile. They may show adults their favorite toys, talk a little while, then go about their own business. These pleasant behavior attitudes are not accidents; they are the result of opportunity for social intercourse and of skillful training.

Good manners and common courtesy will be expressed naturally only if they are a routine part of everyday life. From the flow of consideration from parent to child, the child's capacity for consideration grows. From his consideration for other people, the best kind of courtesy develops.

See also BOOKS FOR CHILDREN; IMITATION; TABLE MANNERS

MARKS *See* SCHOOL REPORT

MARRIAGE *See* FAMILY LIVING; FATHER; MOTHER

MARRIAGE COUNSELOR *See* COMMUNITY RESOURCES

MASTURBATION

In spite of the fears of many parents about the harmfulness of masturbation, there is general agreement among physicians today that it is of no damage whatever. Masturbation does not affect the health, it does not injure the mind, it does not produce acne, and it does not interfere with a child's future ability to have normal sex relations or to have children. The greatest evil results from the sense of guilt aroused because the practice is contrary to parental or other warnings.

Parents should realize that all young children masturbate at one time or another. But parents should be able to differentiate masturbation, which is the handling of the genitals for the pleasurable sensation it creates, from the simple touching of the genitals.

The smallest infant explores his body with his hands, and sooner or later he finds and starts touching his genitals. This is not masturbation, but many parents quickly pull the hands away, expressing their disgust or distaste. And many children, reacting repeatedly to this attitude of their parents, gain in the course of time the impression that there is something "not nice," something taboo, about the genitals. With this impression it is difficult for a child to grow up with a wholesome feeling about sex. When infants tend to reach frequently toward the genital area, however, parents should investigate to see if the diaper or clothing is too tight or if the genitals are irritated.

Usually somewhere between 2 and 4 years of age most children learn that a pleasurable sensation may be derived by touching or handling the genitals. It is normal for children of this age to masturbate and for this activity to give them pleasure.

There are many forms of masturbation. Some children sit or lie rubbing the thighs together and so stimulating the genitals; some children hold soft toy animals or pillows between their thighs and sway themselves from side to side causing genital sensation; some children roll over on soft objects and move around over them; some lie on their stomachs and writhe around on the floor; some masturbate by straddling the leg of a table or chair and move up and down it; many manipulate the genitals manually. There are numerous methods used, but none are injurious unless they cause severe local irritation. The majority of children masturbate when lying in bed, when bored or tired, or when lying on the floor watching TV.

Masturbation, if practiced excessively at any age, is usually a sign of emotional upset. What is meant by excessive masturbation? Masturbation is said to be excessive when a child persists in repeating it to the exclusion of most other normal activities.

This drive toward masturbation, which reaches its maximum intensity between 3 and 6 years of age, subsides greatly and often practically disappears until about 11 or 12, when it reappears gradually, increasing in intensity. During puberty and adolescence masturbation once again must be looked upon as a normal physiological manifestation. The genitals are developing and there is an increased awareness of the pleasure of erotic sensation. At this age, also, parents should avoid threats or any suggestion that might make the child fearful, anxious, or produce in him guilty feelings.

During puberty the child is much more beset by a sense of guilt than previously. Usually, there is a constant battle to overcome masturbation. Such children often express their tension by some substitute activity, such as nail-biting or outbursts of uncontrolled behavior, or they are subject to nightmares or insomnia, or even tics.

Today, many parents are aware of the harmlessness of masturbation, but they are still greatly bothered by it. In such cases, it is advisable to divert the child's attention rather than to show displeasure or to resort to threats or punishment. MILTON I. LEVINE

See also GUILT FEELINGS; PUBERTY; REGRESSION

MATTRESS *See* CRIB; JUNIOR BED; LAYETTE AND BABY EQUIPMENT

MEASLES

Among the so-called childhood diseases there is none more contagious and hence more common than measles (*rubeola*). Because of the general susceptibility of children to measles, it used to be thought that they might just as well be deliberately exposed and "get it over with." Doctors do not advise this procedure now. Measles can bring serious complications, and doctors feel that measles should be thought of as a disease with dangerous possibilities.

A protective vaccine has been perfected and is now available. (Single doses of live measles vaccine may be given with or without gamma globulin, or three single doses of inactive measles vaccine may be given at monthly intervals.) Gamma globulin is often recommended for children under 3 years of age, and for other special cases, to give immunity when a child is exposed to measles or to reduce the severity of the case when he has contracted measles.

Measles, which is caused by a virus, often seems to be merely a common cold at the start. Then the temperature rises and a fine pin-point rash spreads rapidly over the body. White spots appear inside the mouth.

The doctor will advise bed care and often a darkened room because light bothers the patient's eyes. MARIE A. HINRICHS

See also COMMON COMMUNICABLE DISEASES; GAMMA GLOBULIN; SICK CHILD; VIRUS

MEDICAL CARE *See* DOCTOR; MEDICAL SPECIALISTS

MEDICAL CHECKUP *See* PHYSICAL CHECKUP

MEDICAL SPECIALISTS

Good medical care of your baby begins before he is born—when your family doctor confirms that you are pregnant and provides expert prenatal care. Or perhaps he will refer you to an obstetrician—a doctor who specializes in the care and treatment of women during pregnancy, childbirth, and the period immediately following delivery.

After the baby is born, your family doctor may look after his general health or you may choose to place him under the care of a pediatrician—a doctor who has specialized in child health and diseases. Certain ailments may at some time call for diagnosis and treatment by doctors who have specialized in other branches of medicine. Some of the more common designations for specialists and the care they provide are given here.

ALLERGIST: A doctor who specializes in treating patients who are hypersensitive (allergic) to certain substances, such as food, pollen, dust.

CARDIOLOGIST: A doctor who specializes in the study of the heart and in the diagnosis and treatment of heart diseases.

DERMATOLOGIST: A physician who is an expert on the skin and its diseases.

OBSTETRICIAN: A doctor trained in the branch of medicine concerned with the care and treatment of women during pregnancy, delivery, and the period immediately following childbirth.

OCULIST: *See* Ophthalmologist

OPHTHALMOLOGIST: A physician who deals specifically with the structure, function, diseases, and disorders of the eye.

ORTHOPEDIST: A surgeon who specializes in treating deformities, diseases, and injuries of the bones and joints.

OTOLOGIST: A specialist in the branch of medicine dealing with the ear and its diseases.

PEDIATRICIAN: A doctor who specializes in the care and development of infants and children and in the treatment of their diseases.

PSYCHIATRIST: A medical doctor who specializes in the diagnosis and treatment of mental disorders.

SURGEON: A doctor who practices surgery. Unlike an ordinary physician, a surgeon treats disease, injury, and deformity by performing operations that may entail cutting and removing diseased tissue.

See also DENTAL CARE; DOCTOR

MEDICINE CABINET

Some medicine cabinets have a small compartment in an upper corner equipped with a lock and key. Drugs and medicines harmful to children can be stored there safely. Some of the newest medicine cabinets have locking devices that make it virtually impossible for children to open them.

Stocking the Medicine Cabinet

The family medicine cabinet too often becomes a catchall for such oddly assorted items as broken combs, old razor blades, empty tooth-paste tubes, and bent bobby pins. An efficient and well-stocked medicine cabinet will include carefully selected, carefully labeled supplies. With these supplies you will be ready to help a patient until the doctor comes. Also, you will be able to take care of the scratches and bumps, aches and pains, and upset tummies that do not require a doctor's immediate attention.

Box of sterile gauze bandages, 3 inches square
Sterile bandage, 2 inches wide
Sterile bandage, 1 inch wide
1-inch adhesive tape
Sterile absorbent cotton
Box of small prepared bandages
Antiseptic
Petroleum jelly
Aspirin tablets, 5 grains each, for adults; 1¼ grains each, for children

Calamine lotion
Mild laxative
Rubbing alcohol (70 per cent)
Small bottle mineral oil
Small bottle milk of magnesia
Aromatic spirits of ammonia
Small bottle oil of cloves for toothaches
Sodium bicarbonate
Sirup (not fluid extract) of ipecac in case of poisoning

Supplies that may not fit into your medicine cabinet but should be part of a household's medical equipment, *could* include the following:

One pair of splinter forceps
Clinical thermometer (rectal for children under 6)
Medicine dropper
Heating pad
Enema bag
Ice bag
Hot-water bottle
Vaporizer
Eye cup
Drinking straws or glass tubes

Things To Remember

- All poisons, sedatives, or pills containing strychnine, opium, or morphine; all solutions containing wood alcohol; or any drugs that would be harmful to children, including aspirin, should be kept under lock and key. Razors, nail files, nail scissors, and medicines should be kept on the top shelves of the medicine cabinet, leaving the lower shelves for cotton, bandages, gauze, adhesive tape, and other harmless supplies.
- Always throw away prescriptions when the illness for which they were ordered is over.
- Every jar, box, or bottle should be clearly labeled, telling what it contains and what it is used for.
- Identify anything "for external use only," with a nail polish symbol or some such mark that family members will immediately recognize.
- Clean out the medicine cabinet at least every three months, discarding anything useless or spoiled. Empty leftover medicines into the toilet bowl and rinse out the bottles before throwing them in the trash container; destroy pills and capsules similarly. VIRGINIA B. NOVINGER

See also FIRST AID; POISONING AND POISONS

MEDICINE GIVING

Giving medicine to a small child or a baby who is acutely ill can sometimes require a good deal of ingenuity and patience.

First, learn from your doctor exactly how much medicine to give in each dose, how often you should give it, and how long you should continue to give it. Write down his directions. Also, your doctor will usually give you specific instructions on how to give a medication. Be sure to follow these instructions carefully and to let your doctor know if the child has vomited the medicine prescribed or refused to take it. If the child is unable to retain the medicine given by mouth, it may be necessary to repeat the dose or to give the medicine in some other form, such as a suppository or by injection.

A very young baby who is not yet taking solid food will be given medicine in a liquid form only. Your doctor may advise you to mix it with a bottle of formula or in a small bottle of sterile water. When medicine is given in this way, be sure that very little formula is left over so that the whole dose is taken. Under no circumstances should a baby or young child be given pills or capsules to swallow. A pill can become lodged in the windpipe and cause asphyxiation. Always crush pills in a spoon and mix them with water, juice, jelly, or a sweet sirup to make them more palatable. Again, try to keep the total amount small so as to be sure the dose is all taken and will not encourage vomiting. Another way to reduce the chance of vomiting medicines is to wait at least half an hour after a dose before offering any large amount of fluid.

Many medicines such as aspirin are now available in more palatable form for older children. (Such medicines should always be kept in a safe place to insure that your child won't eat them like candy.) RUTH S. KEMPE

See also MEDICINE CABINET

MENINGITIS

Any condition in which the coverings of the brain and spinal cord are inflamed is called meningitis. Although some chemical poisons, such as arsenic, may cause a chemical meningitis, most cases of meningitis are caused by infections—usually bacterial.

Meningitis often begins with a fever and irritability. The child may have had a sore throat, a cold, or some other infection before the onset of meningitis. Gradually, his back becomes stiff, and his neck cannot be flexed forward. If the disease continues, the child may start having convulsions and may lose consciousness.

A child with meningitis should be in the hospital so that an exact diagnosis can be made and effective treatment—usually with sulfonamides—carried out.

Early treatment is highly desirable because it helps to avoid complications. In the days before the sulfa and antibiotic drugs, complications were common; today they are, fortunately, rare. JULIUS B. RICHMOND

See also HOSPITALIZATION

MENSTRUATION

All parents want their daughters to grow up not only accepting their feminine role but enjoying their femininity as well. It follows that all girls should learn to accept menstruation as a normal and necessary part of feminine life, essential to the process of reproduction.

When your daughter is about 8 years old —or earlier if she asks questions—she should be told about menstruation, and it should be presented to her as the wonderful phenomenon it is—a sign of growing up and of a good healthy body.

Unfortunately, too many young girls are fearful of the menstrual periods and are even emotionally upset when they finally menstruate. They have heard their mothers or others refer to menstruation as "having the curse," "being sick," "getting unwell," or "falling off."

Menstruation, a girl should be told, is evidence of an important function of her body —preparation for a special day when she is to be a mother. The explanation is not at all difficult.

You can tell your daughter first about the two ovaries, one on either side of her uterus, or womb, and the vagina. The ovaries produce eggs capable of developing into babies. The uterus is the special place in the mother's body where the baby will grow until it is ready to be born. The vagina is the birth canal, through which the baby is born.

In little girls, the ovaries do not produce eggs, but once a girl has entered puberty, generally by the time she is 12 or 13, the ovaries start producing one egg a month. This egg passes from the ovary through a tube to the uterus. But if a baby is going to grow from this tiny little egg, it must receive food. Everything that grows needs food, and this food is brought to the uterus in the mother's blood.

Once a month, then, an egg is produced by the ovary, and once a month the uterus receives an extra supply of blood to be ready in case the egg is developed. If the egg is not going to develop into a baby, there is no further need for this supply of blood, and it passes out of the body through the vagina. And so this discharge of blood from mature girls and women occurs approximately every month unless a woman is pregnant. During pregnancy and for a month or so afterward, the menstrual period ceases.

Girls entering adolescence can be reassured that it is not unusual for the menstrual cycle to be irregular for a couple of years. After that, it usually develops a cycle of 26 to 30 days, each period lasting as a rule about 5 days.

The cycle, once established, is fairly uniform for each girl, but it may occasionally be thrown off by various happenings. Sometimes excitement or nervousness may cause irregularity. Many girls skip menstrual periods when they are away at summer camp or during their first year at college or at some time when there is a great change in routine.

The amount of blood discharged during menstruation also varies with the individual. The total amount is only a few ounces as a rule and will not make a girl anemic or weaken her. This small quantity of blood is quickly replaced by the body.

During the menstrual period girls can use gauze pads of different sizes and thicknesses to absorb the menstrual flow. The pads are held in place by a narrow elastic belt, called a sanitary belt. Some girls use tampons, small rolls of absorbent material inserted into the vagina. As girls approach their first menstrual period, they may have fears caused by the many old wives' tales they may have heard. Or they may have been told that menstruation is a painful experience—that they will feel weak and that they cannot exercise, dance, swim, take baths, or wash their hair.

Pain does not necessarily accompany menstruation. Some girls do get cramps, but a great many do not. These cramps, if they do occur, usually last only the first day. They are caused by an oversupply of blood in the blood vessels of the uterus, or by a uterus that is out of position. Usually the cramps will be relieved by a pain-relieving medication, a hot-water bottle, and warm drinks. But if the pain is too severe, a physician should be consulted.

Today, physicians consider it perfectly safe for a girl to continue her normal activity during her menstrual periods. She may dance, skate, and ski, and she may wash her hair and take showers as long as the water is neither too hot nor too cold. Most physicians advise against too strenuous activities for the first few days. If tampons are used, a girl may swim at any time during her period, but she should avoid chilling.

Your daughter should be assured that even though she might not feel as energetic during the first days of menstruation, there is no reason at all to be concerned. Menstruation is a sign of normal functioning of her body, not of illness; it is just a means of the body to remove a supply of blood that will not be used.

Boys, too, ask questions about menstruation. "Do boys menstruate?" "Does it hurt?" These questions should be answered truthfully. Explain to them that menstruation is simply a process of getting rid of blood that was ready inside the body with food for a baby. Since men can't have babies inside of them, men do not menstruate. And in most cases menstruation doesn't hurt, at least not like bleeding from an injury. Some girls are uncomfortable, and maybe a little cross, but they go right ahead with school or work or whatever they have to do. MILTON I. LEVINE

See also PUBERTY; REPRODUCTION; SEX EDUCATION

MENTAL DEFICIENCY

Mental deficiency is a condition in which an organ of the human body, the brain, has had something befall it, something that makes it work less well than human brains usually do. This something that befalls the brain can occur either before birth or shortly after birth and may occur from different causes, in differing amounts, and to different parts of the brain. This condition may cause widely varying degrees of inability, all the way from that of the person whose mental lacks are seen only when he is under great stress to that of the one who cannot care for himself at all.

Mental deficiency should not be confused with mental slowness, that is, with intellectual underachievement due to improper or insufficient stimulation or education.

The parents of mentally deficient children often look about for someone to blame. Yet to be realistic, no one should blame anyone. No one should blame himself, certainly not his mate. Both parents and child will do better if the situation is accepted, but accepted hopefully. The parents of a mentally deficient child have many avenues open to them—ways in which they can help their child develop and find happiness, ways in which others—doctors, agencies, clinics, schools—can help them to help him.

Some mental deficiency may be said to be caused even before conception. That is, there is a hereditary defect in a gene which creates a biochemical disorder by failure to use some nutritive properly. These cases occur rather rarely. One such type is phenylketonuria (PKU), a defect in an enzyme that metabolizes protein, the basic material of life; another is galactosemia, a defect of a liver enzyme. When these brain diseases are diagnosed in early infancy and the diet regulated for several years, brain damage may be prevented. In some other conditions caused by a defect in the genes, the nature of the enzyme involved is not yet known, nor is there, as yet, any prevention.

Mongolism is the result of one or more chromosomes in the maternal or paternal cell failing to divide properly before or just after fertilization. This causes structural defects in the rest of the body as well as in the brain so that the mongoloid becomes an easily recognizable physical type.

Cretinism is caused by defective operation of the thyroid gland. Development of the brain can sometimes become normal if adequate amounts of thyroid extract are given.

The most common group of mental deficiencies is that in which the brain is damaged during pregnancy. Infectious diseases such as syphilis and German measles during the first three months invade the fetus directly; kidney infections act indirectly. If the mother lacks proper nutrition, particularly in the protein or vitamin intake, or if there is an Rh blood factor incompatibility, the baby may be born with brain damage. Many of these damaging conditions can be avoided through proper supervision and care by a doctor during pregnancy. This is one of the reasons why the informed pregnant woman sees her obstetrician regularly.

It is no longer thought that difficult deliveries result in much mental deficiency. Where mental deficiency and difficult delivery occur together, it is now believed the child was brain-damaged before delivery began. Infants otherwise normal seem to be largely unaffected.

The earlier in the development of the child that brain damage occurs, the greater is the damage caused. On the other hand, the earlier the damage occurs, the greater is the capacity for recovery. It has been shown that some children, even though they may have major brain injuries, can, with proper care and training, regain much, if not all, the brain's power to function.

Brain damage may interfere with the recording in the brain of what is seen, heard, or felt. It may also interfere with how any information gathered is used for the daily needs and experiences of the individual. And it may interfere with control of the muscles. Children thus affected may be clumsy or lack control or may even have cerebral palsy. All these disabilities may be present, in some degree, in any one child.

Because effects of brain damage vary, care and treatment must be individualized to suit the disability. Many devices for teaching brain-damaged children, many ways of managing them and having them fit happily into their environments, have been ingeniously developed. With proper care, many children with brain damage show remarkable recuperative ability. BENJAMIN PASAMANICK

See also HANDICAPPED CHILD

MENTAL DEVELOPMENT

Of all the many things that interest you about your child, probably nothing interests you more than his mental development. "See how bright and beautiful his eyes are," you say when he stares at you with that deep searching look of infancy. "Isn't he an alert baby?" you say when he watches the mobile of birds above his crib. Then as you see that he can differentiate between members of the family or has begun to have favorite toys, you may wonder what it is that makes people develop mentally, why one child differs from another in his mental growth, how bright your child will be when he is grown up, and what you can do to help him achieve his highest mental potential.

Your child's, and every other child's, mental development includes the ability to learn, to deal with abstractions, and to solve problems or deal with new situations. His mental development also makes it possible for him to take on, gradually but constantly, more difficult and more complex problems.

As an infant your child develops so rapidly, and his competence increases in so many ways, that you really can't judge which of his mental powers is developing the most. By the time he is 3, however, and can express himself pretty well in words, you are able to see what direction his mental development is taking. At this stage in his life his mental development will be shown mostly in language.

Language is of vast importance in all mental development. The young child learns that this object is red and this one is green, this round thing is a ball and this one is a globe. He learns which shapes, colors, sounds, smells, and textures are like others and which are different. Words come to stand for objects. As they do and as he finds out more and more how to substitute these

Watching a mobile above his crib

Mastering a more difficult task

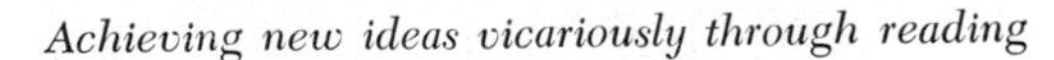

Achieving new ideas vicariously through reading

word symbols for objects and relationships, learning and problem-solving become easier.

If his development is sound and his education effective, he will continue the process of thinking and learning by means of words all his life. And, during all his life, facility in the use of words will play an important part in his mental development.

By the time your child reaches kindergarten age, it is possible to measure, through what you observe about him and through what his teachers observe and test, how well he handles word relationships or how well he can distinguish between likenesses and differences in designs and if he can work with objects in three-dimensional space. These abilities of his are different from the general knowledge and information a child has but do seem to relate to what his learning rate will be, how fast he will gain information, and how much information he can store. Hence, mental development is related in an important way to intelligence and to school performance.

Basic mental abilities, of course, grow and increase—increase in breadth and complexity and in the level at which they are used. Growth rate in mental development is not only rapid in infancy, it also continues to be very rapid throughout the early years. It slows progressively in childhood and adolescence. Although abilities continue to improve for some people during the mature years, there is not nearly so much change proportionately as in the childhood years. Here again, it is important to make a distinction between the *amount* a person knows through the use of his mental abilities and the improvement in these abilities which comes through development and through learning. Increase in amount of knowledge is definitely not the same as increase in ability to learn.

Mental organization probably does not become more complex by an increase in the *number* or *kinds* of abilities present; instead, the person's performance improves to permit him to handle more complex problems. The importance of some abilities relative to others probably changes during growth. For example, ability to tell the difference between objects that are very much alike is an important component in early childhood; abstract thinking becomes more important as a child moves into adolescence.

If individuals with different ability are given similar amounts of training, the differences between them increase rather than lessen. Some few psychologists take this increase in differences to mean that certain aspects of mental development are inborn or that they are related to the nervous system.

A child reacts mentally to insufficient stimulation as he might react physically to insufficient light and food—his potentiality for later development is sometimes permanently impaired. So the opposite side of the question arises: Can mental development be stimulated and can special help raise a child's level of mental growth? The answer is probably yes. Mental life uses concepts, or ideas. At first a child gets his ideas from direct experience, and later he achieves them vicariously through reading. Consequently, firsthand experience with new objects, new persons, and new ideas generally will be very useful. Wide reading plus stimulating, challenging education is valuable in increasing mental development. DALE B. HARRIS

See also CURIOSITY; INDIVIDUAL DIFFERENCES; READINESS; TESTS AND MEASUREMENTS; VOCABULARY DEVELOPMENT

MENTAL HEALTH

Two thousand years ago a man named Socrates combined two small words into a big piece of advice that is treasured to this day: "Know thyself!" The more clearly we understand our own feelings, the better we can build satisfying and lasting relations with other persons. A mentally healthy person is a good friend, a good worker, a good mate, a good parent, and a good citizen. A mentally healthy person is happy, has peace of mind, enjoys even the smallest pleasures, and gains satisfaction in his work and in his play. He gets along with mutual satisfaction with his family, his schoolmates, his business associates, and with people in his community. The emotional well-being of a community, a school, or a place of business depends on the emotional maturity and well-being of the individuals who live and work there.

Life's Relationships

Life, from birth to death, is a series of varying relationships. A person in good mental health is able to find happiness in his relations with at least some of the persons around him, most of the time. But our everyday living is full of problems. It is bound occasionally to inflict on us such psychological pains as anxiety, fear, depression, excitement, and hate in our relations with people. We may show evidences of varying degrees of mental ill health as these pressures enter our lives, but, fortunately for most of us, our less healthy moments are brief and not too disturbing to people around us. Unhappy childhood experiences, emotional blows, or constant pressures, do, unfortunately, disable some of us. It is reassuring to know that nowadays the great majority of individuals who become mentally ill can be restored to health. Mental illness is preventable, treatable, and curable.

To assure our children the good mental health that is everyone's birthright, we must see that they have love, security, protection, and guidance. Each individual wants and needs to believe that he is acceptable to himself, to those he loves, and to those with whom he associates. Childhood experiences add to or take away from our ability to get along with other people. Parents who provide happy, uplifting experiences for their children, who see that the home climate is relaxed and serene (at least most of the time), and who take time to play and work with their children will very likely produce youngsters who have a friendly, a warm, an outgoing approach to life. On the other hand, tense, jittery parents will probably transmit their insecurity to their children.

The little boy who is unable to establish happy relations with his father may go through life resenting authority in any form. The individual who, as a child, was forced to stay dependent long after he should have been looking after himself in many ways, is apt, as an adult, to continue to be dependent on others instead of relying on himself.

Personality

Personality is a delicate and complicated machine. One part of the machine is what we inherit—our capacity to learn and to use what we learn. We probably inherit the capacity to develop certain skills as well. The other part of this mechanism is our environment. Yet it is almost impossible to separate the two forces, for one actually inherits part of his environment. As we grow, and as we form satisfying relations with our parents, our brothers and sisters, other members of the household, friends, and schoolteachers, our personalities grow and are molded. Customs and events in the wider community where we live and grow share in the shaping of our personalities.

Each of us is different from everyone else because of the unlimited number of factors that have a part in our development. But most important to our growing personality is the early immediate environment; especially important are one's parents. For this reason, parents can very well begin planning about the child before his birth. What are the priorities in life? What is important to develop the best kind of family life—and home? What do we need to know to do a good job with our children? Physical development needs care and guidance, too; but a healthy personality depends far more on the care and guidance of the parents.

Making Life Worth While

The greatest satisfactions in life come from our relations with people. A mentally healthy person is able to derive personal pleasure from life. At the same time he can make life worth while for others. Making life worth while for others might be making a home and caring for a family. It might be opening new doors to children as a teacher in a classroom. It might be writing, or painting, or dancing, or assisting in the production of things people need. It might be earning a livelihood for a family or engaging in one of the professions that serve people's material, emotional, or spiritual needs. Making life worth while for others may sound like a nobler calling than most of us follow. Yet in many of the situations in which we gain the greatest satisfaction, mothers, fathers, teachers, and even children are making life fuller and better for those around them.

Our Responsibilities

A mentally healthy person assumes responsibility for his share of a friendship, of his family, of his community, of his nation, and of the world in which he lives. There are those individuals whom one would have to judge mentally unhealthy because they choose to live entirely within themselves. Angry feelings express themselves in any contacts such people manage to make. We can understand these people only when we recognize that, in their earliest days, they did not learn how to be interested in, or to get along with, other people in ways appropriate to their age and to the situation. Learning to get along with people is a slow process. Small children cannot be expected to be good at it. It is at this point that parents, teachers, church officials, and close friends can help a child learn his responsibilities, can help him seek peaceful ways, to assure his entering adulthood equipped with a mentally healthy personality.

Good mental health implies an ability to get along with the world by meeting and conquering obstacles without fighting or fleeing from the real situation. You may become angry when you narrowly miss the train that was to carry you to the country for a weekend visit with friends. But you will not become so angry that you scream at the railroad company, or think the train left early as a plot against you, or go home and sit and sulk all day because your plans were upset. An emotionally immature person might react this way. But one in good mental health would look up the schedule on another railroad, would look into the possibility of going by bus, would telephone the friends concerning the mixup, and would get to the country in due time.

In meeting the demands of life, a mentally healthy person relies more upon his intelligence than his feelings. In making plans or tackling problems, he accepts the world as it is rather than as he wishes it were or fears it might be. He accepts responsibilities and does his best to carry them out.

The ability to fight for principles and convictions helps one to be a constructive person. Mentally healthy people get angry. They sometimes get "fighting mad," but they get fighting mad when there is just and real cause rather than expending unnecessary energy on trifles.

Mental Health Guidelines

There are no simple rules for mental health, but there are some principles that may be applied to one's own experience.

Finding security and satisfaction within this framework is an indication of mental health.

The degree of success with which we meet the realities of health and ill health, economic security and insecurity, and world situations that threaten the well-being of each of us determines our mental health.

Satisfaction is almost akin to happiness, mental hygienists say. If you cannot find satisfaction in the job you must do, you can try to find activities that make up for the things you do not like or cannot change. A mentally healthy person reasons that dissatisfactions are very likely temporary, anyway, and takes things in his stride.

A major goal in becoming emotionally mature is to learn to find more satisfaction in giving than in receiving. We never give up our pleasure in receiving, but as babies, that is all we did—receive. Growing up entails a shift from receiving to giving—along with the satisfaction derived from each of these relationships. If we were fortunate enough to receive love from our parents, we learned slowly to give in return. As we grew, we learned the necessity to give more and more—to friends, to our own family, to the community, to the world. Only as one knows how to give, and with real satisfaction, can he be regarded as mature.

Maturity is easier to maintain if one has a constructive and creative hobby. Unfortunately, there is a tendency on the part of many persons to use their leisure only in seeking entertainment. Our most valuable leaders contribute time, energy, money, and themselves to causes to which they are dedicated. The mature individual has a mission in life bigger than his personal interests.

An essential characteristic of a mature person is the ability to learn from experience. This implies ability to recognize unprofitable and unhealthy behavior.

Under sufficient stress we all develop anxieties. The more mature person learns to work through most of his tensions and fears by developing constructive compromises.

We learn early to love ourselves. If and when we as individuals are able to love our neighbors as we do ourselves, we will be emotionally mature and we will have a happier world in which to live and bring up our children. WILLIAM C. MENNINGER

See also LOVE; IMITATION

MENTAL HEALTH CLINIC *See* CLINICS; COMMUNITY RESOURCES

MENTAL ILLNESS

In the great concern for the mental health of their children, and in the impatience to help with their children's emotional difficulties, parents tend to overlook how new is the idea that children can be mentally ill. As late as the turn of the century there was nothing that could in any sense be regarded as child psychiatry. Only toward the beginning of this century were the first advances made, oddly enough in two rather opposite fields. First, the intelligence test was developed, which enabled testers to separate the normal from the feeble-minded and those otherwise mentally ill. At about the same time, the first juvenile courts were established in which juvenile offenders were handled differently from adult violators of the law. Thus retardedness and juvenile delinquency were the first recognized mental illnesses of children.

Only in the 20's did the child guidance clinic appear, and only in the 30's were any coordinated efforts launched to understand and treat mental illnesses in children. Much confusion—as reflected in such contradictory statements as, "There are no bad children; there are only bad parents," and "Spare the rod and spoil the child"—is natural in a field so new.

But in spite of the brief time since scientific efforts to understand mental illness in children were begun, and despite still widespread confusion, a certain amount of solid knowledge now exists.

To consider mental illness in children simply in relation to those known to be afflicted is misleading. Parents are interested not only in knowing that their child does not suffer mental illness at the moment, they are also equally concerned with keeping his childhood years free of those experiences that may later cause mental illness.

Types of Mental Illness

While the nature and causes of some types of mental illnesses are still not too clear, fortunately a great deal of knowledge is available on others. By and large, all mental illnesses, in child or adult, fall into one of two broad categories. First are the *organic* conditions; that is, types of illnesses which are believed due either to inborn or later acquired defects in the brain or other parts of the central nervous system. These disturbances are in many ways akin to any other sickness of the body. Some are due to injuries before or after birth; others come as aftereffects of virus diseases.

Children, too, can have brain tumors, and so on. There is very little a parent can do if his child is so afflicted, short of seeking the best available medical care and then following the doctor's advice.

Other organic mental illnesses are feeblemindedness and epilepsy. Fortunately for the epileptic child—whose disease was once so dreaded—very good drugs are now available which in most cases control the disease. No drugs have yet been found, however, to help with mental deficiency. But new teaching techniques offer some promise of keeping many mental defectives functioning in society on a restricted level.

Quite different is the story of the *functional* disturbances. They are called functional because, to the best of our knowledge, they are not caused by any disease or any damage to the central nervous system. They are simply a disturbance in the functioning of the mind, though the brain itself is intact. That is, the central nervous apparatus of the child is potentially normal; the trouble is brought about by experiences that prevent the child either from developing or from using his mental capacities to full functioning. There is a great deal a parent can do to help such a child, though again in more serious cases the advice of a psychiatrist is necessary.

While the specific events that may cause functional disturbance are as varied as life itself, the underlying cause is always the same: anxiety. But the anxiety may express itself in the most bewildering variety of symptoms. Exactly how anxiety causes mental illness is not known, but perhaps an oversimplified example may help in achieving an understanding of the process.

Whenever the level of anxiety rises too high, the whole organism becomes flooded with it. If this happens in the child's sleep, for example, he has nightmares. But if, during his waking hours, he experiences nightmarish anxiety due not to any fantasies but to reality or an imagined reality, then life can become altogether a nightmare to him. He may then begin to direct most of his efforts to protecting himself and may end up spending so much time and energy on protective maneuvers that no energy is left for the tasks of normal living and growing up. Just as a child is much more vulnerable to some of the physical diseases than an adult who is in the prime of life, so a child is much more vulnerable to the impact of anxiety. He knows so much less about the world, so much less about how to protect himself and what the consequences of his actions may be, that he can fall into serious errors of judgment. Normal, though unfortunate, events can set a chain reaction of anxiety going in a child. For example, he may think some bad thoughts that he tells no one about. But right after that he may, by chance, fall and break a bone. These two unconnected events he connects and is convinced that if he should ever think such thoughts again, another accident, or worse, will befall him.

This kind of thing happens to many children, and yet sooner or later they overcome their anxiety as they continue to have thoughts that they consider bad, without any evil happening to them. Thus, if lightning does not strike twice, a temporary emotional disturbance will slowly subside all by itself. But if, by bad luck, lightning does strike twice, then as likely as not it will strike still more often. Because the child, trying to avoid the bad thoughts, is even less able than before to pay attention to what goes on around him and may thus have another accident, or what seems to him like an accident.

Just as being physically ill makes a person twice as vulnerable to other diseases, once he is very anxious, any happening will make him more so. Once anxiety has reached a high level, anything goes to prove to a child that he is being punished for his thoughts. Sickness of a parent or a brother or a sister he merely translates to mean that fate made an error and somebody else was punished instead of him. By now he may begin the most elaborate efforts to protect himself. He may force himself to think of nothing but some innocuous subject, such as counting numbers, so that no bad thought can possibly enter his mind. But in doing so, he cannot pay attention to what goes on, and he pays even less attention to life. He may become deathly afraid to go out on the street because that's where the punishing accidents take place. Or he may spend all his time arranging things in a certain order because that seems to offer a magical protection. And if he has always been called a good child when he carefully cleaned up, he will try to pacify fate by always being a good child and may spend his life making things neat in a certain way or thinking about how they should be made neat.

Unfortunately, the variety of such defensive maneuvers is so great that one simple example cannot begin to suggest the wide range of devices a child can hit upon to protect himself from imaginary dangers.

Treatment

Basically, treatment for functional mental illness consists of inducing the child to trust another person, usually his therapist, sufficiently to open up to him about his anxieties. Usually, by the time treatment is sought, things have gotten so out of hand and the child has engaged for so long in so many devious maneuvers to protect himself that, like the child in our example, he no longer knows what the bad thoughts were which he had to avoid thinking at all costs. Or, to put it in technical language, he has repressed the bad thoughts so deeply and replaced them with less dangerous ones, and has done this so many times over, that the thoughts he is presently avoiding no longer have any resemblance to those he repressed in the first place.

To unearth the original bad thought, to convince the child it was harmless and that fate will not punish him for what he thinks—this requires great psychological knowledge and skill. Treatment must be applied in a slow and delicate process of uncovering, of giving reassurance, and of building up security and self-esteem. This, basically, is what psychotherapy entails, though many complicated detours are involved. So parents should not be discouraged if treatment takes a long time or if, after some improvement, the child seems temporarily worse. It may only mean that after one anxiety has been licked, a still greater one was hiding behind it and is now coming to the fore but has not yet been resolved in treatment.

Signs of Mental Illness

So much about the nature of functional mental illness and its treatment. But how is a parent to know if his child is mentally ill or not?

Sometimes the diagnosis between organic and functional conditions is very difficult to make. For example, if a child is, for functional reasons, deeply withdrawn from the world and unable to cope with life, tests may show him to be retarded or feebleminded; actually he may be of superior intelligence but so scared of making any move into the world that he behaves as if he were feeble-minded.

It is much easier to recognize mental illness in an adult. A person who is mentally ill has lost part of or all his grip on himself and reality. He may believe he is the emperor of China. He may engage in fantastic daydreams, disregard social canons and other aspects of reality; he may believe in ghosts, in the evil eye, or that spells have been cast on him; he may feel persecuted by imaginary enemies. But all young children disregard reality at some time or other and believe in evil witches and ghosts. So how do we know when a child is just a youngster with an active fantasy life and when he is mentally ill?

It is much easier to recognize extreme conduct and to understand its significance than it is to be sure about the meaning of actions that are not very definite, that proceed within a middle ground between the extremes of behavior. For example, it is quite easy to recognize imbalance in a child who is always pessimistic and worries himself sick about past, present, and future. Children who see only the bad features of the world have no clear picture of it, but neither do those who cannot see how anything could possibly be wrong. Both these extreme types of behavior are readily understood as signs of emotional disturbance.

While it is difficult to give any guidelines, and while parents should certainly not diagnose the disturbances of their child, they might want to assess whether and to what degree he is disturbed. This does not mean that parents should be constantly on the lookout for signs of disturbance, any more than they should examine their child each morning for symptoms of measles. They do what they can about their child's physical well-being—take reasonable precautions, adopt a positive and unafraid attitude, and if a disease symptom should appear, try to find out what it indicates. Many excellent books are available to help parents judge what behavior they can expect of a child at a certain age—when it is normal to believe in witches and when a belief in ghosts and imaginary enemies has been carried too far. Furthermore, an interested teacher or some other adult with a more objective view than a parent often can see signs in a child indicating a need for a little or a lot of help.

Basically, children are expected to function adequately in three life areas: the home, the school, and in free play with other children. A child who functions adequately in at least two of these areas, and is only moderately disturbed in the third, is not a child to give cause for concern. This statement does not overlook the child who never gives anybody any difficulties, who is always "perfect," who may be cause for concern, because always getting along perfectly suggests that he doesn't dare to assert his independence or initiative. Any parent can expect small disturbances that are short-lived in all three areas of living at one time or another. It is when a child's functioning is seriously impaired in one of the three areas, and when he also has difficulties in the other two, that an expert should be consulted. If a child cannot function in any of the three areas, here sketched only broadly, there is reason for serious concern—and immediate action should be taken.

The mentally ill child, like the physically ill child, needs special treatment. Children who are overly hostile and aggressive, as well as those who are overly submissive, overly fearful, or overly preoccupied with certain anxieties or problems, are children in need of help. So are children who cannot deal with any frustrations except by temper outbursts. And, at an older age, so are those who chronically lie, steal, play truant from school, or run away from home. All these are children in need of help with their emotional difficulties.

When a child shows a mild physical disturbance, his parents likely as not will apply some tried and tested home remedies. The same should be true if there are signs of emotional disturbance, such as when a child takes something (which is not yet necessarily stealing), or when he lies or does poorly in school. Here, too, home remedies should be tried first. Thus, if a child takes things, his life may possibly be arranged so that his desire for additional goods is reduced and the temptation to take things also lessened. Things can be put away, decreasing the temptation to take them. On the other hand, he can be given a chance to increase his ability to control his desires. Such control can be exercised through support and greater supervision, through the introduction of constructive activities, and in a variety of other ways. Similarly, a child who becomes a truant is not just running away from school but is also in search of satisfactions that seem more desirable to him than learning and school. Here, too, a double approach is useful: (*a*) Find out why school seems to be so unpleasant to him that he wants to run away and then try to make school more enjoyable, and (*b*) find out what seems so desirable that he runs toward it and try to enable him to enjoy it without having to become a truant.

Parents of a mentally ill child should try to avoid either a fatalistic attitude that nothing can be done about their child's problems or an overoptimistic view that "he'll grow out of it without help," or "it's just a phase." Even if the child eventually outgrows his difficulty, it doesn't mean that he did not need help at the time. As with physical sickness, many infections go untreated and the patient survives them, but always with some damage to the organism. The organism may thus have experienced some permanent damage that will later on weaken it when other infections occur; it might have been better able to deal with new infections if the original one had been properly treated. Since the same is true of mental disturbances, it is always a good idea to help a child when he needs it.

Here a difficulty arises: If a child is mentally disturbed, his parents may develop strong feelings of fear which block their sound and intuitive reactions. Very often what is disturbing a child is in some way a reflection of emotional difficulty in one of his parents, though in a parent it may never have reached such proportions. For this and other reasons, the emotional interactions between the disturbed child and his parents makes it particularly hard for parents to choose the right course of action and to develop the correct inner attitudes that would enable them to help their child.

Therefore, as with physical sickness, when simple home remedies do not bring the desired improvement and a physician is called, so, too, when home remedies for emotional disturbance bring no results, the expert can be turned to for help and advice. Professional help does not always mean long-term psychiatric treatment. Other people besides psychiatrists often are skilled in evaluating and helping with emotional problems. The family physician and the pediatrician are certainly persons to be consulted, and so are the teacher, the school psychologist, and the school social worker. Many communities, particularly the larger ones, now have community-supported agencies staffed by trained workers who can offer counseling services to a parent about his child's problems. Some of these agencies have people on their staffs who are specially equipped for treating the mentally ill child. In the larger cities, either community-supported child guidance clinics are available or such clinics are attached to the larger hospitals. Neither these services nor the psychiatrist can perform miracles. Psychiatric treatment, to succeed, needs the cooperation not only of the child but also of his family and others with whom he is in close contact.

Very often the treatment of the mentally ill child is lengthy because he is not aware that there is anything wrong with him—nor does he want to change his ways. Therefore, a considerable time of preparation by the professional may be needed to get the child to the point where he himself wishes to do something about his emotional disturbance. Parents must not become discouraged if psychiatric treatment of their child or treatment in a child guidance clinic does not produce results on short order. Usually it takes a long time for a severe emotional disturbance to develop. It may take nearly as long to correct it. But we are fortunate that many mental illnesses of children can now be treated successfully and that much research is going on that should offer more to help in the future. BRUNO BETTELHEIM

See also CHILD GUIDANCE CLINIC; MEDICAL SPECIALISTS; MENTAL DEFICIENCY

MESSINESS

Young children are perhaps never so happy as when they are making a mess. But take heart. Little ones who love to fingerpaint, make mud pies, or dig in the dust usually learn to be neat—eventually.

Children should be allowed to feed themselves with their fingers as soon as they show an interest in touching their food, which, according to some mothers, is much *too* soon. Try to give them bite-size pieces of meat or vegetables, fruit or bread, that they can pick up and eat. Young children will put their fingers in applesauce or chopped spinach; that is how they learn what things feel like.

Children touch wood surfaces, glass, concrete, tile, or metal, and we think little or nothing of it. But many times when young children come into the house with mud or sand or tar or plaster on their hands and clothes, we fuss at them. The wiser course would be to discuss the thing they've gotten into, talk about what tar is and what makes it smell the way it does or how mud is formed, while helping them get cleaned up. Children can learn from messiness, and your cleaning-up chore will not be nearly so tedious.

Many parents are overly concerned that their homes stay constantly neat and clean. They scold when children are messy or when they fail to clean up their rooms. Of course, children have to learn the value of cleanliness and order, but not to the point where these qualities preclude living in a happy, relaxed home.

MIDDLE CHILD *See* BROTHERS AND SISTERS

MILK *See* BOTTLE FEEDING; BREAST CARE AND BREAST FEEDING; FORMULA MAKING; NUTRITION

MILK CRUST *See* CRADLE CAP

MODELING CLAY *See* ART EXPERIENCES

MODESTY

Modesty is of two kinds. There is modesty about one's personality, an attempt to put a true value on oneself and on one's own relation to other people. There is also modesty about one's body that involves respect for one's body, knowing what is accepted social behavior and conforming to what is acceptable. Both kinds of modesty are good attributes for a child to have.

Modesty About Personality

Modest appraisal of self is realistic appraisal. It shows pride and confidence in one's strengths; shows a sense of humility about one's weaknesses. This kind of modesty is evident, for example, in the child who says, "I know I'm one of the best singers in my class, and I like it when the teacher has me sing all by myself. But I got very shy when my father introduced me to a *real* opera singer."

An overmodest child is one who is constantly downgrading himself—belittling his real accomplishments in a way that often annoys and exasperates others. For instance, a charming, attractive, and gifted 16-year-old girl who writes well, is a fine athlete, can play the guitar, and demonstrates real talent for acting in school plays talks constantly about being "stupid, too fat, ugly, and unpopular with boys." This girl has all the ingredients for success, but some emotional problem makes it necessary for her to have a low opinion of herself. Such a young person needs help in finding out why she cannot accept, enjoy, and capitalize on her strengths, why she seems to be constantly seeking failure.

A less extreme and far more natural expression of overmodesty occurs when children, impatient with their own growth, measure what they can do in relation to adult accomplishments and are overwhelmed by their own imperfections. The boy who makes a model airplane and sadly says, "This is nothing," is expressing the realization that his dream is bigger than what he can do; he is fascinated and impressed with remarkable accomplishments in the field of aeronautics and is impatient with his own limitations. Such natural feelings often become the force behind a child's ambition to learn and work and to reach adult goals.

Unfortunately, adults sometimes encourage overmodesty in children by interpreting self-effacing behavior as politeness, "knowing his place," and deferring to adult superiority. If children find such behavior successful in gaining adult attention and approval, they may use it too often.

Modesty About the Body

Modesty is also related to attitudes about one's own body and sexual development. Individual families vary considerably in their opinions about nudity, about open discussion of sex information, about private matters; hence, children deserve guidance in learning what will be considered acceptable behavior both at home and away from home. Children can be taught that appropriate modesty does not mean that there is anything ugly or bad about one's body, about sexual curiosity, about sex development or sexual relations; that these are all normal and good aspects of life, to be discussed in the privacy of one's home, but that inappropriate behavior shows lack of sensitivity to other people's feelings and may result in misunderstandings and unfriendliness.

A typical dilemma faced by parents in this connection is that of a mother who found her 4-year-old son and his playmates "playing doctor" under the front porch. Wanting to help him develop healthy attitudes about his own body and his natural curiosity about sex differences, she calmly told him that he didn't have to play under the porch—he should bring his friends into the house. When neighbor parents heard that the children were undressing in front of each other, this poor, misinformed but well-meaning mother had the wrath of the community descend upon her. What she might have done was to say to her own son privately, "Children your age all wonder about their bodies. You and I can talk about this together, but it is a private matter. People don't go around without clothes on when they visit one another, and you want to learn how to behave so that people will like you and feel friendly toward you."

As children mature, they seem to sense more and more clearly the adult attitudes about privacy; sometimes they even seem to overdo a good thing. The girl who at 2 could not seem to understand any reason for wearing a bathing suit in the back-yard wading pool, screams in horror at the age of 12 if her insensitive brother walks into the bathroom when she's brushing her teeth. The adolescent boy turns crimson if his mother dares to appear in her slip. Most teenagers, self-conscious about their rapid body changes, go through a period of overconcern for privacy before they find the balance of personal good taste and acceptable social custom. EDA J. LE SHAN

See also APPROVAL; NUDITY; PRIVACY; SEX EDUCATION

MOLES

Considered one form of birthmark, moles are black or dark brown spots present in the skin. Large amounts of dark pigment in the cells give moles their color. In some instances, they may be more extensive than just spots or marks and may even cover large areas of skin.

Usually, moles are not harmful and do not change in appearance over the years. In rare instances, however, they can begin to grow and become cancerous. Therefore, if a mole seems to be enlarging—or new ones appear—a doctor should be consulted. A child should be told not to pick at or otherwise irritate a mole, for it is believed that irritation might cause it to start growing. Indeed, if a mole is in a place where irritation cannot be avoided, such as at the belt line or at the edge of the shoe, the doctor may suggest removal. JULIUS B. RICHMOND

See also BIRTHMARK; CANCER

MONEY *See* ALLOWANCE; JOBS

MONGOLISM *See* MENTAL DEFICIENCY

MONONUCLEOSIS *See* GLANDULAR FEVER

MONTHLY PERIOD *See* MENSTRUATION

MORAL AND SPIRITUAL DEVELOPMENT

In every human society parents have the obligation to train their children in those moral and spiritual values which prevail within that society. Parents are also expected to be responsible for the early training of their children in the particular cultural and religious beliefs and practices of whatever social subgroup to which they belong. In highly civilized societies such as ours, in which many people of different national, cultural, and religious origins have come together, it is especially important that parents not only recognize that such differences exist, but that they also teach their children, as far as they are able, to view such differences with sympathy and understanding.

A value is something we hold to be of interest, something we esteem and desire, or believe ought to be. Morals are the customary valuations of right, of good, which are socially expressed in behavior. By "spiritual" is meant the sense or experience of religion and the feeling of relatedness to the whole of animated nature. By development is meant increase in size and complexity of abilities.

The Importance of Sincerity

The first and fundamental thing to know is that the home is the place where moral and spiritual values are principally learned and that the parents are the ones from whom the children learn them. An equally important fact to understand is that these values are learned not by precept but by example. Children learn very early what adults sometimes forget; namely, that what an individual believes is not so much what he says as what he does. And, indeed, what a person does is the only true measure of what he believes. To prescribe one form of behavior for one's children and another for oneself is to teach children the art of hypocrisy. And that, unfortunately, is what many parents teach their children. Hypocrisy is a value that both parents and schools should do their utmost to avoid teaching children.

Many parents, quite understandably, expect their children to be better than they themselves are, and often their expectations of their children tend to be quite unrealistic. It is, for example, disturbing to children to discover that the moral rules which they are expected to obey are often hypocritically unheeded by adults. Let us practice and teach the highest moral ideals, but let us also remember human frailty. Since it is eminently human to err, let us make no rigid demands upon our children that they be impossibly perfect.

Understanding Others

A principal moral lesson parents can teach their children is that of compassion. And a parent can begin by being compassionate himself when dealing with his own children, by being understanding and helpful and forgiving. Compassion means to feel with the other and, while helping the other to understand the wrongness of the act or its motivation, to forgive him it, and thus to help him to avoid such errors in the future.

Compassion banishes every thought of punishment, for punishment teaches children retribution and vindictiveness, not compassion. Corporal punishment actually sanctions violence as a solution of human problems. Instead, children need to be taught inner discipline, not discipline imposed from without,

so that when the occasion arises they will draw upon their inner resources rather than fall back upon infantile destructive devices. In a world in which violence and armed conflict are part of every day's news, it is more than ever necessary to hold true to those values that will always constitute man's best guides in life.

Compassion is not to be confused with an extreme permissiveness. Children want and expect their parents to be firm. Children expect their parents' "Nay" to be as firm as their "Yea." A certain amount of frustration, that is, thwarting of expected satisfactions, is not only unavoidable in life but also necessary, necessary in that one of the earliest and most enduring lessons one must learn in life is the ability to postpone immediate satisfactions for long-term goals.

The Ability To Love

Children are born with powerful drives, not only to be loved, but what is equally important, to love others. One way to define love is to say that love is behavior which confers survival benefits in a creatively enlarging manner upon others. Another way is to say that love is the communication of the feeling to the other of deep involvement in his welfare, of profound interest in his development, the instillation of faith and trust, and the provision of all those stimulations and supports that will minister to the development of his potentiality for being to others what you are in this way being to him. This is love. And of all moral principles and practices, love is the most important, for if a person is wanting in love, it matters little what else he has achieved—he will have a very difficult time as a human being without it. The only way one develops the ability to love is by being loved. And parents—almost exclusively—are the ones who teach children how to love.

Love is the highest form of wisdom and the supreme of moral principles. Love is unconditional and unrestricted. It is the one thing one cannot give anyone too much of. Love should never be made to depend upon the child's doing what is required of him, and love should know no national or racial boundaries.

Religion Begins in the Home

In this world many human beings have become spiritually rudderless. They are tossed about upon an ocean of vicariously experienced emotions in a directionless haphazard manner. These people may sometimes forget that the religions of mankind constitute the great ethical systems of the world, ethical systems that enshrine the hard-purchased wisdom of humanity. Religion is a way of life, and spiritual development is an absorption into feeling, not only of the world beyond the self, but also an absorption of the self in the community of man. Religion is the belief in the relatedness of all living things, not only on this earth but also throughout the universe. And the principle that produces this relatedness in conduct is the principle of love. Each religion has its own way of conveying the lessons it has to teach, and from each religion, and all together, parents may derive great help in helping their children to develop the highest principles of ethical conduct. As the great child educator Heinrich Pestalozzi said, "Love is made up not of words and fancies, but of man's ability to carry the world's burdens, to lessen its miseries, and to soften its distress . . . ." and "The way to Heaven is to do our duty while on earth." Just as love is not inspired by anything but love, so faith has not been inspired by anything save faith. It is the religious feeling of their mentors, their parents and teachers, but principally that of their parents, which calls forth the same feeling in the children.

Unless religion is in the home, it will not be learned at Sunday school.

Through the teachings of religion, children can be given an understanding of the essential community of all living things and of that reverence for life which will cause them to cherish, respect, and protect it under all conditions. Especially can they be given a love for and understanding of their fellow men, for the whole of humanity of which they are a part. Such qualities are not instilled in children through the intense study of holy books; in any event, most children are not ready for the intense study of holy books until they are of high-school age. The feeling of community with all living things and the reverence for life are qualities absorbed from those who exhibit them in their daily lives. It is absurd to expose small children to intense studies of holy books for which they are neither prepared by experience nor ready by capacity to understand—much irreparable damage to spiritual development is often done by such means. On the other hand, children at an early age can be told religious stories in a constructively useful manner and at the same time be initiated into one of the great sources of our cultural background and ethical practices. Every form of bigotry and intolerance should be avoided in such teaching, and, indeed, mentioned and explained only in order to demonstrate them for the cruel errors of judgment that they are.

The Parent—a Spiritual Leader

The best and noblest examples that parents can hold up to the young are not always those of the great spiritual leaders and prophets of mankind, but of themselves. By "best" is here meant the most effective in the sense that children learn best from the most immediate examples. But the examples of the great spiritual teachers of mankind—Jesus, Moses, Confucius, and the lives of contemporary living figures like Albert Schweitzer, and of such spiritual leaders as Gandhi, and of men like Abraham Lincoln, to mention but a few—provide beautiful exemplars of the perfection of human character which human beings can attain and should be encouraged to attain. It is with love, with goodness, that spiritual development is mainly concerned, and through the example of the lives of those who have achieved greatness in love and goodness—and through the lives of parents themselves—much can be conveyed of spiritual development. ASHLEY MONTAGU

See also BOOKS FOR CHILDREN; IMITATION

MOSQUITO BITES *See* BITES, INSECT

MOTHER

It is much easier to learn how to bake a light biscuit than it is to learn how to do what is best for a growing child. That is why child study groups and child development literature have gained so much ground in recent decades. As mothers learn what to expect in a child's growth, they gain confidence in their relationships with their children, they enjoy them more, and they find joy in growing and learning side by side with their youngsters.

There was a time when you knew exactly where to find a mother. Her place was in her home through the centuries that preceded modern times. Traditionally, a mother's role was to bear and rear her children, keep house, and produce almost everything that her family needed to eat and wear. Many women still living can remember the time when most of a family's food was raised and preserved and processed by the mother in the home. The smell of home-baked bread coming hot from the oven, of chili sauce bubbling on the back of the stove, of home-cured ham sizzling in the pan lingers yet in memory. Many an older woman can tell you of making most of her children's clothing as well as her own when her family was young, and her grandmother might remember the spinning wheel, the loom, and the dye kettle that produced the fabrics themselves.

With the coming of industrialization, the homemaker shifted to selecting most of her family's needs from the vast array of goods which flows from mass production. The sewing, cooking, or preserving that a mother does today is no longer necessary but is done because she enjoys doing things that please her family. Freed from making all the things her family needs, today's mother can give herself to the new roles required of her.

Community Activities

By the time children get into school, a mother is drawn into activities within the community. She joins the parent-teacher association and participates in its projects.

She may help with the scout troop or the Camp Fire Girls or some other youth program that means much to her children. She is more active in church and religious affairs while her children are growing up than perhaps she was before they came. She gets interested in politics when a school bond issue is necessary to protect her children's interests or when some other legislation becomes important.

As children grow older, a mother simultaneously plays many roles in the community as she guides her teen-agers through adolescence. She is available to chaperone a party or prepare food for a youth meeting at the community center. She serves as hostess for many an event in her home as she encourages her growing children to bring their friends home rather than meet them outside. She meets other mothers to develop the understandings and codes of conduct that set reasonable standards of teen-age functions. Then as her children grow up and leave home for marriage, college, or work, she is free again to join her husband in companionable trips and excursions, to pursue a hobby, or to pick up the threads of her career.

Companionship in Marriage

Mothers live in two dimensions—as mothers in the mother-child relationship and as wives in the husband-wife relationship. No one denies that being a good mother is important. Increasingly, modern women are discovering that being a good wife is quite as important. A woman is busy as a mother for 20 to 25 years on the average. She is a wife for twice as long in many a marriage. The emotional climate of the home in which the children grow is determined by the kind of companionship husband and wife together establish and maintain over the years.

A mother is wise to help her husband feel that he too is a parent—from the very beginning. As the first child appears on the scene, there is a big difference in whether the mother's attitude toward the father is, "This is *my* baby and you have no part to play in its care," or, "Let's enjoy and care for this little life we have brought into the world together." Talking over the child's development, discussing the youngster's problems, planning together for the child's future—all are ways for keeping the father in focus through the years when children are being reared.

There is a central place for husband-wife interaction that has little to do with their children. When the man of the house comes home discouraged, tired, undecided and upset about his work, his wife may wisely bundle the children off to grandma's for a little while so that she can give her husband the support and companionship he needs. She can go along on a business trip, attend a conference, or take an impromptu excursion that means more to her husband at that time than her 24-hour-a-day service in the home might. Children grow with responsibility and enjoy their parents' confidence and trust. It is a wise woman who realizes that one of her most important functions is to work herself out of her job as a mother over the years.

Being a Good Mother

Research studies show that there are at least two ways of conceiving of one's role as a mother. The traditional conception of the good mother is in terms of keeping a neat, clean house, taking care of her children, and making them mind. In recent years more mothers have come to have a developmental conception of themselves and their children. They emphasize a child's growth and development more than "making him mind." They can let the dusting go to encourage a discouraged family member or to support a project that is important to a particular youngster at that time. They believe in keeping relaxed and cheerful and alive to what is going on around them. The developmental mother keeps growing herself and values the companionship that her development makes possible with her husband and children.

Continuing Education

More mothers read more books and pamphlets now than ever before. Millions are members of parent education classes that regularly study child development, the dynamics of family living, and the growth of parents as persons. Many mothers read not only for themselves, but also with their children in ways that bring more and more of the world into focus in the family.

It is not unusual now for a mother to return to school and complete her education after her own children have become students. High school and college graduations find mother-son or mother-daughter teams getting their diplomas at the same time. After children no longer demand full-time attention, a mother is free to take up her education where she left it years ago. She enjoys broadening her horizons, keeping up with her husband and children, and enhancing her competence as a person. Since she dropped out of school to get married and have a family, her salable skills have grown rusty, and she must sharpen her insights and abilities in order to get the kind of work that her talents and interests indicate. Fortunately, increasing numbers of colleges and universities welcome the mature woman to the classroom. The woman who has borne and reared children of her own brings the kind of wisdom that makes her a good student and a valuable worker in the many fields where such experience is directly applicable.

Business Experience

Business experience tends to be an asset to a mother. Studies of what makes for success or failure in marriage find that women with some work experience before they marry are better adjusted and happier than are wives with no such experience in the business world. The girl who moves directly from the protection of her father's home to that of her husband's lacks the opportunity of finding herself as an autonomous person which the woman acquires on her own, at least for a while. There is nothing quite like earning one's own money to teach a young adult of either sex the value of a dollar as well as how to earn and spend and save money in responsible ways.

The necessity of keeping a schedule, of getting things done on time, and of budgeting one's time and resources which one learns on the job is good preparation for the home management challenges that a family presents. Furthermore, a mother who works some of the time finds, often to her surprise, that household chores and activities with her children become less burdensome when they are interspersed with responsibilities and interests outside the home.

There is mounting evidence that part-time work is especially satisfactory for mothers. Several recent investigations have concluded that a mother who has a part-time job has a better relationship with her children than does either a full-time worker or a mother with no outside responsibilities. A mother who is employed 40 hours a week has little time or strength for the many tasks that await her at home or for the leisurely periods of enjoying her children available to a mother whose work load is lighter.

A full-time homemaker may so make her children her career that she smothers them with more attention than is good for their development or hers. She may so take over the running of the home that her children do not feel that it is their home also, whereas a mother who is employed part time is more able to yield control and to let her husband and children participate and assume responsibility in operating the family home.

Laborsaving Equipment

Modern mothers find laborsaving devices real allies in homemaking activities. In the past, the homemaker spent Monday of every week doing the family wash. By the time she heated the water and scrubbed, rinsed, hung out, and brought in the clothes, she had little energy left for other things. Today, with automatic washers and dryers, a mother may wash several times a week as she goes about doing other things simultaneously. Modern refrigerators, freezers, quick-frozen foods, and prepared products mean that a woman can get an attractive well-balanced meal on the table in a fraction of the time it took her own grandmother. The vacuum cleaner, the floor washer, the modern methods of heating and cooling mean that cleaning the house is not the arduous chore it once was. Miracle fibers have greatly decreased time spent in ironing, sewing, and mending.

With the move to the suburbs has come more out-of-doors living, greater informality, and more participation in food preparation by the man of the house who reigns over the rotisserie, the barbecue pit, or the steak broiler. Children who once resented being "stuck with the dishes" less often mind stacking the dirty dishes in the dishwasher as they help clean up after the family meal. All this can mean greater whole-family participation in a variety of activities, with fewer specialized roles and more overlapping of what used to be clearly woman's work and man's job.

The plethora of new possibilities and new roles now open to women is confusing to many a mother. She no longer feels that her grandmother's roles are adequate for today's family living. She may not feel completely at home in the new roles that she finds herself playing extemporaneously. The courageous, pioneer type mother may glory in the potentialities of her expanding horizons. Others may experience frustration that they cannot be like their own mothers, nor yet resemble their more emancipated neighbors. So they become anxious about just who they are and what they should be doing with themselves as mothers. It is this task of discovering the life style that makes sense for oneself and one's family that is central in motherhood today.

Child-Rearing Challenges

Mothers today approach their motherhood with better education, more experience in business, more mechanical aids, and far more varieties of companionship with other members of the family than traditionally were possible. Mothers now increasingly realize that the way they relate to their children makes a difference in the kind of persons their children become. Modern parents have become aware of the necessity for wholesome, mature, socially creative citizens as vital for the future of our way of life. The 1950 Midcentury White House Conference on Children and Youth and the Golden Anniversary Conference on Children and Youth in 1960 emphasized the urgency of families facing up to their clear challenge as the molders of personality for tomorrow's world.

No other group can perform the family's central function of rearing tomorrow's citizens. Doctors, hospitals, nurses, nutritionists, and other health specialists are valuable resources, but it is the mother in the home who is primarily responsible for her family's health. Schools, colleges, libraries, books, and culture of all kinds basically depend on the mother's ability to funnel through to the children the wisdom and beauty of mankind's accumulated experience. It is the mother, not the psychiatrist, who fosters mental health in the family. No challenge is so great, no task is so important, no satisfaction is so fulfilling as being a mother. EVELYN MILLIS DUVALL

See also CHORES; LOVE

MOTHER-IN-LAW *See* GRANDPARENTS AND OTHER RELATIVES

MOTHER, SEPARATION FROM *See* SEPARATION FROM MOTHER

MOTHER, WORKING *See* WORKING MOTHER

MOTION PICTURES *See* MOVIES

MOTION SICKNESS

Some children have a tendency to develop nausea and vomiting when riding in a car, bus, train, ship, or plane. Although some children may become sick in many types of conveyances, others are bothered by only one or two. The exact reason why one child is more sensitive to motion than another is not known, but children who have more anxiety about traveling seem more prone to motion sickness. If the motion is very bumpy, as in an airplane, almost all children will at some point become sick.

The tendency to sickness while traveling may be reduced by placing the child where he can easily see out of the car. It may also be helpful for him to avoid seats where the motion is accentuated, such as the back of a bus or the tail of an airplane. Drugs are now available which are quite effective in preventing motion sickness. They may be taken in pill form just prior to starting on a trip and may be effective for four to six hours. Such drugs should not, however, be given to children without first consulting your family doctor. JULIUS B. RICHMOND

MOUTH-TO-MOUTH BREATHING *See* ARTIFICIAL RESPIRATION

MOVIES

Nearly all children in elementary school watch films in the classroom, millions see movies at home over television, and about two out of three of these children go to a movie once or twice a month at the local theater. Teen-agers, of course, are inveterate movie-goers, using the movies as a social gathering place for individual or group dates.

Parents can easily control the movie-going of their young child because he goes only when they do. The child of 8 or 9, however, begins to go to movies without his parents, alone or in the company of other youngsters, and often with little or no parental control over what film he sees.

A wide range of film fare is available to young movie-goers, including lavish musicals, westerns, and adult dramas, with their little-understood social problems involving sex and violence, not all of which are labeled, "for adults only." Thoughtful parents realize that they face a serious dilemma. The whole movie question cannot simply be ignored; children need some kind of authority and guidance. The problem becomes: Should parents try to keep tight control over their children's movie habits or should they permit some freedom of choice?

There is no easy solution to this problem. Eventually, parents begin to lose control over movie selection anyway. If too tight controls have been exercised by the parent, if the child's own developing independence has been restricted, he will often go to extremes when he gets some freedom. Films of a type that have been "forbidden" take on an attraction far exceeding their normal interest value—simply because they have been forbidden. Parents who allow their child to choose his own movies are less likely to learn later that he has been defying his parents' wishes and hiding his behavior from them. At the same time, there clearly are movies shown in most communities which offer little or nothing of value to a child. The absence of all restrictions on attendance might expose the child to particular movies that should have been avoided. It is also only fair to point out, however, that a great deal of the content of commercial movies obviously is quite entertaining and is of real educational value.

Some compromise on control offers the wisest path to follow. There is no evidence that movies produce or increase juvenile delinquency, but common sense says that premature exposure to large amounts of violence, sexual activity, and problems of adulthood do not benefit a developing youngster. Some restrictions are necessary, but the fewer placed upon a child, the more likely he is to feel free to talk with his parents. It is most important that parents encourage open and frank communication with their child about the content and meaning of the things he sees. If the child is willing to talk freely at home about what he saw and what he thought it meant, there are fewer grounds for worry. A child gets a feeling of support where it means most if his parents seem to trust him and are sincerely interested in what he is doing and how he feels about things. The loss of this feeling of support represents a much larger danger than any presented by a film.

Restrictions that you might have to make on your child's movie-going can be lessened in at least two ways. First, discussion with other parents often produces agreement on the kinds of movies all will or will not permit their children of a given age group to see. Such agreement reduces the charge from your own child that he is being separated from his friends because they get to do things that he can't do. Second, and equally important, is the possibility of discussion with the management of local theaters. Groups of parents, either on their own or cooperating with civic and social organizations, can influence the theater management to show more appropriate programs at times and on days when the most children go. Parents have considerable influence in this way. It is helpful to remember that most theater managers not only are parents themselves, but that they also are sensitive to the social needs of the community. They will usually make an effort to book the kinds of films that people in the community demand.

The availability of educational movies and projection equipment makes it much easier for parents to let their children see material that is useful and in good taste. Movies are excellent teaching aids. They are likely to attract and keep the attention of the viewer. They bring events and people to life in a way that makes the material enjoyable and easy to remember. You might be surprised at the number of movies you can show for your children at home and the relatively low cost of them. Movies and projectors can be rented in almost any community. A joint showing sponsored by several families can produce social events that are inexpensive fun, educational, and serve to bring family and friends closer together. Family use of movies provides an excellent opportunity to influence young tastes and powers of discrimination without appearing to control a child's own thinking and activities. A good predictor of a child's taste is the old adage, "like parent, like child."

DAVID K. BERLO

Related article in WORLD BOOK: "Audio-Visual Materials"

MOVING TO A NEW NEIGHBORHOOD

Moving from one home to another has become a frequent experience for many American families. Sometimes the move is just to another neighborhood in the same town or city, but more often it involves a real pulling up of family roots and a move from one part of the country to another, or even overseas. If you are faced with the need to move, you will be eager to make it a good experience for your children.

Much will depend upon how *you* feel about the move, for most children follow the lead of their parents. There are always regrets over leaving good friends and a familiar neighborhood where you know the grocery man, the doctor, and the dentist, and are part of your church, the school, and various community activities. These regrets are normal and to be expected. But beyond the normal regrets over leaving the loved and the familiar, the way you act can give to your children either a dread of the unknown or an eagerness to find an interesting and healthy experience in the new life.

A move can be a valuable educational experience for the whole family. Children have to learn how to meet new situations, to adapt to new ways of doing things. Without this ability they will be poorly prepared to meet life in a rapidly changing world. The development of eagerness and curiosity, which makes a new situation a challenge—the encouragement of a genuine interest in finding out about things that are different—is probably better preparation for life than the false sense of security that goes along with the idea that life will always be just as the child has known it.

Tell the Children Beforehand

When the move is decided upon, it is wise to include the children, all except the littlest ones, in making plans. This is one of the ways in which children learn. A matter-of-fact attitude about the move is a good beginning. As one army wife said, "I always tell the children, 'This is what we have to do, so let's do it well.'"

Tell the children why the move is being made, where you are going, and whether it may be for a long or a short time. It is helpful, if it is possible, for father and mother, or at least one parent, to go ahead and actually see what the new situation will be like—the kind of house that will be available, the school facilities, the kind of community in which the family will live. Then the children can be given a firsthand picture of the new community and an idea of some of the advantages and disadvantages to be expected. Whether or not this procedure is possible, get out the maps. Together, find out all you can about the new place or part of the country, or of the world, in which you will be living. Anticipate those less agreeable aspects that might be a problem to the children—differences in climate, in the attitudes or ways of life of the people among whom they will be living and to whom they may have to adapt. Painted all in glowing colors, a move may prove disappointing. A realistic understanding will help the whole family to be prepared to make needed changes in their way of doing things. You will want to interpret local customs and attitudes whenever it is possible to do so, and by your own interest help your youngsters to become absorbed in and fascinated by different ways of doing things rather than to scorn them.

When there are to be real disadvantages or even hardships, as there may be if a family must move to a less well-developed area, it is well to explain to your children what they will find and to give them the feeling that as a family you are able to make the best of things. If family morale is high, children can stand up under many difficult circumstances.

Get into the Swing of Things Quickly

When the family reaches its new home, it is important to feel that you want to become part of the new community right away. For the sake of the children, after the unpacking is done and the house is livable, it is often better to take time to help the family settle into the new life than it is to try to perfect the furnishings and arrangement of the new home. Even before the curtains are up, the children will want to explore the new neighborhood and find other boys and girls with whom to get acquainted.

The first contact usually is with the school. Here is where the life of the children of the community is centered. Some boys and girls have little fear of entering a new group. They are friendly, secure little people who can walk into a new classroom and feel at home in a very short time. Making friends is easy for them. If you have this kind of child, he will probably make friends before you do and will easily make the transition to the new community. But other boys and girls will need more help. If your child is shy or timid or shows uneasiness in the new situation, as many children do, he may need your support as he enters the new school. It would be unfair to send him alone and expect him to face a sea of 30 or more new faces if he is uncomfortable doing so. If your child seems at all reluctant, it is a good idea to take him to the school before the day he will enter and introduce him to the principal and his teacher, and if possible to some of the boys and girls. If your child has school problems, you should ask for an appointment with the principal and teacher before he enters. It is wise to talk quite frankly and honestly with them. If he has had difficulty with any of his schoolwork, if he has physical problems such as poor hearing or vision or poor coordination, or if he has special abilities, the school should know right away so that his needs can be met from the very beginning. Failure to tell the new school of any special problems in the fear of prejudicing the teacher or in the hope that the problems will disappear is not a kindness to your child. Most teachers want to be helpful and can only do their best for a child when they are aware of his particular situation.

In most communities there will be other organized groups who will be eager to help your child feel that he is welcome in his new home. Groups such as young peoples' groups in the church of your choice, Scouts, Camp Fire Girls, 4-H Clubs, and teen-age centers, or the YMCA and YWCA, can be of great help in drawing your boys and girls into activities with others of their own age. Often membership in one of these smaller and more personal groups may make a great deal of difference in the time it takes for your youngster to "settle in."

As soon as possible it is wise to develop a "talking" acquaintance with the neighbors. A friendly attitude toward your new street or community will soon be felt by the neighbors and reflected in their welcome to your children. It is a rare community in which the neighbors will not offer a welcome if you respond to their courtesies. In fact, today, most people have had some experience with moving and establishing their families in a new community and expect to welcome newcomers. Often a kindly neighbor will give a coffee klatch. The fact that you respond to the kindness of neighbors does not mean that you commit yourself to long-term, intimate friendships before you have had time to find out who are the people with whom you are personally congenial, but it does mean that your children will find themselves in a friendly atmosphere and, taking their cue from you, will be better able to meet new boys and girls in a friendly way.

You Can Expect Some Problems

With the best of preparations, however, there will usually be some emotional reactions to be met and understood when children must make a move. What these will be depends upon the kind of child, how old he is, his previous degree of emotional stability, and his previous problems.

A tiny baby or little preschooler will usually take a move very well indeed as long as his parents do not become too rushed or upset so that he feels neglected. The little one will need to have his familiar bed, if possible, his cuddle blanket or favorite doll, some of the toys he is used to, and his customary food. But as long as you are nearby and in sight, and his daily routines are not too disturbed, a move need not be upsetting for a little child. Mother and father are the center of his life. As long as you are there, he is reassured and satisfied.

But as children grow older, it is sometimes more difficult for them to leave behind accustomed activities and special friends. When possible, particular treasures should go along: special collections, books, a much-loved doll, tennis racket, baseball mitt, bicycle. Unless it is impossible, pets should also be included in the family move. If they cannot be taken along, a good home should be found so that the child knows that his dog or kitty or even hamster is being well cared for. Anxiety about the loss of a pet often precipitates a real emotional crisis at the time of leaving. Friends cannot go, but post cards and letters can bridge the gap and, often, visits can be planned and anticipated.

The feelings of children for their friends can be genuine and very intense. A child may be deeply distressed at leaving his best friend, his gang, or his group. This is especially true for older boys and girls of junior and senior high-school age to whom a special friend or membership in a particular group or on a particular team has spelled security and belonging. It often takes time for boys and girls of this age to accept the necessity for a family move or to feel that they will ever be accepted and belong to a new group. A period of loneliness, restlessness, and moodiness may be a reality for some months after the move has been made.

There are two points at which a move seems to be particularly difficult for adolescent boys and girls—when they are in ninth grade and in their senior year of high school. A young person who has looked forward to a last year in his old school may find himself a stranger indeed in the already formed groups of his new school. Membership in some of the smaller, well-organized, and more welcoming groups in the church or community may be helpful.

Friendship groups in the elementary school are usually not so well formed or so exclusive as those in junior and senior high school. If a child has the skill to play games the other children play, he is usually accepted almost casually by those on his block and in the immediate neighborhood. A newcomer can usually find boys and girls to walk to school with and can get to know them in the neighborhood schoolroom as well as on the block. It is easier, also, for the mothers of younger children to get to know each other through informal neighborhood meetings and through the school PTA. Soon the new child is invited into someone's yard, or home for lunch, and friendships begin to develop.

Sometimes a child appears to take a move well and then in a few weeks, when the first excitement is over, seems to slump. There may be real circumstances facing this child which have spoiled his original good adjustment. Perhaps he has not found as many interests in the new neighborhood as he had in the old. Perhaps the new friends are not fully satisfying, or the new teacher or school as stimulating as the ones he has left. A child may be missing an environment in which he was particularly happy. In such circumstances he will need help in accepting his new home. It will be best to help him look at the situation realistically. Accept his feelings and encourage him to tell you about them. Accept the fact that the situation is less than ideal, but do not commiserate too much with him; rather help him to continue to look for ways of making the best of the circumstances as you yourself must do. Talk with the school principal to see if his teachers can help the youngster find more interests or more congenial friends. Encourage him in personal hobbies. If the school should be inadequate, provide him with books and materials that interest him at home. Increase the family trips to places of interest and help him seek for positive things in the environment in which the family must live.

Not All Children React the Same

Children will react differently to a move; it is not always possible to predict just how they will take it. A child who is secure within himself and within the family group, unless the circumstances are unusual, will be able to take a move in his stride, even though he may not at first like the new community as much as the old one. But if a youngster was already unhappy within himself and in his relationships with other people, you may find that his anxiety increases with the move. If the child is truly disturbed and cannot seem to solve his problems, it is usually wise to turn to someone who is trained to help you understand the more fundamental cause of the youngster's unhappiness.

Most youngsters, however, settle into a new community, if not at first, at least within a period of months. Their adjustment is helped considerably if the experience of the move has given the secure feeling that, "Where-ever we live we are a family; we can make a home and meet all kinds of circumstances." This is a fine way to establish the emotional security that will stand a child in good stead all through his life. GLADYS GARDNER JENKINS

See also COMMUNITY RESOURCES; EMOTIONAL DEVELOPMENT; FRIENDS; LONELINESS; POPULARITY; YOUTH ORGANIZATIONS

MUMPS

A case of mumps (infectious parotitis) may occasionally be so mild that it is not recognized. But usually the signs of mumps are so characteristic and so well known that a mother is pretty sure what ails her child as soon as the symptoms appear. The parotid (salivary) glands just below and in front of the ears become swollen and tender. Chills and fever may or may not be present. Most often, one gland reacts this way first, with the other becoming swollen a few days later; sometimes the swelling does not ever affect the second side. The onset of mumps makes it painful for the patient to swallow sour or highly seasoned foods.

Sometimes, though rarely, a child who has had mumps may have a second attack of the disease. When mumps attacks adults, complications can be serious, particularly for adolescent boys and men. Secondary complications may involve the sex glands and sometimes cause sterility.

In some mild cases of mumps the doctor does not insist on bed rest. In a more severe case or with a child past puberty he usually instructs that the patient be kept warm and quiet in bed. MARIE A. HINRICHS

See also COMMON COMMUNICABLE DISEASES; SICK CHILD

MUSCULAR DYSTROPHY

Muscular dystrophy is a disease that attacks the voluntary muscles, such as those controlling arm and leg movements. Often the disease is inherited. It is characterized by a wasting away and a weakness of the muscles. Gradually most of the muscles of the body become affected. Some children are born with symptoms of the disease, but muscular dystrophy does not usually become apparent until early childhood. There is no known cure for muscular dystrophy, but research scientists continue to probe for both its cause and its cure.

Many victims of muscular dystrophy are able to go to school for some time after the onset of the disease; others require more constant care and can be taught at home more easily. There are various kinds of therapy that help to make a muscular dystrophy patient more comfortable and, in some cases, prevent deformities.

Because this disease is at present incurable, the child's happiness and the measure of his physical comfort come first in the minds and hearts of his parents. A happy home, cheerful parents, guests who will keep up the spirit of happiness the parents strive for will help a child who has muscular dystrophy.

See also COMMUNITY RESOURCES; HANDICAPPED CHILD; HOME AND HOSPITAL INSTRUCTION

MUSIC

Music plays an important role in every child's life from the moment his mother holds him in her arms and croons a lullaby. Music is one of the pleasures that bring all members of the family together. Happy experiences with music at home can deepen a child's feelings, stimulate his creativity, develop his taste, and begin a sense of fulfillment that will stay with him for life.

There are no specific, consecutive steps to follow in sustaining a child's love of music, for it is his parents' attitude toward music that counts more than training. If a child feels that his family loves music enough for it to be part of living, and if everyone in his home shares in the enjoyment and relaxation that music adds to family life, he will find it as natural and vivifying as breathing.

Man's primary instrument, the singing voice, can be used by everyone regardless of age—only a few of the millions of adults

who enjoy music perform better than the growing child. Simple, heartfelt songs are the wellspring of music, and natural, spontaneous singing is the common denominator of all music experiences.

Singing together has a way of brightening every day, transforming work into something to look forward to, transforming a pleasure into an unforgettable experience. The child who is slow to move can often be speeded up with a suitable song, and the one who is too full of nervous energy can be slowed down. A simple ditty with lyrics adopted as a family joke relieves tension when tempers are ruffled. Clean-up after a meal or after play is more effectively accomplished if accompanied by singing, as sea chanteys and work songs have proved. But the joy of singing is greatest when song is an end in itself, when the family relaxes together of an evening or whiles away the time in the car on a trip, around the campfire, or on a moonlit beach. This is how music becomes part of a child to stay with him as a sustaining force throughout his entire life.

Where do you find songs that suit these occasions? Mostly in your own background. If you start delving into what you yourself know, you'll come up with more than a hundred titles of songs you remember over the years—nursery songs, camp and community songs, folk songs, hymns and patriotic songs, traditional songs of all sorts, including religious holiday songs. A community song book from the library will refresh your memory. Write down the titles, recapture words and melody, and sing. In little or no time, you'll discover how these songs fit into your family's pattern of living. It is the spirit of a song rather than the literal meaning of its words that makes it usable. Try out a song as you remember it, singing simply and unaffectedly in whatever voice you can muster. Your love of the song is far more important than the way you sing it, for this is what gets across to children, who perceive emotions and don't notice style of performance.

When you have tried out the songs you know, you will want to widen the musical horizon. If you don't read music, the easiest way to learn new songs is by listening to records, which can be bought to build your own record library or borrowed from public libraries. But more challenging and, in the long run, more fun, is to teach yourself to read a melody line. It will take most people only one evening of concentrated work on a keyboard instrument of any sort. If a piano is not available, an inexpensive set of tuned bells will serve the purpose. There are many reasonably priced instruction books on the market to guide you. The best way to practice reading is to examine a familiar song. The mystery of rhythmic and melodic notation will be unveiled along about the third or fourth familiar song you study. Once you have found the key to the code, it will be possible to use many collections of American folk songs to enrich family musical life.

Teachers in the nursery, kindergarten, and primary grades are discovering the value of folk songs at school. They do not hesitate to substitute the name of a child for one in the song or to encourage children to change a line within a familiar tune. This practice can also be followed in the home. Children are highly inventive in making up their own words once they know a song, and they feel perfectly free to improvise a tune to go with an appealing poem or rhyme. Adults would do well to copy the natural creativeness of children.

The sharing of music in the home is a genuine give-and-take between adult and child. There is no audience and no performance as such; therefore there cannot be a critic. With each member making a contribution, music becomes a great equalizer, for no one in the family is in a superior position. What a happy and rare situation for a child. What a delightful recess for a parent.

A musical relationship between you and your child can be further developed through exploring musical sounds and objects right around you. Begin with the ringing, singing, whistling, tapping, and knocking sounds heard inside your house. Listen to pitch, rhythm, and timbre and encourage your child to reproduce them as nearly as possible with his speech organs. Such an exercise has a double purpose: It sharpens and sensitizes the ear and trains the singing apparatus. As the ear becomes increasingly discriminating, crude instruments of rhythm or pitch can be made. The most obvious are drums, made from large boxes or cans, and a row of water glasses tuned to a scale. But the possibilities are endless, as you can see if you study primitive instruments. An interest in sounds can expand to the city streets, the countryside, the seashore, and the woodlands, each area revealing objects that will produce distinctive and rewarding musical sounds. Explore and experiment.

Other more organized trips are also fun. A music store that carries real instruments is a source of never-ending delight for a youngster, who will be welcome in such a place if his interest is sincere. Buying a minor instrument—a tin whistle, an ocarina, a pair of maracas or other percussion instrument, or buying a new paperback collection of folk songs satisfies a child's desire to own things and stimulates family music experimentation.

You can take similar trips to the library, the bell tower of a local church, outdoor community concerts, parades with marching bands, school recitals or performances. Such experiences can give your child a glimpse of the social side of music and proof that music is a pleasure-giver in community life as well as in the home. More formal indoor concerts where the very young child must sit still and be quiet most often bore him and therefore hinder rather than help his musical growth. Musical instruments are explained and illustrated in Volume 8, *How Things Work*, pages 116–141. BEATRICE LANDECK

See also BOOKS FOR CHILDREN; BOOKS FOR PARENTS

MUSICAL INSTRUMENTS

In a family where music plays an important role in everyday life, there is no sharp division between singing and playing musical instruments—that is, if one thinks of man's first musical instrument as the voice. So a child's first instrument to "learn" should be his own voice. Most young children like to sing and can learn to express themselves through song.

But a child's musical expression does not have to be limited to singing. There are easy-to-play instruments that afford pleasure and satisfaction and at the same time provide a sound basis for the study of music. A set of bells in the home, inexpensive to buy and easy to store, encourages picking out melodies by ear or reading simple music, both of great value in musical growth. An instrument that is popular with adults and children alike is the autoharp. It is similar to the zither and requires almost no playing skill, since chords are selected by pressing on buttons marked with the name of the chord. The player then strums the strings and gives an almost "professional" performance.

When a child has played by ear and by note on various easy-to-play instruments and has some definite impressions of music he has heard, he is ready to choose an instrument to study—but the choice must be his own. Children usually like an instrument because of its size, tone quality, or even the way it is played. Boys will often prefer an instrument of the blowing type, and a good way to introduce them to the wind instruments is through the recorder, a kind of wooden flute. Much good music has been written for the recorder, and it may be preferable to a band instrument for some preteen-agers because less breath is required to produce a good tone.

Some children like the harmony of string instruments such as the ukelele, banjo, or guitar. The violin and cello are much more difficult to play, but if a child seems interested in either one, by all means, let him try.

Still other children may prefer a keyboard instrument such as the piano or the accordion. There is more music available for the piano than for any other instrument, and, like the bells, it gives a child a good foundation if he wishes to play other instruments later on.

But suppose none of these instruments interests a child. Then, perhaps, he might like something a little unusual, such as a drum, a tom-tom or Latin-American maracas, or castanets. Or he may even like to make his own instrument of tuned water glasses or bottles. For specific suggestions see Volume 9, *Make and Do*, pages 20–23.

Any musical instrument that a child might choose to play serves a double purpose: It materializes elements of music that are elusive in singing and it gives him pleasure in accomplishment. It also lays the foundation for future study in music. BEATRICE LANDECK

See also BOOKS FOR CHILDREN; MUSIC
Related article in WORLD BOOK: "Music"

MUSIC FOR BABY

It is never too early to start your baby on his way to enjoying music. From the physical point of view, music seems to be the birthright of every newborn: Hearing is the keenest of his senses, and his first voiced sounds are more related to singing than to speech. You can have fun extending your baby's expressive powers while giving him the comfort and joy that musical vibrations convey.

During the first year of their baby's life, both parents have a chance to find themselves musically, too, experimenting with melody patterns in the speaking voice, varying pitch, rhythm, tempo, and intensity, and making up snatches of tunes with appropriate words of endearment or encouragement. One is never self-conscious with a baby, and even the most timid parent will dare to explore his voice range for the infant listener. This kind of musical play is a delightful introduction to music.

You will soon notice that a quiet song has a marked effect on a baby. The custom of singing lullabies is not only international; it goes back in time as far as recorded history. How important it must be then that no child is denied his natural heritage. It doesn't matter what you sing as long as you give your baby the comfort of a quieting song. Everyone knows some lullabies, but if none occur to you when you want to sing to your baby, make them up.

A "live" voice, however inferior in quality, means more to a baby than a voice on a record. One is warm and adaptable to the immediate needs; the other cold, forever fixed and inflexible. But you can profit from records, not only by learning new songs from them, but also by listening to the treatment given a song. When your baby is walking, he may enjoy marching or dancing to recorded music, sometimes joined by other family members in a "follow-the-leader" game.

At an early age, encourage your child to imitate the sounds he hears about him, such as the starting of a motor, the bang of a door, the meow of a cat, or the bark of a dog. Animate his picture books, too, with sounds that belong with the illustrations so that when he looks at them again, he will add his own sound effects. This kind of musical play is the first step in awakening his ears to the music around him. Another kind of musical play with a special appeal for young children is a game of contrasts: high and low, loud and soft, fast and slow, jerky and smooth. These basic music concepts are learned unconsciously as they are enjoyed.

A 2½- or 3-year-old who has been surrounded with music from birth will begin to sing fragments of songs with some differentiation in pitch (not accurate) and will recognize familiar tunes without the help of lyrics. But of far greater importance is the promise that he will feel on comfortable, easy terms with music and look to it for pleasure and refreshment. BEATRICE LANDECK

See also MUSIC; PHONOGRAPH RECORDS

MUSIC LESSONS

A child is ready for music lessons with a professional teacher when he has some familiarity with music and a great desire to pursue it further. Without musical play, casual singing, experimentation with simple instruments, and an awareness of the social side of music, formal lessons become a dry, technical drill. One studies an instrument to extend his ability to express himself. But there is nothing to express until he realizes the existence of musical ideas—his own and others—and has the beginning of a musical vocabulary. Failure in accomplishment is due more to lack of musical background than to the old excuse of disliking to practice.

If you have been unable to provide a natural musical background of singing and simple instruments for your child, let him join a relaxed group where musical play and experimentation are the guiding principles. If no such group exists in your locality, ask the most enlightened music teacher to organize one; he or she is certain to see the wisdom of your suggestion. For one thing, it is only after experience of this kind that a child can make a thoughtful choice of the instrument he wants to study. Do not assume that the piano is the only choice open to him.

The choice of a teacher is also important. In general, children do better, especially in the beginning, if they take their lessons in the teacher's studio rather than at home. There, they usually find various instruments in addition to the chosen one, collections of music to look through, and books about music to borrow, a phonograph and records for demonstration, and perhaps also a tape recorder. This kind of enrichment adds interest to lessons; it also shows the child the many facets of the art.

Another advantage in going to a teacher's studio for lessons is that a child may meet friends and schoolmates who are there for the same purpose. Some teachers offer group instruction for beginning students, ensemble playing for the more advanced, and informal recitals in which parents take part along with the children. This helps to socialize learning and relieves the feeling of isolation that private lessons sometimes give.

You can help your child enjoy his lessons by showing an interest in what he is doing and by continuing your own musical learning. A mother or father who seeks to improve his skills without competing with a youngster serves as a convincing example of the worth of study. In addition, such a parent will better understand the problems with which the child is coping and be better able to judge his progress.

The investment in music lessons and an instrument cannot be protected with watchfulness and anxiety. No one knows how or when musical growth takes place. A child may learn more when he seems to be dawdling or playing at an instrument than when he reads a page of music from the upper left-hand corner to the lower right. Trust in his own way of learning and in his teacher's guidance; let him determine his goals and how best to achieve them.

Practicing

Their child's music practice is often a worry to parents, perhaps because they as children hated to practice and finally gave up lessons rather than go through the agony of being prodded by a parent. Inevitably they suffer regret and sincerely want to give their offspring what they missed. If this description applies to you, why not profit by experience and avoid repeating the pattern with your child? Instead of transferring to the child your own feeling about practicing, rest assured that times have changed and teaching is more stimulating now than it was in your day. An adult's attitude is so quickly conveyed to a child.

Your responsibility about practicing is to plan with your child the time he will use, a time that does not interfere with his outdoor play and that will be free from all household interruption. Let him know that this is his quarter- or half-hour to spend with music, making his own discoveries and drawing his own conclusions without interference.

No matter how well you pave the way, don't expect your child to head straight for the destination. Unless he is a dedicated musician, he may stray from the path, may even prefer a course different from the one you foresaw. That is no cause for alarm; perhaps he is inventing music of the future, which is totally beyond the comprehension of older folk. On the other hand, if after a fair trial he prefers to study another instrument or to give up lessons entirely, neither time nor money has been wasted. There are innumerable outlets for the expression of music when a child's original interest has been preserved. Not all music-lovers are instrumentalists.

BEATRICE LANDECK

See also MUSIC; MUSICAL INSTRUMENTS

MYOPIA *See* NEARSIGHTEDNESS

Your child is ready for music lessons even when very young.

NAGGING

Nagging seldom plays a useful role in any human relationship whether between adults or among adults and children. Two damaging results almost always occur. First, children tend to "tune out" the nagging voice that surrounds them. The adult keeps on talking but the youngster stops listening. This leads to wasted effort on the adult's part. It also holds the danger that children will not be "tuned in" when the adult has something new or really important to say. Secondly, nagging destroys relationships. A child who is constantly pestered by an adult is no longer glad to see that adult; he does not welcome his company or enjoy his presence. This coldness in the relationship can have a serious long-run effect in undermining the very discipline the nagging adult hopes to achieve. The everlasting harping on misbehavior defeats its own end.

Despite the futility and dangers of nagging, and despite our own dislike of being nagged, almost all who live with children are tempted at times to indulge in this vice. When we find ourselves scolding children over and over for the same misdeeds, several possibilities are worth exploring. The persistence of the child's behavior ought to raise in our minds the question: Is this perhaps the right way for a child his age to act? Maybe we are trying to stop, through nagging, normal behavior that is healthy and universal at this stage of development. Or, if this seems not to be the case, we should ask whether the child's persistent act can be a symptom of some fundamentally important need that is not being satisfied in the course of his daily living.

The child's persistence in the face of our obvious disapproval often is an indication of how important that need is to him. Rather than try to scold him out of the symptom, it would be wiser and much more helpful to meet the need. Still another possibility is that we may be relying too much on words alone to change behavior. A young child in particular might need physical help from us to get a job done, or at least our cheerful company. But whether any of these alternatives seems to be the answer, the fact is: The urge to nag ought to warn us that there is something wrong somewhere. Simply talking more seldom helps. JAMES L. HYMES, JR.

See also DISCIPLINE; HUMOR

NAIL-BITING

Children have many ways of revealing that all is not well with their world. Nail-biting is one of these ways. Ear-pulling and hair-pulling or twisting are others. Each gives evidence of a child under strain. Unconsciously perhaps, he is easing his anxious feelings through biting, pulling, twisting.

None of these so-called nervous habits are serious in themselves. In mild form they are to be expected, at some time, in all children. Threats, punishment, and restraints do not help a child. Neither do bribes and rewards. Such devices serve only to focus attention on his mannerism and increase his tension. If by some chance you do stop one kind of jittering, anxious feelings are likely to break out in some other way—unless you can discover what is disturbing your child.

Does he bite his nails only while watching a scary movie or TV program? Less exciting entertainment is an obvious substitute, but it is better for the easily excited child to create his own entertainment. Even better, encourage your nail biter to let off steam, whenever possible, in active outdoor play.

Does homework bring on an attack of nail-nibbling? Now is not the time to call an anxious school child's attention to still another problem. This problem may be solved at least temporarily by a bowl of apples, a pitcher of milk, or even a package of chewing gum, cheerfully offered.

Is school a possible source of tension? Some children fear tests, teachers, failure, the teasing or bullying of other children. Talk to your child's teacher. She may be able to offer an extra bit of friendly encouragement or attention. Or she may find ways to provide opportunities for him to enjoy some measure of success in his schoolwork or to appear important in the eyes of his classmates.

Perhaps the most difficult area for a parent to look for the root of a nervous habit is in the parent-child or family relationship. Are you, by any chance, managing the child within an inch of his life? Does your definition of being "good" really mean being "perfect"? Is a new baby getting all your affectionate attention? Is there quarreling and bickering between parents or other adults in the home? These are hard questions to face, but they are worth facing.

A child needs to know that his place in the family is secure, that he is loved even when his behavior is something less than perfect. A smile, a caress, a word of encouragement at the right moment, a 15-minute romp or storytelling session—these are tangible expressions that can comfort a child and lessen his tensions.

Most of the time nail-biting can be ignored, but not the nail biter.

See also EMOTIONAL DEVELOPMENT; NAIL CARE

NAIL CARE

Nails require regular care to keep them neat. Warm water plus scrubbing with a moderately stiff brush will coax the dirt from under tiny nails. Either a manicure scissors or an emery board can be used to keep nails short. The baby's manicure should be done with a special pair of blunt-edged scissors and may take place at bath time or when he is asleep and not so wiggly. Cut the nails straight across so that they will be less likely to curve into the flesh.

Sharp-pointed scissors should be kept well out of reach of a child and should be used only when his nails are cut by an adult. Even when a child can care for his own nails, an emery board is safer to use. As a hangnail preventive, a child can be taught to push back the cuticle gently with the towel as he dries his hands after washing. As a further step, when cuticles are unusually dry, they can be lubricated with cream in the same way as rough hands, or the fingertips may be allowed to soak in warm olive oil.

A little girl who wants to look grown up can have her nails buffed to a high gloss with the special powder and buffer included in most children's manicure sets. A manicure set sometimes provides the special inducement a child needs to stop nail-biting. At least, it's worth a try. Clear or slightly tinted nail polish is usually considered acceptable for use by girls in their teens. VERONICA L. CONLEY

NAKEDNESS *See* NUDITY

NAMING THE BABY

In the secret world mother and baby share before the miracle of birth, the problem of what to call him is usually solved very simply. She calls him Baby. To others, he is The Baby. But there comes a day when society demands a much more dignified and distinctive name. What shall it be?

A baby's potential appearance, his background, and, of course, his family name must all be given careful consideration.

Family traditions play a large part in naming many babies. "All first boys in our family are named William," one new father says proudly. But mother has something to say about it, too. If parents cannot agree, the father might forever call his son William while the mother calls him George—a confusing situation for the child, his friends, and his school alike.

Naming the baby for a relative is sometimes a favor to the child, sometimes not. Difficult-to-pronounce, old-fashioned names often give a child a lifelong burden. Also, family names used as first names sometimes prove to be the butt of many jokes—Parker Daley, for example, or Hamilton Bone, who will always be Ham Bone.

Will a baby girl's name combine well with the name of the man she marries? Nobody knows, of course, but a simple, conservative name will be more likely to blend pleasantly than one that is odd or too flowery.

Avoid giving children names that are in vogue at any one moment. We may find eight Kathys in kindergarten who will travel the remaining grades in confusion. Naming a child for a famous person may tend to date him or her. For example, Shirleys and Judys came by the thousands throughout the era when Shirley Temple and Judy Garland were child movie stars.

Parents who have planned specifically for either a boy or a girl sometimes relieve their disappointment by using a boy's name for a girl or a girl's name for a boy. Ask a boy who has gone through life as Shirley or La Verne, or a girl called Frankie or Johnnie, what confusion, even embarrassment, they have known.

The sound of a name is important. Avoid a first name with a vowel ending when the last name begins with a vowel—Anna Enders or Leo Allen. The adding of a middle name breaks the monotony of the vowel sequence, Leo John Allen, for example. Family names are often used successfully as middle names and are sure to please family members.

Names that have a rhythm are pleasant sounding. A two-syllable first name combines well with a three-syllable last name—Marlene Anderson or Patrick Allingham. Or the reverse, Patricia Carter or Meredith Johnson.

A family named Lee may use longer first names for its children. The Hendrickson or the Hickenlooper families, however, would do well to stay with John or Jean, Beth or Bart, or any short one-syllable name.

Consider the nicknames your child may acquire. Charles will be Chuck or Charlie; Michael will be Mike; Suzanne will be Susie; Rose will be Rosie. Are you satisfied with nicknames? You'd better be, because despite the family's efforts to call Richard by his name, his friends will most surely call him Dick.

If you call your baby "Princess" or "Skipper" or "Chipper" or "Peaches," the pet name will probably stick. Will he appreciate it later?

Give your child a name he can proudly carry. Parents may well feel pleased when a child says, "I like my name."

NAPS

As your new baby becomes accustomed to his world, he will require less and less sleep during the day. Most children, however, continue to need one nap, usually in the afternoon, until they are about 3 years old. From then on the afternoon nap becomes less frequent and may stop by the time the child is 5. Afternoon naps after 3 years should be short—not more than an hour, lest they interfere with readiness for sleep in the evening. Of course, in times of illness or when for other reasons more sleep is required, a child can benefit from morning as well as afternoon naps. Some parents feel that a long nap right after lunch prevents overtiredness in the evening and actually helps the child to go to bed more readily and to sleep more easily.

Both you and your child will find it helps if daytime sleeping routines follow those of bedtime; that is, getting undressed, using the same crib or junior bed, and having the same favorite toy alongside. A darkened room usually is desirable during the day as well as at night, but no attempt should be made to exclude all light or to avoid all noise. Your baby may be able to sleep comfortably in his carriage either indoors or out. But if he regularly naps outdoors in his carriage, he may resent being transferred to his crib at other times of the day or at night. If sleeping outdoors, he should be protected from insects, dust and smoke, and from people who may keep him awake or awaken him from sleep.

Older children may not be able to sleep but may be willing to play quietly in bed during naptime. If the child is relaxed, he is receiving most of the advantages of a nap. Both the preschool and the school-age child who are supposed to rest during the daytime frequently find relaxation in reading, working puzzles, listening to music, or drawing. When the habit of relaxing follows an established family pattern, children more readily follow suit. A mother who lies down after lunch and a father who does so on weekends encourage their children to nap or rest.

MILTON J. E. SENN

See also SLEEP

NAUSEA *See* FOOD POISONING; STOMACH-ACHE; VOMITING

NAVEL

The navel, or umbilicus, is the point at which the umbilical cord of an unborn baby and the placenta of its mother are attached. The cord is the channel for nourishment and oxygen from mother to unborn child. After the birth, the cord is clamped and cut. The small remnant left at the navel gradually dries up, turns dark, and falls off in about a week. The navel looks a little red for a few days but quickly heals. Until the navel is healed, keep it clean by covering it (and the remnant of the cord) with a gauze pad on which a little alcohol is sprinkled. Any marked redness, swelling, or bleeding around the navel should be reported to your doctor. After the navel is healed, the baby can have a tub bath. From then on, the navel requires no special care.

Very frequently when small babies cry, a small protrusion appears near the navel. This protrusion, called a hernia, comes about because the muscles running up and down on either side of the navel are not yet strong and the connecting tissue has not yet closed. These hernias usually disappear without special treatment or surgery by the time the child is 12 to 18 months old.

A tight belly binder will neither prevent the hernia nor cure it and need not be used. And, of course, the fact that the hernia shows up more when the baby is crying is no reason to believe that he should never be permitted to cry.

RUTH S. KEMPE

See also BATHING THE BABY; HERNIA

NEARSIGHTEDNESS (MYOPIA)

The nearsighted, or myopic, eye is wider in the front-to-back diameter than the normal eye. Just as some people normally grow taller than others, so eyes can also grow to various sizes.

Fortunately, very few children develop a high degree of nearsightedness, although quite a number have mild to moderate disability. The major problem for a nearsighted child is twofold: He does not see clearly and he does not know that he does not see clearly.

To myopic eyes, the world looks like this.

The condition, therefore, is usually discovered by routine testing. It is true that a nearsighted child may hold things close, but so will a farsighted child on occasion. Nearsighted children may also keep their eyelids partially closed to make a tiny slit, a device that enables them to see clearly.

It is important that all children be seen by an ophthalmologist (medical eye doctor) when they are ready for the first grade, sooner if their parents observe suspicious behavior pointing to eye trouble. If nearsightedness is discovered, the doctor will measure its degree and will prescribe glasses. As a child's shoe size changes, so his glasses may need a change in power. The only way a nearsighted child can be assured of correct glasses at all times is to have regular examinations. Your doctor will tell you how often your child should return.

Children who are nearsighted should be allowed to use their eyes as much as they wish. They cannot save their eyes by not using them, nor does use make their nearsightedness worse. Vision is stimulated and its use is learned by practice, much as playing the piano increases facility of the hand muscles. ROY O. SCHOLZ

See also EYE HEALTH

NEATNESS *See* MESSINESS

NEGATIVISM *See* "NO-NO"

NERVOUSNESS *See* ANXIETY

NEW BABY

The coming of a baby into a home is bound to cause a certain amount of conflict. From time to time mixed feelings will be aroused in parents as well as in brothers and sisters no matter how enchanting and welcome the newcomer is.

Most fathers of first babies, for example, have their moments of wondering if their wives will ever again be as considerate and understanding as they were before the baby's arrival. New mothers have their bad times, too, when they feel resentful or depressed about being so "tied down"—or about what seems to them lack of consideration on their husbands' part. And if the new baby is not a first one, the children in the family will inevitably feel on occasion that life was better before the baby came. But once we accept the fact that feelings such as these are universal and are nothing to be ashamed of, that love and resentment often walk hand in hand, it is amazing how much inconvenience we can put up with.

Before the Baby Comes

When do parents start preparing an older child for the arrival of a new baby? Before the mother goes off to the hospital, of course, but the precise when and how depend on the child's age. With very young children—those under 3—we delay as long as possible, since waiting is generally hard on these little ones. Usually we say nothing until they give us the cue, by noticing mommie's changed appearance or her preparations for the baby's coming. But if by the last month of pregnancy the small child still doesn't seem aware of changes, his mother has to take the initiative. She explains that she is growing a baby and she answers any questions this information may lead to. At some point she should inform her child that she will go to the hospital to have the baby, tell him who will take care of him while she is away, and reassure him that his father will be around as usual during this time.

Though no small child likes the idea of being separated from his mother, there are ways to soften this blow. Most toddlers adore talking on the telephone. You might promise your child that while you are at the hospital you will call him every morning and every night. Let him have an opportunity ahead of time to get used to the sound of your voice on the phone. You can call from a neighbor's sometime when your husband is at home.

Some children seem better equipped than others to take a new baby in stride.

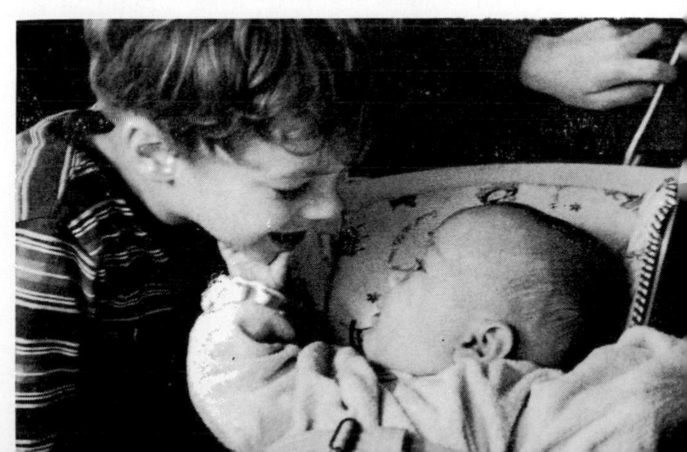

It also helps to plan something special for your child and his father to do during the time you will be in the hospital—a trip to the zoo, the firehouse, or a nearby dairy, a meal out—any treat to look forward to. And you might get or make a present to be given to him when you leave for the hospital.

Preschoolers—children 3 to 6—need to be told earlier in your pregnancy that a baby is on the way, although again not until they notice something is different. A preschooler is usually enormously excited at the prospect of getting a baby, full of questions (which should be answered honestly), and anxious to be involved in readying the new baby's bed and layette. Let him help as much as possible, even if his help is an inconvenience at times. In the process, he gains understanding of the care that an infant needs and so will be better prepared for the demands that are going to be made on your time. After the baby arrives, little girls—and many boys, too—often like to pretend that a doll or a cuddly toy is a live baby and care for it in just the way that mommie cares for the new brother or sister. This game not only occupies them happily but also heightens their sense of being a part of all that is going on. It might well be started before the birth of the baby.

Youngsters of school age, for whom waiting is easier, can be told the news very early, even before you tell relatives and friends. Children enjoy being in on a secret and it helps them to feel grown up. Use their excitement as a springboard for some intimate talk about how excited both their parents were before *they* arrived, what they were like as babies, what it is like to be a parent and watch children grow physically and intellectually. This kind of closeness before the baby comes will reassure your school-ager about his lasting hold on your affections and help him to see life through your eyes later on whenever the going gets a bit hectic.

Return from the Hospital

A word about your return from the hospital: Things usually go more smoothly if the older children are out of the house for school or play when you bring the baby home. You can get the baby settled and then have a good chance to devote a little uninterrupted time to the other children when they return. Usually, the older ones will want to hold the baby the minute he wakes up. Why not let them sit in the middle of a bed or a large chair while you place him in a brother's or a sister's arms? There's nothing like the feel of a newborn to bring out those

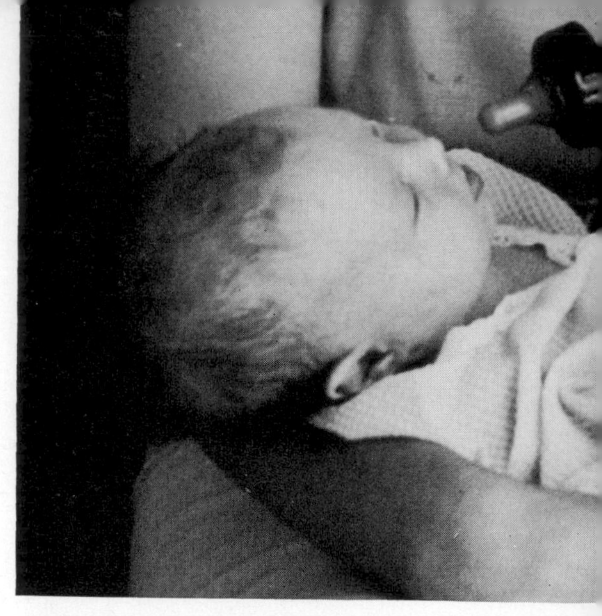

positive emotions of love and protectiveness, even in the very young.

You will soon acquire a knack for handling an infant and an older child at one and the same time. You will learn how to let your older child help with bathing and diapering the baby, how to carry on a relaxed conversation with your eldest while your hands are busy with other work—even, perhaps, how to read a story while nursing your infant.

But don't for a moment think, as some mothers mistakenly do, that if you just manage matters expertly enough, you can keep your older child from ever having any negative feelings about the new baby. That's neither a realistic nor a desirable goal. The way in which these negative feelings show themselves will depend, of course, upon your child's individual temperament—and the emotional climate of your home. Some youngsters come right out with their resentment or jealousy: "I hate my brother!" or "You don't love me any more!" they wail. Be careful to show neither shock nor anger. What is called for is patient reassurance that feeling mad at the baby is understandable—that the lot of an older child is indeed difficult at times, but that it has its compensations, too. Given this kind of sympathy, your youngster will usually become his sunny self in short order. Such incidents may indicate, however, that you need to step up compensations, give special privileges, such as staying up later at night, being read to more, and having more outings with one or both parents.

Other children show their distress in a more roundabout fashion. They may pretend that the baby belongs to another family and has only come to visit. Or they may hug him so strenuously that he cries. Frequently they regress to younger ways of coping with

the world: thumb-sucking, clinging to mommie as they never did before, insisting on having a bottle just like their new brother or sister. A child who has been toilet trained for some time may begin to wet his bed again at night or have daytime accidents. Similarly, a child who has always been happy in school may suddenly decide he doesn't like it and beg to stay home. (There's no harm in letting him do so once or twice.) Again, reassure rather than reprimand, devote more time to your older child, and look for enjoyable activities in keeping with his age and status which will make him feel that being more grown up is fun.

What about the youngster who, his mother insists, "has never shown the slightest sign of being jealous"? Most likely, such a mother is exaggerating. Perhaps she has forgotten certain incidents in the past because her children get along so well today. Some children really do seem by nature better able to make the most of everything that comes their way—to enjoy the good and take frustrations in stride—while others achieve this kind of maturity more slowly, require more help. Or perhaps the mother has never put two and two together: She simply does not connect her older child's nightmares, shyness, trouble at school, or what not with the new baby in the house because the older child is always so sweet with the baby.

This leads to an important question: Should parents be concerned about a youngster who continually shows nothing but affection for the new baby. It is often hard to know. As long as the child doesn't develop problems in other areas, it is best to simply watch and wait. Some youngsters, especially those over 4, are not threatened by an infant; their difficulties come later, when the baby has begun to walk, talk, and get into everything. But parents should ask themselves if their own behavior makes it hard for their children to own up to feelings of annoyance or hostility. Parents might make a special point of letting an older child know that it is permissible to feel things other than love for the baby. For example, a mother could say one day when her youngster is being noticeably affectionate with the baby, "He *is* sweet, isn't he, even if he is such a bother sometimes."

Last, but Very Important

A final suggestion for husband and wife: Try not to be so preoccupied with your children that you neglect each other's small needs. Be a neat wife, with combed hair and straight lipstick when your husband comes home. Put as many of the baby's things away as is possible just before your husband returns. A large cardboard carton or a laundry cart that you can fill and then shove into a closet will let you accomplish this task in a matter of minutes.

Reciprocally, be an attentive husband; bring home flowers now and then or a gay gift, no matter how small. Together, get out by yourselves occasionally—or simply take some time off from parental and household duties to read or chat; it will help both you and your partner to enjoy your children more, and make life increasingly rewarding as your family grows. MARY BIDGOOD HOOVER

See also BROTHERS AND SISTERS; NURSE; REGRESSION; SEPARATION FROM MOTHER; SEX EDUCATION

NEW FOODS *See* INTRODUCING NEW FOODS

NEW NEIGHBORHOOD *See* MOVING TO A NEW NEIGHBORHOOD

NIACIN *See* VITAMINS

NICKNAME *See* NAMING THE BABY

NIGHTMARES

The sleep of a child from 2 to 5 years old is often broken by dreams—sometimes pleasant dreams, but more often frightening, and as real to him as though they were actually happening. Fears and frustrations of the day spill over into the night, resulting in nightmares from which he awakens crying or screaming. Actually, such dreams serve as safety devices for getting rid of feelings he cannot live with, and to that extent they are good. But alone and terrified in the darkness, your child needs all the comfort you can give him.

Waken a child who is having a nightmare, speak to him soothingly, and encourage him to tell you about his dream. He may be too terrified to give more than a garbled account, but listen carefully, for there may be a clue, if not to the cause of this particular disturbing dream, then to other problems that have been troubling him.

It is impossible, of course, to eliminate all worry and anxiety in children, so there can be no way to prevent bad dreams altogether. But tensions in the home over money or in-laws, the arrival of a new baby, or the viewing of scary TV programs can create within a child anxiety that finds an outlet in bad dreams. Perhaps a little more attention to his emotional security will help him to sleep more peacefully. MILTON J. E. SENN

See also ANXIETY; DARK, FEAR OF THE; FEAR; SLEEP

NIPPLES *See* BOTTLE FEEDING; BREAST CARE AND BREAST FEEDING; LAYETTE AND BABY EQUIPMENT

NOISE

Almost immediately after birth an infant responds to sounds. If the sound is of moderate intensity and occurs suddenly, he will probably react with the so-called startle pattern: If lying on his back, he will blink his eyes, extend his arms outward and upward, straighten and then bend his legs. If the noise is loud enough, the startle may accompany or be followed by crying.

A baby's response to varying degrees of noise will depend on how wide awake he happens to be. If he is sleeping soundly, he may not "startle" to a loud noise; if he is sleeping only moderately well, he may startle but not waken.

Parents often worry lest the slightest degree of noise waken their babies. This does not have to be the case, for infants get used to most types of repeated sensory experiences. Thus the baby with a number of noisy older brothers and sisters simply does not "hear" their noise. How much any given noise will disturb a baby will be in part determined by how much that noise stands out from the background noises. It is, therefore, not necessary to go to extremes to reduce ordinary household noises in order for most infants to sleep comfortably. BETTYE M. CALDWELL

See also SLEEP

"NO-NO"

When you say "no," or as you probably phrase it, "no-no," to a little child, it is usually either to protect him or to save some precious object. Whether or not the prohibition will be effective depends on the age of the child, for his response to "no" can vary greatly with his age and development.

Your 9-month-old child can comprehend to some degree what your "no-no" means. It is surprising and gratifying to watch his response to your command. He suddenly stops what he was doing, yet stopping doesn't necessarily mean that he won't repeat the behavior you were objecting to. Nor does it mean that you will stop saying "no."

"No-no" is in fact used so frequently by parents that babies often think it is the signal for a game. A 1-year-old child who hears his mother say "no-no," might conceivably stop his objectionable activity, but he is much more apt to smile or laugh and continue whatever it was he was doing. The parent, too, often joins the fun, delighted with the spunky give and take.

This game, however, soon loses its flavor. By the time your toddler is 15 months old, and you say "no," he may boldly insist on going ahead with his explorations. Try distracting his attention or substituting another activity rather than persisting, for your persistence can lead only to his tears or to an unwarranted punishment. Even a gentle slap on the hand does not accomplish what you want, for the sensitive child may be frightened by the slap and the hardy one only stimulated to repeat the forbidden act.

The child of 18 months is very frequently balky and negative. Furthermore, the more resistant and repetitive his parent is, the more the child will reply in kind. This suggests that guile and a friendly approach from the parent will accomplish more in the long run than parental severity or stubbornness. A stern "no-no" to a child at this age may make him only want to pick up a forbidden object, run away with it, and possibly drop and

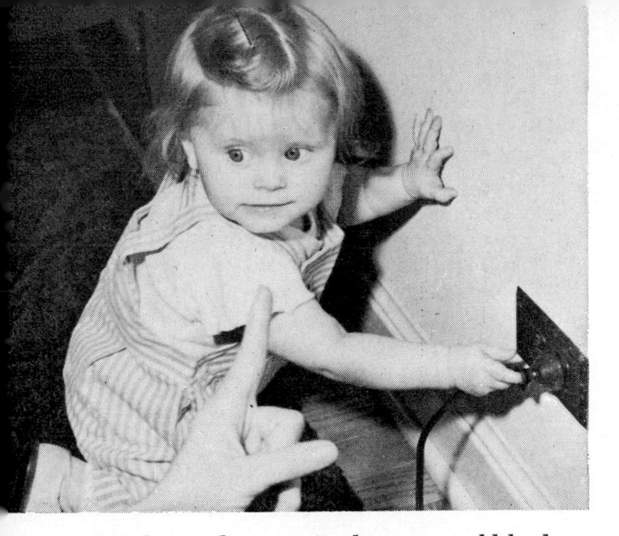

break it as he runs. Perhaps it would be better if the parent picked up the child and laughingly carried him away from the object he was not to touch. True, he will improve by 21 months, when he teases, on purpose, with a charming glint in his eye. A little later the teasing stage, too, passes, and he comes to recognize that certain things should be left where they belong and that certain other things belong to him or to mommy or to daddy. Now he hoards his possessions to himself. "Dat mine," rings through the house. He is the first one to put things back and to be disturbed by change of place. This trend will become even stronger by the time he is 2½ years old.

During his resistant stages a child needs to have his environment simplified. He needs to be kept out of places such as the living room, with its bright temptations. There are other areas that can be adapted more surely to the toddler—the kitchen, his bedroom, and outdoor play space. "No-no" is needed then only when danger lurks. The warning can be very effective if used only in these moments. Otherwise, resort to wiles—substitution, distraction, or simply pick him up and take him to another place. The toddler is pliable if handled skillfully. Lessons you wish to teach him will come later when he is ready.

When he does finally improve, when he has learned not to touch forbidden articles, you may be inclined to credit scolding or punishment. But you would be leaving out of your calculations the power of innate growth. Remember that growth is on your side—everything in due season. And it is the child who often leads the way. He is often ready to obey by the time he is 2 years old. At that age he wants to please. Listen to his query at 2 years: "Dat right?"—and know that many "no-no" battles have been futile and quite unnecessary. FRANCES L. ILG

See also DISCIPLINE; HUMOR

NORMAL CHILD

The most reassuring words that new parents can hear about their baby is that he is normal. He is sound of mind and body. He is not a "blue" baby, his arms and legs and hands and feet are well formed. He does not have a cleft palate. All the interrelated pieces that make up this tiny new human being fit together into a harmonious whole.

A normal child is not the same thing as an average child. In the first place, there is no average child. A child may be of average size or intelligence, but he is always a unique individual who cannot be reduced to an average of all his parts. In the second place, a child may be above or below average in some traits and yet be completely normal.

A child is thought of as not being normal when he falls outside of safe or acceptable limits with respect to some characteristic, either inborn or as a result of illness, accident, or neglect. Perhaps an eye does not function as it should; perhaps he is crippled by cerebral palsy; perhaps he has lost a hand in an accident; or perhaps he has a learning problem caused by unfavorable home conditions.

It is apparent then that the whole idea of normality is based on minimum levels considered necessary for proper functioning. What is known as 20/20 vision remains the standard, whether or not most of the children in a community deviate from it. If a child does not come up to the standard set for vision, speech, hearing, or mental or emotional functioning, he is considered to deviate from normal in some aspect of his growth, development, or behavior. This deviation may be within safe limits or it may be gross. Judgment should be left to the child's doctor.

Parents of children who are normal in every way should rejoice daily. Such children are favored at the outset in the search for full, meaningful, and happy lives. Too many parents are less than content with normality in their child and endanger this precious asset by seeking to have him become something counter to his developing nature. They create unnecessary pressures which, in turn, produce abnormal behavior where none existed before.

Little by little, education is destroying the wall of ignorance and superstition that has kept so many childhood maladies hidden from view. Parents are learning to watch closely for signs of visual or hearing loss, bone or muscle impairment, unusual emotional outbursts, and overly aggressive social behavior. Proper medical care, including psychiatric, often leads to early detection and cure of some abnormality before it becomes crippling. In modern societies, at least, a minor deviation from normal need not distort the life of a child. JOHN I. GOODLAD

See also GROWTH; HEREDITY; MENTAL HEALTH; SOCIAL PRESSURES

NOSEBLEED

A nosebleed may come from a punch in the nose or from the spontaneous rupture of a blood vessel within the nose. The spontaneous rupture may be a result of infection, or it may happen if a child injures himself when picking his nose or poking something into it.

Popular remedies for nosebleed, such as putting a cold key on the back of the child's neck, may be dismissed. For mild nosebleeds the simplest measure is to close the bleeding nostril by applying pressure on the outside with the finger until bleeding stops. A cold, wet towel held on the nose may help. In the meantime, it is best to have your child sit up with his head held backward rather than to have him lie down. Another effective measure is to place a small, tight roll of toilet paper under the upper lip, and thus make pressure on the arteries that supply the blood to the nose.

If the nosebleed does not respond promptly to simple measures, it may be necessary to call for medical aid. Your doctor may simply pack the patient's nose with gauze or, in some instances, he may need to cauterize the small bleeding points. Since a child may lose considerable blood from long-continued bleeding, it is best not to rely on home first aid too long before calling a doctor. W. W. BAUER

See also BLEEDING

NOSE DROPS

A doctor will occasionally prescribe nose drops in the final stages of a cold when a child's nose is stuffy but not in the early stages when the secretions are flowing freely.

Nose-drop preparations may contain ephedrine, a drug that causes the blood vessels in the mucous membranes to shrink, or related compounds in a salt solution. Oily solutions should not be used—they may get into the lungs of babies and young children and cause a chemical pneumonia.

Nose drops or sprays should be used only on the suggestion of a doctor and in the amounts he specifies. Young children can get an overdose of the active drugs in these solutions. And nose drops should not be continued indefinitely. If long-continued use seems necessary, it is better to look for the cause of the difficulty and to see why the condition is not clearing. JULIUS B. RICHMOND

NOSE, OBJECTS IN

Sometimes by accident and sometimes just to find out what will happen, a child puts objects into his nose. If the object can be seen and easily grasped, it can be removed, but if there is bleeding or if the object cannot be seen or easily removed, a physician should be consulted without delay.

It is poor psychology to tell a child not to put things into his nose because he will almost certainly wonder why and be tempted to try. The best way to avoid this problem is to keep small objects away from small children, a feat requiring a fairly high degree of alertness, for children are curious and often very quick. W. W. BAUER

See also ACCIDENT PREVENTION

NUDITY

There are various opinions about whether or not parents should appear in the nude in the presence of their children.

It is evident that there can be no single answer, for a great deal depends upon the age of the child, the casualness of the family, the culture in which the family is living, the feelings of the parents, and the behavior paterns by which they live.

Almost all experts in the field of child behavior and child psychology agree that if a child is under 3, there is probably no harm if he is exposed to the nudity of his parents.

Past that approximate age, however, a child becomes much more impressionable than previously, and unless nudity is practiced in a very casual way, it should not be continued. But even in the most casual families it can be harmful for a child approaching puberty to see the parent of the opposite sex in the nude. It is hard enough for children of this age period to adjust to the sudden surge of new urges without the added stimulation of seeing a display of adult nudity.

There are some parents who make a practice of appearing nude in the presence of their children, believing that by so doing they are encouraging a healthy attitude toward the body. Generally speaking, with the exception of the most casual families, such display is not advisable. Children in their preschool years often become extremely interested in the body, especially the genitals, and parental nudity may prove upsetting.

Then there are a few parents who enjoy displaying their nudity before their children. This is a form of seduction, whether they are willing to admit it or not, something that can be harmful to their sons and daughters.

Small children under the age of 7 should be given an opportunity to see other children of both sexes in the nude. It is important for them to observe the differences between boys and girls and to learn that all girls are built one way and all boys another. MILTON I. LEVINE

See also ATTITUDES; MODESTY; SEX EDUCATION

NURSE

There are two kinds of licensed nurses. One is the registered nurse, or R.N.; the other is the licensed practical nurse, or L.P.N. (sometimes called L.V.N., or licensed vocational nurse).

The R.N. may be trained in a course lasting from two to four years in a junior college, hospital school, or regular college. After graduation she (for most professional nurses are women) must pass state examinations.

The L.P.N. takes a training course of approximately a year and then must pass the state examination for licensed practical nurses.

In addition to licensed nurses there are practical nurses who have had some kind of training and experience but who have not taken state examinations.

Private duty nurses may be obtained from nurses' registries, which are sometimes in hospitals, sometimes are set up commercially, or sometimes maintained by a nurses' association. Private duty nurses may occasionally be obtained through a doctor. These nurses formerly nursed in only one home at a time, but there are now some group nursing plans whereby a nurse may do private duty for as many as four patients in a day.

Public health nurses, although they work in city and county health offices and in clinics, also do a great deal of work in homes. A mother may, for instance, receive training in baby care from a public health nurse at a clinic before her baby is born, may take her baby to a public health nurse in a clinic for shots when he is old enough for them, and may between these clinic visits have the services of a public health nurse two or three times in her home for instruction in formula making and in bathing and dressing her newborn child.

The Visiting Nurse Association is a social agency that provides nurses both for health teaching and for bedside nursing. Services of visiting nurses may be obtained by calling the office of the association, but many patients make their contact with the association through a welfare clinic, hospital clinic, or doctor. The Visiting Nurse Association charges a small fee for services if the patient can afford it; otherwise services are free.

See also COMMUNITY RESOURCES

NURSERY RHYMES

When a mother smiles, pats her baby's hands together, and says,

Pat-a-cake,
Pat-a-cake,
Baker's man,

she is introducing him to a whole world of music, poetry, and language—in fact, the culture of his race. She probably does not think of the implications of her act; her only thought is to soothe or amuse her baby, and she almost instinctively repeats what may have been the first rhyme she heard from her own mother, and that her mother, in turn, heard from *her* mother.

Some of the commonest nursery rhymes are so old that they had spread across the civilized world before the invention of printing. By 1698, when the first collection of nursery rhymes was printed, "Pat-a-Cake" was already old.

If the mother had identified her little rhyme, she undoubtedly would have called it a Mother Goose rhyme. For this is what most nursery rhymes have usually been called in the United States since *Mother Goose's Melody,* or *Sonnets for the Cradle,* was published by John Newbery in London about 1760.

All rhymes known as nursery, or Mother Goose, are not so old, however; many of those most familiar originated with the writers of the 18th century. Most nursery rhymes were originally composed for children, whether rhyming alphabets, skip-rope rhymes, counting-out rhymes (also known as rimbles), riddles, lullabies, singing games, or Mother Goose.

However old they are, and of whatever type, nursery rhymes are as well known and loved today as they have always been. Children learn to recite the melodic words long before they know their meaning, and recite them over and over because of their rhythm and appealing sounds. "Jack Be Nimble" joins "Pat-a-Cake," "To Market, to Market," and many others, the appeal of which lies primarily in their melody and rhythm. Yet an appreciation of these apparently meaningless rhymes is considered basic to an appreciation of the sound of language.

Some of the rhymes tell the first little stories a child hears, and Old Mother Hubbard, Jack Sprat, and Little Bo-Peep are characters who come to live forever in a child's imagination.

The child who knows, "One, Two, Buckle My Shoe," is already on his way to counting —up to 10 at least. Even "Intery, Mintery, Cutery Corn" gives him some insight into simple arithmetic, with its three geese in a flock, one of which "flew east, and one flew west, and one flew over the cuckoo's nest."

A baby is never too young to be sung to or to have nursery rhymes recited to him. The definite rhythm and appealing sounds, coupled with the adult's delight in saying them, make a pleasant play experience for a baby even as young as 6 to 7 months. Later, nothing matches the pride with which the adult hears the timeless words prattled in the child's first talking efforts.

And, because most of the books containing nursery rhymes are profusely, and often charmingly, illustrated, a child profits even more perhaps by developing a long-lasting appreciation of good art and illustration.

For a fine selection of the favorite Mother Goose and nursery rhymes, see Volume 1, *Poems and Rhymes*. ELIZABETH S. MARGULIS

See also BOOKS FOR CHILDREN; READINESS FOR READING; READING ALOUD

Related article in WORLD BOOK: "Nursery Rhyme"

NURSERY SCHOOL

Nursery school is the name for a school for children who are 3 or 4 years of age. It may seem startling to parents to think of 3- and 4-year-olds going to school: They are still such babies; they are too young. Yet one of the new discoveries about children is that 3- and 4-year-olds are quite as ready for school as we have long known 5- or 6-year-olds to be. There are, of course, individual differences; but by 3 or 4 most children benefit by leaving home for a small part of each day. They are ready to learn and to work with children their own age.

Going to nursery school represents the first in a life-long series of separations from the known, the safe, the familiar. Good nursery schools make every effort to insure that this first separation is a happy experience for the child. If the first experience is handled well, a good base has been laid for success in later efforts. Nursery school teachers frequently visit the child at home before school starts. The child and the mother are usually invited to visit school before opening day. All children do not come at once on opening day so that crowds are avoided. Often the beginning sessions are brief so that children can have a short but pleasant taste of school life. Generally, a mother is encouraged to stay with her child as long as needed if he gives an indication of wanting her present. With these few precautions, most 3- and 4-year-olds soon leave their mothers very happily, play hard with their new friends, and rejoin their mothers at the end of the morning. Many times the reunion leads to greater love on the part of both parent and child because of the brief separation.

One of the first advantages of a good nursery school is the opportunity it provides the child for greater independence. Children under 6 especially value independence. They make giant strides in their total development if they experience it. Saying "Good-by" to mother and living for a short part of each day in the world of his own age-mates is one excellent means of enabling a child to feel big and to stand on his own two feet like a separate and growing individual. At school, a child can get any help he needs from teachers, of course, but children make great gains in dressing and undressing themselves and in toileting independently. They choose their own activities and develop them in their own time and way.

Children begin to learn to live, work, and play together. Because they are in a group under skilled supervision, they make progress in taking turns, in settling disputes fairly, and in cooperating throughout the course of the morning. The program is planned to give children an opportunity to use their bodies well. A good nursery school has both indoor and outdoor facilities and gives ample time for climbing, balancing, games, and other activities that build the large muscles as well as time for the development of small muscle coordination.

Nursery school children hear stories and good music. They sing songs and take many short educational trips; they are surrounded by informative and challenging pictures and exhibits. There is ample time for them to ask many questions both of the teacher and of their friends. In all of these ways the great curiosity of young children is stirred, resulting in significant gains in background information and often in language development. The children also have the opportunity to express themselves through block play, sand play, art work of all kinds, and working with

carpentry tools and wood. Outdoors they use such equipment as boards and boxes and big blocks, tricycles, climbing apparatus, wheelbarrows and wagons. The children are almost constantly involved in make-believe play. This does not mean they waste their time, however. Through play, children get the chance to use their initiative, to think and to plan. They develop their attention span and their capacity for problem solving.

The Child Gains as a Whole

It is not easy to separate children's gains into social, physical, emotional, and intellectual compartments because each interrelates with the other. On a trip to the farm, for example, a child who learns how cows are milked often becomes more confident because he is more informed. This confidence shows in his social relationships. As he plays better with children his own age, he is frequently led into wider and more daring physical adventures. All of these advances together strengthen the youngster's emotional tone, his good feeling about himself and about other people in his world.

It is not easy to see a child make a specific gain. The nursery school day is not divided into separate periods for particular lessons, nor does the teacher "teach" the lessons in the usual school manner. Occasionally, the teacher plays a prominent part, as when she is telling a story, leading a brief discussion, or taking children on a trip. Sometimes the teacher plays a very active but inconspicuous part, answering an individual child's question or helping several children think through the best way of solving a problem. Her most important role, however, is in the background, making it safe and possible for children to play. Her greatest challenge is to create an environment, both indoors and outdoors, which sets the stage for children to learn through their own experience and from their age-mates. Young children make their greatest gains through what they do, not through what someone tells them. These are action rather than verbal children at this stage of development.

Parents Have Many Reasons

Parents have many reasons for sending their 3- and 4-year-olds to nursery school. The most common reason is the parent's awareness that children this age have grown to the point where they need more than the home alone can provide. Parents reach out to the nursery school to supplement what they themselves can offer their youngsters. Frequently, parents realize that their child needs more companionship. But an individual child may need more challenge in the use of his body, or more stimulus to stretch his thinking, or more uninterrupted time to work at projects that are important to him.

Parents, as well as children, often gain when a youngster goes to a good nursery school. The mother, for example, might welcome a brief time alone to work on housekeeping, shopping, and other parts of her job. Many mothers report that they are more relaxed with their children and can better enjoy the hours they have together because the child spends his mornings in nursery school. Parents often find out a great deal about their own child and good ways of working with him. Most schools are glad to have mothers observe the teacher at work. They are also glad to have a mother observe her own child in comparison with other children of his age. Cooperative nursery schools, in fact, require mothers to work directly in the school with the children, usually about once a week.

Many parents first think of nursery school when a new child is about to be born into the family. This is seldom the best time for a 3- or a 4-year-old to begin to go to school. When a new baby is due, the older child is more likely to be seeking closer relationships with his parents than to be wanting more experience in independence.

Finding Good School Important

Nursery education is very expensive education. There are almost no public nursery schools. Since they are mainly private schools, the tuition must be high enough to cover a major part of the expenses, if not all. And the expenses are high. Nursery school teachers must be highly trained, holding at least a bachelor's degree in nursery school or early childhood education. A nursery school must be limited to small groups of children. Twenty children should be the maximum size for a group of 4-year-olds; a group of 3-year-olds should be smaller. Even when there are fewer children—and many schools prefer no more than 12 or 15 in a group—there must always be two adults—a teacher and an assistant teacher. Nursery schools need a great deal of equipment because the children almost never work as a total group. They are subdivided by their own choice into working groups of two or three or four, and many children often play alone for part of the time. A good nursery school also needs a generous amount of space, both indoors and out.

Even though the nursery school idea is relatively new, the demand for good schools far exceeds the supply. In many communities nursery schools are not regulated by any public supervisory agency. Schools with low standards can come into being and flourish. Some nursery schools are run by untrained individuals simply for profit. Most of the best schools operate on a nonprofit basis.

Nursery schools should be distinguished from day nurseries or child-care centers. The usual nursery school, created primarily to further the growth and development of children, is in session only a half day, generally in the morning from around 9:00 to 11:30. Day nurseries or child-care centers, created primarily to aid working mothers, must usually serve children through all the hours of the working day, sometimes as long as from 7:00 A.M. to 5:00 P.M. These long hours of separation are a hazard to young children.

Many mothers who work, even some who do not, look for schools for children under 3 years of age. While some universities and research centers have groups for children who are younger than 3, this age is usually considered too early for most children to benefit by group life. Instead of gaining independence, children under 3 are apt to become more dependent. This likelihood is greater, of course, in the day nursery with its long hours, but even nursery school, with its shorter hours of separation, can threaten the under-3 child.

Parents who want a good school and who can afford one should be very careful to make a full investigation before enrolling their child. It is wise to check with the state department of education and the departments of health and welfare to see if the school is properly licensed. A publication that can be used as a helpful guide is *How To Distinguish a Good Nursery School,* published by the National Association for Nursery Education, 155 E. Ohio Street, Chicago 11, Illinois.

JAMES L. HYMES, JR.

See also SEPARATION FROM MOTHER

NURSING

See BOTTLE FEEDING; BREAST CARE AND BREAST FEEDING

NUTRITION

In the midst of plenty, it would seem impossible to have a poorly nourished child. And yet, undernourished children are not at all uncommon, even on farms or in the best neighborhoods. Although these children have no hunger pains, their bodies have "hidden hungers" for the vitamins and minerals that may be lacking in their diets. Knowing that this kind of hunger is possible, no sensible mother subscribes to the oft-heard advice: "Just let a child eat what he wants and he will eat what he needs." Whether a child

YOUR CHILD'S DAILY DIET NEEDS

	2-5 YEARS	5-10 YEARS	10-12 YEARS	12-16 YEARS
Milk	3-4 cups	3-4 cups	4 cups	4 cups
Meat	2 ounces	3 ounces	4 ounces	4 ounces
Egg	1	1	1	1
Fruit				
Citrus fruit	1 serving	1 serving	1 serving	1 serving
Tomato (whole or in juice)	2 servings	2 servings	2 servings	2 servings
Other fruits	1-2 servings	1-2 servings	1-2 servings	1-2 servings
Vegetable, 1 dark green or bright yellow Potato, 1 medium sized	3-4 servings	3-4 servings	3-4 servings	3-4 servings
Cereals and breads, enriched and whole grain	2-3 servings	3-4 servings	3 servings	3 servings

chooses the foods he needs depends upon what the choices are and the conditions under which they are offered. Furthermore, patterns of eating established during his childhood may become permanent, affecting his well-being throughout his entire life.

The secret of good nutrition is to eat a diet comprised of the kinds and amounts of food that contain all the nutrients essential for a healthy body. It is true, as the poem says, "Whatever Miss T. eats turns into Miss T." If eaten in the amounts needed, the food not only becomes Miss T., but it is also becoming to Miss T.

All foods contain nutrients in varying amounts. Each nutrient does for the body a special job that cannot be handled by any other nutrient. Therefore, the absence of any one nutrient causes a deficiency. In addition, some nutrients cannot work alone but combine with others to perform their functions. For example, vitamin A cannot be utilized by the body unless fat is also present. Calcium and phosphorus, essential for bone formation, cannot be absorbed by the body unless vitamin D is present.

A child will not instinctively eat all the right foods his body demands. A mother should know something about good nutrition and the importance of proper foods, make these foods available, and encourage her child to eat them.

There are four basic food groups that contain material for energy and other essential nutrients:

1. Milk and milk products, such as cheese and ice cream, supply calcium, phosphorus, protein, and riboflavin.
2. Meat, fish, poultry, and eggs supply protein, thiamine, niacin, and mineral elements, such as iron and phosphorus.
3. Vegetables and fruits supply vitamins A and C, iron, thiamine, and certain mineral elements.
4. Breads and cereals, in the whole grain and enriched forms, supply thiamine, niacin, riboflavin, and iron as well as protein. Potatoes can substitute for bread.

How much of these foods does your child need? Nutrition authorities have compiled a chart, reproduced here, showing the foods that should be included in the daily diet of every child.

If your child doesn't eat exactly the recommended amounts every day, there is no need for concern. If, however, during a week he eats much more or much less than the suggested amounts, you should investigate the cause. Through regular physical examinations a doctor can determine if the child is well nourished and growing normally.

Of course, a child will also eat foods, mainly fats and sweets, not included in the basic four. In moderate amounts these extra foods are all right, especially because they help to produce energy. But eating large quantities of gravies, rich cream, mayonnaise, potato chips, pastries, and cookies can be disastrous to good nutrition. Too much fat adds calories that, if not burned up, can produce unwanted pounds. An excess of sweets also can result in overweight, and can ruin a child's appetite for more valuable foods.

You should try to discourage a child's taste for sugary and fatty foods, especially when he takes such foods as snacks. Eating between meals is all right—sometimes necessary to keep up a child's energy, but a peanut-butter sandwich or cheese and crackers are much better than rich cookies or chocolate bars.

It's important to store and to prepare foods in ways that will preserve their nutrients. Vitamins and minerals can easily be lost by poor storage and poor cooking methods.

Generally, the longer you cook a food, the more nutrients it loses. For example, vegetables that are still intact and a little crispy contain more vitamin C than vegetables allowed to cook to the mushy stage.

Using large quantities of water in cooking also is a sure way to wash away vitamins. A good rule for conserving nutrients is to cook food quickly in small amounts of water and with a minimum area of the food's surface exposed.

Knowing what foods are nutritious and how to prepare them is not enough. It is a wise mother who understands the social implications of food. When she gives food to her baby who is in pain from hunger, she gives him more than food. Food presented by a giving and loving mother becomes associated with the notion that the world is good; with "mother loves me and the food she gives me makes me feel good." This early association of hunger causing pain, pain leading to food, and food easing pain should be maintained and strengthened. It is weakened when, for example, food is given to a child to relieve his boredom: when a cracker is given to a baby who actually wants only his mother's arms about him.

Gradually, as the child grows older he learns to associate eating with a family whose company he enjoys. His enjoyment reinforces his desire for the food they share and becomes a powerful force in his habit of eating certain foods. Even the patterns of what foods constitute a good meal are a strong force in assuring that these foods will be eaten. Fortunate is the child who learns with his family to eat the needed foods because they are considered a vital part of the meal—for instance, milk with each meal. Thus a mother sets the stage for the formation of good lifetime food habits.

There are many things that can be done to help your young child to enjoy his food. To understand your child and how he feels about food is as important as to understand what foods are necessary.

The first consideration is to make eating so pleasant that your child will look forward to his food. Meals, including breakfast, should be relaxing and tension-free—times for the family to enjoy one another's company.

A child much prefers familiar foods and is hesitant about trying new ones. Therefore, you should present new foods patiently, perhaps several times, until he gets used to them. They should also be presented in small quantities.

A child likes crisp foods such as raw vegetable sticks and cooked vegetables that are still intact. Overcooked, mushy, or watery vegetables are not popular with most children, although mashed ones usually are. If your child doesn't like a certain food, perhaps the texture is bothering him. You might try cooking the food another way.

Most children have a keen sense of taste and smell and therefore shun seasoned foods, often preferring those that seem bland and tasteless to adults. The flavors that seem to be hardest for a child to accept are those of strong vegetables and those of highly acid fruits. For example, a child may not care for cooked dried apricots, but he will eat them if they are covered with a mild custard sauce.

Foods that are steaming hot or ice cold may cause a child to reject them. He tends to like foods that are lukewarm.

A child also likes foods that he can handle easily—foods that he can eat with his hands and foods that are cut into bite-size pieces.

The color of food also makes a big difference to a child. He may exclaim, "Oh, dinner is yellow today!" Or, "I want some pink ice cream!" Making food visually appealing often entices a child to eat it.

Sometimes you can get a child to eat food by serving it in an intriguing manner or in a novel dish. Such devices are all right as long as the child doesn't come to depend on them entirely.

A well-nourished child will not only give you pride in a healthy youngster, but also the satisfaction that you have established good eating patterns that he will follow his entire life.

MIRIAM E. LOWENBERG

See also APPETITE; EATING PROBLEMS; GROWTH

OBEDIENCE

A child must be taught to respect and to respond to the demands of people in authority. Initially these authorities are the child's parents. As the child grows older, he must be ready to give the same positive response to teachers in school and to other duly authorized adults. Such obedience is only one aspect of the larger problem of learning good discipline. It is an important aspect, however, because there are times even in a democracy when quick compliance with commands is essential.

There are no important differences in procedure between the teaching of discipline and the teaching of obedience. All the teaching techniques contributing to the development of good discipline simultaneously contribute to the development of obedience.

Some Pitfalls

Difficulties arise, however, if parents fail to realize that obedience is only one part of discipline. An overconcentration on obedience can lead to an unwise and too heavy reliance on punishment as a method of teaching discipline. A youngster will respond through fear when a powerful adult issues a specific command. If good behavior always depends on fear of an adult, however, the same child may prove quite undisciplined if no adult is present or if the youngster senses that he can continue, unpunished, what he is doing. Fear of punishment plays some part in the development of total discipline; but love—quite a contrasting emotion—plays a much more basic part. When obedience is the only goal, there is the danger that parents will also expect quicker results than are possible. In the healthy development of a well-disciplined child, obedience is not normally one of the first achievements. Younger children are less able to be obedient than are older children because of their search for independence and self-awareness. Two-year-olds, for example, are normally much more willful and more determined to have their own way than are 4-year-olds or 6-year-olds. One-year-olds are much more egocentric and concerned with their own interests than are 5-year-olds or 7-year-olds. The adult's role in teaching obedience as a whole must allow for the immaturity of these younger children. Great gains can be made during their early years in laying the foundation for good discipline, but obedience as such is not apt to emerge early (unless one places an unusually heavy reliance on fear).

The adult who wants quick results can become dissatisfied with his child, and this dissatisfaction can lead to an intensification of punishment. Both of these outcomes complicate the job of building a complete and sturdy sense of discipline.

There is also the danger of overtraining for obedience. Even though children must become obedient, they must also retain a capacity for rebellion. None of us want citizens who are totally dependent on authority and who have no capacity to think for themselves. Our rejection of blind conformity is important in our political and economic life. Even in military life there are occasional situations when the individual must be on his own, not dependent on commands but capable of thinking. The danger of overtraining for obedience is lessened if one sees obedience in the setting of teaching good discipline as a whole.

Some Aids in Teaching Obedience

Even though obedience begins to emerge in a child's behavior only after two or three or four years of growing, situations inevitably arise in the early years when parents begin to teach it. Whenever we begin to teach obedience, whether in the early years or later, the first step is to be clear in our own minds on what we want. We must be convinced that whatever we are insisting on is right. We must feel that it is our job as parents to demand it. We must be certain that we have the power to achieve the desired result. If we say "Come," we must mean *come* and must be solidly sure that the child will, without any doubt, *come!* We must never talk to the wind or talk just to hear ourselves or talk not caring whether anyone is listening. We must intend for the "Come" to be heard and to produce action.

At the very beginning of obedience training, however, we cannot expect that our word alone—no matter how deeply felt or clearly stated—will be sufficient. That result will be achieved through long years of education, but not at the very beginning. A 2-year-old child, for example, will probably need a preparatory warning that the command will soon be forthcoming. He will undoubtedly need some action from us to give the word more reality than simply a sound in the air. We may have to stand near him when we give the command or perhaps head in the direction we want him to come. We may even have to take him by the hand or good-naturedly lift him up so that he comes on our legs instead of his own. The goal is to give as little support as is needed, but at the same time as much support as is necessary so that, without fail, "Come" actually means that the child comes. If one recognizes that this learning is a difficult and new learning for a child, "Come" need not lead to a battle. Like all good lessons, it ought to have a tone of good will rather than of antagonism, a spirit of pleasure with the child's growing accomplishments rather than of despair at his failures.

Initially the child's impulsiveness and his deep concern for independence may make it difficult for him to respond perfectly, but children have no more deep-seated need than to please their parents. They want, above all, to do what we expect of them. When this is not the trend in their behavior, something may be wrong. Adults may be expecting more obedience than the child is yet capable of. They may be giving less support than he needs at this point in his learning of obedience. Or, despite our commands, we may actually feel unsure of what we are asking or uncertain that the child will respond. It is also easy to confuse a child's normal and healthy behavior, stemming from his search for selfhood, with disobedience. Some pondering as to why and some puzzling over next steps are usually more constructive than the automatic assumption that more pressure on the child is the only answer. Children are not serfs or slaves or puppy dogs. They can grow to be as obedient as we adults are. But because they want our love so badly, they should become increasingly obedient and they should be increasingly able to respond to our words alone if we can find the right ways of living with them. JAMES L. HYMES, JR.

See also DISCIPLINE

OBSTETRICIAN *See* MEDICAL SPECIALISTS

OCULIST *See* MEDICAL SPECIALISTS

OLDER PARENTS

Most Americans marry in their early twenties and have all their children within the next few years. But many men and women, for one reason or another, are older when their children come. These older parents have the advantage of being more mature and are, therefore, more able to assume responsibility for the care of their children. They may have wanted children for a long time and so welcome them with even greater eagerness than younger parents do.

On the other hand, older parents may find it harder to understand their growing children because of the larger-than-usual gap that exists between the generations. Also, medical reports show that an older mother may have somewhat more difficulty giving birth to a first-born child than a younger woman does.

Still another problem that older parents face is that of sheer physical stamina. It is taxing at any age to keep up with the vigorous activities of growing children. But none of these problems of older parents are insurmountable. Each can be faced and met as one of the challenges of life.

The older mother and father may find child-study classes particularly helpful, not only in understanding their own children, but also in associating with other parents whose children are about the same age. The child of older parents will find companionship in nursery school and kindergarten where teacher conferences can be especially valuable in interpreting the child to his parents and in keeping them more flexible.

Older parents who very much want to have children, often enjoy their parenthood more than young parents whose children come almost before the home is ready for them. As in so many areas of life, it is the attitude toward an experience, whatever it may be, that makes it either a burden or a satisfaction. EVELYN MILLIS DUVALL

See also BOOKS FOR PARENTS; PARENT EDUCATION

OLDEST CHILD *See* BROTHERS AND SISTERS

ONLY CHILD

Despite an increase in the number of larger families, approximately one out of every six couples in the United States has an only child; about one out of every 20 children is an only child. Because there is considerable social prestige associated with large families these days and because of the often exaggerated warnings that only children tend to be lonely, spoiled, or selfish, parents of only children frequently show undue concern and anxiety.

What Research Says About "Onlies"

The truth of the matter is that an only child has as good a chance of growing up to be a happy, well-adjusted person as a child from a larger family. Many studies have been undertaken to determine whether or not there are typical personality patterns among only children. None of the popular stereotypes have been borne out by this research; the results do not indicate that "onlies" are more spoiled, more selfish, or less sociable.

If parents of an only child feel guilty or deprived, if this circumstance cannot be accepted as a fact of life, their child will, of course, be influenced adversely. Where parents are able to meet the special needs of their only child with realistic optimism, there is no reason why the child cannot have a rich, happy, and productive life. There are many perfectly good and valid reasons for having an only child, including such considerations as health, economic limitations, age, and personality needs and interests of parents.

All children are "onlies" in certain ways and at certain times: the eldest, the youngest, the only one at home when others are away. All children have special problems in growing up: shyness, loneliness, disobedience, jealousy, fears. In each family situation parents try to develop the necessary skills to meet the challenges they are confronted with, and just as other parents must evaluate the special characteristics of their family life, so parents of an only child have certain factors to take into consideration.

Many parents tend to be somewhat anxious and overprotective with a first child; when the second comes along, they know what to expect and may become more relaxed. But parents of only children remain "new parents." They have less opportunity to make comparisons, to learn from experiences at different age levels; they are focusing all their love and attention on one child. They may be somewhat overwatchful; their devotion may be too concentrated, too intense, all because they are making a greater emotional investment in one child. Unfortunately, the result may sometimes be overindulgence and overprotection.

Parents Should Avoid Extremes

On the other hand, just to avoid these difficulties, some parents lean over backwards, controlling themselves to the point where they actually provide too little support, supervision, and understanding. To avoid either extreme, parents can be watchful that they provide opportunities for growth, that they encourage increasing independence and don't hold on too tight, while at the same time they keep in mind the fact that children grow slowly and need patience and guidance. It is often helpful to take stock by watching other parents with their children, by observing one's own child in his relations with others outside the family, and by having consultations with his teachers and other adults who come in contact with him so as to maintain a broader perspective on his growth, his needs, and his strengths.

Parents of an only child are frequently warned not to spoil their child. They are told that he may become selfish and self-centered by being overindulged. And some parents are inclined to overreact to this often exaggerated warning and demand an unrealistic stoicism from their child. Spoiling really means depriving a child of his self-respect by not giving him the opportunity to find out what his own strengths and resources are. Children want to be able to *give* and to *do,* and self-confidence develops as a child is permitted to test himself. Too many possessions, too little freedom, may hamper the development of one's own resources. On the other hand, children need love and approval and time to grow; all children go through periods of selfishness, of irresponsibility, and parents must continually seek a balance between what they give and what they can expect from their child.

When Comparisons Are Unfair

Adults tend to be the pacesetters for only children, who frequently measure their growth and their worth by the adults around them rather than by comparing themselves with other children their own age. Such unfair comparisons may make for unrealistic standards, too severe a conscience, or feelings of inadequacy. The child who learns slowly or has an occasional temper tantrum or is shy thinks he's unworthy because he is comparing himself to his parents, who seem all-wise, in control of their impulses, and socially poised. Such a child is not aware of the fact that he is just about like any other child of his age. He also judges himself by how he is treated. If his mother is angry with him, if his father seems disappointed in his ball-throwing skill, the child thinks there is something wrong with himself—he doesn't have the opportunity to see that his parents would behave in the same way with other children. It is important for parents to help their only child look upon his development with more kindness and forgiveness. They can tell him about their own shortcomings as children; they can talk quite directly about the fact that children cannot expect to be little adults but need time to grow.

An only child sometimes seems very sophisticated; he tends to have a large vocabulary at an early age and often appears advanced in social relations with adults. It is sometimes difficult to remember that such appearance is usually a pseudosophistication based on mimicry, on being with adults much of the time; actually, "onlies" may be quite immature in understanding the words they use or in social relations with their age-mates.

Feelings of rivalry and competition that children with brothers and sisters may work out with one another frequently are worked out with the parents of an only child. His normal jealousy and rivalry are toward his parents; they may have to be more aware and sensitive. And they may have to help their child develop satisfying relations with other adults and children so that he will not interfere with the privacy of his parents' marriage relationship.

Opportunities to play with other children and to get to know other families can help an only child attain a natural and wholesome childhood. Other children can be invited on family trips, on picnics, or to participate in special events with the only child. Visits to relatives and friends with larger families can be planned. Nursery schools, day camps, or sleep-away camps when a child is old enough can provide opportunities for learning to live with others. And a pet can be important to an only child especially; it can provide him with something outside himself and his parents to love and care for.

Because parents want their only child to have friends, they may overdo a good thing and leave him with little or no time alone. Such parents should not forget that an only child has one great advantage over other children: Aloneness without loneliness is often the most fruitful road to creativity, imagination, and resourcefulness.

All children feel envious of other families at some time in their lives; the grass is always greener somewhere else. "Onlies" may at times wish for a larger family, but just as frequently their observations of their friends' troubles with pesky little brothers and bossy older sisters will make them feel very smug about being an only child. If parents don't feel unduly alarmed by their child's occasional discontent and if they can permit him to express himself freely, they can help him accept reality and work with it.

The fact of being an only child does not account for success or explain failure; "onliness" is simply one of many factors in a child's life to which parents can bring sensitivity, understanding, and imagination. In the deepest sense, each member of a family is an "only"—precious and unique—adding his own flavor and color to life. EDA J. LE SHAN

See also CAMP; LONELINESS; NURSERY SCHOOL; OVERPROTECTION; PETS; PLAY GROUPS

OPERATION

Many an adult looks back on one particular childhood experience, his tonsillectomy, as a nightmare. He entered a hospital almost totally unprepared for all the new and terrifying things that were to happen to him, for his well-meaning but misguided parents had thought they were making things easier for him by sparing him the truth about his coming operation. Such treatment could cause a child to have a lasting fear of hospitals and doctors.

Fortunately, today's young patient can have a totally different hospital experience. His parents, his surgeon, and the hospital staff are now aware of the importance of emotional preparation before surgery. A child is told calmly and frankly what to expect at the hospital and, of course, why the operation is necessary. Nowadays he is not nearly so surprised or frightened by nurses and technicians, masks, or operating room procedures because all this has been described ahead of time.

If your child is going to have an operation, here are some suggestions for helping him. Although these suggestions relate to tonsillectomy because it is the most frequent operation of childhood, they can be modified to suit the specific needs of other operations such as hernia, eye squint, or even emergency appendectomy or heart surgery.

1. Tell him that operations are sometimes necessary to improve the health of children and adults. You might point out some member of the family or some friend who has benefited by an operation.

2. Avoid constant adult discussion of his forthcoming operation. Don't let him see your anxiety or he will worry, too. It is better not to tell a young child the exact date of his operation.

3. Because it is the unknown that frightens children, try to anticipate and explain those things at the hospital that might confuse or frighten him. Don't burden him, however, with unnecessary or too vivid details. Tell him that:

- His tonsils and adenoids must be removed so he will have fewer colds and sore throats.
- The operation itself will not take long and will not hurt because he will be given something to smell and, after a few deep breaths, he will be fast asleep until the operation is over. When he wakes, you will be there. (More and more hospitals are encouraging parents to remain in their child's room for the duration of the hospital stay. Your presence will contribute greatly to his feeling of security.)
- In the operating room there will be other doctors and nurses to help his own doctor. Their white masks are for the patient's protection. The nurses not only assist the doctor but also help to make the patient more comfortable.
- He might get an injection before the operation.
- He will wear a funny little white jacket, something like the one the doctor wears.
- He will not have breakfast before the operation. Children feel more comfortable afterward if they have not eaten.
- At the hospital he may be required to sleep in a crib or a bed with sides on it. But he may take his favorite stuffed animals or other bed toys with him.
- His throat (or whatever part of his body is involved) will hurt after the operation, but it will get better and better every day.

4. After the operation don't make your child suppress his feelings about it if he wants to talk, complain, or play hospital, doctor, or nurse.

5. If your hospital does not have the facilities for parents to stay overnight in private rooms or wards, give your child special assurance that you will be thinking of him every moment and will be eagerly waiting to take him home.

6. Once he is home, don't treat him like an invalid. Your love, attention, and praise are important, but don't keep harping on the operation. As soon as he feels able, let him get back to a normal routine.

If you tell your child the truth ahead of time, not only will he benefit physically from surgery, but an operation can also become a constructive and important experience in his development and a source of pride in his own accomplishment.

Some of the essential principles for preparing your child emotionally for surgery are incorporated in a child's picture storybook entitled, *A Visit to the Hospital* by Francine Chase.

LESTER L. COLEMAN

See also CONVALESCENT CHILD; HOSPITALIZATION

OPTHALMOLOGIST *See* MEDICAL SPECIALISTS

ORGANIZATIONS *See* AGENCIES AND ORGANIZATIONS; COMMUNITY RESOURCES; YOUTH ORGANIZATIONS

ORTHODONTICS *See* DENTAL BRACES

ORTHOPEDIST *See* MEDICAL SPECIALISTS

OTOLOGIST *See* MEDICAL SPECIALISTS

OVEREATING *See* OVERWEIGHT

OVERPROTECTION

No one denies that most parents have the best of intentions toward their children. They love these small people, they want them to be comfortable, not to suffer, to grow up safe, to enjoy the world, and to be largely unaware of the world's complexity, cruelty, and coldness. Many parents, in trying so hard to be good to their children, do less than good to them; in trying to protect their children enough, they protect them too much. But, you ask, what possible harm can come out of protection; why try to stop anything as natural as a parent wanting to take proper care of his child? The answer lies not in the word *protection*, but in the word *over*.

The chief danger of overprotection is that it lessens a child's chance of becoming an independent, resolute, adequate human being. It stifles his belief in his own powers and diminishes the courage and resources he will need to stand up to the demands of adult life. An overprotected child is afraid to do what is possible and right for him. He tends not to trust himself in new experiences and, thus, often does not do so well in school and social life as he could. Sometimes, on the other hand, an overprotected child takes too many risks just to prove he can be free of his parents. As adults, such overprotected people tend also either to be too rebellious or too cowed and are, in either case, defeating themselves.

Parents overprotect for a number of reasons. In general, mothers are more apt to overdo the job than are fathers, perhaps because mothers are with their children more and have the responsibility for the daily safety of their sons and daughters, perhaps because a mother is more likely to view her children as part of herself. Then, too, a mother is usually judged by how happy, safe, healthy, and successful her child is. A father is judged mostly by his success when he is on the job.

A particular type of mother, by the nature of her physical constitution and experiences, is "fiercely maternal." These women are often strong, rather dominating; they are sure they know what is best for their families. They may marry rather weak men. Then, often disappointed in their husbands, they may pour all their need to love, direct, and protect onto their children, especially onto their sons.

Parents are tempted also to turn to their children for comfort when tragedy strikes the marriage. After a death or a divorce, the child sometimes becomes the focus of too much attention. Or parents are tempted to overprotect the only child, who is often the center of parental love, concern, and ambition.

Many parents immediately feel guilty after becoming angry with a son or daughter. It is normal to be irritated at the natural problems of living with the young. But because most fathers and mothers have been taught to believe that it is wrong to resent a child, their negative feelings disturb them. Out of their guilt they seek atonement by overdoing the kindly, protective parent act. For instance, a father who sees his 10-year-old son hacking away at the back steps with a hatchet may well react with rage; he has the sudden impulsive wish that the youngster would let the hatchet slip and cut himself, just to teach him a lesson. This impulse is followed by guilt and shame, and, to undo the wicked feeling, the father rushes out to confiscate the hatchet because "it is too dangerous." He may go on to make his son promise not to use the hatchet again until he is 16. Without parental guilt, the child would be punished for chipping the steps and then taught the proper way to use a hatchet.

Some overprotection seems to spring from the child himself, for certain children are unusually dependent from infancy on. A child may be exceptionally sensitive partly because of his body build or he may be psychologically sensitive, easily upset. Sick children need a great deal of care, and it is a temptation for parents to overdo the job. Some national and religious groups with a long tradition of a close, protective family life where the mother is the central figure have a tendency to overprotect their children.

A decidedly overprotective parent is unrealistically anxious about his child's safety, health, achievements, and social acceptability. Often a parent will realize his tendencies and will try to change but will be unable to do so without the help of some family counselor—a psychologist, a psychiatrist, or a social worker.

Youngsters who have felt too much parental anxiety and overprotection often become overanxious about themselves. They may feel that they will never be good enough to satisfy their parents or to face the world. They may have exaggerated fears and difficulty in schoolwork and in learning new skills. They are frequently timid, given to persistent nightmares, and sometimes have aches and pains without a physical basis. Some overprotected children show a wild disregard for danger in an attempt to conquer their basic fear. Behavior of this kind may, of course, sometimes spring from other causes; it is a sign that something may be wrong but not necessarily that a child is overprotected. Some of these symptoms may appear, for instance, under temporary stress, such as when moving to a new neighborhood.

It is hard to know just how much protection is required. The modern world *is* full of real dangers, and a child must develop many skills to live in it. Parents need a large reservoir of inner strength and faith not to overprotect their cherished sons and daughters.

The trick is to know when your child is ready for new experiences. With each passing month an infant or toddler is able to handle activities for himself that he could not before. He learns to climb with comparative safety; he learns that stoves are hot; he learns that knives are sharp; he learns to stand up for his rights on the playground. He learns these things if parents can let him find out by *guided* experience. *A healthy child has a natural drive for self-preservation.* With experience he learns what is painful and what is pleasurable. He avoids pain and seeks pleasure. There is pleasure in running, climbing, sliding, swinging, and generally exercising his body and mind. There is pain in falling, getting hurt, overeating, and so on. Parents have a double role: to stand by and guard their child from serious hurt and at the same time to count on the caution that most youngsters develop to save themselves.

Parents accomplish a great deal when they teach a youngster to cope with his environment. They can teach him many ways of self-reliance, including how to cross the street, how to turn on electrical appliances, how to use matches, how to avoid walking on thin ice, how to climb without falling.

Not *everything* can be learned by doing. Parents, by acting in a reasonable manner themselves, demonstrate that parental judgment can be trusted. By putting trust in their child's instinct for survival and his growing know-how, they demonstrate that he can trust himself.

The best armor a child can have is knowledge, experience, and self-confidence, plus his own natural drive for survival. As youngsters grow, they can handle more and more of life's hazards for themselves. Parents are called upon for great flexibility so that they can assess the reality of dangers and can give increasing freedom as their child grows in skill and knowledge. A flexible parent can admit a child's constantly increasing competence. The more confidence a parent has in himself, the more he can give his child increasing independence. CATHERINE S. CHILMAN

See also INDEPENDENCE

OVERTIREDNESS

Babies and young children become overtired, or fatigued, as easily as adults do—and for much the same reasons. Overstimulation, insufficient rest, and oncoming illness can cause a youngster to become fatigued.

A young baby shows fatigue by crying and fussing. His arms flail the air and he cannot seem to get comfortable. Often you can help him to relax by swaying his bassinet or carriage, cradling him in your arms and rocking him, or even walking with him.

An older child may whine and resist sleep when he is fatigued. If you give him a warm bath, read a story to him, or gently rub his back as he lies in bed, you may succeed in calming and soothing him.

Prevention, of course, is the best cure for fatigue. Don't permit others to jounce, talk loudly to, or tickle your baby. Don't play with, tease, or scold a small child just before bedtime.

Regular mealtimes and regular naptimes and bedtimes in his own bed will help insure pleasant days and peaceful nights for your child. MILTON J. E. SENN

See also NAPS

OVERWEIGHT

A child is said to be overweight when he weighs more than the "average" child of his age and sex, as measured by a standard age-height-weight table. When a child is considerably overweight, parents are concerned about some "glandular disorder." In rare instances there may be a disorder of the pituitary, thyroid, or adrenal glands, and this kind of abnormality usually can be detected rather readily by the child's doctor. In some families there is a tendency to overweight so that heredity may account for the excessive weight. In most overweight children, however, excessive eating is the cause of excessive weight. They are consuming more calories than they are burning through body activity.

Parents may wonder whether overweight is harmful. A few extra pounds probably are not, but if a child is quite heavy, he may develop some disturbances at the growth lines of his long bones or difficulties in heart function. Excessive weight also interferes with normal physical activity, and the child may have psychological difficulties, possibly complicated by teasing playmates.

A child who is overweight should be under the care of a doctor, who will, if necessary, prescribe a suitable diet. Unwise dieting may easily harm a growing child. JULIUS B. RICHMOND

See also APPETITE; EATING BETWEEN MEALS; SPECIAL DIETS

PACIFIER

As its name implies, the pacifier is used to induce a state of peace in young babies. It consists of a small plastic or rubber nipple attached to a flat disk that keeps the infant from swallowing the nipple. The pacifier offers no nourishment, yet often seems to soothe an irritable or a colicky baby or to placate a hungry one. It also offers the infant an opportunity to satisfy his need for sucking —a very strong need in infants—and thereby possibly to discourage the development of thumb- or finger-sucking.

Over the past several decades, pacifiers have been in and out of favor. Many parents who object strongly to having a child suck his thumb are not too distressed by the substitution of a pacifier. They feel that they can offer the pacifier as they wish, whereas the thumb is always at the baby's disposal. But even those parents who favor the pacifier may not like to see it used beyond the first year. One disadvantage of the pacifier is that a baby may have trouble keeping it in or near his mouth, and thus become agitated rather than soothed. But to put a pacifier on a ribbon or string around the baby's neck or wrist in order to keep it handy is dangerous.

Many dentists who believe that thumb-sucking can have a bad effect on the teeth or jaw approve of the pacifier since it does not push against the teeth. BETTYE M. CALDWELL

See also BABY; SUCKING; THUMB-SUCKING

PAIN *See* APPENDICITIS; COLIC; GROWING PAINS; RHEUMATIC FEVER; STOMACH-ACHE

PAINTING *See* ART EXPERIENCES

PANTS, WATERPROOF *See* WATERPROOF PANTS

PARENT EDUCATION

It is a strange fact that few of us have had any special training for the most important job we ever undertake in our lives: raising our children to be happy and effective human beings. In a real sense, we are all amateurs in the one job in which we would like to have the very best skills. Some few lucky people have the opportunity for some pre-parental education through home economics and other classes in high schools and in college. Such courses are rare, however, and are seldom taken by boys. Most of the parent education we receive we seek for ourselves and usually after the birth of our first child.

One important goal of CHILDCRAFT, of course, is to help parents do the right thing for their children. Each year many books are published which are written specifically for parents. These are available in public libraries and some, like Dr. Benjamin Spock's famous *Baby and Child Care,* are available in inexpensive paperback editions. The U.S. Department of Health, Education, and Welfare, through the Children's Bureau, also publishes sound and inexpensive books on children. The best known are: *Prenatal Care, Infant Care, Your Child from One to Six, Your Child from Six to Twelve,* and *The Adolescent in Your Family.* These are all available from the Government Printing Office, Washington 25, D.C. Many parents also find it useful to subscribe to a magazine about children. *Parents Magazine* (Bergenfield, New Jersey) and the *PTA Magazine* (700 North Rush Street, Chicago 11, Illinois) are widely read.

Parents of very young children often receive much help on child growth and behavior from their pediatrician. For parents of preschool children participation in a nursery school, especially in a cooperative nursery school, can become an important source of better understanding. Active membership in a PTA, in nursery school or kindergarten, or in elementary school is another very helpful way of becoming a better parent.

Most conscientious mothers and fathers seek all the help they can get from every source. Parents today are eager to learn the newest and best ways of living with children. Their search usually reveals that there is no one single "approved" technique for handling every situation with children. Human behavior is too complex for one simple answer; children and parents and families are all too individual. Consequently, it is not uncommon for all parents to have moments when they feel very unsure. It seems that the more they know, the less they know! The various professional experts on child rearing sometimes disagree, too, which adds to the confusion, but they are agreed on one point: At any one time, each parent must do what makes sense to him, whether or not the action jibes with "the book." Children are not helped when parents become so unsure of themselves that every action is tinged by uncertainty and hesitancy. Any new ideas coming from any parent education source make their best contribution when parents thoroughly understand them and make the ideas their own. Parents must act toward their children on the basis of what they have come to believe, not simply because the book or the expert says so. JAMES L. HYMES, JR.

See also BOOKS FOR PARENTS; FATHER; MOTHER; PARENT-TEACHER ASSOCIATION; PATIENCE

PARENT-TEACHER ASSOCIATION

Your membership in the PTA, as the National Congress of Parents and Teachers is familiarly known, can become a three-way stretch involving you, your child, and his teacher—a stretch because each grows a little through his contact with the others.

It can stretch you by increasing your knowledge of what is going on in your child's school and in his classroom; how the school differs from what you were brought up with; how much your child is like others his age; how much your pleasures and rewards, your problems and difficulties, resemble those of other parents. It can stretch your child through his pride that you play a role in the place where he spends most of his day, his confidence that what he does there is important to you, his ability to talk to you more about his school day because you know what he is doing there. And it can stretch the teacher by assuring her that she is working with parents who care, that her attempts and problems and successes are appreciated. Her teaching may improve because of you.

The PTA is a voluntary educational organization, open to anyone, with nominal dues for its more than 12 million members. Although an elementary school PTA serves an entire school, it can have sections for parents of preschoolers. There are also high school PTA's. And there are more than 20,000 PTA parent education study groups. The organization publishes *The PTA Magazine* to provide its membership and the public at large with reliable information about child psychology, education, health, and home-school cooperation. Besides working to meet the needs of children in its own school and community, the PTA works to strengthen education and child welfare in general. PTA's have, for instance, contributed nearly 5 million dollars for scholarships to young people interested in teaching and related careers. The state and national PTA's, to which every PTA member automatically belongs, have initiated state and national measures to advance the education and welfare of all the nation's children.

In your child's own school the PTA can do many things that no single individual or loosely organized group could do. It can help improve school health services. It can foster children's interest in books through book fairs and by helping to establish a central school library. It can, because it represents so many parents in the community, set up a parent-student social code governing dating, teen-age smoking and drinking, and dress and behavior at parties. As a community group with strength and backing, the PTA can influence the kinds of movies shown at local theaters, can promote traffic safety, and can have a large voice in legislation and taxation for schools.

If yours is a lively group, enthusiastic new members are always welcome and needed. If it is an inactive or a disgruntled group, even a single interested and hard-working new member may supply the lift to launch a productive program and the power that will make it go places. EVA H. GRANT

See also HOME-SCHOOL RELATIONS; SCHOOL TEACHER

PARTIAL SIGHT *See* HANDICAPPED CHILD

PATIENCE

Patience is not only a virtue—it is an essential of parenthood.

All other forms of life mature more quickly than does the human child. A puppy becomes a dog in a jiffy, a calf becomes a cow almost overnight, a chick becomes a chicken in a brief passage of time. The newborn child must pass through infancy, toddlerhood, the preschool years, early childhood and middle childhood, preadolescence and adolescence —a span of 20 years or so—before he has the capacities of a mature human being. Furthermore, a child must acquire an extensive backlog of experience and knowledge before he can live well as an adult. There can be no short cuts, no speed-ups. Time—time for growing, time for knowing—is a basic ingredient. Adults must be willing to give the child the time he needs.

Only in the prenatal period do growth and change take place at a really rapid rate. During the first year of life, the human body changes and "improves" more slowly but still rather rapidly. From then on, growth takes place more and more slowly. The child cannot speed up his growing; the adult has to adjust his expectations—and his patience.

No child's progress toward maturity is a smooth, even, steady step-by-step progression. The child who can walk goes back to crawling at times. The child who has some dry nights at the beginning of his toilet training has other nights when he wets. Preadolescents typically are more messy and careless than they were during earlier years.

Children have resting points, or plateaus, in their growth, too. Many children, for example, say a few words somewhere around the end of the first year and then for months seem to add hardly any new words to their vocabularies. Each "plateau period," though it seems to be a stop in development, actually lays the foundation for the next steps in growth.

All children also act in many ways that are important to them developmentally but which do not seem like signs of progress to adults. The 2-year-old, for example, may bite another Two. Biting is hardly nice, yet it is a part of the child's progress toward becoming more social and toward beginning to explore ways of living with other people. Around 4 years of age many youngsters typically use insulting names and make up sing-songs that involve toilet talk. Such verbal spouting looks like a worsening of behavior. Actually it represents an important step forward in the child's ability to substitute words for physical blows.

The fact that large gains in growth so often come in disguised form is a great challenge to patience, yet a glance backward makes patience easier. A 2-year-old, for example, may seem "bad" most of the time. He is into everything, constantly on the go, full of strong feelings, unmindful of your words. Yet think of what he was like two years ago! A 6-year-old may irritate you by talking too much, by interrupting, or by squirming in his chair at dinner. To feel pleased about him and to restore your patience, take the time to realize how far this child has come since he was 2.

The child who is rushed suffers in many ways. He can lay only a skimpy foundation for his later growth. He often feels that his parents are dissatisfied with him as he is, a disastrous feeling. He often experiences needless failure and frustration as impatient adults try to speed up his achievements. Patience from adults—giving a child the time he needs to live his life fully, at his natural pace, each day, at each stage of his development—means stronger children and happier parent-child relationships. JAMES L. HYMES, JR.

See also READINESS

PEDIATRICIAN *See* DOCTOR; MEDICAL SPECIALISTS

PEDIATRICS CLINIC *See* CLINICS

PERIOD *See* MENSTRUATION

PERMANENT WAVES

If your very young daughter begs for a permanent wave, or if you yourself have begun to think about one for her, three questions will probably occur to you. How safe is a permanent wave for my child? How will her hair look afterward? What about introducing a youngster to a sophisticated cosmetic process so early in life?

To the third question you will have to supply your own answer, based on your feelings about naturalness versus artificiality and on your daughter's temperament and needs. If she feels she has to have the permanent just to be like her friends, maybe this is the time to suggest to her that complete imitation isn't always necessary. If she wants a permanent because she feels she is unattractive, maybe it will provide a boost in confidence. But also, perhaps, there is some more basic way to bolster her confidence. As for your personal reaction, only you can decide whether you are among the many parents who feel that a child's loveliness is in clean, shining hair, kept that way with soap and water and brushing, or among the growing number who accept permanent waving for their daughters as a way to add body to the hair, to make it more manageable, and to increase the girl's attractiveness.

How her hair will look after the permanent has no positive answer, either. At best, a child's hair is more difficult to curb than an adult's, and skill in giving a permanent is required for good results. Strength of waving solution, length of exposure, and neutralization are major factors in success. A well-trained beautician with knowledge of the unique demands of permanent waving for children might be the best person to give your child her first permanent.

Your question about safety to your child's skin and hair can be answered with facts. Thousands of permanent waves are given to children each year with few untoward reactions. This is reassuring evidence that permanent waving is safe for the average child if caution and skill are used in giving the permanent. But the horny surface layer of a child's skin is thinner than that of an adult, and the likelihood of irritation by the chemicals used for a permanent is greater. Therefore, whether your child is given a permanent either at home or by a professional beautician, certain minimum precautions should be respected: (1) Keep waving solution away from eyes, ears, nose, and off the skin; (2) keep waving lotion and neutralizer out of reach during the process; (3) discard unused solutions; and (4) do not permit a permanent to be given when there are abrasions or scratches on the scalp.

If you use a home permanent, select one intended for children. Most manufacturers, in making up their products, conscientiously take into consideration the problems of children's hair so that both formula and directions for use are modified to promote safe and successful hair waving. VERONICA L. CONLEY

PERMISSIVENESS

The word "permissiveness" is used to describe an attitude of tolerance on the part of parents or teachers toward a child's normal and healthy behavior. It indicates gladness on the adult's part that the child is acting as he is and a full acceptance of the behavior as good and right for the child. It means that the child is not reprimanded, scolded, or stopped in any way from doing what he is doing. Rather, he is allowed or "permitted" to behave in his own way provided, of course, that the behavior is normal and healthy for his age. Usually this permission is not conveyed specifically by words but more by an accepting attitude. Sometimes the permission is conveyed to the child by the simple fact that his parents ignore what he is doing and refrain from any effort to stop or redirect it.

Permissiveness is interpreted by some people to mean that whatever a child wants to do is all right. They equate permissiveness with the absence of all prohibitions. Parents who are permissive are understood to be parents who never say "No." Most psychologists, however, would not describe such complete freedom as "permissiveness." They would probably describe it as "license" or "indulgence" or as being "overly permissive." Letting a child do whatever he feels like doing is not considered a helpful or constructive adult role. Permissiveness, rightly defined, is limited to an acceptance of normal, healthy behavior. Such easy-goingness has great value for children. It also makes the life of parents and of the family as a whole more enjoyable and pleasant.

Sound permissiveness is based on knowing the behavior that is characteristic of each stage of development. Such knowledge enables parents to draw a line when their child's behavior is not age appropriate. Then their role is not to be permissive but to do something. Exactly what they do must in turn depend upon the reason for the child's inappropriate behavior. But one thing is clear: Since the reason for it is *not* the stage of growth the child is in, his parent's action should *not* be to ignore or tolerate such behavior. Parents might respond by diverting the child, or by talking with him to teach him a better way of acting, or by punishing him, or by changing the environment. All these and other approaches are active approaches, designed to change a child's behavior. When a child is acting his age, however, the goal is not to change him but to let him be himself, to let him do what he has to do because of his particular age. Permissiveness—tolerance, gladness—is a quiet, accepting way that achieves this important goal.

It is important for children of all ages to have the opportunity to live fully whatever age they are. Each stage of growing makes its contribution toward the ultimate development of a strong and healthy personality. A normal, healthy infancy lays the base for a normal, healthy toddlerhood. A normal, healthy span of early childhood years lays the base for good health and good performance during the school years. A child cannot skip any part of his growing up without in some way weakening the whole structure of his life: The youngster misses the joys and satisfactions that should have been his during that skimped period of development. The strengths that period could have built into him are not present in their fullest. Permissiveness—letting a child live the normal life that is right for his age—guards against these two serious losses.

Whether or not they use the word, probably all parents and teachers today are more permissive than adults in the past. We know more about how children grow and develop. We are more willing to adjust to childhood needs. Without even thinking about it, we are all more tolerant of the normal activity and noise of children, of their energy and their curiosity, of their healthy eagerness to talk and ask questions, of their strong social urges to have friends. Both schools and homes have become more gentle places where children feel more free to be themselves. Adults have greatly benefited by the gradual change from the time when children were "seen but not heard." Parents today become more fully parents; they know their child as he really is. Teachers today have more live relationships with children and find more satisfactions in their work because they are dealing with responsive, free humans. Very few people would want to go back to the time when children were not permitted to be children but were expected instead to plunge directly into the quiet, staid ways of adulthood.

Great difficulty with permissiveness arises, however, over specific acts. The fact is that at every age some few characteristics that are normal and healthy, contributing to a child's development, are nevertheless annoying or troublesome for an adult. "Normal" behavior, right for the age, is not necessarily always the same as comfortable behavior, easy for an adult to live with. Very young babies quite normally spit up and drool, but wise parents do not blame the baby or go to great lengths to stop him. They know the behavior will change as the child grows. They adjust their own adult behavior to fit the baby's behavior. And so, at every age, some characteristic child responses call for the adult to make the adjustment.

Two-year-olds, for example, are characteristically more stubborn than they were as babies or than they will be later on. Around 2 years of age children are first struggling to build their self-awareness. This important development leads inevitably but temporarily to an increase in willfulness. Twos, to give another example, do not share their toys easily for the same basic reason. Overpossessiveness is one way in which they express their new self-awareness. Youngsters around 4 years of age characteristically show their independence in some extreme verbal mannerisms. They are more apt to talk big or to call names or to experiment with language that they somehow sense is not quite "nice." And so, at every age, in some few ways—yet ways important to the child—youngsters' normal reactions can be hard for some adults to tolerate. The more one knows about development and the behavior that is common to *all* children at various stages in growing, the easier it is to be permissive. The more one can see the contribution to development that the behavior makes, the easier it is to be permissive.

Permissiveness must be a comfortable, free response on the part of an adult. You cannot be "permissive" because the book says you should. Permissiveness is an attitude of gladness that a child is acting healthfully, exactly as he should for his age. It is an attitude that stems from a basic confidence that, although the child acts a certain way now, he will grow and his behavior will change as he grows. Children are very sensitive to how adults feel, even more so than they are to what adults say. If a child senses that his parents are displeased with his behavior but are quiet because they think they "should" tolerate it, he does not gain strength. The "permissiveness" is not genuine. The child is more apt to feel that he is pushing his parents around. He becomes frightened and unsure by their silence rather than feeling support and reassurance. We must know with a good deal of certainty what behavior we feel good about and then permit it wholeheartedly. Also we must never hesitate not to be permissive when our feelings point clearly in that direction.

JAMES L. HYMES, JR.

See also APPROVAL; DISCIPLINE; OVERPROTECTION; RULES AND REGULATIONS

PERSONALITY *See* MENTAL HEALTH; TESTS AND MEASUREMENTS

PERTUSSIS *See* WHOOPING COUGH

PETS

Among the blessings of growing up on a farm, surely none is more to be treasured than the privilege of having pets.

Almost from babyhood the farm child knows both the sound and the feel of dogs and puppies, of cats and kittens.

By the time he is drinking from a cup, he has exchanged moo's with the giver of his milk, squeals with the source of his breakfast bacon, and baa's with the ewe whose rejected lamb will send shivers of delight up his spine when it tries to suck his exploring fingers.

Then there are the creatures of wood and field. When he can climb, the farm child knows how many eggs are in the oriole's pouchlike nest; when he can roam, he knows where the mother rabbit has dug her burrow and how many bunnies are in it. He knows, too, when the mower has destroyed all but one of the furry family. Holding an orphaned wild thing to his cheek, he experiences for the first time the sad sweetness of compassion. Thus the miracle of birth and death are woven into the fabric of the farm child's life —and something more: He learns early that responsibility is more than a word; it is a daily deed. The strong protect the weak, even as his parents protect and care for him.

City and suburban children should not be denied the privilege of playing with and caring for pets, although ownership may be limited by conditions beyond parental control. Leases often ban pets, but the sternest of landlords usually will overlook a guppie, a guinea pig, or a parakeet. Many children, denied their own pets find satisfaction in visits to the zoo and in animal stories on television and in books and magazines.

Where there are no restrictions on pet ownership, the kind selected will depend upon the size of the home, the age of the

child and, of course, the personal preference (sometimes, the allergies) of the family.

In general, adults should forego the dubious pleasure of presenting a child with a delicate or baby animal at the height of Christmas or birthday festivities. Many small animals, perhaps separated from their mothers for the first time, are very much like human babies. It is cruel to introduce such creatures into a strange environment at the very time when neglect, if not mistreatment, is almost inevitable. A gift-wrapped collar and leash, for example, might well be used to herald the arrival of a puppy when calm and order have been restored.

A very young child cannot be expected to know how to handle and care for a new pet. Tail, legs, and ears, understandably, are convenient "handles," and eyes are made for affectionate poking. Now is the time to show the young explorer how to lift his tiny pet, how to pat and praise, and how to play so that mutual love and trust are firmly established forevermore.

Now is the time, too, to teach a child respect for the rights of animals of all ages and sizes—the right to rest quietly in a place of its own; to eat and drink undisturbed; to be protected from illness and danger. But never should a child be permitted to help with a sick animal or to intercede in a dogfight.

In the joy of acquiring a new pet, most children will agree readily to assume responsibility for care. But parents, particularly mothers, might as well be prepared to take over on those mornings when the school bus arrives before the overshoes are found or when extracurricular activities interfere after school. These things happen to adults, too, and who doesn't appreciate a helping hand?

Certainly, it is parents' responsibility to see that local laws are adhered to, including, in the case of dogs, licensing, leashing, curbing, and immunization against rabies. Here in itself is a splendid example in good citizenship which a child can readily understand.

Both the tangible and intangible values that pet ownership offers children are recognized by educators. The facts, skills, habits, and attitudes learned by children from their experiences with pets are being utilized by teachers to help children develop their abilities in reading, writing, oral language, arithmetic, and artistic expression. Indeed, by means of a classroom pet, teachers are helping children to compare ways of caring for their own health and appearance and to understand the relationship between pets and people, especially their mutual dependency and their affection. PATRICIA M. CHESLEY

See also CRUELTY; RESPONSIBILITY

Related article in WORLD BOOK: see specific animals, such as "Dog"

PHENYLKETONURIA (PKU) *See* MENTAL DEFICIENCY

PHONOGRAPH RECORDS

A child's record library should be as well chosen as an adult's. Haphazard purchases, listened to once or twice and then discarded, lower a child's standards of listening as well as diminish his respect for property. Let quality rather than quantity be your guide in building a record library.

It is time-consuming, however, to preview even a small portion of the many records on the market. Reliable reviews keep one abreast of new record releases, and standard items can be chosen from catalogues available in record shops and libraries or directly from the manufacturers. If you are planning to build a record library for your child, it would be worth the trouble to study catalogues and read the descriptions of the records. Decide on three or four that seem the most promising and go to a shop or library to listen to them. Build a collection gradually in this way, buying only one or two at a time. Folkway Records, 121 West 47th Street; the Children's Record Guild, 100 6th Avenue; and the L.P. Sales Corporation, distributors of Wonderland Records, 235 West 46th Street, all in New York, New York, publish catalogue listings. Their productions are appealingly varied and tasteful.

When you borrow records from a library, be as discriminating as you would be in making any choice that involves taste. Putting on a record or turning on the radio or television amounts to inviting performers into your home as guests. Since records are usually a child's introduction to professional music, they have an important part in developing his taste in music.

Children beyond nursery age will also enjoy some of the records played by adults in the family—folk songs of all nations, show tunes, lighter classics, and certain selections of concert and opera music. Such listening provides another way children can share the pleasure that music affords. BEATRICE LANDECK

See also MUSIC

PHYSICAL CHECKUP

Of course a mother takes her child to the doctor's office when she suspects he is ill or when he has suffered an injury. But an equally important aspect of the general health supervision of an infant or a child is his physical checkup. Such checkups let the doctor see whether growth and development is proceeding normally and that no abnormalities have developed.

During the first year of a baby's life, the physical checkup should be performed once a month. This checkup provides an opportunity to see whether the baby's nutrition is adequate. He is weighed and his length is measured. The doctor usually measures the growth of the head, too, in an effort to determine whether the brain is growing and developing normally. He checks the function of the heart and lungs and notes the size of organs in the abdomen. Development of the baby's nervous system is also checked by noting when he starts to smile, when he can coordinate the movements of his eyes, when he can hold his head up, and when he starts to sit, crawl, and walk. Hearing and seeing abilities are evaluated. And the various shots to prevent infectious diseases are begun during these visits.

In the second year of life, since the child has begun to walk, special attention is given to the alignment of his feet and legs. During this period, visits to the doctor should be at least every three months.

After the second year, it is generally recommended that physical checkups be made at least twice a year. At the time the child enters school, he should have a physical checkup that includes attention to hearing, vision, speech, the heart, and the bones and joints to be certain that he will be able to keep up with and benefit from the school program.

As the child approaches adolescence, his doctor will be interested in seeing that growth and sexual development are normal. At this time it may be well to let the child see the doctor alone so that any questions concerning development may be discussed privately. If an adolescent's food intake is not adequate for his rapid growth, as is sometimes the case, the doctor's examination may reveal this inadequacy.

As part of the physical checkup, regular dental visits are in order. A child should start seeing the dentist at 2½ or 3 years and every six months thereafter. During adolescence, it is desirable that he see his dentist every three months, since this is a period when cavities may develop very rapidly.

Physical Checkup Calendar

First year:	Once each month
Second year:	Once every three months
Childhood:	Twice yearly
	Special examination at start of school
Dental:	Every six months starting at age 2½ to 3 years
	Every three months during adolescence

JULIUS B. RICHMOND

See also DOCTOR; FAMILY HEALTH RECORD

PHYSICAL DEVELOPMENT *See* GROWTH

PHYSICAL HANDICAP *See* HANDICAPPED CHILD

PHYSICIAN *See* DOCTOR

PIGEON TOE

When a child walks with his toes pointing together and the heels outward, he is said to be pigeon-toed. A mild degree of this condition is not uncommon before walking is well established. If it is not corrected by the time walking is well established, some wedging of the child's shoes may be required.

Sometimes a pigeon-toe position indicates a problem in bone alignment of the foot, and plaster casting is required. If there is any question about your child's foot health, consult your doctor. RUTH S. KEMPE

See also KNOCK-KNEE

PIMPLES

Small elevations occurring at the pores of the skin surface are called pimples. They usually develop because of an increase in the secretions that come onto the skin surface through the pores of the glands of the skin. The increase in secretions usually occurs at the time sexual changes are developing in adolescent boys and girls. At such times, the pores may become plugged and the skin will then have "bumps"—or pimples. If many pimples are present, the condition may be called acne. Pimples should not be squeezed, for delicate skin tissues may be destroyed, and scars may form.

If pimples come on unusually early, under 8 years, the child should have a medical examination to rule out abnormality of the endocrine glands. JULIUS B. RICHMOND

See also ACNE; COSMETICS

PINK EYE *See* CONJUNCTIVITIS

PINWORM

The eggs of pinworms gain entry into the gastrointestinal tract, usually from some contact with a person who is infested with the worms and has the pinworm eggs on his or her fingers. These worms are so named because they are long and thin and resemble the shape of a pin. They are whitish in color and may sometimes be seen protruding from the anus of the child or in his stool. They are usually present in very large numbers in the intestines—occasionally so much so that they may plug the appendix and set up an inflammation for which an operation may be necessary. The most common symptom, however, is intense itching about the anus, which causes the child to scratch the area severely. The itching becomes worse at night after going to bed.

The condition is highly contagious, and if one child is found to have pinworms, the entire family should be examined, for often all members will be infested. Treatment should be attempted only under the care of a doctor. JULIUS B. RICHMOND

PLACENTA *See* REPRODUCTION

PLASTIC SHEETING *See* LAYETTE AND BABY EQUIPMENT

PLAY

Play, far from being an aimless and unnecessary activity, is a child's way of experimenting with his environment. In fact, some people have said that play is the "business" of babies.

It takes a while for your baby to realize that he can grasp the bright bauble that he has followed with his eyes. His first physical contact with a desired object causes so much excitement and pleasure that he indulges in random movements of arms and legs—and the precious toy is gone. He has accomplished an important step when he learns that he can hold on to something in his hand and still wiggle his arms and move his legs.

In a similar way, a baby experiments with moving his body. He raises his head and even finds ways of turning himself around in his crib to get a better view of his world. Long before he can crawl, he can wriggle himself around the crib. Next, he begins experimenting with sitting up and, later, with standing. He becomes more aware of things and tries to touch and grab what attracts his attention. Touching and tasting are his first methods of finding out about things. He is a true scientist, discovering how things feel and taste and what he can make things do. He

learns that some things are soft and cuddly and other things make noises. He discovers that pushing his toys off the tray of his high chair will create a delightful bang. He enjoys the sound his rattle makes when he shakes it and he is puzzled when he doesn't get the same result by shaking his woolly dog. He tries banging things together and knocking them against the sides of his crib or playpen. Long before he has learned words, he imitates sounds and actually carries on an unintelligible but animated and earnest conversation. He learns to throw long before he can catch, and he is intrigued by things that come and go. His game of hide-and-seek is another step in finding out about things. At this early stage manipulation is the important part of his activity. This is the period when the wrapping paper and the box may be more fascinating than the toy that came in the box.

Finding out about the world around him continues to be an important part of a child's play as he gets older. Walking, running, and climbing are exhilarating. For apartment-house children who use elevators, steps have a great attraction. A child starts with push toys and then learns to pull, to dig, and to throw. Soon he learns to ride a kiddie car, a tricycle, and finally a bike. A young child accustomed to automation may climb into a wagon and wait expectantly for it to move. He may get out and push it, climb in again, and look around to see what is wrong. He has recognized the gross similarity of a wagon and an automobile, but the presence or lack of an engine is beyond his ken.

The Values of Play

Many and varied activities are important in developing the large muscles of a child's arms and legs. Gradually he begins to gain control of the finer muscles of hand and eye; his movements become less clumsy and jerky and there is better coordination. As he handles many different kinds and sizes of materials, he begins to learn about color, size, and shape. He observes that some things move more easily than others; some things can be poured and others can be piled. Words take on meaning as he experiments with objects that are heavy or light, soft or hard, rough or smooth. Some things are bigger or higher than he is. Some things remind him of other things and he sees relationships between various types of objects.

Imagination in Play

The type of activity carried on by children in their play is largely an imitation of what they see adults do. They imitate gestures and movements, and their first sounds, other than crying, duplicate the sounds they hear. As soon as they begin to walk, they will try to dust and sweep as they see adults do. Little girls prepare and serve food and feed their doll babies. If there is a baby brother or sister, they will try to feed him. Putting the doll to bed and taking it up again begins very early. Little boys drive imaginary cars and trucks; they pilot airplanes. A telephone very early becomes a favorite toy, and in households where a great deal of reading is done, a 2-year-old may hold a book and pretend to read. Youngsters of 3 or 4 will scribble on a page, giving a good facsimile of handwriting, and then turn to an adult and say, "Read me my letter." Do not let him down. Use your own imagination and you will be justly rewarded by his pleasure and satisfaction in your understanding of his efforts.

Children's imagination has no limits. Objects seldom represent the same thing twice. What may be a collection of rocks to you is some delectable food to "cook" on an improvised stove. A series of chairs can be a train, and an inverted crate makes a wonderful cave. It is therefore important to provide flexible play materials that can be converted to many uses. Through this imitative and imaginative play a child expresses his ideas and his feelings. When he plays with other children, he tries out his ideas on them and learns also how other people think and feel and react to what he does and says.

It is through this type of play and manipulation of material that the child increases his knowledge and understanding. As he grows older, he needs new materials and new challenges. Children up to 3 years of age like the sociability of playing where there are other children, but they do not play together in the way older children do. It is important that the littler ones are protected from the overstimulation of older children who use a young child like a toy or a puppet.

Other Values in Play

Play has another important function for adults as well as for children. It is a wholesome outlet for aggressive feelings. The strain of a day at the office can be relieved by attacking an innocent golf ball. The number of kindly family men who never miss a boxing match is another indication of the way some of us work out our aggressive feelings, even though vicariously, through the television screen. With children, because of their small size and limited physical strength, play serves a very useful role in acting out feelings of impotence and anger. When a 4-year-old climbs to the top of a jungle gym, he suddenly finds himself looking down upon the adults whom he usually sees at knee level. He may chant, "I'm the King of the Castle and you're the dirty rascal." There is no offense implied—he is just feeling a new sense of power. He also gets a feeling of importance when he is an airplane pilot or a spaceman or the daddy of the house. His imitation of adult gestures and tones of voice are often as revealing as they are accurate. A little girl knows she must be kind to her baby brother. She goes through all the appropriate motions when she is with him. Her resentment at the time mother spends on this helpless intruder, however, can be harmlessly worked out with her baby doll, which she feeds lovingly but finds very "bad" and in need of frequent hard spankings.

Play and the Family

Just as a baby learns to love and trust adults through the love and care of his mother, so a child learns to adjust to other social groups by his experience in the family. He learns to share and to accept other people by playing with brothers and sisters and by being with the other people in the household. Since play and recreation are important for both adults and children, the space and opportunity for these activities must be provided in the home today. It is also important to recognize that while there are many kinds of recreation in which the family can share, it is important not to be so carried away by "togetherness" that no space or time is allowed for the pursuit of individual activities or for permitting certain members of the family group to follow interests that do not involve the entire family. An older boy who is working on a hi-fi set can be justifiably annoyed by having his young brother or sister come in and meddle with his materials. Children must learn respect for things that are important to other members of the family. Fine chisels from father's woodcarving set should not be used to pry open cans or to remove nails when a small boy wants to construct a space ship out of a fruit crate. Similarly, respect should be accorded this same boy's rock collection, which is *not* just a "collection of dirt." ADELE FRANKLIN

See also GROWTH; IMAGINATION; IMITATION; PLAY GROUPS; TOYS AND PLAY EQUIPMENT

PLAY-ACTING *See* DRAMATICS

PLAY EQUIPMENT *See* TOYS AND PLAY EQUIPMENT

PLAY GROUPS

Playing alone is fine, and necessary—part of the time. But all children need group play, too. A child should play as much as possible. Play serves many purposes in the life of a child.

Much of a child's creative play will be done alone. Group play encourages a child to use his big muscles as he runs, jumps, skips, hops, climbs, and marches. As children play together, they find out a great deal about getting along with each other. You can talk until doomsday about sharing and cooperating or about standing up for one's rights or about the unpopularity of the bully, but these things take on real meaning for a child only when he has opportunities to see how they work—or don't work—in his own experience.

If your preschooler seems bored or if he has no playmates in your immediate neighborhood, perhaps you and two or three other mothers could start a cooperative play group. The back-yard play group is the simplest example of such a venture. One mother found in her town a woman who had had training and experience in nursery education and who was willing to give counsel to the proposed play group. Three other mothers living near and needing companionship for their preschool children readily agreed to take turns, one morning each week, in caring for the four children involved. Each took on a morning in her own home and yard. They found that each home could provide some special interest or activity for the children. One yard had an excellent tree for climbing, one a fine sandbox, another easels and art materials, and the fourth home had suitable records and costumes for dancing and dramatic play.

The professionally trained and experienced woman agreed to take the fifth morning. Her wide experience equipped her to provide a rich variety of activities in music, storytelling, cooking, dramatic play, art, and nature experiences. The other mothers visited her group as they found time and learned from her.

No fees are involved in this kind of project. The play group is planned and staffed by mothers. Fathers may be called upon to build furniture or play equipment, to keep toys and equipment in repair, and to paint playroom walls and scenery.

If you plan to start a play group, it would be wise to consider carefully the people you would like to include. Select parents who will get along well together and who will share the work. Only adults who genuinely love children, their own as well as other people's, should be included. Children are quick to recognize the mother who takes her morning with them merely as a duty.

Mothers who have worked in play groups are enthusiastic about the benefits of such a plan. These mothers find they have more time for other members of their families and more time with their husbands, plus a little time for outside activities. The children, of course, will gain in many ways. Their craft skills will improve and they will learn to get along with other children before being plunged into kindergarten. ADELE FRANKLIN

See also DRAMATICS; TOYS AND PLAY EQUIPMENT

PLAYING HOOKY *See* TRUANCY

PLAYMATES *See* FRIENDS

PLAYPEN

Your baby's playpen should be selected with an eye to the space available in your home. There are several styles and sizes of this basic piece of baby equipment. The playpen you select should have a finish that is smooth, nonsplintering, and nontoxic.

Some playpens are constructed of sturdy nylon webbing, secured top and bottom to tubular steel frames. The webbing gives as the baby moves against it, and the mesh is fine enough so that toys cannot fall out of the pen, nor can pets get in. Pads are available for various shaped playpens. These pads tie at the corners to keep them from moving or lumping.

Begin to use your playpen when the baby is between 3 and 4 months old, before he has had an opportunity to become accustomed to unlimited freedom. Here he will creep, crawl, sit up, pull up, and even walk in due time. Put him in his playpen for short periods of time, even allowing him to take his nap there occasionally, first making sure there is no draft.

The mobility of a playpen makes it possible to move it from room to room with you as you go about your household tasks, or if you find keeping the playpen in one room works best for you, be sure to check on the baby frequently. Let him hear you and see you often so he won't think of his playpen as a prison. And never put him in his playpen for punishment. In warm weather he will enjoy having his playpen on the porch or on the lawn.

Playpens that fold away for storage make ideal cribs for a traveling baby.

See also ACCIDENT PREVENTION; CREEPING; FRESH AIR; TOYS AND PLAY EQUIPMENT

PNEUMONIA

Inflammation of the lungs, regardless of cause, is called pneumonia. Although some instances of pneumonia are caused by chemicals such as toxic fumes and oils, or other foreign materials such as foods accidentally taken into the windpipe, or trachea, most are caused by infections and can come from many types of bacteria and viruses. Tuberculosis once caused pneumonia frequently but fortunately does so much less commonly now. Many instances of pneumonia occur as complications of other diseases such as colds, influenza, and measles.

The child with pneumonia usually breathes very rapidly and sometimes with a grunting sound. He develops a cough, but in young infants the cough is often not very forceful. Fever is usually present but may not be as great in young infants. The child usually is listless and, in severe cases, appears desperately ill.

A baby or child ill with pneumonia should be under the care of a doctor. Hospitalization is often necessary, for the child may need oxygen and intravenous fluids. Except for pneumonia caused by viruses, sulfa and antibiotic drugs are effective and usually shorten the length of the illness. JULIUS B. RICHMOND

See also COLDS; SICK CHILD; VIRUS

POETRY *See* BOOKS FOR CHILDREN; BOOKS FOR PARENTS; READING ALOUD

POISONING AND POISONS

If you have a child 5 years old or younger, the chances of his eating, drinking, or inhaling some poisonous substance are extremely likely. Some 500,000 children each year succumb to their natural curiosity to touch, feel, and taste enough deadly compounds to kill 500 children and put many others in hospitals.

Bad smells and horrible tastes as adults know them are unknown to children. The child who refuses his milk or his orange juice may gulp ink or lighter fluid with gusto. Left to their own devices children will eat or drink not only ink and lighter fluid, but also glue, crayons, paint, solvents, matches, medicines, reducing tablets, sleeping pills, turpentine, bleach, and countless other common everyday household necessities.

The kitchen, bathroom, and bedrooms of your home are the most likely places for poisonings to occur. Household cleansing agents and solvents, and even insecticides, are stored in kitchen and bathroom cupboards easily accessible to children. In bathroom medicine cabinets are kept tins, tubes, and bottles containing powders, lotions, and pills. Bedroom night tables are likely to hold tranquilizers, sleeping pills, and aspirin, any one of which, if taken in sufficient quantity, can be fatal to a child. Children see their parents take medicine and mimics that these little ones are, they also take the pretty-colored pills. But mother's medicine is often baby's poison.

Of all medications, aspirin causes the greatest number of child poisonings. The adult tablet is four times the strength of a child's dose. If a youngster eats several adult-size aspirin tablets or a large number of children's size, he is in grave danger. The child may not seem ill immediately because the results of aspirin poisoning can be delayed. Several hours later the child becomes listless, breathing is rapid and deep, headache and hearing disturbances occur. In very serious cases delirium, convulsions, and coma may occur. *Every child who unnecessarily takes aspirin should be seen by a physician.* Get him to your doctor or to the nearest physician if yours is not available. No time should be lost in starting treatment of a stricken child, for delay can complicate successful therapy in serious poisoning cases.

In addition to keeping lethal compounds in plain sight or in cupboards without locks, parents often make it even easier for children to drink or eat these substances. Mother may empty the half cup of bleach from its big, cumbersome bottle to a soft-drink bottle for easier handling and storage. But her toddler, happily exploring a cabinet, knows only that this kind of bottle yields a delightful bubbly soda pop—or does it? Kerosene used for heating or cooking may also be the culprit in a poisoning accident. The drip cup near the heater catches dripping kerosene, but it is also tempting to a thirsty or curious child. Sometimes a weed killer is mixed in a teacup and then left on the back steps. A child finds it, sips it, and may die an agonizing death.

Chipped paint is fascinating to some small children. They pick at blistered paint on walls or furniture, eat it, and become ill. Old paint

• Keep calm.

• Call your physician or take the victim to a hospital emergency room or to the nearest poison control center.

• Carry out first-aid measures, but do not waste time trying first one thing and then another. If someone else is available, one person should apply first aid while the other calls the doctor.

• Save the container to help the physician identify the poison.

FIRST AID IN POISONING ACCIDENTS

It is *extremely important* to know that the treatment given a victim of a poisoning accident will vary according to the type of poison taken.

IF A CHILD

SWALLOWED POISONS

Do not cause vomiting if the patient—

- Is unconscious or in a coma
- Is having fits (convulsions)
- Has swallowed a corrosive substance that burns the mouth or throat (toilet bowl cleaners, lye, ammonia, bleach)
- Has swallowed a petroleum product (kerosene, lighter fluid, paint thinner, furniture polish)

Make the patient vomit in all other instances of swallowed poisons.

- Have him drink some water or milk.
- Keep his mouth open with a spoon handle. Place him face down with his head lower than his hips.
- Tickle the back of his throat with your finger. If you cannot get him to vomit within a few minutes, lose no more time. Get medical attention *at once.*

may contain lead. If a youngster persists in eating paint chips, he is in real danger. (The symptoms of chronic lead poisoning are colic, pallor, weakness, constipation, and cramps. In acute lead poisoning there may be nausea, vomiting, muscular weakness, and pain in the legs, severe headache, convulsions, and coma.) If any of these symptoms occur, take your child to your physician or to the emergency room of the nearest hospital.

Cleanliness is part of our culture. We have many products that help us achieve this goal. Metal polishes, drain and bowl cleansers, waxes and polishes, bleach, ammonia, are all in daily use and in constant reach of children. Many parents are unaware of, or disregard, the warnings on these caustic substances. Soaps and detergents are usually stored in low cabinets where youngsters can easily reach them, as are dangerous furniture polishes and waxes. Parents seldom realize that the kerosene-like solvent in these waxes and polishes is a very dangerous ingredient. Happily, ingredients in cleansing creams, beautifying lotions, and hair tonics usually are not harmful and therefore seldom cause serious illness in children. But the insecticides, weedicides, herbicides, and rodenticides that are used so frequently to keep homes and premises free of insects, weeds, and mice are real killers. And, *eating* or *drinking* these substances isn't the only way to become poisoned. Some of these products can be absorbed through the skin. Prolonged inhalation of their vapors may also be harmful. *Read all warnings on these containers and follow the manufacturers' directions.*

REMEMBER

- Store medicines after each use. Do not leave them in convenient places about the house, including your purse.
- Flush unused pills and liquids down the toilet.
- Do not put household cleaning products in teacups, drinking glasses, soft-drink bottles, or food containers.
- Do not leave cleaning cloths or sponges saturated with furniture polish or other cleaning fluids lying about. Babies love to chew on these, with serious results.
- Check the basement and the garage regularly to be sure no one has left poisonous products within reach of small children.

Prevention is the key. *Protect* a very young child, but teach him, as he grows older, that it is dangerous to eat or drink or smell strange liquids or powders he may see about the home or yard. Teach him to ask you about each new thing. But, at the same time, adults must remember that curiosity is part of the normal development of a young child. Thus it is up to parents to keep a watchful eye over small children and, also, to keep everything that might harm them out of sight and out of reach. Older children in a family can be enlisted as "private eyes" to help protect the little ones. IRVING SUNSHINE

See also ARTIFICIAL RESPIRATION; EMERGENCY; EMETICS; FOOD POISONING

IS POISONED

INHALED POISONS

- Carry patient to fresh air immediately. Don't let him walk.
- Loosen tight clothing around neck and chest.
- Apply artificial respiration if breathing has stopped or is irregular.
- Keep patient quiet and warm.
- Get medical attention *at once.*

SKIN CONTAMINATION

- Flush affected skin area immediately with lots of water. If the poison is oily, or does not wash off with water, cleanse thoroughly with soap and warm water, then rinse freely.
- Remove contaminated clothing.
- Get medical attention *at once.*

POISON IVY, OAK, AND SUMAC

Three common and closely related plants that give serious skin rashes to most people upon exposure are poison ivy, poison oak, and poison sumac.

Perhaps the most common of these is poison ivy. Most often encountered as a creeping vine, it can appear also as a bush or shrub or as a tree. Poison ivy is characterized by three leaves on one stem. The leaves are sharply pointed, with slightly notched edges. The surface of the leaves is shiny and the stems have a reddish tinge. In winter the plant bears white berries. Children who spend a great deal of time outdoors, especially in woods and fields, or those who help with gardening should be helped to familiarize themselves with the appearance of this plant. Merely touching the leaves is usually sufficient to cause an eruption. The small blisters may appear after a few hours or a few days. They are caused by an irritating oil contained in the plant. Few people are immune.

If you have reason to believe your child has touched poison ivy, immediately wash his hands and any exposed portions of the skin thoroughly in a rich and generous lather of mild soap. Rinse with plenty of water and lather again, and rinse again. Do not rub too hard. Do not use brushes, sponges, or other rough or harsh materials. Do not use strong soap.

The rash is characterized by a series of small spots and blisters that itch furiously. Scratching them spreads the eruption and should, therefore, be avoided. Clothing that has been in contact with ivy may be just as irritating as the ivy leaves themselves and should be washed or cleaned before being worn again.

Home treatment is usually unsatisfactory. Salves and oily substances spread the irritating oil to new areas of skin. It is best to see a physician at once for the quickest results. In extreme cases of poison ivy susceptibility, immunizing injections have sometimes been recommended, but ordinarily it is best simply to try to avoid contact with the ivy.

Poison oak and sumac are less commonly contracted because they are less likely to be handled. In areas where these plants are prevalent, a child should become acquainted with their appearance and avoid contact with them. Otherwise, the precautions are the same as for poison ivy. W. W. BAUER

See also FIRST AID

Poison oak

Poison ivy

Poison sumac

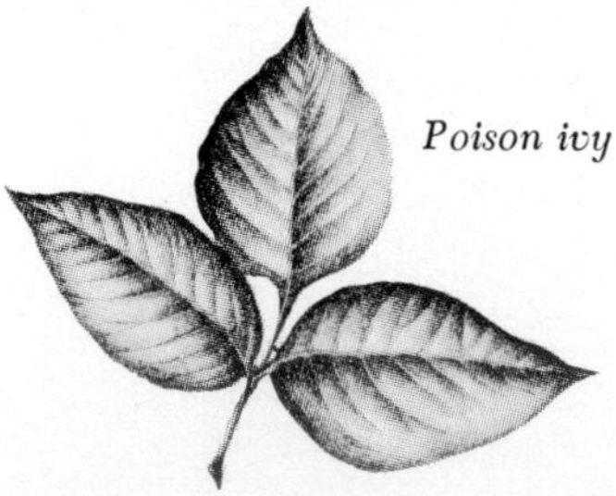

POISONS *See* POISONING AND POISONS

POLIO

Polio, also known as poliomyelitis and as infantile paralysis, can be a disease serious enough to cause death or paralysis. But paralytic polio is no longer the widespread threat it once was, largely because of the Salk vaccine with which literally millions of children and young adults are now inoculated.

The Salk vaccine is frequently given to infants along with their diphtheria, whooping cough, and tetanus shots. In this way protection against polio can be obtained with fewer skin punctures and undesirable reactions and less pain. Sabin oral poliovaccine has also been found to be safe and effective for children. Your doctor should be consulted about when he wants to begin and how often he wants to give your child protection against polio.

The improved care now given to polio patients is another reason for fewer deaths and less crippling from the disease than formerly. Also, gamma globulin given to patients who have contracted paralytic polio tends to make the disease less severe.

The onset of polio may be sudden and the symptoms may at first resemble those of a common cold. There may also be fever, chills, sore throat, headache, severe intestinal upset, stiff back, or muscle spasms in the neck or thighs.

Even if preventive shots have been given, a child with polio symptoms should be seen by his doctor immediately. MARIE A. HINRICHS

See also COMMON COMMUNICABLE DISEASES; GAMMA GLOBULIN; SICK CHILD; TYPEWRITER

POLITENESS *See* MANNERS

POPULARITY

It is a very pleasant thing to be popular. To be sought after, to be given tokens of being liked, to have one's choice of companions—these are signs of popularity. Toward this envied state innumerable adults unceasingly push their offspring, never questioning its desirability. The thoughtful parent, however, will have several questions. Is popularity really an unqualified good? What is popularity worth when compared with other values such as integrity, peace of mind, and solid achievement? And if popularity needs to be deliberately sought, can it really be achieved? These questions need to be considered seriously because of the desperate emphasis on popularity found in so many American homes. Mothers seem to be particularly afflicted, and the intensity of their concern, especially about their daughters, is pathetic.

Popularity during childhood is likely to be a shifting state. A child may be popular and outgoing at 5 but ignored and lonely at 10. Secondly, popularity may depend on how long a child has been in the group. If his parents move frequently, he may not have enough time to establish his position. A good deal depends, too, on the kind of group to which he comes. One with several solidly entrenched popular leaders may be harder to break into than a loosely organized group.

Since the qualities needed to achieve popularity often vary with the group, parents might do well to ask themselves whether they would want a child of theirs to be popular in all groups. In some groups of 10- and 11-year-old boys, defiance of adults, minor delinquencies, and dangerous "stunts," such as hitching rides on the backs of trucks, form the basis for group activity. To be popular in such a group, a boy would not only have to "go along" with the others, but also outdo them. Certain girls' groups may dictate that the members worship the latest teen-age entertainer, slavishly follow the latest teen-age fad, and spend very little time on schoolwork. The serious student is not a likely candidate for popularity in such a group.

To gain acceptance in some groups, intellectually superior children have deliberately made errors in schoolwork, adopted slipshod speech, and pretended interests to conform to the fads of the crowd. Whether popularity is worth the price of dishonesty and denial of self is doubtful.

Even assuming that there is a group acceptable to parents, there is still no formula that will assure a child's popularity in that group. In general, popular children seem to be comfortable in their own skins and with their age-mates. They are usually well-coordinated physically so that they are good at active games. They make advances to others easily, and they are usually not great individualists, nor far ahead of their group in intelligence. They accept teasing with good grace and a sense of humor. And reasonably good grooming is often a characteristic of popular children. Above all, they tend to be self-confident, serene individuals who do not doubt their reception by others.

The child who is not popular may be unsure of himself and anxious. Upbraiding him or urging him to do what he cannot do will only make him worse. It is important to remember that popularity is not an all-or-none thing. It is a matter of degree, and a child may be better off with less popularity among his age-mates but with more respect shown him as an individual in his home.

Preoccupation with being popular is likely to be a sign of insecurity, whether it occurs in children or in adults. If popularity does not come spontaneously, more attention should be paid to the underlying causes and less to the outward signs. RUTH E. HARTLEY

See also ACCEPTANCE; SOCIAL DEVELOPMENT; SOCIAL PRESSURES

POSSESSIVENESS

Adults have every reason to expect children to be possessive. After all, we live in an acquisitive society and make little or no effort to conceal the delight and pride we enjoy in the fact of ownership. Our response to a new Easter hat, new suit of clothes, dishwasher, or automobile becomes our children's response to their newly acquired possessions. They act like us, only more clearly so, because of their basic naïveté. This very same characteristic—their lack of experience—may easily distort their sense of values. Almost always, a child's early values depend more on what a thing means to him than on what it means to others. He may, for example, enjoy the noisy tissue paper and colorful box more than the costly present that came in it. Even more important, a child often invests what is his with some small part of himself. What may be inanimate objects to adults are often endowed by the child with special symbolic meaning and are therefore more a living part of him than adults realize. Extreme possessiveness thus signifies the clutching dependency of an insecure child. If he appears ungenerous, helping him feel more certain of our love will dilute his possessiveness back toward normal. ALLAN FROMME

See also IMITATION.

POSTER PAINT *See* ART EXPERIENCES

POSTNASAL DRIP *See* SINUSITIS

POSTPARTUM BLUES *See* DEPRESSION

POSTURE

A toddler has a long body and a big head in proportion to his arms and legs. He walks on a broad base. His abdomen is prominent, his feet look flat, and there is usually some bowing of the legs. At this age, as he also does later, the child adopts the posture and way of moving that keep his body in proper balance. Preaching posture has no value during the preschool years and may only confuse a child.

The skeleton the child is born with is the most important factor in his posture. He may inherit his father's round-shouldered posture or the ramrod stance of his grandfather. Some children have relaxed muscles and ligaments, which may result in knock-knees or bow-legs. Other children are firmly and tightly built; even when at rest they do not slump. A child with a chronic fatigue will likely slump and sag. Unusual tallness may make an adolescent walk with shoulders slumped.

There is, also, a direct relation between the development of muscular strength and co-ordination and the establishment of good posture. In no small degree the maintenance of good health, working efficiency, and attractive appearance throughout life depend upon good carriage. Good posture is achieved through the balanced action of the muscles controlling the head, neck, trunk, hips, and feet. The vigorous and varied play activities of later childhood include the coordinated use of the whole body in many different positions. These activities contribute directly to developing good posture.

Parents will be wise not to nag their child to "Stand up straight!" and "Square your shoulders!" A child with the double problem of bad posture and nagging parents is likely to slump and sag all the more. Children often will listen to a doctor and will participate in good-posture campaigns at school more readily than they will respond to parental insistence.

See also GROWTH; NUTRITION; PLAY

PRACTICAL NURSE *See* NURSE

PRAISE *See* APPROVAL

PREADOLESCENT CHILD

Preadolescence is the time when, as some say, "The nicest children behave in the most awful way." It is also a highly significant period in the life of your child.

The preadolescent is a volatile, changing individual who is beginning to free himself from the adults in his life, but he is not ready to go as far as he thinks he wants to go on his own. He is extremely interested in and influenced by children of his own age. Although he is growing more slowly now, he is always hungry. Preadolescents, especially boys, are exuberant and full of boundless energy that they work off in sports and competitions. Curiosity, rambunctiousness, and poor manners are characteristics of boys of this period; the girls tend to be lady-like, feminine, neat, and tidy.

A child between the ages of 9 and 12 is a preadolescent. Slight changes in body build occur in both boys and girls at this period. Limbs lengthen; bones harden (and break more easily); blood pressure increases; pulse rate decreases; more food is necessary and is consumed accordingly. Muscle tissues increase and the child grows stronger. Your boy is almost twice as strong at this time of his life as when he was 6. Your girl, although increasing in strength, is somewhat weaker than a boy her age. Until the age of 10, boys on the average are slightly taller than girls; but from then on until they are about 15, boys are somewhat shorter than girls. The same kind of difference is found in weight: Girls are slightly lighter than boys until about 11; after 11, for a time, boys may weigh less than girls.

Motor coordination has improved so that the preadolescent is able to cope with more complex activities. Baseball, football, swimming, and tennis, as well as carpentry, leatherwork, and model building, can be handled with increased ease.

Although most preadolescent children do not grow facial hair, experience voice change, breast development, or menstruation, some do. Some children may show these changes at 12 and some as early as 10 or 11. Considerable variation among children in their rate of growth and development is a perfectly normal result of individual differences.

Hail, Hail, the Gang

The period of preadolescence has been characterized as the "gang" period. Age-mates, or peers, have an increased importance. Boys and girls get deeply involved in social relationships with children their own age. Friends are everything, and parents may sometimes feel left out.

Your preadolescent child seeks this type of social life with his friends because of his growing independence from adult authority. He wants to be a person in his own right and to spend his time with other children who accept him on his own merits. The group gives children relationships in which they learn to get along each with his or her own sex, learn what the values and attitudes are about being a boy or a girl. This "gang" experience also provides the security of a group. It gives the preadolescent a sense of belonging, which in turn helps him to master certain childish fears. The group of his age-mates has practical advantages as well. With them your child now has companions with whom to carry out projects or play team games.

The apparent loyalty of children to their group makes many parents fear that they have lost control—that their child has thrown them over for his friends. Unless parents look beneath the surface for the real meaning of preadolescent behavior, they may be both bewildered and hurt. Worse, unnecessary conflicts are bound to develop. Preadolescent children are likely to resent adult supervision if it seems to be denying them independence. If, however, supervision stays within the limits of the child's own sense of justice and fair play and does not represent a display of power, he is more likely to accept guidance by parents or other adults.

Preadolescent Versus Adult

A child's social development also is shown in his dealing with authority. In our society a person has to grow away from parental and adult domination to an independent and self-controlled life. If your child is to make a good transition from childhood to adulthood, he has to have opportunities to make his own decisions, to learn from his own mistakes, and to develop a sense of responsibility. The preadolescent takes strong steps in this direction. He rejects many standards of adults. Boys in particular substitute sloppiness, disorder, and disobedience for their previous cleanliness, orderliness, and obedience. They are often teasing, discourteous, scuffling, rebellious, inattentive, careless, untidy, tardy, and disobedient. Girls at this period are not quite so trying, for they achieve prestige with their friends by being tidy, neat, friendly, and pretty. Boys seem to prefer other boys who are unkempt, boisterous, and aggressive rather than those who are submissive, too clean, and reserved. The preadolescent behaves in the same way both at home and at school. In both places he is striving for greater self-expression and for power over his own life.

The differences among preadolescents and other age groups, and the differences between preadolescent boys and preadolescent girls, are not accidental. Boys and girls behave as they do because each sex has a different developmental need. The boys have to free themselves of mother domination and to reaffirm their maleness, while the girls need to strengthen their feminine identification.

Boys and girls need to free themselves from adult supervision. This is an important step toward achieving maturity, toward being in control of their own destinies.

Another characteristic of the preadolescent period is the increased separation of the sexes in keeping with our society where we have strong sex typing, with markedly different expectations for boys and for girls. Boys prefer to be with boys; girls with girls. The differences between boys and girls in physical development and in values make for this separation. Boys are more pronounced in their desire for segregation than girls, perhaps because boys have greater difficulty in throwing off the feminine influence of mothers and women teachers—relatively pervasive influences in their lives at this time.

Moral Standards Are High

Rejection of moral standards at this period does not necessarily mean that your child is losing his sense of right or wrong. Quite the contrary. During the period of preadolescence, a child shows marked increase in moral growth and begins to incorporate ideas of right and wrong as a part of himself. Heretofore he tended to accept ideas of right and wrong from his parents, teachers, and other people important to him; he thought of standards as arbitrary and not within his control. Now he gains the feeling that right and wrong come from within himself. This gives him a sense of strength and flexibility and understanding. He feels free to make changes in the rules, depending on the requirements of the situation. He also has a strong sense of justice, sometimes sternly held. Unfair actions of parents and teachers are noted and talked about when he is with his friends. The preadolescent child can become irritated with adults when they act unfairly.

In the area of values and ideas of right and wrong, the preadolescent frequently comes into conflict with his parents. The child may see that the values and standards of his parents or teachers differ from those of the children he goes with, and to him these children are terribly important. He is, therefore, caught in a conflict of interest and loyalty. At times the opinions of his age group win out over the judgment of the parents. Parents should be extremely sensitive to this point and not make issues over

some of these differences unless they are of cardinal importance, unless they affect their child's health and welfare, or are contrary to the family's basic moral standards. Many of the differences may be quite minor and may best be ignored. If they cannot be ignored, wise parents will at least forgo a frontal attack in favor of joint action with other parents, perhaps following suggestions offered by the school guidance counselor.

Horizons Are Broadening

When your child was small, he had to use his energies to learn how to control many of his aggressive impulses. Now his energies may be released for more constructive social and intellectual activities, may pour out to broaden and expand his horizon. He can now push out of consciousness his aggressive and hostile impulses so that he is more able to function in a realistic way, able to repress and postpone some of his wishes. Preadolescent children, for example, are able to learn to save money in order to buy something. They are also able to accept promises of something in the future. This new-found ability to postpone desires enables a child to get along much more easily with adults and so win their approval.

Since the preadolescent child is going through changes in his relationship with authority and is showing increased resistance to socialization, he displays some of the rebelliousness and outbursts that are later found among adolescents. He is unstable; his moods change. At times he may appear eager to do something, but he may shift almost immediately to "laziness" and lack of interest. He develops feelings of resentment and blows up sometimes without provocation.

He also is not always equally mature. On some days maturity will vanish and childish antics and behavior will reappear. Boys at this age are usually expected to give up crying or showing "childish" fears. But they cannot always do so. Although girls seem able to express some of their aggressions in words, boys still fight and scuffle. The preadolescent may want very much to be grown up, but he still is not ready to give up some of the ways of childhood, ways that have spelled security to him.

Intellectual Development Is Swift

Intellectual growth during preadolescence is pronounced. Preadolescents are becoming more and more adult-like in their thinking. Their capacity to distinguish between what is real or what is imagined is increasing. They are moving rapidly away from imaginative play to more realistic group activities like sports and crafts. They are better able to understand cause-and-effect relationships, the *how* things happen and the *why*. Their fears are more realistic. Instead of worrying about the danger of imaginary characters, they are more concerned about bodily injury, fire, and war. They have greater ability to think in abstract terms, to make wider generalizations. They are now ready for play and recreational activities that involve science, technical matters, and physical problems. Their interest in reality makes them less interested in people than in their pursuits and hobbies, but they are still learning about people because they and their friends engage in their special activities together.

Other intellectual characteristics also develop rapidly in the preadolescent. Adults are able to generalize, draw inferences, and see relationships. Now preadolescent thinking begins to take on these characteristics.

Preadolescent humor involves jokes or riddles that tend to deal with issues of "smart" or "dumb." The intent is to show how smart the child is compared to others. The jokes now are of the moron kind. "Why did the moron put hay under his pillow?" "To feed the nightmares." The jokes are short and have abrupt conclusions.

Attitudes toward intellectual matters will vary with the family and social background of the child. In those homes where intellectual curiosity is valued and where there is ample opportunity for its expression, the child will have plenty of chances to try out his new knowledge. He has by this time mastered the skills of basic reading and can read freely on his own. His reading provides new information, opens up new vistas, and gives him some needed escapes.

Through his reading and increased knowledge, through his curiosity and eagerness, your preadolescent may begin to engage in a variety of hobbies or projects. Sometimes they are beyond his ability and skill, so his enthusiasm lags. His interest in discovery, coupled with his limited skills, may also cause him to shift from one project to another.

His activities are sometimes chosen to conform to what he thinks is appropriate to his sex. A boy may love to dance but may avoid dancing because he thinks it is sissified. A girl may enjoy playing baseball but may be embarrassed to be seen playing a boys' game. But many activities are chosen simply because they appeal to that sex—boys turning, for instance, toward science or mechanics, girls toward music or sewing.

One of the topics of conversation among preadolescent boys and girls within their own groups is the opposite sex. The fact that they prefer to be with their own kind at this stage of life does not mean that they are uninterested in sex. If children by this age have received no adequate sex information, their curiosity may be very high. They want to know about the facts of reproduction and the roles of fathers and mothers. The preadolescent's ability to assimilate information and to understand cause-and-effect relationships now make it easier for him to understand what he is told. The attitudes these children develop toward sex depend in large measure on the way they are informed and the attitudes shown by respected adults in their lives.

Parents Have Problems, Too

The preadolescent has a desire for self-expression. Parents and teachers desire obedience. These two opposite wishes set off many conflicts, particularly between adults and boys. Children of this age are frequently referred to child guidance clinics for overaggressiveness, disobedience, and stubbornness. Perhaps not nearly so many need to be. This period is distinguished by authority conflict, and parents and teachers should be aware that it is characteristic. The child has enough inner conflicts and struggles not to have to take on needless outside ones.

But these conflicts do pose disciplinary issues. As new types of situations arise, the parent is faced with new problems. Among these is the need of the child to make his own decisions—to go to a movie, choose an item of clothing, join a club. Yet too many choices can create difficulty.

The parent can try very hard to understand and then limit the number of choices to those the child is mature enough to handle.

Children at this age are inclined to feel misjudged, so that parents are called upon for great tact in making requests or critical comments. For example, as a child becomes more inclined to be independent and to assert himself, obedience to parental requests—such as to go to bed—may indeed be maddeningly slow. Wise parents will try to be patient and control themselves; they will realize that they cannot achieve immediate compliance. Parents should also be aware that at times their child will not hear them because he is too absorbed in something he is deeply involved in doing.

The supreme test for parents at this period is to set limits and at the same time show an understanding of their child's desire and necessity to be a free agent. Parents can let some things pass and avoid unnecessary arguments. Parents who understand their child's needs at this period and realize the growing pains he is experiencing not only will help him pass through this phase, but also will give him strength to handle problems arising during his adolescence and, finally, in his adulthood.

The greater the preadolescent's opportunity to strengthen his sense of male or female identity, the greater his chance to learn how to get along with age-mates, make decisions, and achieve a sense of self-competence, the easier will be his adolescent adjustment and his big step into adulthood. IRVING E. SIGEL

See also AGGRESSIVENESS; GROWTH; MORAL AND SPIRITUAL DEVELOPMENT; PATIENCE; PUBERTY; REGRESSION; SEX EDUCATION; SOCIAL DEVELOPMENT

PREGNANCY *See* PRENATAL CARE; PRENATAL IMPRESSIONS; REPRODUCTION

PREMATURE BABY

Almost one out of every ten babies is born early—before his body is completely ready to cope with life outside his mother's body. Not all the causes of premature birth are known, but complications of pregnancy are the most common cause. Premature births tend to be somewhat more frequent when the mother does not have good prenatal care.

The "official" definition of prematurity is that the baby weighs less than 5½ pounds, but most babies between 5 and 5½ pounds do not have much difficulty and usually require little special care. Small premature babies who weigh from 2 to 4 pounds need a great deal of special care in order to grow healthily. The organ systems of the premature's body have not had enough time to mature in the protection of the mother's body so that they can function well. The baby is born before he is really ready to breathe, able to keep warm and to eat and digest his food without extra help. Fortunately, doctors have been able to learn a great deal about the problems premature babies have and to overcome many of them. The small premature baby needs to be in a highly protective environment. Usually, such a baby is kept in an incubator where the temperature, humidity, and oxygen are carefully regulated.

A premature baby's digestive system is not usually ready to digest the kind of formula the full-term baby gets. His feedings are carefully calculated to give him just the right amount of calories and fluids. He is fed small amounts and fed much more often in order to keep his metabolism regulated with the least waste of energy on his part. Often, small babies are fed by a tube that is kept in place in the nose and goes down into his esophagus (food tube). In this way a small and rather weak baby doesn't have to waste energy in sucking and he can be fed often without being disturbed.

These special ways of helping a premature baby overcome his disadvantage take a great deal of work and expert knowledge on the part of hospital personnel. That is why premature babies sometimes must remain in the hospital for awhile after the mother goes home.

What about the premature baby when he is ready to come home? Does he still need all this special care? Does he catch up with other babies? A premature baby is not sent home from the hospital until he is big enough and mature enough in his reactions to do well with the kind of care a mother can provide at home. When he does come home, he can be cared for in pretty much the same manner as the average newborn baby. He may still require fairly frequent feedings and a formula specially suited to his needs. For some time he may still need a little bit more protection from exposure to temperature extremes and to infection than does the average baby. The premature baby is behind the full-term baby in his development if the date of his birth is taken as the starting point. But if the head start a full-term baby has is discounted, the delay in development of a premature baby usually is less obvious. This difference gets progressively less as time goes by and is not at all apparent after a year or two. RUTH S. KEMPE

See also BABY; FORMULA MAKING; IMMUNIZATION; INCUBATOR; PRENATAL CARE; PRENATAL IMPRESSIONS

PRENATAL CARE

The most important duty of expectant parents is to secure good medical care for the mother, for medical supervision is the best insurance for a healthy and happy pregnancy and delivery. As soon as you suspect that you are pregnant, visit your family doctor or an obstetrician or a prenatal clinic.

During the first six months of pregnancy the doctor usually advises a visit once a month, more frequently throughout the remaining three months. Many women take a small notebook to jot down the month-by-month instructions given by their doctors.

Each pregnancy is different. One woman will be given a diet including larger quantities of calcium; another will require less calcium and more iron. One woman will need to lose weight, while still another may be encouraged to gain. A well-balanced diet is of great importance to baby's good health —and helps to keep the mother well and comfortable, too. The expectant mother should be extremely cautious about taking any drugs not prescribed by her doctor. He will give advice on all phases of pregnancy, advice that should be followed carefully.

Many women hesitate to go to a doctor as soon as they should because they fear the complete and intimate examination the doctor will perform. This hesitation is unwise. Often, a nurse will see you first, especially in a clinic, taking notes of your family history, past illnesses, what sort of work you have done, your husband's health history, and so on. The nurse will do all she can to prepare you for the doctor's examination, putting you at ease and reassuring you of the routine nature of the examination. She will then ask you to undress, giving you a large sheet or a robe to put on.

The pelvic examination need not be uncomfortable if you will follow the doctor's advice. He will tell you to relax and to breathe through your mouth. From a vaginal examination the doctor will be able to tell the size and shape of your uterus, and almost exactly how far along your pregnancy is. He will take measurements at this time which will tell him whether the birth canal is large enough for a normal delivery.

At the time of this first examination the doctor will want a urine specimen and will probably take a blood sample. The blood will be tested for several things, including anemia. The doctor will also want to know your blood type. He will examine your eyes, ears, nose, and throat for any signs of infection; he will take your blood pressure and will listen to your heart and lungs. He will also examine your breasts.

The examinations that follow the first thorough one are much shorter and less exhausting. The doctor will probably check your blood pressure and weight gain each month, talk with you about diet, and he will always be ready to answer your questions about the baby's growth and development. Doctors welcome questions from a mother-to-be, even though many of these questions begin, "You'll probably think this is silly, doctor, but . . ." No question is silly to your doctor. He is sympathetic to the problems of pregnant women and is eager to help make your pregnancy a happy and comfortable experience.

The father of this baby-to-be should be included in all phases of the prenatal period. One of his first concerns will be the expenses involved and a frank talk with the doctor will be in order, probably at the time of the first visit. Early discussion of family finances paves the way to a smooth and pleasant relationship between doctor and patient.

The father will have other questions about how he can help his wife through this period of waiting. The doctor can give him much good advice on this score.

The physical and emotional aspects of pregnancy are understandably bewildering to a first-time father, and husbands also need some encouragement along the way. This encouragement he can get from the doctor, but since reproduction is a family affair, it is a wise wife who makes an effort to understand and sympathize with her husband's concerns.

Be obedient to your doctor's instructions during pregnancy. Keep yourself occupied, maintain a happy outlook, and prepare yourselves and your home to welcome this new member of the family.

See also BLOOD TYPE; BREAST CARE AND BREAST FEEDING; PRENATAL IMPRESSIONS; ROOMING-IN

PRENATAL IMPRESSIONS

Almost before your pregnancy is apparent, well-meaning friends, storekeepers, and sweet old aunts will shower you with all sorts of myths and superstitions that might shadow your pregnancy if you were not the sensible person you are. You, of course, will never believe that if you want a boy all you have to do is eat peanuts and drink alkalies; or, if a girl is your desire, you must eat sweets and acids. You will not believe that if your right ovary hurts, you will produce a boy, and if the left one hurts, you will have a girl.

You will give no credence to the statement that wearing high heels during pregnancy causes cross-eyed children, nor that if you eat lobster, you will mark your baby.

Neither has it been proved that if you listen to piano concertos all day, or read poetry, or walk through art museums gazing at paintings, your child will be talented in one or more of these areas. You will gain a measure of calm, and your days will be serene only if you yourself enjoy these activities. If you do not enjoy them, you may only be bored. In either case, the baby will be what he will be, despite piano, poetry, or paintings.

Any mark that your baby may have—and most all babies born are completely normal and free of malformation or disfiguration—will be entirely coincidental. You may have developed a craving for strawberries during pregnancy. If your baby is born with a small strawberry mark on his right shoulder, be assured it was not your eating the fruit that caused the mark. If your baby has a tiny, hairy mole on his back, it is not because you were frightened by a dog or a cat.

See also PRENATAL CARE

PRESCHOOL CHILD

The term "preschool child" usually applies to youngsters who are no longer infants but not yet in first grade. Many a so-called preschooler goes regularly to school, however, as a nursery school child or kindergartner. Broadly, then, the term leaves out the thought of school and describes the child between the ages of 2 or 3 and 6.

Development of the child during the preschool period continues the advances made during infancy and early toddlerhood and also moves him on into new ways of behaving. Most of all, the preschool child still counts on kindly adults to be willing to do the countless things that he cannot do for himself. This warm, close, supporting adult-child relationship is still the most significant fact in his life.

Through the way in which his parents and other adults treat him, the preschool child is continuing to learn his basic attitude toward all people and toward authority: whether human beings generally are good, whether he can trust them and count on them, whether they are "after" him or "against" him, whether he has to be wary of them. Simultaneously, through the same relationship, the preschool child is continuing to build up feelings about himself. If his experiences are such that he feels enjoyed, appreciated, gently and well cared for, a child builds an image of himself as a good person: Important people like me; I must be likable. If a child is constantly reprimanded and always in trouble, he tends to build a picture of himself in the opposite direction: People are not good to me; I must not be a good person.

Preschool children can be deeply upset by the displeasure of parents. They cannot shrug off the severity of reprimands and threats as school-age children are able to do. They are more apt to exaggerate the parents' displeasure and often worry more than one intends they should.

The Seesaw Between Two Needs

Two conflicting concerns characterize the preschool child: a need for dependence and a great capacity for independence. Children go back and forth between the two needs. Parents must be very flexible. When a child is acting big, showing his eagerness to stand on his own two feet, it usually is wise to give him as free a rein as possible. But when a youngster shows that he wants sympathy, company, reassurance, or help, it is good to shift gears and accept his obvious need for dependence.

Behavior at bathtime is a good example. The preschool child often loves to soap himself and even to try to dry himself. He can play alone in the bath for long stretches of time. On other days the good-natured company of a parent seems very important to him. He relishes being bathed, the rough-housing fun of being dried, the conversation of his adult companion, the closeness of the whole experience.

Bedtime is another period of the day when children typically act big or little, often unpredictably. They may insist on undressing themselves, on toileting alone, on climbing into bed. They feel so big they even brush off adult attempts to speed up the process by helping. Yet the same children in a jiffy may respond eagerly to the comforting routine of the bedtime story and insist on being tucked in and kissed. Big as giants one moment, they want to hold on to the precious company of mother or father for a few seconds more just when adults least expect it.

Despite his conflict about dependence, the preschool child is, of course, markedly more independent than he was. One way he shows this independence is in developing his physical skills. He loves to run, to balance, to hop, to jump—all as extensions of his walking ability. He thoroughly enjoys new ways to move, tricycle riding, and pulling, pushing, and riding in wagons. Climbing, whether it be a tree or monkey bars, has a very special appeal to him.

Preschool children also continue to increase their fine muscle control and their use of hand and eye together. They can manage more and more of eating, dressing, and toileting by themselves. They can master more and more of the everyday objects they meet. Most fives, for example, can build tall towers of blocks, placing one block on top of the other very precisely, with a fine feel for the balance involved. But 5-year-olds find many tasks still beyond their capacities.

Even 6-year-olds are still struggling to master many small muscle skills. Knots give them real trouble; tying bows can be a laborious process; cutting their dinner meat usually calls for more control than even they have. In general, however, the preschool child gives an impression of competence. He handles his body well, loves to use it, and he is eager to take on tasks that involve it.

A Highly Social Age

During the preschool years, playmates of the same age become increasingly important. Most children are highly social by age 3. Their days are richer, more full of challenge and excitement if they can be with age-mates. For all of her importance, mother now must share with children a place in the preschool child's world. By 4, sometimes even before, a child often has a special friend, his favorite in nursery school or in the neighborhood. These friendships change from time to time, but preschoolers reach the point in development when they love to play together and look forward to company of their own fully as much as adults anticipate seeing their good friends.

Sometimes during these years boys prefer to play only with boys, and girls with girls. More commonly, however, boys and girls enjoy the same activities together and tend to show relatively little awareness of playing in a mixed-sex group or a one-sex group. The number of children does matter, however. Children from 3 years upward can learn and live quite happily in a school group of about 12 to 15 for 3-year-olds, 15 to 18 for 4-year-olds, and 20 for 5-year-olds. Within these numbers, however, the preschool child always settles down to a small group of two or three. It is too much of a strain on his social and emotional development for him to be one of the whole group for any continuous length of time.

Two-year-olds and young threes are not yet sure enough of themselves or sure enough of the other fellow for very peaceful living. They are not even completely aware that people are different from things. Not uncommonly there is some exploratory hair-pulling and poking into eyes and ears, almost as if the child were trying to discover the unique nature of this other object. Children this young are very possessive when they first play together, finding it beyond them to share with the other fellow. It is not uncommon for such young children to defend themselves vigorously when they feel threatened, sometimes biting and kicking. Conflicts are common, but seldom as serious as the screams or tears make them sound. Usually, life picks right up and goes on happily again as soon as each child has what he wants. Physical aggression markedly lessens by age 4 and age 5, although arguments and name-calling usually arise as new elements in children's social living.

Intermingled closely with social development is another major advance of the preschool years: the development of language. By the time a child is about 3, his mother will report that her child has become a chatterbox who never shuts up.

The preschooler does not simply chatter, however. His amazing vocabulary growth includes the use of all parts of speech, a gradual increase in the length of sentences, and a great improvement in the clarity of what he says. Language development and social development now seem to aid one another. All preschool children still fight at times, of course; if they are greatly provoked, even fours and fives may bite and kick. But they gradually learn to settle their differences and their disputes by compromise and words.

To adults, the great growth in speech made by preschoolers can be troubling. Youngsters seem to talk too much. They almost always interrupt because what they have to say is still the most important thing in the world to them. They often talk too loudly. Not infrequently, around age 4 or so, they are apt to go on a jag of name-calling and of experimenting with nonsensical singsongs.

One other occasionally annoying characteristic of the preschool child's language is his never-ending stream of questions. His inquiries become more complex from about 3 years of age on. "Why?" and "How come?" increase as he tries to understand relationships, how things work, and what those things are for.

The child's constant questions reflect another side of preschool development: his intense curiosity and deep thirst for knowledge. The youngest preschoolers especially use all their senses—touching, tasting, smelling, as well as hearing and looking—to explore their world. But children in the whole age range are seldom content to take another fellow's word for something; they want to find out for themselves. Gushy, messy, dirty textures have a very special appeal. So do any objects that have some of the same characteristics as the children themselves: noisy, fast-moving, busy, and big-seeming. It is easy to dull the intellectual curiosity of these young children by a steady flow of "Don't touch," "Stand back," "Watch out," and by ignoring their many questions. These children are scholars at heart. They thoroughly enjoy stories, conversations, and looking at pictures. They make great gains if they have the opportunity to go on short trips to see steam shovels, animals, planes, and other community sights close-up and firsthand.

The Importance of Play

Language and social development, an increasing store of knowledge, a growing attention span, a vastly improved physical coordination, all combine in what is the most distinctive characteristic of the preschool child: He is highly imaginative. He has a very special capacity to make-believe and to pretend. He can take on any role that suits his fancy. He can pretend any object is what he plays it is. The child himself can become a baby or a cowboy; a chair can become a horse or a plane or a prison. To the casual adult looking on, the preschool child seems to spend all his time "just playing." The play of the preschool child is far from a waste of time, however. It is highly significant activity that teaches important emotional, intellectual, and social lessons. Wise parents foster dramatic play and are in no hurry to see it end. They find time to let the child have first-hand experiences on which this unique outflow of imagination is based. They provide the raw materials, such as paints and blocks and sand and creative toys, through which it flows. And they arrange for the companionship of other children which best stimulates imagination.

Some Common Problems

Preschool children challenge the patience of adults. Although they make somewhat fewer physical demands on parents than they did during infancy and early toddlerhood, although their temper tantrums decrease and their blatant stubbornness lessens, these children are far from being angels. Big as they seem in comparison to a short time ago, and big as they themselves often feel, they are still little children. They lack an adult sense of time; they dawdle when eating or dressing and seem to be distracted by what adults think are unimportant things. Despite their moments of liking to help set the table or straighten up a room, they are still messy and often leave a trail of possessions behind them.

One new way in which they assert their independence is to express strong preferences for a particular glass or plate, for instance; or to develop a sudden new strong dislike for some particular food. Their wishes frequently do not make sense to adults who forget that the real wish is to be big; the specific wish is simply a means toward that important end. Their great energy can be tiring to their elders, and their sudden exhaustion when all their energy is used up can be irritating. These children still have a strong need to be the center of attention; they are seldom placid companions when company drops in, or on shopping trips, when visiting, or in any situation where there is nothing for them to do. Although often full of bravado, they can become suddenly afraid of the dark. Sometimes they begin to have nightmares and to imagine perils that do not exist.

Preschoolers are in an in-between age—not totally dependent, not totally independent —a mixture of both, sometimes all in a few moments. It is easy to overestimate what these children can do and to expect too much. It is also easy to underestimate them and to open up too little physical challenge and too little social and intellectual stimulation. Your best safeguard and guide is to keep your eye on your child, to judge from his behavior how he is feeling at the moment—big, brave, and bold, or like your little baby—and to enjoy him as he is. JAMES L. HYMES, JR.

See also CURIOSITY; GROWTH; IMAGINATION; INDEPENDENCE; KINDERGARTEN; NURSERY SCHOOL; READINESS; SOCIAL DEVELOPMENT; VOCABULARY DEVELOPMENT

PRESCRIPTIONS

Directions provided by the doctor for the prevention or treatment of an illness are called "prescriptions." At the top of the prescription form you may notice an ℞, representing the Latin word for recipe, meaning in medicine "take." Doctors used to write their prescriptions in Latin, but today most of them use English except for a few signs and symbols instantly recognized by druggists. Most prescriptions are for medicines, but prescriptions may also be given for diet, physical therapy, eyeglasses, and exercises.

In recent years prescriptions for medicines have tended to contain fewer ingredients than formerly because of the considerable increase in the number of "specific treatments" available for many diseases. Thus, antibiotics for the treatment of specific types of pneumonia, for example, have reduced the need to prescribe a number of different medicines for a patient. Insulin, vitamins, and specific hormones are all examples of specific medicines.

Care should be taken to have prescriptions filled by a qualified pharmacist and to follow to the letter the doctor's instructions for giving the medicine, for accuracy may be of the greatest importance in obtaining the desired good effect. In prescribing for children, the doctor pays particular attention to providing instructions that will enable parents to get their child to take the medicine.

Today's pleasant-tasting medicines for children also carry a hazard, for if medicine has a good flavor and children can get access to it, they may consume large amounts and develop severe reactions as a consequence. It is important to remember that practically all medicines are harmful if taken in larger amounts than prescribed. All medicines, including aspirin, therefore should be kept out of the reach of children, preferably in a cabinet with some kind of lock that cannot be opened by a young child. It is better to discard a medicine after the patient has recovered, for the same medicine will probably not be useful again, and often it will deteriorate on standing. It is *never* wise to give medicine prescribed for one member of the family to another whose symptoms seem to be similar. JULIUS B. RICHMOND

See also DRUGS; MEDICINE CABINET

PRESSURES *See* SOCIAL PRESSURES

PRICKLY HEAT

Although prickly heat is most common in hot weather, it may also appear in the winter if babies are clothed too warmly or if the room is too warm. Prickly heat is a skin condition in which there are elevated and reddened pin-point spots, and the surrounding skin is reddened. The condition tends to occur in such areas as the groin folds and neck folds in fat babies and children, areas in which there may be an accumulation of perspiration or irritation.

Prickly heat may cause considerable itching and scratching, and the skin might become quite raw, irritated, and infected. It is therefore well to try to clear the condition promptly. Cleanse the skin frequently and gently with warm water and mild soap, and avoid clothing that may irritate the affected areas. Exposure to the drying effect of air can be quite helpful. Obviously anything that keeps the baby comfortably cool will be helpful also. Medicines and powders are usually not necessary if the child can be kept cool and clean. If prickly heat is difficult to clear up, a doctor should be consulted. He may suggest a weight-reducing program if the child is too heavy. JULIUS B. RICHMOND

See also OVERWEIGHT; RASH

PRIVACY

"Leave me alone, Mom," may be an ugly sounding phrase, but whether the child says it aloud or only thinks it, there are many, many times when he means it from the heart.

Privacy says to the child: I am me, myself; I don't have to be supervised by a grownup; for a little while I don't want to be interrupted by what somebody else wants me to do for him; I am alone; I am free; I can think my own thoughts; I can do what *I* want to do.

Everyone needs such privacy, some more than others, of course. Even a nursery school child doesn't always want to tell what he did there. He may want to feel that the teacher belongs to him alone or he may feel that he wasn't up to the other children in his finger painting. At any rate, he doesn't want to discuss certain areas of his small world, and he shouldn't be forced to.

The preadolescent, with his increasing sense of individuality, needs both physical and psychological aloneness now and then. His world is beginning to be a world of children his age; it is with them that he wants to have private plans, conversations, and discussions. It is with friends his age that he has his secret clubs, passwords, handshakes, and secret codes.

Parents sometimes feel a sense of rebuff: "What does that child mean, keeping secrets from me when he knows he can always count on me for everything?" Sometimes it is a sense of rejection or suspiciousness the parent feels: "What can children that age possibly be up to in that musty old attic?" Here is where a parent has to hew a careful line. Children still need adult supervision and guidance; there is no doubt of that, but they also need a chance to begin to make many of their own choices. They need, too, the knowledge that their parents believe in them, trust them, and respect them. Every step on the way toward this knowledge gives them an increase in confidence and hence more ability to make their choices well.

Wherever parents can succeed in respecting the privacy of a preadolescent, they will have made a gain. An adolescent is going to need even more privacy than a preadolescent, and if he can count on his parents to give it to him, he will be easier to live with, less touchy, less defensively standing his parents off.

The need for privacy expresses itself in a variety of places. A child wants to shut the door of his room; he wants to be alone in the bathroom; he wants to be alone even perhaps in the presence of others. Privacy is not only physical. A child who shares a room can still withdraw to his part of it and feel alone if allowed to do so. His thoughts, his daydreams are his own and he does not want to share them. If he does, he will let his parents know. If he does not, persistent questions about what he is doing or thinking will only bring out the typical adolescent response of "Nothing."

Perhaps the cardinal principle for the parent of the adolescent is the same as that for the parent of the kindergartener: Know him, sustain him, trust him, and let him have the privacy he shows he needs. IRVING E. SIGEL

See also INDEPENDENCE; MODESTY

PROBLEM CHILD

All parents have problems at one time or another in helping their children to grow up. Growing up isn't an easy process at best, either for children or for their parents. At every step of the way children have to learn many things. Even in infancy they have to learn to wait to be made comfortable or to be fed; the first days in which the whole world revolves around them are soon over as parents begin to fit the new baby's care into the life of the rest of the family.

Children have to learn to move out of themselves and gradually to master the world around them. Slowly they learn to be more independent, yet they still need the love, the care, the protection appropriate to their age. As they come to act on their impulses—to do, to learn, to assert themselves, to compete, even to fight—they must learn to control these feelings, not bottling them up but rather directing them into channels that are acceptable to those around them. Each child faces an enormous life task: to develop from a passive, dependent and yet impulsive baby to a healthy, active, responsible child and young person who is able to get along with his family, his friends, his teachers, and other adults; to function successfully in work and play; and to find his place and his values as he moves toward his own adulthood and adult relations.

Each Phase Has Its Problems

But this task isn't accomplished smoothly or evenly. Different phases of growth have their particular hurdles, which are basically present for everyone but which each child must work through in his own way. On the other side, mothers and fathers vary enormously in their responses to their children at different stages of growth and vary, too, in their ability to understand and to help their children to meet the crises that characterize these different stages.

Take, for example, an active, curious 2-year-old who is "into everything" and who hasn't yet been able to learn not to run out of the front door whenever it is open. His behavior is quite normal for his stage of development, but it presents some difficulty for him because he is always being scolded and pulled back into the house. It is also difficult for the mother who doesn't understand that this behavior is natural and even desirable as part of a child's growing wish to use his body and to explore the world; she has not yet learned how to help him direct his energies into safe outlets that will give him other satisfactions. So, while his behavior presents a problem for him and his mother, he can in no sense be considered at this point to be a "problem child."

Before giving such a label to a child of any age, one would have to consider his behavior against the backdrop of the ordinary but quite usual emotional ups and downs of different ages and the developmental tasks that go with them, the special circumstances in which he finds himself, the kind of child he seems to be, and the help he is getting from his parents.

Is a child's behavior in keeping with his age and the demands of his particular stage of growth? Or is he somehow stuck in a rut, struggling too long and too hard to accomplish something that should already be part of his emotional equipment.

Developmental Tasks

Even to begin to answer these questions, parents should become familiar with the characteristics of the different stages from infancy through adolescence, as described in such books as Stone and Church's *Childhood and Adolescence* or Erikson's *Childhood and Society*. Parents should watch their child—but not hang too closely on every little thing he does—to see whether he is moving ahead over a period of time. And within broad limits, they should compare his behavior with that of *many* children his age—and not just his cousin Bill or his older brother Marvin. Here, as with physical growth, one must recognize the wide range of individual differences that seems to be absorbed in time. The crux of the matter lies in such questions as: How much deviation is permissible? When is a child's behavior really out of bounds?

Parents can be reassured that if a child has a real problem, there is usually a gross deviation that parents themselves often sense without anyone having to tell them. For example, today many parents recognize that a child who is wetting his bed at night when he is 3 has not yet learned to control his urinary functions but may be expected to do so shortly. If, however, he is still wetting his bed when he is 8 or 9, he is struggling with a real problem for which he probably needs special professional help. A child of 3½ or 4, or even 5, who has some difficulty in parting with his mother when he first goes to nursery school or kindergarten is probably behaving as many children do who have had little experience in being away from their parents or in being with other children. If, however, a girl of 7 or 8 goes into a panic when her parents go out at night, leaving a responsible person with her in the house, she may be showing some deeper fear for which she needs help.

There May Be Backsliding

These examples merely suggest some of the developmental tasks that children have to learn at appropriate times. There may be some fluctuations and backsliding, but it is reasonable to expect that children should be dry at night by the time they are 4, and they should surely be able under normal circumstances to "separate" from their parents, at least for brief periods, by the time they are 5 or 6.

Is the child's behavior in keeping with, or to be explained by, external circumstances? By now, many parents have come to expect that a boy or a girl of 2 or 3 who has achieved some measure of independence and more grown-up behavior will act like an infant again if a new baby comes into the family. Other parents are not prepared for this behavior and fail to see that it is the new situation that pushes the child back. He somehow senses that if he acts like a baby, he, too, will get the same attention and fussing-over that the new baby is getting. Fortunately, with a little encouragement these children soon give up their renewed wetting or their wish to have a bottle and move back to acting their age, especially if they get the satisfactions that go with being a little older and being able to do more things.

An older child—of 8 or 9, perhaps—may have excessive nightmares or seem to go off into a world of his own after the death of a near relative. Here the loss may bring more than a feeling of sorrow; it may also be a real threat, reviving in the child fears of personal danger to himself which he had probably struggled with earlier in his life and already had brought under some reasonable control. In such a case, the child is reacting understandably to what has happened. He needs help in facing the situation, perhaps by being encouraged to talk about it with his parents or some other understanding adult. But his behavior is not a sign in itself of a problem for which there is no obvious cause and which therefore may be connected with deep inner conflict.

Is a child's behavior in keeping with the kind of child he seems to be? Even from the moment of birth children seem to have distinctive temperaments all their own: Some are more active and alert than others, some are more responsive or outgoing or quiet or happy-go-lucky. Temperaments do change to some extent as children hit new stages of growth. This is especially true of preadolescence and adolescence, when physiological changes appear to bring with them dramatic changes of mood and behavior which make young people difficult to live with and even more difficult to understand. Except during these periods of change, however, by and large parents know what to expect of their children if they have watched them thoughtfully. Any *drastic* and prolonged change in temperament or behavior may well be a sign of some inner disturbance that represents a real problem.

Has the child been given enough—but not excessive—help from his parents in moving ahead from one stage of growth to the next? Children can't be expected to grow up on their own, though some children seem to accomplish this feat in the face of what would seem to be insurmountable difficulties. A child needs parents who can encourage him, when they sense he is ready, to give up his baby ways, to become more independent, to be more like the grownups he loves and needs. On the other hand, he is not helped by parents who push him too fast, expecting more of him than he can possibly do. He needs parents who will stand by while he makes mistakes, who will pick him up and comfort him and help him start over again, and who are ready *themselves* to give up having him dependent on them as he was when he was younger. A child who has been given this kind of help should be better able to step out on his own. If he still has difficulty doing so, his behavior takes on a different meaning and may, again, be a problem in the deeper sense.

These criteria are merely suggestions for parents to use as preliminary guidelines. Obviously they overlap and must be considered together. Usually, one sign alone does not necessarily mean trouble; it is the over-all pattern and combination of signs that indicate when a child has a real problem. Usually, when he does, *he* is troubled and so is his family.

If in Doubt, Seek Help

And so if you are puzzled as to what lies behind your child's behavior, if you are in any doubt at all as to whether your child has a real emotional problem, you should seek professional help, just as you would for a physical problem. Parents should know that in many communities there are professional people specially trained to evaluate and to help them with their children's emotional problems and their own. They are there to be of service.

ALINE B. AUERBACH

See also BOOKS FOR PARENTS; CHILD GUIDANCE CLINIC; EMOTIONAL DEVELOPMENT; GROWTH; MENTAL HEALTH; REGRESSION

PROMISES

Promises should be sparingly made and scrupulously kept, but sometimes even the best promises have to be broken—for very important reasons.

Promise only when you're pretty sure you can do what you promise. Try not to let anything make you break that promise. But if you have to, explain the reasons to the child and make good on the promise as soon as you can.

"But you promised, Dad, honest you did," wails a boy as his father explains that a business emergency has just come up and he won't be able to take him fishing as he had promised. "I know I promised, Son," answers father, "but sometimes promises have to be broken, especially when more important things interfere. Let's go next Saturday instead."

You may be sure that son will remind dad of the promised outing several times during the week—too many times, dad may feel. Children seldom let grownups get away with failure to live up to their promises.

Are we always so persistent about helping children live up to the promises *they* make?

When your daughter promises to pick up her things "as soon as I finish my puzzle," do you see that she does, or are you so busy that you forget until you stumble over the mess after she has gone to bed and then pick it up yourself?

Your son promised to mow the lawn "this weekend," but Sunday afternoon comes, the lawn is still unmowed. His friends swarm around urging him to go swimming with them. What does a parent do? That depends on what you are trying to teach him. Hard though it may be, it's a part of our duty as parents to teach our children that promises can be broken only for *very* important reasons. MAY REYNOLDS SHERWIN

See also RESPONSIBILITY

PROMOTION *See* ACCELERATION

PROSTRATION, HEAT *See* HEAT EXHAUSTION

PROTEINS *See* NUTRITION

PSYCHIATRIC CLINIC *See* CLINICS

PSYCHIATRIST *See* MEDICAL SPECIALISTS

PSYCHOLOGICAL TESTS *See* TESTS AND MEASUREMENTS

PTA *See* PARENT-TEACHER ASSOCIATION

PTOMAINE POISONING *See* FOOD POISONING

PUBERTY

Puberty is not an age; it is a period of development. Both boys and girls, in puberty, begin to take an interest in the opposite sex. Both grow greatly in height. Both develop underarm and pubic hair. Boys also grow facial hair in puberty, their muscles develop, their voices deepen, and seminal emissions occur. Girls' breasts develop, their hips widen, and menstruation begins.

There is no answer as to just when a child will enter puberty. One girl may start developing at 9½ years, another, just as normal, at 14 years. Boys may begin their pubertal development at any time between 12 and 15 years.

Many children are upset because they develop earlier or later than their friends. Even those boys and girls who develop at the time most do, become increasingly concerned and uneasy about their bodies and bodily development. They observe the changes that occur in their bodies, and they begin to encounter new desires and new urges. They are constantly worried: "Am I normal?" "Am I developing as I should?"

During this period of development your children will need a great deal of reassurance from you. Tell them ahead of time about bodily changes they can expect. Let them know, also, that the new sex urges and desires they experience during this time are experienced by everyone growing up and are entirely normal. MILTON I. LEVINE

See also GROWTH; MENSTRUATION; SEX EDUCATION; TEEN-AGER

PUBLIC HEALTH NURSE *See* NURSE

PUBLIC LIBRARY *See* LIBRARIES

PUNISHMENT

Punishment is the infliction of pain to teach a child that a particular kind of behavior is undesirable. The varieties of possible punishments are almost numberless, much too varied for description. Probably the most common form used is physical pain—a spanking or a slap. Confinement is another widely used type of punishment: "Go to your room." "Go to bed." Depriving a child of a prized pleasure is also a popular approach: "No more TV." "No allowance." "No more movies." "No dates." A common thread runs throughout all techniques: This pain will teach you not to act that way in the future.

Many parents have a guilty feeling that punishment is an "old-fashioned" method, one not in line with the recommendations of today's experts. There is no basis for this feeling. Punishment is a legitimate technique for teaching discipline. It is, however, only one of many possible techniques and is not a cure-all. Punishment has its strengths and limitations and weaknesses.

Punishment is best suited for teaching highly specific lessons and lessons that must be mastered quickly. These strong points—specificity, speed—are at the same time punishment's great limitation. Punishment usually does not give a child a reliable base on which he can build generalizations about how he should act in somewhat different situations in the future. It can be used effectively to teach, "Don't touch this particular object" (a glass bowl, for instance), but it would not be a sound approach for teaching caution in general or respect for property or any other broad goal. Punishment might be used appropriately for teaching "Don't hit this particular child," but it would not be effective for teaching courtesy or cooperation or any of the general values involved in living well with people.

A Tricky Technique

Punishment is a very tricky teaching technique. This fact is often overlooked because punishments are as available as the tip of a tongue or the palm of a hand and because we are all familiar with them through our own experiences in growing up. Probably the least skilled of us resort to punishment most frequently. Yet because it opens up so many hazards, punishment probably should be used only by people who are expert in understanding children. For the unwary, it can cause trouble that might not be anticipated.

One of the hazards of punishment lies in the fact that it tends to stop a particular symptom of trouble without in any way helping to correct the basic cause of the trouble. Many adults mistakenly take this as a virtue. They say of punishment, "I tried it and it works." It does "work," but it may end thumb-sucking, for example, only to have the child substitute nail-biting or daydreaming or masturbation as his symptom because the root of the trouble, the child's insecurity, has been untouched. Frequently, the new symptom is less obvious than the old, which greatly complicates the job of recognizing that a child needs help.

Another hazard stems from the fact that punishment is a very personal teaching method. A child may learn to behave well as long as his punisher is in sight, but there is no guarantee that he will continue his good behavior when he is on his own.

Still another difficulty arises from the tendency of children to build defenses against punishment. After a time, some youngsters do not care whether or not they are punished; they may even choose to take the punishment rather than change their behavior. Parents who rely on punishment find that they must constantly increase the severity of it, hurting more and hitting harder in order to be effective. This "escalator effect" opens up still another danger. An occasional punishment will hardly do any lasting damage, but a steady and increasing reliance on punishment can damage the relationship between parent and child, eventually undermining the very basis for good behavior.

Since punishment is only one of many methods of teaching discipline, it is not imperative that every child be punished to insure that he will become a good citizen. Some parents rely very little on punishment because it is such a tricky method with unpredictable results. Such parents do not allow their children to "do anything they want to" or "get away with everything." There is a difference between stopping a child quite firmly at any given moment from doing what he is doing, and taking the next step of punishing the child. Wise parents recognize that many possible "next steps" are open to them. They try to think through which of the alternatives is most likely to produce a lasting and constructive result.

There is no reason why any parent should shrink from punishment when, in his best judgment, that seems the best of the alternatives. It usually is best to punish at once if punishment seems the wisest teaching technique to use rather than to postpone action "until father comes home" or until anger has subsided. A quick response increases the likelihood that a child will accept the justice of the punishment and that the learning will be directly connected with the bad behavior. It is obviously wise, too, not to punish to excess. A punishment must hurt to be effective, but if it hurts too much, it is apt to breed resentment and rebellion.

There is some tendency to think of punishment as the last resort. If a child persists in misbehaving, despite efforts to reason with him and other approaches, we are apt to think that we have no alternative but to punish. This is seldom the wise solution. The child who is punished most is apt to need it least. The chances are that the cause of his frequent misbehavior is not simple ignorance of how to act, and that the solution is not a punishment to teach him and teach him quickly. The real reasons for persisting bad behavior are apt to lie elsewhere. Anyone who finds himself punishing frequently or being pushed into punishment as a last resort would do well to stop and look again at the child, asking why he behaves this way and what approach is most likely to get at the root of the trouble? JAMES L. HYMES, JR.

See also DISCIPLINE; GUILT FEELINGS; MORAL AND SPIRITUAL DEVELOPMENT; OBEDIENCE; RESENTMENT; SLAPPING; SPANKING

PUS *See* ABSCESS; BOIL

QUARANTINE *See* COMMON COMMUNICABLE DISEASES; SICK CHILD

QUARRELING

A quarrel among children may be anything from a flash of name-calling, scarcely interrupting their play, to a longer argument involving a few blows as well as words, and ending with the indignant departure from the scene of one or more participants who vow never to speak to each other again. That vow is usually broken before the day is over.

Quarrels within the family or the neighborhood may have a number of meanings. Remarks that might appear to sound the knell of a friendship may be only the 4-year-old or the 8-year-old equivalent of an adult's "I couldn't disagree with you more."

Children are inept at getting along together. They have little capacity to wait. The present moment is one of burning intensity. Everything matters so painfully much. Then, too, they have rigid, but incorrect, ideas of what is "fair" and what is "mean." The smallest offense, therefore, can raise a disproportionate protest.

Who shall gain possession of a toy, who shall be "first," or what constitutes being a "liar" or a "baby" may be the immediate cause of a quarrel. Underneath this surface cause may lie the need for the youngster to prove to himself and to the world that he can get his way and that he is not weak and defenseless. Deeper still may lie smoldering embers of other hurts, real or fancied, easily rekindled by the present contention. That is why both parties to a quarrel often continue their accusations and ill feelings after they have forgotten why they fell out in the first place.

What is done to stop a dispute is far less important in reducing the number of acute arguments between children than what is happening in each one's daily life. A contentious child often feels—justifiably or not

—that everyone is against him. He is always ready to start the fight lest someone get the best of him. A child who has been teased, ridiculed, or yelled at much of the time or who has heard adults communicate chiefly in abusive language will tend to follow that pattern in his relations with other children. The most amiable of youngsters may become quarrelsome if he is not feeling well, if there has been some upsetting event in his life, or if he is worried about something "bad" he has done or even thought of doing.

A youngster who finds satisfaction in at least some parts of his daily life, who has a warm relationship with one of the adults around him, is not likely to be unduly quarrelsome. Opportunities to work off strong feelings in active play are an aid to living comfortably with oneself and others. If a child is dealt with consistently and firmly, he is helped toward being sufficiently at peace with himself so that he is not impelled to start a fight over every trifle. Yet even a happy child growing up in the most favorable conditions will get involved in squabbles with his brothers and sisters and with his playmates from time to time.

Most disputes are settled without adult intervention, especially among children over the age of 6 or 7. It is the parents who may not survive the clamor. If one child seems to be getting the worst of it continually and it is necessary to step in, be sure you hear all sides. There always are at least two. You can often help even the younger ones arrive at a more equable solution of the incident by asking, "Can you think of a better way to settle this?" It may also help the aggressor to save face—which he may badly need to do—to state calmly, "Next time you will find a better way." Emphasizing that the desirable thing is to find a way out of difficulties gives the children a clue for future operations—not that the clue is always followed. You give the 3-, 4-, and 5-year-olds a hint for the next time, too, as you explain, perhaps for the hundredth time, about taking turns. Suggesting something for a youngster to do while waiting for the desired turn is often useful. If the quarrel is of the "She can't come in. We're playing cowboys. We don't need her" type, you can often cue the rejected one in by inventing a part for her to play.

Among the children in the family it is often a temptation to blame the older ones or the eldest when quarreling breaks out. Small brothers and sisters have their own ways of provoking a controversy, and their seniors cannot be expected to exercise forebearance forever.

The ounce of prevention is worth many pounds of cure where children's disputes are concerned. If you listen to what is afoot, you may discover when and why quarrels occur. Then you are in a better position to forestall them. Sometimes children in the family have frequent controversies just because they have been too much in one another's company. The same thing can occur among children on the block. A brief separation, not as a punishment, but as a refreshing break, may improve the relationship markedly. An afternoon or a day or two spent in another activity or another setting gives everyone a fresh start.

Sometimes two or more younger children will play together quite happily for an hour or two, and then trouble begins. Their mothers may then agree to send home or call home their youngsters before their tolerance for one another's society has been completely exhausted.

Hunger and fatigue are prime causes when friends—or brothers and sisters—fall out. A glass of fruit juice or a cracker before tempers become frayed may save the day. A quiet time with records or books before the zero hour arrives is good prevention, too.

It must be admitted that sometimes one child does seem to foment bickering in a group of three or four who without him get along quite well. Perhaps he is not really "a bad influence" but just too old or too young for the others. Some children who appear to be insufferably bossy do quite well when a legitimate outlet for their desire to dominate is provided. Some who appear to be bullies respond to kindness from adults. Often, two or three children who are quarrelsome one season may get along quite nicely a few months later. If it really seems necessary to discourage certain combinations, try letting those children be together again after a time.

If quarreling is a child's *only* way of making contact with others, and if he has troubles at other times as well, then we may wonder if he needs some help from a professional person skilled in treating disturbed children.

Experiences of many kinds contribute to a child's ability to get along with others. Learning to end a quarrel, to make a fresh start, to accept compromises are all a part of growing up. Quarrels do not need to be banned, just kept within bounds. EDITH G. NEISSER

See also AGGRESSIVENESS; DISCIPLINE; HOSTILITY; JEALOUSLY AND RIVALRY; LISTENING TO CHILDREN; SHARING; TEASING

QUESTION ANSWERING *See* CURIOSITY; SCIENCE; SEX EDUCATION

RABIES *See* BITES, ANIMAL

RASH

Any eruption on the skin may be called a rash. Rashes are commonly associated with communicable diseases, such as measles, chicken pox, and scarlet fever; with contagious skin diseases, such as impetigo, scabies, and ringworm; or with allergy, as in hives or penicillin reactions. Some rashes result from heat or irritation by clothing or chemicals in contact with the skin; some may result from insect bites. Rashes like acne come in part from hormonal changes going on within the body, while other rashes seem to be caused by emotional changes and disturbances. A rash is rarely caused by drugs like aspirin or by poisons like arsenic.

Since it is difficult to tell a mild, relatively harmless rash from a serious one, it is wise to call a doctor if your child develops any kind of rash. JULIUS B. RICHMOND

See also ACNE; ALLERGY; COMMON COMMUNICABLE DISEASES; IMPETIGO; POISON IVY, OAK, AND SUMAC; RINGWORM; ROSEOLA INFANTUM; WATERPROOF PANTS

READINESS

Parents and teachers recognize that the child who is eager to learn, who has an inquiring mind, who is emotionally secure, and who is physically fit learns more efficiently than the child who does not possess these qualifications. And a child who is "ready" to learn tends to gain more from new experiences than one who is not. How, then, can parents determine when a child is ready for a given task?

The word "readiness" has been used mainly in connection with the learning of school subjects—reading readiness, arithmetic readiness, and so on. Parents and teachers will be helped if they keep in mind that readiness is important for the learning of any complex task, whether in school, in the home, or in the community. A child learns to pick up his toys, make a purchase at the store, take a trip alone, or operate an electric train. Readiness for tasks like these is just as much a part of a child's development as readiness for schoolwork.

Studies of reading and arithmetic readiness have shown that a child's age in years is not a very useful measure for deciding when he is ready for a given task. In fact, no simple factor such as mental age, age in years, or maturity of the body should be used as the only guide in determining readiness. Only the various strengths and abilities of each individual child should be taken into consideration.

We might say that a child is ready for a new experience when he is interested. We might assume that interest develops in each child at his own rate without much influence from experience. In the past, some people have suggested that all a parent can do is to wait until the interest appears and then provide materials to encourage the child's further interest.

But more recent studies of interest have shown that the experiences parents and teachers provide can have a great deal to do with the development of interest. For example, when a child feels that an activity will help him to become a person who can do something worth while and that it will earn him the respect of his friends, he will very likely be interested in learning. But, if he feels the activity will make him seem babyish or silly or if he feels his friends will not respect his efforts, he will avoid the activity in favor of something more satisfying.

Grownups have learned that immediate satisfactions and conveniences are only a part of the picture. Something is worth while for adults if they think the immediate effects and long-run results are in some kind of balance. Mature adults consider both long-term and immediate effects.

A child, however, will tend to emphasize only immediate results. His limited experiences make it difficult for him to think of results very far in the future. Here it is that parents can provide opportunities for their child to observe and experience some of the long-run as well as the immediate effects of learning new activities and gaining new experiences. Parents do not have to stand by and wait for a child's interest to develop on its own. Instead, parents can be alert to existing conditions and can provide new experiences designed to develop new interests. A child who has never seen water colors could not know what fun it is to paint. A child who has never seen sand would not know the joy of building sand castles.

A kindergarten child who is asked to perform simple counting or measuring tasks at home in connection with home or school projects or who is encouraged to make occasional purchases at the store, including making change, will very likely achieve higher scores on beginning arithmetic tests than a child who has not had these experiences.

Alert parents will think of many such tasks: "Count the rooms in our house." "Count the number of chairs we have." "Here is 50 cents; buy a loaf of bread and bring back the correct change." "Count the books to find out how many shelves we need." "Measure the living room to see how much carpet we will have to buy." The list is endless and the rewards many for the child who is encouraged to use his mind and his body to gain new interests and experiences. Your child wants to become a real person and he wants to be respected. And perhaps, most of all, he wants to respect himself.

Readiness, then, assumes a child has the necessary abilities to perform a task, an interest in doing it, and a feeling that what he is doing is significant. Readiness is also dependent on the child being free from serious worry or conflict. A child who feels insecure, worried about family conflict, or who feels that his parents do not love him will tend to use most of his energy to overcome these problems. He will be less ready to take on a new experience.

Parents and teachers can plan ahead to help a child build the necessary background and abilities so that he may be ready to master a new task. Consider the electric train. Most parents can foresee the time when their son will want an electric train. A year or so before providing him with this complicated and expensive equipment, parents might buy a simple, battery-operated train, with wires, track, buzzers, bell, and picture diagrams. The child can learn what a completed circuit is, how connections have to be firm and clean. He will learn how to lay track, how to couple cars, and he can acquire a healthy respect for the electricity that will operate the train he is to have when he is older.

A child must be provided with the proper background to insure his readiness for school. Some children, unprepared for the confusion of the first days in school, never completely adjust to the new environment.

The problem of helping a child to be "ready" for a complex experience continues throughout his development. Children develop at such different rates that it is not possible to say that at 4 or 5 years of age a child is ready for one experience or at 7 years he can handle other experiences. There is no substitute for treating each child as an individual when it comes to getting him "ready" and for determining when he is "ready."

The whole problem of readiness involves the parent in developing a method that can be used for any complex experience his child will be called upon to master. Parents can look ahead and ask themselves:

- What complex experiences will our child be called upon to master by virtue of his growth and the culture in which he lives?
- What can we provide as background to help him feel challenged and not defeated by these experiences?
- How can his home environment help him to obtain this background?
- What will he need by way of knowledge to help him master these tasks and how can his home environment help him?
- Is he fearful, worried? Does he have hostilities that will drain his energy?
- How can we, in our home, help him to be emotionally secure?

Parents who take the time to answer these questions, who will look ahead to the needs of their children, and who will provide them with a background in support of those needs will undoubtedly send children into the world who are "ready" to cope with unfamiliar situations. RALPH H. OJEMANN

See also EMOTIONAL DEVELOPMENT; GROWTH; INDIVIDUAL DIFFERENCES; MENTAL HEALTH; READINESS FOR SCHOOL

READINESS FOR READING

Does the term "reading readiness" sound mysterious to you, almost frightening? It need not. For although the educator may mystify you by talking about readiness, he means no more than you do when you say, "It's time, I think, for a tricycle." Your remark means that you believe your child's legs can reach the pedals, his arms the handle bars, and that he is grownup enough to be willing to ride off a bit ahead of you or to dawdle along behind. Your remark also means that he knows the difference between a sidewalk and a street and that when you say, "Stop at the corner," he will understand what you want him to do. In other words, you know your child's physical being, his emotional maturity, his degree of experience, and his mental capacity.

You are not likely to put your child on a tricycle simply because he is the age of some cousin or neighbor who rides one. You are going to wait until he is "ready" because then he can sit on his new toy eagerly and can expect to ride it fairly well. You do not want him to become discouraged and to lose interest, for you have already found out, in other of his activities, that once he doubts his ability to do something, he has a much harder time learning to do it.

And so it is with learning to read. Reading ability does not come about automatically just because a child is at the age to start first grade. The ability depends on how well his eyes, ears, and powers to think have developed. It also depends on certain things he understands and certain things he is able to do because he has had a prereading program in kindergarten and the first grade. It may even depend on the child's emotional state. Yet given the right combination of all these factors, your child may undertake reading with meaning and an expectancy of success. He is ready.

Today the importance of *readiness* in learning to read is much better understood than it was when many present-day parents went to school. Then, no one thought much about preparation for reading. Reading began for all children when they started first grade. Many youngsters learned to read, of course, but there were others who either failed first grade or who never did learn to read so well as they might have, simply because their teaching began too early.

Even some of today's poor readers prove that their reading problems began because they were pushed into the deep water of reading before they were ready to swim. Little is gained, but much is lost by insisting that a child take on the complex task of learning to read before he is ready to be successful in it.

What Does It Take—To Learn To Read?

Many things. First of all, a child must be as free as possible from physical defects that stand in his way. He should be able to see well and hear well everything that is written or spoken. He should also be robust enough to attend school regularly, to learn new words and master new skills as the teacher presents them, for if he isn't physically up to regular attendance, he will be struggling continually with what he has missed as well as with the new.

The mental level of the child, also, is related closely to readiness for reading. Reading is a complex mental task. It requires memory, reasoning ability, word understanding, and general comprehension. Since these are all intellectual factors, a child with a high mental level is ready for reading earlier than a child with a lower level. The child with the lower level will likely need a longer period of preparation for reading. He will not get much out of reading instruction until he has enough mental maturity to understand what he is being taught.

The learn-to-read task also demands a normal degree of emotional balance. Any condition that takes away from the well-being of a child and leaves him unhappy, insecure, or frustrated may serve as a block to learning. For instance, suppose that soon after a child begins to learn to read at school his family acquires a new member—a baby sister. The attention and affection that had been his alone are now being divided with someone else who seemingly has taken his place. The older child's attempts to solve this baffling problem have left him insecure and frustrated, and he has little desire to concentrate on the job of learning to read. As far as he is concerned, winning a secure place in the family is more important anyway.

Or imagine, perhaps, a somewhat shy and withdrawn youngster, new in the community. When he starts first grade, he finds himself with 29 other children he has never seen before, along with a teacher who is busy every minute. Since the teacher cannot give the newcomer the time and attention he is used to at home, and since he finds it hard to make a place for himself with the group, he, too, has difficulty keeping his mind on the work of learning to read.

But Readiness Is Learned, Too

In the days of not-so-long-ago, reading instruction began on the opening day of school in September. Many parents can recall the beginning first-grade "chart class," where they met the words, *cat, rat, mat, sat,* and *Nat.* True, many youngsters learned to read by putting these words together in sentences, but many did not, because at their stage of development they simply could not understand the process of reading.

Today's reading teacher begins her first-grade work with a prereading or reading readiness program. This program is made up of many different activities all of which lead a child toward being able to do things he could not do before. For example, after returning from the morning play period, some children were anxious to talk about a milkweed pod that the night's frost had opened. The children had blown the seeds into the air and watched them parachute to the ground. The teacher suggested that they might like to write about what they had seen.

So the children dictated and the teacher wrote on the blackboard.

The Milkweed

We found a milkweed pod.
The frost had opened it wide.
We saw the seeds inside.
We blew them into the air.
The seeds went up, up, up.
Then they came down, down, down.

Dictating this "experience story," as it is called, developed some very important understandings necessary for the beginning of reading. First, the children noticed that their teacher wrote the sentences on the blackboard from left to right. As she read the story back to the children, she moved her hand under the lines in the same direction. They were being helped to learn that reading is always done in a particular direction. Their spoken language became a series of marks on the blackboard which the teacher called words. Some of the words looked the same, and each time she read them, they said the same thing. In this observation the children learned important characteristics of words. Even in the planning stage of the story the children's discussion gave them exercise in use of words and added new words to their vocabularies.

But although blackboard exercises and other informal types of activities are important in developing readiness, there are certain skills and abilities that may be more efficiently increased through prepared materials, commonly called the "readiness book." Likely this will be the first schoolbook the children receive, but unlike the chart or primer with which many parents began their reading, the readiness book contains little, if any, actual reading. Instead, there will be pictures that call for careful attention to details, which is exactly the same kind of attention the children will need in noting the differences between words. There will be pictures for the child to "read" and discuss in his group. Pages will stress memory, or attention to sounds in words, or eye and hand coordination, or relationships among many kinds of pictured objects.

As an example of how this method works, the children may be given a book with a series of pictures of a boy and a girl going into a store. There are no words and so the school children make up a story out of what they see. They must advance beyond the stage of merely saying, "There is a man in the store," to the concept that the man is selling something, that a package is being wrapped, perhaps for a birthday party. They are asked to discover the differences between quite similar objects, two hens facing one way and one another way, just as later they will have to be able to distinguish the differences between *m, n,* and *r.* A young child needs all these learning experiences as stepping stones to reading.

Besides the experience activities and the prepared prereading program, there are other devices to help children walk the reading road with ease and enthusiasm. The teacher has them play games that develop coordination and call for careful attention to directions. She reads aloud stories and poems, some of which may be dramatized with puppets the children make themselves so that they become more adept with spoken words and develop confidence in doing things with their group. In fact, from the time the youngsters come to school in the morning until the bus rolls away in the afternoon, the major portion of the day is spent, one way or another, in developing those abilities that are essential in learning to read.

Every Child Can Read—When He Is Ready

In due course, some of the youngsters will be ready to make the transition from prereading to reading. But in a good school each child will be asked to make this transition when he himself has the most chance of being successful at it. For the difference between success and failure, enjoyment and dislike, continued progress and frustration is based on the thoroughness and fitness of the prereading program.

Under such a proper prereading program, every child has the chance to come to the place where he is thoroughly prepared to step into the magic circle with confidence. No matter what his age or capacity, if the child can be brought to this threshold, he should read easily and naturally.

When Will He Be Ready?

The question of when a child will be ready to read is not easily answered. Some children are well advanced on the road to reading by the time they enter the first grade, some even before that time. They come from homes where there is a good environment for reading. There are books and magazines, both children's and adults', in abundance. The "story hour" has been a daily feature; books in this kind of home are a source of enjoyment and information, and the children come to school with an interest in reading and a strong desire to learn. If they need glasses, they have been properly fitted, and if they have hearing problems, parents are

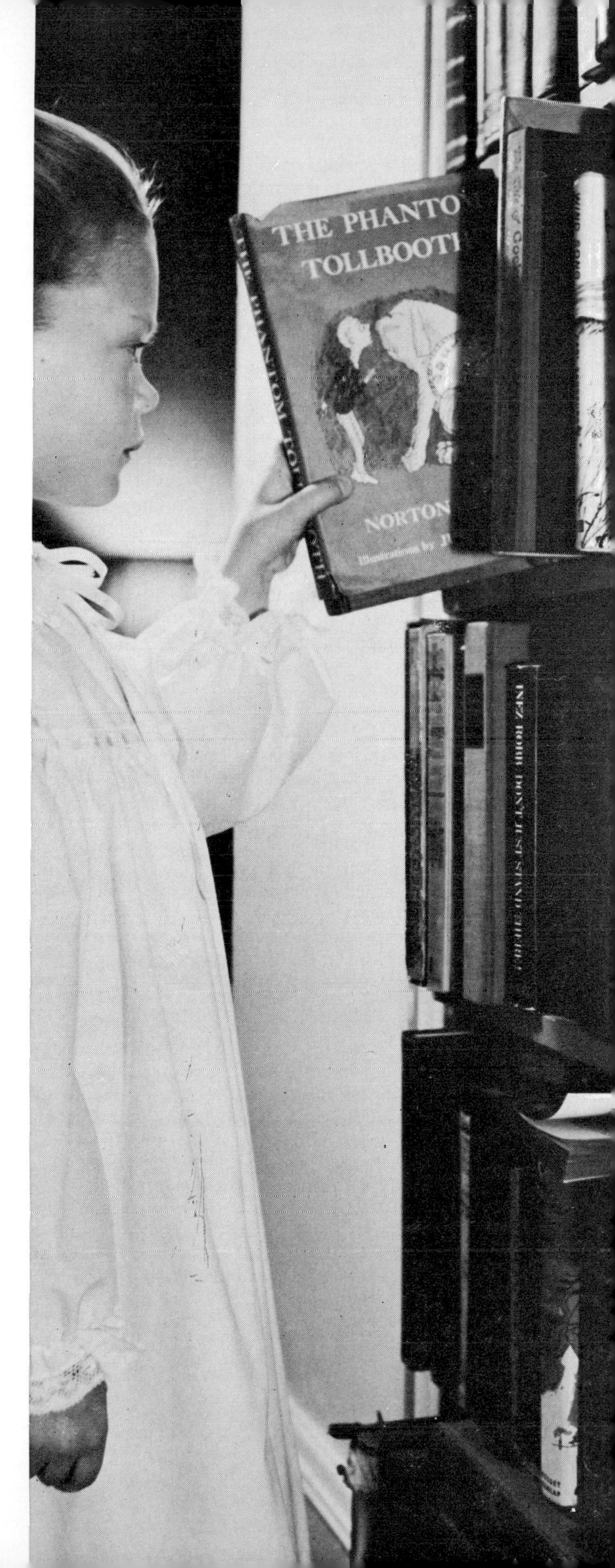

aware of them and have sought help. They get adequate nutrition and rest; hence, they are wide awake, energetic, and able to concentrate for sustained periods. They have no major emotional problems and they find the school experience an exciting adventure.

After a relatively short period of readiness activities these more advanced children are ready to go on, and their teacher will start them reading. In fact, it is not unusual for some 6-year-old children to be well started in reading. This is not because they have had formal teaching at home, but because they are naturally curious about their verbal world and have developed a reading vocabulary from cereal boxes, signboards, television commercials, and the captions below the pictures in their storybooks.

Quite the contrary is true of other children who come from less stimulating environments, who have physical, social, or emotional limitations, or who are all-around slow developers. These children will need more time to be allowed to grow up and will need a lengthened readiness period.

Thus no one can determine readiness by a date on the calendar, but only and always by the level of development of the child himself.

But this is the way children grow and progress—not only in reading, but also in piano playing, sewing, or building model airplanes. Some will get there rapidly, some slowly, and others at an average rate. Understanding parents will make their expectations for their child fit what the child himself is like. They will neither push him into water too deep for the novice swimmer nor overprotect him in the wading pool; they will let him have normal growth.

What May Parents Do To Help?

There are many things that parents may do to contribute to their child's reading readiness. In the first place they may create a rich reading environment in the home. This means surrounding the child with books—picture books, books of nursery rhymes, and collections of stories of all kinds. Birthdays and special days will provide an excuse, if one is needed, to add another book to a growing collection. Public libraries usually have a good department for children. There are a number of excellent children's magazines carrying a continuous stream of good material. Even before a child can read he will get a thrill out of a regular monthly magazine addressed to him.

A story period, perhaps at bedtime, can be the bright spot in the day's activities. Here in quiet and peace, parent and child may enjoy together a lilting poem or a thrilling story. There is no better way to create an interest in good literature or to stimulate a desire to be on one's own in this exciting venture.

Equally important is a rich and varied experience to provide background for reading. Translated into everyday activities, this means taking ample time to answer your child's countless questions as completely as possible and in his language. It means, too, taking advantage of all kinds of opportunities for new experiences, such as family excursions to a nearby park, zoo, farm, city, fire department, or airport. These experiences bring out questions and discussions that give significance to reading.

Then, too, a child needs the opportunity to play with other youngsters and to learn how to get along with them before he goes to school. Learning to read will require a great deal of group activity, and a youngster has to be prepared for the give and take of a group. Moreover, he needs to be emotionally weaned from his home ties so that he can go to school in the morning with a feeling of confidence and security; the home's emotional umbrella should gradually be taken down to enable a child to learn to meet cloudy skies on his own.

The precocious child, the "rapid learner," creates special problems of his own. Quite likely this child will be one who has shown an interest in reading at an earlier age than 6. He imitates his parents by pretending to read. "Tell me what it says," is his byword as he points to the cereal box or signboard.

By all means the wise parent will answer his child's many questions. When he asks what a word says, he should be told. In a short time he may be remembering the words and putting them together in phrases and sentences. The point is that there is a difference between satisfying a child's normal curiosity about words and their meanings, curiosity expressed because he is interested and ready, and deliberately setting about to teach the child to read because the parent thinks he should be ready. The former procedure is desirable and good. But teaching a child to read is a professional task that requires training, experience, and skill. This delicate and important job should be done by the professional, who has the preparation, time, and patience to devote to it.

Readiness—a Cooperative Process

Watching a child learn to read is an exciting experience for parents—as exciting as the actual learning to read is for the child. The parent's role in a child's learning is major, for in a real sense the child has been traveling the readiness road from the day he was born, and most of the road has been traveled under the guidance and direction of the home.

It is the home, therefore, that lays the foundation of readiness in terms of interests, understanding, attitudes, and physical, social, and emotional well-being. The teacher takes this foundation and builds on it specific reading skills and abilities. Thus home and school, in an attitude of mutual confidence and respect, guide a child toward reading success. A. STERL ARTLEY

See also BOOKS FOR CHILDREN; INDIVIDUAL DIFFERENCES; MAGAZINES; MENTAL DEVELOPMENT; READING ALOUD; READING DIFFICULTIES; STORYTELLING

READINESS FOR SCHOOL

Starting to school for the first time is a major adventure and a dramatic change from past living for all children. Most youngsters take this challenge comfortably and easily in their stride, whether at age 3 when they may enter nursery school, at age 5 when they enter kindergarten, or at age 6 when they begin first grade. From about 3 years on, a child is curious about the wider world outside his home. He is eager to work and play with friends his own age. He is sufficiently sure of himself, and trusting of other adults, not to feel threatened by spending a part of each day away from his mother and under the supervision of a teacher.

A child's normal growth in language, in attention span, in wider social interests, in curiosity, and in independence is the major force that lays the foundation enabling him to welcome school without undue strain. There are, however, a few measures that parents can take which make it even easier for a child to move on into school life without unhappy upsets. Most of these measures fit quite naturally into the standard home activities of the preschool years.

Making the Transition Easy

It helps, for example, if the leave-taking for school—whether at age 3, 4, 5, or 6—is not the first time that a child has been away from home without mother. Those children who have gone to the store with a neighbor or who have eaten lunch at a friend's house or who have visited nearby relatives often have no problem in leaving the home base to move on into a classroom.

It helps, too, if children have had experiences in accepting someone other than their own parents as authorities. A child who has known good baby-sitters during his preschool years, for example, will probably have less trouble in accepting a teacher who is not his own mother. Children who have played with their friends in a neighboring back yard or a living room down the street, responding to whatever mother was in charge of the play, have laid a foundation for working with a teacher.

There are useful steps that parents can take in the period just before the actual start of school. One is to introduce a child to his new teacher. In many communities, although not all, it is possible for mother and child to visit the classroom before school opens. Such a visit gives a youngster the advantage of starting to school with a feeling that the new adult in his life is not a total stranger. It also builds a very helpful sense of familiarity with his new setting and prevents the first day of school from being a shock.

Many teachers are glad to visit the child in his own home before school begins, especially if parents extend the invitation. This intimate relationship with the teacher, no matter how brief, is another aid in making the start to school a pleasant and easy one. The child sees that his parents and his new teacher are friends who can talk together easily. He begins to feel that the teacher is his friend, too.

This basic relationship between friendly adults and a child is the foundation on which a sound beginning of the school years is built. The relationship begins with good feelings between parents and their child within the home. The child who knows that he can count on his parents is quite willing to believe he will be able to count on his new teacher. In his mind there is a readiness to accept all adults as good people who will help him if he needs help.

Three- and 4-year-olds going to nursery school for the first time will almost certainly be accompanied by their parents to and from school. Especially with this age, but even with fives and sixes, it is usually wise for parents to be prepared to stay at school with their children on the first days if that seems necessary. Some schools do not want parents to hover around. More and more schools, however, are recognizing that the separation of the child from his home does not have to take place in one fell swoop. The goal is not to pile on so many new experiences that a youngster is overwhelmed. Amid the new faces, a new room, a new bathroom, a teacher who is known but not yet an intimate, a new building, all the new sounds and rules, the comforting presence of mother can be the one little support a child needs to take all the newness in his stride.

Many nursery schools arrange for car pools to bring children to school. Others provide buses, and there often is bus transportation to kindergarten and first grade. An individual child who is unusually sure of himself may be able to cope with these new experiences, along with the total new experience of the school itself. But if a parent can find the time on the first days to come along, especially if a child gives any indication at all of wanting company, opening day is sure to be more happy and more comforting, and future upsets often can be avoided. Later, when some of the newness has worn off, going alone or going by bus or car pool can be a real step toward full independence.

Most children beginning kindergarten or first grade know other youngsters in their neighborhood who will be their classmates. This situation may not be true when children enter nursery school or when a family is new in a community or when a child has no playmates near him. It does help a child to make a good adjustment if, in addition to knowing his teacher, he sees other familiar faces around him. If a child has no friends in his class, it is wise for parents to invite one or two future classmates to play or for lunch so that their child can begin school knowing some of the children with whom he will work.

Some Safety Precautions

Since kindergarten and first-grade children will soon go to school and return alone, they need some specific instructions about the trip. Children walking to school, for example, need to make the trip with their parents before school opens so that they can learn the route thoroughly. They need specific instructions about staying on the sidewalks. They should know how to cross streets safely: stop at the curb, look to the left and to the right, wait until the road is completely clear or until they are given the signal to cross. Several trial runs with a parent as the friendly instructor, and one or two trips alone with the parent watching from a distance, can build the necessary competencies into 5- and 6-year-olds.

Children who travel alone should be taught to go directly to and from school without stops or side trips. They should be taught never to accept rides from strangers or even to stop to talk with strangers. Such instructions need not be given in a frightening manner but matter-of-factly as part of a child's solid learning about his new role and his new responsibility. Five- and 6-year-olds should know their own names and addresses before coming to school. A nickname is not enough. A child should be able to say clearly his full name and street address.

Good Natural Living the Best Preparation

Apart from this safety instruction there are no academic skills or special information that children should know ahead of time. Of course some children know how to count or know colors even before they come to nursery school. A few children can write their names and read simple words before kindergarten or first grade. If any of these learnings are acquired in the simple course of family living before school begins, fine and good. But you do not need to teach your child specific lessons of this kind in order to send him off to school "well prepared." The teacher's job is exactly the same as the parent's job: to teach each child what he is ready to learn when he is ready to learn it. Some children have a great curiosity to learn some of this material at home before school begins, and they should not be held back. Other children, who may be equally able, have no interest in this information before they come to school and they can be hurt if pushed ahead.

Much more important than any specific lessons geared directly to schoolwork are all the natural experiences of good preschool home living. From infancy on, for example, all children are ready to hear stories and to listen to music. All children are ready to talk to adults and to learn from listening to adults. All children are ready for short trips away from home, out into the community: for bus rides, for visits to stores or to a railroad station or an airport, for trips to a river to see the boats or to a farm to see the animals. Such experiences bring in a flow of ideas and impressions to children which are important for their own sake during the preschool years; they also stimulate curiosity and whet an interest in learning.

As the school years approach, some parents unwisely use school as a threat with their children. It is not uncommon to hear adults say: "You had better be good because when you get to school the teacher will make you . . . ." "You'd better stop what you are doing because the teacher won't let you . . . ." Parents need not go out of their way to talk at great length about the joys of going to school. In fact, too much happy-talk can make a child suspicious that school may not be as much fun as people say it is. It certainly is a mistake, however, to give the impression that school is a prison. Helping a child to feel ready for school is the simple task of building on his natural curiosity and anticipation without undue fuss and bother and surely without instilling in him needless fears and anxieties.

Despite the natural anticipation and readiness of most children, it is not unusual for all youngsters to have some qualms once school has begun. Every single day is not necessarily a happy day. Although most children basically like school, they have some moments in almost every day when things do not go their way, some times when there are conflicts with the teacher or more often with their classmates. These temporary upsets can show themselves in direct questions from children: "Do I have to go to school?" Sometimes they show themselves indirectly through unusual dawdling or through stomach upsets and other minor illnesses. It is important for parents to know their child's teacher well enough to communicate this kind of information easily and quickly. Parents and teachers who work as a team almost always can straighten out the difficulty with no major trouble.

Helping a child get ready for school is only one part of the job that must be done as children grow older. Parents must also get themselves "ready for school." We must be honestly glad that a child has reached a more independent stage in his development. We must be glad that his life is opening up to include the new, thrilling experiences that a good school can bring. Sometimes, unconsciously we are sorry to see our children grow up. Youngsters sense these hesitancies and, especially in the nursery and kindergarten years, often use them to magnify any misgivings they themselves are feeling.

Schools Must Be Ready for Children

Almost all children from 3 years of age on are ready for school, but not all schools are ready for them. A 3-year-old can do very well in a nursery school that is geared to the capacities of threes in its equipment and program and expectations. A 5-year-old can do very well in a kindergarten that is right for 5-year-olds. But even a child as mature as a 6-year-old can fare very badly in a first grade that is better suited for 8-year-olds. Fives can be very unhappy in kindergartens that are more like first grades. Schools must be ready for the children who come to them.

Unfortunately, many schools today are overcrowded. Some of them demand more sitting, more quiet activity, and more conformity than many children are comfortably able to give. Some kindergartens and first grades put a stronger emphasis on reading, writing, and paper-and-pencil work than many children are able to cope with so early in their growth. It can take a long time for a community to build good schools if it does not have them. The basic ingredient is usually money, a community's willingness to tax itself so that it has the funds to hire enough well-trained teachers, to insure well-equipped classrooms, to maintain classes small enough so that teachers can use their training to best advantage.

It is too late for parents to inquire into the quality of their schools when a child approaches school entrance age. About the time a child is born is not too early to begin this kind of inquiry. JAMES L. HYMES, JR.

See also INDIVIDUAL DIFFERENCES; MUSIC; PHYSICAL CHECKUP; SCHOOL-AGE CHILD; SEPARATION FROM MOTHER

READING ALOUD

A pleasure shared is a pleasure retained. A book read aloud in a family group will be remembered years later, not only for the book's content, but also for the way some loved voice sounded, the way someone made a character come alive, the hilarious mistake someone made in pronunciation.

Schoolteachers know that the child who has been read to enjoys the sound of words. To such a child, words on the printed page are not fearful obstacles to be conquered but are instead keys to adventure and humor.

Through the experience of books read aloud, a child's curiosity is piqued, his knowledge is increased, and he begins to appreciate the beauty of phrase and thought in his mother tongue.

Reading aloud begins with the infant to whom words are meaningless but whose small body will sway to the rhythm of the nursery rhymes read or sung by his mother. A comfortable lap, a relaxed attitude, and a book with gayly colored pictures about something familiar to him will provide a child with an open door to the literature of childhood and eventually to the great literature of the world.

All too often, reading aloud ceases when a child begins school or as he grows older. Yet, reading aloud could be continued profitably for as long as the family remains a unit. Many of the classics are difficult for young children to read, and yet their story content will be appealing.

Not only can the contents of books be shared, the actual reading aloud can be shared, too. Parents will no doubt do much of the reading, but each member of the family, according to his capabilities, can have the satisfaction of learning to read aloud with expression and feeling. By reading aloud a child practices sounding words correctly, he learns to interpret characters, and he gains the confidence that accomplishment in any art provides.

It will be easier for your child to read aloud in school and to participate in assemblies and other school events if he has had the opportunity to learn to read aloud in his family group.

Excellent reading material for children on all age levels includes folk and fairy tales, the myths of the ancient world, the poetry of childhood, and the many stories of realistic adventure and family life. Some public libraries publish special book lists for family use. And in CHILDCRAFT you can find reading material for children in Volume 1, *Poems and Rhymes;* Volume 2, *Stories and Fables;* Volume 11, *Scientists and Inventors;* Volume 12, *Pioneers and Patriots;* and Volume 13, *People To Know.* ELIZABETH H. GROSS

See also BOOKS FOR CHILDREN; FAIRY TALES; LIBRARIES

READING DIFFICULTIES

The joy and exhilaration of reading come to a great many children as they go through elementary school, for they have learned to read quite well. But for some children the job of learning to read involves so much pain, and the skill they acquire is so slight, that even though they graduate and enter high school, they may remain poor readers.

The reading difficulties of these children disturb their teachers and parents. Yet it is the children themselves who suffer most—they are frustrated; they have come to dislike reading, either for information or pleasure. Lacking reading skill, they often are denied success in other subjects where they are talented, for they cannot read well enough to understand the text. They are also helpless unless some school or teacher or parent recognizes and understands their problem early enough to get at the root of the trouble and start them on the way to successful reading.

There is usually no single cause for a child's reading difficulties. Some factors are within the child and some factors are in the educational setup to which he is exposed. These are the common causes to be found within the child:

Lack of readiness for reading. Even though a child may be the same age as other children who are learning to read, he may not have matured enough to be taught reading just then or have the abilities and understanding that are needed for beginning reading success. It is of interest that boys have a disproportionate number of reading difficulties and, on the average, read less well in the early years.

Inadequate oral language development. Reading is a process of recognizing printed symbols that stand for spoken words and of attaching meaning to the symbols. Therefore, to learn to read, a child needs an adequate vocabulary and a familiarity with spoken language. But many children come to school from environments that fail to give them the background they need.

Emotional problems. Reading, or any other activity requiring a high level of concentration, thinking, and remembering, is difficult to master if most of the learner's mind and energy are being used to cope with personal problems. Rivalry with a brother or a sister, problems the family is having, frequent change of schools, or feelings that he himself is not up to standard, all have been found to stand in the way of a child's reading success.

Neurological problems. A few children are unable to associate meanings with the printed symbols. This inability possibly is the result of some kind of damage to the brain before or after birth, an accident, or a disease.

Reduced physical vitality. Insufficient rest and improper diet may prevent a child from giving his undivided attention to learning. Chronic infection and frequent illness often result in absence from school at the time important material is being learned.

Slow learning rate. Some children naturally learn more slowly than others. Their slowness may be due to a variety of reasons, including their degree of intelligence. The slow learner will read less well than others in his class, although in terms of *his own* capacity for learning he may be achieving well. Children in a family tend to show resemblances in the way they grow in reading. Thus, delayed and early starts are characteristics of families. Some children who start late show later spurts in learning.

Vision and hearing. Proper functioning of eyes and ears is basic. Frequently, undiscovered or uncorrected trouble in seeing or hearing is a huge barrier to reading success.

These are the common causes of reading difficulties to be found in the school.

Inadequate reading instruction. Unfortunately, some schools employ or are forced to employ teachers who are poorly trained or who are using inappropriate methods. Teachers of reading must have the best initial training and preparation and must also be given opportunities to keep learning while they teach so that they can keep up with new ideas and developments.

Inadequate teaching materials. Schools may lack well-developed and up-to-date teaching materials, library books, magazines, and reference sources. Without good materials the teacher finds it difficult to start reading interests or to keep them going. The child whose school lacks the books he needs not only misses the enjoyment that comes from reading, but he also does not get enough reading practice.

Large classes. The teaching of reading requires a great deal of small group and individual instruction. Where classes are too large, the teacher has little time or opportunity to work with an individual child on his particular problems.

In many cases of reading difficulty the classroom teacher may be able to give the necessary type and amount of corrective help. If your child's problem has existed for some time or if complex causes are present, discuss the situation with his teacher or in a parent-teacher-principal conference. It may be necessary to take the child to a reading clinic or child study center where his difficulties can be diagnosed and corrective or remedial work given to him. A. STERL ARTLEY

See also BOOKS FOR PARENTS; CLINICS; EYE HEALTH; FAILURE, FEAR OF; HOME-SCHOOL RELATIONS; MENTAL DEFICIENCY; READINESS FOR READING; SLOW LEARNER

RECKLESSNESS

It is often difficult to make an accurate distinction between recklessness and a child's natural instinct to be active, to try new things, to develop new skills, to be adventurous and curious. Yet it is important to make the distinction since parents want to protect their children from real danger and, at the same time, permit them to learn new skills through experimentation and direct experience.

There are a number of clues for judging whether or not a child is reckless. When a 2-year-old runs onto the road, or a 3-year-old blithely walks into the ocean, he is not reckless; he is simply ignorant of the dangers involved. His parents know this and see to it that he is protected from the consequences of his immaturity and inexperience.

A child is not reckless if he has an awareness of what is involved in an experiment and is able to proceed cautiously. A 4-year-old who makes his first try to climb to the top of a jungle gym has already had experiences with balancing, climbing, holding on tight, and looking down from high places; he has already been on a slide, jumped from the porch steps, balanced on a swing. His wish to do something new includes an understanding of the skills he will need. Beyond this awareness, how does he proceed? Does he try to climb halfway up first, or does he try for the top the first time? A tightrope walker who starts his first lessons on a high wire, far above the ground, is reckless; if he had practiced for a long time on a rope near the ground, he would not be reckless. Some children who seem the most daring are really just very well coordinated; they know what they can do, and when they say they are ready to try something new, they really are ready, for they have proceeded with care. Although they may be constantly trying new things they are not reckless.

Much recklessness is motivated by reasons other than just wanting to learn and grow. There is a difference between the child who loves to climb a tree for the fun of it and the child who climbs on a dare, to gain attention and admiration from his playmates. There is a difference between the youngster who wants to try to swim across the lake and back to challenge himself and to develop his skills and the child who tries to accomplish this feat in order to gain approval from a father who admires such prowess more than anything else his child might do. When children seem to be struggling for success primarily to gain approval, attention, or acceptance that they have not achieved in other ways rather than for enjoyment of the activity, they are more likely to become reckless and take unnecessary chances.

Some children are not merely reckless occasionally but have repeated accidents of a relatively serious nature. Accident-proneness is usually associated with deep and often complicated needs that are not being met in more constructive or positive ways. Here, the wish for attention, for comfort, for dealing with inner anxieties by getting oneself hurt are likely to be so complex that expert help and guidance may be necessary in order to help a child find healthier satisfaction of his emotional needs.

Adult supervision and a relatively safe environment can minimize hazards, but the only way to grow is to try new things; the only way to overcome inexperience and ineptness is to practice some more. Children have to be permitted to take some chances—there is no way to avoid danger completely at any time in one's life. Parents can minimize the inevitable bumps and scratches by protecting their very young child from doing what he cannot yet understand, by helping a more aware child learn caution and patience, and by trying to help a child of any age to increase his skills—not to prove himself to others, but for his own pleasure and satisfaction. EDA J. LE SHAN

See also ACCIDENT PREVENTION; APPROVAL; CHILD GUIDANCE CLINIC; DISCIPLINE; PROBLEM CHILD

RECORDS *See* FAMILY HEALTH RECORD; PHONOGRAPH RECORDS

RECREATION *See* PLAY; SOCIAL DEVELOPMENT

RED BLOOD CELLS *See* ANEMIA; BLOOD COUNT

REFERENCE BOOKS *See* BOOKS FOR CHILDREN

REGISTERED NURSE *See* NURSE

REGRESSION

Regression is a technical term that means to turn back to something that is simple and familiar—to return to some earlier way of behaving. Regression is the opposite of growth. A 5-year-old, placed in kindergarten the first day of the new term, shows growth by a readiness to be independent and he becomes absorbed in his classroom activities. Another child, who appears to be equally independent, breaks down and cries as his mother is about to leave. Previously, he had played in the park unaccompanied by his mother, slept overnight at friends' homes, but now he suddenly feels as dependent on mommy as he did when he was 2½ or 3. This is regression.

Slipping backwards is a most common occurrence, not only in the lives of children but in the lives of adults as well. Growth is by no means an uninterrupted series of improvements. Nor do we constantly maintain the level of the growth achieved. Our level of maturity can be toppled by illness, failure, or disappointment. How far it topples and for how long depends on the quality of our emotional adjustment. A child who has learned to keep his bed dry for more than two years may begin bed-wetting all over again following his keen, though privately felt, disappointment over the invasion of the family by his newly born brother or sister. Any child's more recently acquired habits may give way under pressure to return to some less grown-up form of behavior.

Adolescence in general is a good case in point. Early in the teens, children face considerably more pressure than they have for several years. Not only are they confused by the physiological changes taking place inside them, but also society has begun to impose roles upon them which they alternately reject and desire. The result is that adolescents are frequently awkward mixtures of grown-upness and babyishness. Among the common manifestations of regression are crying; masturbation; argumentative, cantankerous attitudes; and unrealistic daydreaming.

Regressions are an inevitable part of growth, and a sensitive parent does not scold a child out of them. The trick is to help one's child maintain the best possible picture of himself even through his illness, failure, or disappointment. Concentrating one's efforts on the regression itself—whether it be bed-wetting, crying, or unreasonable fears—is not nearly so rewarding as helping the child think well enough of himself not to hesitate to be grown up. ALLAN FROMME

See also EMOTIONAL DEVELOPMENT; JEALOUSY AND RIVALRY; READINESS

REGULATIONS *See* RULES AND REGULATIONS

REJECTION

Rejection is a frightening word. Even adults feel uncomfortable and unhappy at being rejected by those they care for. Think how much stronger this feeling must be in little children. And it is so easy for a child to feel rejected. Let a new baby come into the home, or let more attention be given a brother or a sister, or let a visiting child be admired, and that cold, lonely feeling of being pushed away takes over. No wonder rejection has been blamed for many of the ills of childhood.

Most parents do not reject their children. They do not neglect them, punish them severely, or show active dislike in other ways. But to a child, a parent may seem to show rejection—by criticizing, by demanding better schoolwork, or by comparing the child with others to his disadvantage. And a child may also think he is being rejected when his parents are too busy to help when he asks for help, when they reproach instead of sympathizing if he has had a hard time, when they are too preoccupied with their own anxieties to understand *his* feelings. Whenever a parent's or a teacher's behavior seems to deny a child's right to have limitations, to make mistakes, and when adults withhold appreciation of the abilities he does have, he may feel rejected.

Real or fancied, rejection has drastic effects. Basically, it makes a child reject himself and distrust others. A youngster who feels left out cannot develop the spontaneity and outgoingness that are signs of well-being in childhood. Once having experienced rejection, he expects more of the same. He advances toward the world with his guard up or retreats from it to protect himself from further hurt.

When parents or other persons important to a child seem dissatisfied with him or belittle and shame him, he feels there must be something wrong with him. If he is constantly criticized, he cannot figure out exactly how he falls short or how to remedy the situation, since whatever he does seems wrong. He develops a general distrust of himself and apprehension about other people. He may give way to excessive daydreaming and cling constantly to any adult who will be kind to him. These behaviors do not attract others and the child may find himself doubly rejected—by his age-mates as well as his parents. Under these conditions he may give up the battle altogether and become a recluse.

Some children meet rejection in the crude forms of neglect and harsh punishment. These children often react by becoming braggarts and bullies. They may turn the tables and themselves reject everything their elders stand for. From such children develop many of society's incorrigibles and delinquents.

Rejection is not, of course, an all-or-none affair. Every parent rejects some childish behavior or fails to realize some need a child may have. All parents feel momentarily irritated by their children's demands when tired or preoccupied. Yet these occasional lapses do not seem to produce ill effects when a child is basically accepted as a *person* with needs and limitations of his own.

It is necessary at times to refuse to accept some kinds of behavior to guide a child to more mature levels. Such refusal is not rejecting a child. Children often feel rejected if their parents do not take the trouble to make clear to them what is and what is not acceptable behavior. RUTH E. HARTLEY

See also ACCEPTANCE; APPROVAL; SELF-CONCEPT; SOCIAL DEVELOPMENT

RELATIVES *See* GRANDPARENTS AND OTHER RELATIVES

RELIEF BOTTLE *See* COMPLEMENTARY FEEDING

RELIGION *See* MORAL AND SPIRITUAL DEVELOPMENT

REPORT CARD *See* SCHOOL REPORT

REPRODUCTION

In the human being, as in almost all other animals, new life begins by the joining of two cells—the egg from the female and the sperm from the male. The eggs are produced by the ovaries of the mother, and in the human being are spherical and about 1/125 inch in diameter. They cannot move or swim by themselves.

The sperm are produced by the testes (testicles) of the father. Under the microscope the sperm appear like tiny tadpoles, with oval heads, narrow necks, and long threadlike tails. The sperm cells are approximately 1/500 inch in length and swim about, with tails moving rapidly. They swim in semen, a fluid produced by special glands in the male.

There are two ovaries in every woman. They are in the lower abdomen, one on either side, and are about the size of an almond. Leading from each ovary to the uterus is a narrow tube, the Fallopian tube. When an egg is developed and leaves the ovary, it is sucked into the Fallopian tube and moved toward the uterus (womb). It takes approximately three days for the egg to pass from the ovary through the tube to the uterus.

During the sex act, millions of sperm enter the uterus of the woman. Many of them swim into the Fallopian tubes. If an egg cell is present in one of these tubes, a sperm cell can enter the wall of the egg and unite with it. This uniting of the egg and the sperm is called fertilization.

Now the egg, containing qualities of both the mother and the father, is capable of developing into a baby. The fertilized egg is then moved down the remainder of the tube and into the uterus where it attaches itself to the inner wall. The inner wall of the uterus is well supplied with blood vessels, but at the time an egg is produced by an ovary, an extra amount of blood is brought to this area to nourish the egg if it is fertilized.

The fertilized egg, attached to the nourishing wall of the uterus, begins to develop. First, it divides into two cells. Then these two cells divide, and all the new cells continue to divide and divide. At first there is just a mass of cells of no particular shape, but after several months this mass begins to take on the appearance of a human body.

As the baby develops and grows in size, a round, flattened organ called the placenta is formed on the wall of the uterus where the egg first became attached. The placenta is composed of small blood vessels of the mother intermingled with small blood vessels of the baby. The placenta is connected to the navel of the baby by a cord, known as the umbilical cord, which contains the blood vessels of the baby only. Both the placenta and the umbilical cord are extremely important, for it is through them that oxygen and food are brought from the mother to the baby, and waste products carried from the baby's body.

While the baby is in the mother's uterus, it lies within a sac of fluid that serves as a protection for the baby, preventing the baby from being bumped or jarred and maintaining a temperature that is always warm and stable.

The baby develops within its mother's body for a little over nine months. At the end of this time the muscles of the uterus start to contract, causing the mother slight cramplike pains in the lower abdomen. At first these contractions occur at intervals of approximately 30 minutes, but gradually they occur closer and closer together, and the pains become more and more severe. The muscles of the uterus are contracting to force the baby out of the mother's body through the vagina. This process of forcing the baby out of the uterus is called "labor," and the pains, "labor pains." Labor may last only an hour or two, or even 36 hours or longer. MILTON I. LEVINE

See also BIRTH; HEREDITY; MENSTRUATION; PRENATAL IMPRESSIONS; SEX EDUCATION

RESENTMENT

A child who believes he has been wronged feels resentful. This feeling does not last so long as hostility nor go so deep as anger or hate. Also, resentment can be dealt with more easily than hostility, for the hurt is still new and open to soothing discussion.

The resentful child has been treated badly according to his lights, and his resentment is normally followed by angry behavior of some kind. If resentment is a judgment, "I have been wronged," it is followed usually by the question, "What do I do about it?" This question requires a rethinking of the original judgment itself. A punished child is usually resentful at first and then, after some preliminary expression like griping, crying, muttering under his breath, stomping off, or slamming a door, he begins to think it over. If he has been wisely punished, he usually comes to the conclusion that he had it coming: He had better take it and try not to let it happen again. Thus, it is not the resentment but how it is handled by a child that becomes the more important issue for mental health. In fact, had the punished child no feeling of resentment at all, it is likely that the punishment was not very well designed. If a child's resentment is produced by an adult, the adult should have a good reason for his action, one that the child can understand; otherwise, the second step—thinking it over and positive handling by the child—will not take place. If, for instance, a child is talked down to or treated like a baby or handled authoritatively just to show who is boss, there is no normal, healthy way for him to modify his feeling, and the feeling may turn into a way of thinking, or remain and harden into hostility. DAVID WINEMAN

See also ANGER; HOSTILITY; MENTAL HEALTH; PUNISHMENT

RESOURCEFULNESS

The child who can stand on his own two feet, the child who is resourceful, is a happy child and an effective child. He will help others, he will find life smoother, and he will be able to cope with this world as he finds it. Parents' role in helping to strengthen a child's resourcefulness is relatively easy because this quality is one that youngsters prize for themselves.

When we hear a child say, "I can do it . . . I'm old enough . . . Let me!" we should heed him. The 2-year-old's first attempts to dress himself may yield pants on backwards or a sweater on upside down, but the child's eagerness to try is important and deserves encouragement.

Don't underestimate your child's abilities. The 5-year-old can wield hammer and saw; the 8-year-old can use a screw driver, a wrench, and a brace and bit. The 9- and 10-year-old can work with a power jigsaw after his father has given him careful safety instructions. At every hand there are tools

Don't underestimate your child's abilities.

and instruments children can control. The 4-year-old can use the wall can opener; the 6-year-old can operate an inexpensive camera; the 8-year-old can very efficiently clean your rugs with the vacuum cleaner. Children can make many decisions, too. A 3-year-old can decide whether to go to a friend's house or stay home, what toy to play with, and what book he wants to look at.

Children grow in resourcefulness as parents expose them, in easy stages, to the wonders of the world about them. Give your young children varied experiences—riding in an airplane, a car, a bus, a tractor, a train, a boat, an elevator, an escalator, even a ski lift.

Encourage your child to ask questions. The child who knows how, when, and of whom to make an inquiry or a request in a clear and friendly way has a valuable social tool at his command. Let your child speak for himself. When the dentist, the camp director, the teacher, or the policeman on the corner speaks to your child, let him handle his own reply. Allow your child to run any errand he possibly can. Let him lick the stamps and mail your letters; let him return his own books to the library.

Our goal, as parents, is to give our children enough help to make them feel comfortable. You cannot push children. You cannot brush away shyness. You cannot force children to speak up when they feel better being quiet or force them into situations where they feel ill at ease.

But there are errands, there are trips, there are tools, there are jobs that make a child feel big. If you open up opportunities adjusted to his age, your child can get the thrill he wants —a sense of being resourceful, increasingly able to cope on his own with life's many challenges. JAMES L. HYMES, JR.

See also INDEPENDENCE; RESPONSIBILITY

RESPECT *See* OBEDIENCE

RESPONSIBILITY

The true meaning of responsibility goes deeper than remembering to hang up one's coat. The word itself is composed of two words—"response" and "ability." Responsibility, then, means being able to respond of one's own accord to the needs of others. It is learned gradually through many kinds of experiences rather than through the repetition of uncongenial tasks.

Foundations for being a responsible person are laid long before words have any meaning to a baby. As he is cared for consistently and gently, a baby discovers that his mother is to be relied upon to make him comfortable. Human beings find out how people are expected to behave as they copy the actions and feel themselves a part of, or identify with, those they love.

When a mother leaves a 2- or a 3-year-old with a neighbor for a few hours and says, "I'll be back before suppertime," and then returns as she promised, her youngster gets the feeling, deep inside himself, of the meaning of dependability, although he could not put the feeling into words. Parents who behave in a responsible manner and give their sons and daughters opportunities to practice being dependable are likely to bring up responsible individuals. Of course, lapses from the ideal are to be expected while children are growing up.

Different kinds of responsibility are appropriate in each phase of development. The earliest steps a youngster takes in that direction are those of dressing and toileting himself. The feeling, "I can do something about this," also contributes to responsibleness. This feeling is fostered as adults around him guide him toward solving situations without losing his temper or without demanding that someone "fix it." Encouraging statements along the line of "See if you can find a way; you're good at that," or "What do you think you can do?" further a 3- or a 4-year-old's resourcefulness when a toy car will not fit into the garage built for it out of blocks or when the cover on the doll's bed won't stay tucked in. To stand by while the child finds a way may be necessary, for a small child needs the reassuring presence of someone more knowledgeable than he while he resolves his dilemma.

A young child usually delights in setting the supper table, bringing in the morning paper, or doing anything that makes him feel important. A few years later—just about when parents think children should be capable of taking on more extensive daily chores—boys and girls are becoming absorbed in

activities with their playmates. They have little time for or interest in anything beyond their own concerns. Yet it is through what is often dismissed as "just play" that a keener understanding of the need to be responsible and the capacity to act in dependable fashion develops.

"I promised. I gotta be there. The whole team'll be waiting for me," or "But, Mother, the girls are counting on me to do it. You always say we shouldn't let people down. If I don't make the sandwiches for the picnic, I'll spoil it for everyone." These situations and similar ones are evidence that a youngster is learning to live up to his commitments. Parents who support a son's or a daughter's desire to act responsibly in his relations with friends often find that the housekeeping and baby-tending tasks on which the older generation lay such stress are carried out more willingly.

A young person is demonstrating a high type of responsibility if, sensing that mother is tired, he volunteers to do, or quietly takes over, an extra job. Spontaneous hospitality to the guests of any member of the family, unsolicited but well-timed assistance to brothers or sisters, using initiative in helping someone, or resolving a difficult situation are proofs that a child has a healthy sense of responsibility, even though he has to be reminded that this is his week to take out the garbage.

Children can develop a wider sense of responsibility as they are maturing if parents, schools, and leisure-time agencies all emphasize how much the agreeableness and, indeed, the safety of everyone's life depend on each person doing his share. Youngsters can be shown the necessity for keeping parks, beaches, and woods clean and free of litter. They can be taught how to take care of library books and to return them on time. If

safety hazards exist, children can learn how and to whom to report them. Public property belongs to everybody and therefore everyone wants it to look nice. Children who get the idea that they play an important part in maintaining the common good are on the road to responsible citizenship.

The feeling that one helps to take care of persons in trouble, even though they are outside the family circle and not known personally, comes about through the example of parents who give time and effort to humanitarian causes without thought of reward. Children, too, can exercise this kind of social responsibility through church groups, scout troops, 4-H Clubs, Camp Fire circles, and other youth-serving agencies. Community service programs in these organizations go beyond money raising, but they are planned so that the children make a useful contribution through something they create.

A concern for the needs and feelings of others is rooted in sturdy self-respect. "I am the kind of person who lives up to my promises," and "I can do something to help," are attitudes that lie at the root of being a responsible individual. EDITH G. NEISSER

See also IMITATION; INDEPENDENCE; MORAL AND SPIRITUAL DEVELOPMENT

REST

There are times when rest is the only cure for a child's fretfulness, restlessness, and contrariness. If your child has been ill, you will want to see that he gets additional rest. Before going out in the evening with the family or if the child is going to be up late for *any* reason, a rest in the afternoon will refresh him so that the evening's activity will not be too tiring. An older child, a kindergartner, or a first grader usually will profit by a rest period after school if he comes home exceptionally tired or cross.

There will be times when your child will resist a rest period. He will think of all sorts of reasons why he should not rest. "I'm not tired," he may say. But if you will insist that he lie down for a while in a quiet, well-ventilated room, allowing him to have a favorite toy or blanket in bed with him, he may end up actually enjoying his rest. A warm midday bath may help to relax him, and if he is put into his pajamas, he will probably snuggle down in bed willingly. If mother can lie down at the same time, a child often will be more cooperative about resting.

Children inevitably pass the stage of napping in the afternoon and consider it babyish. When this time comes, try calling the nap a "rest." Many times the rest turns into a nap, but the child, being eased into resting, feels no resentment since he wasn't forced to try to sleep.

Children who are taught to rest their bodies when they get tired instead of driving on without rest and relaxation are not likely to become harried adults who *cannot* relax and pace themselves to productive living. If mother will take her cue from her children and rest when she insists that they rest, she will find her child-rearing task a much easier one. MILTON J. E. SENN

See also NAPS; SLEEP

RESTLESSNESS *See* FIDGETING

RETARDATION *See* MENTAL DEFICIENCY

REWARDS

Children experience three kinds of rewards for accomplishment. The first is a deep sense of inner satisfaction when they respond well or come up to approved standards. In this instance children reward themselves. Their inner pleasure is a very strong force spurring them to continue to act in the same good way. Second, children experience praise and approval from parents and teachers when they do a job well. Such simple, honest appreciation, directly related to the job that has been done, is another booster shot. It, too, increases the likelihood that the child will continue in his good ways. The third type of reward is the bonus, or bribe, usually unrelated to the behavior itself: "If you will be quiet for five minutes, I will buy you some chewing gum." "If you will get all A's, I will give you two dollars."

The bonus—or bribe—reward can be, at times, a useful way of controlling children. Unlike the first two types of rewards, however, it tends to involve parents in some tricky pitfalls. There is the danger that children will learn only to please adults who give rewards rather than to please themselves. This can mean that, when no adult is present or no added reward is forthcoming, they will not try. There is the danger, too, that adults will need to "jack up" the reward higher and higher to have a continuing influence in determining behavior. These same dangers can occur when adults overpraise and are overly lavish in their enthusiasm.

There is a real place for sensible praise for a job well done. There is no harm and occasionally some good in the rare use of an added extra tangible bonus when it seems to be called for to spur on some highly specific kind of behavior. But the first kind of reward—the child's inner satisfaction with his own growth and own achievement—is the safest reward. It is the reward most apt to insure that a child will perform to his maximum capacity. JAMES L. HYMES, JR.

See also ALLOWANCE; APPROVAL

RHEUMATIC FEVER

Parents are often frightened by the mention of rheumatic fever, a disease that involves inflammation of the heart's valves and the heart muscle. Although the disease is certainly a serious one, parents should remember that cases of rheumatic fever vary tremendously in severity, and that some are so mild that the heart and its valves survive an attack without any demonstrable change.

Rheumatic fever usually follows a streptococcal sore throat. Many different kinds of streptococci are found in the throat, but a specific germ, the *beta* hemolytic streptococcus, is the cause of rheumatic fever. While accurate statistics are not available, it is estimated that about one "strep throat" in a hundred results in an attack of rheumatic fever.

Shortly after the throat infection has cleared up—or sometimes as long as two weeks later—the child may have vague pains in the muscles, often erroneously called "growing pains." The pains may become more intense, and the joints painful and swollen. At the same time, inflammation involves the heart's valves and the heart muscle. The inflamed valves become permanently wrinkled and puckered. Inflammation of the heart muscle, or myocarditis, eventually results in replacement of a few muscle cells by fibrous, or scar, tissue. It is obvious the muscle cells that have become scarred lose some of their power to contract.

Rheumatic fever differs from infectious diseases such as measles or chicken pox, which produce immunity in the body and do not recur. The child who has had an attack of rheumatic fever is actually more susceptible to recurring attacks, each of which causes further damage to the heart valves. Eventually, so much scarring of the valves occurs that operative correction becomes necessary. All valves in the heart may be affected, but the mitral valve between the left auricle and the left ventricle is the one that is usually most seriously deformed. This valve may become so puckered and shrunken that blood can scarcely be forced through it—a condition known as mitral stenosis. Fortunately, operative correction of mitral stenosis has proved very successful during the past 15 years. Recurrent attacks are avoided by prevention of streptococcal sore throats.

Every child who has had an attack of rheumatic fever should receive daily a dose of penicillin, or sulfadiazine, or have an injection in the buttocks of a long-acting drug once a month. Protective treatment has to be kept up for at least five years—often until the patient is about 21 or even older.

But the best way to fight rheumatic fever is to prevent it. Every child who has a sore throat should have a throat culture. If streptococci are found, antibiotics (penicillin and other similar drugs) should be given immediately before the germs have a chance to attack the joints and the heart.

Research workers in many institutions are seeking a vaccine that will prevent rheumatic fever. It is not unlikely that such a vaccine will soon be available. WILLIS J. POTTS

See also COMMUNITY RESOURCES; HANDICAPPED CHILD; HOSPITALIZATION; SICK CHILD

RH FACTOR

The Rh factor is a chemical substance that most people have in their blood. It gets its name from rhesus monkeys, in whose red cells it was first discovered. If the factor is present, blood is Rh-positive; if absent, Rh-negative. In simple terms, Rh-positive blood possesses a substance that Rh-negative blood does not. Both types are equally normal and healthy, but the two types do not always intermix safely in transfusions. Danger of complication has been largely eliminated, however, by tests that insure that the patient gets the proper Rh blood.

The Rh factor is inherited. The child of an Rh-negative mother and an Rh-positive father may be Rh-positive. Under certain conditions of mother-baby blood interaction, the unborn baby's Rh-positive blood may cause the mother's Rh-negative blood to produce antibodies against the Rh factor. These antibodies may then return to the baby's circulation to clash with his blood cells, make them clump together and clog small vessels, and exert other destructive actions. Depending upon the severity of reactions, the infant—commonly called an "Rh baby"—may die before birth or be born with very mild or very severe jaundice and anemia. The opposite condition, that is, an Rh-positive mother and an Rh-negative baby, rarely causes trouble. Thus, blood typing of parents can be very important because it gives warning of possible Rh difficulties, even before the baby is conceived.

An Rh-negative woman with an Rh-positive husband can often have two and frequently three healthy babies because antibody production may be so slow that these first babies escape its effects. But, if an Rh-negative woman has been transfused with Rh-positive blood prior to pregnancy, even years before in girlhood, her blood already contains antibodies that may react dangerously with her Rh-positive baby's blood. If such a sensitized woman is given transfusions of Rh-positive blood, her existing antibodies may cause hazardous clumping reactions with the donor's blood. A general rule is that a woman who is Rh-negative should not be transfused with her husband's Rh-positive blood.

With correct and immediate treatment, a seriously affected "Rh baby" can usually make a good recovery and be normal. Doctors can detect Rh incompatibilities by simple blood tests that measure the levels of threatening antibodies. If levels rise threateningly, the doctor may induce early labor and be prepared to give the baby transfusions if necessary.

Sometimes it is imperative that transfusions (occasionally, total transfusion—complete replacement of the baby's blood) be given immediately after birth. Transfused blood must be Rh-negative since Rh-positive blood would be destroyed. Equipment, typed blood, and skilled hands must be ready.

None of these things may be useful or available unless the mother has consulted a competent physician early in her pregnancy. The best protection against the heartbreak of an "Rh baby" is competent prenatal care and confidence in the physician. DONALD G. COOLEY

See also BLOOD TYPE; PRENATAL CARE

RIBOFLAVIN *See* VITAMINS

RICKETS

Rickets is a disease that occurs as the result of insufficient vitamin D. The bones of a child with rickets do not calcify, or harden, adequately and bony deformities may result. Severe rickets causes deformed ribs and pelvic bones and bowed legs. Because premature or small babies and children undergoing rapid growth are most susceptible, preventing rickets during infancy and early childhood is an important concern.

Although vitamin D enriched milks and foods are available and although enough exposure to the ultraviolet rays of the sun can prevent rickets, neither of these sources should be relied on completely. Daily vitamin D should be given to all babies and young children. RUTH S. KEMPE

See also NUTRITION; SUN BATH

RINGWORM

When fungus, similar to molds, infects the skin and sets up a chronic inflammation, the resulting condition is called ringworm. Ringworm usually appears on the scalp but can occur on the skin of other areas. When a ringworm infection occurs on the feet, it may be called athlete's foot. The infection usually comes from contact with another infected child. When a number of children are living together, the infection may spread to many of them. Ringworm causes considerable itching and, hence, considerable scratching. If the condition is not controlled and if the scratching continues, the skin may become infected with bacteria, and the child may become quite ill. Scarring may result as the spots heal. Hair in the affected area may fall out so that the rest of the hair appears to be growing in patches.

Treatment should be directed by a physician. Some antibiotic drugs do not have an effect on the ringworm fungus, but they may be quite helpful in clearing up the bacterial infection. New antibiotic drugs have become available recently which promise to be much more effective. X-ray treatment for ringworm should be avoided.

A child with ringworm should be cautioned about scratching the infected skin area and about the possibility of spreading the condition, either to other parts of his own skin or to other children. JULIUS B. RICHMOND

See also RASH

RITUALS

Sometimes an anxious child tries to protect himself from imagined danger by doing certain things in a specific way. The regularity and preciseness make him feel safe.

A good example is the bedtime ritual, when a child may arrange his shoes and stockings in a definite, identical manner every night or place toys in certain places, or prescribe the way his parents should act—so many

"Step on a crack, break your grandmother's back."

bedtime stories or good-night kisses or glasses of water.

These little rituals, in themselves harmless, are usually a passing phase and should not be condemned or punished. Probably, good-humored acceptance is your best policy. If parents take this kind of behavior too seriously, their child may feel they, too, are frightened and dependent on these outward signs of safety. But parents should make it clear that nobody *has* to do those things.

Actually, rituals are a throwback to primitive ways of getting in good with the gods. They survive in superstitions such as, "Step on a crack, break your grandmother's back," or "Load of hay, load of hay, make a wish but turn away," which children still practice without belief in their magic. Similarly, both children and adults may "knock on wood" or pick up a ladybug or a bent pin for good luck without belief in that magic either.

Rituals are likely to accompany a child's dawning conscience and his efforts to be good. They develop usually when he is about 3 years old, and may persist long after that, even to school age. If they do continue to the extent that they become compulsions and the child seems more and more obsessed by them, it is wise to consult an expert. Slavish devotion to highly developed rituals is a handicap to learning. The child who must do things always in a certain way has lost his freedom of choice in action and thought. His way may possibly be efficient and useful, but the very fact that he is inwardly compelled restricts his development and his personality. HELEN ROSS

See also ANXIETY

RIVALRY *See* JEALOUSY AND RIVALRY

ROCKING SELF

Many babies seem to enjoy rocking themselves. Some do it by tucking their knees up under them as if they were about to crawl, but then instead of crawling they stay in the same position and rock back and forth. Others, when held in a sitting position, either in someone's lap or in one of the infant seats offering loose body support, move torso and head back and forth as though in a rocking chair. It is natural for parents to be disturbed and bewildered by this activity, which, to them, is senseless. Rhythmic movements, however, like head-banging, are not uncommon in young children. Chances are the head-rolling, jouncing, or swaying will appear briefly in the developmental stage and eventually disappear.

Rocking usually starts, if it is going to start, sometime during the latter half of a child's first year. The habit may appear briefly and never recur, or it may wane only to reappear with greater intensity during the second year. It also tends to occur when the baby's sensory system is "tuned down"—that is, immediately preceding or following sleep or even during sleep. Also it seems more apt to occur when the infant is in his crib.

A baby who gets up on all fours and rocks in his crib is likely to bump into something—usually the head of the crib. Then he not only seems to enjoy the rocking, but the bumping, too. It is not uncommon to find a baby who sucks his thumb, rocks, and bumps his head against the crib all at the same time. And the crib that once seemed stationary may yield to the pressure and begin to "dance" about the room. Some infants actually rock so hard against the crib that they develop bumps on their heads. Thus it is easy to see why parents can be both annoyed and frightened when a baby rocks and bumps.

Occasionally, the baby ceases the rocking just as he began it—for no apparent reason at all. Occasionally, also, parents may help to stop the habit. If the baby is one who rocks himself as he goes to sleep, the mother may gently straighten him out and pull him down from the top of the bed, or she may try to pat him to sleep. In some cases, turning the baby over on his back and gently holding him in that position may help. If such mild techniques do not work, the best solution is to make rocking less fun for the infant and, at the same time, make sure that less actual harm could result. Pad the head of the crib with foam rubber or with a sofa cushion that is carefully anchored so it cannot fall on the baby and threaten his air supply. Such padding takes away from the baby both the sound and the touch that he seems to enjoy in the rocking motion. Or perhaps the mother might allow the baby to fall asleep in her lap a few nights or she might try sleep garments that give him a little less freedom of movement. Too much restraint, however, is not recommended.

BETTYE M. CALDWELL

See also HEAD-BANGING AND ROLLING

ROOMING-IN

Rooming-in is a plan of hospital care for newborn babies and their mothers in which the baby spends at least part of the day in his crib by his mother's bedside. The main purpose of the plan is to allow mother and infant to feel comfortable with each other and to help both mother and father develop confidence in the care of their baby before taking him home.

An ideal rooming-in plan offers a homelike atmosphere where mother and baby may receive the personal attention they need from a nurse who is always on hand to take care of them as long as they are together. Such a plan allows greater flexibility than the usual hospital system permits and helps the mother develop confidence in herself for her new parental responsibility. The supportive help offered by a rooming-in nurse may be particularly helpful to a mother who wishes to breast-feed her infant.

In one sense, rooming-in is an old plan of care for infants because when babies were born at home, they were placed in cribs where they could be seen and tended by their mothers. It has now been demonstrated that some of the advantages of home maternity care can be safely provided in the modern hospital setting.

No special facilities are necessary as long as there is room for the baby's crib by the mother's bed and space for a nurse's station adjacent to the rooming-in unit. Different hospitals have different rooming-in plans according to the size and arrangement of rooms, the number of nurses available, and the ideas of doctors and nurses in charge of the maternity service. In some hospitals, mothers and infants are roomed together soon after birth, in some not until 12 or 24 hours afterwards, or later if the mother does not feel well.

Very few hospitals have rooming-in service available for all mothers. Usually only part of the maternity floor is reserved for mothers who want rooming-in, and usually the babies are taken care of in a nursery at night.

A mother, insecure about taking care of her first-born, has much to gain from rooming-in. Rooming-in establishes a natural, friendly, cozy situation where the mother picks up and fondles her baby as she wants to and feeds him when he needs feeding. The mother with her baby near her has an opportunity to become used to this small new human being. She can begin to sense what his cries mean, can observe how he looks when he sleeps and breathes and wiggles normally. With a hospital nurse to demonstrate child care, to answer questions, and to offer suggestions, the mother can recover from her fears of the child's fragility and can discover that she herself is not as incompetent as she thought she was. She can feel free to ask for advice and help on any matter from doctors and nurses. She can leave the hospital assured that she knows how to hold her baby, feed him, change him, generally make him comfortable.

Even the old hand, the mother who has previously had children, generally derives much benefit from a rooming-in plan. Her days in the hospital are her one chance to concentrate solely on the new baby without the distraction of having to give time and attention to the other children.

Rooming-in is also an advantage to the father. He, too, can hold the baby when he visits, can begin to know him as an individual and not as some abstract joy and remote responsibility.

There are advantages for the baby, too. He is guaranteed more experienced care when he goes home than he would have had otherwise; he will already be familiar with the feel of his mother's arms; he will have been exposed to less danger of infection in the hospital by not being near so many other babies; he will have been fed and changed on a schedule adapted to his own needs. Even with a rooming-in plan, the general hospital timetable is, of course, followed for mealtime, nap time, and visiting hours, but there is a comfortable degree of latitude. Babies who are with their mothers and are fed soon after they indicate hunger, cry relatively little. For this reason, and because nothing has to be done at any exact time, the baby benefits from the peaceful atmosphere of the rooming-in unit.

Some mothers do not ask to use a rooming-in plan for fear they will not get enough rest. The fear is based, usually, on a misunderstanding of the type of care that will be offered, a belief that they will be left alone to take care of the baby without help from nurses. The belief is unfounded, for nursing and medical supervision are very important parts of the rooming-in plan.

Many mothers who have had babies in the two types of hospitals—one where only nursery care is provided for the infant and the other where rooming-in care is provided—have said that they felt more rested and contented with the baby beside them than in a room where the baby was brought in only at feeding time. In many hospitals, mothers can hear the babies crying in the nursery; each mother is sure that it is her baby crying, that he is not getting proper attention, and she worries. With her own baby beside her, a mother feels contented and assured, not disturbed by the crying of other babies.

If you are to have a baby and think you want rooming-in, the best thing to do is to talk it over with your doctor. Find out whether the hospital or hospitals he is associated with provide rooming-in care and what his attitude is toward it. Then abide by whatever he suggests. If you discover that your community does not yet offer rooming-in, and you feel that it should, you and your friends with similar ideas may perhaps be able to interest hospital boards or administrators in such a plan before the arrival of your next baby. EDITH B. JACKSON

ROSEOLA INFANTUM

Some people call this disease baby measles, but really it is not related to measles at all. Roseola infantum is a virus disease that usually occurs between the age of 6 months and about 2 years. It is often mild enough to be nearly missed as an illness. The characteristic story is fever for three to four days, followed by a sudden drop in the temperature to normal or below. At that time, the child feels quite well and a rash appears for a few hours. The rash shows up as small, light-red, raised spots, mostly on the chest and face.

Most of the difficulty with roseola infantum comes in diagnosing the disease and in dealing with the effects of the fever. Because the baby may feel quite irritable with the high fever or may in rare cases have a convulsion caused by fever, it is sometimes difficult to be sure at first that he does not have some other more serious illness. There is no specific treatment for the disease itself except fluids and aspirin if the fever is very high. So that another more serious illness is not missed, the diagnosis should be made by the baby's doctor, who will also recommend appropriate treatment. RUTH S. KEMPE

See also TEMPERATURE; VIRUS

RUBBER PANTS *See* WATERPROOF PANTS

RUDENESS

A child who is rude is usually making a bid for attention. The particular rudeness may be an impertinent remark to a parent, such as "You talk like a dope!"

A parent has several possible responses to such behavior. He may agree, he may demand an apology from the child, or he may punish him. Actually, if the child is usually well behaved, the best thing may be to ignore the remark, for being rude is not so much the words a child uses as the feeling behind the words.

If a child really does need more attention than he has been receiving, or if he needs only to try out the sounds of defiance, or if he feels he has a just cause, he may burst out with an untypical rude comment.

Discipline, if needed, should vary according to the age of the child and his knowledge of acceptable and unacceptable behavior.

Usually, if the punishment is fair, a little will go a long way—denial of some privilege or expected treat can bring about improvement in behavior.

A child will not develop much idea of social courtesy or self-control unless limits are set as to what he can or cannot do. Consistency is the keynote when disciplining a child for displays of rude behavior.

See also DISCIPLINE; MANNERS

RULES AND REGULATIONS

The rules and regulations that govern the operation of a family, of a classroom, or even of some specific event such as a trip ought to be clear-cut and definite so that a youngster knows what is allowed and what is prohibited. Children of all ages find it hard to function at their best in an atmosphere of great uncertainty and indefiniteness. Children develop their powers by testing the limits of a situation. If they find that there are no limits, or that they can wangle exceptions by playing one adult against another, or bring about a change in the rules and regulations simply by putting up a little fuss, they become baffled and unsure. Youngsters may not like the limits that are set, but if those limits are held firm, children take some firmness into themselves.

Of course, it is not possible to have rules and regulations that govern every possible situation. The events of family life, and of all human relationships, are too unpredictable. Nor is it desirable to have so many rules and regulations that the law does all a child's thinking for him, leaving little to his own judgment. A few basic, sensible rules and regulations make it more nearly possible for people to enjoy living together. Too many rules and regulations, an overwhelming emphasis on what can't be done and what mustn't happen, take all the fun out of living.

While rules and regulations should hold firm as long as they apply, they should also change from time to time. As youngsters grow, their areas of freedom should expand. Children should have some voice in the establishment and in the continuous change of the limits from their very early years on. Initially their "voice" will have to be an unspoken one. Parents must judge from children's behavior whether a particular rule is a good one. In general, any rule that is a constant source of friction and conflict probably needs re-examination. As children get older, beginning perhaps around 5 or 6 or 7, it becomes increasingly possible for them to enter into discussions of rules and regulations and take part in their modification. Children will always obey better those laws that they have had a part in establishing. JAMES L. HYMES, JR.

See also DISCIPLINE; FAMILY DISCUSSIONS; INDEPENDENCE; PERMISSIVENESS

RUNNING AWAY

A child carrying a suitcase repeatedly passed the same street corner. This activity aroused the interest of a friendly policeman, who asked, "Where are you going, Sonny?" The youngster replied, "I'm running away, but I'm not allowed to cross the street."

Many escapes from real or fancied difficulties at home are just about as serious as that. The child is making a gesture of defiance and he wants as much attention as possible. There is often a good relationship between child and parent when such antagonistic ideas can be freely expressed. It's wise to take threats or even the packing of an overnight bag with calm. "If something is wrong, let's talk about it," is a possible approach to a discussion in which it can be made clear that running away does not solve problems. It is *not* wise to offer to help your child pack, as some parents have done. This implies an acceptance of the child's leaving, which is more than he wants. He may be operating on a fantasy level, but it does not help him if you join him.

Older children, in trouble in school or unhappy at home, may make sincere attempts to run away and even succeed for a time. This behavior is a serious matter and should be treated as such. It may be that the child wants to punish his parents in a dramatic way. But it may also be that he is quite earnestly running away from something that is, to him, intolerable. Perhaps he exaggerates the unfairness of his parents or teachers and his own misery, but he most certainly is not a happy child. Severe punishment for such behavior will defeat its own purpose by giving him added reasons for wanting to escape from a situation where he feels unwanted and misunderstood. Perhaps his parents have been too strict, perhaps they have expected achievement of which he is not capable. In any case, both the child who runs away with serious intent and his family need the experienced advice of a guidance counselor or psychotherapist. It is unlikely that the average parent can figure out the problem alone, and the child needs to be helped to discover ways of moving from immature, unsuccessful solutions to more effective ones. IRMA S. BLACK AND JOAN W. BLOS

See also CHILD GUIDANCE CLINIC; TRUANCY

RUPTURE *See* HERNIA

SAFETY *See* ACCIDENT PREVENTION

SAINT VITUS'S DANCE (CHOREA)

Chorea is commonly called St. Vitus's dance. The child with chorea has uncontrollable, jerky body movements. He may appear to be making faces. Muscular movements may be mild and few, or severe and many. When chorea is severe, the muscular jerking may cause the child to fall out of bed. Sometimes it is advisable to hospitalize the child to insure proper protection and care. Occasionally, chorea may be confused with severe tics, and the doctor might need to observe the child for some time to be sure just what his true condition is.

Chorea has been thought to be one form of rheumatic fever. Since the heart may be affected in rheumatic fever, a child with chorea should be examined carefully for this possibility. In many instances, however, no evidence of rheumatic fever is found and the real cause of chorea remains obscure.

There is no specific treatment for chorea, although many medicines have been tried. Of course, if rheumatic fever is diagnosed, the child should be treated for that condition. Generally, a child with chorea is kept in a quiet place, since excitement tends to aggravate the jerky movements. Sedatives may be helpful in keeping him quiet. The attack usually lasts about six weeks and gradually subsides, leaving no apparent damage to the nervous system. JULIUS B. RICHMOND

See also RHEUMATIC FEVER; TIC

SANITARY NAPKINS *See* MENSTRUATION

SANTA CLAUS

Today much is said and written about various customs surrounding Christmas. Santa Claus especially commands the attention of children, and many parents are at a loss as to how they can properly explain this mystic being to their little ones when they begin to question his existence.

There comes a time in the life of almost every child when he discovers father dressed as Santa or questions how this person in the toy department can be Santa when he just passed another Santa standing at the entrance, ringing a bell and collecting coins in a kettle.

If the child is disillusioned, he will possibly question more important truths later on. So it is wise to have an intelligent answer and explanation ready when the occasion requires it.

The explanation set down here has appealed to many parents and seems to satisfy the questionings of their children.

Actually, Santa Claus once lived. Historically, he was St. Nicholas, Bishop of Myra, who died in A.D. 343. Our Santa Claus is but an American distortion of the old Dutch name, Sant Nikolaas, which meant St. Nicholas. If you say "St. Nicholas" very fast, you'll see how the name "Santa Claus" came about. This goodly man was and is the patron saint of children. He was born in Patara, not far from the Port of Myra on the shore of the Mediterranean Sea, directly north of Syria and the Holy Land. Many lovely tales are told of this saintly bishop, and from them have evolved the customs of hanging up the Christmas stocking, the giving of gifts at this season, and other joyous practices. His red bishop's robe and his white beard naturally are copied by those who imitate him at Christmastime. St. Nicholas is remembered by Christians in the church calendar on December 6.

Now with this historical background, what must we tell children about the present-day Santa Claus when they see numerous men dressed as Santa and inquire as to which is which? Let us be truthful and say that these men are dressed to represent Santa, as an actor in a play may represent another person. Just as a young Christian girl may act the part of the Virgin Mary in the Christmas play, or a doll may be used to represent the Christ Child in a Nativity story, so do many fathers and others dress in the traditional garb of Santa to represent him at this joyous season.

We can also tell them that the good St. Nicholas, when he lived, was most kind and generous to children; that he distributed to them candy and toys and other things that delighted the hearts of the little ones. His spirit of generosity and love toward others has come down to us as a great example of devotion to Christ, and people emulate his deeds when they observe Christmas.

The child can be taught these truths, and as he matures there is nothing to undo, no shock to overcome, no misrepresentation to clear up. He will know from the very beginning that Santa (St. Nicholas) actually lived on earth and helped teach God's law to be kind and good and loving. And we are thankful for all he did to make us more aware of our duty to our fellow men. Many countries follow the tradition of Saint Nicholas and Santa Claus. You can find illustrations and descriptions of them in Volume 5, HOLIDAYS AND CUSTOMS, pages 12–13. A. ELLISTON COLE

See also MORAL AND SPIRITUAL DEVELOPMENT

Related article in WORLD BOOK: "Christmas"

SAVINGS *See* ALLOWANCE

SCALD

A scald is a burn by hot liquid or, occasionally, by escaping steam. Scalds have all the characteristics of burns and should be treated the same way. Scalds are typically household injuries. They often happen to children who upset or fall into containers of boiling liquid being used for cooking, cleaning, washing, or even bathing.

Pan handles should not project over the edge of the stove, but the best protection against scalds is to keep small children out of the kitchen or the laundry area by a gate across the door. The safest way to draw a hot bath is to draw the cold water first and then add the hot water until the temperature is right. W. W. BAUER

See also BURN

SCALES *See* LAYETTE AND BABY EQUIPMENT

SCARLET FEVER

In spite of the "wonder drugs" that now make cases of scarlet fever less severe and of shorter duration, scarlet fever is still not a disease to be thought of lightly. There is no effective preventive measure and there are no successful vaccines. The Dick test may be used to determine whether or not a child is immune to scarlet fever. Contact with a known case or carrier should be avoided by the child who is not immune. Contact with linens or objects used by a person with scarlet fever should be avoided, too.

Symptoms of scarlet fever come on suddenly in the form of fever, chills, sore throat, and headache. The first symptom is sometimes sudden vomiting. The characteristic rash appears a day or two later. It is deep red, with tiny raised spots close to each other. The tongue becomes red and rough-looking. After the rash fades, the skin, even of palm and soles, usually peels or flakes off.

A doctor should advise not only the care of the patient, but also the form of isolation to protect other people. MARIE A. HINRICHS

See also COMMON COMMUNICABLE DISEASES; SICK CHILD

SCHEDULE, FEEDING *See* FEEDING SCHEDULE

SCHOOL *See* CURRICULUM; KINDERGARTEN; NURSERY SCHOOL; READINESS FOR SCHOOL; SCHOOL-AGE CHILD

SCHOOL-AGE CHILD

It is simple, when looking at one's 10-year-old, to see how much he has changed since he was 6. It is not so easy, looking at him when he is 6, to realize how much he will have changed by the time he is 10. But it is important that the parents of a child entering school be able to look ahead, that they be aware of the many changes that will occur in their child during the early school years.

At 6 a child is not only immature physically, mentally, emotionally, and socially, he is also at a starting point in developing the many skills, attitudes, and ideas he will need in school. The next few years will reveal a close interrelation between his physical, mental, emotional, and social maturing and his advance in skills, attitudes, and ideas.

Enormously energetic, the school-age child thrives on a variety of physical activity.

Six to Ten, Physically

The physical immaturity of children just entering school is such that they lack certain physical readiness for the school tasks ahead of them. For instance, hand and eye coordination is not nearly so good as it will become. (Nor will the large muscles be fit for all they will be able to do later on.) But the child from 6 to 10 usually will be enormously energetic and will take on a variety of physical activities that use and strengthen his muscles and that develop his muscular skills. This activity comes naturally to both boys and girls of the 6 to 10 group. If girls choose different ways of working off their energy than boys do, it is more because of social custom and what is expected of them by parents and teachers than because they have different built-in preferences.

The 6- to 10-year-old, on the whole, tends to be healthy and robust although he quite likely will have some of the childhood diseases. He will be hungry for meals and in between meals. He will lose his baby teeth and gain some of his permanent teeth. He will not have great dramatic spurts in height and weight but will generally grow rather steadily. Of course, children this age will vary greatly in height and weight and physical speed and dexterity. Parents who realize how great the variance in maturity can be and allow for it can more happily accept a child who is shorter or taller or heavier or lighter or clumsier than his fellows, and can help him find the physical activity and physical achievement so necessary to his well-being.

The intensely active 6- to 10-year-old wears himself out, and he needs physical rebuilding—a great deal of sleep, times of quiet play and work, and plenty of nourishing food. He won't be able to meet these needs himself—his parents will have to guide and assist him.

Six to Ten, Mentally

The child from 6 to 10 who is in sound physical and mental health wants to learn and achieve. Much learning and achieving are asked of him, both in and out of school. When he enters school, he undertakes to meet one of the biggest challenges of the developmental periods, the mastering of the symbolic aspects of his culture—to read, to write, and to work with numbers. Mental growth is not nearly so rapid as it was earlier in his life and it will not go along in even, gradual steps. All children will not undertake their new learning tasks with the same ease, even though they may be the same age, and they will show varying readiness in all the school skills. Hence, it is most unfortunate for the mental development of a child if he is compared with other children his age. His developmental age, not his chronological age, should be the important factor in planning and aiding his mental development.

A parent who wants to assist his child's mental development is most likely to be successful if he is acquainted with the fundamental principles of development. Growth unfolds in an orderly, predictable sequence through which all children seem to proceed. The rate of development varies from child to child, however. The best clue to his readiness will be found by close observation of him and by following his natural and spontaneous interests. Some children will read faster, earlier, and with greater comprehension; others will have early success with numbers. Every child has periods of rapid mental growth and intervening periods of steady, slower growth. A child himself may be the one who knows best what he is able to accomplish at certain periods in his development. Pushing by an adult can bring just the opposite of the desired effect, can set up opposition and resistance, which may in turn greatly lessen a child's intellectual curiosity. On the other hand, encouragement without pushing is highly desirable. Encouragement implies that the parent accepts the child as he is and has faith in him. Encouragement also involves providing a wide variety of educational experiences that fit in with his abilities and give him a chance to be successful.

The mental development that takes place in the 6-to-10 period is extremely significant. It lays the foundation for success in future work, both in school and in life in general. Although parents cannot alter their child's heredity, and heredity certainly appears to play some part in determining a child's general level of mental development, they can influence his environment and, hence, influence the growth of his natural mental powers and capacities. The family's attitude toward books, and educational experiences and the family's problem-solving approach are all witnessed by the child. Cultural and creative activities in the home encourage a child to develop such interests. Opportunities to communicate through letters and a family newspaper provide real reasons to develop skill in communication. Family meetings that provide opportunities to discuss problems and resolve issues are also part of an atmosphere that can stimulate mental growth.

Six to Ten, Emotionally

One of the standards by which to measure emotional growth is how much a person is directed by his own reasons and how much he is still directed by the reasons others keep giving him. The 6-to-10 youngster is on his way toward being a self-directed person. At

The healthy child from 6 to 10 who is in sound physical and mental health wants to learn and achieve. Much learning and achieving are asked of him, both in and out of school.

Fear, jealousy, and anxiety are all important emotions of the school-age child.

times he would like to be one. At other times he needs all the backing and direction he can find. His moments of being self-directed become more frequent as he goes along. He wants to be assured of his parents' continuing interest and attention, but he also likes to express and act upon his own preferences and tastes concerning people and activities and objects.

Thus the 6-to-10 youngster enters this period in his life with many hesitations and with uncertain feelings. Many children show a certain amount of regression—they want to master the skills of school, but they are also hesitant at times to give up certain of the advantages of babyhood and immaturity. Individual differences in emotional behavior are great. But the child himself indicates the way in which he is trying to manage his world and his problems. If, for instance, he is making unhealthy use of the defense mechanisms —forever giving logical-sounding reasons for his acts rather than real reasons or if he tends usually to blame another for what happens to him—instead of having a problem-solving approach, he indicates some signs of emotional difficulties. A parent may not always know what the exact difficulty is, but he can remind himself again that a child's fundamental emotional needs are love, security, belonging, recognition, and independence. And after he has reminded himself, an attempt to supply the child with a proper balance of what he needs will assist all the developmental processes.

A child's emotions are different in a sense from those of an adult, for the child is frequently very open in expressing his emotions; he is intense and may have many more emotional displays than an adult would.

Parents are presented a variety of emotional problems to deal with. Fear, anger, jealousy, and anxiety are all important emotions of the school-age child. His emotional growth can be aided by parents who understand why he is performing as he is and how best to cope with his behavior. This means having a policy, dealing with the child consistently, letting him know that limits exist, letting him experience a balance between parental firmness and parental kindness. It also means letting the child experience certain logical and natural consequences of his misbehavior, letting him feel his parents' attitude of encouragement, letting him become part of an atmosphere of mutual respect. No parents who are less than superhuman can do all these things all the time, but those who can develop a definite philosophy about bringing up children, who can replace words with actions and policies, and who can be aware of a child's purposes, goals, and needs will have gone a long way toward nourishing their child's emotional growth.

Six to Ten, Socially

A child of preschool age will often seem to be playing with other children when what he truly is doing is playing where they are and with the same collection of toys while he simultaneously pursues his own thoughts and plans. A child of school age begins to be ready to be more fundamentally a part of a group. The group he becomes a part of will usually be a small one, consisting of one or two other children at a time, even though he may be a member of a large school class. Usually, too, he will not notice or care particularly whether he is playing with children of his own sex or of the opposite sex. As he advances through school he will want to, and be able to, play or work with more children at a time, and he will be apt to seek out playmates of his own sex.

The change to a larger group indicates his ability to cooperate, his understanding of teamwork. As he grows in understanding of teamwork, he somehow manages to understand competition, too. When left to choose what he would like to do, he very frequently finds an occupation that involves working with and being pitted against; that is, he will play on a team and he will try to win.

It is increasingly important to the 6-to-10 child to feel that he is a part of his own age group. He wants very much to have friends. He wants to choose his own friends and to choose them for his own reasons. As he becomes more and more involved with playmates of his age, the group has more and more influence on him. Children his own age teach him their standards of fairness, of sharing, of taking turns; they teach him their beliefs about right and wrong, what they think is acceptable and unacceptable. His parents' standards still carry enormous weight, but the standards are questioned, are held up to be examined in the light of the standards of his schoolmates.

So it is, too, with what goes on in the homes of his friends. He notices the ways in which his friends live and how those ways differ from his own. He questions why they do as they do, and what may be better about their way than his way. He becomes less convinced that his parents are always right.

The need to belong to a group different and separate from his family group often finds a satisfactory outlet in organizations such as Cub Scouts, Brownie Scouts, or the junior YMCA and YWCA. One of the many advantages of this type of group is that a child can feel himself involved in child-selected activities while he also has the assurance and protection of adult supervision. Many children, during the early years of school, also like to form their own private clubs, finding two angles of club activity equally fascinating—inclusion of themselves and exclusion of some other child.

It becomes increasingly important for the 6-to-10 child to feel a part of his own age group.

A child who enters first grade without previous school experience is presented with a new social environment and a series of social challenges unlike any he has had before. At home he was usually in an atmosphere in which it was pretty well taken for granted that he belonged and was accepted. This gave him a certain security. Certainly at home he has had to adapt to parents and to brothers and sisters, and he has had challenge and interaction by being in contact with the other children in his family. But the home situation is unlike the challenge and interaction provided by contact with 25 or 30 classmates his age.

School also provides a social challenge for a child, for he must not only work with the other children, but he must also learn to know the teacher and her ways and try to adapt and adjust to her. This is not easy. A child who has had frequent contacts with children his own age before entering school has an advantage when it comes to his social adjustment at school. He will also be more ready for the adjustment if he has experienced some situation, such as a Sunday school or nursery school, where he was one of many children under adult supervision.

Every child needs to learn to live with himself and society. In the elementary school years he comes to grips with certain work and social tasks. The home can help most by the type of support it provides, for the family atmosphere gives a child his first experiences in social living and his most indelible impressions of what social living involves. It is from these experiences and impressions that his style and pattern of life emerge. Parents, naturally, play an important role in their child's evaluation of self and society—what is called the life style. In the child's social adaptation, as in all other phases of his development, the parents' acceptance of the child can make him feel that he is adequate and that he has achieved. DON DINKMEYER

See also ADJUSTMENT; BOOKS FOR PARENTS; GROWTH; HOME-SCHOOL RELATIONS; IMITATION; MENTAL DEVELOPMENT; READINESS FOR SCHOOL; VOCABULARY DEVELOPMENT

Related article in WORLD BOOK: "School"

SCHOOL FAILURE

"I flunked."

This sad sentence has been spoken too many times. It has caused too many tears and too much self-recrimination, too much resentment, too much surrender. These evils have affected both the failed child and his parents.

Failure—its causes, its results, and what adults can do to prevent it—needs to be examined. School is usually a child's first out-in-the-world testing ground. His success in school is apt to feed his personality; his failure can very well wither it.

What Causes Failure

Almost all children have some tensions and fears when they know they are about to be examined or given tests. Some can overcome the nervousness, rise to the occasion, and do their best. With many others, not only on tests but also in daily classroom work, fear of failure causes failure. Some children worry enough so that they do not do quite their best; others, particularly those with oversensitive feelings, are so frightened at the thought of failure that they "freeze" and come out far below their best.

Fear is, of course, only one of many reasons for poor schoolwork. A few children fail because they do not try hard enough; perhaps they are not encouraged by parents or teachers to put forth their best efforts, perhaps they are bored with work that is too easy for them, or perhaps they have a vague, uneasy feeling that the work is too hard and so give up before they start.

On the other hand, some children may try very hard, may have ability, and may still fail to meet the requirements of their grade. These children may be handicapped by poor day-to-day study habits or they may never have been taught how to prepare for a test. Some children, although they are making an honest, worthy effort, actually are working at cross-purposes because they were absent or not paying attention when an assignment was explained. They think they understand what has been assigned them to do, but they really do not understand.

Some children fail to do their required schoolwork because of poor health. Through frequent absences they miss many explanations of new ideas and new processes—and they flounder. Illness has probably lowered their vitality, too, making it harder for them to keep up with healthy, vigorous children.

The child is not always the source of his own failure. The home that permits a child to put schoolwork aside for less important activities is not being fair to that child and contributes directly to his chance of failure. A parent who has no interest in his child's school tasks may create a like disinterest on the part of the child. And, if unsupervised television viewing takes precedence over lessons, success in school will be more difficult. Well-selected TV programs, however, often can enrich and contribute to learning.

Teachers can contribute to failure, too. Those teachers who set impossible tasks for children, those who show a lack of interest in helping a child when he is having difficulty, or those who don't encourage him when he is doing his best will increase the likelihood of work that is under par.

Some teachers expect all children to measure up to the same standards; they assign to the less able child work that is too difficult for him and do not give the brilliant child sufficient challenge. Under these circumstances it is certain that some children will fail.

A good many failures in school arise out of the inevitable human problem of individual differences—differences in capacity, in maturity, in temperament. Some children unquestionably do not have the mental ability to learn what other children learn—they will neither keep up nor catch up. Other children will fail because they are asked to learn something they are not yet mature enough to understand. Almost any classroom will contain a wide range of mental ability, from the very dull to the very bright. Yet some schools by tradition have a standard for each grade. While many children will meet such standards, some will not and will have to repeat. Teacher, principal, and parent will possibly all have part in deciding on the "repeats." They will doubtless soften the blow as much as they can for the child who will not be allowed to pass.

Results of Failure

By whatever name you call it, failure means defeat to a child. If he knows that he is not doing well during the school year or is left behind at the end of it, he thinks of himself as a failure, and something unfortunate happens to his outlook on school and learning. From then on, it will be harder than ever for him to do his best, not to be afraid, to dare to think, to enjoy his work.

For the child who knows he has failed, there is often a damaging loss of self-respect. Some degree of success is a necessary ingredient of self-respect, and nobody should be asked to go through life feeling that he is incapable of doing much of anything well.

A further result of failure in school is this: Parents sometimes lose their respect for a child or their faith in his ability to succeed in any activity or subject. And so, a vicious circle is formed in which the child thinks less well of himself and consequently does less well.

Two opposed systems of promotion have not been entirely successful. One system promotes all children at the end of each school year whether or not all have done the required work. The other keeps a child in the same grade, year after year, until he has completed that grade's requirements. Under the 100 per cent promotion plan, some children who might have learned enough to catch up had they been taught more slowly —had they been given one extra year in a grade—are rushed into permanent confusion. Under the opposite system, that of long retention in one grade, a child becomes too large physically and too mature socially for the other youngsters in his class. He becomes discouraged, restless, and hence a problem to himself and others. The good modern school uses an in-between policy. Such a school requires some children to repeat a grade, but it does not have them repeat it indefinitely. And it tries to give each child who has been held back some other forms of activity in which he can feel successful. In other words, the modern school has accepted the fact of individual differences and tries to shield a child as much as possible from the harmful effects of failure. Many schools are studying ways of organizing their classes so that each child can progress continuously according to his abilities. Some educators are suggesting that promotion be made at longer intervals than one year, and that a child's adjustment to school programs receives continuous study.

How To Help Prevent Failure

A competent teacher not only recognizes that children are different, but he is also prepared to vary his teaching as best he can in accordance with his pupils' individual rates of development, scaling the learning tasks of children to somewhere near their ability. In first grade he will encourage the bright children to begin reading at once, let the average proceed at an average rate, and reassure the slow that it is all right for them to wait a while. Also, when a child fails in spite of all child or teacher can do, he will base his recommendation as to whether or not the child should repeat a grade on what may do the most to prevent the child's future failure.

It is important that parents understand the difficulty teachers face in trying to eliminate all failure. So long as there are wide differences in children, it will be impossible to force them into standard molds without either the mold or the child giving a bit. Teachers generally believe that parents would prefer to have the school yield a little rather than to have their children faced with the fearful stamp of failure.

Parents can help to lessen failure in other ways than by a passive understanding of the problem. For a variety of reasons children seldom work up to capacity. Merely expecting a child to do well spurs learning. But expecting does not mean pressuring; it is, rather, an easy acceptance that work will go well. Interest in a child's work on the part of his parents reinforces that child's interest. Keeping in touch with the school so that there is an awareness of poor work when it begins may keep a situation from getting out of hand.

Giving a child good study conditions at home helps learning. A desk of his own in some quiet corner of the house, established rules about turning on the television or radio and about study before engaging in other activities all help a child to work to capacity.

If the work is poor, however, parents should take pains to discover any possible cause. A thorough physical and psychological examination will determine whether the cause of poor schoolwork might lie in health or emotional factors. An individual intelligence test sometimes will reveal facts about mental capacity that the group tests did not.

After all the information—physical and psychological—is in, a conference with the teacher and principal should result in some agreement concerning the welfare of the child. If the record shows that he is doing the best he knows how and that it would be better for him to stay in his present grade another year, both child and parents should have ample time to get used to the idea. All the facts that he can understand should be shared with the child and the reasons for nonpromotion explained. If low ability is the cause of his failure, parents should try to face the bitter truth that their child does not possess the necessary mental capacity. Then it is only humane to help the child live within his capacities. It is also humane to help him find some field in which he will do well enough to feel satisfied with himself—some hobby, some home or school responsibility, a sport or a craft.

In any graded schools where there are standards for advancement from grade to grade, some children will inevitably fail. Failure that comes from poor work habits, indifference, or lack of attention can very often be corrected and overcome. In many cases, so can failures that arise from poor health and emotional disturbances. But a lack of mental ability must be patiently tolerated, with both the school and the home prepared to give a little for the sake of the child. Such "giving" by the school does not mean lowering the standards of the school program, but rather modifying it according to the needs of the individual child. Failures due to lack of ability cannot be eliminated, but the severity of their bad effects on children can be reduced. A sympathetic teacher and an understanding parent, working in harmony and working with the child, can assist him in growing with some feelings of success. WILBUR A. YAUCH

See also FAILURE, FEAR OF; HOME-SCHOOL RELATIONS; SLOW LEARNER; STUDYING; TESTS AND MEASUREMENTS

SCHOOL LIBRARY *See* LIBRARIES

SCHOOL MARKS *See* SCHOOL REPORT

SCHOOL RELATIONS *See* HOME-SCHOOL RELATIONS

SCHOOL REPORT

Some kind of reporting to parents has always been a function of schools in this country. In the early days of organized schools a teacher reported to the parent by giving a child a percentage grade (87 per cent, 65 per cent, etc.) in each of his school subjects, often based on how well the student did with his final examination paper. Unless the parent happened to talk with the schoolmaster in church or at a community social, this grade represented all a parent ever knew of his child's success—or failure—in school.

After the turn of the century teachers began to translate percentages into letter grades —A, B, C, D, F, but what these grades meant in percentages was usually included— A = 95–100, B = 85–95, and so on. Then, after World War I, came the system of E, G, F, P, standing for the marks, Excellent, Good, Fair, Poor. Some schools also tried describing behavior traits with such comments as, "gets along with others," "finishes his work without prodding," or "has difficulty with arithmetic." Later on, some schools omitted reporting grades in favor of letters from the teachers describing each child's progress.

Teachers and school administrators have not tried to create new ways of reporting just for the sake of being different; they have made a tremendous effort to improve ways of letting parents know how their children are getting along in school.

The big problem teachers face in reporting to parents, whatever the form, is the difficulty in being fair. Even though the teacher has taken great pains to measure your child's work accurately, there is still the difficulty in deciding how to grade him in relation to other children's work. Shall the teacher use the standard of performance in that class as the basis, or the standard of performance of all children over the country in this grade or at this age? If the level of performance of the local grade is used, and if your child happens to be an average one in a group of bright youngsters, his grades will be discouragingly low. If he is a bright child in an average group, he will find it ridiculously easy to get high grades.

On the other hand, what if the teacher uses national standards? The school might be in an area where all the children come from underprivileged or foreign-language homes. Even though these children do extremely well under the circumstances, their achievements are likely to be lower than children who come from more privileged homes. Thus, nearly all the children are condemned to low grades no matter how hard they try. Or, take the reverse. Suppose the teacher's class is made up of children whose parents can provide them with many fine cultural advantages. If the children are compared with average ones, they will automatically get higher grades without half trying. It is easy to see how these children could quickly develop lazy work habits. Any way the teacher turns, he runs into difficulties in grading those children who are either bright or dull or those who have unusual cultural advantages or unusual educational lacks.

While schools will continue to struggle to find better methods of reporting, most of them have concluded that there is no better way than to talk to the parent face to face. The teacher can describe the work the child is doing, show examples of it, and be able to tell parents directly and clearly whether or not the child is doing as well as he is capable of doing. In turn, the parent can immediately ask the teacher any questions that will help to answer the question, "How is my child doing in school?"

Parents who have taken part in these parent-teacher conferences feel that they are worth while, but some still want a more formal report. Many schools are now doing both. The conference is held whenever either the parent or the teacher feels that it is necessary, but the formal report card is sent out regularly, usually twice a semester. This combination is fairly satisfactory, although it by no means solves all the problems of fair and accurate reporting, many of which are probably built-in and will always be there.

Report cards also help in reaching the critical decision—to pass or not to pass. Usually, those children who might possibly be failed fall into two groups: those who do not try hard enough and those who, even though they try, do not make high enough marks. In either case, the teacher has to make a decision based on what is best for the child. Flunking brings discouragement and frustration. Being too easy, letting unqualified pupils pass, encourages lax habits of study, and so most 100 per cent promotion policies have been given up because they tended to make children feel that concern about their schoolwork was unnecessary. WILBUR A. YAUCH

See also HOME-SCHOOL RELATIONS; SCHOOL FAILURE; TEACHER CONFERENCE

SCHOOLTEACHER

Children spend so many hours in school during their growing years that schoolteachers become very important people in their lives. Teachers are important as instructors of children's minds. They have an equal importance as human beings who help to shape children's values and feelings and total personalities. Fortunately, most teachers have professional preparation for the important job they do. Their education as teachers prepares them in the areas of knowledge that they will teach to children, in modern teaching methods, and in the field of child growth and development. All teachers must be licensed to teach by their state department of education. A bachelor's degree with an approved program of professional training is the usual minimum requirement for full licensing. Because of the shortage of teachers today, some hold only emergency licenses; such teachers are required to continue their professional study by attending summer school or evening classes. All teachers, even those fully licensed, are also required to continue their studies in order to keep abreast of new developments in their field. Many states and school systems are today encouraging teachers to work toward advanced degrees by providing salary incentives.

Finding and Holding Good Teachers

Gradual improvement in some of the working conditions for teachers in recent years has attracted more able people to teaching as a career. The starting salaries for new teachers have increased across the country; in almost all school systems today, women are allowed to continue teaching after marriage; and most communities have dropped many restrictions that in the past narrowly controlled the private lives of teachers. The security of their jobs is well protected by tenure laws. The setting in which they do their work is often an attractive and pleasing one, as communities continue to build modern and efficient schools.

There are, however, various unsolved problems that operate to keep able people out of teaching. The maximum salary that teachers can earn is usually low compared to that paid to other college-educated professional workers. Male teachers, with families to support, have difficulty in living on a school salary, and many of them take a second job in order to maintain the standard of living they desire. The scarcity of male teachers in the elementary school leads some able single women to seek employment in fields where the two sexes are more evenly distributed. Many dedicated teachers also become discouraged because of large class size, lack of materials, and lack of encouragement to do all the things for the children that their professional training and their idealism lead them to want to do.

Teaching is a very tiring and demanding job. The usual elementary schoolteacher is with his or her group of children, constantly responsible and constantly alert without a break, throughout the entire school day. The teacher must be prepared to respond at every second with the greatest flexibility and sensitivity to varied unpredictable demands: with sympathy, with sternness, with praise, with reproof, with information, with encouragement. The teacher must be constantly alert to the movements of the total group of children and to the behavior of each individual within the group. Many people in other occupations regard the school day as a short working day, overlooking the never-ceasing pressures on the teacher every minute in that day. And many are unaware that a teacher's work seldom ends with the end of school. Extracurricular responsibilities, preparation for the following day's teaching, correction of tests and of homework, work with individual children, getting to know parents, and taking part in school-related community activities add many hours to every teacher's work load.

Teaching is a field of public service. Despite the improvements that have been made, the financial rewards from teaching will never equal those that are possible in activities centered around private profit. The reward that supplements every teacher's cash salary is the satisfaction that his work brings. Those who choose teaching must find a deep measure of satisfaction in their work, or two alternatives are likely to arise: They will either leave schooling for other work that offers more of a cash reward or they will remain but gradually lose their spark and enjoyment. Under both alternatives, children are the losers. They do not have the chance to associate with creative, challenging adults during their school hours.

Parental Support for Good Teachers

Parents determine in two ways the quality of the teachers with whom their children live. As citizens they determine the community and state tax rate, which in turn fixes the beginning and the maximum salaries for teachers, the class size, and the amount and quality of teaching materials available. Equally important, parents play the major role in making possible other less tangible satisfactions that skilled professional workers seek.

Many school systems today have teacher recognition days, special ways of honoring retiring teachers, and other similar official acts to reward the dedication of good teachers. As important as these are, they probably do not count as much as the more intimate, almost day-by-day, personal relationships between parents and teachers. Public ceremonies cannot make up for the feeling some teachers have that parents simply send their children to school as if the teacher were a "baby-sitter"; that parents are quick to believe any criticism of teachers and teaching; that they listen only to a child's side of any conflict that may arise; that they are slow to praise and stingy in expressing appreciation for a school's good work; that parents expect the school to carry the full load of educating children rather than to supplement the home's continuing efforts. When these complaints are true, parent antagonism or apathy or aloofness throughout a year can never be atoned for by some one gracious public act. Dedicated, idealistic, conscientious teachers will use their professional skills more fully for children's benefit in a climate where parents, each parent in his own way, take the initiative in expressing their awareness of the key role that teachers play in their children's lives, and bring to their relationships with teachers attitudes of interest, of patience, of understanding.

JAMES L. HYMES, JR.

See also HOME-SCHOOL RELATIONS

SCHOOL TESTS AND EXAMINATIONS

Teachers have to know how well or how badly each individual child, and the class as a whole, are getting along in schoolwork. And tests tell them.

Tests show the teacher whether a child remembers what he has been taught, whether he understands the material, whether he can apply the knowledge he has gained, whether he can follow directions.

Tests are also useful to show whether it is the teaching or the child that is weak. If the whole class is doing badly in the same subject, then something must be wrong with the way the teacher is teaching that subject. Or perhaps there is something wrong in the teaching methods set up by a particular school. If only one child is doing badly, then, obviously, it is the child and not the method that needs bolstering.

A test may simply be a spelling list or a group of arithmetic problems given the child as homework. Or the teacher may give in class little informal tests he makes up, such as a spelling quiz, a few questions on recent work in history or geography, or a theme in English.

A teacher may use one test to find out several different things. For instance, a theme might be assigned in order to find out how well each child is learning to write, what his problems in English usage are, the quality of his thoughts, how much he knows about a given subject, and which of his mistakes in writing are common to the children of his class.

There are other quite different kinds of tests that your child will probably be given throughout his school life:

Diagnostic tests. These reveal how strong or weak a child is in a particular part of a school subject. Through such tests a teacher learns what to emphasize for a particular child and what to emphasize for the class.

Interest inventories. These are lists of items children are asked to check as "liking" or "not liking." The results, which reveal a child's real interests, often lead toward helping him to decide on a career.

Aptitude tests. These show what a child is especially good at doing. They show what talents or abilities he should concentrate on to his profit. Often, but not always, interest inventories and aptitudes point in the same direction.

Sociometric tests. These tests show what friends a child has and how well he is accepted in his group. They frequently point out to a teacher how he can help a child in his relation to others.

Some of these tests do not seem to have a great deal to do with schoolwork. Actually, however, they do, for the teacher who knows some of a child's interests, social problems, and bents can build on this information to improve that child's scholastic work.

One of the best tests is nothing more than the keen observation of an experienced teacher. Over a period of years he has developed a general notion of what work can reasonably be expected of children of a given age. He measures a child's performance against this general standard and can determine whether that child is doing as well as he is capable of doing.

Tests will do more than simply check on a child's work. Just knowing that a test is to be given will often spur him on to greater effort. Then, too, when a child has passed a test well, he gets a boost in confidence, which tends to make him do better the next time. Even if he has not done remarkably well, he will be spurred toward better work if he can see a gain from test to test.

You undoubtedly would like to know what you can do to help your child make better scores on tests. Obviously, on subject matter and skill tests, the child who keeps up in his daily schoolwork is bound to do better than one who waits until the last minute to study for tests. Last-minute cramming is fine for review or for finding out what he has missed as he went along, but information gained solely this way is soon forgotten. Encourage your child to do his daily assignments to the very best of his ability. When he comes home with an assignment or a test to prepare for, you can help most by going over the material with him and helping him to understand it. Make sure he does it himself, though, and that he leans on you only for your listening ear and sustaining presence.

Of course, in diagnostic and guidance types of tests, any help from you would destroy their value. They are intended to find out what is needed to make your child a better balanced person. WILBUR A. YAUCH

See also SCHOOL REPORT; STUDYING; TESTS AND MEASUREMENTS

SCHOOL VACATION *See* VACATION, SCHOOL

SCIENCE

Your young child plays in a world of sights and sounds, of tastes and smells, and of temperatures and pressures. It's a world where darkness sweeps away everything but the feel of things. Where sharp chirping sounds seem to come from rocks. Where most of the flowers wear perfumes. Where leaves are crisp and crunchy, but some of them taste horribly bitter. Where little things fly and crawl, and some give hot and painful stings.

Some things crawl and others squish. It's a world to be curious about, to ask questions about, to experience—with ears, nose, tongue, fingertips, and toes.

It's a world to be curious about.
It's a world to ask questions about.
It's a world to experience.

In his play, your child does ask questions, and he finds many of the answers for himself. He experiences with his ears, his nose, his tongue, his eyes, and his fingertips. This experience answers some questions about the world around him.

This experience—of asking questions and of finding answers to them—is the experience of science. We adults look at the products of science. We look at the fat books packed with knowledge, at the machines throbbing with power, at the intricate processes of manufacturing and medicine, at the tons of chemicals put to thousands of uses. We look at all these products and more, and we are baffled by the complexity of science.

But science is a process, too. It is a way of doing things. It is a way of finding answers to questions. It is a problem-solving process.

Little children seem to understand this process. They ask questions about the nature of things—about the properties, the structures, and the behaviors of living and nonliving things. They ask questions about causes—about the ways in which one thing is related to another. They ask questions about the way things will be in the future. And for many of these questions, they get answers. They get these answers freely, privately, and unconsciously. They get them while they play.

Now, scientists work. They work to solve problems about the nature of things—problems in observation. Scientists work to solve problems about causes and relationships—problems in explanation. They work to solve problems about future behaviors or events—problems in prediction. Let us see what the work of science has in common with your child's play.

Problems in Observation

"How deep is a puddle of water?"
"What's a flower made of?"
"Does grass burn?"

These are the kinds of questions your child asks. And he answers them quite naturally. He wades into the puddle of water. He tears to shreds some of your choice blooms. He sticks grass into a fire. You may frown upon his methods—or the results of them—but his methods are scientific.

"How deep is the ocean off the coast of Norway?"
"How many petals has this hybrid rose?"
"What is the melting point of this metal?"

These are the kinds of questions a scientist might ask. And he answers them the only way he can. He sails into the ocean. He tears to shreds the rose. He sticks the alloy into a furnace.

To solve these problems, a child and the scientist must observe; they must use their senses. It is what they see and hear and feel and taste and smell that give them facts about the world. Of course, the scientist uses tools—microscopes, telescopes, electric meters, radiation counters—to sense things that his natural powers are too limited to sense. These tools are extensions of the senses, so to speak—they help the scientist to make observations. But a child can learn to use them.

The scientist usually tries to find out "how much" or "how many," so he counts or measures with tools. A child does not think to do these things, but he can learn. Tools are essential in scientific work, but the scientist does nothing more than observe with them.

Problems in Explanation

"Why does popcorn pop?"
"Why does iron get red when it's hot?"
"Why are living things wet inside?"

These are questions that require an explanation. A child cannot answer these questions by direct use of his senses—nor can the scientist. It is by observing that they have noticed likenesses or differences that they do not understand. The causes or relationships are hidden—they cannot be observed.

To answer these questions, a child does what comes naturally: He daydreams. He builds fantasies. He guesses. And this, too, is the scientific method: The scientist daydreams. He speculates. He guesses. He formulates a hypothesis. The scientist, of course, has more knowledge than the child, and he has more regard for sound logic. A child does not mind logical inconsistency. But still, a guess is a guess—the method is the same.

But the guess is not enough. It must be tested. The test is made by experimentation, and in experimentation, the child and the scientist go directly to nature to make observations. This time, they observe with a purpose. A child might think that popcorn has a tougher, thicker skin than other kinds of corn. He'd bite or break open the kernels and look at the skins. If the hypothesis is wrong—and it often is—he'll make others and test them.

Now, neither the scientist nor the child can be sure that he has the final answer to an explanation problem. He can test many hypotheses, but he can never escape the nagging doubt. He'll always wonder if he might have tested one more hypothesis. Your child will form his own private conclusions, but the doubt will linger and he may come to you with it. His eternal why-why-why questions may unnerve you, but he needs the assurance you can give him. He needs to know if the world he sees is the same as the one you see.

Problems in Prediction

"Will an egg get hard if I bake it in the oven?"

"Will this plastic melt if I heat it?"

"Will this twig grow if I plant it?"

These are questions about the future. A child isn't sure what will happen, but he has a store of facts from past observations, and he has developed a few theories about how things work. Now he is willing to try his general ideas—to see if he can tell what will happen in specific instances.

To answer these questions, he must make predictions and test them. He expects a baked egg to get hard because fried and boiled eggs get hard. He expects this piece of plastic to soften because it looks like the kind of plastic that has softened. He expects the twig to grow, because he's seen new plants started from slips. But not until after he tests each prediction will he know if his general ideas fit these specific cases.

The scientist has a broader background than the child. The scientist has more facts obtained by observation; he has more theories that have sprung from problems in explanation, but the scientist, too, must test his predictions. Of some predictions he can be quite sure, but not of others: The sun has always come up, so it is quite safe to say that it will rise tomorrow, too. But he can not be so sure that tails will turn up on the next toss of the coin; there's only a 50–50 chance that it will. So, the scientist needs mathematics—statistics and probability theory—to help him to describe predictions—to help him to say how sure or how unsure he is that a specific thing will happen. With or without mathematics, predictions depend upon knowledge of facts and theories, and both the child and the scientist try to make predictions when they think they know enough.

For Your Child

Your child's world is an immediate world —limited to his own neighborhood. His understanding of the world is limited by the experiences he has there. You can find ways to broaden his experience—with stories, trips, books, and interesting people to talk with.

With broader experience, he can build better daydreams for the things he tries to explain; he can rely upon more facts and more theories for the things he tries to predict.

Such books as the three science volumes in CHILDCRAFT, Volume 3, *World and Space;* Volume 4, *Life Around Us;* and Volume 8, *How Things Work,* will help to take your child beyond his back yard. The large, realistic pictures will let him see many things that he needs to see—hidden things, small things, fast-moving things, faraway things. The words will help him to sense these new things; familiar tastes, smells, sounds, and textures help him to experience a vivid new world. Against this background, you won't have to be concerned whether or not your child will become a scientist. You need not yield to the pressure for more and more men and women of science. You need not "push" him too early into a laboratory. For if your child's curiosity and imagination have been cherished and whetted, he will carry them into his classrooms and find fulfillment in whatever career he chooses—when the right time comes. WILLIAM S. VASILAKES

See also BOOKS FOR CHILDREN

Related article in WORLD BOOK: "Science"

SCOLDING

What good (if any) does scolding a young child do? One good guess is that scolding will not accomplish precisely what his parents hoped for. For example, there is much discussion about whether valuable objects in the house should be put out of the toddler's reach. Some parents say that they will not move objects because they want their child to learn from the beginning that the parent is boss and that there are some regulations to which even a very young child must conform. So, every time the child reaches for a forbidden object, the parent scolds gently with "No, no" or "Bad boy," and perhaps reinforces the "no" with a spank on the hand or the bottom. The parent has a purpose for this mild physical punishment and scolding: to help the child learn which acts are permitted and which are forbidden, which objects he may handle and which he must leave alone. Yet it is questionable if the child understands what the scolding or the spanking means. The message might get across quite differently and the baby could easily believe that his parents scold him because they do not want him to have what he wants, that it is wrong to explore the environment, and that curiosity gets one into trouble. The baby's interpretation is, of course, wrong—but that is irrelevant.

Often parents, in their attempts to be fair and yet firm with their children, will scold a child and then explain lengthily and, probably as far as the child is concerned, incomprehensibly, why the behavior was wrong. But a young child cannot usually respond to such a barrage of words. It is probably better, therefore, in using scolding as a teaching technique, to minimize it until the child knows exactly what is being said to him. Let your child know by example and a few simple words what is expected of him. If he violates the rules, do not be too upset. Harsh scolding and punishment seem often to crystallize the behavior you dislike rather than to remove it. It is better to give in a little once in a while than to win a skirmish and lose the game. BETTYE M. CALDWELL

See also DISCIPLINE; "NO-NO"

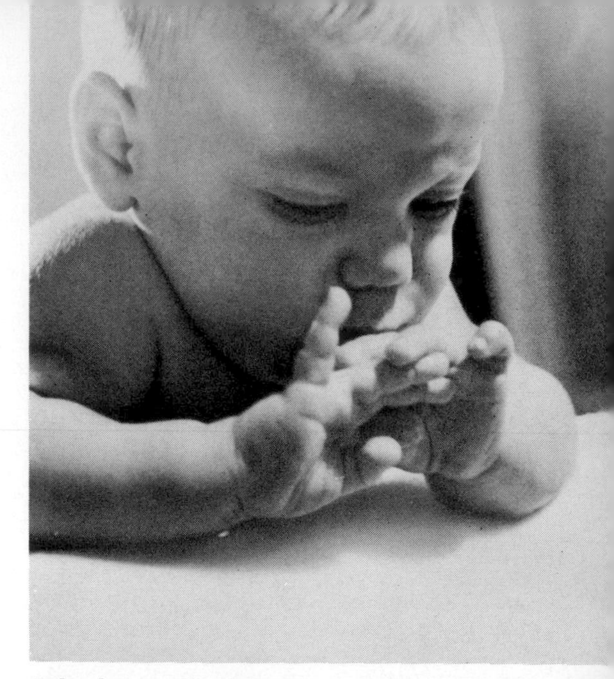

Baby discovers his fingers.

SCRAPES *See* CUTS AND SCRATCHES

SCRATCHES *See* CUTS AND SCRATCHES

SEAT BELTS *See* ACCIDENT PREVENTION

SECOND LANGUAGE *See* TALKING

SECRETS

Your 2-year-old puts his sticky little face up close to your ear and whispers a stream of meaningless words—his secret. All this is in imitation of older children, who have secrets among themselves, sometimes giggly ones, sometimes serious. Wherever there are children, there are secrets, sometimes between two "best friends," sometimes among the members of a "secret" society.

So you might as well play the game as a child does, taking your mood cue from him, and hope that at adolescence, if you are lucky, your child will trust you with some of his really serious "secrets." From your example of trustworthiness will grow the child's ability to keep his word when he promises not to tell a soul. MAY R. SHERWIN

See also CONFIDENCES; PRIVACY

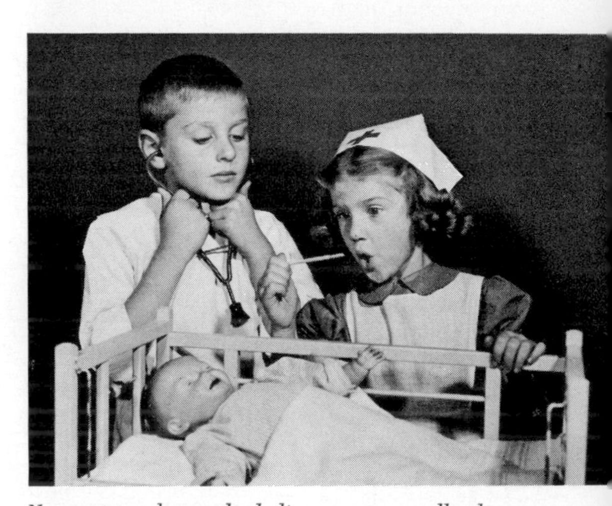

Youngsters play make-believe games endlessly.

And a little boy imitates his father.

SELF-CONCEPT

A baby "new to earth and sky" has no concept of himself. In fact, he has no concepts. One of the first concepts or ideas he begins to form is that of himself.

There are three interrelated aspects of the self-concept—physical, social, and personal.

The Physical Self

The physical self-concept develops ahead of the other two. A baby gradually becomes aware of himself through the feelings he gets from his body. He gains a sense of the positions and movements of his body. First, he discovers his fingers and then his big toe and he explores them with his mouth, where his sensations are keenest.

Eventually the child forms a picture of himself which he remembers and adds to. Most people have some early memory of themselves, as though they were looking at a picture. For instance, the historian Henry Adams tells us of his first memory of himself, "sitting on a yellow kitchen floor in strong sunlight."

This picture of the physical self continues and develops, partly because we have mirrors and are able to see physical images of ourselves. Most of us have a favorite physical image of ourselves, and we try to dress and carry ourselves so as to be like this image. We even prefer a front view rather than a side view, or the other way around, and we tend to stand so as to get the favored view when we look at ourselves in a mirror.

Also we have an image of our voice, but we never really hear ourselves as others hear us unless we can listen to our voice when it comes from somewhere else than our own mouths. The invention of tape recorders has allowed many of us really to hear our own voice. Some people are pleasantly surprised when they hear their voice and others are disappointed. In either case their self-concept grows a little through this experience.

The Social Self

The social self is the self as a person among persons. It grows out of living with other people. It starts with the mother and child, who form a social world of their own. They learn to smile at each other and to make other gestures that mean something to them. Soon they learn to talk with each other.

Then the baby begins to talk to himself. At this point his social self has definitely come into being. As the psychologist puts it, the child becomes an object to himself. "Sally sweep the floor," says the little girl to herself as she sweeps with a toy broom. Or "Sally is naughty," she says when she spills water on the floor. The little girl is putting herself in her mother's position and looking at herself. She has begun to see herself as others see her. She will never acquire this ability completely, as the poet Robert Burns noted when he said in his Scottish dialect:

Oh wad some power the giftie gie us
To see oursels as others see us!

And a homespun philosopher, Strickland Gillilan, advised:

Just stand aside and watch yourself go by;
Think of yourself as "he" instead of "I."

Young children discover their social selves partly through games. They play make-believe games endlessly, pretending that they are "mother" or "father" or "the doctor" or "the teacher." A 3-year-old picks up a black leather bag and struts around the house with it, saying "I'm the doctor."

Probably language is necessary for discovering one's social self. Therefore, it is not likely that animals have social selves.

The boy of 2 years is told by his parents, "What a big boy you are!" or "Sammy is a big boy," and at the same time they smile at him and give him a hug or a kiss. Then he says to himself, "Sammy is a big boy," and he feels good about himself. Or, if he drops a glass on the floor and it breaks, he may say "Sammy bad," as his mother sometimes says. But his mother may pick him up and kiss him and say, "Yes, Sammy is bad but he won't do it again, will he?" and Sammy will say, "Sammy won't do it again."

The little girl plays with her dolls and talks to them like a mother. Thus she practices being a mother. The little boy picks up a stick and makes a noise like a machine gun and says, "I'm a soldier."

Thus children try on a number of roles for fit, as it were. They see themselves as various people, but often as people who take care of them and give them rewards—such as their fathers and mothers and big brothers and sisters. They also stop seeing themselves as certain people when punished for acting like these people or trying to take their roles. Thus a boy who goes around with a stick hitting people and saying, "I'm a giant," may be punished by his mother, and therefore may not repeat the misconduct. What might have been a part of his social self is nipped in the bud by his mother.

But the little boy who has grown accustomed to sitting on a potty, one day goes into the bathroom and stands to urinate, saying, "I'm Daddy." This makes him proud of himself, and his mother may reward him further by saying, "You're a big boy now."

Children do not really confuse themselves with other people in this process of building up a social self. Thus a little girl said to her mother, "You're so lucky because you can be with you all the time." She knew her mother was one permanent self, and she was another, although she might play at being her mother.

By the time a child is ready for school, he has a pretty well-defined social self. A boy has learned to see himself and to expect himself to behave like a boy and not a girl. He also has made up his own special combination of his father, mother, big brother, the doctor, a policeman, and other characters that he has played at being.

By this time a boy or a girl is a unique combination of people—like pieces of other people but not completely like any other one person, except that identical twins sometimes have social selves that are very similar, as are their physical selves.

The Personal Self

The third aspect of the self-concept is the personal self. It is hard at first to distinguish from the social self, and it grows out of the social self. It was beginning to appear in a boy aged 3 years and 9 months who said, "I'm a big boy." He was asked, "Who told you that you are a big boy?" and he replied, "Myself told me."

The personal self, sometimes called "the spiritual self," has three parts—the conscience or moral self, the ideal self, and the sense of identity. These come into existence during childhood and the teens, and they go on developing through life.

Probably the personal self develops through a process of "identification," which has been much studied and much discussed by psychologists. Identification is a process of *acting like another person*. It starts before the age of 2 as a child gets the habit of imitating his mother because she rewards him for such behavior. She rewards him for smiling when she smiles and for repeating sounds that she makes. The rewards she gives him are food, hugging and kissing, and later on such rewards as saying, "Sammy is a good boy."

A child also learns to imitate his father and perhaps older brothers and sisters who are often with him and can reward him. The act of imitation is unconscious and becomes a deep habit, which affects the way he walks, talks, and later on the things he likes and dislikes, the way he meets people and gets along with them, and so on. We do not know why the child tends more to imitate the parent of the same sex than the parent of the opposite sex.

Among other things, a child imitates or takes into himself the warning or scolding or praising voices of his parents. If they punish him either by spanking or by scolding when he hits his little brother or when he takes cookies from the cooky jar, he learns to punish himself in his mind for doing these things, and he learns to avoid doing these things most of the time so as to avoid having to punish himself.

By the age of 5 or 6, a child has taken into himself enough of the warning and punishing voices of his parents to control himself most of the time and to keep himself from doing what he knows is wrong. He has developed a *conscience*. The strength of his conscience depends on the combination of love and of discipline or punishment his parents have given him. If they have not given him love, he does not learn to imitate them. If they have not scolded or punished him, he does not have their scolding or punishing voice in himself. If they have punished him too severely and have not given enough love, he may not identify with them.

Thus a child's conscience depends in a complex way on the treatment given him by his parents and other people who act like parents toward him. His conscience goes on developing through childhood and through the rest of his life, but the basic sense of moral self-control and self-discipline develops in these early years.

The ideal self is also a result of identification. A child develops a concept of himself as he ought to be, or as he would like to be. By the time he is 7 or 8 years old, he can tell you about his ideal self. If you ask him, "What kind of person would you like to be?" or "Whom would you like to be like when you grow up?" a child under 9 or 10 quickly says that he would like to be like his parent of the same sex or sometimes like a grandparent who has taken care of him. Then he goes through a phase of wanting to be like some glamorous or romantic person, such as a movie star or an astronaut or a professional ball player. By age 14 or 15 he outgrows this stage and generally wants to be like a real person whom he knows—usually a young adult who is attractive to him—sometimes a teacher, or a club leader, or a neighbor, or a younger brother or sister of his father or mother. Then a good many teen-agers decide they want to be like a combination of real people or to be like an imaginary person who has a combination of good qualities.

Thus the ideal self goes through a series of changes as a boy or girl grows up. Everyone has his own particular sequence or combination. For instance, a 13-year-old girl said, "I guess I want to be a singer. Somebody in front of people so they can see me. You know my father is on television." Here was a combination of father and a glamorous person.

A 16-year-old boy wrote: "When I grow up, I would like to be a medical doctor and I want to work hard and discover something. I want to be liked by all people, be good-looking, have a good wife, and take part in the things of the community to better it in any way I can. I would want to have a good social standing."

A 12-year-old girl wrote the following little essay on the topic, Am I an Imitator?

"I imitate etiquette from my mother. She taught me all of my manners. I try to draw my pictures in school like Barbara. I put my hat on like Doris. I copy my clothes clashes from Lois. I imitate my hair styles from many moving picture actresses. I choose my own clothes though and I'm a Christian because my conscience tells me to. I make my bed in the morning the same way Eleanor does because when I first came up to the Busy Bees room she was the one who showed me how. I imitate very many people, but I mostly get my ideas out of my own head."

The personal self is rounded out during the late teens by the achievement of *identity*. A boy or a girl becomes an adult more by achieving an identity than by going through the physical changes of the teen years.

When a person has achieved identity, he is one and the same person at all times and places. He carries a sameness within himself and presents himself to others as always the same person. He has answered for himself the questions: Who am I? What are my goals in life? What kind of person will I be one year from now? Five years? Ten years?

Thus the self-concept of the baby grows into the self-concept of the competent young man or woman, depending at every stage on how he is treated by his parents and others who are near and significant to him. Although the self-concept is a product of living with other people, it is different from any one of these people. The young man or woman is a little bit of all the people he lives with and also a person in his own right.

Importance of the Self-Concept

What does the self-concept do for a person? Why is it important? It does three important things for him. First, it helps him to become self-consistent—a person who is the same next week or next year as he is today. Second, it gives a person moral character. Third, it makes a human being into a real individual, different from all others.

Who is responsible for the child's self-concept? Mainly the mother and father in the first years of his life, and they are always important through the whole period of growing up. But teachers and club leaders and other adults have a part in his self-concept, as do his friends.

A person should come out of the process started by his parents as a competent, self-directing individual, captain of his life, though not responsible for the process that made him what he is. ROBERT J. HAVIGHURST

See also IMITATION; LOVE; MORAL AND SPIRITUAL DEVELOPMENT

SELF-CONSCIOUSNESS

The discomfort of self-consciousness is a familiar sensation, for most people have experienced some agonizing moment of self-consciousness and everyone has experienced mild but disturbing moments of it. Yet it is practically impossible for parents always to foresee when or how self-consciousness will strike their child, either as an awareness of his physical self or as to what he is as a person.

A young child can have moments when he doesn't want his mother to make him feel different from his friends or when he doesn't want his friends to be aware he has a mother at all, someone who can scold him at will and give him positive directions what to do.

A preadolescent has many ways of being self-conscious. He tends to be sensitive and embarrassed about being criticized in public, feeling occasionally that the attack is unjust. Or, since he is now increasingly aware of right and wrong, he may feel that some of his own thoughts are wrong and that he is being criticized for these. He can become miserably self-conscious if an adult makes fun of his plans and projects; the plans may be too complex to carry out, but he wants to learn this for himself. He is, however, mainly self-conscious about what children his own age think of him and how they react to him, even to the extent of suffering sometimes from being well dressed when others are not. If a girl is taller or fatter than her friends, or a boy more scrawny than his, self-consciousness may be acute.

Parents can be helpfully reassuring if they stay within strictly realistic limits, if they have a sense of humor without bite, and if, when it seems right to them, they let their child have things and take part in activities like those of his friends.

The self-consciousness of an adolescent is merely a huge extension in scope and pain of what it was before adolescence. Anything and everything can bother the young person this age—what he does and says and thinks, how he looks, how his parents look, what they think and say and do. He still wants to be like the other fellow. He doesn't want grownups reminding him that he is growing up, that he is awkward. He doesn't even want to be reminded that he is self-conscious. His parents will step on his toes many times, but soon he will learn that they don't intend to, that most of their trampling is accidental. Eventually he will learn that his parents were once self-conscious, too. IRVING E. SIGEL

See also AWKWARDNESS; SHYNESS AND TIMIDITY

SELF-DEMAND SCHEDULE *See* FEEDING SCHEDULE

SELF-FEEDING

The human infant has to depend on his parents for a long time. Unfortunately, some parents enjoy and encourage a child's dependence when they should welcome his attempts at self-sufficiency.

One of the early signs of independence comes when a child tries to feed himself. First, he reaches for the bottle when you bring it to him. Next, he holds the bottle and eventually shoves it away when he has had enough. As he is allowed to, he assumes some responsibility for feeding himself.

At about 12 months (give or take two months) a child usually shows rapidly increasing independence. He may push the spoon from your hand and clumsily try to feed himself. During this stage patience is necessary, for allowing a child to assume some responsibility is tremendously important in his development. Mothers should actually encourage self-feeding, although it is much easier to retrieve the spoon and do the job neatly. But the mother who understands the urge for independence will not interfere; she will simply stand by. Most babies even at 12, 18, or 24 months get too tired to feed themselves enough to satisfy hunger, so a mother must take over where baby willingly leaves off.

How can you help your child learn to feed himself?

- Watch for ways to encourage his early efforts.
- Prepare for spills and protect surroundings so when baby drops food on himself or on the floor, cleaning up is easy.
- Show that you accept and approve the procedure, even though baby's first clumsy efforts to feed himself are unsuccessful. If you understand that learning takes place when the learner feels successful, you will praise a successful effort even if he gets only a small amount of food.
- Give your child silverware that fits his small, chubby hands. Short, dull-tined forks with stubby handles and shovel-shaped spoons with shallow bowls are available in less expensive materials as well as in sterling silver. These utensils were designed by the staff of a well-known child development institute and are well adapted to an infant's uses. Plates for young children should be somewhat deep and have sloping sides to push a spoon against. Shallow soup bowls may be even better than plates. Glasses and the handles of cups should be easy for a child to grasp.
- Prepare foods that a child can eat easily. Cut his food in bite-size pieces. "Soupy" food should be thin enough to drink. Servings should be small so that he does not grow discouraged. MIRIAM E. LOWENBERG

See also EATING PROBLEMS; INDEPENDENCE; MESSINESS; TABLE MANNERS

SELFISHNESS *See* POSSESSIVENESS; SHARING

SELF-RELIANCE *See* INDEPENDENCE

SENSITIVENESS

The ability to respond feelingly to people, the sun, music, books, art can be one of the great joys of life. People sensitive in this way can be delightful to be around. But people can be sensitive in other ways, too; they can be easily crushed, easily hurt, react intensely to even unintended criticism. When this kind of sensitiveness becomes quite strong, it is not delightful to be around.

The excessively sensitive child is one to whom the heart goes out. He seems so handicapped, so restricted. His fear of being hurt causes him to miss much of the joy of everyday personal encounter and relationship.

Why is such a child so careful to avoid being hurt? Why does he react so extremely hard to even a little tension or difficulty? Essentially, his reaction is a matter of self-protection. Everyone tends to protect his weakest spots or those he believes are weakest. And, unfortunately, the busier a person is defending his tender spots, the less efficient and less effective he becomes. For example, when the sensitive adolescent reacts to adult scolding that has shown up his immaturity, he usually gets into further trouble through his moodiness or hostility.

Children will, at times, go to great lengths to avoid situations that threaten their feeling of adequacy and their sense of personal worth. They will sometimes pretend to be sick or even play hooky to protect themselves when they have been doing poor schoolwork. Is there any adult, for that matter, who has not tried to impress others in areas where he feels seriously inadequate?

Since children are naturally less accomplished than adults, they are just as naturally more sensitive. With more tender spots they are likely to bruise more easily. As they grow older, learn more, do more, they gradually grow stronger psychologically, but growth is bound to be a slow and probably an uneven process. Thus, to some degree, sensitiveness in young children is to be expected, just as a gradual lessening of sensitiveness is expected as the years go by. As children develop and as their personalities grow stronger, they will be better able to resist threat. Individuals will differ, however, so that in some youngsters this kind of growth occurs quite readily; others require more support and reassurance before the "skin begins to thicken."

Excessive sensitivity, particularly in one general area, is a sign of weakness or tenderness in that area. A child may not actually be aware of what he needs, for it is quite natural to suppress certain unpleasant facts about oneself; yet in many instances, if a parent can find out what the child feels he lacks, and supply it, the sensitiveness may decrease greatly. If, however, efforts to help the child in this way are not successful, if severely excessive sensitivity continues, parents should seek professional guidance and counseling for their child. ARMIN GRAMS

See also CHILD GUIDANCE CLINIC; EMOTIONAL DEVELOPMENT

SEPARATION *See* DIVORCE AND SEPARATION

SEPARATION FROM MOTHER

Every reasonably healthy child has a strong urge to grow up and become independent. Yours has, too. If each time your telephone rings your toddler comes up with some pressing demand for your attention or if every time you leave him at home with someone else he frets or protests or even screams, you may doubt that he has any urge toward maturing. But he has. The difference between him and an adult is his lack of experience on which to build faith—to him, when you are out of sight you are all-gone, all-gone forever as far as he knows.

Even though your child will eventually want to be independent of you and even though you want to help him along that road, he is not going to achieve independence at the same age nor in the same way as any other child. His ability to get along without you is one phase of his development, but it is only one. His emancipation will depend on what kind of child he is and on the circumstances of his life.

You have seen children under the socializing influence of brothers and sisters or of neighborhoods where there is much friendly visiting back and forth. You have also seen "only" children who live in apartment buildings where they have little contact with either child or adult neighbors, and you have possibly noticed marked differences in these various children and their dependence on their mothers. But you may also have noticed that all clinging or relinquishing does not depend on environment. A child's readiness to be more on his own is influenced equally by his own personality, his responsiveness to the atmosphere around him, his natural sensitivity to words and sights and sounds, his natural awareness of people and of change.

There is no question that an infant needs the loving closeness of his mother and that the toddler needs the chance to follow her around. Yet it is good for both mother and child if there is some sort of gradual weaning, both physical and psychological. Thus, many pediatricians who are strongly in favor of breast feeding also recommend a bottle once a day—to relieve the mother and to prepare the child for future independence.

Similarly, the infant whose daddy shares some of the routines of baby care will probably be less dependent on his mother, but it is important for this sharing not to be so constant as to blur for the child the differentiation of each parent's role.

As your child leaves infancy, it is only natural that he will sometimes get the feeling of being left out. He knows that family activities continue after he goes to bed; he knows his parents have interests in other people and in activities in which he cannot participate. Parents, of course, do have other interests—they need to have them—and every child must learn to accept his parents' temporary turning away from him as one of the facts of life. But you can smooth his path to this knowledge. In the first place, don't leave him without telling him you are going. Tell him also that you will return. Sometimes it will help to say that you will bring him some simple surprise or that he will find something special under his pillow in the morning. Your tone about departure can be casual and your tone about return can be cheerful. Even silliness helps sometimes with a slightly older child. "See you later, alligator," not only has the light touch, but also has the emphasis on your reunion.

Many children, even quite little ones, like to be told specifically about timing. "I'll be back before lunch," or "I'll see you at bedtime," you say, and they are much more satisfied about your leaving. If you make such a contract, keep to it and be there when you say you will be. Occasionally, but not until after the child has learned he can depend on your return, you may want to arrive a little late on purpose. Such deliberate lateness serves to help him become more flexible, less apt to panic, and it also helps to keep you from feeling enslaved. Some children are helped by having their mothers telephone from "away"; others can be upset by the loved voice sounding strange through the receiver and by the fresh reminder that mother is not there.

Dissimilar reactions to similar circumstances is another proof of the importance of knowing your own child and using this knowledge to decide how to help him. Perhaps one of the ways to gain knowledge of him is to try different approaches to see what works best.

One way to help him learn about leave-taking is this: Let your child do the going away; have him depart from the house with a grownup and leave you behind. He should be going somewhere he wants to go, toward an experience he will have a good chance of enjoying. Your good-by to him can be casual.

Finally, there comes a moment for more decisive handling. You know your child and you know he is ready for a new phase. You can say, "No fussing this time—I'm sure that you can manage," and he understands that you expect some rather grown-up behavior. Chances are, he will respond to your expectation and have a very good feeling of what a wonderful person he is.

Some children, of course, do not grow out of their dependence on their mothers enough to accept even temporary substitutes or to enjoy playing or eating when she is not around. For these children, and for their mothers, it is often sensible to seek some form of professional help.

There is another type of child, however, who continues to regret his mother's departure, but he still leads his own healthy, active life with other children. A child like this is probably a very sensitive person, one who will mature fully and have warm, good relationships in his grown-up life. With him you can appreciate how much relationships mean to him and perhaps also find ways of softening the stress of separation without belittling it or denying its reality.

And what about your side of the coin—separation from your child? A woman who has fully enjoyed being a mother, with its warmth and challenges and satisfactions, is neither unusual nor neurotic if she suffers a few pangs as her child needs less of her comfort and protection. Acknowledge these feelings honestly without letting them spill over into an unhealthy clinging to your child and they will do no harm. Perhaps you can even deliberately begin to make yourself less competent or companionable to him. You may soon find more lasting satisfaction in the further unfolding and maturing of his personality.

GWENDOLYN B. ZEICHNER

See also BABY-SITTER; BROKEN HOME; FEAR; INDEPENDENCE; NURSE; READINESS; WORKING MOTHER

SERVICE AGENCY *See* FAMILY SERVICE AGENCY

SEX CURIOSITY *See* SEX EDUCATION

SEX DIFFERENCES

A newborn child is immediately called boy or girl according to his primary sex characteristics. In the male these are the penis and the scrotal sac (scrotum) containing two testicles (testes). The testicles have been within the baby's abdomen during most of his life within the mother, and in most instances have descended into the scrotal sac by the time the baby is born. Occasionally, one or both testicles are still undescended at the time of birth. Most of these descend within the first few years.

The sex organs of the female baby are almost entirely within the body. At birth the vulva, composed of folds of skin (the labia) separated in the middle, is visible below the abdomen and between the legs. The cleft between the labia leads internally to the vagina and uterus. At the upper end of the cleft is a little mound of erectile tissue called the clitoris.

Both boys and girls continue to grow, but there is no change in their sexual development until they approach puberty. Then the hormones of the sex glands cause the appearance of what are known as secondary sex characteristics.

In boys entering puberty (usually between 12 and 15 years of age), there is a marked increase in the size of the penis and testes. Secondary sex characteristics also appear. Hair grows over the lower abdomen, under the arms, and then on the sides of the face and chin. A boy's voice changes gradually from the high pitch of childhood to the deeper voice of approaching manhood; his shoulders widen, his muscles develop.

Two other important signs of approaching maturity also appear in boys. There are occasional erections of the penis and the outset of "seminal emissions," which usually occur during sleep. These emissions are evidence that certain glands in the boy are now secreting semen, the substance in which sperm cells swim. When an excess of this fluid is formed, it must pass from the body and does so through the penis. Because these emissions occur during sleep, they are sometimes called "wet dreams." They do not occur at regular intervals, as does menstruation.

In girls entering puberty the breasts develop, the hips widen, hair appears under the arms and on the lower abdomen, and there is a general rounding out of the body, caused by the deposition of fat tissue. Menstruation occurs usually between 10½ and 15 years of age, usually when the breasts are already fairly well developed and pubic hair has appeared on the lower abdomen.

In early puberty there is a rapid growth in the height of both boys and girls. As a rule, puberty starts a year or two earlier in girls. At 12, girls are almost always taller than boys. But if you observe the same group of boys and girls when they are 14, you will find that generally the boys are of equal height or taller. Girls grow in height until they are approximately 17 years old, whereas boys continue to grow until they are about 20 or 21 years old.

It is very important that parents inform their children of the various changes that will take place as they enter and go through puberty. Growing children must not be taken by surprise, especially in the matter of menstruation or seminal emission. Those who have not been so informed will often be deeply upset by these changes, fearing that they are sick or that something is very wrong with them. Children should also be told that all boys and girls do not mature at the same rate. Some may start developing as early as 10 years, while others, just as normal, will start developing as late as 14 or 15. The age of entry into puberty is usually related to the family background.

But physical differences are not the only differences between boys and girls. There are definite differences in interests and attitudes which make them fulfill their respective sex roles. Children do not develop these values by themselves. Impressions each child gains of a boy's role and of a girl's role are largely determined by his family, his home, and his environment.

Generally, there are very few differences between the two sexes in their attitudes and patterns of play up to the approximate age of 5 years. But as boys and girls reach 6 and 7, their parents begin to exert a very deep, special influence upon them. A boy looks to his father for an ideal of what a man should be like, what a father and a husband should be like. And a girl looks to her mother for her model of womanhood, of a mother and a wife.

But all the time boys and girls are forming their conception of their own sex, they also are forming their ideals of the other sex. And again, their parents are their most important models. Both father and mother should encourage their children in attaining their sex roles. Mothers, as well as fathers, should show an interest in their sons' masculine pursuits and attainments, and fathers, in turn, should admire the feminine qualities, interests, and attainments of their daughters—their pretty dresses, the way they fix their hair, the cakes and cookies they make.

By the time boys and girls reach 7 or 8 years of age, their interests usually become very divergent. Boys begin to idolize heroic figures—baseball players, prize fighters, television cowboy heroes—who represent real masculinity to them. On the other hand, girls have their own feminine idols and activities. They develop hobbies, form clubs, and read girls' books. The boys are noisy and usually aggressive. The girls as a rule assume more feminine characteristics and attitudes. Boys go with boys and girls go with girls during this school-age period. Girls have no part in male society and vice versa.

As children approach puberty and begin to develop the physical characteristics associated with this period, they also begin to develop new desires, interests, and urges. During the period of prepuberty almost every boy and girl has a close buddy of his or her own sex. These close friendships are important, for as a boy or a girl begins to find an interest in the opposite sex, an opportunity is afforded to discuss with a friend of like sex problems of this new relationship.

As a child enters puberty, interest in the opposite sex becomes more vital, accompanied by impelling new desires and urges. Both boys and girls should know that these new feelings are normal, natural, and to be expected. They are an important part of growing up.

And throughout puberty, parents should continue, as in the years before, to assure their children of their love and support. It is a prime responsibility of both mother and father to make their children feel that they are wanted for what they are—that they want their daughters to be girls and their sons to be boys, and that they value both equally. MILTON I. LEVINE

See also GROWTH; HEREDITY; IMITATION; PUBERTY

SEX EDUCATION

Education about sex is a gradual process and it cannot be accomplished in one or two easy lessons. Facts must be presented gradually in keeping with the changing needs and curiosity of a growing child. If parents want to give their child balanced and healthy attitudes toward sex, they must accept as perfectly normal and natural his questions about the birth of babies, his curiosity about the parts of the body, about the differences between boys and girls, about relationships between men and women.

Those First Questions

Somewhere between the ages of 3 and 6, almost all children will start asking their first questions concerning sex. Your answers to these questions—what you say and how you say it—will make a difference in the child's future sex attitudes. Your answers will also help determine whether he will continue to turn to you for sex information or will seek it elsewhere through less desirable channels.

In answering the sex questions of a child under the age of 6, give him the information he requests and no more. But at all ages there are three cardinal principles to be remembered:

Always use the correct language or terms.
Always tell the truth.
Never put off answering.

It is necessary to use correct terms in order to avoid giving your child the impression that there is something different, something wrong, something taboo about the genital system.

It is necessary to tell him the truth because, eventually, someone else will supply him with information—perhaps not always correct information. When he learns that you have deceived him in your answers, he will mistrust you and will cease to come to you with his questions.

It is necessary to answer when he asks a question because that is when he needs the answer. Delay may also give the impression that you find the subject distasteful or taboo.

Where Do Babies Come From?

Usually the first questions are brought forth by the expectation or arrival of a new baby in the home or neighborhood. "Mommy, where do babies come from?" Answer: "From their mommies." That's all that is asked and the answer is complete. Nothing further need be added until the child asks the next question, which may come days or weeks later: "Where in their mommies?" And the answer: "From a place inside here, below the mommy's stomach." It is important to specify "below the stomach" because of the confusion many children develop when told that a baby develops within the mother's stomach. A little child, who is almost always literal, may picture the baby in the mother's stomach, sitting in the midst of a mass of food.

The child should then be told that a baby develops from an egg. The term "seed" so often used is not recommended, since children associate seed with a plant or a tree, whereas an egg is associated with something that is not rooted, but has freedom of movement as they have.

"Where did the egg come from?" is usually the next question. And the answer: "All baby girls are born with these eggs in their bodies, but the eggs cannot develop into babies until the girl is grown up."

And then comes that question so difficult for most mothers to answer: "How does the baby get out?" The mother can answer that there is a special opening, called the vagina, through which the baby is born. This opening is between the legs. This opening is not for urine nor is it for bowel movements (misconceptions that many children carry into adult life). If, however, your child then asks, "Well, let me see it," his request should be denied. Such an experience is very upsetting to little children and may disturb them for a long period afterward. A simple sketch can be made showing the baby in the body of the mother and the opening through which the baby is born.

Children under the age of 5 will rarely ask about the father's part in the birth of a baby. But when they do, they should be told about the sperm from the father which joins with the egg in the mother so the baby that develops will have qualities of both parents.

"But how does the sperm go from the father to the egg inside the body of the mother?" is frequently asked. The reply should not be complicated or detailed. Usually the answer that the sperm goes out of the father's body through the penis and into the mother's body through the vagina is sufficient and satisfying.

Actually, it is not easy for most parents to answer such questions in a casual manner, for most people have been brought up in homes where they could not speak freely or openly about sex.

Put Your Child at Ease

Don't worry if occasionally you make mistakes in the way you answer a question. The important thing is that your youngster should feel free to come to you with his questions. If he has gained this confidence, there will be many opportunities for you to make up for past mistakes.

The preschool child is also usually curious about the differences between boys and girls.

He often wonders if girls can become boys and vice versa. He should be told that sexually all boys are built alike and all girls alike. He should learn that the differences between the bodies of a male and a female exist because the sex organs serve different functions. Very often a little girl is envious of little boys because they have penises. But this envy can quickly be turned to pride when she is impressed with the fact that girls are built as they are so that they can bear babies—boys can't.

Observing Differences

A small child should have the opportunity to see other children of both sexes nude. Two important purposes are served: He will be able to observe the differences between the sexes and to see for himself that all boys are formed one way and all girls the other. Of course the opportunity to learn the difference in sexes is comparatively easy in homes where there are children of both sexes. But what can be done where there are no children of the opposite sex at home so that the opportunity to see differences is both casual and natural? A mother can invite some playmate of the opposite sex to stay overnight or to spend a weekend. Or she might take a child to see a newborn baby or an infant of the opposite sex and let the child stand by while the diaper is being changed or the baby is having a bath. Another suggestion is to enter the child in a good nursery school, for most nursery schools have toilet rooms where youngsters have the opportunity to observe one another. There is usually an adult present in the toilet room to answer questions as they arise.

Curiosity Diminishes

When children are approximately from 6 to 11 years old, boys have a tendency to go with boys, girls to go with girls, and interest in the opposite sex is at a minimum. However, although sex curiosity is considerably diminished in this period, a child will continue to ask about birth, reproduction, and growing up if he has found his parents ready and willing to answer his questions. With the child in this age period, your discussions on subjects relating to sex can be much fuller. If you find the subject difficult to handle, there are well-written and well-illustrated authoritative books and pamphlets available to be read with your child.

Girls of 8 years and older should be told about menstruation. They should be given the knowledge that menstruation is a sign of growing up and the sign of a good healthy body. Care should be taken not to present the subject in a way that might create fear. Avoid terms such as "the curse," "getting unwell," and "falling off."

If a Child Is Not Curious

Sometimes a child asks no questions about sex and reproduction. In such a situation when he reaches 7 or 8, find opportunities to open a discussion on the subject. A mother cat with her kittens or a dog with puppies, or, better still, a pregnant animal around the house can open up a discussion on babies and how they are born. A trip to a farm or to the zoo may also present such opportunities. You can also read to your child one of the excellent books on the subject, appropriate for his age level.

Where There Is Reluctance

Often a child's reluctance to ask questions about sex stems from some previous experience where a question was not answered or where the child was told or was made to feel that the subject was not a nice thing to discuss. It cannot be emphasized too strongly that your child should be made to feel free to come to you with these questions. And he should know that his questions will receive prompt, truthful, satisfying answers.

During the period of prepuberty (approximately 12 years of age) boys and girls have a tendency to keep apart. There still is, however, sex curiosity rather than sex attraction. Both boys and girls attempt to appear mature at this age by using dirty language and telling dirty stories. During this time your child needs companions of the same sex with whom to discuss and exchange his ideas on all subjects. This companionship and sharing of "secrets" tends to relieve feelings of guilt.

Gradually as the shift in interest veers toward the opposite sex, the child's close ties with companions of his own sex are resolved. He or she is beginning to enter puberty, with its new interests, desires, and urges.

A Healthy Attitude

Parents should always remember the importance of giving their children healthy attitudes toward sex. The child who grows into manhood or womanhood lacking in sex education or with incorrect knowledge will find himself seriously handicapped in sex attitudes and, later on, in marriage and also in parenthood. MILTON I. LEVINE

See also BAD WORDS; BOOKS FOR CHILDREN; BOOKS FOR PARENTS; CURIOSITY; MASTURBATION; MENSTRUATION; NUDITY; REPRODUCTION; SEX DIFFERENCES

SHAMPOO *See* HAIR CARE

SHARING

Many parents feel that it is vital that a child be able to share. Even the very young child who does not do so readily is regarded as a nuisance in the playground and, what is worse, a blot on the family escutcheon. Parents often become agitated when their child won't let others use his things, and they angrily confront the hapless youngster with alternatives, bribes, admonitions, and warnings, leaving him confused, concerned, and more resistant than ever.

The first consideration is the age of the child. Learning to share is one of the major tasks of the period when a child is 3, 4, or turning 5 years old. The 2-year-old, who has just about learned what "mine" means, is not ready to let a beloved object become "his" even temporarily. The 3-year-old is probably beginning to develop the emotions and ideas needed for comfortable sharing, but they are not likely to be reliable parts of his psychological apparatus as yet. That is why on some days he can, but on other days, cannot, accomplish social transactions with ease. To be able to share voluntarily, a child must have begun to understand group relationships. He must be able to look ahead and trust that what he now gives up will soon be returned and he must also be ready and willing for mutual exchange.

Parents who remember these things are not so upset when their very young child wants to hold onto what is his *even*—and this incongruity is hard for grownups to understand—if he is not using it. Instead of feeling that the child is selfish and that selfishness is undesirable in any form at any time, these parents know it as a perfectly natural state in the development of a healthy sense of the self. They draw consolation, and the important ability to be patient, from the ironic fact that children who are allowed to keep their own things at a stage of development when they need to do so, are the very youngsters who are most likely to be able to lend to others later on. With good conscience it then becomes possible to say to a would-be borrower, "I'm sorry, but that pail belongs to my little boy and he doesn't want anyone else to use it." Or, "I can give you some of *my* clothespins, but these are just for him." As a child grows, his experience and observations (particularly if his family is one in which possessions per se are not regarded as too important) and his feelings about himself and others will make him ready to take an active and effective part in social interchange.

By the time a child is 4 or 5 years old, he has become accustomed to having friends; he can appreciate fairness when he sees it. He is honest enough to know that sometimes he likes to use things belonging to others, and even his hazy sense of time suffices to convince him that when his mother says he will get a possession back "soon" or "later," she really does not mean "never." Unfortunately, but very naturally, the fact that he is ready and able to share does not mean that he is always glad to do so. Parents can, at this point, help.

A practical idea for the mother of a young child is to have a few duplicate toys on hand so that if a visiting child clutches her child's toy broom, for example, there is another available. The same thing is true of such inexpensive items as pails and shovels, beads, and balls. Often a related toy may be offered to the protesting child. If your child is sweeping, suggest that the visiting child use the toy carpet sweeper. A new and even better game may develop.

Another way of promoting sharing is to suggest an activity in which the cooperative use of things is involved. Perhaps your child has a new and prized doctor kit. His visitor may be fascinated by it, but she may also consent to tie on one of daddy's handkerchiefs and act as nurse. Or she may be the

The 2-year-old who has just learned what "mine" means is not ready to let a beloved object become "his," even temporarily.

mother of the doll patient whom your child "examines." Later on, it is likely that the junior M.D. will be willing to let his playmate take the temperature of, or administer play medicine to, an ailing Teddy bear. Taking turns, exchanging items, setting up play situations in which "some of his and some of yours" are used are all valid forms of sharing and sometimes allow a way around a difficult situation.

Of course, there are some situations in which a child cannot be expected to share a toy. A little girl may have a doll that is simply too precious to be given into another's hands; a boy may not be able to lend a new and wondrous dump truck; his parents have told him this truck must be used knowingly or it will break. It is appropriate to protect a child's strong feelings and sufficient to indicate that later—oh, perhaps when another doll has become favorite or the truck is no longer new—the toys will be available for use by others.

As is true of most aspects of personality, the capacity to share with others is not an isolated trait but is instead shaped by intellectual, emotional, and social experiences. If he has learned to share, you may be sure your child has also learned many good things en route. IRMA S. BLACK AND JOAN W. BLOS

See also SOCIAL DEVELOPMENT

SHEETS *See* LAYETTE AND BABY EQUIPMENT

SHOCK

Shock is a condition resulting from a blow that may be either physical or emotional. Severe injury such as a broken bone may cause shock. So may bleeding, major burns, severe pain, or infection. Fear or other strong emotions also may bring on shock.

In many injuries, such as severe burns, the patient's state of shock is more dangerous than the actual injury. It therefore often becomes more important to treat the shock than to deal with the injury, unless bleeding from a wound is contributing to shock.

Symptoms of shock are weakness or fainting; pallor; cold, clammy skin; weak, irregular, or "fluttering" pulse. Nausea and vomiting are common.

A child who has sustained shock should be put at rest. Lay him flat and keep him warm, but not excessively warm. Usually a blanket under and around the patient is enough. Only if his body is extremely cold to your touch should artificial heat, such as hot-water bottles or electric pads, be used. Be careful not to burn him. A physician should be called, not only to treat the shock, but also to treat the underlying condition.

If the child is old enough and sufficiently conscious, hot, strong coffee or hot tea may be given as a stimulant. Alcoholic beverages should not be offered unless advised by your doctor.

A child recovering from shock, whatever the cause, should be kept in bed until all symptoms or signs of weakness have disappeared or until the doctor says he may be allowed to get up. W. W. BAUER

See also FIRST AID

SHOES *See* WALKING

SHOTS

There are three kinds of shots: (1) preventive, to avoid a disease; (2) curative, to rid one of a disease; or (3) desensitizing, to decrease allergies such as hay fever and asthma. Shots are of value in many diseases.

Preventive Shots

Children today usually are given their first series of preventive shots early in life. It is customary to start the initial dose of triple antigens (the substances used to make preventive shots) against diphtheria, whooping cough, and tetanus when a child is a month and a half to 2 months old. In recent years it has become customary to give poliovaccine against infantile paralysis at the same time. The polio shot is either injected separately into another spot or it is already mixed with the other three antigens and is given as a quadruple shot.

Immunizing all at once against these three diseases and polio is most desirable. Doses are usually given at monthly intervals when a child is having his regular checkup. Combined shots are great timesavers for parents and doctors. Combined shots are also better for a young child because of the fewer times he has to experience the discomfort of a needle prick and his possible fright. Fortunately, reactions after a triple or quadruple shot are seldom worse than when each antigen is injected separately.

Reactions are usually trivial and do not last long. When fever or undue redness occurs, it is usually within the first 24 hours, and discomfort seldom lasts longer than a few days. After your child has had a shot, it is prudent to keep him quiet and out of the hot sun. Offer water repeatedly and keep covers and clothing to the minimum compatible with comfort. When you have questions, by all means phone your doctor. Even if he only repeats what he has already told you, his reassurance is comforting.

If your doctor does prescribe aspirin, be sure the supply is safely put away.

Immunity is not attained until a month after all the shots of the first series have been given. And even after the first series it is important to see that the child has his periodic booster shots.

Occasionally, a physician decides not to give the triple or quadruple shots but to immunize against each disease separately. This procedure might very well be the case with a premature baby. The prematurely born are more likely to run a somewhat higher fever or have other undesirable reactions to shots. Some doctors prefer to delay immunization until these infants are older and stronger, to give fractional doses, or to give whooping cough shots first. Occasionally, a doctor may give smaller doses of whooping cough vaccine, with a complete series of triple or quadruple antigens later on.

Curative Shots

Antibiotic drugs like penicillin not only cure but also often prevent serious complications; they are frequently lifesaving. It is often better to give these antibiotic drugs as shots rather than by mouth because a dose that is injected puts the drug into the blood stream much sooner where it can more effectively fight the disease. When given by mouth, the doses must be divided—given at from two- to eight-hour intervals, perhaps at the very time the patient is sound asleep. Also, regardless of how well the taste is disguised, children often refuse to take a second dose or they vomit the medicine.

Desensitizing Shots

Some children are allergic to one or several substances from which they cannot constantly be protected, such as dog hair or ragweed. For such a child, a doctor may recommend desensitizing shots. These shots are sterile solutions made from the offending material and injected into the child in small, increasing doses. As a result of these repeated shots the child's body is able to manufacture a protective substance that lessens the allergic reaction.

Your attitude and that of the doctor and nurse can influence the effect on the emotional child who is fearful of the shot he is to get. When an older child asks, "Will it hurt?" everyone should be truthful. You might tell a frightened toddler that it will hurt a tiny bit, but not much; that the doctor is his friend and wants to keep him well; that the child's friends have had shots. Your infant's crying can be prevented or minimized if you can be seen by him, if you can lean over his face and possibly whisper into his ear at the very moment of the prick. If this effort to comfort him fails, the next time you might try to press a hand or foot gently at the instant, then pick him up promptly before crying sets in and fondle and gently jostle him to divert his attention from the site of pain.

Whenever a child is known to be allergic, forewarn your doctor because penicillin and other drugs may cause undesirable reactions, especially when a child has eczema, hay fever, or asthma. LOUIS W. SAUER

See also IMMUNIZATION; NURSE

SHOWING OFF

Everyone knows that some degree of showing off is natural to childhood—a way to get attention and recognition. But not everyone realizes that showing off is also an attempt to cover up or control feelings of uncertainty, shyness, and overexcitement.

Normal or not, however, showing off can get out of hand and leave both you and your child emotionally exhausted. When things go too far, you may have to step in and call a stop. But you can also avoid excessive showing off by knowing what situations will overstimulate your child in this direction and by doing some advance planning. For example, if doting grandparents and aunts and uncles come for Thanksgiving dinner, and all through the day make a fuss over adorable and beautiful 3-year-old sister, 9-year-old brother is more than likely to let out a war whoop by midafternoon and show off with whatever antics he can dream up, to get a little of the spotlight himself. If he can be prepared for some of what may happen, and if he can be given very special responsibilities and opportunities, the 9-year-old may not feel quite so upstaged by his sister's feminine wiles. He could make holiday decorations or place cards for the table; he could help with some of the cooking. He could be in charge of games and entertainment for younger cousins. He might write a story to be read to the family after dinner. He might be in charge of serving canapés or after-dinner candy.

The child who shows off with other children, who seems to get "all wound up," overexcited, and silly at a birthday party, may be covering up his embarrassment at not knowing quite how to behave. Maybe he needs some assistance in thinking about what he can do that his friends will enjoy. Opportunities to practice social skills help children to become more sure of themselves, less overexcited, more able to take part in social activities without having to show off. Often, special talents and hobbies can help a child channel his natural desire for attention and recognition. A child can, for instance, feel legitimately important and successful if he is allowed to present a short original play to company on special occasions, or to invite special grown-up guests to his room to see the chemistry experiment, photography project, or stamp collection he is working with.

Unfortunately, parents sometimes encourage tendencies to show off by urging a child to perform before company when he really doesn't want to. "Say that little poem you learned," they urge and, turning to the guests, "You *must* hear this; it's so cute," or "What is the point of going to ballet class if you never want to dance when we ask you to?" There is a difference between pushing a child into performing and helping a child who wants to be "included in" find constructive ways of participating.

Showing off is usually at its height when children's feelings are the most two-sided. For instance, boys approaching puberty, still feeling unsure and uncertain, but experiencing the unmistakable stirring of interest in the opposite sex, will try to prove their manliness by wild and raucous deeds of glory, while girls will seek the attention of boys by the giddiest giggling and the most painfully naïve maneuvers. Nature takes care of this kind of showing off, for as these boys and girls mature, they become more poised, and the showing off gives way to much more subtle and sophisticated methods of communication. Yesterday's somewhat hysterical show-off becomes tomorrow's suave man of the world, and we parents, unreasonable beings that we are, will probably miss the noise and excitement.

EDA J. LE SHAN

See also EXTROVERT-INTROVERT; PUBERTY

SHYNESS AND TIMIDITY

Shyness and timidity are usually not noticed in the first two or three years of life. A toddler is usually shy until he has had a little experience with people beyond his immediate family, but he overcomes this shyness easily when he discovers friendliness around him. An unfortunate encounter may give him a setback until he finds out that not all people are unfriendly. He then begins to be discriminating.

Shyness shows up more clearly when a child joins a play group or goes to school. Then parents begin to get anxious that their little one is not going to get along well with his fellows. Often he is shy merely because he has been an only child and simply does not know yet how to act; the social world is new. This kind of shyness, however, is seen less often today than in the past. Children go to nursery school, parents in a neighborhood combine to care for the children in groups, television brings a secondhand knowledge of the world. Normally, even an only child becomes a member of the child community, whatever it may be, at an early age.

When timidity and shyness do not gradually disappear, look for anxiety and discouragement. When unfortunate experiences have made a child afraid of what may happen, or when he is constantly scolded for what he does, or when he is spurred on beyond his capacities, he is likely to withdraw into himself. To avoid fear and discouragement, he tries not to get into situations that may turn out to be unpleasant.

If a child has been in an automobile accident, he may try to avoid going out in the car. If he has overheard his parents saying he will never be good at sports, he may feel so humiliated that he will retire from all competitive games.

The opposite may happen too: In a child's eagerness to please, he will deny his fear and make a show of bravery. Just why one child responds with shyness and another with bravado depends on many circumstances. Behavior is rarely explained by one incident. Bravado is one method of trying to overcome anxiety. People often try to hide their timidity by aggressively trying everything and boasting of their prowess when at heart they are frightened.

To force a child to repeat a frightening experience may easily make him more frightened than ever. It is an outmoded notion that repetition of fright will clear up the trouble. We try to heal a bruised arm by resting it; we do not bruise it again. Emotional wounds need rest, too.

A common belief is that if a shy boy tries harder, he will become a manly one, and parents are often tempted to put the heat on. But there is a danger. To pretend bravery when one is quaking inside requires great psychic energy, maybe more than the timid child can muster up. It is not fair to the child to press him.

A child who has made a good showing for a long time may suddenly change in behavior or he may become physically ill under too much pressure. The body responds as well as the mind.

To force a timid child to be aggressive is beginning at the wrong end of the trouble. It is far better for parents to ask themselves, "Why is this child timid?" and "What can we do to remove or lessen the cause?" Kindly encouragement and reassurance will go a long way, but unless the reasons for shyness are understood, the problem remains.

When parents get disturbed about a child, it is a good idea for them to look into their own attitudes. Are they afraid their child will turn out to be like someone in their own families who remained a passive weakling all his life? Are they objecting to a weakness in their child which they themselves have or a trait of their own which they do not admire? What do they want their child to become? Parents are likely to see their child as an extension of themselves. Often, a child is expected to achieve what his parents did not. But their child may be quite different from his parents in temperament and capacity.

It is important to recognize that not all shy children will be misfits or failures. Quiet, thoughtful, creative people are much needed in the world today.

Another common difficulty for a child is disagreement between his father and mother. The mother may try to shield her boy from the demanding ideals of the father and indulge his anxious withdrawal from sports. Or it may be the other way around, for mothers can be aggressive also in their wishes for their children. If parents differ in their standards for their child, then he is thrown into a conflict and finds it hard to know which path to follow.

Shyness is not a disease in itself to be quickly cured by a prescription of kind words. It is a symptom of anxiety that can become chronic and get ingrained into the character. As would be the case with a physical symptom, thoughtful parents get at the cause. Sometimes an expert can help parents see where the trouble lies and guide them in wiser handling. HELEN ROSS

See also ANXIETY; CHILD GUIDANCE CLINIC; COURAGE; EMOTIONAL DEVELOPMENT; STRANGERS, FEAR OF

SICK CHILD

Children dislike being sick. Illness ties them down; it keeps them from doing so many fascinating things. Little ones feel miserable; they cry, they want constant attention, and most children, when ill, revert to babyish ways. In his feeling of discomfort the child really needs once more the solace that is usually granted only to babies. Your little boy will want to curl up in your lap because it feels good to be held close to someone he loves. Your little girl will enjoy being pampered—having her hair combed and brushed, her face washed, and her body powdered.

After a brief illness, the need for extra attention and the dependent, babyish ways of behaving tend to disappear as the youngster feels better. In a long illness, an important part of convalescence will consist of helping the child come back to the stage of development expected of him at his age.

Illnesses and accidents often mean a great deal more than just danger to a child's health. They are often real annoyances to parents. Sickness often tends to occur at just the wrong time in family planning. Parents must realize that it is not mean or wrong to admit that the illness is inconvenient. But it is important not to take out feelings of annoyance on a sick child. Parents who have guilt feelings about their child's illness, combined with feelings of annoyance at the interference with vacation or party plans, often find caring for the child difficult. Admit your annoyance; be frank about it, though never resentful, and the task will be easier to accomplish.

When your child is to be confined to bed for some time, his room should be as uncluttered as possible. It should be kept clean and well lighted, making use of daylight whenever possible. (Ideally, the temperature should be between 68° and 72°F.) The room should be well ventilated. Place the child's bed near a window, if there are no drafts, in order that he may enjoy looking at what goes on in the outside world. The use of a drawsheet on his bed, such as hospitals use, will make bed-changing much easier. A draw-sheet is simply a large sheet folded in half, the long way, and tucked across the lower bed sheet, extending from the child's shoulders to below his knees. It can be changed when necessary without disturbing the lower sheet, the rubber sheeting (if used), or the mattress covering.

Medicines should be kept out of a child's reach and given according to the doctor's orders. If the child is to be in a reclining position, it is important that he be well propped from behind. Soft pillows do not give him the support he needs, but a back-rest, possibly with a pillow over it, will help make him comfortable. A small bedside table to hold a box of tissues, a book or two, a radio, a mirror, or a favorite game will put these things at the child's hand and save mother many trips to fetch and carry. A serving tray with legs that fit over the child's lap not only will make mealtimes more pleasant, but will serve also as a game or handiwork table when the small patient feels better.

A sick child usually enjoys his bath. If the illness is long, the soothing ministrations of his mother or the nurse will be a high point in his day. To avoid chilling, bathe the child, a part at a time, keeping the rest of his body covered with a large bath towel or bath blanket. Always be sure to dry his skin thoroughly. If you have time, your young patient may enjoy having his back rubbed with whatever solution your doctor suggests, possibly half alcohol and half water, to help prevent bedsores if bed confinement is to be prolonged. A little talcum powder after a back rub is soothing, too.

It is extremely important that you understand clearly all instructions given by your child's doctor. Write down the times at which medication is to be given and all instructions about diet and special treatments. Go over with the doctor the daily routine, and if you have any questions, be sure to get answers to them. Sometimes it helps to prepare a written schedule of your day. A mother who is to take care of a sick child and who has the care of her home and other children will have to plan skillfully to include time for all her duties.

It must be remembered that a sick child needs rest and quiet as part of his physical care; he needs comfortable, clean, cheerful surroundings; he needs loving care and gentle diversions. He does not need stimulating conversation, a steady parade of visitors, or constant amusement.

Never burden a child with the details of his illness. Instead, always give him the feeling that he is steadily going toward better health. "If you rest quietly, you will feel better," or "If you do as the doctor says, you will get well faster." Avoid threatening him with becoming sicker. Never blame your child for his illness even if he did go out in the rain without his raincoat and rubbers the day before he became ill.

If a child is seriously ill, perhaps has had hospital care and is now at home for a long convalescence, mother may need help in caring for him. Many communities have a community nursing service, which is available to provide home care for the sick. Your public health department may have visiting nurses who will come to your home to bathe the child, give injections, change dressings, and in many other ways help the mother who bears the major share of a sick child's care. Often the cheerful presence of a nurse helps a child get well faster and certainly eases the mother's burden. HENRY H. WORK

See also COMMON COMMUNICABLE DISEASES; CONVALESCENT CHILD; DOCTOR; HOME AND HOSPITAL INSTRUCTION; MEDICINE GIVING; NURSE; SPECIAL DIETS; STERILIZING; TEMPERATURE

SILLY TALK *See* BAD WORDS

SINGING *See* MUSIC

SINUSITIS

An inflammation of one or more sinuses is called sinusitis. The sinuses are air pockets surrounding the nose and, like the nose, are lined with mucous membranes. Tiny openings into the nose are the sinuses' only means of drainage.

Since the sinuses are connected with the nose, they often become inflamed when a child has a cold or other inflammation of the mucous membranes of the nose. If drainage of mucus from the sinuses is blocked, inflammation usually results. Presence of pus may cause a child to have severe, throbbing pain over one or both cheeks or he may have a severe headache without being able to say just where the pain is. He may be fearful and will stop playing and doing the things he usually enjoys. In chronic sinusitis the symptoms may not be so severe, but a child may have a nasal discharge, perhaps with a foul odor; he will lack energy and he may complain of frequent headaches.

A child with sinusitis should be under the care of a doctor. JULIUS B. RICHMOND

See also NOSE DROPS

SISTERS *See* BROTHERS AND SISTERS

SITTER *See* BABY-SITTER

SKILLS *See* ABILITIES; CREATING; TESTS AND MEASUREMENTS

SKIPPING GRADES *See* ACCELERATION

SLANG

The main trouble with slang is that it deprives user and listener alike of the satisfaction and efficiency of exactness in thought and speech. "Tommy stinks," "This spinach stinks," are remarks that do not specify what is wrong with either Tommy or the spinach. They are "counter-words," general terms without reference to exact meaning.

It is reassuring to realize that there are fads in words just as there are fads in fashions, and that the life-span of most novelties is brief. Often children take on the speech habits of their friends or of admired older children by way of demonstrating that they are "in." The child does not think of these habits as slang—he has simply heard a new word or phrase, finds it useful or dashing, and adopts it. He does not check each new word he acquires in the dictionary—if indeed he is old enough to use a dictionary.

When your child's slang bothers you, about the best thing you can do is to try in as many ways as possible to increase his exposure to good speech. If you find yourself careless in speech, you can try to correct your own speech. Reading aloud may enormously increase your child's awareness of the loveliness and precision of language well used; so will listening to you and to good, vigorous speakers on radio or television. Antidotes, to be effective, must, however, be offered without preachment or overemphasis.

The direct approach may sometimes be useful. "What do you really mean about Tommy?" (or the spinach) may cause a child to reflect and to state his case against either with more thoughtfulness and accuracy. If some particular word gets maddeningly monotonous (icky, stinky, kookie—for instance), you might suggest, "I know your friends say that, but I wish you'd find another word when you're talking to me."

No matter how one looks at it, however, slang is a minor problem. And it may be a sobering thought for a mother to remember that her cheery "Hi!" and "OK" were considered beyond the pale of proper usage not long ago. IRMA S. BLACK AND JOAN W. BLOS

SLAPPING

Slapping is used very commonly to control the behavior of children, yet it has grave weaknesses that ought to make us use it very sparingly. Slapping seldom builds within the child an understanding of why his behavior is not desirable. The youngster learns primarily that his specific action results in some pain and disapproval. He has little opportunity to learn the general principles that can guide his action in future and somewhat dissimilar situations. A child will also be troubled by the anger he senses within the adult. He may stop the behavior for the moment but feel less sure of his relationship with his parents. In the long run this uncertainty weakens discipline and is apt to produce a less well-behaved rather than a better-behaved child.

It is unwise to slap children who are less than a year old for any reason. Infants are so very dependent on the good will of their parents that slapping can be much too threatening. As children grow more into their own self-awareness, it again becomes increasingly hazardous to slap. Older children resent this punishment because it is such a personal affront—an attack on their own feelings of selfhood. This resentment can lead to a result exactly the opposite from the one sought.

While always unpredictable in its results, slapping is somewhat less hazardous when used very sparingly with children old enough to walk and yet not old enough to understand involved explanations. Though it is difficult to specify exact ages, such a description probably applies more to children between 12 and 24 months than to any other age range. The activity and mobility of these children can lead them into situations such as exploring the stove or stepping from a curb into the street. Then a slap on the hand and its consequent pain may be the best way of stopping the action for the moment. Such a rare slapping best accomplishes its momentary purpose if it is done at all, not as the response of an angry adult expressing frustration or fear, but as the response of a thoughtful adult attempting to teach a child an important specific lesson. JAMES L. HYMES, JR.

See also DISCIPLINE; PUNISHMENT; RESENTMENT

SLEEP

The amount of sleep your child *requires* varies with his age and the state of his health. The amount he *gets* depends on your attitude as well as on the way you handle sleeping routines and arrangements.

Young babies need more sleep than older children. There is no schedule of hours-of-sleep-needed according to age, and if there were, it might not be right for your child. Variations exist in the amount of sleep needed by different children just as they do for adults. Needs change from time to time, depending on many factors.

Your newborn needs more sleep and spends more time sleeping than he ever will again in good health. In the first few days after birth, he may sleep as much as 23 hours. His sleep, often accompanied by much restlessness, is broken up into short and long periods. He is aroused mainly by hunger and by other pain or discomfort.

After the first few days he seems to be able to spend more time awake or in semisleep as he becomes hungry, eats, and is kept awake by routines of bathing and body care. By 6 weeks to 2 months both baby and mother enjoy his waking moments; he smiles socially, coos, and responds to playful overtures. As he grows older, he has longer periods of wakefulness, but within a 24-hour period there are a number of sleep times that vary from half an hour to several hours. Gradually a pattern is formed, usually one that finds your baby sleeping from early evening into early morning, with one or two naps in the forenoon and at least one nap in the afternoon.

Before the first birthday, most healthy babies whose hunger is satisfied, are willing to sleep, without interruption for a feeding, from early evening—seven o'clock—to five or six in the morning. There are a few babies who, without signs of misery or discomfort, sleep considerably less than the average and continue to require less sleep all their lives. The sleep pattern each child adopts may be constitutional with him. If your child seems healthy, happy, and rested, he is probably getting enough sleep.

Your preschool child sleeps fewer hours in 24 than does an infant because his body requires less sleep. Training and learning experiences help him to stay awake much longer. In fact, his life may become so interesting that he is stimulated to the point where both the amount and the quality of his sleep suffer. When he is overtired, he may resist going to bed and may have difficulty going to sleep and sleeping peacefully.

Your school-age child should be able to sleep soundly soon after going to bed. Both homework and the family pattern of living influence his bedtime. Some children feel tired enough to go to bed as early as 8:30 P.M. The school-age child's sleep may cover eight to nine hours. As he grows into the junior high period, homework and extra curricular activities force him to stay up later. Then he may sleep later the next morning.

Some parents take their children's sleep very seriously. "Early to bed" is a household rule and may result in their children getting more sleep than they actually require. There is no magic number of hours, such as 8 or 10, which can be said to be the sleep allotment for all children of a given age, although 8 to 10 hours is ordinarily considered necessary for the good health of school children. Children, like adults, can become accustomed over a period of time to less and less sleep without showing signs of fatigue. On the other hand, children, like adults, can be trained to sleep more. If your child has been ill, for example, he may need more sleep, at least until he has regained his former good health. Sometimes children use sleep, often unconsciously, as a means of escape from situations that are distasteful to them: Dread of school, fear of failure, fear of neighborhood bullies can cause a child to resist getting up in the morning.

Environment

Proper sleeping arrangements can help a child to fall asleep and sleep peacefully. Your infant requires a crib to confine him and to keep him from falling out of bed. A smooth, moderately hard, flat mattress, without pillows, is favored for the first three years of his life. Pillows and bedcovers present hazards in the crib of a baby, who may cruise around and get so tangled up that he has trouble breathing. And if the crib is free of too many bedclothes, you can more easily recognize distress signals.

A young baby or toddler cannot be expected to lie under bedcovers for long periods of time. Keep him warm and snug in sleepers or a sleeping bag of weights appropriate to the temperature. Even preschoolers continue to appreciate one-piece pajamas with feet in them for winter wear. Too much clothing and cover is almost as bad as too little, for an overheated child will surely be restless. In warm weather, your baby requires nothing more than a diaper and a lightweight shirt.

Contrary to popular belief, it isn't necessary, or even desirable, to open your child's bedroom windows wide in the wintertime. Sleeping rooms ventilated through open doors are better than those made cold and drafty by outside air currents.

Your baby will easily become accustomed to falling asleep in the midst of normal activity, either indoors or out, but he should, of course, be protected from harsh and unnecessary sounds. If sleeping outdoors, he should be protected from insects, dust and smoke, and people who might disturb him. Although sunshine and fresh air are required for human growth and health, in infancy they are not necessarily provided in a more wholesome fashion outdoors than in the house. Sunbaths before an open window on days when the temperature is comfortable are fine, but when it's cold or windy, babies should be kept out of direct contact with air currents coming through open windows.

The toddler and school-age child may be able—may even prefer—to sleep in semi-darkness, but darkness should not be forced on the child who is afraid. Some children have trouble falling asleep in the daytime after daylight saving goes into effect, but as a rule they adjust in a week or two.

Sleep in Parents' Bedroom

There is general agreement that an infant, from the newborn on, should not share his parents' room. If for some reason it is necessary for you to keep your baby in your room at night, plan to discontinue the arrangement as soon as possible before he becomes so used to being near you that he cannot be weaned without a struggle. An early morning romp in his parents' bed is a joyous occasion for any child, but it is never wise to take a child into your bed for the sake of providing a sense of security. For a short time, such togetherness brings mutual comfort, but few children are willing to return to their own beds when the moment of fear has passed. In fact, a struggle is likely to develop which the child may win by raising such a fuss that he is permitted to stay—clear admission on his parents' part that his fears are justified. Even in times of physical illness or periods of special fearfulness, it is far better for you to encourage and comfort your child in his own bed, in his own bedroom.

Movement and Posture

Babies and older children move frequently in their sleep. Healthy young babies make trembling and sucking movements with their lips; their eyelids flutter; their hands and feet twitch. They whimper as if talking in their dreams. Their breathing is normally fast and irregular.

Not only do the infant and toddler sleep restlessly at night, cruising from one part of the crib to another, but they assume postures that seem most uncomfortable. Neck turned sharply to one side, arms and legs bent acutely on chest and abdomen, legs extended beyond cribside—these postures are usual, normal, and healthy for most infants and young children, as are the knee-chest position or lying face downward with mouth and nose to one side. These face-down positions are safe if there are no pillows or loose bedclothes around to interfere with breathing; such postures even help drain secretions from the nose and throat of the child who is suffering from a cold.

Dreaming

When your young child's sleep is restless and he talks and cries out, you can be sure he is dreaming. If he is going through toilet training or starting nursery school, his dreams may be frightening and he will seek comfort from you. He may want you to come to his bedside for cuddling or rocking. He may settle for a few reassuring words and a drink of water, or he may demand that a light be left on close to his bedroom for the rest of the night. The contents of his dreams often seem irrational. For example, he may find animals friendly and acceptable during the day, but fierce and frightening in the night. His dreams may be accompanied by bed-wetting or soiling.

As a rule the preschool child is not able to remember his dreams, whereas his school-age brother may not only remember, but also be willing to discuss the nighttime activity with you, complete with details of the frightful episodes he experienced. Many times, these dreams are carry-overs from things witnessed or participated in the day before—television and radio programs, fights at school, or other disturbing adventures. Let him talk out his dreams, particularly those that are upsetting. Not only will such unburdening do much to prevent recurrence, but even more importantly, clues concerning the worry and tension spots in his life may be revealed.

Rituals and Routines

Everybody goes through some kind of ritual in preparing to go to sleep. It may be elaborate, or it may be the simple ritual of undressing, taking a bath, brushing teeth, and getting into a comfortable sleeping garment at a certain time each night. The small child who has become accustomed to a certain routine will continue to demand it. He may want you to read a story out loud, or he may get a favorite doll ready for bed, kiss everybody good night, recite his prayers, and wait for you to tuck him in, in a special way. Young children not only accept routine readily, they crave it. It gives them a sense of security and makes them happier than a series of irregular and unpredictable performances. Routine need not be rigid or punishing or threatening, and certainly there should be no implication that going to bed is unpleasant. Going to bed can become a game in which your child enjoys an opportunity to learn new skills—to undress himself, arrange his clothes, and take a bath. Whatever routine is adopted should not be too long, too exciting, or too complex. If your child is uncooperative at times, it may be that he has had too long a nap in the afternoon. In this case, if you postpone bedtime somewhat—but not indefinitely—or change or prolong the routine, you offer him a practical flexibility that fits better into his readiness for sleep. Some children regularly fight going to bed. They demand a drink, to go to the toilet, another story, and then another drink. Anger is useless. If you are able to limit the ritual, yet keep a healthy flexibility, you will find that your child responds to limitations set and a consistent attitude: He will do less arguing and will be more willing to part with you and go to sleep.

Prayers at bedtime are traditional in many families. Saying his prayers can bring reassurance to a child when he separates from his parents and enters that unknown land of Nod. Most toddlers go to bed with a toy, a favorite blanket, or some object that represents security to them. To other children, thumb-sucking offers bedtime security. Sometimes parents, feeling that their child is now a "big boy" or a "big girl," attempt to stop these bedtime habits. There really is no need to worry, because a child, after about the age of 4, is able to assume increasing responsibility for putting himself to bed; he relies less and less on rituals and routines with his parents. MILTON J. E. SENN

See also ANXIETY; FEAR; NAPS; NIGHTMARES; REST; WAKEFULNESS

SLEEPING SICKNESS

Encephalitis, commonly known as sleeping sickness, is a disorder in which inflammation of the brain causes the child to sleep almost constantly. Other symptoms involving the nervous system may be present, such as paralyses, convulsions, and tremors. Sleeping sickness is caused by a virus often transmitted by mosquitoes or other insects. Or it may accompany such infections as measles or influenza. Preventive measures include vaccination for measles and influenza and insect abatement programs.

Care of a child with this disorder is extremely difficult, especially when he is in a period of sleep. He must then be fed artificially, usually through a tube passed through the nose or mouth into the stomach. At present there is no known treatment for sleeping sickness, although in some instances the patient gradually does develop consciousness and recovers. JULIUS B. RICHMOND

See also SICK CHILD; VIRUS

SLOPPINESS

When we look at a very young child covered with dirt, and with his clothes in disarray, we see an engaging tot in need of a bath and clean clothing. But when we see a school-age child in similar condition, we are very likely to dub him "sloppy." There are children, some say boys especially, who just can't seem to keep shirts or blouses tucked in, shoelaces tied, and socks pulled up.

Then there are the fads that catch a school child's fancy. Both boys and girls may wear long, loosely woven sweaters or sweat shirts pulled down over their hips. For years girls have worn their father's or brother's shirts, sleeves rolled up, shirttails out. Whether children adopt these fad fashions because they are comfortable or in defiance of adult restrictions imposed on them as to what is right and wrong, is debatable. But the fact that "everybody does it, mother," is a pretty stiff argument in the child's favor.

Time, however, is always on the parent's side. The little girl who wants to wear boys' blue jeans and doesn't care whether her pigtails are ever brushed out and replaited, and the boy whose face is always dirty, whose hair is a mess, and whose clothes look as if he has slept in them, eventually make an abrupt about-face. They are likely to be as fastidious when they get to sixth or seventh grade as they were sloppy in the early grades.

Many times, parents are too strict about neatness as it applies both to appearance and to housekeeping. Children will rebel against constant commands, demands, rules and regulations. In their rebellion they will take up the same fads and fancies of those children whose parents take a more lenient attitude toward occasional lapses.

SLOW LEARNER

Slow learners are found in nearly every classroom. Yet many people, among them both parents and teachers, have mistaken ideas about what a slow-learning child is, what he is not, what causes him to be mentally slower than the average child, and what can be done to help him achieve his potential.

What Is a Slow Learner?

A slow learner is a child who scholastically lags behind children of his same age. He is definitely not in the mentally retarded category, but at times his intellect may be below average. In some instances, his intellect is above average, but he shows a delayed start in reading and in other school achievements. Often he is capable of doing better work than he does. Certain environmental factors, including emotional problems and cultural deprivation, may be blocking his learning.

A slow learner can be normal in emotional, social, physical, or motor development. On the other hand, he may also be characterized by lateness in walking or talking, short attention span, limited imagination, slow reaction time, weak memory, shyness, dependence, low tolerance for change in situations and people, impulsive behavior, lack of self-confidence, fearfulness, confusion, inability to foresee the consequences of his acts, and poor physical development and health. One or more of these traits in a child, of course, do not mark him as a slower learner. If a large number of the traits are present, however, they are signposts for parents pointing to a child's need for special help.

If a child's IQ (intelligence quotient) score is below normal, it is well to remember certain things.

IQ tests have limitations and are certainly not infallible. The tests cannot measure intelligence directly. They measure ability to perform tasks that are believed to require intelligence. The validity of the tests depends on several factors, including the type of test itself, the testing personnel, the child's interest and self-reliance, and to a great extent the cultural quality of his home background.

Contrary to popular belief, a child's IQ is not determined at birth and fixed for life. This idea was formerly popular, but educators now know that the IQ can and does often change as a child grows older. Often it rises—more drastically in boys than in girls.

It is important, however, to realize that many slow learners have a below-average intellectual ability that can never be changed. On the other hand, some children acquire a tendency to learn more slowly than their ability would predict. Some causes for this type of slow learning are:

- Low socioeconomic homes
- Lack of cultural opportunities
- Physical handicaps
- Poor health
- Language differences
- Family emotional problems
- Absence of motivation

In some cases, if the cause of slow learning is found and modified, the child can reach a higher achievement, perhaps even up to the normal range.

Whether the slow learner can be helped depends largely on the causes and the length of time his problem has existed. Another complication is that there is never one environmental cause for slow learning; there is a combination of reasons which work together to retard the child.

Accept Him as He Is

The best way to treat the academically slow child—whether his capacity be permanent or changeable—is to accept him as a human being, who, like all human beings, has his own unique potential. Encouraging him to live up to *his* potential, not to that of others, is the important goal. Essentially, he has the same needs as other children. He must have a sense of accomplishment in order to maintain his self-respect. Putting together a simple puzzle can be as sweet an accomplishment to him as controlling a tricky gas is to a young Einstein.

Parents who set realistic goals for a slow learner will praise him for his achievements because they are *his*, although they are considerably less than those expected of other children. It is undoubtedly even more important to express pride in the slow learner than in the fast one, for the child left behind in the classroom may feel an insecurity that unless combated can severely damage his self-esteem.

A slow-to-learn child demands much patience from adults because he is a doer rather than a thinker. He is a child of habit, not of reason. He must be *shown* what to do, not told what to do. Sometimes he needs to do things over and over before he becomes efficient. A parent can help him practice until he meets with success. Early successes in his life are crucial, for they give him motivation to try more difficult tasks.

Many children who have trouble with schoolwork also have trouble organizing their lives. They can't seem to get up at a certain time, dress in time for breakfast, or get to class or meetings on time. A child must meet these important obligations if he is to live with others satisfactorily. He should learn to assume responsibility for his own acts. Giving him an alarm clock that he can set to get up and then reset for breakfast may remind him. If despite assistance he still doesn't arrive at places on time, he should pay the consequences. He can be late for school. He can miss the bus headed for a class outing. He may be miserable, but he will learn lessons that no amount of talking would teach him.

One mistake parents often make is to protect their child from the "harsh world." They may do everything for him, watch over him constantly, give him undeserved praise. Such treatment is as detrimental as neglect is to the slow learner's development. Overprotective parents make him unnecessarily dependent and may degrade the ability he does possess. A parent should try to realize that a child who thinks slowly *can* think, and one whose sensitivity is slowly aroused still *can* have it aroused.

A family's acceptance of a slow-learning child is essential for his adjustment. Threats to that adjustment are bright brothers and sisters who look down on him, parents who deny or ignore his limited intellect, insist on high vocational aims, or disguise their rejection of him by being overly protective.

It is often difficult for parents to believe the slowly emerging truth that their cherished first-born not only won't be a doctor but he may not even finish high school. But parents must honestly try to submerge their feelings, for the child can sense his parents' disappointment. It may cause him to become emotionally disturbed, to do even poorer work in school than he is capable of, and to resort to excessive daydreaming, withdrawal, temper tantrums, or other antisocial behavior. Parents who accept their child's limitations from the very first by giving him toys and books geared to his intellectual level set the pace for his adjustment at school.

Cooperation with School Essential

Parents and schools should cooperate in establishing the appropriate place for the slow learner in the classroom. Usually, he is in rooms with normal children his own age. Sometimes he is put exclusively with other slow-learning pupils. Some children actually are more comfortable and perform better in slower groups. Others do better in some subjects when they are seated with faster learning classmates.

Schools every year are intensifying efforts to educate the slow learner. They know his problems—that he may feel insecure; his self-respect may be in jeopardy because of his competition with brighter children, and his scholastic achievement may be only a small part of his life.

Through experimentation, schools are trying to solve problems relating to the slow learner. Parents who want these problems solved and who give intelligent, quiet backing to the school's efforts are of monumental assistance. WILLARD ABRAHAM

See also ACCEPTANCE; APPROVAL; HOME-SCHOOL RELATIONS; OVERPROTECTION; TESTS AND MEASUREMENTS

SMALLPOX

Everyone is susceptible to smallpox (variola). But in countries where the use of vaccination against smallpox is almost universal, the disease is extremely rare. In such countries immediate and thoroughgoing isolation of those few who do contract smallpox also helps prevent spread of the disease.

A parent should not rely on a child's one vaccination but should have him revaccinated (with a successful "take") every five years.

Smallpox is spread by a virus, through direct contact with the coughing or sneezing of the smallpox patient, or the pus from his sores, or by contact with articles he has used.

Smallpox generally starts suddenly as a severe chill, and with fever, vomiting, or convulsions. There may also be severe pains in head and back. Red spots appear a few days later, first on the face and arms, then on the lower areas of the body. Later, these spots change to blisters filled with pus.

A patient with smallpox should, of course, have the best possible medical care. And because he is contagious until all sign of his scabs has disappeared, he should be rigidly isolated. MARIE A. HINRICHS

See also COMMON COMMUNICABLE DISEASES; SICK CHILD; VIRUS

SMOKING

By the time they are 9 or 10 years old, many children have tried puffing on a cigarette, although serious smoking does not usually set in until the early teens. It is thought by some that children of nonsmoking parents are less likely to smoke than are children of parents who smoke. Girls, particularly, are influenced by their mothers' role.

Smoking as a habit springs from the very normal need of the young to conform to the social behavior of the group. If everyone else in the crowd smokes, the pressure to conform is almost unbearable for some children. Stern parental disapproval often drives these children to smoke in secret, thus adding a sense of guilt to their feelings of inadequacy and rebellion.

How can parents who do not want their children to smoke—at least until they have achieved maximum growth—help them?

One thing can be said with certainty: Threats are useless and bribes are worse. Much depends on the quality of understanding and love that exists in the family unit. If the attitude of the parents has been one of trust and confidence that the child, as a self-respecting individual, will live up to his own estimate of himself, chances are good that he has achieved enough sturdy independence to resist group influence when it conflicts with his own ideas. Moreover, the lines of communication are open. Talking things over is a cherished family tradition.

In an atmosphere of mutual trust and affection, the whole problem of smoking can be examined: what tobacco does to the body, especially to that of a would-be athlete; smoking and scholastic achievement; smoking and femininity; smoking and cancer; how much smoking costs. These are practical considerations that have nothing at all to do with touchy areas like "right and wrong," or freedom of individual choice, or even old-fashioned versus modern.

See also FAMILY DISCUSSIONS

SMOTHERING

Smothering is medically known as asphyxia. It is also called suffocation and asphyxiation. It consists of depriving the tissues of necessary oxygen. And it may result very quickly in unconsciousness or even death.

One way smothering comes about is by the actual cutting off of air, as may happen in a variety of situations: when a child remains underwater and drowns, when he is accidentally locked in an old refrigerator or trunk, when he is lost in a cave or an excavation, or when he is buried under a landslide or in the collapse of a pit or trench.

An infant can be smothered by blankets or pillows (or by thin plastic, which of course should *never* be used as a protective covering about his crib or as a toy). Children have been strangled by poorly designed harnesses intended to keep them in chairs or automobile seats and, on rare occasions, by devices intended to keep them covered in cold weather. But the supposedly common disaster of infants being accidentally smothered by adults with whom they are sleeping is not common, and many infant deaths once attributed to smothering have been found due to an insidious type of virus pneumonia.

Another way smothering may come about is by a deficiency of oxygen in the air. Such smothering may occur when open-flame heating units, such as coal stoves, oil stoves, or gas stoves, are operated in close, unventilated spaces, as in trailers or small cottages. All open-flame heaters should be properly vented to the open air. And air-conditioning systems should have frequent safety inspections.

When a child is apparently asphyxiated, the first thing to do is to give him air. The mouth-to-mouth method of getting air back into the lungs is preferred. Every family should be equipped with the proper size of mouth-to-mouth resuscitation tube. Then send for a doctor immediately and keep the child warm and absolutely quiet. W. W. BAUER

See also ACCIDENT PREVENTION; ARTIFICIAL RESPIRATION

SNACKS *See* EATING BETWEEN MEALS

SNAKEBITE *See* BITES, ANIMAL

SNEEZING

Most small babies sneeze occasionally without having a cold. A baby cannot clean his nose of dirt, lint, or mucus in any other way than by sneezing (nor should his mother try to do so with a swab), and so he will be apt to sneeze whenever a particle of foreign material is lodged in his nose. Usually, a mother can tell whether or not her baby is getting a cold because there will be more mucus discharge than just the drop or two accompanying the sneeze. Also, a baby with a cold is more apt to be irritable, to have more trouble eating, and to show other signs of illness.

Lint is a frequent irritant in a baby's nose, but if you wash new blankets and baby clothes before using them, you can make them lint-free. RUTH S. KEMPE

SNUGGLING *See* CUDDLING

SOCIAL DEVELOPMENT

Social development starts with an infant's interest in himself and proceeds to reach outward to all those around him. A very young child is not even aware that others exist. When he begins to recognize their existence, he sees them only as extensions of himself. From this recognition to real interest in others as separate individuals is a long journey.

The stations on this journey can be summarized very briefly. Social development begins with a baby's first social response to those who take care of him. At about 5 months he begins to smile at friendly faces. He also begins to make sounds if someone talks to him and to try to touch and grasp people. He pokes his fingers into eyes and mouths, twists noses, and yanks at hair. These are all friendly social approaches.

Between 5 and 8 months most babies begin to distinguish strange from familiar faces. At this time, many babies shrink from strangers; some babies may even cry at the approach of people they have seen often before. A child's rate of development and experience with people are factors in the length of time this behavior may continue. Babies from small families with limited contacts may show more fear for a longer time than babies from large families. Some infants never seem to go through this fear-of-strangers phase. In any case, this kind of fear is temporary, but while it is in process is not the best time to begin leaving the baby with strange sitters.

Between 6 and 10 months parents will notice several other changes in their child.

More elaborate social interplay with adults and older brothers and sisters emerges. He waves bye-bye, plays peek-a-boo, nuzzles, and bumps heads. These games become tricks by which he can get attention. A baby also begins to notice other children his age and may explore them by poking at their eyes or trying to bite them. He is not much interested in them as persons, however. If they get in his way, he shoves them blithely aside. Playthings are still more interesting than playmates.

When a child is about 2 years old, he begins to notice other little children, but he is not yet ready to play with them. It is usual in a group of 2-year-olds for each child to play with his toys in his own way in the presence of the others. He may briefly do what another does, but the concept of cooperation is still beyond him. This period of parallel play is, however, extremely important as a preparation for real social exchange later. When a child begins to show preferences for individuals and to develop brief friendships, short visits with another child are in order.

At 3 and 4 years of age parents can expect strong but temporary attachments to other children. Give-and-take develops, and a child can begin to cooperate with others, to learn social techniques, and to become part of a group. Instead of strike and grab, a child can now learn to wait for his turn, offer something in exchange for a toy he wants, use words instead of fists.

By the age of 4, small, exclusive cliques may begin to develop, and a new child may have a hard time breaking into these social knots. Now is the time for finding ways for the newcomer to fill some need of the group.

From about 5 or 6 years, boys and girls tend to play in separate groups. Intense attachments of the "sweetheart" variety may, however, continue between individuals. Although some girls may continue as tomboys right through the school years, most girls congregate in all-female cliques, occupied with skating, jumping rope, jacks, collections of various sorts, and table games. Boys move further and further into the world of popular sports—baseball, basketball, football—and thus further away from the company of girls.

At about 10 or 11 years, as children near adolescence, they seem to create a society of their own, pointedly keeping adults out, much to the hurt bewilderment of many a parent. At this stage of their development, children need places where they can have meetings without interference or interruption. A "club room" tactfully provided in the home, with plenty of cookies, milk, and soft drinks available, will help to guarantee the social success of a child at this period. Both boys and girls need a chance at group privacy, where "secret" rituals can be carried out and group projects planned. Girls tend to maintain their ties with adults more than boys do at this time, but both boys and girls need freedom from adult "snoopiness."

The basic ingredients for a satisfying social life are spontaneity, self-confidence, good physical skills, some sensitivity to others, and a dash of generosity. The ability to stand up for oneself is also important. To be socially successful, children have to be able to defend themselves and to insist on their rights. Children who cannot defend themselves often are the victims of teasing and bullying. Shyness, fearfulness, and lack of self-confidence, which frequently result in rejection by a group, may indicate that expert help is needed. Your child's teacher or doctor should be able to recommend the local agency or organization that will prove the most helpful to the child unable to deal successfully with personality problems that threaten his social adjustment.

The child who feels comfortable and accepted at home moves toward other children with confidence and spontaneity. But most children differ in the number of friends they need. One friend at a time seems sufficient for some; other children like to move in swarms. Parents and teachers must consider a child's individual needs in order to decide whether his social development is proceeding smoothly. RUTH E. HARTLEY

See also ADJUSTMENT; EMOTIONAL DEVELOPMENT; INFERIORITY COMPLEX

SOCIAL PRESSURES

From kindergarten through college a child today advances from group to group, and at each stage he is under pressure to adapt to some undefinable ideal of American manhood or womanhood. His adjustment to the group is taken as a measure of his mental health. His popularity and the number of friends he has are examined as clues to his future. He is conscientiously prodded to conform to the manners and customs of groups of children his own age.

The child's parent may feel too subdued by this pressure, by the real tyranny that the youngster's age group exerts, to object. ("I don't agree, but I don't want my child to feel different.")

As early as age 7 or 8 the child himself not only is familiar with the efforts to make him part of a group, but also is aware of the problems that come with having his time overscheduled. A child of school age may within one week go to Cub Scouts, Little League, a music lesson, a dancing class, Sunday school, and a birthday party. It is not unusual for a child of 10 to have all his after-school hours planned for him. Nor is it unusual for him to react like a harassed and overworked businessman and to feel guilty when he gets an hour alone—to ask sadly on Sunday afternoons, "What's there to do?"

The world of these striving, frantically busy children becomes a burlesque of the adult world. Watching them, adults can see some of the things that are wrong with their own world, just as they can see themselves when their very young children play dress-up, when their little girls parade like mother before a mirror, and when their little boys imitate father's sternness and infallibility. The speeded-up pace of the child's life, his uneasiness over solitude, his clinging to the standards set for his group, his very early dating, and his great need to be popular become for the adult a mirror of adult strivings.

Is the number of groups one belongs to, an adult asks himself, a guide to what one is worth as an individual? Is conformity—the degree to which one individual is like the group—the measure of good emotional health? Does conformity help a child to develop intellectually? Is the enjoyment of solitude a sign that a child doesn't know how to get along with people? Is popularity a sign of "good adjustment"? Is a boy more or less masculine or a girl more or less feminine because he or she receives much or little attention from the opposite sex?

The child whose opinion of himself depends mostly on the changeable ideas of children his own age cannot get a very firm picture of what he is really like. Nor can he discover what he himself believes and stands for if he never has time alone to question what other people believe in and stand for. He has to accept blindly, without question. It is true that every child must learn to conform somewhat to society as a whole, but if there is too much demand that he conform, he and others like him are in danger of losing individuality. And individuality has been rightly cherished for generations in America because criticism, opposition, and originality are basic in developing leaders and intelligent citizens.

Adjustment to the group is not in itself a measure of mental health. If "adjustment" means that a child is a reasonable and acceptable member of his age group, that he is able to establish real friendships among the children he knows, then this fitting in with the group can be taken as one of the signs that he is developing well. But if adjustment means passive compliance with the standards and opinions of peers, we may question the mental health values of such an "adjustment." There are times when opposition to group opinion is necessary, when a child has to take the risk that other children will disapprove of him for some of his personal opinions. If a child can stand up for what he personally believes in, even though other children may not agree, he may be showing more strength than if he were completely "adjusted."

Should a child's popularity be a measure of his mental health? Not necessarily. In the best of cases a child's popularity may mean that he is an attractive person, that he makes others feel comfortable, exhilarated, and happy. Although these are splendid qualities, they again cannot be taken alone to mean that he is developing in the best possible way. Sometimes a child's driving need for popularity merely means that he is afraid no one really loves him, that he isn't worth being loved, and if this is the case, he has to keep testing to quiet his doubts. Sometimes, too, a very popular child is one who avoids close friendships and prefers instead surface friendships with dozens of youngsters.

Is too much importance given to cultivating charm, poise, sex appeal, "a good line," and other ways of winning over people, and does this importance make children believe that feelings between people are matters of mechanical control? Lasting human relationships must grow out of the ability to love. The child who has one or two close friends and has kept them a long time has perhaps shown more capacity for friendship than his much admired schoolmate who is constantly adding new friends to his circle.

Boys and girls in their early teens are not helped in their attempts to get along with one another if they are forced to feel that wide popularity is a proof of masculinity or femininity. What they need instead is some assurance from their elders that a masculine man and a feminine woman have many qualities that actually have little to do with dazzle.

And if parents feel that they cannot in good conscience let their child be a slave to the standards of other children, that extreme conformity is stifling, and that children need education in the true meaning of relationships with others—what can they do? They can disagree with what most people say and then tell their child what they themselves believe, of course.

"But won't he feel different? Is it good for him to feel so different from others?"

Perhaps parents have worried too much about the problem of being different. The little girl of 11 or 12 who is not permitted to use lipstick ("But all the other girls in my class do!") will undoubtedly feel different, but it is not likely that the difference will hurt her in any lasting way. And it may be a positive help for her in those turbulent years of puberty to feel the strength of her parents' authority. The 14-year-old boy who prefers his basement laboratory to escorting a 13-year-old girl to a dance may be considered "different," but if he feels the support of parents who allow him to be himself, the basement lab may fulfill more of the 14-year-old's needs than a social life for which he is not yet ready. The 12-year-old girl whose parents do not permit her to have dates may feel set apart from girls who are allowed dates. She may also be secretly relieved to have her parents make this decision for her, for if she is like most normal 12-year-old girls, she has already discovered that she is not yet ready for courtship. SELMA FRAIBERG

See also MENTAL HEALTH

SOCIAL WELFARE AGENCIES

The term Social Welfare Agency applies to numerous organizations whose primary purpose is to help and guide individuals and families with problems that cannot be solved within the family itself or with the help of the family physician, minister, or trusted friend. Individual and family problems having to do with marital adjustment, budgeting, chronic illness, housing, job finding, and medical care are among those most often brought to social welfare agencies. These agencies also help groups toward improvement of a community, and tend to raise standards and improve living conditions in an area. For example, recreational and educational facilities for children and adults are studied and improved. Also, a social welfare agency, working with a lay group, may aid a community center in a fight against juvenile delinquency.

Some people feel that to go to a social welfare agency is asking for charity. Others have the notion that this kind of agency exists to help only emotionally disturbed children and adults. Neither attitude is correct. An individual or a group able to pay for the service may contribute to the agency, but those unable to pay are given identical attention.

Practical human improvement is the goal of social welfare agencies. They help both individuals and groups.

See also COMMUNITY RESOURCES

SOFT SPOTS

At birth, a baby's skull may have as many as six soft spots, or fontanels. Generally, only two can be felt. These are simply areas in the baby's skull where the bones have not yet developed. In place of bone, the fontanels are covered by a very tough membrane. Gradually through the months these soft spots disappear as the skull bones grow and harden. The largest soft spot is shaped like a diamond, about 1 to 1½ inches on a side, and is just in front of the top of the skull. The fontanels vary in size in different babies but usually are hard to find by the time the baby is a year old.

Although it may seem as though the brain is unprotected in these softer areas, the tough membrane is actually very strong and gives adequate protection. Mild shampoos and ordinary handling of the head and scalp will do no harm at all. RUTH S. KEMPE

See also BABY

SOLIDS *See* INTRODUCING NEW FOODS

SORE THROAT

A common ailment of children, sore throat varies from mild soreness to severe pain, with inability to swallow. A doctor should be called if the child has fever or if his throat is more than mildly sore. Sore throat is also a symptom of streptococcic infection of the throat, "strep throat," which usually responds rapidly to penicillin.

Since rheumatic fever sometimes follows streptococcic infection, it is important that strep throat be treated promptly. The doctor by examining the child's throat can decide whether or not to use antibiotics in treatment. Gargling or other types of local treatment of the throat are generally not recommended by doctors for children. JULIUS B. RICHMOND

See also COMMON COMMUNICABLE DISEASES; RHEUMATIC FEVER; VIRUS

SPANKING

Spanking is one of the most common forms of punishment experienced by young children. As youngsters move into the school years, and certainly as they become adolescent, spankings usually cease and other forms of punishment are increasingly relied on, usually the deprivation of some pleasure. Unfortunately, spankings hold more danger for the very young child, on whom they are commonly used, than they would for the older child, on whom they are seldom applied. The young child is uniquely dependent on the love of his parents. This fact, plus the difference in size between the parent and the young child, can give a youngster an exaggerated and frightening impression of the significance of the spanking. It is especially unwise to spank children under 3 years old, and only slightly less hazardous in the 3-to-6 age range. During this whole age-span, some other technique for teaching good behavior and discipline probably will produce better results in the long run, with fewer risks involved.

It is sometimes said that one should not spank in anger and that there are virtues in a cooling-off period. If a spanking is to be used at all, probably it ought to be administered right at the time of the infraction rather than postponed. The fact that the parent is angry at the moment is not so important a consideration as the advantage in having the child learn that his behavior was not good behavior at the very moment when he has done something wrong. There are, however, no special techniques for administering good or bad spankings. The important question is not one of technique or timing. It is whether or not a spanking of any kind is the most effective way of teaching the lesson that must be learned. Just as spanking is only one form of punishment, so punishment is only one means of teaching good discipline. The real skill of the "teacher" lies in choosing the method best geared to producing the good behavior that is desired. JAMES L. HYMES, JR.

See also DISCIPLINE; PUNISHMENT

SPASM *See* SAINT VITUS'S DANCE; TIC

SPASTIC PARALYSIS *See* CEREBRAL PALSY

SPECIAL DIETS

Rely only on a doctor to prescribe a special diet for your child. It's sad enough for an adult to adopt the bizarre menu of the food faddist, but it can be disastrous for a growing child.

If your physician does advise a special diet, be sure to ask questions and understand all points. Know explicitly why the diet is being used and how you can best carry it out. Minor points are important, for they can very often determine the outcome of the treatment.

Is the quantity of food eaten important? (It often is.) If so, how can you keep a record of what the child eats? If your physician advises a gelatin dessert, does he mean one made from plain, unsweetened gelatin or from prepared sweetened products? How urgent is it to follow the diet closely? Most special diets depart only slightly from normal ones. In some metabolic diseases, however, where the child's body can't handle certain component materials in foods, it is vitally important to follow the dietary prescription to the letter.

If there are choices among foods, use those the child prefers, especially if he must remain on the diet for a long time. Some mothers let the child who can understand assume some responsibility for eating needed foods and avoiding others. Most children respond well to this trust placed in them. An older child often can help plan what he will eat. Helping to make such decisions gives him incentive to carry them out.

The palatability of foods in special diets is of utmost importance—more so than in food for the normal individual. The pleasure you will receive from having your child eat what he is asked to makes careful preparation well worth your effort. For instance, a white cream soup, beautifully smooth and served in a colorful bowl or cup, with a bright garnish, usually appeals to a flagging appetite. Also, it helps to remember that a sick child's appetite is fickle and not really under voluntary control. MIRIAM E. LOWENBERG

See also ALLERGY; NUTRITION

SPECIALISTS *See* MEDICAL SPECIALISTS

SPECIAL SCHOOLS *See* AGENCIES AND ORGANIZATIONS; HANDICAPPED CHILD IN SCHOOL

SPEECH DIFFICULTIES

Many children have troubles of various sorts in learning to speak well. Parents can do much to help normal development and to prevent defective speech by speaking well themselves and by having a home atmosphere in which the child is encouraged, but not unduly pressured, to speak correctly.

All types of speech defects occur four or five times as often among boys as among girls. These defects are of two main types: functional and organic. The functional disorders are those in which the child is not using his normal speech apparatus correctly. Organic speech defects, which fortunately are rare, may be caused by deafness; malformation of the mouth, such as cleft palate; or some form of brain damage, such as cerebral palsy or aphasia. A child with a physical defect hampering his speech always needs expert help to teach him to speak as well as he possibly can.

Children who are normal physically may still have difficulty in learning to talk. If a child is not talking by the usual age, it is advisable first to rule out a hearing difficulty. Excellent techniques are now available for testing the hearing of even young infants. Hard-of-hearing children always have to be taught by special methods. Their speech training must be started early to save the tone of their voices. Most states provide for the special education of deaf and hard-of-hearing children, even those of preschool age. After communication is learned, many deaf boys and girls often are able to join regular school classes.

Mental retardation and generally slow development may also account for delayed speech. Not all children who are late in talking are mentally retarded, but all mentally retarded children are slow in speech development. The child may be talking as well as he can for his general developmental level and will probably talk in time. A child psychologist can evaluate the child's developmental history, alertness, learning ability, gesture language, and desire to communicate, and can often give helpful suggestions to promote earlier speech. He can also direct parents to further sources of help.

The emotional atmosphere of the home, especially the child's relationship with his mother, is very important. Some mothers do not show their love in ways that make their children feel secure. Although they may give excellent physical care, these mothers do not find it easy to teach children to talk and may need help to do a better job. Counseling for the mother and a play group for the child often help solve the problem. Children who withdraw and who show no desire to communicate with people have serious emotional problems and are definitely in need of help from experts.

By far the most common type of speech difficulty is prolonged baby talk. Very early most children make sounds that are something like real words. Adults accept these sounds as names for objects and people and encourage the child to practice and improve. The child needs a good model to imitate; he needs to be listened to carefully and encouraged to use all parts of his speech mechanism correctly. Grownups should not repeat the child's "cute" baby talk back to him. The more the child hears correct speech and is expected to try to speak clearly, the sooner he will talk well. Children first learn the beginnings of words, then the middle parts, and finally the sounds at the ends of words. Some of the sounds learned relatively late are the "s," which is often pronounced "th" in the typical lisp, and the "r" and "l." Most children perfect their articulation as they gain in self-confidence. The child who does not articulate reasonably well by the time he is 8 years old may need the help of a speech therapist. If emotional problems are causing him to cling to his baby speech, psychotherapy before or along with speech therapy may be necessary.

Voice disorders, such as chronic hoarse, husky voice, usually caused by strain and overuse, and weak, whispered, or breathy speech are rarely found in children. When a child does exhibit any of these disorders for which no organic basis can be found, anxiety is usually the cause, and speech therapy, psychotherapy, or both are recommended. Disorders in the rate of speech such as talking too fast or too slow, as well as difficulties brought about by foreign dialect, also respond well to expert speech therapy, especially before adolescence.

Because of the importance of good speech for mental growth and for good schoolwork, and because speech difficulties have so many causes, any child with a speech difficulty should have expert study and help as early as possible. Excellent facilities are rapidly becoming available not only in the schools, but also in community mental health clinics, speech and hearing centers, rehabilitation centers, and child guidance clinics throughout the country. DOROTHEA MC CARTHY

See also ANXIETY; COMMUNITY RESOURCES; STUTTERING; TALKING

SPENDING MONEY *See* ALLOWANCE; JOBS

SPIDER BITE *See* BITES, INSECT

SPIRITUAL DEVELOPMENT *See* MORAL AND SPIRITUAL DEVELOPMENT

SPITTING UP

Almost all babies spit up a small amount of food, at least occasionally, after eating Usually, spitting up does not mean that anything is wrong but rather is an entirely mechanical problem of air in the stomach or of a too-full stomach. The amount spit up, usually not more than a teaspoon or two, is apt to look like more than it really is. Babies are most likely to spit up when they are bringing up a bubble of air or immediately after being laid down in the crib. Be careful, therefore, about getting up a good air bubble. Lay your baby gently down on his stomach or right side after feeding him.

A great deal of spitting up or vomiting in larger amounts and with force should be discussed with your doctor. RUTH S. KEMPE

See also BABY; DROOLING; GAGGING; VOMITING

SPLINTER

Splinters are usually of wood, metal, or plastic. A splinter usually penetrates the upper layers of the skin only, and lies embedded there. By pressing on nerves underneath, it can be very painful and annoying.

A splinter is usually easy to remove, but first, wash the area with warm water and soap and then sponge it with 70 per cent alcohol. Using a sharp needle, also previously sterilized with alcohol, the splinter can usually be picked out with little or no difficulty. A further application of alcohol and a dressing for 12 to 24 hours is usually all that is necessary. If inflammation begins or if it is apparent that the splinter has not been completely removed, the child's physician should be consulted. W. W. BAUER

SPOILED CHILD

A "spoiled child" is usually a child who has been given too much of the wrong things and not enough of the right ones. The expression is unfortunate because, as commonly used, the term "spoiled child" refers to an unpleasant, unfriendly, irresponsible child who "has too much of everything"—too many toys and other material possessions, too many privileges, too much freedom. In one sense this description may be correct because the child we see seems on the surface to be indeed spoiled. What is far more important, but not so apparent, is the fact that the child is without the guidance, the controls, and the opportunities he needs to develop his inner resources.

The spoiled child lacks the security of adult supervision and attention—the things that mean genuine love and respect in a child's life. It is these missing ingredients that make such a child disliked. It is also these missing ingredients that make him dislike himself. A more accurate description of a spoiled child would be that he is an unhappy, uncertain, insecure child, deprived of the things he needs the most.

For example, the little boy who lives down the street seems to have every toy ever invented; all the other children in the neighborhood are green with envy. He has a fire engine that really runs; he stays up as late as he wants; he can watch any amount and kind of television. He bullies the smaller children; he is fresh to adults; he is constantly boasting about his possessions and showing off. But as it turns out, he is also the little boy whose parents are on the verge of divorce. They are absorbed in successful business careers and have little time for him. He is left in the care of a succession of baby-sitters and maids. Too immature and emotionally unstable to meet their child's need for emotional support, and guilty over their neglect, his parents have taken the easy way out of responsible parenthood and have substituted "things" and unlimited freedom for guidance, discipline, and love. Such a child is more to be pitied than censured.

Another example is the 16-year-old who drives his own sports car and recklessly endangers the lives of others. He never studies and is failing in his schoolwork. He smokes and drinks. He encourages his companions to disobey parental rules and school regulations. He is a social menace, undisciplined and overindulged. But upon looking deeper, we find that his father died several years ago. His mother, always a weak and dependent person, has never recovered sufficiently from her own loss of support and comfort to take control of this boy and his two younger sisters. Such mothers cannot say "no" to their children because they have never really grown up enough themselves to behave like responsible adults. They justify their indulgence and their inability to maintain controls by saying, "But they are poor, fatherless children—they deserve to be pampered a little now and then."

Still another example is the 5-year-old who is waited on hand and foot by two doting parents. The child wears elaborate and expensive dresses all the time; she is driven to and from her school, just five blocks away; her back yard has more play equipment than most nursery schools, and she is not allowed to play anywhere else. She runs to her mother with every little problem and tells on her playmates continually. She has only to say, "I can't," to have her parents do for her something she is old enough to do for herself. It turns out that this little girl's parents were in their middle 40's when she was born; they had yearned for a child for so long that they could hardly believe their good fortune. Their daughter is a most precious treasure. As older parents are prone to be, they are overprotective and overanxious. They have not permitted their child to test her own strengths, to face the realities of life, and to learn ways for meeting the normal challenges of childhood. She has too much protection, supervision, and assistance; what she doesn't have is any real self-confidence or pride in herself. She has not had the opportunities to try her own wings, to experiment, to learn and grow through the normal adventures of childhood.

"Things" in themselves cannot spoil a child. He needs an environment that provides the tools of growth, that stimulates creativity, curiosity, learning. It is only when "things" stifle rather than free a child's growth, it is only when they serve as substitutes for affection that they become a hazard.

Freedom cannot spoil a child when it is given wisely and in relation to a child's readiness to use it. The freedom to test, to experiment, to make choices is a necessary part of maturation, an essential of growth. The important concern is to provide this freedom as a result of careful thought rather than indiscriminately, to see that it is used rather than abused.

Love can never spoil a child, for love, in its best sense, is the feeling for another human being which makes him feel valued as a person. Genuine parental love permits a parent to say "no!" to a child, clearly and forcefully, when the best interests of the child are threatened. Such love is not afraid or apologetic or guilty. It is the kind of love that encourages growth, reinforces and strengthens a child's own capacities to mature. Parental love that is wise, responsible, and freely given makes a child feel that he is wonderful and special and that he deserves the attention, the guidance, the direction that will help him become a friendly, resourceful, responsible adult.

The "spoiled child" may appear to live lavishly and freely, but he knows in his innermost being that he would not be given possessions and freedoms that are not good for him if he were truly valued as a person. He would gladly relinquish these "things" if someone only loved him enough to say "no" when it would help him. EDA J. LE SHAN

See also DISCIPLINE; LOVE; PERMISSIVENESS

SPORTS *See* ATHLETICS

SPORTSMANSHIP

A definition of sportsmanship usually includes the ideas of being a good loser, abiding by the rules of a game, refusing to take unfair advantage of an opponent, being a generous winner, and showing modesty in good fortune and kindness to the loser.

Parents usually expect sportsmanship too early. To begin with, most children do not really understand how rules work until they are about 10 years old. And even more years are needed before children can put themselves in another person's place, rejoice with an opponent when he wins, and help to bolster the ego of the loser.

Sportsmanship develops with maturity and with the inspiration of a good model. Before a child can be a good loser, he must have the experience of being a winner. If he is to treat others fairly and with generosity, he must himself have been so treated. It also helps if he witnesses adults who are close to him treating each other fairly and generously.

If parents can emphasize the *fun of playing* rather than the importance of winning, they can help their child. If, in their own games within the family, losses are accompanied with "better luck next time," and a real chance for the child to win is given "next time," losing will become bearable. When a child is very young, everyone should have a chance to win during any session of play. Later, as skills and understanding increase, winning or losing can be left to chance or skill, but no child should be put in the position of losing every time. RUTH E. HARTLEY

See also ATHLETICS; COMPETITION

SPRAIN

Sprains may occur in any joint but are most common in the ankle, wrist, knee, and shoulder. They may result from a strong, sudden wrench or from jumping or falling from too great a height. They occur frequently in athletic competition.

A sprain is the tearing of ligaments—the tough bands of fiber that connect bones—or a sprain can be the separation of muscle tendon from bone. Sprains may occur with or without fracture of the bone.

The usual result of a sprain is a rather rapid swelling when fluid and perhaps blood accumulate in the tissues. There is extreme pain, especially when effort is made to use the joint.

The immediate first-aid procedure is to put the injured limb at rest and to apply cold water or, if available, ice. This treatment reduces swelling. A physician should be called and the child taken to the hospital for X rays to find out whether bones have been broken and for proper treatment of the sprain.

For severe sprains it may be necessary for the youngster to wear a brace for a time, but permanent bracing tends to weaken the muscles concerned. Heat, massage, and hydrotherapy may be necessary following some sprains.

There is a common superstition that a sprain is worse than a broken bone. This belief is only a half-truth. A severe sprain of a big joint may be worse than a minor fracture. A bad fracture of a large bone is far more serious than a sprain. W. W. BAUER

STAMMERING *See* SPEECH DIFFICULTIES

STANDING *See* WALKING

STEALING

A little child who takes something that belongs to someone else rarely has any idea that this is considered a reprehensible act. Someone will soon tell him so, of course, and then he will know, but the chances are that he still won't know *why* stealing is bad.

A small child will have difficulty comprehending the meaning of personal possession, but he can at least understand why he wouldn't want someone to be taking his things. From here he can project to an understanding that other people don't want him to take theirs.

A child's own reasons for stealing seem perfectly logical to him. A little friend has two toy cars; he has none, so he may as well make off with one. A brother takes his mittens and doesn't give them back, so turn about is fair, even if it means taking father's best scarf. Mother has a purse full of coins, and his friends want candy from the store. Money is a means of buying things, and his friends will like him better if he can provide a treat for them.

These are all rather innocent forms of stealing, and you can deal with them on their own level. Severe scolding is not the answer. Humiliation certainly isn't; neither are threats and prophecies of an unhappy future. You can and should ask him to give back what he took, but he doesn't have to be made to suffer as he returns it.

Stealing by older children is a different matter. Here you are dealing with a problem and you want to get at the root of it: What makes him feel he has to steal? Again severe scoldings, dire threats, and refusing him your affection and support will not effect or speed his cure. Also it is a good idea to remember that some errors of behavior are natural expressions of growing up.

The older child who steals money to buy treats for his friends is really trying to buy friendship and so must feel that he is not desirable enough in his own right to be able to win friends without bribery. Stealing may also be an attempt to get even with someone whom the child thinks has a more favorable position. Stealing may be a way of proving to his friends that he is not a weakling, not afraid to steal. Stealing may be done because the child is terrified not to do what some commanding companion asks him to do. Stealing may be for swagger or a thrill when the ordinary occupations of his life seem dull. Stealing may be done to prove to himself that he can be deft and clever in one area at least.

One form of stealing which bothers parents very much is that done by children from good homes and in the best communities. Maybe these children are not getting the satisfactions they need in life despite their good clothes and their more than adequate play equipment. Maybe they are being given just "things" in place of attention and respect. Maybe they are asked to spend too much time at home alone without parental supervision. Or maybe the opposite is true; possibly every moment of these children's days is so well planned and their days so well ordered that they have no chance to do anything on their own and are rebelling through stealing.

The reasons for stealing often may not seem to relate directly to anything. A child may resort to stealing to solve some personally upsetting situation by acquiring "things." It would almost seem that he expects to feel more secure by having a large quantity of things for himself. This is often the hardest kind of stealing for parents to handle, and one that sometimes requires professional help. Punishment only makes matters worse.

If you can think of stealing not as a crime but as a symptom of a larger problem, you will have taken the first step toward helping an ailing child.

A. WHITTIER DAY

See also CHILD GUIDANCE CLINIC; DISCIPLINE; HONESTY; PROBLEM CHILD

STEAMING

Steaming is often recommended by a doctor as an aid in diseases that cause breathing difficulties—bronchitis, croup, laryngitis, whooping cough, and other acute respiratory infections. The steam seems to relieve the congestion in bronchial tubes and nasal passages and to make breathing easier. The steam will also, at times, lessen inflammation.

The simplest way to provide steam when needed is with an electric steamer. Some of these are so small as to be almost useless, but the ones of adequate size are extremely effective. In some cases, the doctor will advise adding medication to the water in the steamer.

A homemade steamer, or vaporizer, may be constructed by placing a kettle or an open pan on a hot plate. If you have been told to have the steam go directly to the child's bed, you can use a blanket to make a tent, supporting the blanket with a chair turned upside down or with an opened umbrella, and can then funnel the steam through an opening in the tent. Often, though, sufficient steam is supplied by having the steamer close to the bed and letting the steam wander throughout the room.

It is necessary to be cautious about several matters when using steam. Steam can cause bad burns, so the child must not be too near it. Every precaution should be taken about fire hazards from the hot plate or about scalding hot water that might be tipped over. The child must not be allowed to get too wet from the steam nor to perspire too much from the heat of a room full of steam.

See also SICK CHILD

STEPBROTHERS AND STEPSISTERS

Many times, two people marry who each have children of their own. Their family then includes, "my children," "your children," and eventually "our children."

In such cases, of course, favoritism is to be avoided whenever possible. It is not necessary, however, to neglect one's own children in a bend-over-backwards effort to help the *other* parent's children adjust. To do so may be confusing and damaging for all the children involved.

Adjustment is speeded up when each parent, besides considering the family as a whole, considers the special needs and tastes of each member of the family.

Parents will do well not to demand that stepbrothers and sisters show great love for one another. They may properly ask, however, that each child show consideration for every other child, and that respect be shown for possessions and privacy. The parents, too, will respect the children's rights.

A parent who gets the support and affection of his spouse makes a good parent and builds a happy home. Happy stepparents usually will have happy stepchildren.

See also BROTHERS AND SISTERS; STEPPARENTS

STEPPARENTS

In "real" parenthood, as most parents know, love grows and deepens with the years, as the child and the parent build on memories. This pattern is true in stepparenthood, too. And in either kind of parenthood there are moments of doubt and discouragement. In stepparenthood, particularly, when the role of a parent is new, and the problems, instead of appearing gradually, come all at once, the stepparent may feel completely inadequate to handle his role. The new parent may actually feel dislike for the children or anger at his new spouse and perhaps feel jealous of the real parent's relationship to a child. And yet, despite all the old fairy tales, stepparenthood can be a richly rewarding experience.

When you become a stepparent, you must be willing, if necessary, to change some of your ideas about children. You may have theories on child care, some of them hangovers from your own childhood, some from observing other children. You may have dreamed rose-colored dreams about marriage and parenthood. You've dreamed of having your own children, one by one, and getting acquainted with them gradually. But stepparenthood is really "stepped-up" parenthood, and it involves a great deal more than just being a parent.

For example, if you are a stepmother married to the father of one or more children, you may be worried about doing the right thing with the youngsters. You are also worried for fear that what you do to the children will make your husband less fond of you. You feel that, to keep your husband's love, you must not be a stepmother, but a "supermother." Tensions build up between real parent, stepparent, and child. In stepparenthood, the happiness of the husband and wife relationship often depends on the parent and child relationship.

There are certain problems that may face a stepparent. These problems will frequently show up, no matter how good the stepparent may be.

A child may:

- Be deeply hurt if he has lost a parent by death or divorce
- Be openly rebellious and sulky
- Have school problems
- Have difficulty learning to read
- Show a marked resistance to schoolwork
- Steal small things from other children or his parents
- Tell "tall tales"
- Want many things
- Refuse to discard anything
- Become unduly concerned about money as a possession.

When one or more of these problems occur, it is the real parent's and the stepparent's task to find out *why* a child acts as he does. The child must never be considered "bad." His behavior is not bad, nor is it the fault of the stepparent. The family doctor or a behavior clinic may be helpful if parents face severe problems in helping the child adjust to a stepparent. A child's willfulness or bad temper is a sign of profound feelings of unhappiness, and he knows no way to express himself other than through aggressive and objectionable behavior.

If a stepparent comes into a home where a child has been cared for by a number of other strangers prior to the arrival of the new parent, or if a child has been ill, or if there has been tension attendant to the divorce of his parents, there may well be many anxieties on the part of the child before the advent of a stepparent. To the child, the stepparent is just another stranger.

Stepparents must not expect statements or demonstrations of love from children, especially in the beginning. A child, who at first does not really know whether or not he loves his new parent, will eventually come to think of the parent as a close and good friend if, from the beginning, *fairness* has been the keynote of the relationship. This fairness has to be shown again and again and perhaps stated openly. You will not demand obedience simply because you are the boss, but because you have to help all the persons in the house live happily together.

As a stepparent, when you impose certain rules or make certain demands, you may meet with fairly active resistance on the part of the children. But, even real parents meet this resistance. If bad feelings come out in the open, so much the better. There will be less buried resentment to clear up in the future, and there will be more face-to-face honesty in your relationship.

With any child, but especially with a stepchild, the most important thing you can give him is the feeling that he helps to govern and discipline himself. Give him the feeling that he can choose things. Help him to see that the world is not slowly closing in on him in a "squeeze play." Instead of saying, "Put out that light because I say so," it is better to say, "When you have finished that page, call me and I will come to tuck you in and to put out the light."

Tensions will be eased, the child will feel responsibility, and a last cozy "good night" session will precede his going to sleep.

A child who has been hurt has a sense of the world's harshness. Remember, the world is *people*. The world is *you*, at the moment, and only you can help the child see that it is not necessarily all harsh.

To help your stepchild adjust:

- Respect his possessions.
- Remember that his treasures are valuable to him, even though you think of them as junk.
- Go easy on changing things around, especially in the child's room.
- Try to let him know about household events or changes before they happen.
- Don't be trigger-quick about saying, "No!" or "Do it!"
- Make room for the child's friends.
- Remember that firmness does not mean harshness.
- Make all rules as simple and as flexible as possible.

The parental love and affection you possess and which you want to give to a child cannot be lost by the addition of the word "step." Most of the child's attitude will come from you—if you feel apologetic and guilty about your status, he will wonder why. If you are happy about your position, if you love the child, then "step" is a pleasant name.

It is the child's right to know the facts. If you want to keep his confidence, never put yourself in a position where he can say, "You fooled me. You didn't tell me the truth."

The role of stepparent can be rewarding; it can be fun. There can be satisfactions in this position that even a real parent cannot know. It is a challenge, an opportunity to help mold a young life, and a chance to be both mother or father and good friend at the same time.

MARY H. FRANK

STEPSISTERS *See* STEPBROTHERS AND STEPSISTERS

STERILIZING

In every home there occasionally will be a need to kill germs by sterilizing. Different methods of sterilizing are used according to the place or article to be sterilized. You can sterilize with heat; that is, fire, steam, heated air, and boiling water. You can sterilize with chemical germicides; that is, antiseptic ointments and liquids. You can sterilize by washing with soap. Sometimes, as with diapers hung out to dry in the sun, the sun alone will do all the sterilizing that is needed.

A needle that will be used to probe for a splinter can be sterilized by putting the point of the needle directly into a flame. Cloth or gauze for bandaging can be sterilized by ironing. Cloth can be sterilized by washing if the water is hot enough. Instruments can be sterilized in steam. Some liquids, including water and milk, can be sterilized by boiling them. Glass containers in which liquids are to go can be boiled to make them sterile. Hands can be made sterile by sufficient cleansing with the right kind of soap or by being dipped in germicidal solutions. A thermometer can be sterilized in alcohol or with soap and water. Wounds can be at least partially sterilized with medicines made for this purpose, and can be safeguarded by having sterile dressings applied by a person with freshly washed hands.

Mothers most often begin their sterilizing chores with the baby's formula, using one of the two popular methods described in FORMULA MAKING. The mother of an infant also sterilizes the water he drinks, boiling it for three minutes and then pouring it into bottles that have been boiled previously.

Some of the most important and demanding sterilizing takes place in the sickroom. The object of such sterilizing is to keep the illness the child has from spreading to other people and to keep the sick child from picking up any additional disease. Sickroom sterilizing practices are described in COMMON COMMUNICABLE DISEASES.

STINGS *See* BITES, INSECT

STOMACH-ACHE

Although stomach-ache is one of the commonest of symptoms among children, the diagnosis of the exact cause is not a simple matter because of the many possibilities. Therefore, if your child has a stomach-ache, consult the doctor right away to find the cause and prevent development of complications. Do not give food or drink and do not give a laxative or a cathartic.

Stomach-aches often result from having eaten too much, from not chewing food well enough, or from some irritating food. The child may have nausea, vomiting, and even diarrhea. Stomach-ache pain is usually cramping and tends to come on in waves.

During the course of many infectious diseases, a child may complain of stomach-ache, and his complaint should not be disregarded. Measles and chicken pox patients, for example, may develop an abdominal pain—and it may turn out to be a symptom of appendicitis, which is often a complication of these diseases. A cold or a sore throat is sometimes accompanied by abdominal pain. This pain is usually thought to be caused by swollen lymph glands in the abdomen, but again pain may be a symptom of appendicitis or some other complication.

A stomach-ache that is at first generalized in a child's abdomen, and then in a few hours localizes to the right lower abdomen, may indicate appendicitis. The doctor should see this child early. Some children have frequent stomach-aches not well localized to any one portion of the abdomen, and detailed observation may become necessary.

Emotional difficulties may be the cause of stomach-ache in some children. For this reason, parents should be alert to the circumstances under which a child complains and discuss them with the doctor. If a stomach-ache comes on after losing a game, or after a quarrel with a playmate, or after being disciplined at home or school, the child may need psychological help. JULIUS B. RICHMOND

See also APPENDICITIS; COLIC; COMMON COMMUNICABLE DISEASES; FOOD POISONING

STORYBOOKS *See* BOOKS FOR CHILDREN.

STORYTELLING

"Tell me a story, Mommy."

This request can lead you into some of the most pleasant hours of your life with your child.

Many a professional storyteller has an inborn talent, but almost anyone who enjoys a good story and the melodious sound of words and a rapt audience can master the art.

Selection of the story is of the greatest importance. Choose only a story that you enjoy and look forward to telling. Folk tales are easy to tell. Since these stories were kept alive orally for centuries, they are brief; they have well-organized plots and well-defined characters. Many times they include a touch of humor; and humor delights children.

Children of nursery age like the simplest tales, such as "Goldilocks," "Little Toot," and "The Pancake" in Volume 2, *Stories and Fables*. In these stories, action is rapid, plots are simple, and there is repetition in both word and deed. As the child grows older, the element of magic, the deeds of princes and princesses, and the villainy of ogres and witches become more spellbinding.

For some people, learning a story is difficult; others can commit one to memory with a few readings. If you want to tell a particular story, read it over and over, preferably aloud. Absorb its flavor, visualize its setting and characters, outline in your mind the logical sequence of events, and memorize an apt turn of phrase or a few specific words that if said in other ways would cause the story to lose its charm. Ordinarily, a story should not be memorized word for word, for then you may tell it in a stilted way or you may forget a word or a phrase and flounder. Writers such as Hans Christian Andersen, Rudyard Kipling, and Howard Pyle are the exception to this rule, for their choice of expression is so precise that to tell their stories in words other than their own destroys the beauty of their writings.

The storyteller is not an actor, but rather the re-creator of a story for an audience. Spontaneous gestures may add to the telling, but planned dramatization calls attention to the action and detracts from the story. Try at all times for intimacy in telling your story, for each child should be able to feel that the story is being told directly to him. Look always into the faces of your audience.

Be certain that your voice carries to each member of the group. A loud voice is not necessary; rather, a soft voice well projected is best. Avoid monotony in the telling. But also avoid changing your voice to represent different characters unless you are skilled in voice use. An attempt at complete voice changes may result in distortion and absurdity. Few storytellers should try dialect unless they are masters at it. The pitch of the voice, varying from loud to soft, will heighten the suspense and action in many stories. Pause briefly at the proper time to create suspense, emphasize action, and recapture the attention of your audience.

There are plenty of books available for you in which folk and fairy tales, myths and legends, have been retold for children. Or you can tell, with much pleasure and profit for your child, stories of your own experiences when you were small or tales you create. You can read stories that you can retell about famous people in Volume 11, *Scientists and Inventors,* Volume 12, *Pioneers and Patriots,* and Volume 13, *People To Know.*

Your child, too, should be encouraged to tell stories in the family group. Although he will be inexperienced at first, the opportunity to use his imagination and compose stories or to tell his own versions of well-known tales will teach him to speak better and to hold the attention of an audience. Through storytelling he will acquire a skill that will bring him much enjoyment as he grows older.

Two books upon which storytellers depend for inspiration and guidance are Ruth Sawyer's *The Way of the Storyteller* (Viking Press), and Marie Shedlock's *The Art of the Storyteller* (Dial Press). ELIZABETH A. GROSS

See also BOOKS FOR CHILDREN; LIBRARIES

STRABISMUS *See* CROSS-EYE

STRAIN

The term "strain" is really an indefinite one which may relate to sprains or to actual muscle injury, as in the case of the so-called charley horse. When a muscle or a joint has been subjected to unusual stress, there may be soreness and tenderness to touch without actual severe damage to tissues such as may occur in sprains and charley horses. As a rule, all that a mild strain requires is rest and, perhaps, the application of heat or warmth for comfort. After suffering a strain, protect your child for a time against strenuous activity of the muscles involved. W. W. BAUER

See also SPRAIN

STRANGERS, FEAR OF

An infant, happy and secure with his mother, usually enjoys the arms of any grown-up person who likes babies and knows how to cuddle them. But as he becomes more aware—about the end of the first year—he begins to show unwillingness to make up to strangers. He is learning that people are not all the same. This is progress. He must now learn that "strangers" are not necessarily harmful, a lesson that is easier for the child who has known consistent kindness than for the one who has suffered neglect or abuse or maybe has suffered an accident when he was not with his mother or father.

When a child is old enough to go to school or to the store alone, it is natural for his mother to extend her protection by warning him against strangers; this precaution is good to the extent that she does not make her child fearful of everyone. It is indeed difficult to know how far to go. Most parents, fortunately, know instinctively how to handle this problem. It is impossible to cover every situation that might occur with a stranger, and to try to do so would only make a fearful, inhibited child. The friendly child regards others as friendly, and he extends the boundaries of his personality by getting to know all kinds of people. HELEN ROSS

See also ANXIETY; FEAR; SHYNESS AND TIMIDITY

STREP THROAT

A specific bacteria, the streptococcus, causes the type of sore throat referred to as strep throat. With strep throat, the child usually has fever, loss of energy, considerable soreness of the throat—especially on swallowing—and swelling of the lymph glands of the neck. Gray or whitish patches may be seen on the tonsils. A culture made from secretions in the throat is often helpful to the doctor in making his diagnosis.

Strep throat is contagious and a child who has it should be isolated from others; his dishes should be sterilized until the condition clears. Fortunately, it is now possible to clear the streptococci from the throat quite readily by giving penicillin. Since strep throats may precede rheumatic fever, nephritis, and other disorders, parents should be alert to the possible dangers and seek prompt diagnosis and treatment. JULIUS B. RICHMOND

See also COMMON COMMUNICABLE DISEASES; RHEUMATIC FEVER; SICK CHILD; SORE THROAT

STROLLER *See* LAYETTE AND BABY EQUIPMENT

STUBBORNNESS

A 10-year-old boy stubbornly refuses to put away his pajamas and make his bed.

A girl of 6 becomes stubborn about drinking her milk.

A youngster in junior high is stubborn about turning off television and getting his homework done so that he can go to bed on time.

Stubbornness can be extremely annoying to parents, but a certain amount of it is inevitable and even very useful.

Naturally, a 10-year-old will forget his chores some of the time, because that's just the way 10-year-olds are. But he can learn that each person in a family has to accept some responsibilities. Some degree of flexibility may show the girl who refuses milk that adults are not always rigidly stubborn themselves; her pediatrician may say that she actually requires less milk or that supplementary calcium or certain cooked foods can provide the nourishment she needs. Compromises may have to be worked out for the TV adherent: less viewing on school nights, an opportunity to stay up later over weekends, or TV watching only after the homework has been completed. Perhaps the child really does not need so much sleep now; if so, and if his parents concede, a half-hour's grace will make him feel more like cooperating.

On the other hand, there are kinds of stubbornness that parents wish to encourage. It is terribly important, for instance, that a pretty 7-year-old walking home from school stubbornly refuse the overtures of a persuasive man who urges her to come with him for some ice cream. Or, if a gang of friends decide it would be fun to break some basement windows in the neighborhood, parents will be proud and delighted when their child stubbornly refuses to go along with the idea. It is even important that a child sometimes stubbornly require proof before accepting everything an elder says—insist that his father's answer is incorrect on a science assignment, perhaps, for it may be that father hasn't kept up with the latest information on electronics and the child is right. In all these situations children are using judgment, and judgment often involves stubbornly refusing to accept another person's point of view or behavior. This kind of stubbornness is vital if children are to become responsible citizens, thinking for themselves and not being blindly swayed by anyone in authority. The uncomfortable fact is, however, that discernment and good judgment come only with practice, and parents are the people children have the most opportunity to practice on.

Children can learn a great deal from their parents about the appropriate times for stubbornness and the equally important times for flexibility. A group of mothers defy authority and set up a "baby carriage brigade" at a school crossing where a child has been killed because there was no traffic light. They are taken to court for causing a public disturbance and stubbornly refusing to give in. They get their light, and their children learn that sometimes, out of a deep conviction, a person must stand by what he believes to be right. In a moment of awful anger at a child, a mother says that his punishment will be cancellation of an imminent birthday party. Then she realizes that this punishment was too extreme and unfair. Instead of rigidly maintaining her authority, she admits to the child that she was wrong, and reverses herself, and the child learns the important lesson that the person who can admit a mistake is a strong person and one worthy of respect.

Adults who want their children to settle problems reasonably have to forego the luxury of being unreasonably stubborn themselves. They have to be objective in reconsidering a decision and willing to conciliate through arbitration. EDA J. LE SHAN

See also DISCIPLINE; HUMOR

STUDYING

Many a father attributes his bald spot to the same destructive element on which his wife blames her first gray hairs—home study. It is not their own studying that ages parents, of course; it is the studying that the school asks their child to do outside of school hours. Parents know the work has to be done. They don't know how to get it done. They try to invent magic formulas to make the study time profitable, and they find that there is no magic except the miracle of human differences: No two children are exactly alike. Still, children are enough alike so that all home study may be considered from two basic points of view: How a student can get the most out of it and how parents can help.

A Child's Responsibilities Toward Study

A child can and should take on many of the responsibilities of home study for himself. First of all, he should understand his assignment. If he can pay full attention when the teacher describes the work to be done and if he writes down what is expected of him, he will certainly be much better off. Then he must have a place to study. If he has no room of his own, help him set up a special place for himself within a room. A desk, a proper chair, a light by which he can see well are all essential. Parents should provide the equipment, but the child can keep his desk in order and see that supplies are at hand. Paper, pencil, and books should not have to be looked for at study time; they should have a constant place and be readily available.

A time to study is as important as a place. A young student can vary the time occasionally but vary it always from a well-established basic schedule. And he should be reasonable, alternating periods of hard concentration with breaks for stretching, snacks, or brief conversation. He should also learn gradually to pace himself so that he can switch quickly from one assignment to another when he begins to bog down and waste time or so that he can recognize when an assignment is too difficult for long concentration.

Each child must learn to rely upon himself while he does his homework. It is nearly impossible for two children to study together. First one and then the other thinks of something he must say, and concentration disappears, time goes, and the homework remains undone.

How Parents Can Help

Parent participation is one of the basic ingredients for a successful study time. Your attitude and interest can provide the delicate balance between success and failure. Children seldom exceed the expectations of some adult in whom they have confidence. Expecting too much, however, can set up its own barriers. Parents help their child when they know his limitations as well as his capabilities.

Parental help can start with listening to the assignment. Sometimes having to state what he is to do clarifies the work in the child's mind. It is important that parents know whether a child has work to do that is easy, simple, and clear, or whether he is struggling with something that is complicated and difficult. Other home activity for the child can be modified to fit the situation. Parents can also certainly encourage orderliness and routine, both in study time and in study place.

Children who do not have to go to public libraries or to the home of a friend for basic reference material have more time for study. Each home should have, if possible, sources of basic information. Encyclopedias provide the best information on a wide range of topics. Other reference materials can be added. Simple picture files or a box of pictures can be kept for report and notebook illustrations.

When a child is working on a long-range assignment, parents should keep some check on how the work is going so as to avoid frantic rush and unhappiness the night before a report is due. They can show their interest by locating sources of information or by collecting illustrations from which the child can select.

During their child's study time, parents should choose home activities for themselves which will not distract him. If he is easily distracted or is working on a difficult assignment while they listen to an intriguing TV program toward which he keeps an ear cocked, it is only natural that he will do less than his best. Parents can expect better homework from their child if while he studies they read, prepare for church or club responsibilities, or stay far enough away to avoid distracting him.

Parents prove to their child that achievement and progress in school are important to them as well as to him when they express an interest in what he is doing, give an occasional word of encouragement and merited praise, expect the best within realistic limits, and see that work that is supposed to be finished is finished. R. VAN ALLEN

See also BOOKS FOR CHILDREN; HOME-SCHOOL RELATIONS

STUTTERING

Stuttering, or nonfluent speech, is one of the hardest speech defects to overcome. Although it is not necessarily inherited, it tends to run in families and is found more often in families in which left-handedness and twins occur. Some children stutter from the very beginning of connected speech. Others begin when they start to school, when a new baby arrives, after an accident, or at adolescence. The earlier stuttering begins, the harder it is to treat.

Stutterers usually are well above average in mentality. They have much to say, but they are shy, timid, and sensitive. It is hard for them to make friends and to socialize. They often have trouble with colds and allergies and tend to be rather clumsy and awkward. Their speech is hesitant; they repeat the first syllable of many words several times or they may completely block on a word and grimace in their efforts to talk. The severity of the defect varies greatly from one child to another, and from time to time in the same child. Once a child becomes aware that he is a stutterer, he lives with the constant fear that he may block while speaking. Real emotional acceptance of himself as a stutterer often improves his speech.

The causes of stuttering are not definitely known. Many young children are labeled stutterers by parents who are overanxious about speech and make their children tense when they try to talk. No one is completely fluent at all times. Around 3 years of age, when children are thinking faster than they can talk, most normal children repeat about every fourth word. If a child is not at this time given excessive attention by tense adults with very high standards, his speech usually becomes normally fluent.

Many stutterers have rather deep personality problems. Stuttering boys usually have mothers who are dominant, possessive, yet critical, and fathers who play the more passive role in the family. These boys often become confused in finding their proper role in life. While outwardly conforming, they may deeply resent their mothers. Their speech often improves remarkably when they are away at camp or boarding school, yet their mothers are rarely able to permit such separations. Adolescent stutterers who do break away from home early, often improve greatly in their speech, but many are never able emotionally to cut the apron strings. The picture is less clear for girls who stutter, but it is likely that they have disturbed relations with their fathers.

The theory that an enforced change of handedness from left to right is responsible for stuttering has not been clearly proved. Cases of this sort are a matter of record; yet many children have had handedness changed without developing stuttering, and many stutterers have never been left-handed. It is not advisable to run the risk of forcibly changing handedness, but mild efforts to teach right-handed habits are all right.

Stuttering can be learned by imitation of a stuttering father, uncle, brother, sister, or cousin. Since the imitator is not usually a true stutterer, separation from the primary confirmed stutterer usually enables the imitating child to clear up his speech. DOROTHEA MC CARTHY

See also ANXIETY; LEFT-HANDEDNESS; TALKING

STY *See* EYELID, DISEASES OF

SUCKING

When a newborn baby is placed at the breast or given a bottle soon after birth, he is usually ready to do his part with strong sucking movements. Rather shortly thereafter, he begins to make such sucking movements in anticipation of being fed, as one of the signals that he is hungry. He will also suck vigorously on other objects—his fingers, his thumb, his wrist, or as much of his hand as he can get into his mouth. Sometimes, however, he tries to suck at a time when he is unlikely to be hungry and by doing so seems to say he has learned that sucking not only brings him food, but that it also is pleasurable. Many infants habitually suck their thumbs by the time they are 3 months old, and it is not uncommon for a baby to be born with one thumb slightly reddened and enlarged, suggesting that some sucking may have occurred in the uterus.

It used to be common practice for babies to receive most of their food via sucking for the entire first year of life. In some countries they still do. But today there is a tendency for supplementary foods to be introduced at a very early age. Most infants, therefore, are receiving semisolid foods by 3 months of age or even younger, and many babies are taken off the bottle altogether by the time they are a year old. This means in general that babies do not have as much opportunity to suck as was formerly the case.

Some people think that an infant has a basic sucking drive. According to this theory, it is, therefore, unwise to limit a baby's sucking experience since, if he does not get enough sucking while taking in food, he will find other means of gratifying this powerful instinct. There is some evidence that thumb-sucking develops from too early frustration of a child's sucking drive, but there is also evidence that if sucking is encouraged too long, the drive is strengthened rather than eventually weakened. Such contradictions indicate that it is probably best for a mother to take the middle of the road: to give her young baby ample opportunity to get his food by sucking while gradually encouraging him toward other ways of eating. This approach should give him the most security and minimize the likelihood that he will need to take to other kinds of sucking. BETTYE M. CALDWELL

See also BABY; BOTTLE FEEDING; BREAST CARE AND BREAST FEEDING; PACIFIER; THUMB-SUCKING

SUFFOCATION *See* SMOTHERING

SUGAR *See* FORMULA MAKING

SULKING

You've heard parents and teachers make the comment: "I can stand anything but sulking." And yet these are the very adults who may stimulate and encourage sulking because they don't permit a more vigorous, direct expression of hostility or annoyance.

Often children whose feelings have been hurt or who feel that they have been treated unjustly may express their annoyance by retreating into an aloof and silent huff that we label sulking.

Usually these sulks will pass fairly quickly if the adult doesn't react to them too sharply. Overeager or annoyed responses of nagging or coaxing a child to stop sulking will be less effective than will recognition that everyone feels out of humor once in a while and that a child in a sulk will "come out of it" without any dramatic reprisal or lecture.

The child who is not permitted to hit or kick or bite or even to say "bad words" to express his anger may resort to sulking as a passive way of expressing his resentment toward grownups.

Chronic sulking can be fairly effective (from the child's point of view) if it is sufficiently annoying to an adult. It is less effective if adults can truly ignore—not *grimly* ignore—it. Sulking loses its punch and satisfaction when it attracts no response. The child who tends to prolong his sulking moments may need some help to jar him out of his mood. With some children, a mildly humorous approach may be effective and diverting, but whatever is done or said must not be construed as ridicule. "You look mad as a hatter; where's your hat?" or "You look cross as a bear, but I don't hear you growl."

Sometimes a redirection of interest and attention may help the child to move out of a sulk. "When you finish feeling grumpy, let's make some cookies."

But more important than diverting or ignoring is the need to discover the reason for sulking and to help your child so that he will not be bogged down by his anger. Encourage him to talk about what bothers him. Help him to feel safe to express his feelings of resentment or annoyance.

Sulking is a rather soggy way of responding to an unhappy situation. Most children will like being helped to find other more direct ways to work out their feelings of being hurt. EVELYN BEYER

See also ANGER

SUMMER CAMP *See* CAMP; DAY CAMP

SUN BATH

A sun bath is a pleasant way to give your baby vitamin D and to make him look healthy and tanned. Sun baths are not absolutely necessary, however, if your baby is getting an adequate supply of vitamins, nor should you rely on the sun to give him all the vitamin D he needs, especially during the wintertime when sun bathing is more difficult to arrange.

Babies can start being exposed to the sun by the time they are 3 or 4 weeks old. Be very cautious at first because a baby's skin is delicate and will burn easily. Give the sun bath in a sheltered spot where there is little wind and use a blanket or playpen or carriage to protect your baby from the ground. At first, two to three minutes while he is lying on his abdomen and about two minutes while he is lying on his back will be safe. This can be increased gradually day by day if the baby tolerates it well and you are sure he will not burn. If his skin becomes at all reddened, discontinue the sun baths for a few days and then resume them more slowly. Warm sun and freedom from all clothing usually help most babies to enjoy these periods very much. Sun in the eyes is, however, annoying and troublesome to a baby, so you will want to shield his eyes. Later, when he is moving about, have him wear a bonnet or a cap if he finds the sun in his eyes a nuisance.

During the winter months give your baby his sun baths close to noon, the time when the most ultraviolet rays are present in sunshine. Place him in front of an open window in such a way that the sun falls directly on him, for ordinary window glass filters out the ultraviolet rays and will destroy the benefit of the sun. Drafts can usually be avoided by opening the upper half of the window and having the room door closed. The room, of course, should be comfortably warm.

Older children love the sun, too, and can take it a little more easily. But every summer it is wise to remember that exposure to the sun should be gradual so that painful or serious sunburns don't develop on the first warm day. Be especially careful where reflection from water increases the likelihood of burning. RUTH S. KEMPE

See also FRESH AIR; SUNBURN

SUNBURN

Sunburn is the skin's reaction to the ultraviolet rays of the sun or of artificially created rays from a sun lamp. The first reaction of sunburn is reddening; more severe sunburns may go so far as to blister. Sunburn seldom, if ever, reaches the third-degree burn stage.

Children with fair skins and especially those with red hair are more prone to sunburn than brunettes, but any skin will burn if the exposure is sufficiently prolonged and severe. Even a tanned skin can burn. Fair-skinned children when sunburned are more likely to peel and burn again than brunettes.

Closely related to sunburn is burning from so-called skyshine, which occurs on hazy days when sunlight is deceptively weak. Don't permit your child to stay too long in the sunshine, especially on the beach. Reflected rays from the water intensify the effect of the sun and may cause a severe burn. A medically recommended suntan oil will give some protection. W. W. BAUER

SUNSTROKE *See* HEATSTROKE

SUPPOSITORIES

Suppositories are small cylindrical objects about 1 inch long and ¼ inch thick which can be inserted into the rectum. There are two kinds of suppositories. The more common ones are made of soap or glycerine and are used to stimulate a bowel movement, especially if the baby seems to be having some discomfort. It is wise not to use suppositories at all except on the advice of a physician and never habitually because routine use interferes with normal bowel function.

The second kind of suppository is one especially made to contain a medicine that is not easily taken by mouth. Since the purpose is to have the medicine absorbed from the rectum, you must be sure to insert the suppository above the muscle ring at the rectum opening. Holding the baby's buttocks close together for a few moments will usually prevent him from expelling the suppository. If it is expelled, wait a few minutes before trying again very gently. RUTH S. KEMPE

SURGEON *See* MEDICAL SPECIALISTS

SURGERY *See* OPERATION

SWALLOWING THINGS

Children have a natural tendency to put things into their mouths. It's instinctive, like the instinct to suck. But this tendency can cause concern when a child swallows things never intended to nourish him. You protect him best when you keep small objects away from your small child. A string of beads, for example, may be dangerous if the string breaks and the beads come loose. Your button box, if kept within reach, is attractive to a small child. Toys with detachable small parts, especially glass eyes, buttons, bells, or other objects, should not be given to children, nor should any toy that might break into fragments that could be swallowed or breathed into windpipe and lungs.

Real danger comes when a child swallows an open safety pin, a carpet tack, or some similar sharp object. Even so, don't panic, for there is a fair chance that the object will pass without harm into the stool. It is common practice to feed a child bread, mashed potatoes, or other starchy substances when he has swallowed an inedible object. These foods may aid passage through the stomach, and they certainly do no harm.

If your child has swallowed a dangerous object, it is wise to consult your doctor immediately. He may advise an X-ray examination. Until the object is recovered, the child should be watched for symptoms of pain or abdominal distress. Parents should make every effort to remain calm, or at least to appear calm, so that the child won't become alarmed.

As soon as your child is old enough to understand, encourage him to give to you any undesirable object that he may happen to find. You can then thank him, without undue fuss, and substitute a more desirable tidbit. And remember, children are great imitators of their parents. The alert child who observes his mother holding open safety pins in her mouth, or his father sprouting tacks from between his lips, will duplicate the deed at the first opportunity. W. W. BAUER

See also ACCIDENT PREVENTION

SWEARING *See* BAD WORDS

SWIMMING

A young child's introduction to water, in his bath as a very young baby and later in a wading pool or a lake, may be a very frightening experience if it isn't handled carefully. All small children are distrustful and fearful of large bodies of water at first acquaintance, but almost all children learn to love the water. In fact, parents must be extremely careful, because children soon exhibit too little fear and may place themselves in dangerous situations.

It takes time, patience, and understanding, but all children *can* learn to swim and, certainly, all children *should,* even those with certain physical handicaps. Lessons should not be too long, the child should not be allowed to become frightened, and the teacher, whether parent or professional, should not show impatience. Lessons should begin by allowing the child to learn at his own pace to like the water. Be sure he feels secure by supporting him in the water. If he knows he is safely supported, he can learn to kick and move his arms; he gets great fun out of his splashing, and at the same time he learns basic swimming movements. Later, he can kick while holding on to your hands and still later, while holding on to a kickboard.

Swimming itself involves putting the face into the water. It is never wise to hurry a child into this phase of swimming instruction. Let him feel completely safe. Show him how you can go under water and come up again. Hold him by the hands when he first ducks his head under water and let him see that it is fun. Avoid such expressions as, "Don't be afraid." You will build your child's confidence by showing him that you are confident, that you are having fun, and that you are enjoying this swimming experience.

After your child has learned to keep his face under water without fear, you will want to teach him to float. Floating on his face is the first step. Help him to learn to float by holding him up in the water; let him feel that the water will support him if he will let it. He will also have to master the techniques of breathing, the next step in learning how to swim. Show him how to blow bubbles by breathing out correctly under water.

Diving from the side of the pool should not be attempted until the child has learned to breathe properly in the water. Few teachers recommend diving from a board before a child is 7 or 8 years old. He should never be allowed in deep water until he can swim at least 20 yards with ease and has demonstrated that he is confident and at home in the water.

While swimming is one of the most healthful and enjoyable of all sports, it should be remembered that water can be dangerous. Children should never be allowed to forget the rules of water safety. They should be taught never to swim alone, never to swim in unsupervised waters, and never to take chances.

Parents have serious responsibilities where their small children's swimming is concerned, a responsibility that grows with the popularity of home wading tanks and swimming pools. Be sure you are right beside your child or watching him closely from a short distance. And this means never taking your eyes from him. A small child can drown in seconds, quietly and quickly. A parent who is not ready to devote his entire attention to a child while at the beach should not take that child to the beach.

Some children swim instinctively. In some cases this instinct does help a child to swim, but parents should not rely on instinct to keep a child above water if he should fall in. Even natural swimmers will profit from good training in swimming techniques.

An older child can learn to swim by imitating others, but he can learn earlier, quicker, and better with lessons. These lessons can be provided by the parent, but unless you are entirely at ease and competent in the water, and will use extreme patience, it is better to have the teaching done by a professional.

The YMCA or YWCA in your community probably offers swimming instruction, both individual and group. Your Red Cross chapter also will refer you to qualified instructors. Children may earn the Red Cross "Beginner's Certificate." ROBERT A. MCGUIGAN

See also ARTIFICIAL RESPIRATION; COMMUNITY RESOURCES

Related article in WORLD BOOK: "Swimming"

SWOLLEN GLANDS

Enlargement of lymph glands—located in the neck, the arm pits, at the elbows, in each groin, and in the abdomen and chest—is usually spoken of as swollen glands. The lymph glands are made up of lymph tissue and have as their function the protection of the body from infection. Thus, when the throat or tonsils are infected, the lymph glands of the neck swell; when an infection occurs on the hands or arms, the lymph nodes in the elbow and arm pits swell; with an infection on the leg, those of the groin swell.

In most infections affecting the entire body, such as measles, scarlet fever, and typhoid fever, the lymph glands of the entire body are swollen. In some infectious diseases, like German measles and glandular fever, the lymph nodes have a tendency to become quite large and to remain so for some time. In rare instances, the lymph glands swell because of abnormal growths within them, similar to tumors. It is advisable to consult a physician when a child's lymph glands are enlarged. Since most lmyph glands swell in connection with infection, the treatment usually is directed toward clearing the infection.

When shots are given to protect against various diseases, the lymph glands in the area usually swell. This is normal, for these glands play an important role in developing resistance to disease. JULIUS B. RICHMOND

See also ADENOIDS; COMMON COMMUNICABLE DISEASES; GLANDULAR FEVER; TONSILS

TABLE MANNERS

When children begin to eat at the table, manners soon become a family concern. Good table manners are important, of course, but it is useless to think about them until a child has learned to eat easily all by himself. At 2, 3, or even 4, a child does not have the muscular coordination to be neat and efficient in eating. A messy face, a spotted bib, an overturned milk mug are to be expected.

This is the time for a child to learn to like to eat. Manners can and should come later—3-year-old manners for threes; 5-year-old manners for fives. And there's a difference. From time to time a child can be told when to use a fork or a spoon, and when fingers are permissible. He will have to be told, too, not to speak when his mouth is full. But it is far more important that mealtime be a happy time, with emphasis on the people present.

Because a hungry child cannot wait patiently for food to be served, many a family meal gets off to a crying start. How much better it is to let him begin his meal early, with a glass of milk or a piece of buttered bread. In fact, his whole main course can be readied and set before him before the adults are served.

A small child should not be expected to sit quietly through a meal geared to adults, but there is no harm in giving him a choice—to sit at the table as long as he wishes or to go off to play when he has finished. Choice may also be given him as to when he wants his dessert—as soon as he finishes his main course or when the family is served. Both the early start, about which the child should be informed in a quiet, friendly way, and the chance to exercise choice in two situations—when to leave the table and when to have his dessert—will help the child to behave pleasantly.

If tension at dinner is usual despite planning, 15-minute rest periods before dinner for parents, as well as for children, often make mealtimes far more pleasant. Relaxation improves manners—and digestion, too.

As with other social graces, most of what a child learns about table manners will come through observation of his parents.

See also MANNERS; MESSINESS; SELF-FEEDING

TAKING TURNS *See* SHARING

TALENTED CHILD *See* ABILITIES; GIFTED CHILD

TALKING

Learning to talk is a most important part of a child's mental growth. A normal child acquires speech skills rapidly during his early years, first responding to familiar voices by cooing and babbling. The baby's first sounds are usually vowels—"ah-ah" or "ooh-ooh," to which he later adds consonants to form his first real words. These may be "mama" or "dada," "baby" or "kitty." He is most likely to try to talk when he sees someone he loves, when another child snatches his favorite toy, or when he is otherwise emotionally excited.

After building up a fairly large vocabulary of name words for the people and things in his world, baby puts phrases together by adding action words: "Baby fall down," "Mama go." He later adds descriptive and connecting words to form short sentences, even with phrases: "Tommy is a good boy," "George ran and jumped in the pool."

The mother is normally her child's first language teacher and her manner and attitude can do much to further and encourage his desire to communicate. Children who grow up in a family advance more rapidly in speaking than do children who live in institutions. Children who have the most contact with adults, such as only children, usually develop speech most quickly. Twins, who always have to share their mother, are likely to talk late.

A baby should be talked to from the very beginning in kindly, loving tones. It is good for a mother to talk to her infant and to make believe he already understands. She should treat him and respond to him as a person, and not as something merely to be fed, bathed, and put to bed. Mothers who enjoy their babies and talk to them in affectionate tones do much to promote good speech at an early age. Before a child is a year old, he should be read to from books and talked to about the stories; he should see the pictures and be permitted to touch them. Thus he will be helped to attain language growth in a pleasant and happy manner.

Children who talk early are almost always bright and usually will do well in school. Late talking is sometimes, but far from always, a sign of mental retardation, emotional disturbance, deafness, or hearing loss. Some late talkers, however, actually turn out to be gifted. The variation in the ages at which children begin to talk is so great that no definite rule can be set down. But because of the importance of speech for a child's mental development, and because many speech difficulties are not outgrown but require special training, parents would be wise to seek professional advice for any child who is not talking at all by 2½ or 3 years of age. Many child guidance clinics, speech and hearing centers, and rehabilitation centers do excellent work in helping very young handicapped children to speak before they reach school age.

Talk a Lot, Talk a Little

Girls usually talk a little earlier and in more advanced ways than boys, but boys often acquire larger vocabularies, possibly because they are usually given more freedom to explore. There are no differences between boys and girls in the amount or rate of talking. Most adults are amazed to learn that normal 3- and 4-year-olds use between 10,000 and 20,000 running words in a single day and that the vocabularies of children on entering school amount to several thousand different words.

It is important that children hear the language spoken correctly at home and have a good model to imitate. Parents should speak to a child in complete sentences rather than to blurt out quick, one-word answers. Many parents unwittingly hamper their children's language growth by understanding their gestures too well for too long. Parents who refuse to respond to hand or facial gestures and insist that their child speak to indicate his needs can often bring about rapid growth in talking. Parents and older brothers and sisters sometimes find it "cute" to repeat a child's babyish words back to him. If "toilet" is called "toidey" by a child's family, it may be years before the child finds out the correct way to say toilet. Families that absorb the child's baby talk and acquire a whole new lingo themselves are hindering, not helping, his language growth.

Some children walk before they talk; others do not. If a child should talk first, he may suddenly stop increasing his vocabulary for a time as he masters the task of learning to walk. Many children talk to themselves at first, or *about* themselves, using "me" or "I" excessively as they speak, but gradually they learn to use speech in a social way to communicate with others.

It is hard to say when a child uses his first word with meaning. It is necessary to listen for him to use the word again and again to be sure he uses it regularly to mean the same person or thing, and not for anything else. Usually, this attempt comes in the last quarter of the first year of life when a normal child probably has about three such words in his vocabulary. As soon as a child learns a new word, he can be helped to spread his knowledge of it. For example, when he learns that a chair is called "chair," all the other chairs in the room can be named so that the word becomes attached, not to just one particular chair but to all kinds of chairs. A child's thinking is at first very concrete. He understands uses of objects and their qualities, but he cannot classify them or understand formal definitions until much later. Educated adults sometimes find it difficult to be simple and specific enough to be good language teachers for young children who cannot understand abstract ideas until they are a little older.

Don't Be Anxious

Parents should not become overanxious about their child's speech. In spite of its importance, there should not be tension or anxiety associated with the beginnings of speech. A calm, relaxed attitude without undue pressure for perfect speech is best for your child's language development. It is far more important to preserve his desire to communicate than to have him attain perfection in speech at an early age. If he wants to call his aunt "Ammarjie," let him do so. He will find out quickly enough that she is Aunt Marjorie, but to insist he say the two words clearly too soon will only cause tension.

Children's ideas tend to run ahead of their ability to talk. It is quite normal for 3-year-olds to hesitate and repeat many words in their efforts to express themselves. If a child does not learn to use his speech as an attention-getting device with tense, overanxious parents, many speech problems can often be avoided.

The child who speaks fluently, in reasonably correct and complete sentences, usually gets off to a good start in reading and the other language arts when he goes to school. Children who have not developed good speech in the preschool period may have to delay the learning of reading until after they have had more experiences to talk and read about and until they know how a sentence is put together. If the home provides a good foundation in listening and speaking, the school can usually do a good job in teaching the other language arts of reading, writing, and spelling.

A Second Language

In many families today, a child may hear more than one language, or because of travel and residence abroad, a second language may be introduced at an early age. Opinions differ on the matter of when and how to introduce a second language with the least confusion to the child. In general, it seems better to delay the second language until the first one is under fairly good control. It seems to work out best if the child hears each language from only one member of the family rather than a mixture of the two from the same person. The second language is learned better, and with little or no accent, if it is heard and used conversationally when a child is at an early age.

When a second language is learned in the family for cultural reasons, there is usually no problem. But if a child learns only a "foreign" language at home from parents who themselves do not learn the language of the community, and the child has to learn the language of the community only at school, he may be handicapped for the first several years he is in school. Many schools are now introducing a second language in third or fourth grade for children who have no problems with language. Such programs are proving quite successful and should do a great deal to overcome the language barriers for the next generation.

DOROTHEA MC CARTHY

See also COMMUNITY RESOURCES; IMITATION; INDIVIDUAL DIFFERENCES; SPEECH DIFFICULTIES; VOCABULARY DEVELOPMENT

TAMPONS *See* MENSTRUATION

TANTRUM *See* TEMPER TANTRUM

TARDINESS *See* DAWDLING

TATTLING

Tattling has a variety of meanings depending on the needs of the talebearer and his phase of development. Unacceptable as it may be by adult standards, in children, tattling is usually only a clumsy attempt to deal with a difficult situation.

When a 3- or a 4-year-old tearfully announces that a playmate or a brother or sister has grabbed his toy, pushed him off the swing, or refused to let him be the pilot of an imaginary airplane, he is saying in effect, "I'm up against something too hard for me to handle. I need help." A definite suggestion about where to find another toy, how to take turns on the swing, or the fun of being a passenger on the airplane often points the way.

Gradually, you can put the responsibility for handling such minor crises on the youngster by saying something like, "What do you think you can do about it?"

The 5-, 6-, or 7-year-old who is bursting with self-righteousness as he rushes to tell you that wrongdoing is afoot, frequently is merely trying to reassure himself—and you—that he knows what is right. His own impulse to indulge in this particular kind of mischief has so recently been conquered that a tender conscience can only be soothed by proclaiming innocence. The parent who calmly takes the stand, "I'm glad you know what's right. Perhaps you can help the other children find a better way," strengthens that budding conscience.

No parent would turn a deaf ear to a child's account of companions who were playing with knives or matches, locking doors, or roller skating in the middle of the street. Reporting potentially dangerous activities shows a commendable sense of responsibility and is different from carrying tales just to get someone in trouble—granted that the motives of even the best 6- or 7-year-olds may be mixed. We help boys and girls distinguish between sensible reports of danger and malicious tattling as we let them know they can always tell us what is troubling them without fear of reproof. But we also let them know that our response to the news that brother has taken more than his share of cookies will hardly be comparable to our reaction to the news that sister is jumping on the roof of a parked automobile.

In order to guide a child out of his tattling tendencies, we may need to look beyond the immediate incident. Does the inveterate tattler need more enjoyable, comfortable relationships with his parents and with others in and outside the family? If he is given the feeling through the way he is talked to, listened to, and spoken of that his parents have confidence in him and consider him a lovable person, he may have less need to become an informer in order to prove he is "good." Some children, when they acquire enough skill to hold their own or sufficient enthusiasm for at least one game, sport, or hobby, have a happier time with other youngsters and find less to criticize in their behavior.

When you are discouraged about talebearing, keep in mind that in a few years you will probably be saying of this same tattler, "I can't get a word out of him about his friends or what they are doing." The years of "informing" are brief, and then the children ally themselves perhaps all too closely with their contemporaries.

EDITH G. NEISSER

TEACHER *See* SCHOOLTEACHER

TEACHER CONFERENCE

Beyond any question, the most satisfying way to get a full report on your child's school life is to talk face-to-face with his teacher.

In contrast to report cards and written reports from the school, a conference provides an opportunity for a more leisurely and thorough examination of all aspects of a child's performance in school. A conference enables parents to raise questions about anything and everything they would like to know, instead of being limited to whatever happens to be included in the written report. A conference contributes to good and complete understanding because it provides time for questions to be thrashed out thoroughly. It usually enables the teacher to make her points more clear by illustrating them with examples of a child's work: his art products, test papers, written reports, and the like. Much more so than either report cards or a written report, the conference makes possible two-way communication and the sharing of ideas. Parents and the teacher can make a joint plan for their next steps to further a child's development.

Conferences Take Time

Although parent-teacher conferences have such strong virtues, few school systems have as yet found ways of capitalizing on these strengths and of making conferences their major means of reporting to parents. The greatest obstacle is lack of time. Obviously, teachers cannot work with children in school and simultaneously talk with parents. One way or another, additional time has to be found. Some conscientious teachers confer with at least some of the parents after school hours, in the evenings, or on weekends. These conferences place a great burden on the teacher. Some school systems close school for a day or two at some time in the school year so that all parents and teachers can talk. Under these conditions conferences usually must be rigidly scheduled and often hurried. The time pressure sometimes makes them less satisfactory than they could otherwise be. Occasionally, school systems hire substitute teachers to work with the children, freeing the regular teacher to confer with parents. But with so many parents to see, the pressure of time usually still remains. Proba-

bly the ultimate solution lies in a major lengthening of the school year so that school for children can be closed for longer intervals, enabling parents and teachers to talk together without actually decreasing the amount of school instruction that youngsters receive. The problem of providing enough time for parents and teachers to talk is not one that professional educators can solve alone. Parents who are eager for an opportunity to confer with teachers without pressure will have to play a leadership role, one that encourages schools to create new schedules that will provide the hours needed for these adult meetings.

Objections to Conferences

Most parents who have taken part in parent-teacher conferences even under today's conditions have found them highly satisfactory. Some, however, find objections. Many of today's adults were brought up on report cards, and consequently they may leave a conference dissatisfied because the points covered were not pinned down to specific grades. Even though mothers and fathers may have learned a great deal about their child's behavior in school, they sometimes feel as if they have not. Other parents dread talking with their child's teacher. Again, their own childhood experiences probably play a part. Historically, parents were called to school only when something had gone wrong, and so today some parents anticipate that fault-finding will be the major tone of a conference with the teacher. A few parents even approach conferences with chips on their shoulders, determined to find fault first before the school can have its say. And, even under the best of conditions, conferences cannot be held as often as report cards can be sent home. Some parents feel that they do not get information as frequently as they would like from conferences alone.

Schools have tried in various ways to allay some of these objections. Many schools use a mixture of reporting methods. They continue with monthly or six-week grades, but they also hold parent conferences either in the middle of the school year or at the end of the year. Not uncommonly, some kind of written report is sent home before the conference as a basis for the discussion, or afterwards to supplement and reinforce what has been talked about. Schools have also taken steps to set at rest any needless fears about conferences. Many schools have conference rooms where parents and teachers can talk more comfortably than in the classroom with its austere teacher's desk. The fact that the conferences are for all parents—not only those whose youngsters may be having some trouble in school—has also helped to lessen tension.

"Conferencing" Is Not Easy

It never is easy for parents and teachers to talk about a child. The problem is simpler with the rare child whose work is excellent, whose social adjustment is all one could ask, who presents no difficulties of any kind. But this situation is highly exceptional. Almost every youngster has some areas where his performance could be improved if the adults working with him at home and at school could hit upon a better plan for his guidance. Inevitably, discussion of these problem areas seems to imply some criticism, either of the home or of the school. And most of us, whether parents or teachers, find it hard to cope with what seems like criticism. A good conference requires tact on the part of the teacher, not pushing too hard into areas where the parents may not yet be ready to think clearly. A good conference requires faith in the teacher on the part of the parents, a real conviction that the teacher wants only the best for the child and, like the parents, is seeking that best. This mutual maturity on the part of both parents and teacher is not easy to achieve.

Conferences usually succeed better if groundwork has been laid for them. It helps greatly, for example, if the parents have had an opportunity to observe their child at work in school before the conference is held. Such observations are usually easier to arrange with the early childhood age range than with older children. But whenever possible, they do make it easier for parents and the teacher to talk together and plan together. They have each had the opportunity to see the same thing and their discussion can proceed on a common base.

Conferences succeed better, too, if the face-to-face meeting is not the first time that the parents and teacher have met and talked together. It takes experience in working together before adults can talk easily and with mutual faith and trust. When teachers have had the opportunity to visit homes, to chat informally with parents at PTA meetings and other similar occasions, when the conference is one of many meetings rather than the only one, it is usually more productive. Parents can play a major part in making conferences more useful by taking the initiative in getting to know a teacher well, through many different associations, before the time comes for parents and teacher to talk together.

It is important for both parents and a teacher to be realistic about what a conference can accomplish. One goal is clear: A conference ought to give parents a full and clear picture of their child at school—how he acts, his relationships with adults and children, his areas of strength and of weakness, his progress and his lags. Parents certainly should feel free to ask all the questions that occur to them, never hesitating for fear some question may be "out of bounds." The parent-teacher conference is the home's opportunity to get a firsthand report from the one person who is Johnny on the spot, the classroom teacher. Similarly, the conference can give the teacher an opportunity to round out her knowledge of a child's home life and his out-of-school experiences so that her understanding of the youngster may be more complete. Realistically, however, one conference can seldom cover all the ground that needs to be covered. Both parents and the teacher should feel at the end of a meeting that some useful, clear information has been shared and that the way is open for future meetings and more sharing.

An important part of a conference, however, is not reporting the past but planning for the future. Here, realism is most needed. The teacher has good professional skills and has seen and worked with many children. The parent has an excellent subjective impression of a child. But neither parent nor teacher is a wonder-worker. At any one meeting, neither one may be able to think up a plan, or to put one in operation, which will solve a child's problems. Many a conference must end simply on the note that both parents and the teacher will continue to think and to puzzle. This may be the most satisfactory outcome possible, even though it can disappoint anyone who thinks that life's problems are simple. One of the greatest lessons both parents and teachers have to learn is to be wary of the simple solutions; they seldom get to the heart of the matter. The sharing of information, plus the willingness to continue to think together and to talk together, either formally in a conference or in more informal ways, can lead to better living for a child, even though at the specific moment a conference ends it may seem as if little has been accomplished. JAMES L. HYMES, JR.

See also HOME-SCHOOL RELATIONS

TEAR DUCTS

The tear duct is a small tube leading from the tear sac (inside the lower eyelid next to the nose) to the inside of the nose. The duct's function is to carry away from the eye extra tears that result from crying or from the normal lubrication of the eye.

Some watering of the eyes in early weeks may be excessive tear production caused by silver nitrate medication placed in the baby's eyes at birth. This watering usually disappears in a few weeks as the irritation subsides. Treat only by wiping when necessary with a clean cloth or a piece of cotton.

Persistent watering because of a blocked tear duct should be treated in the same manner—by wiping away the excess secretion after sleep with a small piece of cotton moistened in cool boiled water. When the condition continues after two months or is very severe or is accompanied by irritation and reddening of the eye, the baby's doctor should be consulted. Special treatment, such as probing of the duct, may be necessary. The doctor may suggest massaging of the tear sac gently down toward the nose, but treatment should be attempted only on the doctor's advice. RUTH S. KEMPE

TEASING

Nobody likes to be teased. This is a simple fact we all know, but knowing it doesn't stop us from teasing people occasionally. It must be that, at times, we actually want to annoy others. Yet the teaser will more frequently than not claim that "he meant no harm." If this is so, why does he approach another in this fashion? Basically, what is teasing? Why do we respond as we do?

Teasing is one of the many varieties of aggressive behavior. It is common to both children and adults, and it is mostly oral as opposed to such gross acts of hostility as kicking, punching, and scratching. It differs also from these more overt and physical expressions of aggression in that it is half covered up. In the event of objection, a person doing the teasing can almost always retort by saying, "I was only fooling." A blow or a kick cannot as easily be explained away. In other words, there is something more subtle and sophisticated and even sneaky about teasing as compared with other more undeniable and obvious acts of hostility. Finally, teasing has a more persistent quality. In fact, the repeated harping on something is part of the very nature of teasing. It is much like a blunt drill, which must be applied for a longer period of time before it can be expected to reach beneath the surface.

When we tease others, we are generally aware of our feelings of hostility no matter how mild and benign they may seem to be. Even good-natured teasing is critical and aggressive. Although no harm may be meant, it is a way of getting a rise out of someone. If teasing works at all, it is annoying and generally prompts some kind of emotional response. This reveals the purpose of the teaser more clearly than anything else. The person who teases wants an emotional response as evidence of his influence or effect on the person he teases.

Teasing, then, is a way of reaching out socially and having one's efforts felt. The quality of this effort depends on the kind of person the teaser is. A 9-year-old who has been unhappy about his younger brother's five-year invasion of his family life might tease him unmercifully. Forced to share a social existence with his brother, he expresses his hostility and proves his influence by the visible emotional reaction he brings forth. On the other hand, a grandparent may tease his own grandchild not to annoy him but merely to get him to pay some attention—which can be done only by annoying him.

Sensitivity to being teased is a fairly good over-all index of emotional stability. A child who cries easily will also cry easily when he is teased. A child with a deep sense of his acceptance by the world tends not to believe you when you tease him; he feels you must be joking and laughs it off unless you persist unreasonably. There are, of course, areas of sensitivity in anyone, no matter how well he is adjusted, but even if these tender toes are stepped on, a stable child will show annoyance and not a tantrum.

Teasing of children by children is almost inevitable for the simple reason that children need every means, short of mayhem, of expressing their hostility. A group of children will commonly gang up on some unfortunate victim and tease him until their loyalties shift and some other member of the group becomes the scapegoat. This is all part of the dynamics of group living among children and, as such, normal, even though frequently unjust. It is the persistent use of teasing by a single child which requires special attention. Such a child is essentially a verbal bully who probably is deeply afraid of the loss of his own status unless he constantly proves his influence by upsetting others.

This tendency to bully others is not entirely alien to adults. Even though teasing is not considered to be in good taste among grown-ups, many of them have the unfortunate habit of piquing children very much more often than is good for their relationship with each other. Children all the way up through adolescence simply do not have the sense of humor that adults do. They are seldom amused when they are teased and, before long, begin to reject the adults who tease them. If they are dependent on these adults, considerable conflict results. Teasing, therefore, should be only a very occasional device employed by adults. It is better for parents to explain teasing to their children than to use it. ALLAN FROMME

See also APPROVAL; HOSTILITY; HUMOR; SENSITIVENESS

TEEN-AGER

Some parents dread their children's adolescence. They may themselves have been unhappy at this time of life, or a neighbor's problem or a newspaper story may have raised parental fear that these are going to be difficult years for their son or daughter or for them. Such feelings are really unjustified. Adolescents are people, not problems.

There is nothing inherently ominous about adolescence; it is not inevitably a disastrous period filled with mysterious and baffling problems that defy understanding. In reality, adolescence is no more than an exciting, very interesting, desirable process—the process of becoming an adult. Obviously, we all want young people to grow up.

Growth Is Rapid and Varied

The changes, physiological and psychological, which are desirable and essential parts of adolescence, admittedly may cause trouble just as do those changes that go on as an infant becomes a child or as an adult becomes elderly. But many adolescents go through these processes with little or no trouble to themselves or to others, and it is fair to say that the more fully you understand this process—adolescence—the more it will lose its mystery and the less likely it will be to cause you anxiety. We tend to fear what we do not understand.

What are some of the normal and desirable changes that your young person must go through in the process of growing up? The outstanding physiological one is that of rapid and extensive and varied growth. At no other time of life except during the first year does one grow so much, so fast, and change in so many respects as during adolescence. The most obvious evidence of this growth is the spurt in height and in sexual maturity. The feet are suddenly far from the head, the arms dangle with no place to go, the breasts or genitalia enlarge, and in girls the menarche (menstruation) occurs. These changes bring with them greatly increased nutritional needs—for protein, calcium, iron, and many other food elements—and are often accompanied not only by an incredible appetite, but also by awkwardness and a resultant increase in self-consciousness.

These experiences are normal and will pass: It takes time for young people to adjust to their larger and more sexually mature bodies. But since we do not all grow at the same age or to the same extent, these variations in growth during adolescence may bring anxiety to those who find themselves shorter or taller or more flat-chested or less bearded than their companions. These differences may be a handicap to a teen-ager's athletic or social success, or he may confuse his being different with being abnormal. It is easier for those who grow in an average way, but most of the others are perfectly normal, too, and his doctor can usually reassure the worried one that his growth, though different, is not abnormal. But we do need to remember how important size and maturity are to a young boy or girl and to avoid treating their worries as inconsequential.

Resistance Increases, Too

Adolescents grow in many other respects. Their hearts and many other organs increase in size; these aspects of growth are mostly a doctor's concern. That resistance to many, but not all, sorts of infection normally increases at this time of life is a matter of more general interest. Why this is so is not fully understood, but it is a fact that many children previously frail and subject to frequent colds and sore throats, for instance, now in adolescence became more resistant to them. And a fortunate thing, for the adolescent not only dislikes restrictions, pampering, and being made to feel different, but he also needs to participate in activities that are often strenuous, and perhaps previously denied him, if he is to achieve the recognition and successes that can yield to him the self-confidence he so badly needs. Parents should realize that it is important for their teen-ager to engage in these activities and that if his resistance to infection has increased, they will be much less hazardous to him than they were in childhood.

The psychological processes that go on during adolescence are no less normal or desirable than the physiological ones. It is natural for adolescents to strive for the ability to behave independently. For those who have not as little tots learned that there are limits and who cannot accept controls or who have little confidence in themselves, this striving can be a difficult process. Their efforts may be brash and awkward and may vacillate between demanding more freedom and retreating from the responsibility offered them.

Some parents, those who are insecure themselves or who dread to see their child grow up, may inadvertently make matters worse by alternately thrusting too much freedom on him and then snatching it away. Independence is most smoothly achieved by those young people whose earlier experiences have brought them some confidence in themselves and to whom more and more responsibility and trust have gradually been given over the years.

Young boys and girls now also need to acquire the ability to control their heightened sex drive and to develop attitudes about sex which will be acceptable in the society in which they live. Attainment of these goals can be difficult in a world that has many standards and in which so many adults fail to live up to their own precepts. Those fortunate enough to have lived in stable homes and whose mothers and fathers have set for them good examples of consideration for each other, may be expected to experience the least difficulty in this adjustment.

Attitudes Toward Parents Change

Another process that must go on during adolescence is the change of feelings toward parents into those more appropriate to an adult. It can be a confusing time for your teen-ager and for you—your daughter gives up being a tomboy and strives to become more like her mother; her brother loosens his ties to his mother and tries to become more like his father. Their silence, their avoidance of caresses previously so acceptable, can be upsetting. And should it be difficult for the young person to wish to emulate a parent, the process can be still more troublesome. When over the years, however, relationships between the child and his parents have been good, the transition is rarely difficult.

This transition and other normal processes that go on during adolescence are desirable and not difficult to understand. They proceed with least difficulty when you give the adolescent your respect (though you may not approve his words or his deeds), when you are more quick to listen than to talk, when you ask his opinion at least as often as you advise, when you offer praise as unhesitatingly (and without a qualifying "but") as you criticize, and when you see to it that he has about him the good example of adults he can admire and respect.

It should be remembered, however, that what is done to help the adolescent during adolescence is often outweighed in importance by what he has experienced as an infant and as a child. In adolescence, it is true, much that has been wrong can still be corrected, but young people will be much more effective, much happier, and much better able to weather adversity and the normal changes implicit in adolescence if their early years have prepared them well. To be wanted and to have one's needs gratified as an infant, to experience joy, to be able to express warm feelings and to behave with spontaneity, to learn that there are limits and to accept controls, and to experience integrity in one's home as a little tot; and during the early part of the school years to have those successes that allow one to develop a feeling of competency—these are the major factors that determine the degree of difficulty the normal processes of your child's adolescence will likely present.

J. ROSWELL GALLAGHER

See also ATHLETICS; BOOKS FOR PARENTS; FAMILY DISCUSSIONS; GROWTH; IMITATION; INDIVIDUAL DIFFERENCES; PUBERTY; YOUTH ORGANIZATIONS

TEEN CLUBS *See* YOUTH ORGANIZATIONS

TEETH *See* DENTAL CARE

TEETH AND TEETHING

The first of the primary, or "baby," teeth begin to form within the jaws about two months after conception. At birth, the crowns of all 20 primary teeth and even part of the first permanent molars are forming. By the time a child is 3 years old, he usually has all his primary teeth. By this time, too, parts of more than 20 of his permanent teeth are developing deep in his jawbones.

The first tooth you see in your baby's mouth usually breaks through the gums at about 6 months. Generally, those in the lower jaw erupt first. At 1 year, your child will probably have the four upper and four lower front teeth, called the incisors. The scalloped biting edges of newly erupted incisors will wear smooth with use. The first molars appear farther back in the mouth at approximately 15 months. Then, at about 18 months the canines come through between the incisors and first molars. Finally, the second molars, or "back teeth," usually appear after two years.

Some children cut their teeth early, others late. If your child should be markedly late in cutting his teeth, your dentist or physician should be consulted.

As a tooth comes through, your baby will drool, bite, chew, and gnaw on anything he can get into his mouth. He may also thrust his lower jaw forward and from side to side, trying to make contact with the gum pads in order to help the teeth push through the

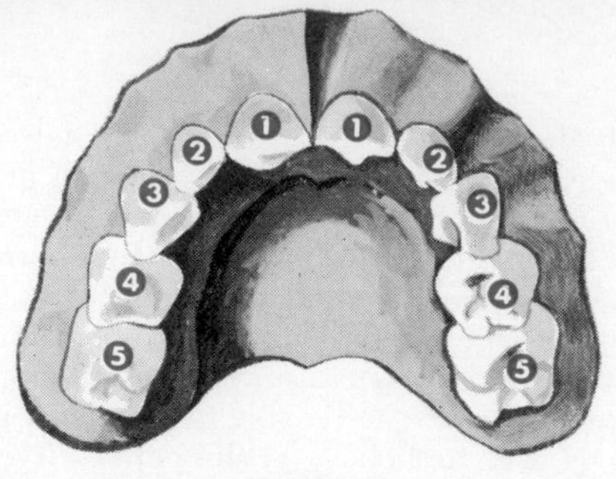

UPPER

1. Central incisor, 6–7½ months; 2. lateral incisor, 7–9 months; 3. cuspid (or canine), 16–18 months; 4. first molar, 12–14 months; 5. second molar, 18–24 months.

LOWER

1. Central incisor, 6 months; 2. lateral incisor, 6–7 months; 3. cuspid (or canine), 14–16 months; 4. first molar, 10–12 months; 5. second molar, 16–20 months.

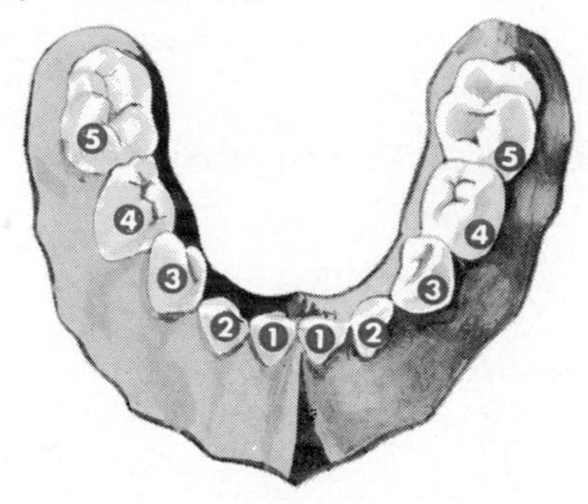

overlying tissue. Teething rings of proper size and firmness may satisfy his urge to bite. Chewing hard foods like carrot sticks, celery, and toasted bread aids teething and jaw development. Your baby will be delighted to use his gums, even before he gets his molars. Babies may be fussy while teething, but it is important that this irritability not be confused with any real signs of illness.

The primary teeth cause more difficulty in erupting than the permanent teeth. This is so because they have to blaze their own trail, whereas most of the permanent teeth follow the path already made by the 20 primary teeth they replace. The 12 molars in the set of 32 permanent teeth have no primary predecessors, but they do not erupt until the child has reached an age when the discomfort is not as annoying. The first permanent molars usually come at about 6 years, the second molars around 12 years, and the third molars (wisdom teeth) after 17 years.

The accompanying diagram shows when a child's temporary teeth can be expected to come in.

ROBERT G. KESEL

See also DENTAL CARE

TELEVISION

The average child spends more time watching television than he spends doing anything else except sleeping or going to school. For this reason, if for no other, parents need to look carefully into what their child is seeing, why he is watching it, and what effect it is having on him.

Most children of 2 or younger don't watch television. But at 3 or 4, the child begins to look at TV about two hours a day. Watching time averages between two and four hours a day, 15 to 25 hours a week. Watching reaches its peak about the fourth grade, and then drops off for most children. Still, the time your child spends watching TV probably is not taken from time spent on homework or reading. Instead, he spends less time listening to the radio, going to the movies, or playing by himself or with other children.

If you wonder how to predict television watching, you might ponder the fact that your watching is the best predictor of all. When the mother and father turn the set on every evening—and leave it on until sign-off—the child tends to watch heavily too. If the parents do other things like reading, playing cards or games, listening to music, or talking, their child does more of those things, too. The best way to reduce or increase your child's time with the TV set is to reduce or increase your own.

Most children under 11 or 12 prefer children's programs, cartoons, and child participation shows. Of course, there is always the western—popular at all ages. The child usually isn't terribly interested in "adult" programs until he reaches the fifth or sixth grade.

Effects of TV

You needn't worry too much about the effects of TV; there seem to be few bad effects and many good ones. Most children are quite able to distinguish between the "real world" of everyday living and the things they see on the magic picture. They probably won't be frightened by cartoon action, even if it is violent. Westerns don't cause them much trouble either. You should worry about a high dosage of "adult" realistic drama and suspense stories. If a child sees people he can identify with, and they get into trouble, he tends to become frightened. In general, stable children are not affected unfavorably by TV. If your child tends to be withdrawn and socially shy, he might be harmed emotionally by a great deal of television.

To some people's surprise, television watching by preschoolers or children in the early elementary grades actually helps intellectual

development. Viewing gives them a larger vocabulary, more experiences to talk about and to be interested in, and a greater awareness of the world. Among older children, this difference between viewers and nonviewers is no longer apparent. But research does seem to indicate that a child of average or a little below average intelligence may actually be helped by TV. For him, it seems to stimulate interest in some things, to cause him to increase reading that is related to the programs he watches, and to help him think more broadly about what he wants to be when he grows up. On the other hand, TV may be harmful to the child of above-average intelligence simply because the time he spends with it doesn't challenge him as much as the same amount of time spent in other pursuits.

The kind of stimulation that TV can offer can be increased and used profitably by parents. Why not encourage your child to read the book, now that he has seen the play on television? Make it easy for him to get printed material related to the material he viewed. Talk to him about what he is seeing, what he is thinking about while the program is going on, his opinion of the program. Such conversation is not only quite satisfying to the child, but also often educational for the parent.

If you're worried about television producing a gang of juvenile delinquents in your own home, you can relax. There is no evidence that television causes delinquency, although many people are firmly convinced that it does. On the other hand, there certainly is no evidence that television viewing reduces juvenile delinquency, either. Of course, television concentrates on the idea that crime doesn't pay. Unfortunately, in many of the good programs, the "badness" of crime is emphasized, but the "goodness" of honesty seldom receives equal attention. Furthermore, "badness" often is quite rewarding during most of the program, and the much-delayed triumph of virtue might give the child the idea that it isn't worth waiting for. Again, a discussion of "good" and "bad" as seen in such a program is probably helpful.

If you use reasonable care, your child's health will not suffer from watching television, either. Some soft light in the room is helpful to his viewing and lessens the danger of his getting overstimulated or frightened by the program itself. TV should not be watched in a dark room.

TV can affect eating and sleeping habits, but not if you exercise reasonable caution. Children who view TV tend to go to bed later than do nonviewers. But viewers tend to go to sleep faster after they go to bed. In the long run, viewers and nonviewers sleep about the same amount.

Children like to watch television while they are eating. A little flexibility on this point won't hurt the child or your family relationships. It probably is not a good idea to sit at the table and watch television. But, if the child is allowed a "night out" once in a while to watch his favorite program (which always comes on in the middle of the meal—no matter when the meal is served), he might be more willing to come to lunch or dinner promptly at other times.

You can also affect taste in your home. Children who are given free rein in their choice of programs tend continually to choose only those that fit their present interests. If you exert some control over viewing, you can broaden your child's interests and stretch his horizons.

No Substitute for Baby-Sitter

If there is one error parents make more than any other, it is that of allowing the television set to serve as a long-term, unpaid baby-sitter. Parents who allow and encourage use of the magic box as a sedative for their child may find themselves with an addicted youngster or one who has rejected the family. Television is no substitute for family activity. Some people might argue that television brings the family together. True, the family often is in the same room watching the same program—but one wonders if they are any more of a family than a group of people in a movie theater would be. Unless care is taken, the family can be split up by keeping it together in front of the television screen.

Guidelines for Parents

As a general rule, you might well keep in mind that a child's view of the world is affected by what he sees. In determining choice of content, you might ask, "Is this the view of the world I want my child to have? Is this what I want him to think fathers are like around the home? Is this the way I want him to think about love, marriage, the business world, and social relationships among people?" If you think about the child's own values, his reasons for watching or not watching, you can use television as an effective and exciting tool of development. Otherwise, the TV set can, in large part, replace the family.

Parents have a great deal of influence over the amount of television watching, the kind of program watched, and the ways in which the child and the family use television. The child reaps social benefits from watching programs that other children watch. One of the best ways to handle the child who says that "all the other kids get to watch that program" is to talk with the the other parents and try to set up agreed-upon guidelines for viewing behavior. You also would be surprised at the influence you hold over the local television station. A relatively small number of organized and aroused parents can exert great power over the timing of particular programs. Parental groups can affect the amount of violence and the kinds of programs that appear at children's peak viewing times. PTA's, church groups, and other organizations can also influence the relationships between home viewing and the school. A young child is strongly influenced by what his parents and teachers feel is good and bad, so the school and church can be used to influence his views on taste and values. Television is an important instrument of taste. The result of a little careful thinking and talking among parents, teachers, and clergy can have considerable influence on the developing values of a child.

A responsible parent recognizes all opportunities to affect his child and family healthily and productively through the way in which television is used. Keeping a schedule of viewing times and program content for the whole family helps a child learn about authority and the necessity for respecting the needs and desires of others. Take care, however, that you are not merely imposing your own values on your child. Turning the set off in the middle of a cartoon program or an action-filled adventure program might not be much of a loss to you; however, it is often very important to a child. It never hurts your relationships with him to try to look at things from his point of view—what's important to him is important to him, even though it might not be to you. DAVID K. BERLO

See also EYE HEALTH; STUDYING

Related article in WORLD BOOK: "Audio-Visual Materials"

TEMPERATURE

The temperature of the human body is normally in the range of 98.6° F. (38° C.). A child's normal temperature will rarely be found to be at *exactly* this point, and variations of several tenths of a degree may be disregarded. The body temperature is usually slightly lower in the morning than in the evening; exercise may raise the body temperature by several tenths of a degree or, if quite vigorous, a whole degree or more. The time to take a child's temperature, therefore, is after he has been at rest for half an hour. When regular daily temperature is being recorded, the time to take it is in the late afternoon or evening.

Premature babies have difficulty in maintaining a stable body temperature and may need to be kept in a heated crib or incubator for some time. Full-term newborn babies also have this difficulty but to a lesser extent.

A body temperature above normal most commonly indicates that some infection is present or is developing in the body. It is important to remember that this raised temperature, or fever, is only a symptom and not a disease and that when fever is present, the cause must be sought. The cause may be a local infection—abscess in the skin or sinusitis, for example, or a general infection—measles, influenza, tuberculosis, typhoid fever. The fever may be low grade, in which case the child may appear to be lethargic, or drowsy, especially in the afternoon; if the fever is above 101° F., a child will usually complain of being ill, be quite lacking in energy, and will want to remain quiet or go to bed. Headache and muscular aching are quite common with high fever.

Regardless of the cause of the fever, if it is high (above 103° F.), some children develop convulsive seizures. But there is great variation in children: Some never have convulsions and others tend to quite readily. It is advisable, therefore, when high fever develops to take some measures, such as cool sponging of the skin or immersion in a bathtub of cool water, and to give aspirin (under the direction of the doctor, of course), to lower the temperature.

Usually parents can tell if their child has a high fever by feeling the increased warmth of the skin. It is better, however, to measure how high the fever is—especially if there is any doubt about whether fever is present. For infants and very young children, it is preferable to take the temperature by means of a rectal thermometer. While the thermometer is inserted for two or three minutes, the parent should remain with the child; otherwise the thermometer might be broken and injure the rectum or anus. For children of school age, an oral thermometer placed under the tongue is best. An oral thermometer should be left in place for at least five minutes, with the mouth closed. If a child is very ill or if his nose is stopped up, oral temperature recording may not be possible. The doctor may then suggest either taking the temperature rectally or placing the thermometer in the armpit and holding it there for five minutes. It is well to be certain that the child whose temperature is to be taken has not been exercising immediately before, that he has not been in the sun or just had a hot bath, and that he has not been drinking warm fluids. Even the chewing of gum may cause a slightly elevated temperature.

To insure accuracy in taking temperatures, the thermometer should be of a good quality.

JULIUS B. RICHMOND

See also COMMON COMMUNICABLE DISEASES; SICK CHILD

TEMPER TANTRUM

A temper tantrum hardly needs definition. It is recognized as a fairly all-over primitive response to frustration. Voice and muscles collaborate to create an explosive picture of rage. Two is probably the peak age for the practice of this particular strategy as a method of expressing dissatisfaction. Usually it will diminish in both intensity and frequency by age 4. By this time other more refined methods of expressing annoyance will have been learned and substituted for the more primitive, infantile temper tantrum.

The parent who is engaged in helping a child to live with his feelings needs to assess the situations that seem to spark tantrums. Are tantrums justifiable from the *child's point of view?* Would a little easing of pressure relieve the need for explosive behavior? Or is the tantrum out of proportion to the cause? Has the child been "egged" into his rage or is he overreacting to a seemingly mild request or expectation or deprivation? If a child explodes because he must put on his boots, his behavior would seem somewhat extreme unless this request is the last straw in a long succession of adult demands.

There is no single simple recipe for effective handling of the tantrum child. Physical restraint is probably least effective; in fact, it is more likely to prolong and stimulate rage. The situation then becomes an endurance battle. Who will win? Permitting the child to gain his end (whatever it may be) is effective only in reinforcing the belief that tantrums get you what you want.

The child in a tantrum is not in a receptive mood to learn much of anything. He needs time to work out of his angry state before he can be approached. A sort of "semi-isolation," without benefit of audience reaction, may help some children. Standing by rather than abandoning an angry child may help him to return to himself more readily.

Most children who are living through the normal primitive tantrum level of expressing their anger will respond to an adult who stands by patiently waiting for the explosion to subside and then moves in to comfort with understanding. This kind of response tells a child that the grownup understands but does not condemn, nor condone, his behavior. It also carries seeds of expecting that the child will eventually be able to learn other more acceptable ways of expressing his needs and wishes.

"I know you feel angry when . . ." and "Someday you can *tell* me what you want—or don't want." The adult who flares back with a tantrum of his own is less likely to be successful in teaching a child to relinquish this primitive method of communicating his feelings.

Commending a child who has learned to substitute more refined modes of expression is also an effective teaching device. "Remember how you used to have a tantrum if you couldn't go outside when you were sick? Now you understand the reason, and you only fuss a little."

The child who clings to tantrum behavior rather than progressing to other less wild and all-over responses to frustration may need a more critical viewing of his needs, his feelings, his satisfactions. Are too many demands and pressures being put upon him? Is he being overindulged? Does he have too many choices—or no choices to make? Does he have to compete (unsuccessfully) for attention or affection? Is he having too much or too little of authority, too many or too few rules, too high or too low expectations? Let us look to our "dosage" of pressure and expectation when the response seems extreme. Occasional temper tantrums are no cause for concern, but the child who persists in resorting to temper tantrums at 4 and 5 needs help, not condemnation. Sometimes parents can be helped by the family doctor to find out the causes of such chronic violent outbursts. Effective treatment or redirection or teaching is more likely to be successful when the reasons for the behavior are probed for and finally discovered. EVELYN BEYER

See also ANGER

TESTS *See* SCHOOL TESTS AND EXAMINATIONS

TESTS AND MEASUREMENTS

More than 130 million tests are given in the schools of the United States each year. This means, of course, that tests are playing or are going to play a very important part in your child's life. He will be given tests to measure his academic achievement, his aptitudes of all kinds, and his personal and social adjustment.

If you yourself understand and respect present-day tests and, most of all, if you take advantage of the information they provide, they can be useful to you and your child as check points in his life as he grows from kindergartner to adolescent and beyond. In many ways, the standardized testing programs serve a purpose similar to the monthly balances you make in your home budget or the daily weighing you do on your bathroom scales.

Why is there all this testing? It is because parents, teachers, and even employers are recognizing that each individual is unique, both physiologically and psychologically. Individualized instruction is important, and psychological tests provide information on which to base such instruction, for tests can show how nearly a child is reaching the goals he is capable of attaining, particularly goals that have to do with thinking.

What Is a Test?

Probably the most useful definition of a test is this: A test is a group of questions and tasks to which your child must respond. In achievement tests your child will be asked to respond to questions involving reading, arithmetic, spelling, grammar, and perhaps questions involving science and social studies as well. In aptitude tests your child will be asked to respond to questions that are designed to predict his probable future success in specific fields such as music, art, foreign language, or mechanics. In personal-social adjustment inventories your child will be asked to indicate how he feels about himself and his relations with other people.

There are many different types of tests: group tests, individual tests, objective tests, projective tests, essay tests, standardized tests, and informal tests.

A group test is any test that is given to more than one child at a time; practically all tests given your child are group tests.

An individual test is any test that is given to just one child at a time. Individual tests are used only in special cases; they usually give highly reliable results, but they are expensive and it takes a great deal of time to give them.

An objective test is any test that is readily scored with a "right-answers key." Examples are true-false tests, multiple-choice tests, and matching tests.

A projective test is a test in which the child "projects" his interests, needs, and feelings. In one widely used projective test, children are shown pictures of life situations and are asked to make up a story about each picture.

An essay test is a test of the child's writing ability. He is asked to write a paragraph or a story, which is then graded for writing style.

Standardized tests are commercial tests that have been developed by professional test builders. Practically all aptitude tests and many achievement tests used in the elementary schools throughout the United States are standardized tests.

Informal tests are those made by the teacher for a particular purpose in the classroom. Usually, they are quizzes on words or numbers and are quite short.

Sometimes you may be confused because several test names are used together. For example, your child may be given a group-objective-standardized test. In simple terms this means that all the children (group) are getting a commercially made (standardized) test of memory or recognition.

Most of the testing done is *achievement* testing. There is also much *aptitude* testing. *Personal-social adjustment inventories* are used somewhat, but they are not well enough developed for the schools to have entire confidence in the results they show.

Why Are Tests Given?

Nowadays, mental health organizations, summer camps, business and industrial personnel offices, and even some day camps and nursery schools give psychological tests. But the school is the unchallenged leader; every modern elementary and secondary school has an organized testing program to study each child's psychological make-up as he goes through school. This information is kept on a cumulative record, begun in kindergarten and continued through high school.

Schools have three major reasons for their widespread use of tests. In the first place, teachers want to know each child's progress in all academic subjects. Achievement tests in the elementary schools emphasize reading, vocabulary, spelling, general language ability, arithmetic computation, and arithmetic reasoning. Tests of this kind, often given in October, are used to show what a child has learned during the previous school year and to plan a program for the year just beginning. Some standardized achievement testing usually occurs between kindergarten and third grade. After that the amount increases greatly, sometimes including not only tests for all the children in a school, but also for all those in a state.

A second important reason for testing by the schools has to do with the need for information about aptitudes. Perhaps you are confused, understandably, between scholastic aptitude and achievement tests. Achievement tests, you will recall, show what a child has already learned. Aptitude tests measure his capacity to learn. On the basis of aptitudes, your child's future academic and later vocational success can be predicted, and his teachers can judge whether he should be able to do well in school, whether he should take a college preparatory course, and even whether he might make a good architect or would do better as a businessman.

By tests, teachers can know more about the emotional adjustment a child is making, a third reason for the school testing program. *Personality tests,* or as they are often more accurately called, *personal-social adjustment inventories,* are usually paper and pencil questionnaires.

These inventories differ from achievement and aptitude tests in that the questions have no right or wrong answers. Each child is given a series of questions to which he is allowed to select one of three answers: "yes," "no," or "I don't know." The questions probe his experiences and feelings, as, for example, "Do you daydream frequently?" and "Do you think that people are often watching you?" His answers are analyzed in terms of feelings, and can be interpreted as insecurity, fear, negativism, and the like.

Unfortunately, the meanings of scores from personal-social adjustment inventories are difficult to determine. In the first place, there is not widespread agreement as to definitions. The author of a test may define negativism differently than you do. In addition, the scores a child makes on the inventories change; they are not reliable. In all probability, the problem here is not in the child but with the test.

These inventories are not widely used in schools. At best they provide only a basis for crude screening of children in terms of emotional stability. If, however, one of these tests should seem to reveal possible signs of emotional difficulties in a child, he probably should be referred to a school psychologist or private clinician, who can come much closer to the true situation than the school tests can. In addition to talking to and listening to both the child and his parents, these professionals give tests designed to reveal a more nearly accurate picture of a child's personality and problems.

About the IQ

The score from a scholastic aptitude test is often called an intelligence quotient (IQ). IQ is figured by dividing the child's mental age by his chronological age and multiplying by 100. His mental age is 8 if his score is that for average 8-year-olds; his mental age is 12 if his score is that for average 12-year-olds. His chronological age is the number of years he has lived. Thus, a 10-year-old child with a mental age of 8 would be 10 into 8, times 100, or an IQ of 80; the 10-year-old with the mental age of 12 would have an IQ of 120.

Your child's IQ is influenced by many things. Heredity, foı example, plays a part. He is born with a certain mental potential. Environment is a very definite influence: If over a long period of time there is not enough

During a child's academic career, as well as in his early professional life, he will meet more and more standardized tests of widely varying kinds.

mental stimulation around him, a child's IQ can be seriously reduced, whereas an environment rich in mental stimulation will certainly increase it.

Health is another factor. Reasonably good health gives him alertness and stamina. A child in poor health may find the scholastic aptitude test exhausting and his score may reflect his fatigue.

Finally, good emotional health is vital. For a child to be able to perform at his level, he needs a positive attitude toward tests and their use. Children who have periods of extreme depression or hostility and who are tested during one of these periods rarely can show their true ability.

The intelligence quotient itself can be changed by a shift in influences. A child taken from an environment where he gets little intellectual stimulation and placed for a long period of time in an enriched environment will often show very noticeable increases in his IQ. Improvement in a child's physical or mental health will very often improve his test scores. Sometimes these improvements are not large and they are not always consistent, but a change for the better will take place. In other words, IQ scores can be raised, but only as the result of unusual improvements in a child's situation and only after these improvements have been going on in his life for quite a while.

How does one interpret the IQ's of a child when his IQ's vary greatly? Say that for several years a child has been taking scholastic aptitude tests with his group and that each time he scores quite differently. The best thing to do is to give such a child an individual scholastic aptitude test. Several excellent ones are available and there are school psychologists or private clinicians trained to administer them. From an individual test you can learn not only your child's IQ, but you can also get a good idea of the variations in his verbal, arithmetic, and motor skills. Thus you find out some of the major reasons for your child's performance in school.

Scholastic aptitude tests often seem mysterious things. Although you can easily see why no child should have advance information about a test, it still is necessary that both you and your child have some idea of the kinds of questions and tasks that make up the typical scholastic aptitude test. For example, you could ask the teacher whether the test will stress motor skills or subjects the children have learned in the classroom.

Children in the last half of kindergarten or in the first half of the first grade are sometimes given a group scholastic aptitude test, known as a reading readiness test. In the last half of the third grade or possibly the first half of the fourth grade, children are given a scholastic aptitude test of the general type. Very likely in the sixth grade there will be another such test. In many school systems a child's cumulative record will contain three scholastic aptitude scores by the time he is ready to enter junior high school.

The Parents' Role Before Tests

You can assist your child greatly if you help him understand the testing situation and his role in it. Three important points to remember are:

1. Help your child to feel at ease about the test. Go to PTA meetings and parent-teacher conferences to find out details of the testing situation. In the standardized test, it is possible to find out what type will be given, the time at which it is to be given, and the reasons for giving it. Your child should, if possible, be informed of these facts. Usually his teacher will do so. But the rapid pace of the typical school plus failure to realize that a child is often not familiar with organized testing programs cause many teachers to overlook telling children about the testing process. You, therefore, can talk over the testing program with your child so that he understands it and fits it into his whole school career. You will thus be giving important support to school and teacher and at the same time you will increase the chances that your child will have a pleasant testing experience.

2. Help your child develop an interest in tests. What you have previously told him about the kind of test and its purposes may already have helped him to look forward to the next test session. But he should also understand that each test is part of a long series with which he will be faced as he goes through school. He can readily understand the parallel between a test to measure his scholastic growth and possible future progress and a physical examination to measure his physical growth and future level of activities. Tell him, too, that test scores can be used to his advantage for many different purposes—for classification, for remedial work, for assigning him the classroom work he needs, and for general guidance of his classroom experiences.

3. Discourage excessive cramming and coaching just before standardized achievement tests. The time to help your child is in the weeks and months before testing. You can do this by showing an interest in his daily school assignments, particularly in the verbal and arithmetic skills. With regular daily study he will feel less pressure, he will learn in a more orderly way, and in the end he will remember more.

Parents' Role After Tests Are Administered

Your child's teacher or principal will probably be glad to discuss test results with you, but it is not altogether easy for a parent to understand what the scores mean. These four steps may help you:

1. Ask to examine the tests or items from similar tests. Study them carefully and answer some of the questions yourself so that you can understand what your child had to answer.

2. Ask how the test was scored and about the units of the test score. The three common units used are percentile ranks, stanines, and grade equivalents. Percentile rank shows how far up from the bottom your child is in relation to a standard group of 100 students of his grade level. For instance, if your child has a percentile rank of 63, he ranks 63rd from the bottom of this group. Naturally, what kind of group he is being compared with makes a difference—is it composed of students in his class or is it based on a state, regional, or national sample? The designation "stanine" comes from the expression, standard nine. Instead of 100 positions, as in percentile ranks, stanines have but nine. A stanine of five is average, one is the lowest, and nine is the highest of the scores. Grade equivalents measure a child's performance in relation to his grade level. Suppose that, in the case of reading, your child is beginning the fourth grade but that his achievement is that of a beginning fifth-grade student. His grade equivalent is 5.0. Another child, also entering fourth grade but with the reading ability of a third grader, would score 3.0.

3. Ask about how your child has done in things other than tests—about his written assignments, his classwork, his deportment, his scores on other recent informal quizzes he has taken. These data often can provide a clue to or reason for your child's test results. For example, achievement test scores and scholastic aptitude test scores should be considered together in order to determine if he is working up to his capacity.

4. Ask the teacher about the exact nature of *new* information now available concerning your child as a result of the test, and be certain that at least the highlights of the new information are carefully explained to him. Remember, however, that the test scores give only a limited picture of any child—on the order of snapshots made by a hurried photographer. Ask the teacher how well the

test serves the purpose for which it was intended, whether the achievement test your child was given is truly like the kind of work he has been doing or whether his aptitude test has proved accurate with other children. In any event, make every effort to find out what the test score showed, whether it told you what you already knew or whether it has given you and the teacher some helpful new information.

Although tests are not perfect, they are becoming increasingly better. No matter what your childhood experiences may have been with tests, it is important now that you cultivate a positive attitude toward them, for your child's attitude will probably reflect your own. Unlike your early school days, however, he is faced with tests that are far more interesting and of much better quality than those you were given. Moreover, during the balance of his academic career, as well as in his early professional life, he will meet more and more standardized tests of a widely varying type. If you can help give him a favorable feeling toward these tests when he is quite young, you will be doing him a service that will last throughout his entire school and business life. J. STANLEY AHMANN

See also HOME-SCHOOL RELATIONS; STUDYING

TETANUS

Tetanus, or lockjaw, is a disease affecting the brain and the nerves. With it, the victim has convulsions, experiences rigidity of muscles, and particularly suffers spasms of the jaw muscles, making it difficult for him to eat. This last symptom has given the disease the common name of lockjaw.

Tetanus is caused by a germ that secretes a powerful poison as it grows. The tetanus organism cannot grow when exposed to air; it requires deep tissue pockets from which oxygen is excluded. Tetanus, therefore, most often develops in puncture wounds or in those where there has been great tissue destruction. A rusty nail puncture is no worse than one made with a clean-looking instrument carrying tetanus germs. The tetanus organism lives in the intestines of domestic animals, and from their droppings it infects the soil. Dirty skin may carry tetanus germs that remain harmless unless they are carried deep into the tissues by a puncture wound. The poison is absorbed by the nerves and travels along them to the brain where it creates the convulsive and spasmodic symptoms.

The best protection against tetanus is tetanus toxoid, an immunizing vaccine given to your infant along with his diphtheria and whooping cough vaccines in a single shot. A booster shot may be recommended when the child enters school. In view of the increasing number of automobile accidents and the possibility of enemy action, tetanus immunization has now been advocated for all persons, including adults.

Tetanus antitoxin is used to treat tetanus after it has developed, but it is much better to be immunized. Tetanus antitoxin is given to nonimmunized persons following injuries.

Any injury of a perforating or punctured nature or any cut that does not bleed readily should be called to the attention of the physician. Meantime, the wound should be cleansed and covered. W. W. BAUER

See also CUTS AND SCRATCHES; FIRST AID; IMMUNIZATION

THERMOMETER *See* TEMPERATURE

THIAMINE *See* VITAMINS

THIN CHILD *See* UNDERWEIGHT

THREATS

Many youngsters are confronted with a steady flow of threats about the dire consequences of their behavior: "If you don't come in right now, I will . . ." "If you don't stop this minute, I will . . ." Such promises of some doom to come, although widely used, are an ineffective means of controlling children's behavior.

When a child's actions have to be stopped or when he should do something, it is much better for a parent simply to say, "No" or "You must," clearly and definitely and firmly. The simple, direct insistence of the adult in authority must be enough to make a child respond. To add a threat to firm insistence adds dangerous complications. In effect, the child is being given a choice. He can continue his misbehavior and pay some price, or he can stop. There should be no such choice if the behavior is wrong. Furthermore, the addition of a threat usually weakens the adult's position. Most children quickly learn that the threats are simply words, not always carried out. The result is that a child stops listening, both to the threat and to his parent's "no's." To safeguard against this negative result, one would have to carry out all threats instantly and without fail. Such a deadly earnest effort, however, would almost surely lead to continuous warfare between parent and child. It could result only in angry and sullen relationships that would destroy the foundation of good discipline. Threats, then, should be saved for those very rare instances when a child really does have a choice and when the adult is fully prepared to carry out his part of the bargain. For all other instances, other methods of teaching obedience and discipline are more apt to pay better dividends. JAMES L. HYMES, JR.

See also DISCIPLINE; GUILT FEELINGS; OBEDIENCE

THRIFT *See* ALLOWANCE

THROAT INFECTION *See* COMMON COMMUNICABLE DISEASES; SORE THROAT

THROWING AND DROPPING

During the time a baby is about 4 to 6 months old, he usually spends much of his waking time struggling to get hold of objects. He will reach toward an appealing toy, miss it, try again, grab hold, pass it from one hand to his mouth to the other hand, then back again. And, after his grasp becomes more efficient, he will often become very upset if an object is taken away from him and can be placated only by receiving something else to hold.

But then it seems as though this phase has hardly begun when he enters an opposite phase. Most things that he gets into his hand are casually dropped or else forcefully thrown to the floor, a particularly intriguing game when mother is close enough to act as a retriever. One by one, all the toys given to him in the playpen will be thrown out; the spoon or, even worse, the full dish of food, may be dropped from the high chair to the floor. Then he may immediately follow with a remorseful or an indignant wail.

This sort of behavior can be most annoying to a busy mother, but like many other things the baby does, it undoubtedly means something in the development of his personality. One obvious use for this pattern of throw-then-wail is to encourage his mother to come near. It is one early version of the thought, "I like you to be near me and to do things for me." Also it seems to serve the function of giving an infant a sense of power: "What I do gets results and makes me important." These are important feelings for an infant to have, and his mother should not let trouble build up around such episodes. If the thrown object is really essential, you can tie a string around it and connect it to the high-chair tray or to the playpen. Or, after several rounds of the game, you can be firm and refuse to play any more. Chances are that the baby will soon think of a more mature way to get your attention or to gain a feeling of power. BETTYE M. CALDWELL

THROWING UP *See* VOMITING

THRUSH

Sometimes, but rarely, a small baby develops thrush, which is a mild fungus infection of the mucous membrane of the mouth. The disease shows as white patches that do not wash away, as milk curds do, with a drink of water. If you think your baby has thrush, consult your doctor. In the meantime, offer the baby sterile water after each feeding. RUTH S. KEMPE

THUMB-SUCKING

Nearly all parents, at some time or another, ask questions about thumb-sucking. They want to know whether it is harmful and, even when they are assured that it probably is not, they want to know how the habit can be forestalled or cured. It is almost as if they feel that there is something faintly shameful, something not quite nice, about the conjunction of small child and small thumb. The larger the child, and hence the larger the thumb, the more embarrassed they seem to feel.

For an infant, thumb-sucking is almost as natural as eating. He can receive food only by sucking. His very life depends upon the desire to suck. Sucking is itself a drive, a basic need. If this need is not totally satisfied at the breast or bottle, he will seek gratification by getting his fingers or thumb into his mouth.

No one can predict how much breast- or bottle-sucking will satisfy your infant, for individuals differ, and what is quite enough for one child is not necessarily enough for another. The clue to how much sucking your child needs, and whether he is getting it, is found in the child himself and in what you notice about his behavior. Perhaps you are rushing him a little, so that his appetite is appeased before his sucking drive is satisfied. He may require a longer period at the breast even though, as is often the case, little milk remains. Or if bottle-fed, he may need only a smaller hole in the nipple of his bottle. On the other hand, your baby may be hungrier than you realize and require more frequent feedings or an enriched formula.

Additional questions that you can ask yourself if you are concerned about thumb-sucking are these:

Is my baby being cuddled enough? Most babies want to be held at times, rocked and snuggled and sung to now and then.

Is he bored? Perhaps he spends too much time alone in crib or playpen and has too few objects to handle and explore. Boredom is as real to a crawler as to an adult, and needs alleviating, too.

Have too many attempts been made to have him feed himself before he is ready to stop being fed—or the opposite? His readiness to feed himself should be honored. Otherwise, he may "give up," permit himself to be fed, and seek solace from his thumb.

Does he have to put up with mechanical restraints to keep his thumb away from his mouth? These restraints will only annoy and anger him and make him more than ever determined to get what he wanted in the first place.

After a child is a year or so old, the sucking instinct becomes less powerful. Now, thumb-sucking may be a carry-over response to hunger or a way to lull himself to sleep. Often he stops sucking his thumb as his sleep habits change. If the thumb-sucking persists after he is 2 years old, it is evidently satisfying some further unexplained need. Perhaps a new baby in the family has made him want to be a baby again, too. Perhaps he is shy when pressured too much by adults or when confronted with new neighbor children. Perhaps thumb-sucking is a way to feel less lonely, perhaps only a request to be hugged.

True, your elders may speak with authority about thumb-sucking, pointing out that their children weren't allowed to suck *their* thumbs. Maybe you can't help being a bit upset by such criticism, but you can remain firm in your resolve to deal with your child's behavior in your own way—to leave him in peace, not to talk about his thumb-sucking too much and certainly not to nag, not to punish or humiliate him. If he is under 6 months old, you can gently remove the thumb once in a while as you hand him a toy. If he is older and uses his thumb more when sleeping than when awake, you can quietly remove his thumb from his mouth. And you can see that he doesn't become overtired or overhungry. Give him as much of your time as you can possibly spare, more physical affection, more play with his father, or more of the company of other children. Praise him whenever he does something well; make him feel, as we all need to feel, as if he is a success.

One of your biggest worries about thumb-sucking may be the effect it will have on your child's teeth and jaw formation. Most dentists and orthodontists now seem to feel that up until the time the second teeth appear, thumb-sucking has no permanent effect on the teeth, mouth, or jaws. But if you are concerned, ask your dentist for his opinion. He will probably tell you that thumb-sucking after a certain age can be a factor in getting teeth out of line—but only one factor—and that the degree of deformity will depend on how long, how hard, and how often a child has sucked his thumb.

A time may come when you feel that the thumb-sucking habit has persisted too long, when you have done all you know how to do about it, when you have outwardly ignored it while trying to discover why your child resorts to thumb-sucking. You know, of course, he is using his thumb for solace, but as solace for what? You are convinced that there is some anxiety in him somewhere, but its exact nature eludes you. You also know that all people have anxieties and keep on having them, but you think that this particular one can perhaps be relieved if you learn what it is. The answer for your child may be extremely simple or it may be something that will need more intensive study. At any rate, this is a good moment for you to seek outside help. Your child's school probably has a guidance department or a teacher who has run into the thumb-sucking problem before and knows where to refer you. Your family doctor or pediatrician can be of great assistance. And these days, a child psychologist or a psychiatrist is often available who will listen to you, listen to your child, and help you both unravel some of the whys and wherefores of thumb-sucking. JANE MAYER

See also ANXIETY; BOTTLE FEEDING; CHILD GUIDANCE CLINIC; FEEDING SCHEDULE; PACIFIER

THUNDER AND LIGHTNING, FEAR OF

It is unfortunate that little children ever have to become afraid of the marvels of nature, like thunder and lightning. Babies aren't, and if parents have no apprehension themselves, their babies will grow into children who enjoy a good thunderstorm. Even when these children hear of damage and destruction, they will likely think of it as faraway and not be concerned unless an unhappy experience comes close. Then their parents can comfort them, show them how to be helpful in an emergency, and how to take precautions for their own safety should they be caught outside in a storm. A simple and accurate explanation of natural phenomena will take some of the mystery out of a storm. The count between the lightning and the thunder appeals to a child's wish for knowledge, and knowledge makes him feel more in control.

At summer camp many children experience their first nearness to nature, which can be thrilling or menacing. Camp directors and counselors have a great opportunity to help children love the elements.

It is probably fear of the unknown which makes thunder and lightning terrifying, just as darkness hides possible dangers. But children should be helped to learn that the unknown is not always threatening; it also harbors the great discoveries and creations of mankind. Children's eagerness to learn should not be clouded by fear. Above all, they should never be told that God is showing his displeasure with them. The causes of thunder and lightning are explained in Volume 3, *World and Space*, pages 288–289. HELEN ROSS

See also COMFORTING; FEAR

TIC

The child with a tic is afflicted with uncontrollable spasms of certain muscles. He may blink his eyes or shrug his shoulders. He may cough or sniffle. His cheek muscles may twitch, his neck may jerk to one side or the other and, in more unusual instances, his entire body may jerk. It is sometimes difficult to distinguish tic from St. Vitus's dance, or chorea, but a tic usually persists, whereas chorea subsides after several weeks. A child with a tic usually has more of these jerky movements when he is tense or emotionally upset.

Children have tics for highly individual reasons, sometimes quite difficult to determine. Although the basis for the development of the tic may be psychological, this does not mean that these children have obvious psychological problems or obvious difficulties in adjustment. But parents are wise to consult a physician as early as possible, since the best results from treatment come about if the child is seen when symptoms first appear. It is well worth following through with detailed care as suggested by the doctor. Often, psychological tests and psychiatric consultation, perhaps in a child guidance clinic, are helpful.

Development of a tic in a child is quite disturbing to parents, but they should try to avoid putting pressure on the child to stop the movements. A child with a tic has no voluntary control, and pressure tends only to make him worse. Parents should also try to remember that the child probably is often teased about his tic by schoolmates and is embarrassed enough by it without the added burden of family criticism. JULIUS B. RICHMOND

See also CHILD GUIDANCE CLINIC; SAINT VITUS'S DANCE

TICKS

Be careful how you remove a tick from a child's body. Working gently and slowly, remove with tweezers or a piece of paper held between your fingers. If you tear the tick loose, its mouth or other body parts may become embedded in the skin. A few drops of turpentine will hasten the loosening process as will application of a heated needle. Scrub the area from which the tick is removed with soap and water for five minutes. If the bite becomes inflamed and swollen, or if the patient has a fever, tell your doctor at once.

TIMIDITY *See* SHYNESS AND TIMIDITY

TODDLER

The toddler is that charming nuisance, that constantly-to-be-guarded marvel, that great hazard to himself—the child between the ages of 1 and 2. Perhaps the one phrase that best describes him is that he is "into everything."

It is not only in walking that the toddler totters. It is in everything he does. He can tumble emotionally over the tiniest rough spot as well as physically on only slightly uneven ground. Fortunately, very slight support gives him steadiness as long as it is given him in a way he can accept. Shifts are unusually quick with the toddler, needing quick responses on the part of adults to stabilize him again.

Perhaps the vantage point from which to view the toddler is midway through—at 18 months—when he is at his toddling best. His very physique is losing its previous top-heaviness. He is on his way to that better balance of trunk and legs when the legs are released for freer and surer movement. The one phrase that best describes him is that he is "into everything."

Keep Him Safe

This all-embracing trend of getting into everything needs its rightful outlets, but it also calls for strong checks and a defining of limits. The toddler is surrounded by many dangers, so he must necessarily be surrounded by many safeguards. The fall down the cellar stairs could have been averted. The invasion of mother's powder and creams (and red nail polish), with subsequent disastrous results, could have been prevented. These dangers are not only to himself. Possessions are in danger; animals can be mistreated; and other children may be treated as inanimate objects, with a bop on the head, a strangling bear hug, or a probe in the eye.

A toddler needs to be both hemmed in and kept out. Within the home an accordion gate provides this restraint very nicely. He sometimes needs a gate on his own bedroom door. He needs one in dangerous places, such as the top or bottom of stairs. He needs one to keep him in the kitchen and out of the living room. And older brothers and sisters might welcome a gate on their doors to keep the toddler out. He will linger on the outside of the gate, accepting any handouts and will watch happily any activity of older children. A closed door is not enough to protect the possessions of the older children because very soon he can turn the knob.

Bathrooms especially need to be safe from him and for him. His zeal to throw things into the toilet bowl and flush them away increases in intensity with just a little practice. Perhaps it is his resistance to toilet training that draws him so strongly to this modern gadget. Or maybe it is his love of water, whose flow he controls with an easy twist of the handle. The contents of a medicine cabinet fascinate him. His very passion for bottles —little bottles, big bottles, any kind of bottle—draws him to this cabinet. And as he becomes more adept at unscrewing or removing bottle tops, he is more liable to sample the contents. Medicines should be kept in a locked part of the cabinet.

Added hazards arise as the young child learns to climb. Stairs can engage him for long stretches of time. Gates have their uses here unless he can be supervised. He is safer and surer on carpeted steps. But he doesn't confine himself to the more usual climbing. He is all too often after things out of reach. He quickly learns where the cooky jar is kept and soon he's clever enough to reach it by piling chair on table.

By the time he is nearing 2 he will likely have a special interest in climbing on top of radiators or furniture to get to window ledges. There is certainly no reason to keep him away from the fascinating sights and sounds out of doors, but windows can and should be barred or kept closed when his play is unsupervised.

A kitchen can be an ideal place for a toddler. There he can watch his mother work, follow her around; but a kitchen has its special dangers from which he needs to be protected. The knife drawer or rack should be made inaccessible. The gas jet handles when he can reach them, should, if possible, have a simple temporary wooden frame built around them. And nothing should be kept under the sink that could possibly poison him in case he decides to sample the contents.

In due time a toddler will learn the danger of fire and that certain things are not to be touched. In the meantime, electric outlets should be covered when they can be, for his desire to poke and pry often stimulates him to find some object such as a hairpin or a bobby pin to probe into the hole. He may feel the shock, but even this may not stop him from trying again.

Outdoors, too, has its hazards, especially when the safety of the playpen has been abandoned. By 18 months a screened-in porch, simply equipped with sandbox and small climbing equipment, can provide safety and the interesting activity lacking in a playpen. The transition to the yard is a bigger step, partly because father may have problems in enclosing the play area. If there is no play area and if mother is not able to keep an almost constant eye on him from her kitchen window, it might be a good idea to tether him to a stretch wire, which can give him freedom of movement but prevent him from wandering off.

No safety device, of course, can take the place of supervision. Supervision may be very demanding on the mother, but it gives the toddler the human contact he needs—his mother's facial expression to tell him "no-no," her warning voice to stop him, her hand to lead him away from harm. He also needs her praise and her hugs to reassure him that all is well.

The Toddler's Day

A mother who wants both her toddler and herself to get the most benefit out of his day might do well to think through his total day in advance. Waking is a happy time for the midtoddler. He romps in his crib. He plays with his stuffed animals. He vocalizes but not in a demanding way. He is usually ready to wait until he is visited, and even then he will continue to play after being changed and given a cracker and a toy. At 15 months he is alert to any household noise and wants to be fetched and taken into the family circle. At 21 to 24 months his one morning desire is to be with daddy in the bathroom, watching him shave. Daddy is very important to him; the ritual of standing at the window watching daddy go is essential. Maybe this ritual serves to keep him assured that daddy will return.

Forenoon is vastly different in different households. But the 15-monther is still not too demanding. After breakfast he will return cheerfully to playtime with his toys in his crib or in his playpen if the pen is placed in a strategic place where he can watch household traffic and activities.

By 18 months he has grown increasingly aware of the activities of vacuuming, dusting, cleaning up the bathroom, cooking, putting away the canned goods, and he can often be included on the edge of these activities without undue effort by his mother.

The older toddler becomes even more imitative. He enjoys working along with his mother, with similar equipment if possible. He becomes familiar with where things are kept and can even fetch and carry. The morning household activities are a happy time for him.

Naps are still an integral part of a toddler's life. He shows his readiness for sleep at 15 months by pulling at his shoes. He is asleep in no time. By 18 months he accepts his nap with good humor and is off in short order. By 21 to 24 months he often delays his sleep with contented play, but he will succumb when tucked in a second time. Naps last two or three hours and the toddler usually awakes refreshed.

The young toddler is exuberant and impatient to get dressed and be off on an excursion. He knows what should happen by what happened yesterday. But the midtoddler lingers over his dressing, wishing to assist. He wants his juice and crackers before setting out for his afternoon excursion. And the older toddler awakes even more slowly; he enjoys lingering over his dressing, choosing his clothes at times and helping to put them on. He likes to be talked to and to talk in answer as much as he can.

The afternoon excursion out into the world is one of the highlights of the toddler's day. He shows rapidly increasing ability in what he has to give to these walks. He is full of shifts at 15 months. Initially, he is content in his stroller, though he may want to get out to push. Then off he goes, if steady enough on his feet, to pick up sticks and stones as gifts for his mother. The 15-monther stops in his play, leans over, looks between his legs, and is a delight to passers-by. He is attentive to all kinds of sounds—dogs barking, hammers pounding, airplanes whirring.

With age he is less distracted and more purposeful. By 18 months he is surer on his feet and insists upon exploring any byways or stairs. He resists having his hand held, but accepts the steadying force of a harness if he is allowed to explore as he wishes. A nearby park will hold the child's interest for a while, especially if there is a sandbox where he can fill and dump. To pick up stones is his delight. He prefers to push his stroller, but he will accept a ride on the home stretch.

The older toddler is more sedate on an afternoon walk. He will even accept a hand or a ride in his stroller. He would prefer to go straight to a park where he may see other children. The older toddler can linger for quite a spell, adding cake-making to his sand play, or watching another child's activity, happy in this new awareness of companionship. A drive in the family car is also to his liking. Here he can be tucked into his special seat or he may prefer the greater freedom of the back seat with its own safety devices. He is interested in the passing scene, in traffic lights and signs, in fire hydrants, and he spots any flag in view.

The end of the day is the last big hurdle for parents. Success or failure can make or break the day for the toddler or for the child of any age. The young toddler can be more readily satisfied with just a short stint in the living room, listening to music to which he can sway, emptying the wastebasket, turning pages in a book. He enjoys bath play most. He needs only a short snuggle session with his father or his mother and then he's off to sleep with ease.

At 18 months the toddler still likes the same prebedtime activities, but now he wants to do more things for a longer time. A doorway swing that can be snapped into place delights him. He searches out his favorite interests in a picture book, maybe pointing out a Teddy bear or a watering can. He loves to dance to music, if only to bend his knees rhythmically. He likes roughhousing with daddy if this is not carried too far. He snuggles into his bed happily after this satisfying play and after saying goodnight to everything and everybody.

The older toddler becomes more selective in his play. He may even listen to a short story told about pictures, or he may enjoy marking on paper with crayons. His bedtime hour is important and should be given freely and willingly. Good, satisfying play and attention send him to bed happier. Then when he calls once too often after he is in bed, a loving, tolerant father can rightfully become a firm father, and the basis for a good working relationship can be established.

The daily routines need not produce the complications they often do if the toddler's growth stage and his individuality are respected. Take feeding, for example. His appetite isn't as hearty as it was when he was an infant. He likes certain foods for a short time and others for a longer period of time. The older toddler as a rule goes on certain food jags. One meal can be very poor in quantity, another very good. Fortunately, one good meal a day is quite enough. Self-feeding, especially finger feeding, is often demanded by the child and should be encouraged. Provide him with implements suited to his stage of growth. Eating will be easier for him if the bowl of his spoon is given a simple 90 degree twist and the handle is arched. The toddler may still be on the bottle, but bottle feedings are usually restricted to naptime or bedtime. Often it is the parent who continues this type of feeding, fearing the toddler won't get enough milk now that he drinks so little from a cup. His daily quota of milk can be supplied easily in such things as cereals and puddings. Cheese can be used as a substitute, and he will eat butter by the handful. There was a time when feeding problems were common. Nowadays, it is mainly the unsure mother who produces a feeding problem.

Fortunately, a similar more relaxed attitude toward elimination training has taken place. Some children train early in the last quarter of the first year. Most often, they lose this early success and then resist sitting on the toilet; they function best, especially for their bowel movements, while in an extended posture—standing up or lying down. Some children function easily after meals. There is no harm in giving training a try, even though success is more common at 2 years or later. A potty chair is preferred by some children to a toilet seat. Training pants are good for an afternoon stroll. But on the whole, this second year is not the time to push training. The child who indicates he has functioned, either by pulling at his pants or by making a related sound, rates compliments as he is being changed rather than recriminations. "Bad boy" is sometimes used so often that a toddler may associate this phrase with the function as he asks to go "bad boy." And if he investigates for himself and ends up with stool smearing, he really is considered a bad boy. Such behavior is quite common at 18 to 21 months. Some toddlers restrict this activity to a single episode. Others persist for a few weeks or longer. Closer supervision is the answer. By 21 months the toddler is often aware of and frightened by what has happened to him; he stands transfixed and screaming until someone comes to rescue him. Successful training is just around the corner. Awareness usually precedes success.

That Toddler Year

Each part of the year from 1 to 2 demands a special attitude of understanding. The attitude of immediacy is necessary for the 15-monther. It is easy to flow with him, to respond to him, to recognize that "no" no longer works. This is the age when the living room may slowly become denuded of loose objects. But the 15-monther's resistances and demands are all in good fun, even to the demand to receive a cooky from the container rather than from someone's hand. He readily accepts most substitutions. He still can play happily by himself and can be confined easily.

But not the 18-monther. This is truly an exhausting age for a parent. The child needs constant supervision and a variety of new stimulations. A mother may gladly accept the relief of a baby-sitter for the afternoon walk. Fathers who provide relief over the weekend will eagerly return to their offices on Monday morning for a rest. The adult's fatigue is emotional as well as physical. Because the 18-monther is so adamant in going his own way, it is often difficult to reverse him. If forced, he stages a sit-down strike. He may come out of this situation if transported bodily in a humorous way. Distraction and substitution still work but not for long. If the 18-monther starts to run away, he may respond well to reverse psychology. Say "Bye-bye, baby," and begin to move away from him. But this strategy should not be carried out to the point of frightening him into thinking that he will really be deserted. His own inadequacy with his toys frustrates him most—they get stuck; he can't manipulate them. Frustrating toys should be put away until someone can play with him and help him solve his problems.

By 21 months the scene has changed markedly. A whole new set of rules needs to be thought through. The child of 21 months knows definitely what he wants, but unfortunately, he may lack the words to express these wants. Maybe he has been given the wrong bib or the wrong spoon. He will cry until his wants are satisfied. He becomes frozen in his desire. Crying is still his best, though often not successful, means of communication. This is not the time for a mother to leave home and go to work unless it is absolutely essential for her to do so. The child needs someone who can read his mind, someone who is living his life fully and intimately with him. Sometimes he can make his wants known by pointing or pulling the adult to the desired spot or object.

By 2 years of age the child will begin to communicate more fully through language. He can communicate even his own feelings. He knows when he has become a "good boy." Those "bad boy" toddler days, made worse sometimes by inadequate planning and insufficient concern for safety and supervision, are almost over.

Mother is very important in the toddler stage. But a rested, alert mother is even more important. Thus, ways and means to relieve mother should be found. The toddler needs her. Other things must go or someone else must do them. It takes planning and thought to figure out the best formula. Place, too, is important. This is not the time to move if moving can be avoided. Perhaps the summer vacation trip should be skipped. Home and routine are highly important to the toddler.

The less complicated life of the outdoors is where the toddler does best. Sticks, stones, water, sand, and snow are all to his liking and should be tapped as they are available. It is the "nearness" and "nowness" of things and time that he needs. FRANCES L. ILG

See also ACCIDENT PREVENTION; CLIMBING; EATING PROBLEMS; GROWTH; SLEEP; TOILET TRAINING; TOYS AND PLAY EQUIPMENT

TOILET, FEAR OF

Toilet training is fairly simple if not started too early and if the mother is patient with the inevitable relapses. Though one can start a child on the nursery chair or directly on the potty, the small toilet seat that fastens on the larger seat is equally good. But there are two warnings about the toilet seat: (1) Don't leave your child unless he is well fastened in, and even then it is better to be near until you are sure he is accustomed to the seat and that he is not afraid of the water, and (2) don't flush the toilet while he is sitting on the seat. Sudden flushing may frighten a child. Occasionally, children are so terrified in this way that they refuse to sit on the toilet for a long time, and continue to be afraid to go to a strange toilet for fear that the same terrifying thing will happen again. Some children's dread of school is based on unhappy toilet experiences there. Under no circumstances is it ever wise to punish a child for resisting or fearing the toilet.

Another frightening aspect of the toilet to the toddler is the very mechanism of it. Something goes in and is flushed away. What he deposits there may seem to him a part of his own body because it comes out of him, and he may get scared about losing other body parts. Though he learns the truth early, he will master the situation sooner if he is not frightened. HELEN ROSS

See also FEAR; TOILET TRAINING

TOILET TRAINING

Each child is different. For that matter, each parent is different, and never were these differences more worthy of consideration than when it comes to toilet training. The system that worked so beautifully with the child next door may be utterly unacceptable to your child and completely beyond the limits of your own patience to carry out. Sometimes there are few or no problems. This happy state is more easily attained by those parents who realize that a toilet training timetable may be followed in general principle only; they vary the program to take full advantage of the child's readiness.

In general, the aim of toilet training is to encourage your child to do what you want him to do so that he will be more comfortable and so that he may know a sense of achievement in conforming to adult-like behavior.

Although a mother sometimes boasts about her ability to catch bowel movements every time her 6-to-12-month-old gives signs of soiling himself, credit belongs to her powers of observation rather than to her training skill. True cooperation from the baby rarely comes before he is 18 months old, and he has his own ways of letting you know when he is ready.

The first sign may be a show of discomfort; he may grunt or squirm or grow red. His readiness may be further identified by his ability to sit unsupported, his interest in the toilet, and his powers of observation. If he has had an opportunity to observe others using the toilet, he will feel encouraged to imitate them and to part with his stools in a receptacle of someone else's choosing.

Timing is important. Choose a period in your baby's life when things are going smoothly and a moment in his day close to the time he normally has a movement. Calmly place him on a baby's toilet seat or a potty chair on the floor. He should be comfortable, with feet touching the footrest or floor. Use words he can understand to tell him that this is the place to have a bowel movement and to

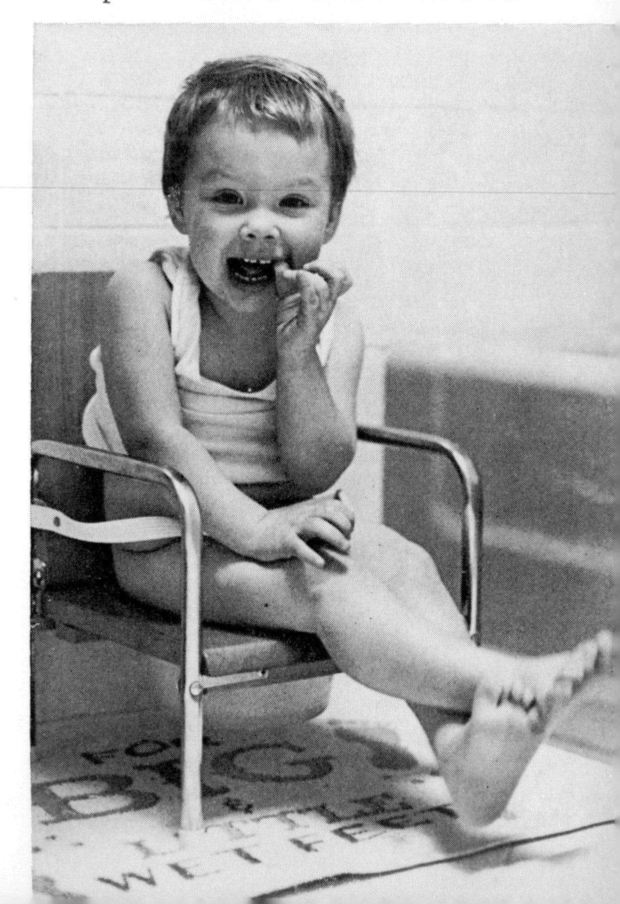

urinate just like big boys and girls and his parents do. Don't ask him to sit there more than five minutes, and at the start of training, one or two sessions a day are enough. When he has success, let him know he has done well and that you are pleased, but refrain from making a big fuss about a normal function. Bribes, of course, are never justified; neither are words of disappointment or anger when the child has not been successful.

Gently clean the genitals and remove the child from the toilet. Then and not until then should the bowl be flushed, lest the noise frighten him. Let him help press the flusher and watch if he wishes. He may be greatly reassured to see the feces disappear without loss of some part of his body.

Successful training is not accomplished all at once. It is a matter of trial and error, usually, for both the child and his parents, but never should you force or punish or coax overmuch. Neither should you discuss the child's success or failure in his presence. To do so may give rise to the notion that training is something special with which he can tease or challenge you.

Girls are easier to train than boys. As a rule, children are not completely toilet trained for bowel movements until sometime between their second and third birthdays. Training pants in the second year instead of diapers encourage a child to use the toilet to avoid the discomfort of soiling and wetting. Bladder control comes later—between the second and fifth birthdays.

Occasional lapses are to be expected (especially lapses into wetting, even in children as old as 8 or 9), particularly when a child is undergoing new and strange experiences, such as nursery school, sleeping in a new bed, or when ill. The wise parent will delay training if any disrupting experience threatens the smooth tenor of the baby's days.

Some balkiness in the use of the toilet is common when the child is old enough and intelligent enough to deliberately withhold stools in order to deposit them where he can play with and smear them. This messy stage is usually temporary which, of course, is small consolation to his mother at the moment. Diversion and substitution are her allies. Give him play materials to substitute for his feces —substances like finger paints and modeling clay, leftover morning oatmeal and soft-cooked rice, or let him make mud pies. Water play in the bathtub will also provide a satisfactory substitute activity.

In cleansing the child who is dirty, either from soiling through toilet "accidents" or in messy play, do not overemphasize the need to be either clean or "good." There should be no equating of cleanliness with "goodness." In his desire to please his parents by becoming toilet trained, the young child may consider himself "bad" when he has accidents. Guilt from these feelings may interfere with successful toilet training and increase the number of episodes of soiling or wetting. Occasionally, children fear being bad or dirty so much that they withhold feces and urine to a point where they become physically uncomfortable from prolonged constipation. Such children become compulsively clean about their bodies and clothing. They wash their hands excessively and demand frequent baths and complete changes of clothing at the slightest smudge of dirt. At the same time, they become finicky about eating food that is soft and odorous because it is "messy."

Bladder training is slower than bowel training, partly because it is natural to empty the bladder more often than the bowels. After 16 to 18 months, babies are able to hold their urine for as long as two hours at a time because their bladders have enlarged and their nervous systems are more fully developed. Ability to stay dry through a nap is further evidence of readiness for toilet training.

In training your child to use the toilet for wetting, it is better to let him wait, within reason, for longer periods of time between visits to the bathroom than it is to take him there too often. As the bladder stretches and becomes accustomed to larger amounts of urine, the child is able to remain dry for longer periods of time—perhaps throughout the entire night.

Training for staying dry at night is accomplished best if you let your child work out his own rhythm of holding his urine for longer and longer periods. If you pick him up often in order to catch him before he wets, you run the risk of conditioning him to hold his urine for a very short time. He will more easily become dry at night, as well as during the day, when his bladder is mature enough to hold more urine for longer periods of time, to be released where he wants it to go, when he gives the signal himself. As a child learns to hold his urine when he is awake, his bladder learns to contain its urine automatically for longer periods at night. This process is normal and natural in the growth and development of every child, but it usually is not accomplished entirely until he is around 5 years old.

Most boys learn to urinate standing up at a toilet soon after they are 3, particularly if they have had frequent opportunities to see other boys void that way. The desire for imitation prompts a small boy to experiment, and he is pleased when he succeeds. Here is another incentive for him to use the toilet instead of holding his urine so long that he wets himself. A strong, secure step-up box placed in front of the toilet may make it easier for him to reach the bowl. MILTON J. E. SENN

See also BED-WETTING; CONSTIPATION; TOILET, FEAR OF

TONSILS

Small pockets on either side of the throat contain the tonsils. The average fully grown tonsil is about the size of a small walnut, but there can be great variation in size. Since tonsils are made up of lymphatic tissue, just as are the lymph nodes found in various parts of the human body, they, too, are thought to help protect the body against infection. The adenoids, which are made up of the same tissue, serve the same function in the nose.

Because of their location at an opening of the body, the tonsils are considered to be barriers to infection. Indeed, this is probably why they are so frequently inflamed; during early childhood most children will have an average of four infections of the upper respiratory tract a year, and each time the tonsils are inflamed. Any inflammation of the tonsils is called tonsillitis, and the severity of the attack usually depends upon the kind of virus or bacteria causing it. In severe attacks the tonsils are quite swollen, red, and may have patches of grayish membrane on the surface. Usually during attacks of tonsillitis, there will be fever and swelling of the lymph glands at the angles of the child's jaws.

Most attacks of acute tonsillitis subside after five to seven days. If the tonsillitis is caused by a bacteria sensitive to antibiotics, a proper drug, such as penicillin for "strep tonsillitis," may shorten the attack and also reduce the possibility of complications of chronic tonsillitis or nephritis or rheumatic fever, any one of which may follow strep tonsillitis.

In severe attacks of tonsillitis, an abscess may develop in the tissue about the tonsils. Or following several attacks of tonsillitis, the tonsils may remain inflamed, and the child may have chronic low fever and constant swelling of the lymph glands about the neck. Such a child may not be growing normally and may be lacking in energy. It may become necessary then to remove his tonsils surgically. If the adenoids are also chronically infected, the doctor may remove them in the same operation, but it is not necessary to remove them at the same time.

Although a common operation, tonsillectomy is not as common as it was many years ago. It can have complications and should not be undertaken without good reason. Since the tonsils are normally quite large in the school-age child, the size of the tonsils—except for rare instances as determined by the doctor—is alone not a good reason to remove them. JULIUS B. RICHMOND

See also ADENOIDS; OPERATION

TOURNIQUET *See* BITES, ANIMAL; BLEEDING

TOYS AND PLAY EQUIPMENT

Children are as different in the way they play and react to play equipment as they are in all the other ways they develop, both physically and mentally. Some children seem born with the agility of little monkeys and they can climb over jungle gym sets with ease. Other children stand and look at the maze of bars in awe, working up the courage to swing or hang by their knees as they see other children do. Even young babies react in different ways to a toy suspended over the crib or the carriage. Some babies reach out to touch the toy; others are content to follow it with their eyes.

Baby's Playthings

Since anything your baby plays with is bound to be put into his mouth, his toys should have smooth surfaces, easy to wash and to keep clean. There should be no sharp edges or detachable parts, such as glass eyes, buttons, and bells. Even though loving relatives and friends shower your baby with elaborate rattles and all manner of gadgets to be suspended over carriage or crib, you have to select and offer him only those playthings that are safe and appropriate.

Too many dangling objects only confuse a baby. Similarly, it is unwise to put a basketful of toys in playpen or crib for him to make his own selection. Since he is unable to choose, he probably will end up screaming in frustration.

Things that are bright and easy to grasp, as well as things that make a noise that is not too harsh or too loud, will attract a baby. He reaches for your beads and earrings and clutches at his daddy's eyeglasses or keys because these objects are bright and colorful or because they jingle enticingly. Among the toys he will enjoy most are colorful dolls and animals made of vinyl plastic, which is flexible but will not crack when bitten into by rosy gums or newly erupting teeth. You can divert his attention from your beads by offering him plastic disks or lightweight wooden beads on a strong cord. He will be enchanted equally by a couple of old door keys (first sterilized) strung on a clean shoelace.

As the small muscles of your baby's hands develop, he will begin to pick up things and put them into containers. He will like small blocks or spools (but not bite-size) that he can put into a pan from your kitchen. It is at this stage that he begins to eat with his fingers because, as every baby knows, spoons are for banging on high-chair trays, not for carrying food to the mouth. Besides, chasing peas and bread crusts with chubby fingers is much more fun!

Boxes that he can open and close easily will entertain him. Many children love to crumble and tear newspapers. As they begin to crawl, they enjoy sturdy wooden toys that they can push along the floor.

Play, at any age, must be fun. Too much stress on order, neatness, cleanliness, and "learning" experiences takes the joy out of play as children should know it.

Outgrowing the Playpen

The playpen, the crib, the carriage, and the high chair provide varied places in which your baby can play until he is 12 or 14 months old. At about this age he will need more activity and he will need more space to develop his growing capacity for play and to satisfy his curiosity about the world he lives in. The playpen has become too confining for prolonged play.

Delightful new experiences await this early toddler. He will enjoy such things as:

Toys with handles that he can push and pull along the floor

A ball that he can throw and chase

Toys to load and unload in toy trucks

Digging in dirt or in sand

Splashing and kicking in the bathtub, surrounded by toys: a sponge to squeeze, boats or animals that float, a plastic pitcher with which to pour

A toy carpet sweeper or broom so that he can "help" mother

The play of children continues to be an imitation of things they have experienced themselves and also of activities in which they see adults engaging. They cuddle and feed a doll or a stuffed animal. The toddler follows mother and "helps" her with the cleaning. He enjoys clambering under tables and chairs to dust furniture legs. Using a toy carpet sweeper, he, too, cleans the rugs. He probably will not stay with the job very long, but he gets a sense of belonging and he actually develops manual skill crawling in and out of small places.

Educational toys for 2- or 3-year-olds have simple parts that fit together and are excellent for these youngsters. Some of these toys have big bolts and locks, gears and wheels; some come apart in several pieces and require a measure of dexterity to reassemble—dexterity a child gains only through practice. But he still likes boxes that fit together and into which he can put things.

Airplanes, spaceships, rockets and missiles, as well as guns of all kinds, are welcomed very early in children's play, partly because of television, partly because of the influence of older boys and girls, and partly because toy manufacturers are alert to the fact that children are eager to imitate the adult world.

Dolls and Housekeeping Toys

Dolls and housekeeping toys are important for both boys and girls of 2 and 3. A cuddly doll almost always is a favorite and may vie for attention with a stuffed animal. Some little girls lose their interest in dolls very early, but with many this interest continues for several years. Even when the dolls themselves may not get a lot of attention, doll dishes and cooking and cleaning materials are used by boys up to 5 or 6, and with girls they may remain popular until the play cooking becomes real cooking.

Durable metal or plastic doll dishes and pots and pans are best for little ones just starting "housekeeping." As a little girl gets older, she may enjoy an attractive china tea set, but for the young child it is well to keep things simple and unbreakable. A toy teakettle or coffeepot that will pour water, a bowl for mixing, and a pot for "cooking" are a few obvious essentials.

Although play at housekeeping is not necessarily confined to one place, housekeeping furniture can stimulate play. Whether this equipment is provided really depends upon the space available in the house and in the playroom. There are attractive child-size cupboards, doll cribs, refrigerators, and stoves on the market, but they are fairly expensive and with little more than nails, hammer, and fruit crates from the supermarket, you can make adequate substitutes.

A fruit crate painted or covered with bright contact paper serves nicely for a dish cupboard. Or lined with cloth and mounted on two boards, the box makes an attractive doll bed. You can construct a usable toy kitchen sink by suspending a small plastic basin between two crates, or make a small stove by painting the burners, the knobs, and the oven door on the tops and sides of one of these versatile crates.

TOYS AND PLAY MATERIALS FOUND IN THE HOME

Many articles found around your house are valuable for play materials. These might include:

A wooden spoon and a metal bowl to imitate mother as she cooks

An old aluminum percolator with its many take-apart pieces

An egg beater, a large bowl, and a small amount of soapflakes and water, which let a 4- or a 5-year-old make fine "frosting"

Empty wooden spools (Perhaps the neighborhood tailor would save some of his big ones for you.)

A deck of cards to line up for sidewalks and roads

Empty cigar boxes with lids glued down to make fine building blocks

An old purse of mother's and some small things to put in and take out of it; a spoon, an empty cosmetic jar, a fat eraser, an old wallet, or a discarded eyeglass case

Collection of big buttons (These can be money, imaginary food, or soldiers lined up.)

Bright-colored cloth for making into play clothes or doll dresses

Sheets and tablecloths for tents and playhouses

An old suitcase to pack dress-up clothes for visiting and for dramatic play

Old clothes, hats, scarves, jewelry, high-heeled shoes for dress-up

Children can learn to make many toys from odds and ends. To stir their imaginations, see Volume 9, *Make and Do,* pages 5–38, 93–108, 193–214, 222–227.

Tools

Young children enjoy hammering and sawing, but this is an activity that needs adult supervision and careful direction. With a lightweight hammer a 3-year-old can safely hammer nails into a board. A real hammer with a securely fixed head is better than so-called toy tools that break easily and do not really function as tools. Small saws satisfy a child's urge to "build something" real. Your child must learn that he should never hold wood in his hand to saw it. The wood must be fastened in the vise of a workbench or with a strong C-clamp on an old table or chair provided for the purpose. He must never saw when other children are near him. Any young carpenter will be thrilled to construct crude boats, trains, or airplanes from scraps of pine or birch, using ¾-inch nails. You can find constructive ideas about the use and care of tools in Volume 9, *Make and Do,* pages 93–108.

Out-of-Doors Play Equipment

If we were to picture an ideal play area for children, we might think of wide green fields or rolling lawns shaded by trees with low-hanging branches. A babbling brook is nearby. There is space in which to wander, a tree to climb, living things to watch, water to dabble in, dirt to dig, and pebbles or plants to collect. The very thought of this idyllic situation fills us with nostalgia. But in crowded cities, finding space for out-of-door play is a very real challenge. To meet this important need, play space is provided in most modern housing projects, in apartment buildings, in health centers, in churches, and in settlements. The play area may be on a roof, in a basement, or in a courtyard.

Modern schools have specially equipped play areas for young children in addition to gymnasiums and yards for older boys and girls. Many parks have special play areas with equipment for young children as well as playgrounds for older boys and girls. Jungle gyms and swings take the place of trees, and a wading pool and a sand pit provide for water and for digging.

In suburban areas and in cities where families own their own homes, space is often pooled to provide a joint play area for several families. These areas may include:

A sandbox or shallow pit, 40 inches square and 6 inches deep, filled with clean sand

A number of sturdy packing cases that have no rough edges and from which any projecting nails have been removed. (These cases may be painted with two coats of flat outside paint for conversion into houses, garages, stores, or any one of countless purposes that pop into children's heads.)

Hollow wooden blocks and smooth boards lend themselves to dramatic play for children age 3 to 9. (Blocks are 12 × 12 × 6 inches deep and 12 × 24 × 6 inches deep. Blocks that are screwed together wear better than those made with plywood. The boards should be 6 or 8 inches wide and 3 to 4 feet long)

A small climbing bar. (Carefully inspect commercial outdoor equipment. Avoid chrome-plated decorations. These bend and break and are a hazard. Be sure that there are no raw metal edges and that bolts in exposed areas are covered with "acorn nuts.")

A swing. (A swing is not advisable, however, in a small area in which several children will be playing.)

A slide. (Stainless steel is preferable because it does not rust.)

A wading pool in warm weather

Tricycles and wagons

Wheelbarrows

Sturdy doll carriages big enough for small children to ride in

Sleds in winter

Safety First

No matter what type of play equipment you buy or are given for your child, the first concern should be for safety. From your baby's first stuffed animal (whose glass or plastic eyes may be attached to sharp, sawlike pieces of metal) to the chemistry set your 10-year-old gets for Christmas, you must be sure it cannot bring harm to your child. Ask yourself such questions as: Are there detachable pieces so small they can be swallowed? Is the finish chemically safe? Is there danger of broken or splintered glass? Are there sharp metal points or wires? ADELE FRANKLIN

See also ACCIDENT PREVENTION; DRESS-UP PLAY; IMAGINATION

TRAINING, TOILET *See* TOILET TRAINING

TRAVELING WITH CHILDREN

Children can give you great fun on a trip.

Children can be a dreadful nuisance on a trip.

These contradictory statements are both true. Which one will be more true when you travel will depend in large part upon you. Fate may once in a while interfere with some of your best plans, but not even the kindest fate can save you if you don't plan.

The where, when, and how of traveling with children certainly have to be planned or you would never get to your destination. And there are other items that demand careful planning—comfort, safety, health, recreation, rest, meals, clothes, and sight-seeing. Your planning doesn't have to be frighteningly formal. Lists will help. Discussions with the children may remind you of some things you might otherwise forget and will also make the children far more interested in the coming trip and hence happier and much more cooperative.

How Will You Travel?

The speed, the good meals, the help of the stewardess, and the general cleanliness and comfort make air travel ideal for a cross-country journey with small children.

If you plan to go by train, a bedroom or a compartment is most convenient. Children may wear a minimum of clothing, can lie down for naps, and have floor area in which to play. Meals can be served in your space or in the diner. Coach travel can also be reasonably comfortable. A child may be allowed to walk about occasionally to stretch his legs and perhaps find a new friend. Most train seats are roomy enough to allow a small child to rest comfortably. A baby will be happier in his own portable car bed.

Bus travel is becoming increasingly luxurious. Some buses are air-conditioned, some have modern washrooms aboard, others make regularly scheduled rest stops, and all make stops for meals. Bus seats are comfortable and can be adjusted for napping. Windows of modern buses are large and glare-proof—good, safe openings onto interesting sights.

The most popular mode of transportation, however, is the family car. The call of the open road appeals come vacation time, and families by the thousands take to the highways in search of something new to do and to see.

On the Road

Try to keep children on a schedule approximating your home routine. Give them three meals a day, a rest in the afternoon, and a regular bedtime, and both you and they are more likely to remain cheerful and relaxed. But do try to spice up routine with unexpected small pleasures.

Plan to make frequent stops to let the children run and play. Get a conversation going about the horses or cows or sheep on a hillside. Read aloud to the children or get them to join in singing songs or reciting nursery rhymes. Plan ahead for little treats and surprises. Dad might say, "At the next town we will stop for ice-cream cones." Or, "We'll all get out and play soon. Help me watch for a park."

End your day's journey by four o'clock in the afternoon. This will give the children time to run off their pent-up energy and time, too, for a relaxing bath and a leisurely dinner. A familiar song or story or prayer and his own favorite bed toys will help a young child go to sleep quickly.

Safe and Sound

Before starting on a trip, call a family conference and map out a safety program. Talk over how and why safety rules are to be obeyed. Dad can explain the mechanics of dashboard controls, gear shift lever, and brake and accelerator pedals. Now is a good time to see that the car first-aid kit is well stocked, that seat belts are installed. A family check list of safety rules might look something like this:

- Fasten seat belts and keep them fastened while car is in motion.
- Keep car doors locked.
- Never put hands, arms, or head out of windows.
- Never throw things out of windows.
- Never play with dashboard controls.
- Never touch the lighter or gear shift lever.
- Never put foot on brake or accelerator.
- Don't pester the driver. (No "Guess who, Daddy?")
- Keep voices low—shrill, loud conversation bothers the driver and may cause accidents.

What Shall We Wear?

Simplicity is the keynote of children's travelwear, with cool, comfortable, lightweight wash-and-wear clothing and jackets and sweaters for changes of climate. Take along cotton T-shirts, and shorts and slacks of jersey, corduroy, or denim for both boys and girls, with a simple dress-up outfit or two for special occasions. Baby will travel most comfortably in his regular sleepwear.

Make use of laundromats en route. There is no need to carry soiled clothing for more than a day or two (Don't forget to take a laundry bag). Mother can do the laundry while dad plays with the children in a park or a playground.

Back-Seat Playroom

If you drive a station wagon, your play space problem is solved by the addition of a foam rubber pad, a crib mattress, or simply a supply of blankets and pillows in the rear of the car.

The back seat of the conventional car can also make a very acceptable play space for children. Put something solid on the floor so short legs don't have to dangle too far, but don't wedge children in between pieces of luggage. In fact, it is much safer to stow heavy suitcases in the trunk or in a luggage carrier.

Portable seats that hook over the car's back seat afford a small child a place to sit where he can see out of the window. A baby rests comfortably in a car bed that hooks between back and front seats. The pockets of a shoe bag attached to the back of the front seat will provide ideal storage space for small toys, children's shoes, maps, cleansing tissues, writing materials, and an occasional surprise treat.

What About Food?

If you carry food, better stick to the "finger" kind: carrot sticks, celery, raisins, popcorn, fruit, plain cookies, and crackers. (Salted crackers are good "tummy settlers" if a child is prone to car sickness.) Packaged cereals in individual boxes, make good snack-time treats. Some families like to carry small cans of fruit juice. A single hole may be punched in the top of the can and the child can drink the juice through a straw.

Be extremely careful about foods that spoil easily in hot weather. Stick to bottled, pasteurized milk, and peel carefully any fruits you buy along the way.

Do feed your children sensibly while traveling. Go easy on sweets. Don't let them eat rich or heavy food. Be firm with relatives and friends along the way who urge children to eat rich desserts or foods to which they are not accustomed. Better to hurt an auntie's feelings than to have to take care of a sick child en route.

If you are traveling with a small baby, his daily formula can be made in advance, bottled, and kept in a portable refrigerator. Or you can take small cans of evaporated milk or a supply of powdered milk, boiled water, and formula sweetener in a sterilized bottle. Since a vacuum bottle cannot be sterilized, do not take milk in this kind of container. Carry sterilized or disposable bottles and prepare each feeding individually. If you use evaporated milk, throw away the unused portion, opening a fresh can for each feeding.

A bottle warmer is a wonderful gadget. Use it to heat canned baby foods and to warm the milk for baby's dry cereal.

If you have any doubts about your baby's travel diet, consult your doctor. Any change the doctor suggests should be given a trial run at home for a week or so before you begin your trip to be sure it will agree with the young traveler.

Many families feed the baby before they go into a restaurant for their own meal. He may then promptly go to sleep—or if he stays awake, he is usually content to sit in a high chair or to lie in his own car bed.

Keeping Children Amused

Your predeparture planning will pay off in keeping traveling children amused. A child over 7 usually will enjoy making his personal scrapbook, pasting in menus, table mats, souvenir pamphlets, and picture post cards. He may want to write a day-by-day commentary on what he sees, including his impressions and his feelings about each place you visit. When two or three children keep such books, they have fun comparing what the others have recorded.

Let each child have his own map. He can circle with crayon the places you stay overnight, the historical landmarks visited. Let him paste a star at your hometown, another star at your destination. He can crayon in the route you follow. He can add up the miles you've traveled each day by checking the figures on the map. Children can learn distances between points and the answer to that often-asked question, "How far is it to the next town?" If dad says he plans to drive 300 miles the next day, let the children figure out where you will likely spend that night.

If you visit the library before you leave on your vacation, you will find books on games especially suitable for traveling—guessing games, number games, games using the alphabet, and rhyming games. Many travel games are also explained in Volume 9, *Make and Do*, pages 257–261. Have a box of small prizes that can be awarded. You might give a child a small cash award occasionally, which he can use for souvenir shopping.

Travel Hints and Helps

- Travel light; take only the essentials.
- Use as many "throw aways" as you can when vacationing. Disposable diapers and diaper liners for baby; paper towels, napkins, and cups.
- Take along a big, heavy plastic tablecloth or two for use as waterproof sheeting at hotel or motel or as a floor cloth to give baby a clean play space.
- For a small child, carry along the toilet seat he uses at home.
- Take a little child's own spoon, dish, and cup.
- Be sure to include a simple first-aid kit with bandages, an antiseptic, petroleum jelly, and aspirin. Ask your doctor's advice about including sedatives and laxatives for the children.
- Take along a "wiggle box." Fill this with little toys and gadgets you've picked up at the dime store or around your home: some familiar toys, new clothespins, pipe cleaners, small building blocks, and little cars. When a child gets wiggly, let him play with something from the wiggle box.
- Don't frown at comic books during your vacation ride. You may not think highly of them from a literary standpoint, but they do keep a child amused when riding for long periods of time.

See also FIRST AID; MOTION SICKNESS

TRUANCY

When a child skips school again and again without his parents' knowing anything about it, he is saying that he is very unhappy or bored. He is saying that he would rather be scolded or punished than stay in the hated place. It is very important for his sake to find out why he tries to solve his daily difficulties by leaving them. Some questions can be asked him on the whys of his behavior, but there are many more his parents and teachers can ask themselves.

Has this child defective hearing, speech, or sight or a generally run-down physical condition that might tire him or make him have trouble understanding his schoolwork? Is he, because of these handicaps, unable to concentrate and always behind in his schoolwork? Is he extremely overweight so that other children ridicule him? Is he forced to wear clothes that make him look different from the other children of his age and grade? Has he a bad scar, an unusual mannerism, or a physical defect? If ruthless children tease him to the point where he simply cannot stand it, he may retreat by playing truant.

Parents and teachers should also ask themselves whether outside pressures are too much. Sometimes parents, because they find their child so wonderful, may think he is brighter than other children and will do better at school than others do. But the child finds out at school that he is actually less bright. He doesn't know how to tell his parents. And they go on insisting that he be top man in everything he tries to do. The pressure becomes too much for him—he takes the only road he can think of and simply stays away from school.

Sometimes a truant's reason for skipping school lies in the fact that he is much brighter than his classmates. He becomes so bored that he stays away. For a child of this superiority it is important to find some way of adding stimulating work to his curriculum.

Truancy may sometimes be simply an adventure to see what happens. Or it may be a show of defiance toward a teacher whom the child feels is unfair or it can be a show of loyalty to another truant whom he admires. A child can play truant as a bid for independence or for recognition as an individual. Another child may find that if he is bold enough to play truant, others in his group will admire him. Or there may be some far more serious, deep-seated problem driving the youngster away from school.

If the reasons for staying away from school are not very important ones, truancy can often be cured by a readjustment of relationships in and out of school, a rearrangement of home or school routines, patient encouragement, affectionate attention, and the granting of greater independence. Where the problems are more serious, parents will need all the help they can get from the school, from the attendance supervisor whose job it is to deal with truancy, and from a child guidance counselor. A. WHITTIER DAY

See also CHILD GUIDANCE CLINIC; FAILURE, FEAR OF; GIFTED CHILD; HOME-SCHOOL RELATIONS; PROBLEM CHILD; SLOW LEARNER

TRUTHFULNESS *See* HONESTY

TUBERCULOSIS

The most important fact for you to know about tuberculosis is that it is contagious. All infants are born free of this disease. They do not inherit it, although they appear to when tuberculosis strikes several members of the same family, as it often does. When a family is tubercular, spread of the disease has been brought about by close contact so that one family member has infected another. A new victim has picked up tuberculosis usually by breathing in or swallowing matter contaminated with millions of tubercle bacilli in the saliva of a sick person.

Children are least likely to get tuberculosis when they are between 2 and 12 years old. Up to the age of 2 they have much less resistance to the germs; there are many active cases in this age bracket and some fatal ones. If a baby is exposed over and over again, as he would be in a home where there is a case of tuberculosis, any normal resistance he might have would be destroyed.

The two main types of tuberculosis are primary infection tuberculosis (when a person picks up the disease for the first time) and reinfection tuberculosis (when he is infected again a second, third, or fourth time). Children who have primary infection tuberculosis show very few symptoms. Sometimes the signs of the disease are so slight that a child can have it without his parents knowing anything is wrong. This statement is not true of children who are reinfected. These children usually have fever, and they lose weight, cough, and show signs of the weakness associated with tuberculosis.

About 95 per cent of those children with a primary infection never become seriously sick. The other five per cent unfortunately develop complications. There can be a generalized spread into the lungs or into the covering of the brain or there can be a general spreading into the blood stream, with germs lodging in any part of the body except the hair and nails. These complications are not easy to cure.

It is tremendously important, therefore, to find out if a child has a primary infection of tuberculosis so that the disease can be treated before complications develop. It is still more important to keep him from being infected with tuberculosis at all. Children should be kept away from infected adults or, if isolation is impossible, the sick person's living should be controlled in a way to keep the children safe.

A common method nowadays of finding out if a child is exposed to tuberculosis is through the tuberculin test. The tuberculosis skin test, as it is also called, offers a simple method of finding those children who have been infected with the tubercle germs.

A drop of tuberculin, which is harmless, is either injected, scratched, or rubbed into the skin. If after two days the spot becomes red and hot, the test is considered positive. A positive test does not mean the child will necessarily become ill, but it does mean that he has been exposed. All positive reactors should have a chest X ray to determine the extent of the infection.

Associates of the child should have chest X rays to determine if they are the ones who have infected him and, in that manner, stop any more infections.

Yearly chest X rays are now a routine part of physical examinations. Free chest X rays are often available to employees by large companies and large tuberculosis organizations. It is a simple precaution for all adult members of a family to have chest X rays at yearly intervals.

Some children who live in areas where there is a great deal of tuberculosis or in a family where there is an active case are given shots so that they will have immunity to a primary infection.

But the most effective protector a child can have is his parents. They can try to keep him in general good health, avoid exposing him to known cases of active tuberculosis, see that he has periodic checkups, and bend some energy toward having the disease stamped out in the community. JULIUS B. NOVAK

See also CONVALESCENT CHILD; HOSPITALIZATION

TWINS

The unique problem in the rearing of twins is the need for unusual emphasis upon individuality—upon "identity." Identity is composed of many elements, all of which go into the making of character. The upbringing of twins, particularly identical twins, is one of the most perplexing and complex problems parents face in dealing with relationships between or among their children.

There are two types of twins—fraternal and identical. Identical twins are those developed from a single ovum (egg) and nourished from a single placenta (the round, flattened organ that forms during pregnancy in the mother's uterus, or womb). Fraternal, or nonidentical twins come from two seperate ova, each of which was fertilized by a separate male cell. Each baby is nourished by its own placenta. Such twins are no more alike in looks and personality than are other brothers and sisters.

Rarely are twins born with equal physical maturity. The smallest and least physically mature twin often assumes the secondary role, which may affect the pattern of their lives as twins grow up together. The stronger, more dominant twin will be the spokesman who announces, "We don't like cereal," or "We need a jungle gym." Later on, as the twins go to school and play outside their home or yard, the weaker or more submissive twin will benefit from new companions. These new friends will help him avoid being dominated by his more forceful counterpart and will keep him from feeling he has always to compete for attention.

Biologically, twins are different, a fact sometimes hard to understand when we are confronted with two look-alikes who use the same mannerisms and gestures and who have the same skin coloration and physical stature. Your aim in rearing twins is to insure each one the healthy, basic character that is his birthright. Extra sensitivity on the part of parents is required, especially when even trained observers cannot tell the twins apart.

Some degree of prematurity is usually present in one twin; sometimes it is present in both. Two completely full-term infants are the exception at birth. Feeding difficulties may occur with the less mature child, and he may be more subject to colds or other illnesses than his stronger twin. When there are other children in a family, parents will find their energy and resiliency taxed as they attempt to answer the demands of all children, assuring each one proper care and attention.

Parents often, knowingly or unknowingly, will expect identical accomplishments from twin babies, when actually the children have quite different needs, highly individual human beings that they are. Often, the less sturdy twin is overly protected at the expense of the stronger one, or just the reverse; the less mature twin is expected to function on the level of the more advanced twin. Parents of twins, it would seem, almost have to forget that the babies are twins except in looks.

If your twins are girl babies, you will probably expend less energy in their care. Boys, being more dynamic, demand more sheer energy for their upbringing, a situation often true, even when babies come one at a time.

Parents, with the best intentions, usually dress twins exactly alike. The children, however, might be happier in the long run if they wore contrasting styles and colors at least part of the time. Wise parents will realize their twins may have different tastes and different responses to fashions and colors. Consequently, to insist that they dress alike often makes it easy for tensions and dissatisfactions to build up between the twins. Other children in the family may resent the extra time and attention paid to choosing identical clothes for twins. If the family will keep in mind the special preferences of each twin, each will feel he—or she—has the right to be an individual. You encourage twins to be individuals, too, when you talk to them and about them by their names and not always as "the twins." Twins occasionally get the notion that they are valued only because there are two of them. Each needs to feel worth while in himself. Different clothes to be admired, different books to read, different conversational subjects, all help twins to attain the identity every child needs.

Twins sometimes take the attention of the entire family, relatives included. You, as the parent of twins, will want to be very sure that your other children are not overshadowed by these little carbon copies you have produced. Your children will love one another, but remember that in children of the same family resentment can also be more intense.

The mother of twin babies is entitled to an extra portion of consideration by her family. The enormousness of her job when the babies are tiny will at times seem insurmountable. The father, the older children, and the relatives who live nearby can help the mother through the first weeks and months by relieving her of some of the physical care of the infants. She will be refreshed by an afternoon away from them or just by the opportunity to take a long nap, knowing that the little ones' needs will be attended to.

Some experts question the wisdom of placing too much responsibility for the care of infants on older brothers and sisters. It would seem, however, that for character formation there is much to be gained by an early sense of participation by all members of the unique family situation involving twins.

In schooling, in the selection of playmates, in play interests, and in the arts, your twins should be treated as if their needs were as different as your children who are not twins. Schooling may pose a particular problem. One of your twins may be quite ready for social and group experiences, and the other may not. In this case the more aggressive twin might be placed in a nursery school or play group while the other is allowed to remain at home until he is ready for these experiences.

We know that twins seem to have simultaneous experiences of a psychic nature as well as similar reactions to disease. They will often incur the same disease although separated by many miles. They also may suffer emotional changes of a similar nature, simultaneously. These similar reactions are more likely for identical twins than for nonidentical twins. Again, as in dress and in schooling, twins, even though reacting in much the same manner, do have differences. Their responses to treatment may be very unlike, and their physical and emotional needs, though strikingly similar, must be treated as individual concerns.

Parents and educators should realize that rearing and educating twins is a challenge that requires cooperation, patience, and continuous teamwork. Above all, using the image of one twin against the other must be avoided. With the best intentions in the world, you may be building up one twin in his own eyes and tearing down their whole relationship in the eyes of the other.

Remember, your twins are not oddities. They are people. They have the right to privacy. Their likes, their dislikes, their loves, and their hates must always be treated individually.

EDWARD LISS

See also FAVORITISM; INDIVIDUAL DIFFERENCES; OVERPROTECTION

TWITCH *See* TIC

TYPEWRITER

An 8- or a 9-year-old child is not too young to be taught to use a typewriter. Several elementary school systems in the country have tried experimental summer typing courses for children this age with great success. Children who learn to type at an early age usually learn to read and to spell more readily and show greater ability to express themselves in writing.

Many high schools recognize the importance of a student's knowing how to type by offering typing programs for incoming freshmen. Students spend two or three mornings a week with a qualified instructor, and it has been found that these children learn to use a typewriter very quickly.

The boy or girl who has learned to operate a typewriter finds greater ease in participating in high school activities—working on school publications, making committee reports, and working on school plays.

Some parents feel that a typewriter is too expensive a piece of equipment to turn over to a child. But if the child learns early that a typewriter is not a plaything, and if time and patience are used in teaching him to use it properly, there should be no problem. A good household rule would be that only one child at a time may have access to the typewriter, and that it has to be put away in its case or covered properly after each use.

Electric typewriters are an invaluable aid to postpolio children who cannot use their arms or hands or to children with other orthopedic handicaps involving the hands, arms, or shoulders. The child is placed before the typewriter, his arms in slings adjusted so that his hands rest over the keys. A whole new world opens to this child as he watches his fingers spell out words on paper.

UMBILICAL CORD *See* NAVEL; REPRODUCTION

UMBILICAL HERNIA *See* NAVEL

UMBILICUS *See* NAVEL

UNDERSTANDING *See* LOVE; PATIENCE

UNDERWEIGHT

Before you worry about what to do about an underweight child, you had better make sure that he really is underweight. The range of so-called "normal" weight for a given age and height is pretty wide; usually a child must weigh a lot less than others his age and height to be classed as underweight. So let your doctor decide whether or not your child *is* underweight. Then he can also look into the cause of the child's weight problem and decide what to do about it.

Perhaps your youngster is eating what seems to be enough, but his foods lack nutritive value. A diet that gives him "less of this and more of that" may be all that is needed to bring his weight up.

A child may, however, be eating good nutritious foods and yet have some chronic disease, such as chronic diarrhea, that prevents his body from absorbing or using food properly. There are also rare instances, such as overactivity of the thyroid gland, where a young body uses food too rapidly.

The most common cause of underweight, of course, is that the child is simply not eating enough. If he does not eat, then reasons for his lack of appetite must be sought. It is important that he be checked carefully to find out whether a chronic illness, such as tuberculosis or chronic tonsillitis or sinusitis, is causing his loss of appetite. Often the doctor will find no physical illness and will then look for the possibility of emotional cause for poor appetite.

Sometimes children lose interest in food because they have had too much coaxing to eat, or they may develop poor eating habits because their eating or not eating is of too great concern to their parents. The eating problems associated with coaxing begin quite often with the toddler. An infant, unless he is physically sick during his first year, usually eats enough. During his second year, as he begins to walk and explore his environment, he may lose interest briefly in food. Unfortunately, at just this time, he also loses the chubbiness of infancy and this loss may cause his parents to believe, mistakenly, that he is not eating so well as he should. If he is coaxed to eat at this time, a chronic eating problem may develop. If not coaxed, he usually starts eating again without any difficulty.

An eating problem may also begin when a child loses his appetite during an acute illness. If at this time his parents are unduly anxious and coax him to eat, he may use eating as a bargaining device to gain other ends in the future or he may develop an aversion to food. Emotional reasons for not eating, however, do not always have their basis in food itself—depression or unhappiness may cause a child to stop eating his normal amount. Once in a great while a child's refusal to eat may become quite extreme and his case may need intensive study and hospital care.

If your doctor tells you there is no cause for concern, yet your child himself still feels he would look better carrying a few more pounds, there are many ways you can help him: You can make some of his foods a bit richer or add attractive extras at mealtimes or see that he eats some weight-building foods between meals. You can try to have him avoid appetite-killing snacks just before meals. You can see that his activities are not overabundant or too exciting, that his TV programs are not too stimulating, that his hours for rest are plentiful and relaxed. You can minimize your child's self-consciousness by seeing that his clothes fit properly, that he is not lost, for instance, in baggy trousers or shirts with too-long sleeves. For your girl child you can choose becoming patterned fabrics and full skirts to make her look a little plumper than she is.

But best of all you can stop talking about weight. Constant reminders about being "painfully thin" or "just skin and bones" do not help an underweight child. Make as few comments as possible and make those few only when they seem to be demanded by the child himself or when they can be discretely and concretely helpful to him in specific situations.

JULIUS B. RICHMOND

See also APPETITE; EATING PROBLEMS; GROWTH; NUTRITION

UNTRUTHFULNESS

Suppose a 6-year-old finds life not very exciting one day. He may come home with a tale of having driven the school bus because the regular driver was busy elsewhere. He tells the story with solemn conviction, but you will recognize it at once for the tall tale it is. You will certainly, however, not consider him untruthful in the usual sense, for a 6-year-old does not yet understand that there is anything wrong in trying to pass off an imagined adventure as a real one. You aren't going to put a label on him, either, and call him untruthful, even in your own mind. So you listen attentively and then give him the good-humored response that this is a fine story, all right, but that you know it is make-believe and so does he. You even tell him that you enjoy make-believe as long as both of you know what it is.

Usually a child will outgrow tall-tale telling in a short time. But if such stories represent a child's effort to get adventure into his life, you could help to provide more wholesome excitement. Perhaps he hasn't enough friends or places to go or perhaps the stories read to him lack imagination and daring.

Older children sometimes lie to escape punishment or to avoid having to own up to a misdeed. Perhaps a youngster accidentally tosses his ball through a neighbor's window. He knows he will be in for it as soon as his misdeed is discovered, and he may pile falsehood upon falsehood in an effort to divert suspicion from himself. You can be kind but also firm in insisting that he acknowledge his guilt and make what amends he can. And you can let him know that accidents happen to everyone and that you are with him in his difficult situation. You can also ask yourself if you have been pretty harsh with him on other misdeeds lately and if this harshness perhaps frightened him into denial.

Lying may also result from experiences or situations that a child considers unfair. In this case, the child is bitter and resentful and is trying to even the score with those whom he feels are "mean" to him. It is important in this kind of trouble that the parent know whether or not injustices exist and to eradicate them if they do. If they do not, parents may need professional help to find out why a child thinks he is being treated unjustly.

No matter why a child lies, you are not going to improve his habits by meting out punishments that are too severe or that do not fit the misdeed. The wrong punishment can only heighten his sense of injustice; severity that goes too far can only make him more prone to lie his way out of trouble.

When an older child lies, it may mean that the pressures and tensions of schoolwork are too much for him. If he tells his parents that his daily grades are good and then poor grades show up on his report card, perhaps his parents have been too demanding. Perhaps the combined demands of having to get good grades, to be a social success, and to be seen with the "right" children are too much of a burden for him to bear. He will lie about where he has been and with whom he has spent an afternoon if he feels his parents would disapprove of his companions. It is far better to relax these pressures; let the child know he is trusted and allow him to make some of his own decisions.

Unfortunately, children will often lie because untruthfulness is what they see and hear. A parent who is concerned about his child's growing tendency to lie can often learn a lot by listening to examples set by adult members of the family.

To be scrupulously honest with them from the beginning of their lives is one of the finest gifts parents can give their children. If children are always told the truth, if their questions are answered clearly and honestly, and if promises to them are faithfully kept, they are quite likely to react honestly to almost all situations. A. WHITTIER DAY

See also CHILD GUIDANCE CLINIC; DISCIPLINE; HONESTY; IMITATION; MORAL AND SPIRITUAL DEVELOPMENT; PROMISES

UPPER RESPIRATORY INFECTION

See BRONCHITIS; COLDS; COUGH

UPSET STOMACH

See COLIC; COMMON COMMUNICABLE DISEASES; FOOD POISONING; MOTION SICKNESS; STOMACH-ACHE

URINARY DISTURBANCES

Children are subject to several types of urinary disturbances. One is lack of control of urination. Some children may continue to wet their beds after other children their age or younger have learned control.

Unusual frequency of urination is another common disturbance. Usually frequency is a symptom of an infection of the urinary tract. Pain, or a "burning" sensation, on urination is often part of this condition, but in an infant, it may be difficult to know of his discomfort since the child cannot use words to tell you. Such a child is often feverish and may be irritable and cry excessively. In any instance of fever for which there is no apparent cause, infection of the urinary tract is a possibility. The doctor can determine that infection is present by examining the urine under a microscope. It may be that some abnormality in the formation of the kidneys, the bladder, the connecting tubes, or the passage through which urine flows from the bladder to the outside is responsible for poor urine flow and infection. Thus when infection of the urinary passages occurs, the doctor may wish to examine the urinary tract very carefully. Many drugs are now available to treat urinary-tract infections. These infections tend, however, to recur, so it is important to try to prevent further attacks.

Blood in the urine is always a matter of enough concern for a parent to consult the doctor. Remember, though, that occasionally the urine may appear to be red after a child has eaten beets. Blood in the urine may occur because of nephritis, infection, or some abnormality of the urinary tract. Occasionally, the amounts of blood are so small that they can be detected only by observing the urine under a microscope or by chemical tests of the urine. JULIUS B. RICHMOND

VACATIONS, SCHOOL

Most children and their parents look forward to summer vacations from school and the relaxed routines of long and languid summer days. Although father will probably have a two- or three-week vacation during which the whole family may take a trip, there will be many other days to enjoy.

It is possible, however, for children to become bored with days that are almost identical and without planned activity. Mothers who want their own summers to be reasonably relaxed and enjoyable, who want father to appreciate having the children at home, and who want their children to gain both a sense of achievement and some good memories from vacation can come nearer their goal if they plan some out-of-routine activities.

To keep young children contented during the summer, each day might well have its high spot—a trip to a children's zoo, a backyard picnic with the neighbors, or a walk to the park or local soda fountain. And, of course, a swim in a nearby pool is usually a prime favorite pastime.

Each week might have a high spot, too, such as a fishing trip on Saturday when dad is home or an excursion to the city toward the end of summer to buy new school clothes. Children get almost as much fun out of anticipation as out of the event itself. So let the children share in your planning.

Some children enjoy a project that occupies them for several days or even weeks. Such children will work toward producing a backyard circus or a country fair, a puppet show, or a magic show. Children will combine talents to make scenery, write scripts, design and sew costumes, sell tickets, and learn their lines or stunts for the big event. A suggestion often is needed from you to get these projects started. Your continued interest and encouragement can also keep them going.

Summer is an ideal time for older brothers and sisters to relieve mother of some of the care of younger children. But older children should not be given responsibilities beyond their years nor be expected to assume full charge of an infant.

Summer days are ideal for reading. Many libraries feature special summer reading programs for children, sometimes offering special inducements to encourage children to read a great number of books.

Religious holidays are usually spent joyously with family and friends. New toys and books, parties and celebrations, take the attention of children, and time passes swiftly. Some families find the Christmas vacation an ideal time for winter sports or sunny beaches and pool their Christmas money to spend the holidays in a different setting.

For all vacations, whether you stay at home or go away, remember that children enjoy being allowed to help in planning their own and family activities, however simple they may be.

See also CAMP; CHORES; DRAMATICS; LIBRARIES; TRAVELING WITH CHILDREN; YOUTH ORGANIZATIONS

VACCINATION *See* IMMUNIZATION

VAGINAL DISCHARGE

A vaginal discharge (leukorrhea) is first noticed when the underclothing of a girl shows whitish stains. This condition may result from an infection, causing the external genital area to be red and inflamed. The condition may also be brought on by rubbing of the genital region. In some instances a foreign object may have been inserted into the vagina. It is, therefore, advisable to have a doctor examine the child for this possibility and to provide proper treatment. He may prescribe antibiotics and bathing of the external genital area.

In girls who are reaching adolescence and who are beginning to undergo sexual growth and development, a slight discharge from the vagina is common and normal. It is well to explain these changes to a young girl and to give her instructions concerning the onset of menstruation. JULIUS B. RICHMOND

See also MENSTRUATION

VAPORIZER *See* STEAMING

VIRUS

A virus is a tiny particle—so tiny that it cannot be seen under an ordinary microscope. Viruses may cause infectious diseases such as infantile paralysis, influenza, measles, chicken pox, smallpox, mumps, and the common cold.

Viruses gain access to the body in various ways—through food or water, inhalation, injection, or breaks in the skin—and when they do, they produce their effect by growing inside body cells.

Some of the effects of specific infections are produced in certain types of cells; for instance, liver cells in infectious hepatitis, brain cells in sleeping sickness, skin cells in fever blisters. As more becomes known about viruses, it is likely that more vaccines and other methods of disease prevention will become available.

JULIUS B. RICHMOND

VISION *See* EYE HEALTH

VISITING TEACHER *See* HOME AND HOSPITAL INSTRUCTION

VISITORS

While your child is young, a great part of your social life is going to include him. When people come to your house to visit or when you go to theirs, your child's needs go on. And unless at these times he is reasonably content, amenable, and agreeable, you are not going to have very much fun. This means that you will have to think of your child, too, as part of the visited or visiting group. It does not mean that you have to think of him as the most important member of the group, but simply that some of his ordinary needs cannot be altogether brushed aside.

Physically, he needs to be fed when he is hungry and get rest when he is tired. Socially, he needs to have someone or something to play with to occupy his attention. Emotionally, he should not feel that he has been rudely pushed out of your life for an interest more vital than he is. He should not feel that you love him only for some accomplishment that you make him parade before others, nor that the only way to get attention is to create a disturbance. And he shouldn't get the idea that total silence is necessarily golden either.

It sounds difficult, but to keep a child contented and agreeable when he is visited or visiting need not be as difficult a job as it seems. Your own response to the situation affects his; if you look forward to seeing family and friends, he probably will, too. You can prepare him for visits by talking about them ahead of time, by letting him help get ready to go out or to receive guests—"We'll make cookies today, so we'll have nice fresh ones when our company comes tomorrow." You can shield him from the too-enthusiastic visitor who wants to hug and kiss him when he is feeling shy. You can muffle your pride in his "genius" and not insist that he sing, recite, or dance unless he wants to. You can remember his age and avoid scolding him publicly just because his table manners are poor or his words are rude; you can wait instead until the two of you are alone, and then give him a quiet explanation of why you expect courteous behavior from him. You can remember, also, what his usual behavior is when guests are not present and not expect him suddenly to be very much more grownup. You can cultivate some friends who have children his own age, so that part of the time, at least, some of the visitors are his. You can let him be host, even to adults, if you suggest tasks that are not too difficult for him to perform. You can have him play quietly in another room *if* he has already learned to play quietly alone when visitors are not present, *if* he has been provided with something interesting to do, and *if* he feels he has free access to you when he is lonely or frightened or bored.

Give visitors and visiting a little thought, a little planning, and you may find that both you and your child will enjoy these social occasions.

See also MANNERS

VITAMINS

The human body needs only small quantities of vitamins, but it needs them very much.

Scientists are still searching for more information about vitamins, but on the basis of present-day knowledge, parents can feel sure that their children can get all the vitamins their bodies need, except for vitamin D, from an adequate daily diet of properly prepared foods. If vitamin D-fortified milk is used, the statement that vitamins can be purchased at the grocery store is entirely true. Millions of dollars are wasted each year on self-prescribed vitamin pills.

Dispensing vitamin pills may give a mother a sense of security that each individual's nutritive needs are being met. The feeling is false, for without professional advice it is possible to give a child too much of vitamins A and D and possibly some other vitamins. Vitamins work in subtle relationships with each other and with other nutrients. Thus the amount of a certain vitamin needed depends on the amount of other vitamins and nutrients in the body—something not always considered in the manufacture of vitamin pills.

In addition, the contents of a vitamin pill are limited to those vitamins that have been discovered and that can be manufactured in pure form. Foods may contain undiscovered but essential food substances. Therefore, you may rely on food to give your child an adequate diet unless his doctor prescribes vitamin supplements. A possible exception is

VITAMINS

NAME OF VITAMIN	FUNCTIONS IN THE BODY	FOOD SOURCES	HOW TO PRESERVE VITAMINS
A	Needed for the health of skin, tissues lining body cavities, glandular cells such as tear glands and glands producing digestive juices; good vision at night; and adequate development of teeth.	Animal foods, such as whole milk, cream, butter, egg yolks, liver, kidneys, fats, and oils from fish. Dark green and bright yellow vegetables, such as kale, spinach, greens of all kinds, carrots, yellow squash, sweet potatoes, cantaloupe, peaches, and apricots.	Fats and oils should be refrigerated to prevent rancidity, which causes destruction of vitamin A. Lips of bottles containing fish liver oils should be wiped clean, so that the oil does not become rancid.
D	Helps body to absorb calcium and phosphorus from the intestinal tract, which is important for normal bone growth.	One serving of salt-water fish (as salmon) contains enough for one day. Otherwise, natural foods are not important sources. Synthetic vitamin D products, vitamin D-fortified milk, fish liver oils are frequently used.	Keep fresh by refrigeration.
C ASCORBIC ACID	Increases resistance to infection. Helps form sound teeth and bones. Necessary for healthy gums and body tissues.	Citrus fruits are the chief source. Tomatoes contain about one-half as much per volume as citrus fruits. Other foods high in vitamin C are: cantaloupe, strawberries, green and chili peppers, pineapple, cabbage, broccoli, asparagus, and greens of all kinds. In general, raw foods contain more vitamin C than cooked foods. Canned and frozen citrus fruit juices, however, have nearly as much vitamin C as the fresh product.	Store foods high in vitamin C covered and in a cool place. Cook vegetables as short a time as possible and in as large pieces as can be managed to get the desired product.
B_1 THIAMINE	Gives body productive energy that it needs. Thiamine is important in maintaining a normal appetite, a healthy mental attitude, and normal functioning of muscles.	Lean pork, dried beans and peas, certain organ meats, nuts, whole grain cereals, enriched cereals and breads. Meat, eggs, milk; some fruits and vegetables also contain enough thiamine to add to the total amount needed in the diet.	Use as little water for cooking vegetables as possible.
B_2 RIBOFLAVIN	Helps carbohydrates to release heat and energy in the body.	Milk; meats such as liver, heart, and kidney; whole grain enriched cereals. Cheese, (especially cottage cheese), eggs, and leafy green vegetables also supply appreciable amounts.	Dairy products should not be exposed to bright sunlight.
NIACIN	Necessary for healthy skin and other body tissues.	Glandular meats, muscle meats, poultry, fish, and enriched and whole grain bread are excellent sources. Some fruits and vegetables also.	Use as little water in cooking vegetables as possible.

vitamin D, which is especially needed by the body when minerals, calcium, and phosphorus are being deposited during the growth of bones. Authorities recommend that children be given a source of vitamin D daily in summer as well as in winter throughout their entire major growth period—up to 20 years. It is good to consult your child's doctor about how much of and in what form to give this vitamin. He may suggest vitamin D-fortified milk, which can be purchased at most grocery stores. One quart contains 400 units of vitamin D—the required daily amount. Since vitamin D, like vitamins A, E, and K, is fat-soluble, it can be stored in the body with cumulative ill effects. So follow the doctor's recommendations carefully.

Vitamin C (ascorbic acid), along with the B vitamins, is water-soluble and cannot be stored in the body in appreciable amounts. One serving a day of a citrus fruit, strawberries, or cantaloupe should insure an adequate intake of vitamin C. Fortunately, since freezing or canning does not materially reduce vitamin C content, both frozen and canned citrus fruit juices fill the requirement also.

Tomatoes and tomato juice are good sources of vitamin C, although only half so good as the same measure of citrus fruits. In other words, one measuring cup of tomato juice will furnish as much vitamin C as one-half cup of a citrus fruit juice. Pineapple juice has about one fourth to one third as much vitamin C as citrus fruit juices. Many other fruit juices contain small amounts of vitamin C.

For the infant who refuses or spits up his orange or tomato juice, the doctor usually prescribes drops that contain vitamin C.

The accompanying table shows the uses by the body and the sources of vitamins about which there is current knowledge. Vitamin K, not mentioned in the table, is often administered to mothers prior to delivery to protect them and their babies, and sometimes to children before surgery to insure proper blood clotting. MIRIAM E. LOWENBERG

See also NUTRITION

VOCABULARY DEVELOPMENT

Words are the names or labels we give to our experiences. Words stand for ideas or concepts. Justice Holmes appropriately described a word as "the skin of a living thought."

Children have mastered some 2,500 words when they enter first grade and will learn 10,000 to 15,000 more by the time they graduate from high school. These are averages; some children will learn many more words, some fewer.

How does the illiterate child learn 2,500 words before he comes to school? How does he increase his vocabulary when he learns to read? Why do some children fail to make the growth in vocabulary of which they are capable? And last, what can parents and teachers do to build an interest in words which characterizes the educated adult?

Children Learn in Many Ways

A child learns in several ways the words he knows before he can read. He learns by observing and playing with blocks and toys, by paints and painting, by listening to stories read and songs sung to him, by going to stores and parks, by trips to the airport and the railway station, by watching TV, and by just hearing other people talk. His parents teach him the great advantage of speaking the name of an object instead of pointing to it. Then he can ask for things even when he can't see them. Names become important. So it's not surprising that we hear children ask, "What's your name?" or "What do you call this?"

But words are more than single, unrelated names. Words belong to groups or systems and we can help our children discover words that belong to the grocery store, to the kitchen, to parts of the body, to places visited on a trip, to people we know, to birds and flowers, to animals and minerals.

There are groups of words that deal with doing, with movement: *run, jump, skip, hop, hurtle*. There are words that describe people: *funny, happy, gay, sad, joyful, pleasant, boorish, saturnine*. Or we may have a group of words that describe things: *black, blue, large, small, huge, microscopic, near, distant*, and so on. We have hundreds of words that deal with time and space: *now, later, birthday, century*, or *inch, foot, mile*. The number system provides an endless series of words that tell "how many."

These groups of words furnish us our mental filing systems. We file certain words as fruits or vegetables, as vertebrates or invertebrates, as arithmetic or science, as plants or animals, as male or female, as oviparous or viviparous. The richer the experience of the young child, the richer his vocabulary.

After gaining more effective control over his environment by adding listening and speaking to observing and doing, a child begins learning new words by drawing pictures, by acting them out, by pretending to be someone else. He learns to interpret pictures when mother and father look at pictures with him and ask or reply to the question, "What's that?"

At first he merely names objects in the picture, enumerates them. Next he describes, and later interprets, what he sees. As he grows older, he not only tells a story about what he saw in the picture but also what he imagined. By talking and listening to members of his family and other people, he learns words as they should be learned—in the context of language.

School Brings New Power

In school he gains new power over words by learning to read and write them. As he becomes a fluent reader, the words in his vocabulary are not confined to those that he has directly experienced; they now include indirect experience with persons, places, and ideas from all over the world.

He also learns that some words may represent more than one idea. *Bark* may be the short, sharp sound that a dog makes or the tough outside covering of the trunk and branches of a tree. Most youngsters know these two meanings before they enter first grade. Later, as they read, they may discover that *bark* also means to scrape the skin from knuckles or shins or it may mean to shout or speak sharply—officers may *bark* their orders. And one day they may come across the word *bark* meaning a three-masted ship.

Some of the words children read will be concrete and tangible, such as *boy, girl, house, arm, book,* and *orange.* Other words will be abstract and intangible, such as *freedom, perspective, sovereignty,* or *decimal system.* Abstract words are meaningful and correctly remembered and used when they grow out of the concrete experiences.

Children will learn that words can play as well as work. Their ears will be tickled with words like *hurdy-gurdy, higgledy-piggledy, zigzag, itsy-bitsy, roly-poly, walkie-talkie, hickory-dickory.* They will learn that some words get their names from the sounds they make: *click, clack, cluck, chickadee, whippoorwill, bobolink, towhee, whiz, buzz, zip, swish.*

Perhaps you have helped your youngster get fun out of puns—a play on the sound of words. A 6-year-old making mud pies by mixing shrubbery clippings with mud told her father that she was making shrubbery shortcake. Many of the riddles enjoyed by children are puns, and both big people and small people enjoy an appreciative audience. Charades are based on puns.

Children will misinterpret or mispronounce words both before and after they learn to read. Some of these errors are very amusing, and home is (or should be) a place where everybody laughs with you and not at you. For example, a puzzled kindergartner asked his mother why the pledge of allegiance called for "liver, tea, and just fish" for everybody. A 3-year-old counted "one, two, three, four, five, six, heaven, sakes, nine, ten."

One 4-year-old child, for example, called yesterday night yester*night* in contrast to yester*day.* His thinking was good, since yesternight, like yesteryear, is a real word used chiefly in a poetic sense. Sometimes children draw wrong inferences, however, as did the boy who thought that an in-law was a good cowboy since an outlaw was a bad one, or the little girl, who, when she finished her meal first instead of last, termed herself a "fast-poke."

As children get older, they learn that they can use the key parts of known words to make new words. By learning how to use prefixes, suffixes, and roots, children quickly multiply the number of words they know and use. They learn the difference between *wash, washed,* and *washing.* They learn to put *dis* or *un* in front of a word to make it say "no" or "not." One 7-year-old said that the new automobiles were "disimproved" and that a deflated tire was "unaired."

Children need help in seeing the roots and prefixes in such words as *auto*graph, *tele*graph, *tele*phone, and *tele*vision. It is valuable in vocabulary building to know that *auto* means "self," *graph* means "write" or "record," and *tele* means "distance." It helps to see the root *onym,* meaning name, in "synonym," "homonym," "antonym," "acronym."

Vocabulary Index to Intelligence

The depth, breadth, and precision of a child's vocabulary is important for two reasons. First, it is the best single index of his mental ability. A high IQ reflects the presence of rich, highly varied, and generalized experience. A low IQ reflects limited experience and limited generalization. Second, words are the best index of our ideas and concepts. Reading ability and success in school correlate highly with vocabulary size. To read successfully, a child must not only be able to pronounce the words he reads but he must also know what the words mean. Otherwise he becomes a "word-caller," saying the sounds of words without sensing their meaning.

To read intelligently about cricket, for example, you must know the meaning of such words as *wicket, stump, bail, bowler, century, midoff, midon, gully,* and *slip.* You can pronounce the words, but they may have little or no meaning unless you have played or watched the game.

Contrast your possible meager knowledge of cricket with your knowledge of baseball terms: *pitcher, catcher, inning, three-bagger, infield fly*. The richer one's vocabulary, the more effectively he can listen, read, and observe. The richer one's vocabulary, the greater the resources he has for building new words.

We know, of course, that some children are abler than others and we must take this factor into account. We can't change the potential with which they were born, but we can certainly develop it to its fullest. Some reasons for underdeveloped vocabulary are noted here and remedial measures suggested.

Children may suffer from lack of rich, first-hand experiences. Perhaps they have not adequately explored their environment through trips, concerts, nature walks, and the making and viewing of collections of various kinds.

Perhaps their attention has not been called to the exciting things happening right under their noses. Have you taken time to show your child a piece of moldy cheese or bread and to explain that he is looking at a collection of hundreds of invisible plants that grow on starch?

Did you ever stick the top of a carrot in water and let your children watch it sprout and grow leaves? Does your child understand how your furnace works, how the water and gas and electricity are piped into your house? We need to train ourselves and our children to be more observant, to take fewer things for granted, and to ask more questions.

Children who have inadequate vocabularies have often failed to read first-rate books and magazines. Persons with an excellent vocabulary tend to be able readers and listeners. Encourage your children to listen carefully and thoughtfully to recordings of folk songs or of children's literature. But reading and listening are not enough. There must be encouragement to talk and discuss. When we talk to our children, do we have interesting things to say or is most of what we have to say a series of do's and don'ts?

Encouragement Is Important

We must also ask ourselves: Do we really encourage our children to converse about interesting things? Do we give them our undivided attention when they talk? Do we ask intelligent questions about their school experiences? Do we let them give us the benefit of their ideas? Encourage your child to be the family "expert" in fields that interest him. Give him close attention and generous praise for the ideas he shares with the family.

What are some specific things that parents and teachers of children should know about the stages in understanding words?

Progress in Three Stages

First, we must never assume that words can be neatly classified as known or unknown. Children's knowledge of words progresses through certain stages.

In the first stage the child has heard or seen the word before but he doesn't know what it means. Adult examples might be words like *empyrean, caryatid, apotheosis, sine qua non*, or *serendipity*.

In the second stage the child knows the word as it appears in certain phrases or contexts, but he is vague about its meaning. Adult examples might be *pied* piper, *fell* swoop, make the *welkin* ring. You know you *bask* in the sun, but can you *bask* in the shade? What does short *shrift* mean literally? We have heard and said, "Eleven, twelve, let them delve," but did we know that *delve* means to dig?

In the third stage the word is well known and the child is able to define it in his terms, use it in its varied meanings. Many children and adults have large numbers of words in the second, or foggy, stage. We could sharply increase our vocabulary if we took the time and effort to develop clear concepts out of ones that are now vague and fuzzy. These "twilight" words can be brought into the bright light of understanding.

The family habit of using dictionaries and encyclopedias to look up an unclear word will increase vocabulary and develop the habit of using reference materials. Encourage the look-it-up habit. Children need to learn that a good question deserves a good answer. Many children don't look up unknown words because it doesn't occur to them that it is important to do so.

Of course, nobody looks up every single word that he doesn't know. Hard reading materials may contain too many of them. But when a member of the family has a word in the second, or vague, stage of learning, that word can easily be made a permanent part of his vocabulary if it is checked on in the dictionary. Many times, of course, the parent is at hand to answer a child's questions about unfamiliar words.

When children learn names of things, dictionaries and encyclopedias help them classify and file these new words in the right families or groups. Children will learn that a whale is not a fish but a mammal, which nurses its young. They can learn that the red berries are found on the *female* holly trees.

Spiders and scorpions are not true insects, but butterflies and moths are.

Parents and teachers can help children to realize that precision in the use of words is as important as the number of words known. Thus we learn the differences between *admit, acknowledge,* and *confess; border* and *edge; oral* and *vocal.* It is also important for children to learn that there are certain unfriendly words: "Scotchman" for *Scotsman,* "Chinaman" for *Chinese,* "Jap" for *Japanese.*

Seize the Right Opportunity

Listening, both planned and spontaneous, offers another way that parents can encourage children to enlarge their vocabularies. It is a good idea to set aside special times each day to read to your children, even when they can read for themselves. Seeing life through another's eyes helps a child to sharpen his own vision and also to enlarge his vocabulary. A wonderful time to introduce stories or poetry is based on opportunity—the time when the story or poem captures the mood of the moment. If a fat, furry squirrel pounces on the windowsill and stares in at your youngster, what a perfect time to introduce the poem "Whisky Frisky," page 108, Volume 1, *Poems and Rhymes,* to help the child hear words that paint a verbal picture of a squirrel and his quick, twirling movements down a tree.

Parents also need to learn more effective ways to communicate with their children. Did you ever hear a parent say, "I just can't get my son to talk to me. He doesn't have anything to say to me." Perhaps the parent has failed to ask the right questions, to keep in touch with the things that are important to a child. Instead of starting the dinner table conversation with, "Well, what did you do in school today?" find out what's going on at school by visiting and by glancing through your child's books and papers. When a first-grader is asked, "Well, did little Sally make any funny mistakes in your reader today?" you're likely to get an answer that can lead to more questions—and a lively discussion. Parents who save interesting ideas from their reading or from the day's activities to add to the conversation also help to improve family communications.

Don't make vocabulary development a grim chore. Remember that vocabulary grows best in the soil of interesting experience. Montaigne's advice given in the 16th century is sound today:

> Half of our life is spent in empty babble. We are kept learning words and stitching them into sentences for four or five years, for as many more in arranging a great mass of them in four or five divisions; and then for another five at least in learning to mix and interlace them in some complicated pattern. If only one has plenty of facts, the words will follow quickly enough.

A rich family life offers the best way to develop a rich vocabulary. So try to see that your family has interesting experiences and encourage individual members to talk, write, and read about these experiences.

Horace's advice for poets is equally good for parents and teachers today: "Instruct with delight." EDGAR DALE AND DOROTHY SHERWOOD

See also BOOKS FOR CHILDREN; MAGAZINES; MENTAL DEVELOPMENT; READING ALOUD; TELEVISION

VOMITING

Vomiting refers to the forceful bringing up of any contents of the stomach—not necessarily food that has been swallowed, for the newborn baby who has never eaten may vomit fluid contents of the stomach.

Vomiting is a very common symptom among infants and children and it seems that many things that upset the child physically or emotionally may bring it on. Thus, any illness associated with high fever—scarlet fever, influenza, or pneumonia—may bring on vomiting; disorders of other organs such as the kidneys may be associated with vomiting. Some children respond to riding in cars, trains, planes, or ships with nausea and vomiting. And children who are acutely upset—after being in an accident, for example —may vomit. Vomiting may be associated with emotional problems of longer duration: for instance, the child who vomits in the morning because he is apprehensive about going to school. For such children, special psychological study may be necessary.

If a child accidentally swallows a poisonous substance, he may vomit. If poisoning is suspected, save some of the vomited material for analysis since it may prove helpful in the treatment of the child.

Conditions within the gastrointestinal tract also cause vomiting. Appendicitis, peptic ulcer, and abnormalities in the formation or position of the stomach or intestines may cause it. Because of its many possible causes and the importance, in many instances, of early treatment, a doctor should be consulted when vomiting occurs. JULIUS B. RICHMOND

See also COMMON COMMUNICABLE DISEASES; EMETICS; MOTION SICKNESS; POISONING AND POISONS; SPITTING UP; STOMACH-ACHE; SWALLOWING THINGS

WAKEFULNESS

COMMON CAUSES

- A room that is too warm or too cold
- Uncomfortable bedclothing
- A new bed; a new room
- A new baby-sitter
- A mother who is in a hurry, irritable, or sick and can't provide customary attention
- Noises that come to the child from another part of the house
- A change of routine in daytime activities
- Starting to a new school
- Getting accustomed to a new baby
- Coming home from the hospital
- Too long a daytime nap or being kept in bed too long at night
- Worries or fears carried over from daytime play and other activities
- Fever, pain, or possibly the development of an illness

When your youngster is wakeful at naptime or during the night, you will want to determine the cause of his wakefulness. Talk to him in a quiet tone, check to see that he is comfortable, alleviate his fears, and assure him of your nearness, and he will usually go to sleep, comforted and soothed by your calm sympathy. MILTON J. E. SENN

See also NIGHTMARES; REST; SLEEP

WALKING

Most babies begin to walk by themselves when they are between 10 and 15 months old. A baby's first steps seem historic, and most mothers remember vividly this important milestone.

Before a baby actually takes his first steps, he has gone through a good deal of experimenting and preliminary trial. After creeping, he usually learns first to pull himself to a standing position by holding onto a convenient table, chair, or playpen rail. Then he learns to shift his balance from one foot to the other while still standing in one place and holding on. Fairly soon he begins to move about, back and forth. Rarely does he loosen his tight clutch on his support because when he does, he is apt to sit down with a bang. Most babies continue to walk about in this way for some days or weeks before really launching out on independent steps.

Finally, the baby begins to take a few steps at a time, with no support whatsoever, probably in what seems to him to be the middle of nowhere. He hasn't learned yet to keep his center of balance slightly to the front and so is apt to shift it back and forth while lurching about in the typical widespread gait of the toddler. Every few steps he loses his balance completely and sits down suddenly. This rarely discourages him, however, and he is up and ready to go again almost immediately.

Once in a while a baby is made so unhappy or frightened by his early falls that he gives up temporarily and goes back to creeping or holding on. Soon, however, his eagerness to master such an exciting accomplishment as walking overcomes caution and he is again willing to take a chance.

A few babies are perfectly content just to sit. As long as such a placid child seems to be comfortable bearing his weight on both legs, the chances are that his slowness in walking has no special meaning. If a baby is much later than 15 months in starting to walk or if he cries and seems uncomfortable when standing or bearing weight on either leg, he should be checked by his doctor to make sure there is no special reason for not being willing to walk.

Most babies look unsteady, and their feet and ankles don't look very straight as they begin walking. It often is a temptation to assume that they would be much steadier if they were put into high shoes with stiff sides and stiff soles to give them lots of firm support. Ordinarily, an inflexible shoe makes walking more difficult. The best way to strengthen the weak ankle muscles and to improve walking is to interfere as little as possible with the natural action of the foot and ankle muscles. A soft, flexible shoe will give protection against cold and rough objects and still allow the freedom of movement that encourages muscle development.

Now that your baby is walking, it is time to toddler-proof your home—to protect him from harm and to preserve your treasured breakables. RUTH S. KEMPE

See also ACCIDENT PREVENTION; TODDLER

WARTS

Small, hard growths on the surface of the skin are called warts. Some warts may become quite large. Warts are seen most commonly on the fingers and hands, but they can occur anywhere on the body. Although warts tend to occur in groups of three or four, there can be many more.

Warts are caused by a virus that seems to grow rather slowly. Children should be cautioned against "picking" at warts, since to do so may cause the virus to spread and increase the number of the warts. The folklore about how warts are acquired and about how to treat them has no basis in fact. Aside from their appearance, and the discomfort produced if they grow at the nail bed, warts do not seem to have any harmful effect on the general health.

There are several effective and painless methods for removing warts, but removal, of course, should be attempted only by the child's physician. JULIUS B. RICHMOND

See also VIRUS

WASP STING *See* BITES, INSECT

WATER, FEAR OF *See* SWIMMING

WATER FOR BABY

Water is a very important part of the fluid intake for all of us. Because a small baby gets his food mostly in the form of liquid and because he can't go to the faucet and casually help himself, we may forget that he often needs a drink of water, too. He especially needs water in hot climates, during hot weather, or if he is not well and has fever. And, just as babies differ in the amount of food they want, they differ in the amount of water they take, both regularly and from day to day.

A mild degree of constipation is one indication that you should offer more water. Also, offer your baby water once or twice a day, between breast or bottle feedings. Most babies will take at least a small amount, perhaps one to two ounces. A good time to offer water is during the baby's wakeful or "fussy" periods, when it is too soon to feed him but when he is apt to be restless.

Water for your baby is boiled and stored in sterile bottles exactly the same way as his formula, if he has one. If you make a formula daily, simply fill at least two additional bottles with water instead of formula. If your baby is breast fed, you should sterilize two bottles with their nipples and put in them 4 to 8 ounces of water that has been boiled for 10 minutes. RUTH S. KEMPE

See also STERILIZING

WATERPROOF PANTS

Waterproof pants are used over a baby's diaper and later over training pants to keep his clothes and bedding dry. These pants are made of rubber, plastic, silk, or nylon; some are made of a plastic-coated fabric; others have a fabric outer layer, with a plastic inner layer. Most mothers consider four pairs of these pants an ample supply.

If a baby's wet diapers have an ammonia-like odor, take particular precautions to avoid diaper rash. Ammonia, formed by bacterial action in the urine, can irritate the baby's skin. And continuous use of waterproof pants may be the cause. If irritation occurs, it is best to let the baby go without waterproof pants for a while to see if the rash clears up.

Waterproof pants are a boon when traveling with a baby. Of course, the same precautions must be taken on trips to keep the baby free from the discomfort of diaper rash as are taken at home. Try to change the diaper frequently so baby will not lie in a wet, too-warm garment.

Use of waterproof pants at night, over two diapers, will usually keep a baby comfortable and his bed dry.

Waterproof pants should be loose-fitting around the baby's thighs and no tighter than necessary at the waistband. Correctly fitted pants permit proper circulation and help to avoid uncomfortable warmth and rash.

See also DIAPER RASH

WAX IN EARS *See* EARACHE

WEANING

Not so long ago, weaning was considered something of a chore to be put off as long as possible. Other kinds of feeding were difficult and unsafe then, and mothers took pride in nursing their babies for 12 to 18 months. Now, weaning any time after 6 months is pretty much a decision of convenience and preference rather than of necessity. Formulas of all kinds are available and easily prepared. In most areas a highly sanitary and pasteurized milk supply is easily available. Canned milks, specially processed cereals, canned fruits, meats, and vegetables in many varieties and of excellent quality can be given to a baby in his early months. Good refrigeration is usually available at home and makes the preserving of all these foods quite safe. The baby of today doesn't have to rely on his mother's breast milk supply to feed him safely for his whole first year. Indeed, by the time he is 8 months old, the modern baby is receiving a wide variety of foods that give the well-balanced nutrition he needs.

This all makes weaning a much simpler and more pleasant process. The decision to wean can be made on the basis of the mother's pleasure in nursing and her baby's interest and pleasure in the breast or bottle.

It is much better to wean gradually, whenever possible, allowing the baby plenty of time to get used to new ways of eating. Abrupt weaning is apt to be upsetting to the entire household and should be avoided unless illness or some other major problem makes it necessary. If the interruption of nursing will only be for a few days, it is sometimes worth while to express milk manually and then resume nursing when mother or baby is well again.

Weaning from the breast can be done to either cup or bottle. Unless a baby is at least 4 to 6 months old, it is rather difficult to change feedings entirely from breast to cup—it is usually easier to wean to bottle feeding. Whether a baby is weaned from the breast to a formula or to plain milk in a bottle is again apt to depend on the age and size of the baby and on his doctor's convictions. By the time he is 6 months old, the average baby can certainly receive plain homogenized or whole milk, especially if he is taking a good variety of solid foods. While a baby is taking a formula, the formula should be made sterile, but plain milk can often be offered without special sterilization if the doctor feels that the home refrigeration is satisfactory.

For the older baby, weaning to a cup is probably more desirable. It is necessary that a baby be able to take large amounts of milk by cup before this form of weaning can be started very seriously. Learning to drink from a cup often takes several weeks, and during this time the baby probably should have most of his usual supply of milk from the breast. Then when milk can be taken well by cup, the process of substituting it for the breast can begin.

There are two ways to substitute the cup for breast feeding. One is to offer the baby as much milk by cup as he will take at each feeding, and then allow him to nurse after the cup. Gradually, he will be willing and able to take more by cup, the amount given by breast will automatically be cut down.

The other way to wean is to substitute the cup for an entire feeding—at first, once a day and then, within a week, twice a day. Gradually, in this way over the course of two to four weeks, substitution for all feedings

It is best to begin substituting the cup for those feedings that come after the solid-food meals the baby receives.

can be made. It is best to begin substituting the cup for those feedings that come after the solid-food meals the baby receives. The morning and evening feedings are usually the ones most desired by the baby and can be changed last. The final feeding of the day often is not well taken entirely by cup, and there is no harm in continuing to offer the breast for a while if you wish. By the time you are down to one breast feeding a day, the baby is getting little milk from nursing anyway, but he is deriving pleasure and comfort from the continued closeness to his mother at bedtime.

Weaning from bottle to cup can be done in the same way as from breast to cup—by offering the cup first at each feeding or by substituting it for an entire bottle feeding.

Weaning from breast to bottle is usually easier and quicker than to the cup since the baby continues to suck in much the same way. Weaning to a bottle is therefore preferable if weaning from the breast must for any reason be done suddenly and quickly or if weaning must be done in the first two to three months. To change from the breast to the bottle, a mother can either substitute the bottle for an entire nursing (which is usually easier) or give first the bottle and then the breast at each nursing.

If weaning from the breast cannot be done gradually, there is often some engorgement of the breasts and discomfort for a few days. The doctor can sometimes provide treatment that will help to cut down milk production. To allow the baby to nurse just long enough to relieve the breast fullness or to express a little bit of milk by hand will also take care of the discomfort. Since breast-milk production depends on regular nursing, the supply will diminish automatically as the baby no longer nurses.

A baby may cling to his evening bottle into his second year and there is no harm in allowing him this comfort. If you feel that your child is old enough to give up his bottle, you can try substitution. Hold him a few minutes while you sing a song or tell a story to provide him with the love and security the bottle has represented. A cup of milk or fruit juice may also help in making him feel well satisfied and happy. RUTH S. KEMPE

See also INTRODUCING NEW FOODS

WEIGHT *See* GROWTH

WELFARE AGENCIES *See* SOCIAL WELFARE AGENCIES

WELL-BABY CLINIC *See* CHILD HEALTH CONFERENCE

WETTING *See* BED-WETTING; TOILET TRAINING

WHITE BLOOD CELLS *See* CANCER

WHOOPING COUGH

All infants should be immunized against whooping cough (pertussis). The disease can be fatal to any child, but the death rate from whooping cough is far higher for children who contract it when they are less than a year old. Immunization is now so effective and widespread that the disease is becoming relatively rare. Occasionally, an immunized child catches whooping cough, but the case is then so light that it is frequently almost unrecognizable.

First signs of whooping cough are increased nose and throat secretions, spells of coughing, usually worse at night, and a slight fever. In about two weeks, the cough develops into the whoop that gives the disease its name. The coughing spell can often cause vomiting.

A child suspected of having whooping cough should be kept away from other children, for infection is largely through direct contact—a spray of droplets from the mouth and nose.

The sick child should always be seen immediately by a doctor. MARIE A. HINRICHS

See also COMMON COMMUNICABLE DISEASES; SICK CHILD; STEAMING

WORK *See* CHORES; JOBS

WORKING MOTHER

One of the most debated questions in family life today is, "Should mothers work?" There can be no single, simple answer. Some mothers should work and some should not. Whether you go out to work depends entirely upon your individual family situation.

Before you go to work you will be wise to consider four questions: Will your working result in a happier child? Will you achieve greater personal satisfaction? Will your relationship with your husband improve? Will there be a more harmonious home life? Of course, there are mothers who *have* to work —widows, divorcées, or women whose husbands are sick or disabled. Each mother will arrive at the answers to these four questions in a different way. Her children and their needs, her own temperament and training, family finances, and family values all will influence her decision.

The Basic Facts

There are certain basic facts that you may want to consider in measuring the wisdom of your own decision:

- A child learns about the world around him through the people who take care of him. His mother is the best possible person to assume this protective role. She usually wants to be with her child most of the time until he is at least 3 years old.
- At 2 a child tests his independence and security. He needs consistent handling by loving people. Restrictions are easier to bear if they come from a mother whom he has already learned to trust.
- At 3 a child is usually ready to include other adults and children in his everyday world. Nursery school at this time can further his development and teach him a great deal.
- The school-age child, between 6 and 12, although he may seem independent and self-sufficient, will need some sort of guidance and care before school, at lunch, and after school. This kind of child care is provided by some local communities. A good housekeeper in the home is ideal if her salary fits into the family budget.
- Children go through difficult phases during which they may revert to babyish behavior. It is advisable not to further upset a child's world by going out to work at such times, or when he is ill. Vomiting, nail-biting, temper tantrums, or just plain whining, if they persist, indicate that all is not well with the child whose mother has gone out to work.
- The kind of care a child needs and the kind of care available in the community will directly influence a mother's decision to take a job outside her home. If a mother must leave a small baby to take a job, she should provide the best mother-substitute she can find. She should seek a woman who will come to the home every day, who will fit into the household comfortably, and

Some mothers have to go out to work. For them, a good housekeeper in the home is ideal.

who will give the baby the same care the mother would if she were there. The alternative is foster day care in someone else's home. This kind of care can be found through a family service agency.

- The attitude of the husband is important, too. He should be in complete accord with his wife's plans to work outside the home. While many able-bodied women juggle child care, husband, and job efficiently, there are times when fatigue and tension threaten the well-being of their children and certainly the wife's relationship with her husband. His understanding cooperation is a bulwark in times of stress.

A Life of Your Own

You may well consider all these points and still have the question, "What about me? I, too, have needs and a life of my own to be lived." The schedule many working mothers plan for themselves leaves little time for recreation, something every mother needs. Your husband is likely to feel pretty much left out of things if you spend all your free time with your children, leaving him to watch television alone. Sometimes it is wise to hire a competent baby-sitter to stay with the children and spend an evening out with your husband, even if you *have* worked all day. Husbands are people, too, remember.

Mother is needed at the beginning and the end of each day.

Planning time with your children, time for a job, and time for your husband will present problems, but many mothers who work find their home life happier, not only for their monetary contribution, but also because the mother feels more of a person and is satisfying her own needs for recognition and intellectual challenge.

The Time To Be There

It cannot be emphasized too often that your children's sense of belonging and security is not dependent so much on the number of hours you spend with them as it is on the quality of the relationship you share. Certain times are more important than others for getting together with your young children:

- Your child needs you at the beginning and end of his day—to help him get dressed for nursery school or to greet his baby-sitter or to help him bathe and get ready for bed.
- If your child has been at nursery school all day, it is important that he have his dinner with the family, not alone before adults gather at the table.
- A sick child needs his mother. He needs someone to comfort him, and nobody can "make it all better" quite as well as his own mother. If you can plan your job so that you can be at home with your child when he is ill, you will find that your youngster is less demanding and happier when he is well.
- A young child wants his mother around for his birthday parties; he wants her to attend school programs in which he has an active part.
- A child wants his mother to share his interests and his hobbies. If he loves airplanes, learn to identify those that fly low over your house. Your child will be thrilled that you share his delight in planes—or cars or boats or stamps.
- A working mother has a special responsibility to become acquainted with her child's teacher. A nursery-school child, especially, needs to know that his mother and teacher are friends and are in agreement on various phases of his care.

When a child is very young and two or three persons are responsible for his care, it is better that *all* persons be in agreement. The child's life will have much more meaning if his nurse, housekeeper, or foster day-care mother *and his own mother* agree on mealtime and naptime routines, discipline, toys, friends, and visiting privileges.

"Things" Aren't Security

It is a temptation to try to make up to your child for your absence by giving lavishly of material things or by requiring him to do very little in the way of chores. To your child, "things" do not spell security. He wants to feel your love and affection through your loving touch as you comb his hair or wash his face and ears. He gains security through your warmth and sympathy as he comes to you with problems. He wants to know in the morning as you and he hurry through breakfast that he is not in the way. He feels better if he knows that taking him to the nursery school is not a big bother to you. Try to make this period a time when you and he can share some experiences. And in the evening when you call for him at the school, he wants to know by your smile and your manner that you are truly glad to see him—that his homecoming will not cause you trouble or interfere with your own plans for the evening.

Patience is a virtue to be cultivated by the working mother, for it will bring innumerable rewards. Children cannot be ignored or put aside. A child who is rushed and whose problems are pushed aside today may require many more hours of time later in an effort to woo back a once lovable and loving little person who has become afraid and angry.

Quality Counts

These problems face you as a working mother. Such problems are common to all children and their parents, but the working mother must be especially aware of them. Because you will have fewer hours to spend with your child, the *quality* of this time together counts for more than the *quantity*. Your child need not be the loser if you plan carefully.

DOROTHY H. BEERS

See also FAMILY SERVICE AGENCY; MOTHER; NURSERY SCHOOL

WOUNDS *See* BLEEDING; CUTS AND SCRATCHES

WRITING

Young children love the sound of words. They will try them out in various combinations—repeating again and again the combinations that especially please them.

As they grow older, this same love for arranging and using words can carry over into their writing. That is—this can happen if children are given sensitive help as they begin to discover the joy in writing creatively.

When a child is a beginner in writing creatively—writing something personally significant to him—it is important *not* to make his writing an exercise in spelling and punctuation. Spell words he asks for, yes, and help him to know the few written signals that mean "stop" (period), "pause" (comma), and "excitement" (exclamation point), but don't interrupt him in his writing to give him this information.

Rather than to correct him, a better way to help him see his writing in correct form is to offer to type a copy of what he has written. Then you can supply spelling and punctuation without saying anything about it. If he asks about some of the marks, such as an exclamation point, that is the time to explain their uses.

Remember always that in creative writing the important thing is to enjoy putting one's thoughts and feelings into words. Your child may want to read to you what he has written as part of this enjoyment. Or he may want you to read it yourself. Then, again, he may want his writing kept entirely private. And this should be up to him to choose.

It is also important to remember that it is not likely that a child will have the technical writing skills for getting his thoughts and feelings down on paper. If he seems frustrated when he tries to do his own writing, offer to do the technical part of the writing for him. Be his secretary, as it were—writing down his story or poem or other thoughts and feelings *just as he tells them.* While acting as his secretary, it may be tempting to suggest changes in what he is dictating, but don't allow yourself to do it. The writing is *his*, and he will soon lose the creative pleasure in producing if it becomes yours. Your best help can come from:

- Enjoying interesting words and combinations of words with him
- Writing his dictation
- Reading and enjoying his writing when he invites you to
- Helping him to make covers for poems, stories, and books
- Respecting his wish for privacy

PEGGY BROGAN

See also HANDWRITING; LETTER WRITING; TYPEWRITER; VOCABULARY DEVELOPMENT

YELLING

Yelling is usually effective as an attention getter. It makes itself heard, however offensive it may be to the receiving ear.

We usually think of yelling as the prerogative of the angry child who wants his anger to be heard. It may also be the way in which an angry or a determined or an annoyed adult expresses his annoyance toward a child. Confusion results when we try to discourage yelling as an effective method of communicating at the same time we are demonstrating the effectiveness by yelling ourselves.

Perhaps instead of yelling, "Stop that yelling!" we might try, "I can hear you better when you speak more softly." Or, "When you yell, it makes me feel like not listening; I don't like the sound it makes." Or, "Please save your yelling for outside; it hurts my inside ears!"

And of course we need to *look* as well as to *listen*. What situations seem to bring forth yelling? Is the yelling an occasional explosive and releasing eruption, or is it a chronic accompaniment to all demands? Is it a calculated destroyer of the peace? Who is yelling, and why?

EVELYN BEYER

See also ANGER

YMCA–YWCA *See* YOUTH ORGANIZATIONS

YOUNGEST CHILD *See* BROTHERS AND SISTERS

YOUTH ORGANIZATIONS

Thousands of boys and girls begin their association with organized youth groups in the early grades. Little girls can become Brownies, the first step to Girl Scouting, when they are 7 or 8 years old. Girls who choose Camp Fire Girls can join the organization as Blue Birds at 7 or 8. Cub Scouts is the portion of Boy Scouting reserved for young boys, who may join this activity when they are 8. Cub Scouts learn skills that prepare them for Senior Boy Scouts, which they may join at age 11.

Some YMCA's have Gra-Y, a club for elementary school children, which precedes their membership in Junior Hi-Y, Hi-Y, or Tri-Hi-Y. Also, YMCA's offer Indian Guides and Indian Princesses, which include boys 6 to 9 and their fathers, and girls 6 to 9 and their fathers.

Young people are eager to plan projects and engage in community service but do not want to go it alone. They want adult supervision. They want the companionship of persons their own age, yet need and appreciate the friendship and guidance of sympathetic adults other than their parents. Youth organizations such as the ones named often provide youngsters with just such an opportunity.

Organized youth activity can help boys and girls learn to get along well together, to engage in shared activities and projects, to accept and discharge responsibility, and, perhaps most important, to learn that there must be followers as well as leaders. The childish code of "me first" will no longer work.

Going to meetings actually builds a child's self-esteem and makes him feel important. He can gain new interests, awards for achievement, a chance to feel independent, and the feeling of being a part of a nationwide organization. The uniform he wears makes him feel set apart, yet a part of his own group.

When choosing a youth group for your child, consider first his own interests. Some organizations stress much out-of-doors activity, others engage in handicraft projects or community betterment projects.

Competent adult leadership is always needed in organized youth activities. But, the parents of children in the group also have a responsibility. Leaders will call upon parents for transportation, food, equipment, and to act as chaperones upon occasion. When a child joins, his membership usually involves his parents, too.

See also COMMUNITY RESOURCES; TEENAGER

ZWIEBACK

By the time he is 6 or 7 months old, your baby probably will enjoy holding a piece of zwieback or toast or a crust of stale bread in his hand and sucking or munching away. Don't be concerned if more crumbs get on his face and in his hair than into his mouth. The satisfaction he gets from this experience in self-feeding and the exercise to his jaws are well worth the mop-up operation. He should not be given breadstuffs while lying down, however, lest he choke on the crumbs.

See also SELF-FEEDING

Illustration Acknowledgments

The publishers of CHILDCRAFT gratefully acknowledge the courtesy of the following artists, photographers, publishers, agencies, and corporations for illustrations in this volume. Page numbers refer to two-page spreads. The words "(*left*)," "(*center*)," "(*top*)," "(*bottom*)," and "(*right*)," indicate position on the spread. All illustrations are the exclusive property of the publishers of CHILDCRAFT unless names are marked with an asterisk (*).

12: John Mechling, Shostal (*)
24: Phiz Mozesson (*)
32–33: Dora Mathieu
36–37: photo by Milo Williams (*); art by Dora Mathieu
40–41: (*top left*) Alfa Studios; (*top right and bottom*) courtesy of Eastern Fine Paper and Pulp Division, Standard Packaging Corporation (*)
42–43: (*left*) Gilmore N. Birklund, (*center*) Kieran Joseph Cassin, (*right*) Sharon Scotte Zeilstra
46: Chicago Chapter, American Red Cross (*)
51: Rus Arnold (*)
53: photo by Torkel Korling (*)
55: Dora Mathieu
57: Rie Gaddis
61: WORLD BOOK photo
66–67: (*top*) Don Stebbing; (*bottom*) Rie Gaddis
74: Dora Mathieu
81: Rie Gaddis
83: photo by Carroll Seghers II (*); art by Dora Mathieu
86–87: Dora Mathieu
88–89: Camp Algonquin, United Charities of Chicago (*)
95: Dora Mathieu
98: Dora Mathieu
100: Dora Mathieu
108: Dora Mathieu
110–111: photo by Nothmann, Monkmeyer (*); art by Dora Mathieu
130: Dora Mathieu
136: Nothmann, Monkmeyer (*)
138–139: art by Dora Mathieu; photo by Rie Gaddis
140: Dora Mathieu
144: Rie Gaddis
151: Don Stebbing
155: American Medical Association (*)
157: Rie Gaddis
164: Dora Mathieu
166–167: Don Stebbing
171: Dora Mathieu
174: Dora Mathieu
178–179: Harold M. Lambert (*)
180–181: Harold M. Lambert (*)
182: adapted through courtesy of Nancy Bayley
185: Rie Gaddis
187: Dora Mathieu
193: U.S. Department of Agriculture (*)
201: Ed Fitzgerald
203: Drinnon, Inc., from National Congress of Parents and Teachers (*)
208–209: Dora Mathieu
211: The National Foundation, March of Dimes (*)
218: Dora Mathieu
221: Don Stebbing
225: Phiz Mozesson (*)
226: Kansas City (Mo.) Public Library (*)
228: Dora Mathieu
237: Dora Mathieu
244: Dora Mathieu
247: Vivienne (*)
249: Rie Gaddis
257: Don Stebbing
261: American Music Conference (*)
265: (*top*) American Medical Association (*); (*bottom*) Don Stebbing
266–267: Rie Gaddis
269: CHILDCRAFT photo
271: Dora Mathieu
273: Don Stebbing
280: Don Stebbing
289: United Press Int. (*)
290: Don Stebbing
292–293: (*left*) Suzanne Szasz (*); (*right*) Eiger, Black Star (*)
302: Dora Mathieu
306: photo, Standard Romper Co., Inc. (*); art by Dora Mathieu
315: Suzanne Szasz (*)
320–321: (*left*) Rie Gaddis; (*right*) Don Stebbing
325: Don Stebbing
331: photos, (*top*) Rie Gaddis, (*bottom*) H. Armstrong Roberts (*); art by Dora Mathieu
332–333: Dora Mathieu
336: Dora Mathieu
340: Don Stebbing
342–343: Don Stebbing
344–345: Don Stebbing
351: (*top*) Vivienne (*); (*bottom*) Don Stebbing
354: (*top*) Johnson & Johnson (*), (*center*) Rie Gaddis, (*bottom*) Harold M. Lambert (*)
364–365: Don Stebbing
387: Dora Mathieu
396: Dora Mathieu
399: Dora Mathieu
405: Rie Gaddis
410: Rie Gaddis
414: Ron Galella, Globe Photos (*)
416: James H. Brown
420: Phiz Mozesson (*)
424: Dora Mathieu
429: Dora Mathieu
442: Don Stebbing
444–445: Rie Gaddis